Major Problems in
American Indian History

MAJOR PROBLEMS IN AMERICAN HISTORY SERIES

GENERAL EDITOR

THOMAS G. PATERSON

Major Problems in American Indian History

DOCUMENTS AND ESSAYS

SECOND EDITION

EDITED BY

ALBERT L. HURTADO

UNIVERSITY OF OKLAHOMA

PETER IVERSON

ARIZONA STATE UNIVERSITY

HOUGHTON MIFFLIN COMPANY
Boston   New York

Editor in Chief: Jean L. Woy
Senior Associate Editor: Frances Gay
Associate Project Editor: Jane Lee
Editorial Assistant: Martha Rogers
Associate Production/Design Coordinator: Lisa Jelly
Senior Manufacturing Coordinator: Florence Cadran
Senior Marketing Manager: Sandra McGuire

Cover Series Design: Deborah Azerrad Savona

Cover Art: Navajo trading post scene. Pictorial Navajo Rug made by Laura and Loretta Nez, grandmother and granddaughter. Courtesy of Cristofs, Sante Fe, New Mexico. Photo by Jerry Jacka.

Printed in the U.S.A.

Library of Congress Catalog Card Number: 00-133872

ISBN: 0-618-06854-6

123456789-CRS-04 03 02 01 00

For Our Friends and Mentors
Wilbur R. Jacobs
and
Allan G. Bogue

Contents

C H A P T E R   4
The Southern Borderlands
Page 93

C H A P T E R   5
The Northern Borderlands
Page 134

CHAPTER 9

Indian Perspectives on the Civil War

Page 276

DOCUMENTS

ESSAYS

CHAPTER 10

Resistance and Transition, 1865–1886

Page 312

DOCUMENTS

CHAPTER 13
World War II, Termination, and the Foundation for Self-Determination, 1941–1960
Page 418

CHAPTER 14
Taking Control of Lives and Lands, 1961–1980
Page 452

CHAPTER 15
Continuing Challenges, Continuing Peoples, 1981–1999
Page 486

Preface

In the preface to the first edition of this volume, published in 1994, we raised several questions including some sparked by current controversies. For example: "Should Native American peoples be permitted to operate casinos on their reservations, even if doing so conflicts with state law? Should non-Indian merchants be allowed to sell replicas of such sacred Indian objects as Hopi kachina figures, originally fashioned exclusively for rituals, when this commercial activity sometimes leads to the theft of real sacred items?"

The years since 1994 have witnessed no resolution to these questions or others. If anything, they have demonstrated that the issues have only become more complicated. What, for example, about Indian casinos situated off of reservations? What about members of other Indian communities carving and selling Hopi kachina figures? Answers to these and other questions reveal significant disagreements between and among American Indians themselves and between Indians and non-Indians about the place and status of American Indians in American life. These disagreements, in turn, reveal a good deal about our different perceptions of the Native American past, present, and future. There are, of course, many Indian pasts and presents. Indian communities vary considerably in the nature of their economies, the size of their populations, and the central characteristics of their cultures. Regardless of these differences, through the centuries Indian peoples have shared a common goal of determining their own destinies. This objective, to be sure, has often conflicted with non-Indian perspectives and priorities in regard to land use, religious practices, educational systems, and other crucial concerns.

The field of American Indian history has undergone fundamental changes in the last few decades. For a long time, most scholars in the field largely ignored the twentieth century. They focused their efforts on understanding federal policies toward Indians and the wars that accompanied both the colonial and national periods of North American history. Relying primarily on materials found in local, state, and national archives, as well as on the memoirs of federal employees including policymakers and military officers, they fashioned a portrait that was useful yet incomplete.

To offer a more thorough perspective, many scholars have turned to what is generally called *ethnohistory.* This blending of anthropological and historical methods permits us to gain a more complete sense of how Indian individuals and groups chose to act. Through field work, oral histories, and traditional tribal narratives, we are starting to fill the gaps in the archival record and to present alternative historical explanations for Indian actions that approximate an Indian perspective.

Because of this approach, students of Indian history today often place more emphasis on what is termed *agency* and less emphasis on what is often labeled *victimization.* That is to say, without denying the terrible traumas and costs of the Indian past, scholars now give greater weight to the ability of Native individuals and communities to adapt, to persist, to survive, and, at times, to prosper. This volume reflects this transition in the field.

In the second edition of *Major Problems in American Indian History,* we have increased Indian voices in the documents and essays throughout. We have taken advantage of the wealth of recent scholarship to incorporate new essays; in fact, 80 percent of the essays are new. Five chapters are completely new and several others are greatly revised with mostly new material. This edition includes a completely new introductory chapter with new essays, and a new chapter on Indian history before 1492. In order to emphasize the Indian perspective on history, we have organized the chapters covering the colonial period around regions (southern and northern borderlands) rather than nations (England, Spain, and France). Chapter 4 on the southern borderlands focuses on the Pueblo Revolt and missionary life and features new documents and essays. Chapter 5 on the northern borderlands is almost completely new, with a focus on women and the fur trade society.

There are new chapters on Indians in the American Revolution, the Civil War, and World War II. Chapter 6 on the American Revolution has been completely revised to focus on the War from Indian perspectives, including documents and an essay by Native Americans. Chapter 9 on the Civil War also includes documents by Native Americans, and Chapter 13 on World War II includes documents by Native Americans on their experiences during the war, their reactions to the government policy of termination, and their efforts toward self-determination during the 1940s and 1950s.

Throughout the book there is increased emphasis on gender, family, and social relations. In addition to the coverage of women during the colonial period, Chapter 7 depicts the experiences of Native Americans in the New Republic and includes documents and a new essay on sex and married life among Indians and Indian-white marriages. Chapter 11 includes Indian reactions to the Dawes Act and the boarding school movement as well as the defense of their land, family life, institutions, and religious customs. Chapter 14 on the 1960s and 1970s is almost completely revised and includes all Native American voices in the documents and new essays on the roots of Native American activism. And Chapter 15 on the 1980s and 1990s is completely new, again with all Indian voices in the documents which cover economic development and continuing challenges. Two of the essays in this chapter are also by Native Americans, including one on intergenerational relations among Indians.

This book follows the same general format as other volumes in the Major Problems in American History series. Each chapter begins with a brief introduction to its topic, followed first by documents and then by essays that illuminate the chapter's central theme or interpretive problem. Headnotes that place the readings in historical and interpretive perspective introduce each chapter's primary materials and essays. Each chapter closes with a "Further Reading" section that lists important books and articles for those who wish to explore the subject in more depth. Sources for all documents and essays are also provided.

In the years since the publication of the first edition, the field of American Indian history has enjoyed impressive development. An increasing percentage of colleges and universities now offer courses in the history of the American Indian or Native American (terms that we use interchangeably). The establishment of H-AmIndian, part of the H-Net (History-Internet) program, exemplifies these developments. Subscribers to this lively list, which can be found at www.asu.edu/clas/history/h-amindian, receive daily summaries of important news from Indian country, raise questions, and participate in engaging discussions about new approaches and methods. Through H-AmIndian, participants from all over the world can communicate easily and frequently about key issues and trends in the field. National Native newspapers such as *Indian Country Today* and *News from Indian Country* also provide important coverage of the current scene.

A number of people have helped us achieve a balanced and wide-ranging collection of documents and essays. Richard Adkins, Willy Bauer (Wailaki), and Brian Frehner, doctoral students at the University of Oklahoma, and Kathy Howard, Richard Kitchen, and Andrea Pugsley, doctoral students at Arizona State University, assisted with research, bibliography, and myriad ancillary details. We would also like to thank the following reviewers who gave us helpful comments on the revision: Colin Calloway, Dartmouth College; Angela Firkus, Cottey College; Emily Greenwald, University of Nebraska; Clara Sue Kidwell (Choctaw/Ojibwe), University of Oklahoma; Thomas R. Maddux, California State University, Northridge; Christopher L. Miller, University of Texas, Pan American; Delores Nason McBroome, Humboldt State University; Richard A. Rose (Cherokee), State University of New York at Albany; Neal Salisbury, Smith College; and James E. Sherow, Kansas State University. Jean Woy, Frances Gay, and Katie Huha of Houghton Mifflin, as well as the series editor, Thomas G. Paterson, kept us on track and gave us invaluable assistance all along the way.

As with the first edition, we dedicate this volume to our friends and mentors, Wilbur R. Jacobs and Allan G. Bogue. Without such teachers and role models, this book would not have been possible.

A. L. H
P. I.

Major Problems in
American Indian History

C H A P T E R

1

Interpreting the Indian Past

◈

Today, most thoughtful people would think that the idea of American history without American Indians was an absurdity. Yet for generations historians of the United States wrote the nation's story as if Indians did not exist, or at best historians marginalized native people as bit players in the great national drama. In U.S. history textbooks Indians emerged only in time to be swept aside by westering white Americans. In the 1960s, the civil rights movement and the growth of political activism among people of color, ethnic groups, and women resulted in a challenge to exclusively Anglocentric history. Yet the writing of Indian history is no simple matter. Until the twentieth century, few Indians were literate, so the record of their activities was based primarily on documents that white observers produced. Indians remembered their past, but in the form of oral traditions. Historians of the American Indian experience often find that their work about the past is important to Indians' aspirations for the future. Consequently, the field is sometimes politically charged in ways that other historical subjects are not. Until recently, there were no Indian historians in academe, and Indian views were only indirectly represented. In the past few decades, this situation has improved so that Indian voices are increasingly heard in classrooms and textbooks, but native historians are still a minority even in the field of Indian history. This chapter poses questions about the state of Indian history and the special responsibilities of historians working in this field.

◈ *E S S A Y S*

The emergence of native scholars has necessarily brought new concerns to the attention of historians. For Indian historians, the past is palpably linked to living people, places, and problems with which they are intimately familiar. Professor Donald L. Fixico, an historian of Creek, Seminole, Sac and Fox, and Shawnee heritage at the University of Kansas, challenges historians to augment their research techniques and analytical conceptions with research methods and ideas that are better suited to Indian history. While incorporating ideas about culture and oral history, historians must consciously remove ethnocentrism from their work, a process that Professor Fixico regards as a moral imperative. Professor Richard White of Stanford University explains the methodological difficulties of studying Indian history. He begins by questioning the assumptions that historians work from. Professor White is particularly concerned with the intersection of Indian history and environmental history, but this essay and the questions it raises are generally applicable to the field of Indian history. These essays raise important ethical and methodological questions about how one studies Indian history. Indeed, if Indian culture is so radically different from European norms, how can we use European ideas and sources to understand Indian history at all?

Ethics and Responsibilities in Writing American Indian History

DONALD L. FIXICO

Researching, writing, and teaching American Indian history in a respectful manner calls for a set of professional ethics and scholarly responsibilities. As scholarship evolves, so must the treatment of American Indian history. Such ethics and responsibilities are not currently defined or recorded in any forum, or in any printed material, although historians previously have considered the importance of a fairer treatment of Indians in writing history. The sensitivity of tribal knowledge, especially that of ceremonials, should compel scholars to publicly acknowledge a code of ethics and responsibilities to avoid exploiting American Indians.

Repatriation, the selling of Indian burial remains and imitations of Indian artifacts, and the publication of sensitive Indian knowledge have resulted in a series of controversies forcing Indians to act against whites, and in some cases against Indians where Indians have desecrated tribal properties. The exploitation of American Indians has never stopped. It began with Indian enslavement when a lost Christopher Columbus landed in the Western Hemisphere. Indians have been victimized through centuries of land fraud and disease, the manipulation of warriors as mercenaries, the abuse of Indian women, and the capture of Indian children to meet enrollment quotas in boarding schools.

This essay acknowledges certain moral ethics and professional responsibilities in this field—American Indian history. First this essay will identify those ethics and responsibilities and then provide arguments to convince historians and others of the importance of upholding such ethics and fulfilling responsibilities pertaining to the proper study and writing of American Indian history.

First of all, the field must be carefully defined so the academy, as well as students and writers, understand what is meant by American Indian history. At this date, only parameters can be argued. Is American Indian history also called Native American history and is this acceptable? Is Indian History the history of Indian people and their nations relating only to other Indian nations? To non-Indian nations like France, Spain, Russia, England, or the Netherlands? Or, only the United States? Is American Indian history the history of a tribe within itself without reference to outsiders? Or, is American Indian history all of these histories *in toto*? Defining the field could be another article as an increasing number of individuals from various fields and backgrounds write about American Indian history.

As a discipline, history is more subjective than some other disciplines in its interpretation and analysis of research. Because of this precarious situation, historians need carefully to consider the moral ethics and professional responsibilities

Donald L. Fixico, "Ethics and Responsibilities in Writing American Indian History," *American Indian Quarterly* 20 (winter 1996), 29–39. Reprinted by permission of the University of Nebraska Press. Copyright © 1996 by the University of Nebraska Press.

inherent in teaching and writing about Native American history. On the other side of this issue, some American Indians feel that the writing of American Indian history, mostly by non-Indians, is merely another example of the exploitative and unfair treatment of Indian people.

An interesting irony has occurred in the historiography of the American experience. For at least a century, scholars, writers, and historians have neglected Native Americans in writing the history of America. Different schools of thought like the Germ theory and Turner thesis have encouraged historians to ignore the original inhabitants of the entire western hemisphere. Why did this happen, if a scholar's professional responsibility is to be objective in researching historical topics? These approaches described the "white experience," as if Indians did not exist. To write a history of the Anglo-American experience is not wrong, but to claim that it represents the entire history of the American experience is a gross mistake.

Historians, in particular, wrote Indians out of their textbooks for whatever insecure reasons of justifying the past actions of America's heroes, racial bigotry, or white guilt. By ignoring the dark episodes of the destruction of Indians and their cultures, historians in effect denied that these ever happened. Nonetheless non-Indians have had to face the issue that American Indians, indeed, have existed in the Americas well before the accidental arrival of Columbus, and that Native Americans are a vital part of the history of this country. Hence, the writing of American Indian history emerged as a body of literature in the early decades of the twentieth century, although historians continued to vilify Indians as "savages" and "devilish heathens" that a glorified United States had to destroy, exalting a false white supremacy over all minority races in this country.

Whether racially prejudiced or guilt-ridden, patronizing, paternalistic, or romantic, Indian history mainly has been perceived from a white perspective, based on the idea that "the conquerors write the history." More than 30,000 manuscripts have been published about American Indians, and more than 90 percent of that literature has been written by non-Indians. To illustrate this point further, a similar percentage of these non-Indian historians have written about writing or studying American Indian history.

The point here is that non-Indian scholars have sought to define the parameters of the field of American Indian history. They have attempted to determine its forms of evidence only as written accounts, professed limited theories, and devised methodologies from a non-Indian tradition. European explorers and military officers recorded accounts of their contacts with American Indians. During the British colonization in the seventeenth and eighteenth centuries, newspapers used negative reports about Indians to sell newspapers. Eager novelists picked up their poisoned pens to embellish on any Indian resistance to intrigue readers with horrific atrocities. In the 1880s, ethnographers recorded notes, wrote articles, and drafted manuscripts describing Indians and their cultures. More ethnographers and anthropologists followed in the late 1880s in desperate efforts to study Native American cultures. These were believed to be disappearing with the buffalo, as the Indian population in the United States declined to 243,000. Careless historians followed ethnographers and anthropologists as a part of the academic community that wrote imbalanced articles and books about American Indians.

Even in the twentieth century, historians have written about the American Indian with very little understanding about "him" (since this was assumed to be a man's history) and the depth of his distinct culture. The ill-trained historian approached Indian history with his or her graduate training for writing mainstream history. Historians borrowed much of their approach from western buffs mostly interested in Indian wars. Next, a small group of scholars emerged to write classical tribal histories. The initial studies were published in the 1930s and 1940s by the University of Oklahoma Press. These works led the way for other presses to produce American Indian books.

The growing scholarly interest in Indians led to a series of conferences in the early 1950s, including the Ohio Valley Historic Indian Conference on November 21, 1953. A number of scholars participated, especially anthropologists involved in Indian claims cases, and this regional conference was expanded into the annual American Indian Ethnohistoric Conference, currently known as the American Society for Ethnohistory. Since then, scholars have struggled to understand the complexity of American Indian history.

In the early 1970s, historians worked to revise the discipline when they recognized that inadequate means were being used to examine Indian history. Historians followed the example of anthropologists using ethnography to study American Indian history. The breakthrough was the distinction of "culture" and the study of it as a part of history. Historians who study Indian history must think in terms of culture, community, environment, and metaphysics.

Ethnohistory has allowed a cross-disciplinary approach using history and anthropology to study American Indian history. Since then, Native American history has been written by geographers, sociologists, and literary writers using a combination of their academic expertise and the tools of historians. The value of the ethnohistorical approach is that it examines society and culture within time periods that also allow it to address historical events. As one ethnohistorian stated, the advantage is that ethnohistory can go beyond the limitations of one discipline by combining two fields. On a cautionary note, another scholar warned that ethnohistory written about American Indians is largely from a western perspective, while continuing to suppress the American Indian point of view.

A revived interest in Indians was aided by Indians themselves during the rise of the Red Power movement during the late 1960s, when frustrated urban Indians organized protest marches for better treatment of Indian people. Indian activism and Indian militancy such as the occupations of Alcatraz (1969), the Bureau of Indian Affairs (1972) and Wounded Knee (1973) renewed public interest in American Indians. This renaissance resulted in the writing of a deluge of Indian literature and history.

American Indian history is often thought of as a history of Indian-white relations. The fact that the Native peoples of the western hemisphere already possessed histories of thousands of years time depth before the arrival of Columbus has had little effect on non-Indians who perceive that only written records comprise history.

Records of relations between the United States and Indian tribes have been numerous and lengthy. The noted Record Group 75 of the National Archives includes more than 11,000 cubic feet of documents collected since 1824 when the Office of Indian Affairs opened. More than 19,000 cubic feet of financial documents from the years 1790–1921 are found under Record Group 217. There are 610 docket cases of the Indian Claims Commission in Record Group 279.

A dependence on documents eliminates other evidence, and precludes other methods and disciplines from interpreting Indian history. This singular, focused approach has produced an interpretation that hinges on the white point of view. It is not a balanced history of American Indians since it yields but one version of a history of two peoples interacting. Rather, it is an Amerocentric interpretation of Indian history, a point of view that is shared by the majority of American historians writing about the United States, Europe, diplomatic, and general history.

As historians employ the methodologies of other academic disciplines, other forms of evidence and data have emerged. For example, cultural items found underground like pieces of pottery or hunting weapons need to be considered by historians writing about tribal camp life as social history. Ceremonial items would compel historians to consider the religious views and tribal philosophies extrapolated from them.

A discussion of what is meant by American Indian history is important in determining the parameters for this essay. American Indian history is not just one history of all Indian people. Actually it is a field of many tribal histories, complicated by their relations with the United States. At this date, 547 tribes in the United States and Native Alaska communities have been federally recognized. The significance here is the importance of "relations" in Indian history. In many case, tribes that had foreign relations with European nations before the American Revolution added another level of historical relations with the United States government after. In this light, this series of relations also should include relations between tribes. Considering Indian history from this approach is primarily one of external relations, and studying the history of relations is like studying diplomatic history or foreign policy. It is from this general view of Indian history that studying the relations from a non-Indian, Amerocentric point of view places American Indians in a marginal history. This kind of myopic history is a violation of professional ethics when scholars are supposed to examine all the evidence and postulate objective analyses. To ignore such narrow interpretations is to further break ethics by choosing not to attempt to balance the historical perspectives.

American Indian history had been viewed as a minority history of less importance by frontier and Turnerian historians who viewed Indians as a part of the frontier, diplomatic historians who claim that Indians are an internal subject, and domestic historians who hid Indians in footnotes and called them "pawns" in the making of American History. Such Amerocentric blindness and academic arrogance ignores Indians, and mainstream historians have elected to exile American Indians to "disciplinary banishment." The repercussions are devastating. Each new generation of students learns a misconstrued history of the Americas. Unless critical revisionist textbooks include a more accurate accounting of the role of American Indians in the history of the Americas, Indians could one day be written out of history. In many colleges and universities, Indian history is not taught, but it is even worse when an uninformed, insensitive scholar attempts to teach Indian history. Fortunately, an estimated 250 scholars teach Indian history as a course or as a part of their course on the American West. So then, the root of bias in mainstream history must rest in the mainstream culture and its conscious and subconscious attitudes towards other peoples' histories. It is ethically wrong to use research to subvert the fair historical representation of other peoples, leaders, and non-mainstream events.

The most important ethical concern is for American Indian history to be included in the scope of the American experience, so that historians would encounter it as a part of their training in graduate school. Indian history should not be regarded as a special or exotic subfield to be pushed aside and ignored. In actuality Indian history has set the foundation of American history. For example, early white settlers adjusted to the environment in ways that Indians had done for centuries. Although the results differed, the environment has had a major influence on all peoples in America. To ignore the historical variable of environment is to view history only from a human perspective, disallowing a broader research focus that includes all factors influencing the facts as they fit together. Unfortunately American mainstream history has placed "man" above "woman" and, indeed, above all other aspects of society, culture, environment, climate, and metaphysical forces.

In brief, ethics in writing Indian history require respect for Native Americans including, preferably, visiting Indian people in their homelands. Interpreting research data and writing to take into account the Indian viewpoint is a most important ethic. After all, Native American history should focus on how and why Indians participated in the American experience. Writing Indian history respectfully also requires avoiding negative terminology such as "savage," "red skin," "Indian plight" and other pejorative names or inappropriate prose that demean Indian people. Writing proper Indian history would include avoiding suppressing Indians, or writing from an Amerocentric view. Finally, ethics would include researching and examining all kinds of evidence, including non-written data.

One significant responsibility of all scholarship is to pursue the unknown, especially as it relates to the known. Specifically, mainstream American history presents "one" perspective, which is the known. However, the known history of this particular mainstream perspective fails to challenge itself to experience the unknown or little-known history of American Indians. This narrow vision of history fails to account for the full American experience. Such mainstream myopia fails to understand the other side of historical issues, other historical figures, and Native peoples and their cultures. It is unethical for scholars to claim they are experts on American history; rather they are specialists.

American Indian communities possess internal histories of relations defined according to their separate cultures. Tribal communities are built on an infrastructure of interrelated societies and roles, such as clans, leaders, warriors, medicinal persons, and others. An important part of this network is the community's relationship with the flora, fauna, and metaphysical spirituality. This network is based on a sociocultural understanding of a religious nature. Such an understanding of the internal history of what has happened within the community remains foreign to the Amerocentric historian. This dimension of Indian history cannot be seriously studied until new tools of historical interpretation and new theories can be developed.

The situation requires a basic understanding of the internal and external histories of Native communities. This process is similar to that of using an understanding of United States domestic history and foreign relations to properly study and teach American History. Understanding both the internalness and externalness of tribal communities—even if the assignment is to study or teach the relations of that tribe at war with the United States—is critically important in presenting a balanced history. Unfortunately, this balanced history has been lacking in the practice of American Indian history.

Historians now have an opportunity to study and learn about the internal nature of Indian communities at the tribal or urban levels. This means using ethnohistory or anthropology to comprehend the cultural development of the community. In considering Indian history in this manner, it is necessary to use introspective analysis of how Indians perceive history with regard to tribal language, values, kinship relations, infrastructure, societal norms, tribal beliefs, and worldview. To further this consideration, historians must be willing to acknowledge other means of analyzing history and other sources of facts. For instance, historians will need to turn to other forms of history such as interviews and oral history.

For many years the debate against oral history has gone on despite Studs Terkel winning the Pulitzer Prize for *"The Good War": An Oral History of World War Two* in 1984. Historians must be ready to accept other kinds of history and must approach other disciplines to understand Indian history. Social and cultural history are germane as is the use of historical archaeology to restructure Indian history and understand the internalness of tribal communities. The problem for those who write about American Indians is that written sources have been produced almost exclusively by non-Indians. The alternative is to use oral history and interviews to acquire knowledge about such internal matters as kinship patterns and political organizations.

The need for ethics and responsibilities in teaching and writing American Indian history increases as more individuals pursue the subject. The significance of this dilemma is accelerated as concern about the global environment causes people to turn to tribal philosophies of environmental caretaking. This movement is evidenced in the misguided New Age movement and recent videos, documentaries, and films about American Indians [e.g., "Squanto" (1994), "Last of the Mohicans" (1993), "Lakota Woman" (1994), "Hawkeye" (1994), "The Broken Chain" (1994), and "Dances with Wolves" (1992)]. Non-Indians are increasingly listening to Indian people as a growing number of Indian communities demand input on these projects. Obtaining a tribal viewpoint, a Native feeling, and the other side of history, and then thinking like an Indian and putting yourself in that other position are mandatory for teaching and writing a balanced history of Indian-white relations.

In summary, the moral ethics of properly working in American Indian history include deliberate removal of ethnocentrism. Improper attitudes have caused scholars to write negative histories about American Indians, or to write arrogant histories in which non-Indians see themselves as superior to Indians for whatever insecure reasons. Proper attitude is ethically to subvert racist analysis and subconscious thought about Indians. Respect toward Indian people and their heritage is ethically important. The next ethical step is consideration of Indian viewpoints, while striving to think as an Indian. Disputing the imbalanced scholarship of the past about American Indians becomes a crucial part of the role of the ethical scholar. Moreover scholars must respect sensitive knowledge about tribal ways and not publish information about certain cultural rituals. The ethic of openmindedness in considering the value of disciplines other than one's own and being open to other forms of historical data is imperative to piece together a truer picture of the Indian past.

Responsibilities for American Indian history include fair treatment in the portrayal of Indians as well as other minorities within the mainstream society, and balanced treatment in the characterization of Indian males and females. Culture is an important concept in correctly addressing Native American history, as well as analyzing environmental impacts on Indian life. The scholar needs to stretch his or her imagination to ponder the depth of tribal ways and values as these influenced human behavior and history. The scholar must consider the worldview of an Indian group to comprehend its members' sense of logic and ideology. In order to accomplish this task, thinking about the "whole" of Indian life is imperative. After this step, it is essential to define the conception of reality constructed by the Indian community. Mainstream conceptions of reality such as those commonly constructed in the contemporary world cannot be used to study the past. The historian has the responsibility to understand the reality a tribe constructed to constitute its historical experiences of the physical and metaphysical as a whole.

Historians who teach and write American Indian history must examine the whole picture in studying Native American societies and cultures. Such a responsibility also involves examining Indian history from the diverse perspectives of white American views including different bureaucratic positions, missionary beliefs, and humanitarian concerns, as well as from the perspectives of the many tribes. All of these views naturally depend on the subject of study, and it bears repeating that a single Indian voice is impractical. Just as one cannot say that there is one European view, neither can one say that there is only one Indian view of history.

The historian's last responsibility in achieving a true balance is to "think like an Indian." While this may seem impractical, studying tribal cultures enables a scholar to understand individual and group behavior within the tribal community. Thinking of a synthetic physical and metaphysical reality allows the scholar to understand Indians as pro-active instead of reactive in respect to historical events. In gaining such a Native perspective it is necessary to use ethnohistorical methodologies to reconstruct history according to how tribal members remember it.

This extraordinary diversity of perspectives illuminates the sociocultural and political complexity of American Indian history from an external point of view. Combining the external perspective with an understanding of an inner perspective balances the equation, resulting in a proper study of American Indian history. Placing both perspectives within the full context of Indian life in relationship to the natural world is the ultimate goal in analyzing and writing American Indian history.

Indian Peoples and the Natural World

Asking the Right Questions

RICHARD WHITE

I

Methodology is at the heart of any historical endeavor because methodology goes directly to the most critical of historical questions: How is it that we claim to know about the past? I will make this more specific. Historians concerned with questions of Indians and the environment have made a series of sweeping claims. They have argued that many Indian peoples had, and some still have, quite distinctive ways of

---

Richard White, "Indian Peoples and the Natural World: Asking the Right Questions," in Donald L. Fixico, ed., *Rethinking American Indian History* (Albuquerque, N. Mex.: University of New Mexico Press, 1997), 87–100. Copyright © 1997. Reprinted with permission.

understanding and culturally constructing nature and that Indian actions, in fact, shaped much of the North American world that whites regarded as wilderness. How is it that they claim to know this?

In answering this question, we appeal largely to our practice. Academic historians assert knowledge of the past because they agree on a set of methods according to which claims about the past can be evaluated and judged. These methods will ideally yield general, but hardly universal, agreement among practitioners as to whether some claims are more valid or less valid than other claims. Arguably, there may be a consensus on historical methodology in general, but the environmental history of Indian peoples is another, quite separate case. Writing an environmental history of Indian peoples involves a hybrid methodology in which the methods of environmental history meet the methods of Indian history (a.k.a. ethnohistory, a.k.a. anthropological history). Ethnohistorical methods of cultural reconstruction, scientific methods of landscape reconstruction, and more conventional historical methods all overlap. The result is often dissonance and confusion.

The most basic tasks of any historical method involve asking and answering questions. In any historical methodology, historical methods are intimately related to historical questions. A methodology stipulates not only how to answer questions, but also how to ask them.

Talking about questions in the abstract is confusing, so let me provide as an illustrative text two very broad questions (hereafter Big Question One and Big Question Two) that recur both in the academic and the popular writing about the environment and Indian peoples. They will provide avenues into this methodological issue and prevent the discussion from becoming overly abstract.

First, how do we know what Indians thought in the past about what we now call nature, and what equivalent or related conceptions of the natural world might Indian peoples have had at various times in the past?

Second, how do we know how Indians acted in the past in regard to the natural world, and what were the consequences of their actions?

In answering the first of these questions historians borrow from ethnohistory; in answering the second, they borrow from environmental history and environmental sciences.

How we ask questions is particularly critical in Indian environmental history. It is a field full of pitfalls: hidden assumptions, questions that are really answers in disguise, and loose and unworkable categories. Any methodology that allows us to answer these big questions must stipulate that we ask the questions in a way that makes more than one answer possible. I will call this basic requirement of asking operational questions (that is, questions open to more than one answer) operationality.

To illustrate operationality and the dangers of bad questions, let's go back to Big Question 1.

1. How do we know about what the ancestors of the peoples we now call Indians thought in the past about what we now call nature and what conceptions of the natural world might these ancestors of Indian peoples have had at various times in the past?

This convoluted phrasing might seem to represent an excess of academic caution, the kind of thing that makes it impossible to get a straight answer out of a professor. But the construction is quite purposeful. I want to frame a question that can be answered while at the same time keeping the major concepts the question employs open to interrogation. I am trying *not* to presume too much in the question. I am, in particular, trying not to presume:

First, that there is a universal and transcendent agreement on what "nature" is and that agreement corresponds to our modern concept of nature.

Second, that modern day Indian peoples are identical with or have the same attitudes of their ancestors.

I am also trying to make clear that I *am* acting on a third assumption: that Indians are a people of history and that their beliefs can be discovered and understood through historical research.

No serious historical methodology can proceed without critically examining the concepts it is putting into play, and few terms in contemporary discourse are more contested than *nature* and *Indians.*

"The idea of nature," Raymond Williams has written, "contains, though often unnoticed, an extraordinary amount of human history." Nature, Williams emphasizes, is an idea that shifts and changes over time. What we choose to call nature is culturally and historically specific. You can touch deer, elk, or rocks, but you cannot touch nature. It is not a timeless concept floating through history. We cannot begin our search for what various Indian groups thought about nature without leaving open the possibility that they did not think about *nature* at all. Certainly, they thought about deer, rain, fog, water, corn, camas roots, and all kinds of other nonhuman objects, but they did not necessarily group them together in the category *nature.* Various Indian peoples certainly might have had equivalent concepts, but if they did, it is the historian's job to demonstrate that they did.

There is a corollary involved in leaving our terms open to inquiry; asking questions reveals that in actual practice our methods do not stand totally separate from our findings. In fact, they constantly inform each other. The framing of our questions and our methodology proceeds in conversation with our research itself.

The second term at issue here, *Indian,* is a good example of this conversation between methods and findings. Much of the older literature proceeded on the supposition that there was a rather unproblematic racial identity and common outlook attached to the word *Indian.* The very concept *Indian* went uninterrogated, and this approach has by now been so roundly attacked that I will not proceed to recount the arguments here.

But if the term *Indian* has been problematized, much popular and indeed much academic history still proceeds on the assumption that there was a coherent "Indian" attitude toward *nature.* J. Donald Hughes writes that "when one asks a traditional Indian, 'How much of the earth is sacred space?' the answer is unhesitating: 'All.'" As an illustration, he cites Chief Seattle. The easy methodological attack on Hughes is his failure to question a source, the supposed speech of Chief Seattle, that is almost certainly a fabrication. But I think the more crucial issue is the easy acceptance of the term *traditional Indian* with all its universalizing tendencies. Having accepted the idea of this pan-tribal traditional Indian, one misses all the specific false notes in Seattle's speech and hears only its resonance with our construction: the traditional Indian. We cannot move from specific studies to universal Indian beliefs. Richard Nelson, for example, although he makes methodological mistakes of his own, carefully emphasizes that he is looking at Koyukon attitudes toward nature in *Make Prayers to the Raven.* Koyukon beliefs cannot stand for the beliefs of all Native Americans regarding the natural environment.

This tendency to universalize and essentialize *Indian* can take quite specific environmental forms. Indians can be constructed, for instance, as the antithesis of history, which, in turn, is constructed as the antithesis of nature. Since a historical methodology presumes a history to study, defining Indians as outside history as we understand it creates a few problems. But according to [historian] Calvin Martin, *Indian* supposedly "subscribed to a philosophy of history, and of time, profoundly different from ours." Our history, according to Martin, ignores the "biological perspective" of Indian history.

Indians look not for history but for the "timeless wisdom of the human species, 'the phylogenetic content of human experience.'" Historians, Martin contends, "need to get out of history, as we know it, if we wish to write authentic histories of American Indians." Historical methodology, I will be the first to admit, is of very little use if one is attempting to get out of history.

I accept none of Martin's arguments or premises, but my point here is not to argue with him but, rather, to turn him to a methodological purpose. Martin's attack on history, is, in fact, itself a history, and shows the difficulties of using history to escape history. He gives a history of the invention of history. Martin finds himself relying on history itself to discredit historical consciousness.

But beyond this, Martin's history shows how not to frame historical questions. Martin phrases his questions in such a way that there can be only one answer. Martin asserts that "real Indians" do not think in linear time, never have and never will. This statement demands a history, for how could we know this is true unless we go back and examine conceptions of time among various Indian groups in the past? The question would be: Are there Indian peoples who think in terms of linear time and conceive of a linear history? For this to be an operational question, there has to be the possibility of more than one answer. But Martin structures his argument as a tautology, for his definition of an Indian is, in effect, a person descended from the original inhabitants of the Americas who does not recognize linear time. Any Indian contaminated with linear thinking is no longer a "real" Indian.

This tactic does not place Indians outside history; it places Martin outside usual historical practice. Unless a statement is posed so that it is refutable, it is not a meaningful historical question.

The first step of any historical methodology, then, is asking operational questions. Let me drive this home with one final example of a bad question: Were Indians environmentalists?

To show why this is a bad question, I'll tell you a story about a seven year old, the son of a friend of my wife. The seven year old is Puyallup; he listens to adults talk about how whites have changed Puget Sound. He thinks about it and what the world must have been like before whites came. Old ways have changed; things once permitted have been curtailed. Before whites came, he decided in the way seven years old decide such things, Indians did not have to drive on the right side of the road. They could drive their cars wherever they pleased.

But asking if Indians could drive on the wrong side of the road before whites came is not much different from asking if Indians were environmentalists. Both assume that a current set of ideas and practices can be read back into the past. A seven year old assumes there were cars, roads, drivers; those who ask if Indians were environmentalists assume there was a "nature" that corresponds to our "nature" and practices that can be evaluated according to our definitions of environmentalism. In both cases very twentieth-century practices and concepts are read back onto the past.

Posing questions is, of course, only the first step. Answering them is the trick. Since Indian peoples themselves have left us very few records, we rely largely on records produced by non-Indians and on much more recent accounts left by Indians. Now given a certain construction of Indian societies, this lack of records from the past is not really an issue. An extreme view, represented by a colleague of mine at the University of Washington, a very good ethnobotanist and anthropologist named Eugene Hunn. According to Eugene Hunn, and to paraphrase an old Who song, a good informant can see for millennia. This same practice is often asserted, at least implicitly, by the description of certain practices or beliefs as traditional. In one form this embrace of tradition is straightforward and regards the past as transparent.

This embracing of an unchanging tradition is, however, so extreme that it virtually negates history itself. It brackets off part of a culture so as to make it immune from the changes affecting everything around it. We have now a considerable literature on the syncretic [combined with new elements] nature of many "traditional" Indian beliefs. . . . [There is a] necessity of recognizing the long time that whites and Indians have been in contact and in conversation. There are numerous outside influences on modern Indian beliefs and abundant evidence that they change over time.

Much more common is a second methodological technique: upstreaming, which is connected with the work of William Fenton. Upstreaming starts from a plausible premise. Current cultural formulations about things such as nature have not been formed from whole cloth. Basic cultural patterns remain constant over long periods of time. They have a history. Therefore we can, in effect, disaggregate current customs, beliefs, and practices and look for replicas in the past. So far so good. When reliable sources at both ends of the time span describe similar practices, we can supposedly use safely more abundant modern information to fill in what we do not know about ancient beliefs and practice.

There are two problems here. First, it assumes that the social group in question (the tribe, or nation) has remained relatively constant. Second, it assumes that if rituals or practices exist across time then the meaning and significance of these practices also exists relatively unchanged across time. Both are problematic.

We cannot assume obvious connections between modern Indian groups and historic groups bearing the same names. Historians have sometimes presumed that any Indian group and its cultural practices could potentially be traced back to an ancestral group living before European contact. Recent work, however, has convincingly demonstrated that many tribes are very much historic creations. They did not exist before contact any more than the modern category *Americans* existed before contact. James Merrell's work on the Catawbas and J. Leitch Wright's history of the Muscogolees are two prominent examples.

But the main problem with upstreaming is that similar words, customs, and practices can hold radically different meanings at various points in time. There is much, for example, that is constant in a Catholic mass, but few historians would argue that we could therefore take the beliefs of modern Catholicism and fix them on medieval Catholicism. We do not attempt to do so because we have abundant sources on medieval Catholicism that both show us that this is not true and make it unnecessary to do so. We, however, lack such sources for many Indian peoples, and so upstreaming has considerable appeal. We would be wise to resist the temptation as much as possible.

I think the basic technique in reconstructing older worlds has to remain very close to traditional historical practice: close reading, evaluation, and contextualization of the records. Our basic rule is to know what they are, why they were produced, when they were produced, and what they represent.

Much of what we then do is a kind of literary analysis, but with a difference. History is an act of interpretation; it is, among other things, a reading and re-reading of documents. Ideally, our methods are always comparative. We compare documents; we read them against each other. We order them chronologically. Deconstruction [a method of literary analysis] is, in a sense, what historians have done for a considerable time. We look for assumptions; hidden threads of connections; we probe for absences.

But in Indian history at the earliest stages we are dealing with an imperial history whose documents are not produced by Indians and which both record the reduction of Indians to a European order and understanding and are one of the means of their reduction. Those documents rarely contain Indian writing, but they often contain Indian voices, or what purport to be Indian voices. We need, of course, to be sure that the voices speaking are, in fact, Indian. Whites often speak through Indians, particularly when Indians speak of nature. From the Adario of the Baron de Lahotan to Seattle's speech, to modern books like the *Daughters of Copper Woman,* we have had a whole array of fake Indian voices as well as the mixed Indian/white voice of classic accounts such as Black Elk.

The lack of "Indian" sources might seem on first glance a debilitating liability, but it can in certain circumstances be a singular advantage. Many of the Indian voices that survive in the earliest and most problematic documents are talking to outsiders in circumstances in which both they and their listeners needed to reach a common understanding. They are engaged in a language that creates what I have elsewhere described as the middle ground.

A large chunk of our early documents, then, are conversations between people who do not completely understand each other. Methodologically this has implications. "To know a culture," Greg Deming has written, "is to know its system of expressed meanings. To know cultures in contact is to know the misreadings of meaning." We are connoisseurs of misreadings. We rarely know Indians alone; we always know them in conversation with whites. During early contact situations we never get transparent accounts that allow us to peer into a world of Indian meanings. We get mutual misreadings which often become a new common reading: a middle ground.

My own operating assumption is that we will never recover a pure Indian past, a purely Indian view of the natural world as it existed before whites, because we are prisoners of the documents. What we have is mixture, impurity, and dirtiness. To seek purity is to create falsity. In Greg Deming's metaphor, this kind of ethnohistorical construction is a history of beaches. We know little of the islands that lie beyond.

But to be trapped on the beach does not mean that we might not at least look into the interior. We have limited lines of sight into the islands. We have what archaeology gives us, but archaeology's ability to recreate worlds of meaning is very limited. A second line of sight comes through language. A third comes through what we might call spatial histories.

Historians have done very little with language because so few historians know any native languages. Our argument has been that there are no, or very few, documents in the language and very often no or very few native speakers are left, so what is the point of learning it? To this, we quite legitimately add a third objection: languages change like everything else. The language recorded at a given point is not necessarily the historical language.

All that is true, but languages usually change relatively slowly. Preserved in the language are conceptual frameworks, categorizations of the world that structure how a speaker perceives and organizes the world. In them are potential insights into worlds we do not know, but to follow them we need linguistic skills that most historians do not possess.

The Lushootseed language of southern Puget Sound, for instance, is now nearly extinct, but in it are clues to a way of viewing and understanding the world. There are native words that serve as straight equivalents for English words, words for porpoise, various varieties of salmon, bullheads, candlefish, and so on, but more revealing are words without direct equivalents. There are words for old salmon that has already spawned and is about to die and what fish in general are called after spawning. There are classifications such as *tataculbix*—large animals—which refer not only to size but to use: large animals are food for the people.

Language connects with a second way of recovering an Indian view of the world that moves behind the documents. Spatial history concerns the movement of people across the land. Metaphorically, Europeans remained on beaches, but in actuality they moved inland. Their records of travel become sources for a spatial history which is not a history of what they discovered, what they believed was already constituted, but instead a history of their movements themselves, of why they went where they did, of how and why they created boundaries. They turned space into place. They constituted a world and as they did so they often revealed another world, another possible organization of space that they were in the process of either destroying or covering over. Where they found Indians, where Indians sought to block their path or steer them, the places Indians had named and occupied before them all emerge in their travelings and can become the stuff of a spatial history critical to environmental history, which always has to be located in space.

Court cases filed by the Hopi and Zuni have provided abundant materials for spatial histories, but as an example of different conceptions of the world that can be partially retrieved let me again turn to Lushootseed. There was in the late nineteenth century a long battle over the name of Mount Rainier. Seattle wanted Mount Rainier; Tacoma wanted, not surprisingly, Tacoma, which was derived from the Lushootseed *teqʷube? Teqʷube?* is usually translated as "permanently snow covered mountain," and it refers actually to all mountains that have this character. Mount Rainier was just the supreme exemplar of a type. But the derivation of the name seems to come from words meaning literally "mountain bearing water." But what does it mean to be a mountain bearing water? A source of rivers? Glaciers? There seems to be a spatial relation here, a history, which sets the landscape in motion. Around such questions can come recovery over an older categorization of the world. . . .

II

The second Big Question—How do we know how Indians acted in the past in regard to the natural world and what the consequences of their actions were?—carries into another set of methodological dilemmas. This question involves correlating what the landscape looked like with descriptions of Indian action. Our descriptions of both actions and landscape are partial, fragmentary, and not completely reliable. Methodologically, this is actually quite comforting. It is the kind of problem historians routinely confront. But historians, in working with this material, do not work alone. Much environmental history is interdisciplinary in the sense that historians use the findings and raw data, and much less often the methods, of other disciplines. Other scholars, in turn, use the data and findings of environmental historians. They misuse our data; we misuse theirs.

Most historians recognize the fragmentary and complicated nature of evidence. We do not treat what survives from the past as if it were in any way a random or scientific sample of documents, let alone that those documents preserve some representative random slice of human behavior. Some scientists in using historical evidence, however, sometimes treat this evidence as if it were, indeed, a random sample of Indian actions. Emily Russell, an ecologist, has, for example, made an argument for a limited Indian use of fire in the sixteenth and seventeenth centuries on the basis of European accounts reporting Indian use of fire. Essentially, she evaluated sources mentioning fire as if they were a sample of Indian activities. Specific mentions of Indian burning were few; therefore, Indian burning was rare. This, of course, does not follow, but it raises an interesting issue. How do we know that Indians all across the continent burned the woods or grasslands regularly if this is not something we can easily demonstrate from the records alone?

To make the case, historians borrow from ecological studies and risk misusing ecologist's sources just as they sometimes misuse ours. We want to determine, if possible, what a landscape that was burned regularly might look like and, if it is possible to determine, whether natural fires alone might produce such a landscape. If, in fact, we find that the landscape described at contact gives signs of regular burning, and we can determine the approximate rate at which natural fires occur, and we have accounts of Indian-set fires, then we can begin to make better claims for Indian actions. If, for example, natural fires are rare but we have accounts of vegetation that thrives in frequently burned landscapes and we have even scattered accounts of Indian burning, then we can suggest that we are seeing a pyrogenic landscape.

There is a second technique. If we can determine when Indian-set fires were eliminated and trace the results of this fire suppression, then we can reason that at least part of the earlier landscape may very well have been the result of Indian burning. To do this, historians need to use specialized studies that include examination of fire scarring, dendrochronology, and repeat photography. All of these methods appear in the literature. We are methodological parasites. Our conclusions depend on feeding off the work of others.

There is a danger involved in this kind of parasitism and historians have already encountered it. We become prisoners of the conceptual framework of those outside our discipline and when their work changes or falls apart, so does ours. A crisis in ecology has had profound effects on environmental history. I will use myself as an example.

In 1980 I published a revised version of my doctoral dissertation with a rather turgid title that I have never been allowed to live down: *Land Use, Environmental and Social Change: The Shaping of Island County, Washington.* The early chapters concern the landscape Indian peoples created in Island Country and how it changed with white settlement. In the book, I used ecological concepts like community, succession, climax, and ecosystem unproblematically, as if they were scientific descriptions of actual things or events in nature. I did this even though within the discipline of ecology, these ideas had already come under attack. Looking back now, I realize that this book and other historical studies were themselves undermining such ecological concepts even as they relied on them. Historians were describing a human impact upon the natural world—including an Indian impact—so pervasive that it made questions of climax and successions seem abstractions with few equivalents in the actual landscape. The very scope of the changes that I described in the book should have made me more suspicious of what I mistook for unquestioned orthodoxy. Like most scholars, however, I was more polite and less belligerent when intruding upon disciplines other than my own.

Any intersection of the methods of different disciplines is fraught with danger. But there are also considerable opportunities. Historical studies have had a significant impact on ecological studies. Ecologists who once assumed little or limited human impact on environments before the introduction of European agriculture now are much more aware of a wide range of Indian activities from burning to grazing of domestic livestock, to farming. But at the same time the insistence of historians on these activities has undermined their own easy reliance on a methodology borrowed from an old and now obsolete ecology, and has forced them to pay more attention to newer ecological constructions in which stability plays little part and contingency is as prevalent as in history. Historians have to be aware of such changes. Historians of Indian peoples are not ecologists, but ecological studies become one of our major sources in reconstructing Indian actions.

This essay is not intended to be a mere listing of ways that historians reconstruct landscapes and surmise Indian actions, but instead to stress that the techniques for recovering these landscapes, which include dendrochronology, pollen studies, repeat photography, GIS mapping, and numerous techniques that are being developed almost constantly, become a critical part of the methodological tool kit.

This methodological tool kit is inherently unstable. Developing a historical methodology, particularly in an interdisciplinary field, means constant attention to what you are doing and what those in the fields you plunder are doing. Not only do your own findings, and those of your colleagues, influence your methods, but the basic concepts that underlie methods you borrow from other fields can be about as stable as California. Intellectual earthquakes, fires, storms, and landslides can send structures you think secure tumbling down. If interdisciplinary history is not going to be one field borrowing the mistakes of another, we need to be constantly aware of other disciplines. What seems certain is that the methodologies we learn in graduate school will not be the methodologies at the end of our own practice as historians.

◈ *F U R T H E R   R E A D I N G*

Woodrow W. Borah and Sherburne F. Cook, *Essays in Population History,* 3 vols. (1971–1983)

Jennifer S. H. Brown and Elizabeth Vibert, eds., *Reading Beyond Words: Contexts for Native History* (1996)

Donald L. Fixico, ed., *Rethinking American Indian History* (1997)

Guy E. Gibbon, ed., *The Archaeology of Prehistoric Native America: An Encyclopedia* (1998)

Laurence M. Hauptman, *Tribes and Tribulations: Misconceptions About American Indians and Their Histories* (1995)

Frederick E. Hoxie, ed., *Encyclopedia of North American Indians* (1996)

Frederick E. Hoxie and Peter Iverson, eds., *Indians in American History: An Introduction* (1998)

Wilbur Jacobs, *The Fatal Confrontation: Historical Studies of Indians, Environment, and Historians* (1996)

Shepard Krech III, "The State of Ethnohistory," *Annual Review of Anthropology* 20 (1991), 345–375.·

Calvin Martin, ed., *The American Indian and the Problem of History* (1987)

————, *In the Spirit of the Earth: Rethinking History and Time* (1992)

————, *The Way of the Human Being* (1999)

Laura F. Klein and Lillian A. Ackerman, eds., *Woman and Power in Native North America* (1995)

Devon A. Mihesuah, ed., *Natives and Academics: Researching and Writing About American Indians* (1998)

Donald L. Parman and Catherine Price, "A 'Work in Progress': The Emergence of Indian History as a Professional Field," *Western Historical Quarterly* 20 (1989): 185–196

Daniel K. Richter, "Whose Indian History?" *The William and Mary Quarterly* 50 (April 1993), 379–393

Thomas E. Sheridan, "How to Tell the Story of a 'People without History,'" *Journal of the Southwest* 30 (1988): 168–189

William C. Sturtevant, ed., *Handbook of North American Indians,* 20 vols. (1978–)

Russell Thornton, *American Indian Holocaust and Survival: A Population History Since 1492* (1987)

John W. Verano and Douglas H. Ubelaker, eds., *Disease and Demography in the Americas* (1992)

Indian History
Before Columbus

◈

*The ancestors of the American Indians had lived in the Americas for tens of thou-
sands of years before Columbus and other Europeans arrived in the hemisphere,
but only the barest outlines of their past are known, and much of it is in dispute.
While some Indian tribes recorded important events with pictures—rock paintings,
petroglyphs, and drawings—they did not have a written language based on an
alphabet. Nevertheless, all tribespeople had an interest in their past and recounted
the important events of their history in stories that were handed down from generation to generation. These oral accounts do not amount to a complete verbal record
of the pre-Columbian past, but they do convey a sense of Indian history before
1492. Indian oral history also confirms that there was not one unified Indian history, but many individual tribal histories—a reflection of Indian social, linguistic,
and cultural diversity that survives to the present day.*

*To Indian oral accounts we may add the archaeological record. Archaeologists
disagree over the date of the first human arrival in America, and some argue that
people may have come here as early as fifty thousand years ago. Today, most
archaeologists believe that the ancestors of today's Indians came to America from
Asia by way of a land bridge that connected the continents from fifteen to thirty-five
thousand years ago, when glaciers locked up enough of the world's water to lower the
level of the sea. The first Indians hunted big game—wooly mammoths, giant bison,
camels, and the like—that died out when the climate became drier and warmer about
eight thousand years ago. These new conditions obliged Indians to embrace a way of
life based on wild plant foods and small game. More than two thousand years ago
the Indians in the Southwest—some of them ancestors of today's Pueblo Indians—
cultivated maize, beans, and squash. These people built impressive stone and adobe
towns that still exist. Likewise, Indians along the Mississippi River took up farming
and built huge earthen mounds that continue to inspire wonder in the Midwest.
Elsewhere, many Indians came to rely on agriculture, as well as wild plants, game,
and fish. Along with these adaptations to local environmental conditions, there grew
a rich cultural diversity. Hundreds of different languages and tribes as well as scores
of cultures covered the human landscape of North America when Columbus sailed
into view. Recent estimates of the pre-Columbian Indian population range from seven
to eighteen million people north of Mexico, though some scholars continue to argue*

for much smaller numbers. While much is still in doubt, students should understand that millions of Indians lived in today's United States and Canada in 1492, and that they had an American history that stretched back for more than ten thousand years. Truly, the American continent is the native land of the American Indians.

◈ D O C U M E N T S

The documents in this section present diverse native traditions about their origins and relationship to the lands that they call home. In Document 1, the Tewa-speakers (one of the languages of the Rio Grande Pueblos) convey their sense of love and attachment to the land in their beautiful "Song of the Sky Loom." Document 2 is a Maidu account of the creation of the world and its inhabitants. These California people believe that Earth-maker created dry land from soil that he scraped from underneath the nails of Turtle, who dove deep beneath the sea to find this vital substance. Document 3 presents the Skagit version of world creation. Here, we see that the earth is a transitory place and that periodic changes are to be expected. In Document 4, animals helped Mother-Corn to dig the ancestors of the Arikaras out of the ground. Accordingly, the Arikaras regard themselves as part of the earth. We see in Document 5 that the Cayugas of the great Iroquois confederacy thought that animals helped to create the world, thus demonstrating a sense of cooperation and complementarity between humans and animals that is pervasive in Indian thought.

Together, these documents provide a window through which to view the Indian world as they conceived of it before the arrival of Europeans. They did not see with one pair of eyes or come equipped with a single set of ideas about their origins, history, or their connection with the earth. The tribes of America comprised many nations, each with its own homeland, each with a particular view of the world that sometimes conflicted with those of its neighbors. How, one wonders, did diversity affect the Indians' ability to contend with European newcomers?

1. A Pueblo Song of the Sky Loom, n. d.

Oh our Mother the Earth oh our Father the Sky
Your children are we
   with tired backs we bring you the gifts you love

So weave for us a garment of brightness

May the warp be the white light of morning
May the weft be the red light of evening
May the fringes be the falling rain
May the border be the standing rainbow

Weave for us this bright garment
that we may walk where birds sing
   where grass is green

Oh our Mother the Earth oh our Father the Sky

"Song of the Sky Loom," in William Brandon, *The Magic World: American Indian Songs and Poems* (New York: William Morrow, 1971), 49. Reprinted with the permission of Ohio University Press/Swallow Press, Athens, Ohio.

2. Maidu Account of the Beginning of the World, n. d.

All the earth was covered with water, and everything was dark in the beginning. There was no sun, no moon, no stars. Then one day a raft appeared, floating on the water. In it was Turtle. Down from the sky a rope of feathers came and dangled near the bow of the raft, and then a being, who shone like the sun, descended. He was Earth Initiate. When he reached the end of the rope he tied it to the bow of the raft, and stepped in. His face was covered, so that Turtle was not able to see it. In fact, no one has ever seen his face uncovered. Earth Initiate sat down and for a long time said nothing.

"Where do you come from?" Turtle asked at last.

"I come from above," Earth Initiate said.

Then Turtle asked: "Brother, can you not make for me some good dry land, so that I may sometimes come up out of the water?"

Earth Initiate did not answer at once, and Turtle asked, "Are there going to be any people in the world?"

After thinking for a while, Earth Initiate said, "Yes."

"How long before you are going to make people?" Turtle asked.

"I don't know," Earth Initiate answered. "You want to have some dry land: well, how am I going to get any earth to make it of?"

"If you will tie a stone about my left arm I will dive for some," Turtle answered.

So Earth Initiate did as Turtle asked. Reaching around he took the end of a rope from somewhere and tied it to Turtle.

"If the rope is not long enough I will jerk it once, and then you must haul me up; if it is long enough I will give two jerks and then you must pull me quickly, as I shall have all the earth that I can carry."

Turtle was gone for six years, and when he came up he was covered with green slime, he had been down so long. He returned with only a very little earth under his nails. The rest had all washed away.

Earth Initiate scraped the earth out from under Turtle's nails, and put it in the palm of his hand and rolled it about until it was round and about the size of a small pebble. This he laid on the stern of the raft, and went away and left it. Three times he returned to look at it, and the third time found that it had grown very large. The fourth time he looked at it it was as big as the world, the raft was on ground, and all around were mountains.

When Turtle knew the raft was on ground, he said: "I cannot stay in the dark all the time. Can't you make a light so that I can see?"

"Let's get out of the raft, and then we will see what we can do," Earth Initiate replied.

As they got out Earth Initiate said: "Look that way, to the east! I am going to tell my sister to come up."

"The Beginning of the World," in Edward W. Gifford and Gwendoline Harris Block, eds., *California Indian Nights* (1930; reprint, Lincoln, Nebr.: University of Nebraska Press, 1990), 85–88. Reprinted by permission of the University of Nebraska Press. Copyright © 1930 by the Arthur H. Clark Company. Renewal copyright © 1958 by the Arthur H. Clark Company.

Then it began to grow light, and day began to break, and the sun came up.

"Which way is the sun going to travel?" Turtle asked.

"I will tell her to go this way, and go down there," Earth Initiate answered.

After the sun went down it grew very dark.

"I will tell my brother to come up," said Earth Initiate.

Then the moon rose.

"How do you like it?" Earth Initiate asked Turtle.

"It is very good," Turtle answered. "Is that all you are going to do for us?"

"No, I am going to do more yet."

Then he called the stars each by name and they came out.

Then he made a tree, which had twelve different kinds of acorns growing on it. . . . For two days they sat under this tree, and then both set off to see the world which Earth Initiate had made. Turtle was not able to keep up with Earth Initiate. All he could see of him was a ball of fire flashing about under the ground and the water. When they returned from going around the world Earth Initiate called the birds from the air, and made the trees, and then the animals.

Some time after this he said: "I am going to make people."

So he took dark red earth and mixed it with water, and made two figures, one a man and one a woman. He lay down and placed the man on his right side and the woman on his left. Thus he lay all afternoon and night. Early in the morning the woman began to tickle him in the side. Earth Initiate kept very, very still and did not laugh. Soon after he got up, he put a piece of wood into the ground, and fire burst out.

The two people Earth Initiate made were very white. Their eyes were pink, their hair was black, their teeth shone brightly, and they were very handsome. He named the man Kuksu, and the woman Morning Star Woman. . . .

3. A Skagit Belief About the Origins of the World, n. d.

In the beginning, Raven and Mink and Coyote helped the Creator plan the world. They were in on all the arguments. They helped the Creator decide to have all the rivers flow only one way; they first thought that the water should flow up one side of the river and down on the other. They decided that there should be bends in the rivers, so that there would be eddies where the fish could stop and rest. They decided that beasts should be placed in the forests. Human beings would have to keep out of their way.

Human beings will not live on this earth forever, agreed Raven and Mink, Coyote, and Old Creator. They will stay only for a short time. Then the body will go back to the earth and the spirit back to the spirit world. All living things, they said, will be male and female—animals and plants, fish and birds. And everything will get its food from the earth, the soil.

"The Beginning of the Skagit World," in Ella E. Clark, ed., *Indian Legends of the Pacific Northwest* (Berkeley: University of California Press, 1953), 138–141. Copyright © 1953 The Regents of the University of California; © renewed 1981 Ella E. Clark. Reprinted with permission.

The Creator gave four names for the earth. He said that only a few people should know the names; those few should have special preparation for that knowledge, to receive that special spirit power. If many people should know the names, the world would change too soon and too suddenly. One of the names is for the sun, which rises in the east and brings warmth and light. Another is for the rivers, streams, and salt water. The third is for the soil; our bodies go back to it. The fourth is for the forest; the forest is older than human beings, and is for everyone on the earth.

After the world had been created for a while, everyone learned the four names for the earth. Everyone and everything spoke the Skagit language. When the people began to talk to the trees, then the change came. The change was a flood. Water covered everything but two high mountains—Kobah and Takobah. Those two mountains—Mount Baker and Mount Rainier—did not go under.

When the people saw the flood coming, they made a great big canoe. They loaded it with two of everything living on earth, with the male and female of every animal and plant. When the flood was over, the canoe landed on the prairie in the Skagit country. Five people were in the canoe. After the flood, when the land was dry again, they made their way back here.

A child was born to the man and his wife who had been in the canoe. He became Doquebuth, the new Creator. He created after the flood, after the world changed.

When he was old enough, Doquebuth was told to go to the lake—Lake Campbell it is called now—to swim and fast and get his spirit power. But the boy played around and did not obey orders. Coyote fed him, and the boy did not try to get his spirit power. So his family deserted him. When he came home, no one was there. His family had gone and had taken everything with them except what belonged to the boy. They left his dog behind and the hides of the chipmunks and squirrels the boy had shot when hunting. His grandmother left fire for him in a clamshell. From the skins which he had dried, the boy made a blanket.

When he found that his family had deserted him, he realized that he had done wrong. So he began to swim and to fast. For many, many days he swam and fasted. No one can get spirit power unless he is clean and unless his stomach is empty.

One day the boy dreamed that Old Creator came.

"Take my blanket," said Old Creator. "It is the blanket of the whole earth. Wave it over the waters, and name the four names of the earth. Then there will be food for everyone."

That is how the boy got his spirit power from Old Creator. He waved the blanket over the water and over the forest. Then there was food for everyone. But there were no people yet. The boy swam some more and kept on fasting.

Old Creator came to him again in a dream.

"Gather together all the bones of the people who lived here before the flood. Gather the bones and pile them into a big pile. Then wave my blanket over them, and name the four names of the earth."

The young man did as he was told in his dream, and people were created from the bones. But they could not talk. They moved about but were not quite completed.

The young Creator swam some more. A third time Old Creator came to him in a dream. This time he told the young man that he should make brains for the new people. So he waved the blanket over the earth and named the four names of the earth. That is how brains were made—from the soil of the earth.

Then the people could talk. They spoke many different languages. But where they should live the young Creator did not know. So he swam some more. In his dream, Old Creator told him to stop over the big island, from ocean to ocean, and blow the people back where they belonged. So Doquebuth blew the people back to the place where they had lived before the flood. Some he placed in the buffalo country, some by the salt water, some by fresh water, some in the forests. That is why the people in the different places speak different languages.

The people created after the flood prophesied that a new language would be introduced into our country. It will be the only language spoken, when the next change comes. When we can understand animals, we will know that the change is halfway. When we can talk to the forest, we will know that the change has come.

The flood was one change. Another is yet to come. The world will change again. When it will change, we do not know.

4. The Arikaras Describe Their Origins, n. d.

A long time ago, the Arikara lived under the ground. There were four animals who looked with pity upon the people, and these animals agreed to take the people up on top of the earth. These animals were the long-nosed Mouse, the Mole, the Badger, and the Fox. The Fox was the messenger to the people to tell them of what the animals were doing. The Mole was the first to dig. He ran back, for he was blinded by the brightness of the sun. The animals went out. The people came out of the earth, the Fox being in the lead. As the people were coming out there was an earthquake. The Arikara came out. The other people were again held fast by the earth.

These people who came out from the ground then journeyed west. They came to a place where the earth shook, so that there was a chasm or a steep bank. The people waited and cried. The Badger stepped forward and began digging, so that it made a pathway for the people. . . . After all the people had passed the first obstacles they sat down and gave thanks and made offerings to the gods.

Again they went upon their journey, and it stormed. In front of them was a river. They could not cross it, for it was very deep; but a Loon was sent by the gods. The Loon came to the people, and said: "Your mother is traveling in the heavens to help you. I was sent by the gods to open up this river, so you could cross and go on your journey." The Loon flew across the river, flew back, then dived and came out on the other side of the river. The river was opened; it banked up on each side; the people crossed over and the waters came together again. Some people were left on the other side.

Again they journeyed, and they came to a place where Mother-Corn stopped and said: "The big Black-Wind is angry, for we did not ask it to come with us, neither did we make it one of the gods to receive smoke. But," said Mother-Corn, "the Black-Meteoric-Star understands this storm; it will help us." Mother-Corn went on, and said: "Here we are. We must hurry for the big Black-Wind is coming, taking everything it meets. There is a cedar tree. Get under that cedar tree. Get under

"The Origin of the Arikara," in George A. Dorsey, ed., *Traditions of the Arikara* (Washington, D.C., 1904).

that cedar tree," said Mother-Corn. "The Black-Meteoric-Star placed it there. The Star stands solid, for its right leg is cedar; its left leg is stone. It can not be blown away. Get under its branches." So the people crawled under its branches. The Black-Wind came and took many people, notwithstanding.

The people came out, and they went on. They came to another difficulty—a steep mountain bank, and they stopped. The Bear came forth, and said, "I will go through this place first." So the Bear went to digging steps for the people. Steps were made on both sides and the people went across.

After they had been gone for some time, a Dog came up, and said: "Why did you people leave me behind? I shall be the one that you shall kill, and my meat shall be offered to the gods. I shall also fix it so that all animals shall make great medicine-men of you. My father is the Sun. He has given me all this power. I will give my power to all animals, then I will stay with the people, so they will not forget my promise to them." The people were thankful to the Dog.

5. The Iroquois Depict the World on the Turtle's Back, n. d.

In the beginning there was no world, no land, no creatures of the kind that are around us now, and there were no men. But there was a great ocean which occupied space as far as anyone could see. Above the ocean was a great void of air. And in the air there lived the birds of the sea; in the ocean lived the fish and the creatures of the deep. Far above this unpeopled world, there was a Sky-World. Here lived gods who were like people—like Iroquois.

In the Sky-World there was a man who had a wife, and the wife was expecting a child. The woman became hungry for all kinds of strange delicacies, as women do when they are with child. She kept her husband busy almost to distraction finding delicious things for her to eat.

In the middle of the Sky-World there grew a Great Tree which was not like any of the trees that we know. It was tremendous; it had grown there forever. It had enormous roots that spread out from the floor of the Sky-World. And on its branches there were many different kinds of leaves and different kinds of fruits and flowers. The tree was not supposed to be marked or mutilated by any of the beings who dwelt in the Sky-World. It was a sacred tree that stood at the center of the universe.

The woman decided that she wanted some bark from one of the roots of the Great Tree—perhaps as a food or as a medicine, we don't know. She told her husband this. He didn't like the idea. He knew it was wrong. But she insisted, and he gave in. So he dug a hole among the roots of this great sky tree, and he bared some of its roots. But the floor of the Sky-World wasn't very thick, and he broke a hole through it. He was terrified, for he had never expected to find empty space underneath the world.

But his wife was filled with curiosity. He wouldn't get any of the roots for her, so she set out to do it herself. She bent over and she looked down, and she saw the ocean far below. She leaned down and stuck her head through the hole and looked all around. No one knows just what happened next. Some say she slipped. Some say that her husband, fed up with all the demands she had made on him, pushed her.

So she fell through the hole. As she fell, she frantically grabbed at its edges, but her hands slipped. However, between her fingers there clung bits of things that were growing on the floor of the Sky-World and bits of the root tips of the Great Tree. And so she began to fall toward the great ocean far below.

The birds of the sea saw the woman falling, and they immediately consulted with each other as to what they could do to help her. Flying wingtip to wingtip they made a great feathery raft in the sky to support her, and thus they broke her fall. But of course it was not possible for them to carry the woman very long. Some of the other birds of the sky flew down to the surface of the ocean and called up the ocean creatures to see what they could do to help. The great sea turtle came and agreed to receive her on his back. The birds placed her gently on the shell of the turtle, and now the turtle floated about on the huge ocean with the woman safely on his back.

The beings up in the Sky-World paid no attention to this. They knew what was happening, but they chose to ignore it.

When the woman recovered from her shock and terror, she looked around her. All that she could see were the birds and the sea creatures and the sky and the ocean.

And the woman said to herself that she would die. But the creatures of the sea came to her and said that they would try to help her and asked her what they could do. She told them that if they could get some soil, she could plant the roots stuck between her fingers, and from them plants would grow. The sea animals said perhaps there was dirt at the bottom of the ocean, but no one had ever been down there so they could not be sure.

If there was dirt at the bottom of the ocean, it was far, far below the surface in the cold deeps. But the animals said they would try to get some. One by one the diving birds and animals tried and failed. They went to the limits of their endurance, but they could not get to the bottom of the ocean. Finally, the muskrat said he would try. He dived and disappeared. All the creatures waited, holding their breath, but he did not return. After a long time, this little body floated up to the surface of the ocean, a tiny crumb of earth clutched in his paw. He seemed to be dead. They pulled him up on the turtle's back and they sang and prayed over him and breathed air into his mouth, and finally, he stirred. Thus it was the muskrat, the Earth-Diver, who brought from the bottom of the ocean the soil from which the earth was to grow.

The woman took the tiny clod of dirt and placed it on the middle of the great sea turtle's back. Then the woman began to walk in a circle around it, moving in the direction that the sun goes. The earth began to grow. When the earth was big enough, she planted the roots she had clutched between her fingers when she fell from the Sky-World. Thus the plants grew on the earth.

To keep the earth growing, the woman walked as the sun goes, moving in the direction that the people still move in the dance rituals. She gathered roots and plants to eat and built herself a little hut. After a while, the woman's time came, and she was delivered of a daughter. The woman and her daughter kept walking in a circle around the earth, so that the earth and plants would continue to grow. They lived on the plants and roots they gathered. The girl grew up with her mother, cut off forever from the Sky-World above, knowing only the birds and the creatures of the sea, seeing no other beings like herself.

One day, when the girl had grown to womanhood, a man appeared. No one knows for sure who this man was. He had something to do with the gods above. Perhaps he was the West Wind. As the girl looked at him, she was filled with terror, and amazement, and warmth, and she fainted dead away. As she lay on the ground, the man reached into his quiver, and he took out two arrows, one sharp and one blunt, and he laid them across the body of the girl, and quietly went away.

When the girl awoke from her faint, she and her mother continued to walk around the earth. After a while, they knew that the girl was to bear a child. They did not know it, but the girl was to bear twins.

Within the girl's body, the twins began to argue and quarrel with one another. There could be no peace between them. As the time approached for them to be born, the twins fought about their birth. The right-handed twin wanted to be born in the normal way, as all children are born. But the left-handed twin said no. He said he saw light in another direction, and said he would be born that way. The right-handed twin beseeched him not to, saying that he would kill their mother. But the left-handed twin was stubborn. He went in the direction where he saw light. But he could not be born through his mother's mouth or her nose. He was born through her left armpit, and killed her. And meanwhile, the right-handed twin was born in the normal way, as all children are born.

The twins met in the world outside, and the right-handed twin accused his brother of murdering their mother. But the grandmother told them to stop their quarreling. They buried their mother. And from her grave grew the plants which the people still use. From her head grew the corn, the beans, and the squash—"our supporters, the three sisters." And from her heart grew the sacred tobacco, which the people still use in the ceremonies and by whose upward-floating smoke they send thanks. The women call her "our mother," and they dance and sing in the rituals so that the corn, the beans, and the squash may grow to feed the people.

But the conflict of the twins did not end at the grave of their mother. And, strangely enough, the grandmother favored the left-handed twin.

The right-handed twin was angry, and he grew more angry as he thought how his brother had killed their mother. The right-handed twin was the one who did everything just as he should. He said what he meant, and he meant what he said. He always told the truth, and he always tried to accomplish what seemed to be right and reasonable. The left-handed twin never said what he meant or meant what he said. He always lied, and he always did things backward. You could never tell what he was trying to do because he always made it look as if he were doing the opposite. He was the devious one.

These two brothers, as they grew up, represented two ways of the world which are in all people. The Indians did not call these the right and the wrong. They called them the straight mind and the crooked mind, the upright man and the devious man, the right and the left.

The twins had creative powers. They took clay and modeled it into animals, and they gave these animals life. And in this they contended with one another. The right-handed twin made the deer, and the left-handed twin made the mountain lion which kills the deer. But the right-handed twin knew there would always be more deer than mountain lions. And he made another animal. He made the ground squirrel. The left-handed twin saw that the mountain lion could not get to the ground squirrel, who digs a hole, so he made the weasel. And although the weasel can go into the ground squirrel's hole and kill him, there are lots of ground squirrels and not so many weasels. Next the right-handed twin decided he would make an animal that the weasel could not kill, so he made the porcupine. But the left-handed twin made the bear, who flips the porcupine over on his back and tears out his belly.

And the right-handed twin made berries and fruits of other kinds for his creatures to live on. The left-handed twin made briars and poison ivy, and the poisonous plants like the baneberry and the dogberry, and the suicide root with which people kill themselves when they go out of their minds. And the left-handed twin made medicines, for good and for evil, for doctoring and for witchcraft.

And finally, the right-handed twin made man. The people do not know just how much the left-handed twin had to do with making man. Man was made of clay, like pottery, and baked in the fire.

The world the twins made was a balanced and orderly world, and this was good. The plant-eating animals created by the right-handed twin would eat up all the vegetation if their number was not kept down by the meat-eating animals which the left-handed twin created. But if these carnivorous animals ate too many other animals, then they would starve, for they would run out of meat. So the right- and the left-handed twins built balance into the world.

As the twins became men full grown, they still contested with one another. No one had won, and no one had lost. And they knew that the conflict was becoming sharper and sharper and one of them would have to vanquish the other.

And so they came to the duel. They started with gambling. They took a wooden bowl, and in it they put wild plum pits. One side of the pits was burned black, and by tossing the pits in the bowl, and betting on how these would fall, they gambled against one another, as the people still do in the New Year's rites. All through the morning they gambled at this game, and all through the afternoon, and the sun went down. And when the sun went down, the game was done, and neither one had won.

So they went on to battle one another at the lacrosse game. And they contested all day, and the sun went down, and the game was done. And neither had won.

And now they battled with clubs, and they fought all day, and the sun went down, and the fight was done. But neither had won.

And they went from one duel to another to see which one would succumb. Each one knew in his deepest mind that there was something, somewhere, that would vanquish the other. But what was it? Where to find it?

Each knew somewhere in his mind what it was that was his own weak point. They talked about this as they contested in these duels, day after day, and somehow the deep mind of each entered into the other. And the deep mind of the right-handed twin lied to his brother, and the deep mind of the left-handed twin told the truth.

On the last day of the duel, as they stood, they at last knew how the right-handed twin was to kill his brother. Each selected his weapon. The left-handed twin close a mere stick that would do him no good. But the right-handed twin picked out the deer antler, and with one touch he destroyed his brother. And the left-handed twin died, but he died and he didn't die. The right-handed twin picked up the body and cast it off the edge of the earth. And some place below the world, the left-handed twin still lives and reigns.

When the sun rises from the east and travels in a huge arc along the sky dome, which rests like a great upside-down cup on the saucer of the earth, the people are in the daylight realm of the right-handed twin. But when the sun slips down in the west at nightfall and the dome lifts to let it escape at the western rim, the people are again in the domain of the left-handed twin—the fearful realm of night.

Having killed his brother, the right-handed twin returned home to his grandmother. And she met him in anger. She threw the food out of the cabin onto the ground, and said that he was a murderer, for he had killed his brother. He grew angry and told her she had always helped his brother, who had killed their mother. In his anger, he grabbed her by the throat and cut her head off. Her body he threw into the ocean, and her head, into the sky. There "Our Grandmother, the Moon," still keeps watch at night over the realm of her favorite grandson.

The right-handed twin has many names. One of them is Sapling. It means smooth, young, green and fresh and innocent, straightforward, straight-growing, soft and pliable, teachable and trainable. These are the old ways of describing him. But since he has gone away, he has other names. He is called "He Holds Up the Skies," "Master of Life," and "Great Creator."

The left-handed twin also has many names. One of them is Flint. He is called the devious one, the one covered with boils, Old Warty. He is stubborn. He is thought of as being dark in color.

These two beings rule the world and keep an eye on the affairs of men. The right-handed twin, the Master of Life, lives in the Sky-World. He is content with the world he helped to create and with his favorite creatures, the humans. The scent of sacred tobacco rising from the earth comes gloriously to his nostrils.

In the world below lives the left-handed twin. He knows the world of men, and he finds contentment in it. He hears the sounds of warfare and torture, and he finds them good.

In the daytime, the people have rituals which honor the right-handed twin. Through the daytime rituals they thank the Master of Life. In the nighttime, the people dance and sing for the left-handed twin.

◈ *E S S A Y S*

The essays below encapsulate what archaeologists have pieced together from the physical remains of Indian communities that existed hundreds of years before Columbus arrived in the western hemisphere. Neal Salisbury of Smith College provides a continental overview that shows broad trends in pre-European American history. These developments set the stage for the conquest that followed the Columbian discovery. They also demonstrate that like all human histories, Indian history was dynamic. Far from being isolated bands of hunters with no knowledge of other peoples, Indians communicated and traded over long distances. Salisbury pays special attention to the mound cultures that arose in the Mississippi Valley in pre-Columbian times. Some scholars have argued that the great Mississippian cities, like Cahokia, were influenced by Mexico, but other investigators dispute this interpretation of the archaeological record and argue that these spectacular developments grew out of Woodlands Indian traditions that were nearer at hand. Stephen Plog's essay takes a closer look at the remarkable urban settlements in the Southwest, precursors of today's Pueblo Indians. The Anasazi, Hohokam, and other Southwesterners built formidable towns and irrigation works based on agricultural crops and techniques that Indians pioneered in central Mexico. They established elaborate religious rituals and developed an impressive artistic tradition that persists today. Whatever the origins and influences of these communities they are impressive reminders of the complexity of native cultures and extent of their attainments. What might Indian societies have looked like if Europeans had not ventured to America until 1692?

The Indians' Old World

Native Americans and the Coming of Europeans

NEAL SALISBURY

Scholars in history, anthropology, archaeology, and other disciplines have turned increasingly over the past two decades to the study of native peoples during the colonial period of North American history. The new work in Indian history has altered the way we think about the beginning of American history and about the era of European colonization. Historians now recognize that Europeans arrived, not in a virgin land, but in one that was teeming with several million people. Beyond filling in some of the vast blanks left by previous generations' overlooking of Indians, much of this scholarship makes clear that Indians are integral to the history of colonial North America. In short, surveys of recent textbooks and of scholarly titles suggest that Native Americans are well on their way to being "mainstreamed" by colonial historians.

Substantive as this reorientation is, it remains limited. Beyond the problems inherent in representing Indian/non-Indian interactions during the colonial era lies the challenge of contextualizing the era itself. Despite opening chapters and lectures that survey the continent's native peoples and cultures, most historians continue to represent American history as having been set in motion by the arrival of European explorers and colonizers. They have yet to recognize the existence of a North American—as opposed to English or European—background for colonial history, much less to consider the implications of such a background for understanding the three centuries following Columbus's landfall. Yet a growing body of scholarship by archaeologists, linguists, and students of Native American expressive traditions recognizes 1492 not as a beginning but as a single moment in a long history utterly detached from that of Europe. These findings call into question historians' synchronic maps and verbal descriptions of precontact Indians—their cultures, their communities, their ethnic and political designations and affiliations, and their relations with one another. Do these really describe enduring entities or do they represent epiphenomena of arbitrary moments in time? If the latter should prove to be the case, how will readings of Indian history in the colonial period be affected?

Neal Salisbury, "The Indians' Old World: Native Americans and the Coming of Europeans," *William and Mary Quarterly* 53 (July 1996), 435–458.

Far from being definitive, this article is intended as a stimulus to debate on these questions. It begins by drawing on recent work in archaeology, where most of the relevant scholarship has originated, to suggest one way of thinking about pre-Columbian North America in historical terms. The essay then looks at developments in several areas of the continent during the centuries preceding the arrival of Europeans and in the early phases of the colonial period. The purpose is to show how certain patterns and processes originating before the beginnings of contact continued to shape the continent's history thereafter and how an understanding of the colonial period requires an understanding of its American background as well as of its European context.

In a formidable critique of European and Euro-American thinking about native North Americans, Robert F. Berkhofer, Jr., demonstrates that the idea of "Indians" as a single, discrete people was an invention of Columbus and his European contemporaries that has been perpetuated into our own time without foundation in historical, cultural, or ethnographic reality. On the contrary, Berkhofer asserts,

> The first residents of the Americas were by modern estimates divided into at least two thousand cultures and more societies, practiced a multiplicity of customs and lifestyles, held an enormous variety of values and beliefs, spoke numerous languages mutually unintelligible to the many speakers, and did not conceive of themselves as a single people— if they knew about each other at all.

While there is literal truth in portions of Berkhofer's statement, his implication that Indians inhabited thousands of tiny, isolated communities in ignorance of one another flies in the face of a substantial body of archaeological and linguistic scholarship on North America and of a wealth of relevant anthropological literature on nonstate polities, nonmarket economies, and noninstitutionalized religions. To be sure, indigenous North Americans exhibited a remarkable range of languages, economies, political systems, beliefs, and material cultures. But this range was less the result of their isolation from one another than of the widely varying natural and social environments with which Indians had interacted over millennia. What recent scholars of precolonial North America have found even more striking, given this diversity, is the extent to which native peoples' histories intersected one another.

At the heart of these intersections was exchange. By exchange is meant not only the trading of material goods but also exchanges across community lines of marriage partners, resources, labor, ideas, techniques, and religious practices. Longer-distance exchanges frequently crossed cultural and linguistic boundaries as well and ranged from casual encounters to widespread alliances and networks that were economic, political, and religious. For both individuals and communities, exchanges sealed social and political relationships. Rather than accumulate material wealth endlessly, those who acquired it gave it away, thereby earning prestige and placing obligations on others to reciprocate appropriately. And as we shall see, many goods were not given away to others in this world but were buried with individuals to accompany them to another.

Archaeologists have found evidence of ongoing exchange relations among even the earliest known Paleo-Indian inhabitants of North America. Ten thousand years before Columbus, in the wake of the last Ice Age, bands of two or three dozen persons regularly traveled hundreds of miles to hunt and trade with one another at favored campsites such as Lindenmeier in northern Colorado, dating to ca. 8800 B.C. At the Lindenmeier site, differences in the flaking and shaping of stone points distinguished regular occupants in two parts of the camp, and the obsidian each used came from about 350 miles north and south of Lindenmeier, respectively. Evidence from a wide range of settlement sites makes clear that, as the postglacial warming trend continued, so-called Archaic peoples in much of the continent developed wider ranges of food sources, more sedentary settlement patterns, and larger populations. They also expanded their exchanges with one another and conducted them over greater distances. Highly valued materials such as Great Lakes copper, Rocky Mountain obsidian, and marine shells from the Gulf and Atlantic coasts have been found in substantial quantities at sites hundreds and even thousands of miles from their points of origin. In many cases, goods fashioned from these materials were buried with human beings, indicating both their religious significance and, by their uneven distribution, their role as markers of social or political rank.

While the Archaic pattern of autonomous bands persisted in most of North America until the arrival of Europeans, the complexity of exchange relationships in some parts of the continent produced the earliest evidence of concentrated political power. This was especially so for peoples who, after the first century A.D., developed food economies that permitted them to inhabit permanent, year-round villages. In California, for example, competition among communities for coveted acorn groves generated sharply defined political territories and elevated the role of chiefs who oversaw trade, diplomacy, and warfare for clusters of villages. Similar competition for prime fishing and trading locations strengthened the authority of certain village chiefs on the Northwest Coast. Exchange rather than competition for resources appears to have driven centralization in the Ohio and Illinois valleys. There the Hopewell peoples imported copper, mica, shell, and other raw materials over vast distances to their village centers, where specialists fashioned them into intricately crafted ornaments, tools, and other objects. They deposited massive quantities of these goods with the dead in large mounds and exported more to communities scattered throughout the Mississippi Valley. Hopewell burials differentiate between commoners and elites by the quantity and quality of grave goods accompanying each. In the Southwest, meanwhile, a culture known as Hohokam emerged in the Gila River and Salt River valleys among some of the first societies based primarily on agriculture. Hohokam peoples lived in permanent villages and maintained elaborate irrigation systems that enabled them to harvest two crops per year.

By the twelfth century, agricultural production had spread over much of the Eastern Woodlands as well as to more of the Southwest. In both regions, even more complex societies were emerging to dominate widespread exchange networks. In the Mississippi Valley and the Southeast, the sudden primacy of maize horticulture is marked archaeologically in a variety of ways—food remains, pollen profiles, studies of human bone (showing that maize accounted for 50 percent of people's diets), and in material culture by a proliferation of chert hoes, shell-tempered pottery for storing and cooking, and pits for storing surplus crops. These developments were accompanied by the rise of what archaeologists term "Mississippian" societies, consisting of fortified political and ceremonial centers and outlying villages. The centers were built around open plazas featuring platform burial mounds, temples, and elaborate residences for elite families. Evidence from burials makes clear the wide social gulf that separated commoners from elites. Whereas the former were buried in simple graves with a few personal possessions, the latter were interred in the temples or plazas along with many more, and more elaborate, goods such as copper ornaments, massive sheets of shell, and ceremonial weapons. Skeletal evidence indicates that elites ate more meat, were taller, performed less strenuous physical activity, and were less prone to illness and accident than commoners. Although most archaeologists' conclusions are informed at least in part by models developed by political anthropologists, they also draw heavily from Spanish and French observations of some of the last Mississippian societies. These observations confirm that political leaders, or chiefs, from elite families mobilized labor, collected tribute, redistributed agricultural surpluses, coordinated trade, diplomacy, and military activity, and were worshipped as deities.

The largest, most complex Mississippian center was Cahokia, located not far from the confluence of the Mississippi and Missouri rivers, near modern East St. Louis, Illinois, in the rich floodplain known as American Bottoms. By the twelfth century, Cahokia probably numbered 20,000 people and contained over 120 mounds within a five-square-mile area. One key to Cahokia's rise was its combination of rich soil and nearby wooded uplands, enabling inhabitants to produce surplus crops while providing an abundance and diversity of wild food sources along with ample supplies of wood for fuel and construction. A second key was its location, affording access to the great river systems of the North American interior.

Cahokia had the most elaborate social structure yet seen in North America. Laborers used stone and wooden spades to dig soil from "borrow pits" (at least nineteen have been identified by archaeologists), which they carried in wooden buckets to mounds and palisades often more than half a mile away. The volume and concentration of craft activity in shell, copper, clay, and other materials, both local and imported, suggests that specialized artisans provided the material foundation for Cahokia's exchange ties with other peoples. Although most Cahokians were buried in mass graves outside the palisades, their rulers were given special treatment. At a prominent location in Mound 72, the largest of Cahokia's platform mounds, a man had been buried atop a platform of shell beads. Accompanying him were several group burials: fifty young women, aged 18 to 23, four men, and three men and three women, all encased in uncommonly large amounts of exotic materials. As with the Natchez Indians observed by the French in Louisiana, Cahokians appear to have sacrificed individuals to accompany their leaders in the afterlife. Cahokia was surrounded by nine smaller mound centers and several dozen villages from which it obtained much of its food and through which it conducted its waterborne commerce with other Mississippian centers in the Midwest and Southeast (see Map 2.1).

At the outset of the twelfth century, the center of production and exchange in the Southwest was in the basin of the San Juan River at Chaco Canyon in New Mexico, where Anasazi culture achieved its most elaborate expression. A twelve-mile stretch of the canyon and its rim held twelve large planned towns on the north side and 200 to 350 apparently unplanned villages on the south. The total population was probably about 15,000. The towns consisted of 200 or more contiguous, multistoried rooms, along with numerous kivas (underground ceremonial areas), constructed of veneered masonary walls and log beams imported from upland areas nearly fifty miles distant.

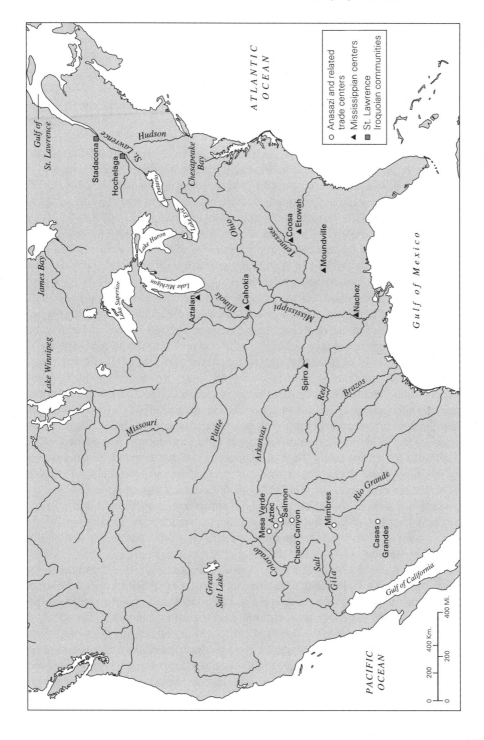

Map 2.1   Selected Native American centers in North America, ca. 1250.

The rooms surrounded a central plaza with a great kiva. Villages typically had ten to twenty rooms that were decidedly smaller than those in the towns. Nearly all of Chaco Canyon's turquoise, shell, and other ornaments and virtually everything imported from Mesoamerica are found in the towns rather than the villages. Whether the goods were considered communal property or were the possessions of elites is uncertain, but either way the towns clearly had primacy. Villagers buried their dead near their residences, whereas town burial grounds were apparently located at greater distances, although only a very few of what must have been thousands of town burials have been located by archaeologists. Finally, and of particular importance in the arid environment of the region, the towns were located at the mouths of side canyons where they controlled the collection and distribution of water run-off.

The canyon was the core of an extensive network of at least seventy towns or "outliers," as they are termed in the archaeological literature, and 5,300 villages located as far as sixty miles from the canyon. Facilitating the movement of people and goods through this network was a system of roads radiating outward from the canyon in perfectly straight lines, turning into stairways or footholds rather than circumventing cliffs and other obstacles.

What archaeologists call the "Chaco phenomenon" was a multifaceted network. Within the canyon, the towns controlled the distribution of precious water. The abundance of rooms reinforces the supposition that they stored agricultural surpluses for redistribution, not only within the canyon but to the outliers. The architectural uniformity of towns throughout the system, the straight roads that linked them, and the proliferation of great kivas point to a complex of shared beliefs and rituals. Lithic remains indicate that the canyon imported most of the raw materials used for manufacturing utilitarian goods and ornamental objects from elsewhere in the Southwest. Particularly critical in this respect was turquoise, beads of which were traded to Mexico in return for copper bells and macaws and to the Gulf of California for marine shells. The Chaco phenomenon thus entailed the mobilization of labor for public works projects and food production, the control and distribution of water, the distribution of prestige goods of both local and exotic origin, and the control of exchange and redistribution both within and outside the network. In distinct contrast to Cahokia and other Mississippian societies, no evidence exists for the primacy of any single canyon town or for the primacy of certain individuals as paramount leaders.

Given the archaeological record, North American "prehistory" can hardly be characterized as a multiplicity of discrete microhistories. Fundamental to the social and economic patterns of even the earliest Paleo-Indian bands were exchanges that linked people across geographic, cultural, and linguistic boundaries. The effects of these links are apparent in the spread of raw materials and finished goods, of beliefs and ceremonies, and of techniques for food production and for manufacturing. By the twelfth century, some exchange networks had become highly formalized and centralized. Exchange constitutes an important key to conceptualizing American history before Columbus.

Although it departs from our familiar image of North American Indians, the historical pattern sketched so far is recognizable in the way it portrays societies "progressing" from small, egalitarian, autonomous communities to larger, more hierarchical, and centralized political aggregations with more complex economies. That image is likewise subverted when we examine the three centuries immediately preceding the arrival of Europeans. In both American Bottoms and the San Juan River basin, where twelfth-century populations were most concentrated, agriculture most productive, exchange most varied and voluminous, and political systems most complex and extensive, there were scarcely any inhabitants by the end of the fifteenth century. What happened and why?

Cahokia and other Mississippian societies in the Upper Midwest peaked during the late twelfth and early thirteenth centuries. Data from soil traces indicate that even then laborers were fortifying Cahokia's major earthworks against attack. At the same time, archaeologists surmise, Cahokia was headed toward an ecological crisis: expanded settlement, accompanied by especially hot dry summers, exhausted the soil, depleted the supply of timber for building and fuel, and reduced the habitat of the game that supplemented their diet. By the end of the fourteenth century, Cahokia's inhabitants had dispersed over the surrounding countryside into small farming villages.

Cahokia's abandonment reverberated among other Mississippian societies in the Midwest. Fortified centers on the Mississippi River from the Arkansas River northward and on the Ohio River appear to have been strengthened by influxes of people from nearby villages but then abandoned, and signs from burials indicate a period of chronic, deadly warfare in the Upper Midwest. One archaeologist refers to the middle Mississippi Valley and environs during the fifteenth century as "the vacant quarter." A combination of ecological pressures and upheavals within the alliance that linked them appears to have doomed Cahokia and other midwestern Mississippian centers, leading the inhabitants to transform themselves into the village dwellers of the surrounding prairies and plains observed by French explorers three centuries later.

The upheavals may even have extended beyond the range of direct Mississippian influence to affect Iroquois and Hurons and other Iroquoian speakers of the lower Great Lakes region. These people had been moving from dispersed, riverside settlements to fortified, bluff-top villages over the course of several centuries; the process appears to have intensified in the fourteenth century, when it also led to the formation of the Iroquois and Huron confederacies. The Hurons developed fruitful relations with hunter-gatherers to the north, with whom they exchanged agricultural produce for meat and skins, and Iroquois ties with outsiders appear to have diminished except for small-scale interactions with coastal peoples to the south and east. Across the Northeast, political life was characterized by violence and other manifestations of intense competition. Whether the upheavals in exchange ties occasioned by the collapse of Cahokia were directly linked to the formation of the Iroquois and Huron confederacies, as Dena Dincauze and Robert Hasenstab have suggested for the Iroquois, or were simply part of a larger process generated by the advent of farming and consequent demographic and political changes, the repercussions were still evident when Europeans began to frequent the region during the sixteenth century.

Violence and instability were also apparent across the Southeast. Unlike in the Midwest, where enormous power had been concentrated in a single center, southeastern Mississippian societies were characterized by more frequently shifting alliances and rivalries that prevented any one center from becoming as powerful as Cahokia was from the tenth to thirteenth centuries. A pattern of instability prevailed that archaeologist David Anderson terms "cycling," in which certain centers emerged for a century or two to dominate regional alliances consisting of several chiefdoms and their tributary communities and then declined. Whole communities periodically shifted their locations in response to ecological or political pressures. Thus, for example, the great mound center at Etowah, in northwestern Georgia, lost its preeminence after 1400 and by the time of Hernando de Soto's arrival in 1540 had become a tributary of the nearby upstart chiefdom of Coosa.

From the mid-twelfth century through the fourteenth, the demographic map of the Southwest was also transformed as Chaco Canyon and other Anasazi and Hohokam centers were abandoned. Although southwesterners had made a practice of shifting their settlements when facing shortages of water and arable land and other consequences of climatic or demographic change, they had never done so on such a massive scale. Most archaeologists agree that the abandonments followed changes in the regional cycle of rainfall and drought, so that agricultural surpluses probably proved inadequate. They point to signs that the centralized systems lost their ability to mobilize labor, redistribute goods, and coordinate religious ceremonies and that such loss was followed by outmigration to surrounding and upland areas where people farmed less intensively while increasing their hunting and gathering. Trade between the Southwest and Mesoamerica was disrupted at the same time, though whether as a cause or an effect of the abandonments is unclear.

Most Anasazi peoples dispersed in small groups, joining others to form new communities in locations with sufficient rainfall. These communities are what we know today as the southwestern pueblos, extending from Hopi villages in Arizona to those on the Rio Grande. These dispersals and convergences of peoples reinforced an emerging complex of beliefs, art, and ceremonies relating to kachinas—spirits believed to have influence in both bringing rain and fostering cooperation among villagers. Given their effort to forge new communities under conditions of severe drought, it is not surprising that southwestern farmers placed great emphasis on kachinas. The eastward shift of much of the southwestern population also led to new patterns of trade in which recently arrived Athapaskan speakers (later known as Apaches and Navajos) brought bison meat and hides and other products from the southern Great Plains to semiannual trade fairs at Taos, Pecos, and Picuris pueblos in exchange for maize, cotton blankets, obsidian, turquoise, and ceramics as well as shells from the Gulf of California. By the time of Francisco Vásquez de Coronado's *entrada* in 1540, new ties of exchange and interdependency bound eastern Pueblos, Athapaskans, and Caddoan speaker on the Plains.

When Europeans reached North America, then, the continent's demographic and political map was in a state of profound flux. A major factor was the collapse of the great centers at Cahokia and Chaco Canyon and elsewhere in the Midwest and Southwest. Although there were significant differences between these highly centralized societies, each ran up against the capacity of the land or other resources to sustain it. This is not to argue for a simple ecological determinism for, although environmental fluctuations played a role, the severe strains in each region resulted above all from a series of human choices that had brought about unprecedented concentrations of people and power. Having repudiated those choices and dispersed, midwestern Mississippians and Anasazis formed new communities in which they retained kinship, ceremonial, and other traditions antedating these complex societies. At the same time, these new communities and neighboring ones sought to flourish in their new political and environmental settings by establishing, and in some cases endeavoring to control, new exchange networks.

Such combinations of continuity and change, persistence and adaptability, arose from concrete historical experiences rather than a timeless tradition. The remainder of this article indicates some of the ways that both the deeply rooted imperatives of reciprocity and exchange and the recent legacies of competition and upheaval informed North American history as Europeans began to make their presence felt.

Discussion of the transition from pre- to postcontact times must begin with the sixteenth century, when Indians and Europeans met and interacted in a variety of settings. When not slighting the era altogether, historians have viewed it as one of discovery or exploration, citing the achievements of notable Europeans in either anticipating or failing to anticipate the successful colonial enterprises of the seventeenth century. Recently, however, a number of scholars have been integrating information from European accounts with the findings of archaeologists to produce a much fuller picture of this critical period in North American history.

The Southeast was the scene of the most formidable attempts at colonization during the sixteenth century, primarily by Spain. Yet in spite of several expeditions to the interior and the undertaking of an ambitious colonizing and missionary effort, extending from St. Augustine over much of the Florida peninsula and north to Chesapeake Bay, the Spanish retained no permanent settlements beyond St. Augustine itself at the end of the century. Nevertheless, their explorers and missionaries opened the way for the spread of smallpox and other epidemic diseases over much of the area south of the Chesapeake and east of the Mississippi.

The most concerted and fruitful efforts of the interdisciplinary scholarship entail the linking of southeastern societies that are known archaeologically with societies described in European documents. For example, Charles Hudson, David Hally, and others have demonstrated the connections between a group of archaeological sites in northern Georgia and the Tennessee Valley and what sixteenth-century Spanish observers referred to as Coosa and its subordinate provinces. A Mississippian archaeological site in northwestern Georgia known as Little Egypt consists of the remains of the town of Coosa; the town was the capital of the province ("chiefdom" to the archaeologists) of the same name, containing several nearby towns, and this province/chiefdom in turn dominated a network of at least five other chiefdoms in a "paramount chiefdom." These conclusions would not have been as definitive if based on either documentary or archaeological evidence alone.

Coosa, as previously noted, attained regional supremacy during the fifteenth century, a phase in the apparently typical process whereby paramount chiefdoms rose and fell in the Mississippian Southeast. But Coosa's decline was far more precipitate than others because Spanish diseases ravaged the province, forcing the survivors to abandon the town and move southward. By the end of the sixteenth century, several new provincial centers emerged in what are now Alabama and western Georgia, but without the mounds and paramount chiefs of their predecessors. As with earlier declines of paramount chiefdoms, a center had declined and, out of the resulting power vacuum, a new formation emerged. What differed in this case were the external source of the decline, its devastating effects, and the inability or unwillingness of the survivors to concentrate power and deference in the hands of paramount chiefs. At the same time, the absence of Spanish or other European colonizers from the late sixteenth century to late seventeenth meant that the natives had a sustained period of time in which to recover and regroup. When English traders encountered the descendants of refugees from Coosa and its neighbors late in the seventeenth century, they labeled them "Creek."

Patricia Galloway has established similar connections between Mississippian societies farther west and the Choctaws of the eighteenth century. She argues that the well-known site of Moundville in Alabama and a second site on the Pearl River in Mississippi were the centers of chiefdoms from which most Choctaws were descended. She argues that, unlike Coosa, these centers were probably declining in power before the onset of disease in the 1540s hastened the process. Like the Creeks, the Choctaws were a multilingual, multiethnic society in which individual villages were largely autonomous although precedents for greater coalescence were available if conditions, such as the European presence, seemed to require it.

As in the Southeast, Spanish colonizers in the sixteenth-century Southwest launched several ambitious military and missionary efforts, hoping to extend New Spain's domain northward and to discover additional sources of wealth. The best-documented encounters of Spanish with Pueblos—most notably those of Coronado's expedition (1540–1542)—ended in violence and failure for the Spanish who, despite vows to proceed peacefully, violated Pueblo norms of reciprocity by insisting on excessive tribute or outright submission. In addition, the Spanish had acquired notoriety among the Pueblos as purveyors of epidemic diseases, religious missions, and slaving expeditions inflicted on Indians to the south, in what is now northern Mexico.

The Spanish also affected patterns of exchange throughout the Southwest. Indians resisting the spread of Spanish rule to northern Mexico stole horses and other livestock, some of which they traded to neighbors. By the end of the sixteenth century, a few Indians on the periphery of the Southwest were riding horses, anticipating the combination of theft and exchange that would spread horses to native peoples throughout the region and, still later, the Plains and the Southeast. In the meantime, some Navajos and Apaches moved near the Rio Grande Valley, strengthening ties with certain pueblos that were reinforced when inhabitants of those pueblos sought refuge among them in the face or wake of Spanish *entradas*.

Yet another variation on the theme of Indian-European contacts in the sixteenth century was played out in the Northeast, where Iroquoian-speaking villagers on the Mississippian periphery and Archaic hunter-gatherers still further removed from developments in the interior met Europeans of several nationalities. At the outset of the century, Spanish and Portuguese explorers enslaved several dozen Micmacs and other Indians from the Nova Scotia–Gulf of St. Lawrence area. Three French expeditions to the St. Lawrence itself in the 1530s and 1540s followed the Spanish pattern by alienating most Indians encountered and ending in futility. Even as these hostile contacts were taking place, fishermen, whalers, and other Europeans who visited the area regularly had begun trading with natives. As early as the 1520s, Abenakis on the coast of Maine and Micmas were trading the furs of beavers and other animals for European goods of metal and glass. By the 1540s, specialized fur traders, mostly French, frequented the coast as far south as the Chesapeake; by the 1550s or soon thereafter, French traders rendezvoused regularly with Indians along the shores of upper New England, the Maritimes, and Quebec and at Tadoussac on the St. Lawrence.

What induced Indians to go out of their way to trap beaver and trade the skins for glass beads, mirrors, copper kettles, and other goods? Throughout North America since Paleo-Indian times, exchange in the Northeast was the means by which people maintained and extended their social, cultural, and spiritual horizons as well as acquired items considered supernaturally powerful. Members of some coastal Indian groups later recalled how the first Europeans they saw, with their facial hair and strange clothes and traveling in their strange boats, seemed like supernatural figures. Although soon disabused of such notions, these Indians and many more inland placed special value on the glass beads and other trinkets offered by the newcomers. Recent scholarship on Indians' motives in this earliest stage of the trade indicates that they regarded such objects as the equivalents of the quartz, mica, shell, and other sacred substances that had formed the heart of long-distance exchange in North America for millennia and that they regarded as sources of physical and spiritual well-being, on earth and in the afterlife. Indians initially altered and wore many of the utilitarian goods they received, such as iron axe heads and cooper pots, rather than use them for their intended purposes. Moreover, even though the new objects might pass through many hands, they more often than not ended up in graves, presumably for their possessors to use in the afterlife. Finally, the archaeological findings make clear that shell and native copper predominated over the new objects in sixteenth-century exchange, indicating that European trade did not suddenly trigger a massive craving for the objects themselves. While northeastern Indians recognized Europeans as different from themselves, they interacted with them and their materials in ways that were consistent with their own customs and beliefs.

By the late sixteenth century, the effects of European trade began to overlap with the effects of earlier upheavals in the northeastern interior. Sometime between Jacques Cartier's final departure in 1543 and Samuel de Champlain's arrival in 1603, the Iroquoian-speaking inhabitants of Hochelaga and Stadacona (modern Montreal and Quebec City) abandoned their communities. The communities were crushed militarily, and the survivors dispersed among both Iroquois and Hurons. Whether the perpetrators of these dispersals were Iroquois or Huron is a point of controversy, but either way the St. Lawrence communities appear to have been casualties of the rivalry, at least a century old, between the two confederations as each sought to position itself vis-à-vis the French. The effect, if not the cause, of the dispersals was the Iroquois practice of attacking antagonists who denied them direct access to trade goods; this is consistent with Iroquois actions during the preceding two centuries and the century that followed.

The sudden availability of many more European goods, the absorption of many refugees from the St. Lawrence, and the heightening of tensions with the Iroquois help to explain the movement of most outlying Huron communities to what is now the Simcoe County area of Ontario during the 1580s. This geographic concentration strengthened their confederacy and gave it the form it had when allied with New France during the first half of the seventeenth century. Having formerly existed at the outer margins of an arena of exchange centered in Cahokia, the Hurons and Iroquois now faced a new source of goods and power to the east.

The diverse native societies encountered by Europeans as they began to settle North America permanently during the seventeenth century were not static isolates lying outside the ebb and flow of human history. Rather, they were products of a complex set of historical forces, both local and wide-ranging, both deeply rooted and of recent origin. Although their lives and worldviews were shaped by long-standing traditions of reciprocity and spiritual power, the people in these communities were also accustomed—contrary to popular myths about inflexible Indians—to economic and political flux and to absorbing new peoples (both allies and antagonists), objects, and ideas, including those originating in Europe. Such combinations of tradition and innovation continued to shape Indians' relations with Europeans, even as the latter's visits became permanent.

The establishment of lasting European colonies, beginning with New Mexico in 1598, began a phase in the continent's history that eventually resulted in the displacement of Indians to the economic, political, and cultural margins of a new order. But during the interim natives and colonizers entered into numerous relationships in which they exchanged material goods and often supported one another diplomatically or militarily against common enemies. These relations combined native and European modes of exchange. While much of the scholarly literature emphasizes the subordination and dependence of Indians in these circumstances, Indians as much as Europeans dictated the form and content of their early exchanges and alliances. Much of the protocol and ritual surrounding such intercultural contacts was rooted in indigenous kinship obligations and gift exchanges, and Indian consumers exhibited decided preferences for European commodities that satisfied social, spiritual, and aesthetic values. Similarly, Indians' long-range motives and strategies in their alliances with Europeans were frequently rooted in older patterns of alliance and rivalry with regional neighbors. Such continuities can be glimpsed through a brief consideration of the early colonial-era histories of the Five Nations Iroquois in the Northeast, the Creeks in the Southeast, and the Rio Grande Pueblos in the Southwest.

Post-Mississippian and sixteenth-century patterns of antagonism between the Iroquois and their neighbors to the north and west persisted, albeit under altered circumstances, during the seventeenth century when France established its colony on the St. Lawrence and allied itself with Hurons and other Indians. France aimed to extract maximum profits from the fur trade, and it immediately recognized the Iroquois as the major threat to that goal. In response, the Iroquois turned to the Dutch in New Netherland for guns and other trade goods while raiding New France's Indian allies for the thicker northern pelts that brought higher prices than those in their own country (which they exhausted by midcentury) and for captives to replace those from their own ranks who had died from epidemics or in wars. During the 1640s, the Iroquois replaced raids with full-scale military assaults (the so-called Beaver Wars) on Iroquoian-speaking communities in the lower Great Lakes, absorbing most of the survivors as refugees or captives. All the while, the Iroquois elaborated a vision of their confederation, which had brought harmony within their own ranks, as bringing peace to all peoples of the region. For the remainder of the century, the Five Nations fought a grueling and costly series of wars against the

French and their Indian allies in order to gain access to the pelts and French goods circulating in lands to the north and west.

Meanwhile, the Iroquois were also adapting to the growing presence of English colonists along the Atlantic seaboard (see Map 2.2). After the English supplanted the Dutch in New York in 1664, Iroquois diplomats established relations with the proprietary governor, Sir Edmund Andros, in a treaty known as the Covenant Chain. The Covenant Chain was an elaboration of the Iroquois' earlier treaty arrangements with the Dutch, but, whereas the Iroquois had termed the Dutch relationship a chain of iron, they referred to the one with the English as a chain of silver. The shift in metaphors was appropriate, for what had been strictly an economic connection was now a political one in which the Iroquois acquired power over other New York Indians. After 1677, the Covenant Chain was expanded to include several English colonies, most notably Massachusetts and Maryland, along with those colonies' subject Indians. The upshot of these arrangements was that the Iroquois cooperated with their colonial partners in subduing and removing subject Indians who impeded settler expansion. The Mohawks in particular played a vital role in the New England colonies' suppression of the Indian uprising known as King Philip's War and in moving the Susquehannocks away from the expanding frontier of settlement in the Chesapeake after Bacon's Rebellion.

For the Iroquois, such a policy helped expand their "Tree of Peace" among Indians while providing them with buffers against settler encroachment around their homelands. The major drawback in the arrangement proved to be the weakness of English military assistance against the French. This inadequacy, and the consequent suffering experienced by the Iroquois during two decades of war after 1680, finally drove the Five Nations to make peace with the French and their Indian allies in the Grand Settlement of 1701. Together, the Grand Settlement and Covenant Chain provided the Iroquois with the peace and security, the access to trade goods, and the dominant role among northeastern Indians they had long sought. That these arrangements in the long run served to reinforce rather than deter English encroachment on Iroquois lands and autonomy should not obscure their pre-European roots and their importance in shaping colonial history in the Northeast.

In the southeastern interior, Vernon Knight argues, descendants of refugees from Coosa and neighboring communities regrouped in clusters of Creek *talwas* (villages), each dominated by a large talwa and its "great chief." In the late seventeenth century, these latter-day chiefdom/provinces forged alliances with English traders, first from Virginia and then from Carolina, who sought to trade guns and other manufactured goods for deerskins and Indian slaves. In so doing, the Creeks ensured that they would be regarded by the English as clients rather than as commodities. The deerskin trade proved to be a critical factor in South Carolina's early economic development, and the trade in Indian slaves significantly served England's imperial ambitions vis-à-vis Spain in Florida. After 1715, the several Creek alliances acted in concert as a confederacy—the Creek Nation—on certain occasions. As a result, they achieved a measure of success in playing off these powers and maintaining neutrality in their conflicts with one another. While much differentiates Creek political processes in the colonial period from those of the late Mississippian era, there are strong elements of continuity in the transformation of Mississippian chiefdoms into great Creek talwas.

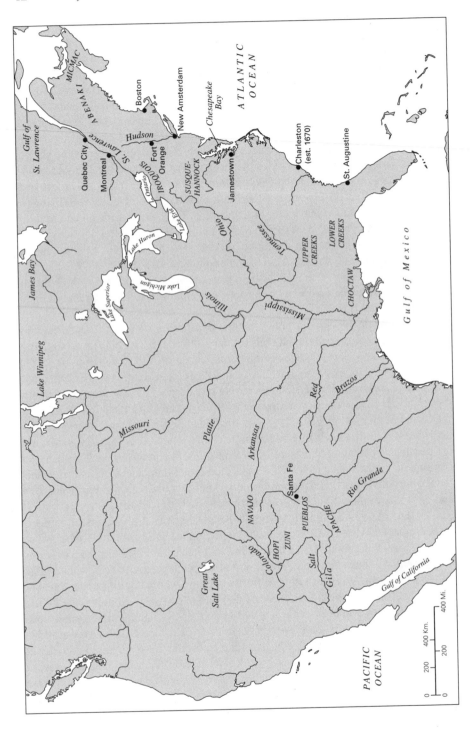

Map 2.2   Selected Native American centers in North America, ca. 1645.

In the Southwest, the institution of Spanish colonial rule on the Rio Grande after 1598 further affected exchange relations between Pueblo Indians and nearby Apaches and Navajos. By imposing heavy demands for tribute in the form of corn, the Spanish prevented Pueblo peoples from trading surplus produce with their non-farming neighbors. In order to obtain the produce on which they had come to depend, Apaches and Navajos staged deadly raids on some pueblos, leaving the inhabitants dependent on the Spanish for protection. In retaliation, Spanish soldiers captured Apaches and Navajos whom they sold as slaves to their countrymen to the south. From the beginning, the trading pueblos of Pecos, Picuris, and Taos most resented Spanish control and strongly resisted the proselytizing of Franciscan missionaries. From the late 1660s, drought and disease, intensified Apache and Navajo raids, and the severity of Spanish rule led more and more Indians from all pueblos to question the advantages of Christianity and to renew their ties to their indigenous religious traditions. Spanish persecution of native religious leaders and their backsliding followers precipitated the Pueblo Revolt of 1680, in which the trading Pueblos played a leading role and which was actively supported by some Navajos and Apaches.

When the Spanish reimposed their rule during the 1690s, they tolerated traditional Indian religion rather than trying to extirpate it, and they participated in interregional trade fairs at Taos and other villages. The successful incorporation of Pueblo Indians as loyal subjects proved vital to New Mexico's survival as a colony and, more generally, to Spain's imperial presence in the Southwest during the eighteenth and early nineteenth centuries.

As significant as is the divide separating pre- and post-Columbian North American history, it is not the stark gap suggested by the distinction between prehistory and history. For varying periods of time after their arrival in North America, Europeans adapted to the social and political environments they found, including the fluctuating ties of reciprocity and interdependence as well as rivalry, that characterized those environments. They had little choice but to enter in and participate if they wished to sustain their presence. Eventually, one route to success proved to be their ability to insert themselves as regional powers in new networks of exchange and alliance that arose to supplant those of the Mississippians, Anasazis, and others.

To assert such continuities does not minimize the radical transformations entailed in Europeans' colonization of the continent and its indigenous peoples. Arising in Cahokia's wake, new centers at Montreal, Fort Orange/Albany, Charleston, and elsewhere permanently altered the primary patterns of exchange in eastern North America. The riverine system that channeled exchange in the interior of the continent gave way to one in which growing quantities of goods arrived from, and were directed to, coastal peripheries and ultimately Europe. In the Southwest, the Spanish revived Anasazi links with Mesoamerica at some cost to newer ties between the Rio Grande Pueblos and recently arrived, nonfarming Athapaskan speakers. More generally, European colonizers brought a complex of demographic and ecological advantages, most notably epidemic diseases and their own immunity to them, that utterly devastated Indian communities; ideologies and beliefs in their cultural and spiritual superiority to native peoples and their entitlement to natives' lands; and economic, political, and military systems organized for the engrossment of Indian lands and the subordination or suppression of Indian peoples.

Europeans were anything but uniformly successful in realizing their goals, but the combination of demographic and ecological advantages and imperial intentions, along with the Anglo-Iroquois Covenant Chain, enabled land-hungry colonists from New England to the Chesapeake to break entirely free of ties of dependence on Indians before the end of the seventeenth century. Their successes proved to be only the beginning of a new phase of Indian-European relations. By the mid-eighteenth century, the rapid expansion of land-based settlement in the English colonies had sundered older ties of exchange and alliance linking natives and colonizers nearly everywhere east of the Appalachians, driving many Indians west and reducing those who remained to a scattering of politically powerless enclaves in which Indian identities were nurtured in isolation. Meanwhile, the colonizers threatened to extend this new mode of Indian relations across the Appalachians. An old world, rooted in indigenous exchange, was giving way to one in which Native Americans had no certain place.

Towns, Mounds, and Kachinas

STEPHEN PLOG

Abandonments at the end of the 13th century transformed the social landscape of the Southwest. The once vibrant cliff dwellings of the Kayenta and San Juan regions became vacant and mute. The more numerous surrounding settlements, both large and small, on mesa-tops and in other settings were also deserted. Not a single Mogollon or Anasazi inhabited vast areas once densely settled—including all of southern Utah and Colorado and much of northeastern Arizona and northwestern Mexico. Overall, the center of social gravity shifted decidedly to the south and east, with the Phoenix Basin continuing to be a key region and the Rio Grande Valley, the Zuni region of west-central New Mexico, and the Casas Grandes area of northern Mexico evolving into important centers. The Hopi area, once on the southern edges of the Anasazi territory, became isolated in the northwestern corner of the Pueblo world. This redistribution of people was simply one aspect of a complex process of metamorphosis that affected almost all the Southwest during the late 13th and 14th centuries.

Even in the southern and eastern areas where overall population grew, the number of inhabited villages actually dropped as the local people and any newcomers coalesced into large towns. Some of these towns were no larger than Cliff Palace or Sand Canyon Pueblo, but others approached a dimension that matched, and in many cases exceeded, the largest settlements of the preceding millennia. The greater number of people living in some locales meant more mouths to feed, more people to organize, more conflicts to resolve, or, from the point of view of aspiring leaders, more allies to recruit and more labor to exploit.

Stephen Plog, "Towns, Mounds, and Kachinas," in Stephen Plog, *Ancient Peoples of the American Southwest* (London: Thames and Hudson, 1997), 154–179. Reprinted by permission.

Community cycles: boom and bust in the Rio Grande Valley

When we examine a small region, such as the Rio Grande Valley, it becomes clear just how intermittent and episodic was the pattern of coalescence characteristic of the late 13th century and after. . . . Despite the presence of one of the few large rivers in the Southwest that carries water throughout the year, the valley was thinly populated before about AD 1000. Human numbers grew during the next two centuries, but Anasazi villages remained scattered in comparison with neighboring Anasazi and Mogollon areas. That pattern changed, however, in the late 12th and early 13th centuries as people moved into the area from the west and northwest and their numbers were augmented by indigenous population growth. The somewhat later pattern of development in the Rio Grande Valley is also shown by the late rise of pueblo architecture. By the end of the 13th century, pueblos with 10–50 rooms were unexceptional and a few had 100–200 rooms or more. Sometime during the 14th century, many areas of the Rio Grande Valley witnessed an even greater increase in population, but the exact timing of this growth varies throughout the Rio Grande region.

Yet between these phases of expansion and coalescence there were puzzling episodes of abandonment. Take Pot Creek Pueblo, near Taos in northern New Mexico, eventually a 250–300-room settlement loosely arranged around a central plaza with a large kiva [ceremonial chamber]. Anasazi settlers built a few rooms in the 1260s, many more in the 1270s, scarcely any during the 1280s, and none at all in the 1290s. They then renewed their building activity in the 1300s, an effort that continued into the next decade at a rate suggesting that new groups moved into the pueblo. By the 1320s Pot Creek had been abandoned, less than 70 years after it had first been settled.

Two similar cycles of expansion and decline characterized the occupation of Arroyo Hondo, an even larger pueblo located about 4.3 miles south of modern-day Santa Fe, along a tributary canyon of the Rio Grande. Analysis of the tree-ring dates shows that the initial settlers built at least a single roomblock by AD 1315 and then over the next 15 years quickly erected one of the largest pueblos anywhere in the Southwest, ultimately 1,200 two-story rooms distributed among 24 roomblocks arranged to define 13 plazas of roughly similar size. This precipitous growth was followed by an even more rapid decline. By the mid-1330s the pueblo was almost, if not completely, deserted. A second cycle of growth and decline commenced during the 1370s and 1380s when a group of new residents initiated a second but much smaller pueblo of 200 single-story rooms. They stayed until at least AD 1410, when a devastating fire destroyed much of the pueblo, incinerating racks of stored corn cobs.

These relatively short-lived occupations by large numbers of people, along with the rapid nature of both growth and decline and evidence that groups cooperated in the construction of several roomblocks, show how fluid the social landscape was in the 14th and early 15th centuries. People moved together, *en masse,* in a manner similar to some of the earlier population shifts in the middle of the 12th century. Groups who once formed communities of smaller, discrete villages, joined others to form new, larger pueblos for short periods of time. The somewhat different dates for the growth and decline of Pot Creek Pueblo and Arroyo Hondo suggest that this social fluidity lasted for a century or more. Many groups must have traveled considerable distances. For example, over 125 miles separates the Mesa Verde of southwestern Colorado from the nearest areas in northeastern Arizona or northwestern New Mexico where Anasazi settlement continued at the beginning of the 14th century. Such unprecedented journeys would not have been made without preparation, provisions, and prayer offerings.

Farming, food, and famine?

Why did people abandon sites like Arroyo Hondo, leaving behind the hundreds of rooms they had labored for years to construct? One reason is that inhabitants of these larger settlements faced greater difficulties in accumulating sufficient food.

Despite the presence of a large, perennial river, agriculture in the Rio Grande Valley is not without its risks. Average annual rainfall is below the minimum required for maize at all but the highest elevations, and growing seasons at those upper elevations are shorter than the 120 days maize needs. To minimize the risk of crop failure, Anasazi settlers adopted a diverse range of agricultural practices. Irrigated fields along the Rio Grande were complemented by fields in upland regions in which a variety of water and soil conservation methods—check dams, terraces, gridded fields with stone borders between individual plots, and stone walls to direct run-off to the plots—were employed to maximize soil moisture. Yet we know that these techniques were not always sufficient, as studies of the food remains and burials at Arroyo Hondo show.

Even the best agricultural land around Arroyo Hondo was not very productive. Probably no more than 400–600 people could have been fed during the average year, and it would have been difficult to accumulate adequate reserves in good years to allow everyone to survive when harvests fell short in consecutive bad years. The recovery by archaeologists of starvation foods such as cattails, cholla cactus, and grass seeds indicates that the residents of Arroyo Hondo did in fact face periods of hunger. These famines caused many residents to suffer from growth problems or afflictions such as iron deficiency (anemia), infections, and fractures. About 15 percent of the people had bowed long bones, a product of periodic or endemic malnutrition. Infant and child mortality was very high—26 percent died before reaching their first birthday and 45 percent before the age of five. Average life expectancy for all inhabitants of Arroyo Hondo was only 16.6 years, the shortest period discovered for any group of prehistoric Southwestern people. Life expectancy was so low and infant mortality so high that it undoubtedly hindered the functioning of the community.

The abrupt florescence and decline of large settlements such as Arroyo Hondo and Pot Creek Pueblo also typified many other areas of the northern Southwest during the 14th and early 15th centuries. In some cases, growth of towns was associated with a rise in the number of people, as in the Rio Grande Valley, but elsewhere population often declined overall. In the Cibola region of west-central New Mexico the ancestors of the Zuni reached a peak population of *c.* 9,300 in 17 pueblo towns near the end of the 13th century. Yet only 6,500 people remained in 10–11 towns in the mid-14th century, possibly followed by an even more rapid drop to 900 people in the last half of the 14th century, and then a subsequent recovery. The growth of large towns was thus not necessarily a product of rising population levels.

Nor were all large towns short-lived. The Hopi region of northeastern Arizona witnessed a striking rise in the size of individual settlements in the late 13th century as groups from surrounding areas moved into the region. Some of the larger towns such as Awatovi and Oraibi housed as many as 500 to 1,000 people and, more importantly, some of them remained major settlements for several hundred years. Awatovi was a thriving community when the Spanish entered the Southwest in the 16th century and remained so until the first few years of the 18th century. The Hopi still inhabit Oraibi today, the longest continuously occupied settlement in the United States.

Why did some communities endure while others collapsed? Although successes and failures at harvest time are part of the answer, conflict between settlements must have played its part as well.

Warfare and defense

Ethnographers have noted there is considerable evidence that conflict was once a much more important component of Pueblo life. For example, in oral traditions village defense is often given as the reason for admitting new groups to Hopi settlements:

> The Kokop people are said to have reached Oraibi after they had formerly lived in a home situated far to the northwest. At first Matcito refused to admit them to his pueblo, so they circled to the south of the mesa and made a temporary settlement there. From time to time their leaders beseeched Matcito to allow them to move into the village, offering to be his 'hands'(warriors), but the chief remained obdurate. In revenge, the head man of the Kokops secretly sent word to the Chimwava, huge men with gigantic feet, supposedly the worst enemies of the Hopi, inviting them to make a raid on Oraibi. Soon after, the people on the mesa were horrified to find a large host of the dreaded Chimwava marching upon their town. Matcito gathered his men, but realizing that his forces were inadequate, he remembered the Kokops' promises and sent word that the clan would be allowed to reside in Oraibi if it would help beat off the invaders.

Archaeological evidence supports the case for conflict in prehispanic times. In the late 13th and early 14th centuries village plans were increasingly designed in terms of defense. Roomblocks were built at right angles to each other to form open areas or plaza inside the pueblo. Such plazas occur at Arroyo Hondo and Pot Creek Pueblo, as well as hundreds of other pueblos throughout the northern Southwest. Narrow passages restricted access to the plazas. Ground-floor rooms could be entered only using ladders placed in openings in the roof. An individual standing outside the pueblo was thus confronted with solid masonry walls several feet in height. Even if one gained entry to the plaza, the ladders required for further access could be quickly raised from above, providing an additional barrier.

The Spanish found the plaza-oriented village plan an effective impediment during their battles with Pueblo groups. Coronado's exploration of the Southwest in 1540 almost ended during his attempt to storm the first pueblo he encountered, the town of Hawikuh in the Zuni area. The Hawikuhans initially resisted by retreating to the rooftops of their houses: "The people who were on the top for defense were not hindered in the least from doing us whatever injury they were able. As for myself, they knocked me down to the ground twice with countless great stones which they threw down from above, and I had not been protected by the very good headpiece which I wore, I think that the outcome would have been bad for me."

In earlier times the towns would have been protecting themselves against other Anasazi and Mogollon groups, rather than European intruders. Several other pieces of evidence support the case for internecine strife. A few of the large towns were in fact built in highly defensible locations. Best known of these is another pueblo of the Zuni region, Atsinna in El Morro National Monument, a pueblo with 750–1,000 rooms that sits atop Inscription Rock where Oñate and other explorers recorded their presence by carving names and dates in the face of the cliff. Other settlements had wells dug in the central plaza rather than in unprotected territory outside. Skeletal remains show an increase in trauma and violent deaths during this period, including evidence of scalping. Some sites, such as Arroyo Hondo and Casas Grandes in northern Mexico, were severely burnt. And we also have signs that Anasazi and Mogollon settlements were clustered together for defense, with considerable gaps—of tens and sometimes hundreds of miles—left between each cluster. The Hopi, Little Colorado River, and Cibola regions are perhaps the clearest examples of this type of distribution, but there were similar clusters, separated by smaller distances, in the Rio Grande area as well. Both village plans and intra- and inter-regional settlement distributions could thus be explained as efforts to increase protection from outsiders.

Ancestors, clouds, and kachina ritual

Plazas were not simply an architectural effort to restrict access to the pueblo. Some Anasazi and Mogollon people had always used plaza areas for a variety of domestic activities such as food preparation, but during this period we also see the first evidence that plazas became the setting for the public kachina dances that are so well known from historic times.

. . . [K]achinas feature prominently in modern-day western Pueblo (Hopi, Zuni, and Acoma) beliefs and ritual. Kachinas are ancestral spirits that act as messengers between the people and their gods. They also bring rain, themselves forming clouds summoned annually to the villages.

Kachinas are present on earth only half of the year, approximately from winter solstice to summer solstice, after which they return to the underworld through the *sipapu* in the San Francisco Peaks, the entrance through which humans first emerged from the underworld. Individuals dressed in costumes that include a mask impersonate the kachinas during their time on earth, performing a variety of group dances. The Hopi believe that when the impersonator wears the kachina masks, he (and it is always a male) becomes empowered with the characteristics of the spirit being represented and should therefore be regarded as sacred. There are a variety of different types of kachinas and kachina societies among the Hopi, and all individuals are initiated into one of these societies.

Kachina ritual as it is conducted today requires large, public spaces for group dances, and plazas are the typical setting. Plazas, as we have seen, developed in the late 13th and early 14th centuries, and there are other changes at this time—particularly in ceramic decorative styles and the introduction of kiva murals—suggesting that modern Pueblo rituals had their origin during this period.

As regards ceramics, in the first half of the 13th century, the Rio Grande Valley, the Cibola and Little Colorado regions, the Hopi area, and the Mogollon Rim country all quickly came to share a similar style of vessel decoration despite the considerable distances between each area. That style, a radical departure from those of earlier periods, was characterized by birds and human figures in addition to geometric designs, by asymmetric patterns, and by a change in the focus of decoration from the walls of bowls to the center. Vessel color ranged from yellow to orange to red, with designs painted in both black and red.

Patricia Crown studied the representational forms on such vessels and she concludes that most are symbols of the earth, sun, weather phenomena, or fertility. The commonest icon is the snake or serpent, often depicted using elongated triangles with hooks (fangs) at the apex, an eye inside the triangle, and a curving horn or plume emanating from the back of the triangle. Pueblo groups today believe that the horned serpent controls flooding and rain and both the icon and its interpretation are reminiscent of Quetzalcoatl, the plumed serpent of native Mesoamerican religions. Crown suggests that the serpent and other representational symbols express and reinforce concepts of the universe, afterlife, weather control and fertility that were central to the religious beliefs of the Southwestern societies.

The centrality of these concepts is supported by the occurrence of the symbols in a variety of contexts other than ceramic vessels. Archaeologists have discovered similar patterns of decoration painted on the walls of a few 14th- and early 15th-century kivas at half a dozen pueblos in the Little Colorado River Valley, the Hopi region, and the Rio Grande Valley. Several layers of murals are sometimes present, a result of the annual or seasonal replastering of kiva walls typical of certain ceremonies, a practice recorded among some historic-period Pueblo groups. At Awatovi and Kawaika-a in the Hopi region, the archaeologist Watson Smith recovered fragments of more than 200 individual murals from approximately 20 kivas. Smith believes that the painted designs supplemented, and sometimes substituted for, the wooden altars characteristic of Hopi kiva rituals when they were last observed by outsiders in the early 20th century. These murals not only contrast with the rare examples of earlier kiva decorations—dominated by simple geometric designs— but also illustrate a greater variety of subjects than those on contemporary ceramic vessels, including plants, animals, anthropomorphs, and altars. Perhaps the single most significant motifs are the anthropomorphs with features characteristic of the kachinas of historic Pueblo groups.

The kiva murals, the rapid appearance of the new decorative style on ceramics, the introduction of large plazas, and changes in burial practices all suggest that Pueblo ritual was transformed during the late 13th and 14th centuries in the northern Southwest. Among the most significant changes was the development or elaboration of kachina ritual. Some scholars believe that kachina ritual provided a sort of social glue, bonding together people within a pueblo because everyone must cooperate for the ceremonies to be conducted properly, and membership in kachina societies crosscuts the discrete and potentially divisive clans and lineages. Certainly the public nature of the kachina dances in the open plazas suggests an increased emphasis on public affirmation of conventions of proper behavior. Kachina rituals helped reinforce the norms of social behavior. Such an emphasis in these late prehispanic times would not be surprising given the concurrent evolution of larger and socially more diverse villages where increased tensions and conflicts were likely and where cooperative behavior was needed for the village to survive.

Another noteworthy aspect of the archaeological evidence of kachinas, that contrasts somewhat with the historic focus of kachina ritual, is the depiction of shields and hostile encounters in a few of the kiva murals. Some of these simply illustrate two figures confronting each other, but in one mural from a kiva at Kawaika-a, 'the ultimate act of warfare is very realistically portrayed, for here the victorious champion, with shield borne before him, stands over the vanquished foe, who has fallen backward, pierced by an arrow or spear. The particular kachinas most likely depicted in early kachina murals and rock art are also associated with warfare in modern Pueblo ritual, often sanctifying warfare (in some oral traditions kachinas assist Pueblo groups during conflicts, for example) or commemorating important encounters. Thus, kachinas initially may have had a dual role as warriors as well as rainmakers. To propose that both increased cooperation and increased conflict characterized the 14th and early 15th centuries in the northern Southwest may appear contradictory, but these patterns are not irreconcilable. A greater emphasis on ritual and cooperation within villages is often associated with social tensions between villages or regions; an emphasis on internal unity is a logical counterpart of the risk of threat from others.

Green stones for red feathers: trade and elites in the Southwest

Trade in a variety of goods demonstrates the strong and multifaceted relationships between regions, in combination with the ties suggested by similarities in ceramic decoration with kiva murals. Turquoise, parrot feathers, cotton and cotton cloth, shell, buffalo hides, obsidian, and pottery are a few of the many items exchanged by the ancient Southwesterners. Certain groups specialized in the production of particular goods. Inhabitants of settlements along the Little Colorado River near the modern town of Winslow, for example, may have specialized in cotton farming, trading either raw cotton or textiles for other commodities. The long, 172-day average growing season around Winslow would have provided an excellent environment for cotton cultivation as long as the Little Colorado River provided sufficient irrigation water. Plant remains from two of the pueblos, Homol'ovi II and III, demonstrate that cotton was a primary agricultural plant, close to maize in importance, and more abundant than in any other area of the Southwest. Although cotton was grown elsewhere, including the gravel mulch fields of the Rio Grande Valley, the residents of the Homol'ovis and the Hopi villages may have been the primary providers of raw cotton and finished textiles; we certainly know that the Hopi played that role when the Spanish arrived in the 16th century. . . .

The Casas Grandes polity.   The clearest picture of the range and amounts of goods being traded among Southwestern communities comes from northern Mexico. Roughly 150 miles south of the U.S.-Mexican border lies the spectacular pueblo of Casas Grandes (also known as Paquimé), once the nucleus of probably the most developed and centralized polity in the prehistoric Southwest. Prior to the growth of Casas Grandes, the people of this region had lived in small, agricultural villages. Here, in the early 13th century, people began building a unique settlement that differs in many ways from most Southwestern pueblos. A contemporaneous population explosion also occurred in the surrounding hinterland. The town, occupied for several centuries, reached its zenith between *c.* AD 1300 and 1400, with remodeling of residential areas and construction of most of the ceremonial mounds and public space.

Casas Grandes is noteworthy in several ways. With over 2,000 pueblo rooms in several discrete roomblocks constructed of adobe, the settlement was the largest that ever existed in the prehistoric Southwest, its resident population numbering in the low thousands. Public ritual architecture included at least 18 morphologically unique, earthen and stone mounds concentrated in the northwestern part of the village. These ranged from a roughly circular platform, 13 ft (4 m) high with a stone façade and staircase, to irregular shapes that in at least one case the excavator, Charles Di Peso, suggests depicted a bird. The Paquimans also constructed three ballcourts, all of which are I-shaped in a manner typical of ballcourts to the south and unlike those previously discussed in the Hohokam region of southern Arizona. The town's water supply system is unique in the New World. A canal network carried water from warm springs 2.2 miles to the northwest. The main canal fed into a reservoir with a settling tank from which small, stone-lined channels took water into the roomblocks; an outflowing sewer and ditch systems removed fluids from the rooms. All of these characteristics suggest a populous, well-planned, and integrated town.

It is the artifacts and animal remains, however, that above all distinguish Casas Grandes from its contemporaries and demonstrate its role as a trade center. Excavations uncovered a total of 322 scarlet macaws (*Ara macao*), an exquisitely colorful parrot native to the humid Gulf Coast region of Mexico, 81 green military macaws (*Ara militaris*) native to the forested regions of southern Sonora and Chihuahua, and 100 macaws that could not be identified as to species. These are tremendous numbers given that fewer than 200 scarlet macaws are known from all other Southwestern sites, of all time periods combined, and that only a portion of Casas Grandes was excavated. Even more infrequent elsewhere, but abundant in several plazas at Casas Grandes, are breeding and nesting boxes—sets of contiguous adobe compartments that were covered with mats and had round, doughnut-shaped stone circles with plugs that served as front entrances to the pens. The pens, along with the presence of macaw eggs, nestlings, and birds of all ages confirm that Casas Grandes was one of the northernmost breeding locations currently known. The Paquimans also bred turkeys. Pens for those birds along with 344 skeletons were discovered during excavations.

At Casas Grandes and at earlier settlements in the Mimbres region, the ancient Southwesterners sacrificed the macaws in the late winter or spring (the vast majority died between 10 and 13 months of age) and then interred the complete skeleton, probably after plucking the long tail feathers that would have been fully formed by spring time. Padre Luis Velarde described a similar practice in 1716: ". . . at San Xavier del Bac [near Tucson] and neighboring rancherías, there are many macaws, which the Pimas raise because of the beautiful feathers of red and of other colors . . . which they strip from these birds in the spring, for their adornment." The tail feathers would have been used for adornment, as noted by Velarde, or for ritual purposes; feathers have been described as "the most basic and widely used class of objects in the entire field of Pueblo ritual." Pueblo people offer prayers by making *pahos,* sticks with feathers attached, and depositing these at shrines and other locations, and they also affix feathers to many ceremonial paraphernalia. (Mimbres bowls from the 11th and 12th centuries depict prayer sticks with attached feathers comparable to those that Pueblo peoples use today, providing a clear prehistoric analog to modern ritual practices.) They place feathers on other objects—from peach trees to rock art—to enhance fertility or to bring rain. Feathers were thus conduits through which petitions could be conveyed to the supernaturals. Colors also symbolize directions among the Pueblos, perhaps adding to the significance of macaw feathers.

Casas Grandes was undoubtedly a major link in a trading network in macaw and turkey feathers that encompassed much of northern Mexico and the South-western United States. Trade in turquoise was also important: in 1536 Cabeza de Vaca reported that the peoples of northern Mexico traded parrot feathers to people who lived in large houses to the north in exchange for green stones. These 'green stones' almost certainly were turquoise which occurs naturally in parts of Arizona and New Mexico. Turquoise was abundant at Casas Grandes, with 5,895 pieces weighing 4.6 lbs recovered during excavations, but these amounts are not as un-usual as are the high frequency of macaws.

Di Peso did find shell in extraordinary amounts at Casas Grandes, almost four million items (counting individual beads) weighing 1.5 tons, all produced from species native to the west coast of Mexico. Prior to the 13th century, the Paquimans buried much of the shell as grave offerings, but later we find almost all of it in three rooms, two in a single roomblock, together with a large concentration of copper artifacts. This suggests that there was some type of central control over the acquisition and distribution of shell and copper, and that a few individuals were able to accumulate significant wealth. The discovery of almost 700 copper artifacts throughout the site and the presence of copper ore indicate that some manufactur-ing occurred at Casas Grandes. As with the scarlet macaws, copper items are cer-tainly known from more northerly sites, but occur in much lower frequencies and without any indication of manufacturing.

Casas Grandes was the center of a polity roughly 40–70 miles across in north-ern and northwestern Chihuahua. Evidence of macaw breeding, similar ballcourts, and a unique type of pottery, referred to as Ramos Polychrome, produced at Casas Grandes tie this region together. None of the villages in the hinterland approach the scale of Casas Grandes—all are smaller and none have any mounds—indicating that Casas Grandes was at the apex of the political and religious organization.

There seems to have been an elite class at Casas Grandes which accumulated and traded these macaw, shell, and copper goods and was buried in the elaborate tombs. Copper, turquoise, and certain types of cotton cloth symbolized high status in parts of the New World when Europeans arrived, and it was often the more powerful elites who regulated access to these materials. Coronado and de Niza's accounts from their travels in northern Mexico illustrate similar patterns.

One mound, at Casas Grandes, seems to have functioned as an elaborate tomb for a few individuals, a significant contrast with normal burials at the site which were in simple pits beneath plaza or dwelling floors. At the base of the ground lay the remains of two men and a woman held, except for their skulls, in unusually large Ramos Polychrome vessels and accompanied by a musical rasp made from a human long bone, a necklace of human phalanges, and other objects. The burials were disarticulated, indicating that the bodies had been laid out elsewhere while their soft parts decomposed, again a departure from the typical mortuary practices at the settlement. Together these patterns evoke an image of a privileged social class who controlled long-distance trade, lived in distinctive residences, and were buried in special tombs.

Scholars commonly acknowledge the presence of such hierarchies in Mesoamerica, but in the Southwest most have argued that Pueblo people were highly egalitarian, with minimal differences in social and political status. They highlight the likelihood of considerable variation in harvests from year to year which they believe would have hindered individual accumulation of food or such items as turquoise and shell. They argue that minimal differences in the amounts of grave goods found with burials support this assertion.

Others have argued, however, that the magnitude of population movement during the late 13th and 14th centuries created opportunities for pioneer groups to control the most productive land, while late arriving groups may have been forced to cultivate less productive tracts. Those who controlled the best lands may have been able to harvest corn more consistently or grow crops such as cotton, providing an advantage in trade with other groups. Hopi oral traditions describe such a process of land allocation as new groups were allowed to settle in existing villages; disparities still exist today in the quality of agricultural land controlled by different Hopi lineages and clans. These disparities may have been enhanced by the inevitable rise in tensions and the need for cooperation whenever larger numbers of people live together. These needs may promote the development of formal offices held by individuals who have the authority to make and enforce decisions. Also, in many of these societies differential ritual education, such as knowledge of the proper ways to conduct various ceremonies, may have been significant in creating and reinforcing social and economic differences, particularly when people believed such knowledge could influence the weather and thus agricultural success. Social distinctions based on knowledge, rather than wealth, will be less likely to produce significant differences in grave goods, making them harder to detect with only archaeological evidence.

Hohokam big houses.   Elsewhere the development of a more privileged class of people is most evident in the Phoenix Basin. It is true that for most Hohokam people the basic fabric of life remained much as before—built around irrigation canals, (a declining use of) ballcourts, and platform mounds, now with residential compounds built on their summits. Nevertheless, we also find evidence for the largest towns ever seen in the Phoenix Basin, far-flung trading contacts, specialized production of particular goods, and large public building projects. The town of Los Muertos, for example, was inhabited by as many as 1,000 people living in 30 different compounds. New polychrome and yellow-ware ceramics appear, similar to, and in some cases traded from, the north, including Jeddito black-on-yellow pottery produced in the Hopi region. Spindle whorls for spinning cotton and possibly yucca fiber commonly occur at platform mounds suggesting that the production of textiles may have been in the hands of specialists, possibly controlled by the elites who live atop the mounds.

Perhaps of greatest significance is the construction of massive tower-like structures or "big houses." At least three of these adobe buildings are known to have existed in the Hohokam region, but the complete base of only one has survived at the site of Casa Grande near Phoenix. Originally this tower had four stories and was constructed on top of an artificially filled first story (thus resembling a platform mound). The residents of Casa Grande erected the structure in a single episode, requiring the procurement of nearly 600 roof beams, each about 13 ft (4 m) long, from woodland areas over 60 miles away, and the excavation of over 1,440 cubic yd (1,100 cubic m) of soil to make the adobe walls. It would have taken at least 15–20 families working full-time for three months to erect the building. In addition to serving as an elite residence, the tower may have functioned as an astronomical observatory. Holes in the walls were probably used to measure the movement of the sun in order to predict solstices and equinoxes and properly maintain the ritual calendar. Once again we find that higher status individuals were central to group ritual.

Conclusions

Some trends in the Hohokam area parallel those in the north, but social differences here and in the Casas Grandes region appear greater than among the Mogollon and Anasazi during the 14th and early 15th centuries. This emergence of higher status individuals and elites characterizes all areas of the New World where civilizations developed, from the Valley of Mexico to the Inca empire of the Andes. It appears to be a significant and necessary transition that accompanies the evolution of more complex societies.

In both the Hohokam and Casas Grandes regions, however, population levels dropped in subsequent periods and simpler organizational patterns again prevailed. In the century following AD 1350, the large towns of the Phoenix and Tucson Basins were abandoned and Casas Grandes was burned. This episode of abandonments, now a recurrent theme of Southwestern prehistory, was duplicated in some, but not all, areas to the north as well. Mogollon and Anasazi groups once again deserted densely inhabited areas, including the pueblos along the Little Colorado River and its southern drainages and large settlements along the Mogollon Rim. Only the pueblos of the Cibola, Acoma, Hopi, and Rio Grande Valley regions endured. It was these settlements that were to witness an even more momentous epoch with the Spanish incursions of the 16th century.

◈ *F U R T H E R   R E A D I N G*

Douglas B. Bamforth, "Indigenous People, Indigenous Violence: Precontact Warfare on the North American Great Plains," *Man* 29 (March 1994), 95–116
Harold E. Driver, *Indians of North America,* 2nd ed. (1969)
Brian Fagan, *Ancient North America,* 2nd ed. (1995)
———, *The Great Journey: The Peopling of Ancient America* (1987)
Peter Farb, *Man's Rise to Civilization: The Cultural Ascent of the Indians of North America,* 2nd ed. (1978)
Robert F. Heizer and Albert B. Elsasser, *The Natural World of the California Indians* (1980)

Frederick Webb Hodge, ed., *Handbook of the American Indian North of Mexico,* 2 vols. (1907–1910)

William Hodge, *The First Americans: Then and Now* (1981)

Francis Jennings, *The Founders of America: How Indians Discovered the Land, Pioneered in It, and Created Great Classical Civilizations, How They Were Plunged into a Dark Age by Invasion and Conquest, and How They Are Reviving* (1993)

Jesse D. Jennings, ed., *Ancient North Americans* (1983)

Alvin M. Josephy, Jr., ed., *America in 1492: The World of Indian People Before the Arrival of Columbus* (1992)

Alice B. Kehoe, *North American Indians: A Comprehensive Account* (1981)

Harriet Kupferer, *Ancient Drums, Other Moccasins: Native North American Cultural Adaptation* (1988)

Jerald T. Milanich, *The Early Prehistoric Southeast: A Sourcebook* (1985)

Wendell H. Oswalt, *This Land Was Theirs: A Study of North American Indians,* 4th ed. (1988)

Stephen Plog, *Ancient Peoples of the American Southwest* (1997)

Carroll L. Riley, *Rio del Norte: People of the Upper Rio Grande from the Earliest Times to the Pueblo Revolt* (1995)

Karl H. Schlesier, ed., *Plains Indians, A.D. 500–1500: The Archaeological Past of Historic Groups* (1995)

C H A P T E R

3

Indians and Europeans Meet

◈

*Five hundred years ago, residents of the Caribbean islands saw on the horizon
ships unlike any they had ever seen or imagined. These vessels carried Christopher
Columbus and his men, who claimed the islands for Spain and called the inhabitants "indios" because they thought that they had found the East Indies off the
coast of Asia. Columbus died devoutly believing in his immense geographical error,
but his name for the native inhabitants of the Western Hemisphere remains as an
ironic monument to Columbus' unrealized search for a shortcut to the riches of
Asia. Scholars argue about the meaning of the European conquest that Columbus
inaugurated. And in 1992—the five-hundredth anniversary of Columbus' voyage—
some Indians argued that genocide of native peoples was the principal legacy of the
Columbian encounter and its aftermath. Certainly, the European conquest of America
set off a vicious cycle of population decline among the indigenous people of America
that may have amounted to as much as a 90 percent reduction. Most of the population
losses came from the impact of epidemic diseases that Indians had not been exposed to
before 1492. Smallpox, measles, bubonic plague, and other Old World maladies swept
off large numbers of Indians at a single stroke and left native communities weakened
and vulnerable. Yet Indians did not merely fade away when Europeans arrived. They
adjusted to new conditions of life and, when conditions were favorable, asserted a
measure of control in the New World that Indians and Europeans together created.*

◈ *D O C U M E N T S*

When Columbus arrived in American he expected to find Asia and its riches. Instead,
he encountered the Carib people on San Salvador island. In Document 1, a letter to the
Spanish monarchs, Columbus describes the Caribs, explains their ignorance of European weapons, and says that they would make good servants. Spaniards also hoped to
convert Indians to the Christian religion, but religious conversion was not an altogether
voluntary experience, as Document 2, the "requerimiento" (or requirement), shows.
This remarkable text not only required Indians to give up their religion and to submit to
Spanish authority, but made them responsible for any death or damage to themselves
if they refused. In 1573, King Philip II abolished the requerimiento and condemned the
use of force against Indians, but Spanish military and religious conquest continued to
go forward together. By 1519, Spanish explorers were expanding their grip to the
American mainland. The Spanish rapidly conquered the formidable Aztec empire,

consolidated their gains, and explored northward to what they hoped would be a "new" Mexico, a country as rich in silver and gold as the Aztec city states. In Document 3 a Spaniard describes the Rio Grande pueblos, which were impressive but did not contain the mineral riches that Spaniards hoped for. The account of Jacques Cartier in Document 4 contrasts sharply with that of Columbus. Here, we see Micmac Indians in the Gulf of Saint Lawrence region clamoring to trade furs for French metalware in 1534. In Document 5 Powhatan, the most important leader of Indians in Virginia, speaks in favor of peaceful relations with the English while complaining of the newcomers' aggressiveness. Finally, Document 6 is the Pilgrim William Bradford's account of the first treaty of peace with the Wampanoags. At first contact, European and Indian needs and expectations varied widely, but ultimately Europeans prevailed throughout the hemisphere. Could these early encounters have resulted in mutually beneficial relationships, or were Europeans destined to overcome Indians from the start?

1. Columbus on the Indians' "Discovery" of the Spanish, 1492

"I [Columbus wrote], in order that they might feel great amity towards us, because I knew that they were a people to be delivered and converted to our holy faith rather by love than by force, gave to some among them some red caps and some glass beads, which they hung round their necks, and many other things of little value. At this they were greatly pleased and became so entirely our friends that it was a wonder to see. Afterwards they came swimming to the ships' boats, where we were, and brought us parrots and cotton thread in balls, and spears and many other things, and we exchanged for them other things, such as small glass beads and hawks' bells, which we gave to them. In fact, they took all and gave all, such as they had, with good will, but it seemed to me that they were a people very deficient in everything. They all go naked as their mothers bore them, and the women also, although I saw only one very young girl. And all those whom I did see were youths, so that I did not see one who was over thirty years of age; they were very well built, with very handsome bodies and very good faces. Their hair is coarse almost like the hairs of a horse's tail and short; they wear their hair down over their eyebrows, except for a few strands behind, which they wear long and never cut. Some of them are painted black, and they are the colour of the people of the Canaries, neither black nor white, and some of them are painted white and some red and some in any colour that they find. Some of them paint their faces, some their whole bodies, some only the eyes, and some only the nose. They do not bear arms or know them, for I showed to them swords and they took them by the blade and cut themselves through ignorance. They have no iron. Their spears are certain reeds, without iron, and some of these have a fish tooth at the end, while others are pointed in various ways. They are all generally fairly tall, good looking and well proportioned. I saw some who bore marks of wounds on their bodies, and I made signs to them to ask how this came about, and they indicated to me that people came from other islands, which are near, and wished to capture them, and they defended themselves. And I believed and still

---

The Indians Discover Columbus, in *The Journal of Christopher Columbus,* edited by L. A. Vigernas (London: Anthony Blond & The Orion Press, 1960), 23–24.

believe that they come here from the mainland to take them for slaves. They should be good servants and of quick intelligence, since I see that they very soon say all that is said to them, and I believe that they would easily be made Christians, for it appeared to me that they had no creed. Our Lord willing, at the time of my departure I will bring back six of them to Your Highnesses, that they may learn to talk. I saw no beast of any kind in this island, except parrots." . . .

2. Spain Requires the Indians to Submit to Spanish Authority, 1513

On the part of the King, don Fernando [Ferdinand], and of doña Juana, his daughter, Queen of Castile and Léon, subduers of the barbarous nations, we their servants notify and make known to you, as best we can, that the Lord our God, Living and Eternal, created the Heaven and the Earth, and one man and one woman, of whom you and I, and all the men of the world, were and are descendants, and all those who come after us. But, on account of the multitude which has sprung from this man and woman in the five thousand years since the world was created, it was necessary that some men should go one way and some another, and that they should be divided into many kingdoms and provinces, for in one alone they could not be sustained.

Of all these nations God our Lord gave charge to one man, called St. Peter, that he should be Lord and Superior of all the men in the world, that all should obey him, and that he should be head of the whole human race, wherever men should live, and under whatever law, sect, or belief they should be; and he gave him the world for his kingdom and jurisdiction.

And he commanded him to place his seat in Rome, as the spot most fitting to rule the world from; but also he permitted him to have his seat in any other part of the world, and to judge and govern all Christians, Moors, Jews, Gentiles, and all other sects. This man was called Pope, as if to say, Admirable Great Father and Governor of men. The men who lived in that time obeyed that St. Peter, and took him for Lord, King, and Superior of the universe; so also have they regarded the others who after him have been elected to the Pontificate, and so it has been continued even until now, and will continue until the end of the world.

One of these Pontiffs, who succeeded that St. Peter as Lord of the world, in the dignity and seat which I have before mentioned, made donation of these isles and *terra firme* [mainland] to the aforesaid King and Queen and to their successors, our lords, with all that there are in these territories, as is contained in certain writings which passed upon the subject as aforesaid, which you can see if you wish.

So their Highnesses are kings and lords of these islands and land of *terra firme* by virtue of this donation; and some islands, and indeed almost all those to whom this has been notified, have received and served their Highnesses, as lords and kings, in the way that subjects ought to do, with good will, without any resistance, immediately, without delay, when they were informed of the aforesaid facts. And also they

Spain Requires the Indians to Submit to Spanish Authority, 1513, in Arthur Helps, *The Spanish Conquest in America and Its Relation to the History of Slavery and to the Government of the Colonies* (London: J. W. Parker & Sons, 1855–1861), 1:264–267. This document can also be found in Marvin Lunenfeld, ed., *1492: Discovery, Invasion, Encounter* (Lexington, Mass.: D. C. Heath, 1991).

received and obeyed the priests whom their Highnesses sent to preach to them and to teach them our Holy Faith; and all these, of their own free will, without any reward or condition, have become Christians, and are so, and their Highnesses have joyfully and benignantly received them, and also have commanded them to be treated as their subjects and vassals; and you too are held and obliged to do the same. Wherefore as best we can, we ask and require you that you consider what we have said to you, and that you take the time that shall be necessary to understand and deliberate upon it, and that you acknowledge the Church as the Ruler and Superior of the whole world and the high priest called Pope, and in his name the King and Queen doña Juana our lords, in his place, as superiors and lords and kings of these islands and this *terra firme* by virtue of the said donation, and that you consent and give place that these religious fathers should declare and preach to you the aforesaid.

If you do so, you will do well . . . and we . . . shall receive you in all love and charity, and shall leave you your wives, and your children, and your lands, free without servitude, that you may do with them and with yourselves freely that which you like and think best, and they shall not compel you to turn Christians, unless you yourselves, when informed of the truth, should wish to be converted to our Holy Catholic Faith, as almost all the inhabitants of the rest of the islands have done. And besides this, their Highnesses award you many privileges and exceptions and will grant you many benefits.

But if you do not do this, and wickedly and intentionally delay to do so, I certify to you that, with the help of God, we shall forcibly enter into your country and shall make war against you in all ways and manners that we can, and shall subject you to the yoke and obedience of the Church and of their Highnesses; we shall take you and your wives and your children, and shall make slaves of them, and as such shall sell and dispose of them as their Highnesses may command; and we shall take away your goods, and shall do all the harm and damage that we can, as to vassals who do not obey, and refuse to receive their lord, and resist and contradict him; and we protest that the deaths and losses which shall accrue from this are your fault, and not that of their Highnesses, or ours, nor of these gentlemen who come with us. And that we have said this to you and made this Requirement, we request the notary here present to give us his testimony in writing, and we ask the rest who are present that they should be witnesses of the Requirement.

3. Augustín Rodríguez Describes the Rio Grande Pueblos, 1581–1582

And so they continued up the [Rio Grande] river for twenty days, through eighty leagues of uninhabited country, until they came to a settlement to which they gave the name of the province of Sant Felipe. There they found a permanent pueblo with houses two stories high and of good appearance, built of mud walls and white inside, the people being dressed in cotton *mantas* with shirts of the same. They learned that away from the river on both sides there were many other pueblos of Indians of the

Augustín Rodríguez describes the Rio Grande pueblos, 1581–1582. This document can be found in Herbert E. Bolton, ed., *Spanish Exploration in the Southwest, 1542–1706* (New York: Charles Scribner's Sons, 1916), 145–147.

same nation, who also received them peacefully and gave them of what they had, namely, maize, gourds, beans, chickens, and other things, which is what they live upon. Inquiry being made as to whether there were more settlements of people, by signs the natives replied in the affirmative.

With this information they passed on up the same river, and found many pueblos along the road they travelled, as well as others off to the sides, which were to be seen from the road; and they came to another nation of Indians of different tongue and dress, where they were also received peacefully and gladly by the Indians, who kissed the hands of the religious. These Indians are also clothed and have three-story houses, whitewashed and painted inside; and they plant many fields of maize, beans, and gourds, and raise many chickens.

From there they passed on to another nation, dwelling further up the same river. These were the finest people of all they had met, possessing better pueblos and houses, and were the ones who treated them best, giving them the most generously of whatever they had. They have well-built houses of four and five stories, with corridors and rooms twenty-four feet long and thirteen feet wide, whitewashed and painted. They have very good plazas, and leading from one to the other there are streets along which they pass in good order. Like the others, they have a good supply of provisions. Two or three leagues distant are other pueblos of the same nation, and consisting of three or four hundred houses, built in the same fashion. They dress in cotton like the foregoing nations.

4. Jacques Cartier on the Micmacs Meeting the French, 1534

... The Cape of the said South land was called The Cape of Hope, through the hope that there we had to finde some passage. The fourth of July we went along the coast of the said land on the Northerly side to finde some harborough, where wee entered into a creeke altogether open toward the South, where there is no succour against the wind: we thought good to name it S. Martines Creeke. There we stayed from the fourth of July until the twelfth: while we were there, on Munday being the sixth of the moneth, Service being done, wee with one of our boates went to discover a Cape and point of land that on the Westerne side was about seven or eight leagues from us, to see which way it did bend, and being within halfe a league of it, wee sawe two companies of boates of wilde men going from one land to the other: their boates were in number about fourtie or fiftie. One part of the which came to the said point, and a great number of the men went on shore making a great noise, beckening unto us that wee should come on land, shewing us certaine skinnes upon pieces of wood, but because we had but one onely boat, wee would not goe to them, but went to the other side lying in the Sea: they seeing us flee, prepared two of their boats to follow us, with which came also five more of them that were comming from the Sea side, all which approched neere unto our boate, dancing, and making many signes of joy and mirth, as it were desiring our friendship, saying in their tongue Napeu

Jacques Cartier on the Micmacs Meeting the French, 1534. This document can be found in Henry S. Burrage, ed., *Early English and French Voyages, Chiefly from Hakluyt, 1534–1608*, Original Narratives of Early American History Series (New York: Charles Scribner's Sons, 1906), 24–26.

tondamen assurtah, with many other words that we understood not. But because (as we have said) we had but one boat, wee would not stand to their courtesie, but made signes unto them that they should turne back, which they would not do, but with great furie came toward us: and suddenly with their boates compassed us about: and because they would not away from us by any signes that we could make, we shot off two pieces among them, which did so terrifie them, that they put themselves to flight toward the sayde point, making a great noise: and having staid a while, they began anew, even as at the first to come to us againe, and being come neere out wee strucke at them with two lances, which thing was so great a terrour unto them, that with great hast they beganne to flee, and would no more follow us.

The next day part of the saide wilde men with nine of their boates came to the point and entrance of the Creeke, where we with our ships were at road. We being advertised of their comming, went to the point where they were with our boates: but so soone as they saw us, they began to flee, making signes that they came to trafique with us, shewing us, such skinnes as they cloth themselves withall, which are of small value. We likewise made signes unto them, that we wished them no evill: and in signe thereof two of our men ventured to go on land to them, and cary them knives with other Iron wares, and a red hat to give unto their Captaine. Which when they saw, they also came on land, and brought some of their skinnes, and so began to deale with us, seeming to be very glad to have our iron wares and other things, stil dancing with many other ceremonies, as with their hands to cast Sea water on their heads. They gave us whatsoever they had, not keeping any thing, so that they were constrained to goe backe againe naked, and made us signes that the next day the would come againe, and bring more skinnes with them. . . .

5. Powhatan Speaks to Captain John Smith, 1609

Captaine Smith, you may understand that I having seene the death of all my people thrice, and not any one living of these three generations but my selfe; I know the difference of Peace and Warre better than any in my Country. But now I am old and ere long must die, my brethren, namely Opitchapam, Opechancanough, and Kekataugh, my two sisters, and their two daughters, are distinctly each others successors. I wish their experience no lesse then mine, and your love to them no lesse then mine to you. But this bruit from Nandsamund, that you are come to destroy my Country, so much affrighteth all my people as they dare not visit you. What will it availe you to take that by force you may quickly have by love, or to destroy them that provide you food. What can you get by warre, when we can hide our provisions and fly to the woods? Whereby you must famish by wronging us your friends. And why are you thus jealous of our loves seeing us unarmed, and both doe, and are willing still to feede you, with that you cannot get but by our labours? Thinke you I am so simple, not to know it is better to eate good meate, lye well, and sleepe quietly with my women and children, laugh and be merry with you, have copper, hatchets, or what I want being your friend: then be forced to flie from all, to lie cold in the woods, feede upon Acornes, rootes, and such trash, and be so hunted by you, that I

Powhatan Speaks to Captain John Smith, 1609. This document can be found in Philip L. Barbour, ed., *The Complete Works of Captain John Smith* (Chapel Hill, N.C.: University of North Carolina Press, 1986), 1:247.

can neither rest, eate, nor sleepe; but my tyred men must watch, and if a twig but breake, every one cryeth there commeth Captaine Smith: then must I fly I know not whether: and thus with miserable feare, end my miserable life, leaving my pleasures to such youths as you, which through your rash unadvisednesse may quickly as miserably end, for want of that, you never know where to finde. Let this therefore assure you of our loves, and every yeare our friendly trade shall furnish you with Corne; and now also, if you would come in friendly manner to see us, and not thus with your guns and swords as to invade your foes.

6. William Bradford on Samoset, Squanto, Massasoit, and the Pilgrims, 1620

... All this while the Indians came skulking about them, and would sometimes show them selves aloofe of, but when any approached near them, they would rune away. And once they stoale away their tools wher they had been at worke, & were gone to diner. But about the 16. *of March* a certaine Indian came bouldly amongst them, and spoke to them in broken English, which they could well understand, but marvelled at it. At length they understood by discourse with him, that he was not of these parts, but belonged to the eastrene parts, wher some English-ships came to fhish, with whom he was aquainted, & could name sundrie of them by their names, amongst whom he had gott his language. He became profitable to them in aquainting them with many things concerning the state of the cuntry in the east-parts wher he lived, which was afterwards profitable unto them; as also of the people hear, of their names, number, & strength; of their situation & distance from this place, and who was cheefe amongst them. His name was *Samaset;* he tould them also of another Indian whos name was *Squanto,* a native of this place, who had been in England & could speake better English then him selfe. Being, after some time of entertainmente & gifts, dismist, a while after he came againe, & 5. more with him, & they brought againe all the tooles that were stolen away before, and made way for the coming of their great Sachem, called *Massosoyt;* who, about 4. or 5. *days after,* came with the cheefe of his friends & other attendance, with the aforesaid *Squanto.* With whom, after frendly entertainment, & some gifts given him, they made a peace with him (which hath now continued this 24. years) in these terms.

1. That neither he nor any of his, should injurie or doe hurte to any of their peopl.
2. That if any of his did any hurte to any of theirs, he should send the offender, that they might punish him.
3. That if any thing were taken away from any of theirs, he should cause it to be restored; and they should doe the like to his.
4. If any did unjustly warr against him, they would aide him; if any did warr against them, he should aide them.
5. He should send to his neighbours confederats, to certifie them of this, that they might not wrong them, but might be likewise comprised in the conditions of peace.

William Bradford on Samoset, Squanto, Massasoit, and the Pilgrims, 1620, in William Bradford, *Of Plymouth Plantation: The Pilgrims in America,* edited by Harvey Wish (New York: Capricorn Books, 1962), 72–73.

6. That when ther men came to them, they should leave their bows & arrows behind them.

After these things he returned to his place caled *Sowams,* some 40. mile from this place, but *Squanto* continued with them, and was their interpreter, and was a spetiall instrument sent of God for their good beyond their expectation. He directed them how to set their corne, wher to take fish, and to procure other commodities, and was also their pilott to bring them to unknowne places for their profitt, and never left them till he dyed. He was a *native of this place,* & scarce any left alive besids him self. He was caried away with diverce others by one *Hunt,* a Mr. of a ship, who thought to sell them for slaves in Spaine; but he got away for England, and was entertained by a marchante in London, & imployed to New-found-land & other parts, & lastly brought hither into these parts by one Mr. *Dermer,* a gentle-man imployed by Sr. Ferdinando Gorges & others, for discovery, & other designes in these parts. . . .

◈ E S S A Y S

It is difficult, some would argue impossible, to reconstruct the motivations of American Indians in the era of first contact. Europeans and Indians seldom spoke each others' languages, and after this problem was rectified, they still understood the world in quite different ways. How then can we begin to understand these crucial early decades of mutual discovery? In the first essay, McGill University anthropologist Bruce Trigger explains two different views of Indian behavior—"romantic" and "rationalist." Using historical evidence from early contact events, Trigger argues that Indians acted rationally, often out of economic interest. Is this the only way that the evidence can be interpreted? Are Indian motives easily divided into romantic and rationalist categories? Historian James H. Merrell of Vassar College takes a longer look at the Catawbas' encounter with Englishmen and Africans in Virginia. Merrell traces the profound and subtle adaptations that the Catawbas made in a rapidly changing new world. How does the Catawba experience square with the ideas that Trigger elucidates?

Early Native North American Responses to European Contact

BRUCE G. TRIGGER

No treatment of primitive economics could be complete without some consideration of the religious factor, however brief it may be. . . . It will serve our purpose here if we bear in mind the fact that the efficacy of an implement, for example, was determined by factors which operated from beyond the material world.

The approaching quincentenary of Christopher Columbus's arrival in the Caribbean is stimulating much discussion about how the native peoples of the New World perceived and reacted to European intruders during the sixteenth century. This

Bruce Trigger, "Early Native North American Responses to European Contact: Romantic Versus Rationalist Interpretations," in *Journal of American History* 77 (March 1991), 1195–1215. Reprinted with permission.

occurs as both history and anthropology are being strongly influenced by the resurgence of cultural relativism, which accords to the beliefs transmitted within specific cultures a preeminent role as determinants of human behavior. This view has challenged and largely eclipsed the rationalist claim that human behavior is shaped mainly by calculations of individual self-interest that are uniform from one culture to another. Studies of how native peoples perceived the first Europeans they encountered will probably be strongly influenced by this shift in emphasis. I wish to investigate in this paper whether it is sound to assign cultural relativism a dominant role in the discussion of this issue. To answer that question, I will examine the conflicting claims of cultural relativists and rationalists and the utility of each position for interpreting the historical evidence. I will seek to demonstrate that, while cultural beliefs may have significantly influenced Indian reactions in the early stages of their encounters with Europeans, in the long run rationalist calculations came to play a preponderant role, and I will document how this cognitive reorganization occurred.

Great caution is required in discussing this issue, since only a small corpus of documents furnishes eyewitness accounts of contacts between native North Americans and Europeans during the sixteenth century. Whole classes of encounters that must have been very frequent, such as those involving European fishermen and whalers along the east coast of Canada, went almost unrecorded. Even the most detailed accounts of North American exploration and settlement provide few data from which native perceptions and motives can reliably be inferred. There is nothing comparable to the detailed accounts of the conquests of Mexico and Peru that were written not only by Spanish participants but also by native witnesses and their mestizo descendants. Even in these cases, however, one cannot help suspecting that the native American evidence was strongly colored by a desire to please Europeans. Moreover, all of these historical records are stereotyped in various ways that must be understood before they can be used reliably as historical documents. The archaeological record for the sixteenth century in North America also remains poorly understood. While future findings will prove highly informative about changes in population, settlement patterns, and material culture, archaeology alone is unlikely to reveal much about native American perceptions and feelings. This lack of precise information about so many topics has long invited scholars to impose their own preconceptions on the data, a situation that is likely to continue.

Alternative Approaches

The most persistent manifestation of these preconceptions has been the conflict between romantic and rationalist explanations of human behavior. For over two centuries the romantic approach has emphasized contingently variable cultural patterns as the principal determinants of human behavior, while rationalism has assigned the major role to practical, or universal, human reason. On first inspection, these two views would appear to be complementary rather than antithetical. Although the varied behavior of different groups often appears to reflect idiosyncratic cultural premises, few scholars would deny that rational calculation plays a significant role in human behavior.

Yet the dichotomy between these two positions is intensified by the alignment of romanticism with an idealist epistemology while rationalism is identified with a materialistic one. Even Karl Marx's seemingly accommodating observation, "Human beings make their history . . . not under circumstances chosen by themselves . . . but broadly encountered, given, and transmitted from the past," is ultimately committed to a materialistic epistemology and hence primarily to a rationalistic rather than a romantic view of human behavior.

The long-term alliances between idealism and romanticism and between materialism and rationalism are not historical accidents. Reason always serves some end. It may be used to promote goals that are wholly determined by the idiosyncrasies of a specific cultural system. Alternatively, it may allow the pursuit of more practical goals that sustain or alter a society's relationship to the physical world and that create new patterns for the production, distribution, and control of matter, energy, and information. While no process of reasoning occurs independently of culture, practical reason has the capacity to transcend culture. By mutual agreement the universalistic processes are termed rationalistic, and the privileging of them constitutes the basis of a materialistic view of human behavior. Some societies clearly are more consciously oriented toward such a privileging of practical reason than are others.

Anthropologists agree that individuals are born into cultural traditions that have been shaped by centuries of development, and each of which is unique in many respects. They also acknowledge that cultural traditions are "sense-making systems," systems that shape people's perceptions and values and hence influence their reactions to new experiences in important ways. More extreme versions of cultural relativism maintain that cultural patterns determine human behavior and view individuals as conceptually trapped within specific cultural traditions. These ideas have their roots within the German tradition of romanticism, which began in the eighteenth century; they were transmitted to American anthropology by Franz Boas. Through the advocacy of Victor Turner, Clifford Geertz, and Marshall D. Sahlins, the romantic approach has acquired enormous influence among American anthropologists in the last two decades. The study of behavior has been directed toward the investigation of beliefs and values, and there has been a growing fascination with structuralism, semiotics, hermeneutics, deconstructionism, and radical forms of relativism that deny the possibility of any objective understanding of human behavior. Each of these has played a significant role in making ideas, rather than behavior, appear to be the starting point for understanding human beings. Sahlins has also played a leading role in the application of a romantic approach to the study of early contact between Europeans and non-Europeans.

The major alternative to this romantic view is the rationalistic philosophy that anthropology borrowed from the French Enlightenment. It stresses the universality of human nature and maintains that through the exercise of reason human groups at the same general level of development will respond in a similar way to the same kinds of challenges. Rationalists recognize that many of the problems that confront large hierarchical societies are radically different from those that must be resolved by small-scale ones. While this evolutionary perspective implies that the problems that must be solved change as societies become more complex, it does not posit that the basic methods for doing this change. Instead a rationalist approach sees the ability to calculate that is common to all human beings as playing a major role in shaping the behavior of all human groups and posits that on the basis of such calculations the most important cultural variations and changes can be explained.

The most widely applied of these concepts is the "principle of least effort," which underlies many explanations of economic, ecological, and locational behavior. Game theory provides principles for exploring the management of risk and uncertainty. On the other hand, more specific formulations, such as that of "economic man," although widely applied, have proved much more controversial. In the late nineteenth and early twentieth centuries, racists believed that "primitive" groups were biologically less capable of rational thought and behavior than were "civilized" ones; but anthropologists, both before and since, have stressed the equal intelligence and rational capacity of all human groups. Rationalism underlies all modern cultural evolutionary approaches, which emphasize the uniformity of cultures at the same level of development regardless of the cultural traditions to which they belong. It is also congenial to a materialistic interpretation of human behavior, which assumes that human beings are likely to be most calculating, and hence least culture-bound, with respect to those matters that relate most directly to their material well-being. Although this approach exerted great influence on American anthropology after World War II through the neoevolutionism of Leslie White, Julian Steward, Morton H. Fried, Elman R. Service, and Marvin Harris, its influence has waned in recent years as romanticism has grown increasingly popular.

This debate, while central to anthropology, creates many problems for the majority of anthropologists who are not directly engaged in it. Most of them seek to avoid becoming partisans in a simplistic confrontation between rationalism and cultural relativism. They acknowledge persuasive arguments on both sides but suggest that little is to be gained by drawing too hard and fast a distinction between the "traditional" and the "rational" or that the relative significance of these factors may vary from case to case and hence may be difficult and not very productive to generalize about. Many argue that, especially in spheres of human activity relating to ecology, technology, and the economy, rational calculations involving universal considerations of efficiency and practicality play a more important role than do culturally constrained perceptions of reality, while cultural traditions may play a more important role in determining the content of religious beliefs. While there is much to be said in favor of these observations, they remain at too general a level to constitute an effective alternative position.

There is also considerable uncertainty about what kinds of evidence offer support for a rationalist or a relativist position. This can best be illustrated with an example from the literature on the fur trade, where it is widely assumed that the historical demonstration that native people continued to perceive their trade relations with Europeans much as they had understood exchanges of goods or sharing of resources among themselves prior to European contact supports a relativist rather than a rationalist position. Yet it can be demonstrated that in at least some instances this was not so. Eighteenth-century Hudson's Bay Company officials, who were used to optimizing market strategies, were puzzled that the native people of subarctic Canada traded fewer furs when they were offered higher prices for them. In modern times historians and economists have concluded that in traditional Indian cultures economic behavior was so embedded in social and political activities that it precluded "economic rationality" after contact with Europeans.

More recently, however, it has been recognized that, because there was a limit to the amount of goods that nomadic hunters could carry about with them, it made sense for native traders to collect fewer furs when those were sufficient to satisfy their needs. Under these circumstances, minimizing effort made more sense than maximizing profits. While cultural considerations no doubt played a significant role in influencing the manner in which native Americans and Europeans perceived the fur trade, these rational calculations conform to a logic that is universal rather than culturally specific. This argument is especially persuasive when native cultures that initially had similar subsistence economies but different trading practices are found to have adopted the same fur-trading patterns.

The problem that confronts historians and anthropologists is not simply to agree that relativistic and rational factors both play roles in human behavior but to determine what roles and how those factors fit together in the larger totality of behavior. Romantics tend to believe that early contact between Europeans and native Americans can best be explained as an interaction between cultures, or more specifically between mentalities. In the words of Tzvetan Todorov, contact was primarily "the discovery *self* makes of the *other.*" For rationalists such relations can be accounted for more effectively in terms of economic and political considerations. All of these factors were at work in concrete situations; what is disputed is which, if either, of them more effectively determined what happened. This is not a matter of analytical preference; it addresses fundamental issues concerning the nature of human behavior and how cultural change comes about.

In the rest of this paper, I will attempt to assess the relative value of romantic and rationalist approaches for explaining the behavior of native North Americans in their earliest encounters with Europeans. In encountering Europeans after 1492, native Americans experienced novel challenges of both a practical and a cognitive sort. They clearly had well-established traditions of intertribal diplomacy, which guided their relations with neighboring groups. These traditions combined rationalistic calculations with culturally influenced objectives. At the same time, each culture possessed beliefs about the creation and nature of the universe that, while having adaptive significance, were far more independently determined by cultural traditions than were aspects of culture that were subjected to practical application on a regular basis. With the exception of sporadic contacts with the Norse in Newfoundland and the eastern Arctic, none of the native Americans had ever previously had to deal with anything like the bearded, white-skinned beings who began haunting their seacoasts. The latter's huge ships, abundant metal goods, brightly colored clothes, and thundering guns and cannons placed them in a different category from any known or imaginable native group. So too did the extreme self-confidence and arrogance with which the Europeans frequently conducted themselves. How were native peoples to interpret such strangers as they appeared with increasing frequency along their coasts, giving away trinkets, carrying off native people, and leaving behind unknown diseases, before coming into closer contact as shipwrecked sailors, traders, would-be conquerors, and finally settlers?

First Perceptions

Indian folk traditions, often recorded generations after the events occurred, suggest that native North Americans believed the first European ships they saw to be floating islands inhabited by supernatural spirits and sometimes covered by white clouds (sails) from which lightning and thunder (cannons) were discharged, or else the mobile dwelling places of powerful spirits whom they prepared to welcome with sacrifices, food, and entertainment. These stories indicate that there was much about Europeans that offered itself to supernatural interpretation in terms of native religious concepts.

European records of early contacts with native Americans appear to corroborate the claim that in numerous instances native people interpreted the newcomers as supernatural. The Spanish who explored the settled Caribbean islands in the late fifteenth century were convinced that native beliefs in their divinity were a source of power that they could use to control these people. In 1492 Christopher Columbus concluded that the inhabitants of the Bahamas believed that he had come from the sky. The Spanish recounted natives holding prisoners under water to determine whether Europeans were immortal. Accounts derived from Spanish and Aztec sources provide detailed descriptions of how native religious beliefs played a major role in the subjugation of one of the most populous and complex societies in the New World by a handful of European intruders. The Aztec ruler Moctezuma Xocoyotzin's fears that Hernán Cortés might be the god Quetzalcoatl returning to rule Mexico caused him not to resist the Spanish invasion directly. This in turn facilitated the collapse of the Aztec tributary system and the eventual conquest of their city-state and all of Mexico. It is also clear that Cortés surmised the general nature of Moctezuma's fears and exploited them to his own advantage.

The accounts of the explorations of Jacques Cartier, Álvar Núñez Cabeza de Vaca, and Hernando de Soto described isolated instances when the Indians brought the sick of their communities to them and requested that they heal them. This suggests that these leaders were regarded as powerful shamans, if not as divinities, by native peoples in widely separated parts of North America. Native people are also reported to have worshiped and brought offerings to crosses erected by Francisco Vázquez de Coronado in what was to be the southwestern United States and to a large stone column put up by Jean Ribault in Florida, although it is possible that at least in the Southwest such behavior was motivated more by political than by religious considerations. The account of Francis Drake's voyage to California in 1579 describes the Coast Miwoks as offering sacrifices and lacerating their faces in the presence of the English visitors, despite the latter's efforts to make them stop. In 1587 English colonists in Virginia reported that because Indians had died of illness in each town they had passed through while they themselves had not become sick, they were viewed as the spirits of the dead returning to human society.

Similar incidents continued to be reported on the frontiers of European exploration in North America. Kenneth Morrison believes that early in their encounters the Abenakis (of what is now northern New England) inferred from European behavioral patterns that the Europeans might be the cannibal giants of their mythology. Jean Nicollet was said to have struck terror into the Winnebagos (or some other tribe of the upper Great Lakes region), who believed him to be a thunder spirit when he visited them in 1634. In 1670 Father Claude Allouez was treated as a *manitou* (spirit) when he visited the Mascoutens and Miamis on the shores of the Wolf River in Wisconsin. They made an offering of tobacco and appealed to him for relief from famine and disease. It is recorded that the Ojibwas of Red Lake, Minnesota, thought the first airplane they saw to be a thunderbird, or storm spirit, and rushed to the shore of the lake when it landed in order to throw tobacco offerings on the water.

Europeans were prepared to exploit North American Indian beliefs in their supernatural powers. Sometimes the deaths of early European explorers and settlers were concealed in the hope that Indians might continue to believe that they were immortal. In the course of their *entrada* into what is now the southeastern United States, de Soto and his followers, drawing upon their experiences in Mexico and Peru, claimed that he was the Child of the Sun and in that capacity had a claim upon the obedience of local chiefs.

Many cultural relativists assume that these scattered pieces of evidence provide insights into how native North Americans generally perceived Europeans in the early stages of their encounter. They take it for granted that similar culturally conditioned beliefs determined native responses in many other instances of early contact, but that such beliefs either were less obvious or failed to be recorded by less sensitive or less interested European observers. This is a highly suppositious conclusion. Moreover, most of the native accounts of what happened were recorded long after the event, and many are clearly influenced by European values and religious concepts. While detailed ethnographic analysis has revealed undeniably traditional elements in some of these tales, it is dangerous to overgeneralize from them about how native peoples first perceived Europeans, especially when we consider the great variability in specific beliefs from one culture to another.

The total corpus of documentary evidence that religious beliefs played an important and widespread role in influencing native behavior is in fact very limited. For the most part, native American relations with Europeans are portrayed as having been governed by relatively straightforward concerns with exchange and defense. While some of the survivors of the Pánfilo de Narváez expedition found roles for themselves as shamans and traders among the hunter-gatherers of Texas, perhaps because they were not equipped to play an effective part in subsistence activities, hundreds of shipwrecked Spanish sailors were enslaved by chiefs in Florida. Did this plethora of prosaic accounts result from many European recorders failing to understand Indian behavior? The written historical evidence is inadequate to supply a definitive answer. In those cases where religious behavior is specifically ascribed to native people in sixteenth-century accounts, there is the equally difficult problem of the extent to which European observers uncritically ascribed their own ethnocentric views about non-Christian religious beliefs to native people, thereby either misinterpreting their actions or ascribing religious motives to them in situations where those did not apply.

Fortunately, evidence concerning those native beliefs is not limited to historical records. In recent years George Hamell has carried out an extensive analysis of the basic concepts underlying the traditional religious beliefs of the Algonquian-, Iroquoian-, and Siouan-speaking peoples of northeastern North America, using ethnographic data recorded from earliest European contact to the present day. He concludes that the cosmologies of these peoples equated certain natural materials with physical, spiritual, and social well-being, both during this life and after death. These substances included marine shell, white and red metals (native silver and copper), and white, green, and red crystals and other kinds of stones. Such substances, which came from beneath the earth and water, were associated with such supernatural beings as the horned serpent, panther, and dragon, who were the guardian spirits and patrons of animal medicine societies.

These concepts appear to explain the inclusion of objects made from marine shell, native copper, and rock crystal in native burials of the Eastern Woodlands in prehistoric times. Archaeological evidence of the continuity of these burial practices from the Archaic period to the historical era suggests a persistence of these beliefs for over six thousand years, although intertribal exchanges of shell, copper, and other materials had been at one of their periodic low ebbs in the centuries preceding European contact. Hamell further suggests that the Indians equated European copper, brass, and tin with native copper and silver and equated glass beads with crystals and colored rocks. Because the Europeans possessed such extraordinarily large amounts of metalware and glass beads and came from across the ocean, where in Indian cosmology mythical time and space converged, they were regarded as supernatural beings or the returning spirits of the dead.

Hamell's ideas may account for the historically attested interest of native groups in European copper, brass, and tin objects and in glass beads. They would also explain why copper and brass kettles were cut into tiny fragments and dispersed by exchange among the tribes of the Northern Woodlands during the sixteenth century and why most of these goods are found in burials rather than in abandoned living sites during this period. The renewed emphasis on securing objects made of ritually important substances and burying them with the dead would also account for the increasing intertribal exchange of marine shell during this period. Although marine shell was a North American product, it was as important as copper or crystals in native religious beliefs, and Europeans never provided a satisfactory substitute for it.

In the course of the sixteenth century, the increasing availability of European goods led to greater emphasis in much of eastern North America on east-west exchange patterns, which in some areas superseded the predominantly north-south ones of earlier periods. European goods may also have brought about major changes in native life. The final expansion of the Huron confederacy and the coming together of all the Huron tribes in a small area at the southeastern corner of Georgian Bay (of Lake Huron) by the end of the sixteenth century seems to have been motivated primarily by a desire to have access to the secure trade routes leading by way of Lake Nipissing and the Ottawa River to the St. Lawrence Valley, rather than simply by a need to place more distance between themselves and hostile Iroquoian groups to the south and east. Before Hamell began his research, I had observed that "in the Indian history of [the northeastern Woodlands], trading in exotic goods has often played a role that was out of all proportion to its utilitarian significance" and that "what appears in the archaeological record as a few scraps of metal seems in fact to have been a sufficient catalyst to realize certain potentials for development that were inherent in prehistoric Huron society, but which otherwise might never have come to fruition."

Hamell's research, while neither finished nor free from controversy, suggests that a combination of ethnographic and archaeological data may provide significant insights into how native people perceived Europeans and European goods in the early stages of their interaction. This in turn may assist in interpreting the limited historical texts that are available concerning contact in the sixteenth century. While there may have been considerable variability in the manner in which different native groups interpreted the first Europeans they encountered, the archaeological and ethnographic evidence that Hamell has assembled also suggests that throughout eastern North America there were numerous culturally shared religious beliefs that encouraged native peoples to attribute various supernatural powers to the Europeans.

Seventeenth-Century Pragmatism

In any discussion of how native peoples perceived Europeans, the far more abundant data from the seventeenth century are of vital importance. If native beliefs continued to play a preponderant role in determining native reactions to Europeans so long after first contact, it would reinforce the assumption that they had done so during the previous century. Recent historical and ethnographic research has challenged established rationalistic interpretations of native dealings with Europeans during the seventeenth century. In particular, a growing commitment to romantic and cultural relativist explanations of human behavior has led an increasing number of historians and anthropologists to reject the proposition that European goods had more than symbolic value to native peoples so long as their societies maintained any semblance of independence from European control. Hamell states that he looks to "Northeastern Woodland Indian myth for an explanation of . . . their history during the two centuries following European contact." Calvin Martin has attracted a wide audience with his thinly documented claim that the fur trade developed, not as a result of native peoples' needing or especially desiring European goods, but as a by-product of their declaring war on fur-bearing animals and seeking to exterminate them because they held animal spirits to be responsible for the epidemics of European diseases that had begun in the sixteenth century. William Eccles portrays native cultures as economically independent, resilient, and able to determine their own destinies at least until the British conquest of New France in 1760. Conrad Heidenreich argues more specifically that "it is doubtful . . . that the Huron maintained their relations with the French because they had become economically dependent on European goods." He claims that they had instead become militarily dependent on the French for protection against the Iroquois.

These arguments ignore a solid body of evidence that by the beginning of the seventeenth century the bulk of trade between Europeans and Indians was not in glass beads, other ornaments, and liquor. The first Indians who traded with Europeans may have hung metal axes and hoes on their chests as ornaments and used stockings as tobacco pouches. Yet, by the 1620s, the Montagnais at Tadoussac, near the mouth of the St. Lawrence River, were using large quantities of clothing, hatchets, iron arrowheads, needles, sword blades, ice picks, knives, kettles, and preserved foods that they purchased from the French. For some purposes, especially in wet weather, woolen clothing proved superior to their traditional skin garments. They had also ceased to manufacture birchbark baskets and stone axes. In the 1630s, the Mohawks, who lived close to the Dutch traders at Fort Orange (now Albany), continued to produce their own food but were purchasing a wide range of clothing and metalware from Europeans. By the early 1640s, they owned more than three hundred guns, which had been paid for partly with skins they had seized from neighboring tribes. The Hurons, who lived much farther inland and had considerable transportation problems, were more selective in their purchases of European goods. They were primarily interested in obtaining metal cutting tools. In particular they wanted knives of all sizes, axes, and iron arrowheads. They also purchased guns, when the French were willing to sell them, and copper and brass kettles. The latter were easier to transport than their heavy and fragile clay cooking pots, and when they were worn out, they could be cut up and used as raw material to manufacture metal arrowheads and cutting tools as well as ornaments. In addition, Huron traders carried home glass beads and metal bracelets, which weighed relatively little. They do not appear to have purchased much cloth or many items of clothing, and unlike the coastal tribes, they did not seek alcoholic beverages when they came to trade. In selecting European goods, the Hurons showed a marked preference for tools with cutting edges that were superior to their own and that replaced native implements such as stone axes that took a long time to manufacture.

Among the Huron, Iroquois, and other Iroquoian-speaking peoples, a stone- and bone-based technology did not completely disappear until the late seventeenth century, which is later than G. T. Hunt and some archaeologists have believed. They also continued to manufacture pottery vessels until then, and the arrival of metal cutting tools seems to have resulted in a florescence of bone working. Yet, well before 1650, there was a marked decline in the frequency of stone tools among these groups. This suggests that by 1636 the Hurons were sufficiently dependent on the French for metal cutting tools that one of their chiefs, Aenons, was not exaggerating when he said that if his people "should remain two years without going down to Quebec to trade, they would find themselves reduced to such extremities that they might consider themselves fortunate to join with the Algonquins and to embark in their canoes." It is clear from the context of this report that Aenons was referring to the necessity of securing European goods, not to maintaining a military alliance against the Iroquois.

From the first arrival of the Jesuit missionaries in the 1620s, the Hurons and their neighbors regarded them as shamans. Beginning in the late 1630s, many Indians concluded that these priests were sorcerers or malevolent spirits, who were responsible for the great epidemics of European diseases that afflicted the native people of the region at that time. The Indians probably also continued to believe that the French, who were able to manufacture such large quantities of metal goods, must possess great supernatural power. Yet in their eyes this did not make Europeans intrinsically different from the Indians, who were also able to practice witchcraft and whose amulets and relations with appropriate spirits enabled them to hunt, fish, and move about on snowshoes and in canoes more effectively than Europeans did. Ordinary Frenchmen who traded, traveled, lived with Indian families, and even intermarried with them were viewed as regular human beings. They had been observed to become ill and die, and a few of them had even been killed by the Indians. The slowness of most Europeans to master native languages and skills led many Indians to conclude that on the whole Europeans were slow-witted, which accorded with the traditional Iroquoian belief that hairy people were unintelligent.

The Indians were also appalled by what they saw as the greed, violence, and bad manners of the French, which all were recognizable, if negatively valued, patterns of human behavior. Huron chiefs felt confident of their ability to outwit and manipulate French traders and officials, even when they were becoming politically and economically reliant on them. All of this suggests that by the seventeenth century the fur-trading peoples of the northern Woodlands regarded most, if not all, Europeans as human beings who were different from themselves and in some respects more powerful, but with whom they could interact on a normal basis.

Cognitive Reorganization

It is thus evident that at some point those native groups that initially reacted to Europeans primarily on the basis of their traditional religious beliefs came to regard Europeans as human beings with whom, while continuing to take account of their special customs and sensibilities, they could do business as they did with any other foreign group. The Indians' increasing familiarity with Europeans led to a "cognitive reorganization" in which the rational component inherent in the mental processes of every human being began to play the dominant role in guiding native relations with Europeans, while religious beliefs ceased to play the important part that in many cases they had done in the early stages of the encounter. The key factor in bringing about this transformation was the Indians' observation and rational evaluation of European behavior. This development accords with the general principle that whenever culturally transmitted beliefs are employed to guide human behavior, they are subject to rational scrutiny on the basis of the resulting performance; where those beliefs encourage counterproductive behavior, the evaluation may result in their being rejected, revised, or judged inapplicable. In the case of early encounters between Indians and Europeans, the question remains: Under what circumstances did this cognitive reorganization occur?

Some answers are provided by historical data from the early sixteenth century. When Giovanni da Verrazzano visited the relatively sheltered Narragansetts of southern New England in 1524, he found them anxious to obtain blue beads as well as bells and other trinkets made of copper. They were not interested in steel or iron objects, mirrors, or cloth. This suggests that these Indians were interested only in objects that had precise counterparts in their traditional system of belief and exchange. By contrast, Indians living farther north along the coast of Maine, who presumably had more contact with European fishermen and their goods (they were wearing European copper beads in their ears), were far less trustful of Verrazzano and his crew and would take in exchange for their goods only "knives, fish-hooks, and sharp metal." Likewise, the Micmacs that Jacques Cartier encountered in Chaleur Bay in 1534 not only indicated very clearly that they wished to barter their furs with the French but also sought hatchets, knives, and other ironware, as well as beads, in exchange. The following year the Iroquoians of Hochelaga, on Montreal Island, seemed pleased with any European goods that Cartier gave them, while those who lived at Stadacona, within the limits of modern Quebec City, and who appear already to have had limited access to European goods being traded by Breton fishermen at the Strait of Belle Isle, sought hatchets, knives, and awls from the French, as well as beads and other trinkets.

While the more isolated Hochelagans brought their sick to Cartier for him to heal, the Stadaconans, on being informed by two of their boys (whom Cartier had kidnapped and taken to France the previous year) that the goods he was trading were of little value in his own country, demanded more of those goods in exchange from the French. At the same time it was the Stadaconans who cured Cartier's crew of the scurvy that was afflicting them. Cartier had attempted to conceal their sickness and deaths among his men, not because he believed the Stadaconans thought the French to be immortal, but because he feared they might attack if they realized how defenseless these intruders were. Soon after Cartier's visit, a large quantity of ironware was reported being taken to the Strait of Belle Isle to trade for furs.

These data indicate that while groups such as the Narragansetts of Rhode Island and the Hochelagans of the upper St. Lawrence (who were remote from European fishermen at Cape Breton and the Strait of Belle Isle) were pleased to secure glass beads and copper and tin trinkets, bands that lived closer to these trading areas were anxious to obtain metal cutting tools as early as the 1520s and 1530s. The latter groups also appear to have already adopted a naturalistic view of Europeans. This suggests that if many Indian groups initially viewed Europeans as supernatural beings, upon closer contact this interpretation was replaced by the conclusion that Europeans were human beings like themselves. At the same time, European metal cutting tools came to be universally valued for their utilitarian advantages. While iron knives may have performed no more efficiently than did stone hide scrapers, they cut better and were more durable and easier to keep sharp than were stone tools. Metal tools also performed better as perforators, needles, and projectile points than did the stone and bone tools the Indians had used theretofore. It was for practical reasons that coastal peoples soon were putting iron tools at the top of their shopping lists. Glass beads and scraps of copper continued to dominate the indirect trade with the interior, but by the beginning of the seventeenth century native groups living as far inland as the lower Great Lakes were seeking metal cutting tools in preference to all other European goods. . . .

These observations may help to interpret the records of other major encounters between Europeans and native North Americans in the early sixteenth century. The native rulers who lived in the path of de Soto's pillaging expedition through what is now the southeastern United States adopted various strategies to placate, deflect, defeat, or speed him on his way. Yet overwhelmingly they conducted their relations with him in terms of what must have been the normal idiom of intergroup diplomacy in that region of hierarchical societies. De Soto was treated as a powerful chief with whom an alliance might be desirable or submission inevitable, but only rarely was he recorded as having been approached as a shaman and asked to cure the sick. Moreover, on at least two occasions rulers pointedly rejected claims that he possessed supernatural powers, including the panic-stricken assertion by his successor Luis de Moscoso that de Soto had not died but gone to the sky for a few days to visit the gods. The Indian ruler of Guachoya, mocking the latter tale, promised to offer two human sacrifices in honor of de Soto—a tradition in that area at the burial of neighboring chiefs. It would appear that previous contacts with shipwrecked Spanish sailors, would-be conquerors such as Juan Ponce de León and Pánfilo de Narváez, and colonists such as Lucas Vázquez de Ayllón had provided the native people living on the periphery of this densely settled region with an opportunity to assess Europeans and that the results of their observations were transmitted inland through the diplomatic networks linking adjacent tribes and chiefdoms. Despite the devastating effects of the Spanish plundering and burning of their settlements, the Indians of what is now the southeastern United States quickly took advantage of new resources that were presented to them; hogs, for example, were soon being eaten.

The accounts of Coronado's *entrada* into the Southwest also describe a naturalistic evaluation of Europeans by native people, who at first ineffectually opposed the Spanish invaders and then resorted to accommodative responses until Spanish exactions provoked them to renewed overt and clandestine resistance. Trading contacts with the Indians of northern Mexico possibly provided them with the information necessary to understand in advance what kind of beings the Spanish and their horses were and how they were likely to behave. Echoes of perceptions surrounding the original encounter between the Spanish and Aztecs in central Mexico may have been heard in an allegedly fifty-year-old prophecy of the Pueblo Indians that strangers would come from the south and conquer them, although this prophecy did not stifle resistance as more deeply rooted cultural traditions had done with Moctezuma.

The available evidence for the sixteenth century suggests that, whatever the initial Indian understanding of Europeans, a relatively short period of direct contact between the two groups resulted in a naturalistic interpretation of the newcomers. It also led to a growing demand for some European tools, which were seen as allowing tasks to be performed more effectively than did traditional stone and bone tools. These shifts involved the Indians' rationally assessing the performance of persons and goods and a desire to adopt a technology that would reduce their expenditure of energy on some routine tasks and improve the quality of their products. This technology was adopted as soon as it became available on a regular basis, even though it rendered native groups reliant on European suppliers.

The first impressions that native peoples had of Europeans and the initial strategies that these peoples devised for dealing with them seem to have been strongly influenced by their traditional beliefs. In some situations these strategies crucially shaped relations between the two groups. Where contact remained limited or indirect, initial interpretations persisted without significant modification for long periods As relations became more direct and intense, it appears that these interpretations were rapidly modified by rational assessments of what Europeans were like and what they had to offer. In at least some areas, these assessments spread inland ahead of European exploration. This appears to have happened more quickly in densely settled regions than in more thinly populated ones.

This utilitarian assessment of European technology does not mean that native people did not continue to assign their own social meanings to European goods or that native belief systems did not play a major role in determining how native people viewed Europeans or how European goods were used in religious contexts such as burials. On the contrary, there is evidence that basic native belief systems remained intact for long periods. This does not, however, rule out the importance of a rationalist perspective for understanding major aspects of native behavior, contrary to what more extreme relativists seek to maintain.

Conclusion

It is impossible to understand native American responses to their contact with Europeans in the early sixteenth century without a detailed knowledge of native cultures. Amerindian world views appear to have played an important role in structuring their initial understanding of these encounters, and this in turn influenced how native people behaved in these situations. The little that we know about these world views suggests that they varied from one region or ethnic group to another and that even adjacent, highly similar world views could, depending on historically contingent situations, structure native interpretations of contact in different ways. From the beginning some interpretations of Europeans were probably more "rational" than others.

Nevertheless, in areas where contact became frequent, it does not appear to have been long before all native perceptions and behavior were significantly influenced by rational appraisals of Europeans and what they had to offer. The long-term evidence indicates that economic determinists were not mistaken when they claimed that native people appreciated the material benefits to be derived from many items of European technology and that they sought to utilize this technology even at the cost of growing dependence upon their European trading partners. Native leaders also learned from observation to understand the motivations of the different European groups with whom they interacted and to devise strategies for coping with their demands. Native people were not constrained by their traditional beliefs to the extent that a rational assessment of the dangers and opportunities of the novel situations in which they found themselves was precluded. In general these assessments appear to have been strong enough to survive the psychological disruptions that must have accompanied the unprecedented epidemics of European diseases that afflicted native North Americans in the course of the sixteenth and seventeenth centuries.

If, in the long run, native people failed to devise strategies that could halt European aggression, it was not because they were unable to understand European behavior from a rational point of view. They failed because they were overwhelmed by European technological superiority, by growing numbers of European settlers as their own populations declined because of European diseases, and by increasing dependence upon European technology. They also failed because they were unable to modify their social organizations and values quickly enough to compete with the more disciplined European societies that were seeking to dominate and exploit North America. In North American Indian societies, decision making depended upon a slow process of achieving consensus, while European ones had evolved complex hierarchies of authority and command. Native groups therefore had less political maneuverability and less potential for concerted action when competing with Europeans. The creation of such structures, involving as it did the formation of new institutions and new patterns of behavior, was a slow process, even when the need for change was clearly perceived. Native societies became increasingly dependent upon European ones and were dominated by them because they lacked time to develop the human and material resources required to compete with them, not because of their incapacity to understand in rational terms what was happening to them.

Although the examples in this paper have been drawn from North America, these conclusions should apply equally to relations between European colonists and native groups elsewhere in the Americas and around the world. Giving due importance to a rationalist approach explains why in the course of the expansion of the European world system there has not been more variation in the basic patterns of relations between Europeans and native peoples, and why world systems formulations . . . are possible. Had relations between Europeans and native peoples been determined mainly by their respective ideologies, much more variation could be expected.

While cultural relativists have expanded our understanding of how in the beginning native reactions to Europeans were conditioned by their cultural beliefs, this approach must not undermine our appreciation of the ability of native people to monitor new situations and to devise strategies that allowed them to respond in a rational fashion to the opportunities as well as the disruptive challenges of a European presence. While the importance of native beliefs should never be underestimated, in the long run a rationalist and materialist analysis of cultural interaction seems to explain far more about what happened to native people following European contact than does an analysis that assigns primary explanatory power to their traditional beliefs.

The Indians' New World: The Catawba Experience

JAMES H. MERRELL

In August 1608 John Smith and his band of explorers captured an Indian named Amoroleck during a skirmish along the Rappahannock River. Asked why his men—a hunting party from towns upstream—had attacked the English, Amoroleck replied that they had heard the strangers "were a people come from under the world, to take their world from them." Smith's prisoner grasped a simple yet important truth that students of colonial America have overlooked: after 1492 native Americans lived in a world every bit as new as that confronting transplanted Africans or Europeans.

The failure to explore the Indians' new world helps explain why, despite many excellent studies of the native American past, colonial history often remains "a history of those men and women—English, European, and African—who transformed America from a geographical expression into a new nation." One reason Indians generally are left out may be the apparent inability to fit them into the new world theme, a theme that exerts a powerful hold on our historical imagination and runs throughout our efforts to interpret American development. From Frederick Jackson Turner to David Grayson Allen, from Melville J. Herskovits to Daniel C. Littlefield, scholars have analyzed encounters between peoples from the Old World and conditions in the New, studying the complex interplay between European or African cultural patterns and the American environment. Indians crossed no ocean, peopled no faraway land. It might seem logical to exclude them.

The natives' segregation persists, in no small degree, because historians still tend to think only of the new world as the New World, a geographic entity bounded by the Atlantic Ocean on the one side and the Pacific on the other. Recent research

James H. Merrell, "The Indians' New World: The Catawba Experience," in *William and Mary Quarterly* 41 (1984), 537–565. Reprinted with permission of the author.

suggests that process was as important as place. Many settlers in New England re-created familiar forms with such success that they did not really face an alien environment until long after their arrival. Africans, on the other hand, were struck by the shock of the new at the moment of their enslavement, well before they stepped on board ship or set foot on American soil. If the Atlantic was not a barrier between one world and another, if what happened to people was more a matter of subtle cultural processes than mere physical displacements, perhaps we should set aside the maps and think instead of a "world" as the physical and cultural milieu within which people live and a "new world" as a dramatically different milieu demanding basic changes in ways of life. Considered in these terms, the experience of natives was more closely akin to that of immigrants and slaves, and the idea of an encounter between worlds can—indeed, must—include the aboriginal inhabitants of America.

For American Indians a new order arrived in three distinct yet overlapping stages. First, alien microbes killed vast numbers of natives, sometimes before the victims had seen a white or black face. Next came traders who exchanged European technology for Indian products and brought natives into the developing world market. In time traders gave way to settlers eager to develop the land according to their own lights. These three intrusions combined to transform native existence, disrupting established cultural habits and requiring creative responses to drastically altered conditions. Like their new neighbors, then, Indians were forced to blend old and new in ways that would permit them to survive in the present without forsaking their past. By the close of the colonial era, native Americans as well as whites and blacks had created new societies, each similar to, yet very different from, its parent culture.

The range of native societies produced by this mingling of ingredients probably exceeded the variety of social forms Europeans and Africans developed. Rather than survey the broad spectrum of Indian adaptations, this article considers in some depth the response of natives in one area, the southern piedmont. Avoiding extinction and eschewing retreat, the Indians of the piedmont have been in continuous contact with the invaders from across the sea almost since the beginning of the colonial period, thus permitting a thorough analysis of cultural intercourse. Moreover, a regional approach embracing groups from South Carolina to Virginia can transcend narrow (and still poorly understood) ethnic or "tribal" boundaries without sacrificing the richness of detail a focused study provides.

Indeed, piedmont peoples had so much in common that a regional perspective is almost imperative. No formal political ties bound them at the onset of European contact, but a similar environment shaped their lives, and their adjustment to this environment fostered cultural uniformity. Perhaps even more important, these groups shared a single history once Europeans and Africans arrived on the scene. Drawn together by their cultural affinities and their common plight, after 1700 they migrated to the Catawba Nation, a cluster of villages along the border between the Carolinas that became the focus of native life in the region. Tracing the experience of these upland communities both before and after they joined the Catawbas can illustrate the consequences of contact and illuminate the process by which natives learned to survive in their own new world.

For centuries, ancestors of the Catawbas had lived astride important aboriginal trade routes and straddled the boundary between two cultural traditions, a position that involved them in a far-flung network of contacts and affected everything from potting techniques to burial practices. Nonetheless, Africans and Europeans were utterly unlike any earlier foreign visitors to the piedmont. Their arrival meant more than merely another encounter with outsiders; it marked an important turning point in Indian history. Once these newcomers disembarked and began to feel their way across the continent, they forever altered the course and pace of native development.

Bacteria brought the most profound disturbances to upcountry villages. When Hernando de Soto led the first Europeans into the area in 1540, he found large towns already "grown up in grass" because "there had been a pest in the land" two years before, a malady probably brought inland by natives who had visited distant Spanish posts. The sources are silent about other "pests" over the next century, but soon after the English began colonizing Carolina in 1670 the disease pattern became all too clear. Major epidemics struck the region at least once every generation—in 1698, 1718, 1738, and 1759—and a variety of less virulent illnesses almost never left native settlements.

Indians were not the only inhabitants of colonial America living—and dying— in a new disease environment. The swamps and lowlands of the Chesapeake were a deathtrap for Europeans, and sickness obliged colonists to discard or rearrange many of the social forms brought from England. Among native peoples long isolated from the rest of the world and therefore lacking immunity to pathogens introduced by the intruders, the devastation was even more severe. John Lawson, who visited the Carolina upcountry in 1701, when perhaps ten thousand Indians were still there, estimated that "there is not the sixth Savage living within two hundred Miles of all our Settlements, as there were fifty Years ago." The recent smallpox epidemic "destroy'd whole Towns," he remarked, "without leaving one *Indian* alive in the Village." Resistance to disease developed with painful slowness; colonists reported that the outbreak of smallpox in 1759 wiped out 60 percent of the natives, and, according to one source, "the woods were offensive with the dead bodies of the Indians; and dogs, wolves, and vultures were . . . busy for months in banqueting on them."

Survivors of these horrors were thrust into a situation no less alien than what European immigrants and African slaves found. The collected wisdom of generations could vanish in a matter of days if sickness struck older members of a community who kept sacred traditions and taught special skills. When many of the elders succumbed at once, the deep pools of collective memory grew shallow, and some dried up altogether. In 1710, Indians near Charleston told a settler that "they have forgot most of their traditions since the Establishment of this Colony, they keep their Festivals and can tell but little of the reasons: their Old Men are dead." Impoverishment of a rich cultural heritage followed the spread of disease. Nearly a century later, a South Carolinian exaggerated but captured the general trend when he noted that Catawbas "have forgotten their antient rites, ceremonies, and manufactures."

The same diseases that robbed a piedmont town of some of its most precious resources also stripped it of the population necessary to maintain an independent existence. In order to survive, groups were compelled to construct new societies from the splintered remnants of the old. The result was a kaleidoscopic array of migrations from ancient territories and mergers with nearby peoples. While such behavior was not unheard of in aboriginal times, population levels fell so precipitously after contact that survivors endured disruptions unlike anything previously known.

The dislocations of the Saponi Indians illustrate the common course of events. In 1670 they lived on the Staunton River in Virginia and were closely affiliated with a group called Nahyssans. A decade later Saponis moved toward the coast and built a town near the Occaneechees. When John Lawson came upon them along the Yadkin River in 1701, they were on the verge of banding together in a single village with Tutelos and Keyauwees. Soon thereafter Saponis applied to Virginia officials for permission to move to the Meherrin River, where Occaneechees, Tutelos, and others joined them. In 1714, at the urging of Virginia's Lt. Gov. Alexander Spotswood, these groups settled at Fort Christanna farther up the Meherrin. Their friendship with Virginia soured during the 1720s, and most of the "Christanna Indians" moved to the Catawba Nation. For some reason this arrangement did not satisfy them, and many returned to Virginia in 1732, remaining there for a decade before choosing to migrate north and accept the protection of the Iroquois.

Saponis were unusual only in their decision to leave the Catawbas. Enos, Occaneechees, Waterees, Keyauwees, Cheraws, and others have their own stories to tell, similar in outline if not in detail. With the exception of the towns near the confluence of Sugar Creek and the Catawba River that composed the heart of the Catawba Nation, piedmont communities decimated by disease lived through a common round of catastrophes, shifting from place to place and group to group in search of a safe haven. Most eventually ended up in the Nation, and during the opening decades of the eighteenth century the villages scattered across the southern upcountry were abandoned as people drifted into the Catawba orbit.

No mere catalog of migrations and mergers can begin to convey how profoundly unsettling this experience was for those swept up in it. While upcountry Indians did not sail away to some distant land, they, too, were among the uprooted, leaving their ancestral homes to try to make a new life elsewhere. The peripatetic existence of Saponis and others proved deeply disruptive. A village and its surrounding territory were important elements of personal and collective identity, physical links in a chain binding a group to its past and making a locality sacred. Colonists, convinced that Indians were by nature "a shifting, wandring People," were oblivious to this, but Lawson offered a glimpse of the reasons for native attachment to a particular locale. "In our way," he wrote on leaving an Eno-Shakori town in 1701, "there stood a great Stone about the Size of a large Oven, and hollow; this the *Indians* took great Notice of, putting some Tobacco into the Concavity, and spitting after it. I ask'd them the Reason of their so doing, but they made me no Answer." Natives throughout the interior honored similar places— graves of ancestors, monuments of stones commemorating important events—that could not be left behind without some cost.

The toll could be physical as well as spiritual, for even the most uneventful of moves interrupted the established cycle of subsistence. Belongings had to be packed and unpacked, dwellings constructed, palisades raised. Once migrants had completed the business of settling in, the still more arduous task of exploiting new terrain awaited them. Living in one place year after year endowed a people with intimate knowledge of the area. The richest soils, the best hunting grounds, the choicest sites for gathering nuts or berries—none could be learned without years of experience, tested by time and passed down from one generation to the next. Small wonder that Carolina Indians worried about being "driven to some unknown Country, to live, hunt, and get our Bread in."

Some displaced groups tried to leave "unknown Country" behind and make their way back home. In 1716 Enos asked Virginia's permission to settle at "Enoe Town" on the North Carolina frontier, their location in Lawson's day. Seventeen years later William Byrd II came upon an abandoned Cheraw village on a tributary of the upper Roanoke River and remarked how "it must have been a great misfortune to them to be obliged to abandon so beautiful a dwelling." The Indians apparently agreed: in 1717 the Virginia Council received "Divers applications" from the Cheraws (now living along the Pee Dee River) "for Liberty to Seat themselves on the head of Roanoke River." Few natives managed to return permanently to their homelands. But their efforts to retrace their steps hint at a profound sense of loss and testify to the powerful hold of ancient sites.

Compounding the trauma of leaving familiar territories was the necessity of abandoning customary relationships. Casting their lot with others traditionally considered foreign compelled Indians to rearrange basic ways of ordering their existence. Despite frequent contacts among peoples, native life had always centered in kin and town. The consequences of this deep-seated localism were evident even to a newcomer like John Lawson, who in 1701 found striking differences in language, dress, and physical appearance among Carolina Indians living only a few miles apart. Rules governing behavior also drew sharp distinctions between outsiders and one's own "Country-Folks." Indians were "very kind, and charitable to one another," Lawson reported, "but more especially to those of their own Nation." A visitor desiring a liaison with a local woman was required to approach her relatives and the village headman. On the other hand, "if it be an *Indian* of their own Town or Neighborhood, that wants a Mistress, he comes to none but the Girl." Lawson seemed unperturbed by this barrier until he discovered that a "Thief [is] held in Disgrace, that steals from any of his Country-Folks," "but to steal from the *English* [or any other foreigners] they reckon no Harm."

Communities unable to continue on their own had to revise these rules and reweave the social fabric into new designs. What language would be spoken? How would fields be laid out, hunting territories divided, houses built? How would decisions be reached, offenders punished, ceremonies performed? When Lawson remarked that "now adays" the Indians must seek mates "amongst Strangers," he unwittingly characterized life in native Carolina. Those who managed to withstand the ravages of disease had to redefine the meaning of the term *stranger* and transform outsiders into insiders.

The need to harmonize discordant peoples, an unpleasant fact of life for all native Americans, was no less common among black and white inhabitants of America during these years. Africans from a host of different groups were thrown into slavery together and forced to seek some common cultural ground, to blend or set aside clashing habits and beliefs. Europeans who came to America also met unexpected and unwelcome ethnic, religious, and linguistic diversity. The roots of the problem were quite different; the problem itself was much the same. In each case people from different backgrounds had to forge a common culture and a common future.

Indians in the southern uplands customarily combined with others like themselves in an attempt to solve the dilemma. Following the "principle of least effort," shattered communities cushioned the blows inflicted by disease and depopulation by joining a kindred society known through generations of trade and alliances. Thus Saponis coalesced with Occaneechees and Tutelos—nearby groups "speaking much the same language"—and Catawbas became a sanctuary for culturally related refugees from throughout the region. Even after moving in with friends and neighbors, however, natives tended to cling to ethnic boundaries in order to ease the transition. In 1715 Spotswood noticed that the Saponis and others gathered at Fort Christanna were "confederated together, tho' still preserving their different Rules." Indians entering the Catawba Nation were equally conservative. As late as 1743 a visitor could hear more than twenty different dialects spoken by peoples living there, and some bands continued to reside in separate towns under their own leaders.

Time inevitably sapped the strength of ethnic feeling, allowing a more unified Nation to emerge from the collection of Indian communities that occupied the valleys of the Catawba River and its tributaries. By the mid-eighteenth century, the authority of village headmen was waning and leaders from the host population had begun to take responsibility for the actions of constituent groups. The babel of different tongues fell silent as "*Kàtahba*," the Nation's "standard, or court-dialect," slowly drowned out all others. Eventually, entire peoples followed their languages and their leaders into oblivion, leaving only personal names like Santee Jemmy, Cheraw George, Congaree Jamie, Saponey Johnny, and Eno Jemmy as reminders of the Nation's diverse heritage.

No European observer recorded the means by which nations became mere names and a [collection] of groups forged itself into one people. No doubt the colonists' habit of ignoring ethnic distinctions and lumping confederated entities together under the Catawba rubric encouraged amalgamation. But Anglo-American efforts to create a society by proclamation were invariably unsuccessful; consolidation had to come from within. In the absence of evidence, it seems reasonable to conclude that years of contacts paved the way for a closer relationship. Once a group moved to the Nation, intermarriages blurred ancient kinship networks, joint war parties or hunting expeditions brought young men together, and elders met in a council that gave everyone some say by including "all the Indian Chiefs or Head Men of that [Catawba] Nation and the several Tribes amongst them together." The concentration of settlements within a day's walk of one another facilitated contact and communication. From their close proximity, common experience, and shared concerns, people developed ceremonies and myths that compensated for those lost to disease and gave the Nation a stronger collective consciousness. Associations evolved that balanced traditional narrow ethnic allegiance with a new, broader, "national" identity, a balance that tilted steadily toward the latter. Ethnic differences died hard, but the peoples of the Catawba Nation learned to speak with a single voice.

Muskets and kettles came to the piedmont more slowly than smallpox and measles. Spanish explorers distributed a few gifts to local headmen, but inhabitants of the interior did not enjoy their first real taste of the fruits of European technology until Englishmen began venturing inland after 1650. Indians these traders met in up-country towns were glad to barter for the more efficient tools, more lethal weapons, and more durable clothing that colonists offered. Spurred on by eager natives, men from Virginia and Carolina quickly flooded the region with the material trappings of European culture. In 1701 John Lawson considered the Wateree Chickanees "very poor in *English* Effects" because a few of them lacked muskets.

Slower to arrive, trade goods were also less obvious agents of change. The Indians' ability to absorb foreign artifacts into established modes of existence hid the revolutionary consequences of trade for some time. Natives leaped the technological gulf with ease in part because they were discriminating shoppers. If hoes were too small, beads too large, or cloth the wrong color, Indian traders refused them. Items they did select fit smoothly into existing ways. Waxhaws tied horse bells around their ankles at ceremonial dances, and some of the traditional stone pipes passed among the spectators at these dances had been shaped by metal files. Those who could not afford a European weapon fashioned arrows from broken glass. Those who could went to great lengths to "set [a new musket] streight, sometimes shooting away above 100 Loads of Ammunition, before they bring the Gun to shoot according to their Mind."

Not every piece of merchandise hauled into the upcountry on a trader's packhorse could be "set streight" so easily. Liquor, for example, proved both impossible to resist and extraordinarily destructive. Indians "have no Power to refrain this Enemy," Lawson observed, "though sensible how many of them (are by it) hurry'd into the other World before their Time." And yet even here, natives aware of the risks sought to control alcohol by incorporating it into their ceremonial life as a device for achieving a different level of consciousness. Consumption was usually restricted to men, who "go as solemnly about it, as if it were part of their Religion," preferring to drink only at night and only in quantities sufficient to stupefy them. When ritual could not confine liquor to safe channels, Indians went still further and excused the excesses of overindulgence by refusing to hold an intoxicated person responsible for his actions. "They never call any Man to account for what he did, when he was drunk," wrote Lawson, "but say, it was the Drink that caused his Misbehaviour, therefore he ought to be forgiven."

Working to absorb even the most dangerous commodities acquired from their new neighbors, aboriginal inhabitants of the uplands, like African slaves in the lowlands, made themselves at home in a different technological environment. Indians became convinced that "Guns, and Ammunition, besides a great many other Necessaries, . . . are helpful to Man" and eagerly searched for the key that would unlock the secret of their production. At first many were confident that the "*Quera,* or good Spirit," would teach them to make these commodities "when that good Spirit sees fit." Later they decided to help their deity along by approaching the colonists. In 1757, Catawbas asked Gov. Arthur Dobbs of North Carolina "to send us Smiths and other Tradesmen to teach our Children."

It was not the new products themselves but the Indians' failure to learn the mysteries of manufacture from either Dobbs or the *Quera* that marked the real revolution wrought by trade. During the seventeenth and eighteenth centuries, everyone in eastern North America—masters and slaves, farmers near the coast and Indians near the mountains—became producers of raw materials for foreign markets and found themselves caught up in an international economic network. Piedmont natives were part of this larger process, but their adjustment was more difficult because the contrast with previous ways was so pronounced. Before European contact, the localism characteristic of life in the uplands had been sustained by a remarkable degree of self-sufficiency. Trade among peoples, while common, was conducted primarily in commodities such as copper, mica, and shells, items that, exchanged with the appropriate ceremony, initiated or confirmed friendships among groups. Few, if any, villages relied on outsiders for goods essential to daily life.

Intercultural exchange eroded this traditional independence and entangled natives in a web of commercial relations few of them understood and none controlled. In 1670 the explorer John Lederer observed a striking disparity in the trading habits of Indians living near Virginia and those deep in the interior. The "remoter Indians," still operating within a precontact framework, were content with ornamental items such as mirrors, beads, "and all manner of gaudy toys and knacks for children." "Neighbourour-Indians," on the other hand, habitually traded with colonists for cloth, metal tools, and weapons. Before long, towns near and far were demanding the entire range of European wares and were growing accustomed— even addicted—to them. "They say we English are fools for . . . not always going with a gun," one Virginia colonist familiar with piedmont Indians wrote in the early 1690s, "for they think themselves undrest and not fit to walk abroad, unless they have their gun on their shoulder, and their shot-bag by their side." Such an enthusiastic conversion to the new technology eroded ancient craft skills and hastened complete dependence on substitutes only colonists could supply.

By forcing Indians to look beyond their own territories for certain indispensable products, Anglo-American traders inserted new variables into the aboriginal equation of exchange. Colonists sought two commodities from Indians—human beings and deerskins—and both undermined established relationships among native groups. While the demand for slaves encouraged piedmont peoples to expand their traditional warfare, the demand for peltry may have fostered conflicts over hunting territories. Those who did not fight each other for slaves or deerskins fought each other for the European products these could bring. As firearms, cloth, and other items became increasingly important to native existence, competition replaced comity at the foundation of trade encounters as villages scrambled for the cargoes of merchandise. Some were in a better position to profit than others. In the early 1670s Occaneechees living on an island in the Roanoke River enjoyed power out of all proportion to their numbers because they controlled an important ford on the trading path from Virginia to the interior, and they resorted to threats, and even to force, to retain their advantage. In Lawson's day Tuscaroras did the same, "hating that any of these Westward *Indians* should have any Commerce with the *English,* which would prove a Hinderance to their Gains."

Competition among native groups was only the beginning of the transformation brought about by new forms of exchange. Inhabitants of the piedmont might bypass the native middleman, but they could not break free from a perilous dependence on colonial sources of supply. The danger may not have been immediately apparent to Indians caught up in the excitement of acquiring new and wonderful things. For years they managed to dictate the terms of trade, compelling visitors from Carolina and Virginia to abide by aboriginal codes of conduct and playing one colony's traders against the other to ensure an abundance of goods at favorable rates. But the natives' influence over the protocol of exchange combined with their skill at incorporating alien products to mask a loss of control over their own destiny. The mask came off when, in 1715, the traders—and the trade goods—suddenly disappeared during the Yamassee War.

The conflict's origins lay in a growing colonial awareness of the Indians' need for regular supplies of European merchandise. In 1701 Lawson pronounced the Santees "very tractable" because of their close connections with South Carolina. Eight years later he was convinced that the colonial officials in Charleston "are absolute Masters over the *Indians* . . . within the Circle of their Trade." Carolina traders who shared this conviction quite naturally felt less and less constrained to obey native rules governing proper behavior. Abuses against Indians mounted until some men were literally getting away with murder. When repeated appeals to colonial officials failed, natives throughout Carolina began to consider war. Persuaded by Yamassee ambassadors that the conspiracy was widespread and convinced by years of ruthless commercial competition between Virginia and Carolina that an attack on one colony would not affect relations with the other, in the spring of 1715 Catawbas and their neighbors joined the invasion of South Carolina.

The decision to fight was disastrous. Colonists everywhere shut off the flow of goods to the interior, and after some initial successes Carolina's native enemies soon plumbed the depths of their dependence. In a matter of months, refugees holed up in Charleston noticed that "the Indians want ammunition and are not able to mend their Arms." The peace negotiations that ensued revealed a desperate thirst for fresh supplies of European wares. Ambassadors from piedmont towns invariably spoke in a single breath of restoring "a Peace and a free Trade," and one delegation even admitted that its people "cannot live without the assistance of the English."

Natives unable to live without the English henceforth tried to live with them. No upcountry group mounted a direct challenge to Anglo-America after 1715. Trade quickly resumed, and the piedmont Indians, now concentrated almost exclusively in the Catawba valley, briefly enjoyed a regular supply of necessary products sold by men willing once again to deal according to the old rules. By mid-century, however, deer were scarce and fresh sources of slaves almost impossible to find. Anglo-American traders took their business elsewhere, leaving inhabitants of the Nation with another material crisis of different but equally dangerous dimensions.

Indians casting about for an alternative means of producing the commodities they craved looked to imperial officials. During the 1740s and 1750s native dependence shifted from colonial traders to colonial authorities as Catawba leaders repeatedly visited provincial capitals to request goods. These delegations came not to beg but to bargain. Catawbas were still of enormous value to the English as allies and frontier guards, especially at a time when Anglo-America felt threatened by the French and their Indian auxiliaries. The Nation's position within reach of Virginia and both Carolinas enhanced its value by enabling headmen to approach all three colonies and offer their people's services to the highest bidder.

The strategy yielded Indians an arsenal of ammunition and a variety of other merchandise that helped offset the declining trade. Crown officials were especially generous when the Nation managed to play one colony off against another. In 1746 a rumor that the Catawbas were about to move to Virginia was enough to garner them a large shipment of powder and lead from officials in Charleston concerned about losing this "valuable people." A decade later, while the two Carolinas fought for the honor of constructing a fort in the Nation, the Indians encouraged (and received) gifts symbolizing good will from both colonies without reaching an agreement with either. Surveying the tangled thicket of promises and presents, the Crown's superintendent of Indian affairs, Edmond Atkin, ruefully admitted that "the People of both Provinces . . . have I believe [*sic*] tampered too much on both sides with those Indians, who seem to understand well how to make their Advantage of it."

By the end of the colonial period delicate negotiations across cultural boundaries were as familiar to Catawbas as the strouds [coarse woolen goods] they wore and the muskets they carried. But no matter how shrewdly the headmen loosened provincial purse strings to extract vital merchandise, they could not escape the simple fact that they no longer held the purse containing everything needed for their daily existence. In the space of a century the Indians had become thoroughly embedded in an alien economy, denizens of a new material world. The ancient self-sufficiency was only a dim memory in the minds of the Nation's elders.

The Catawba peoples were veterans of countless campaigns against disease and masters of the arts of trade long before the third major element of their new world, white planters, became an integral part of their life. Settlement of the Carolina uplands did not begin until the 1730s, but once underway it spread with frightening speed. In November 1752, concerned Catawbas reminded South Carolina governor James Glen how they had "complained already . . . that the white People were settled too near us." Two years later five hundred families lived within thirty miles of the Nation and surveyors were running their lines into the middle of native towns. "[T]hose Indians are now in a fair way to be surrounded by White People," one observer concluded.

Settlers' attitudes were as alarming as their numbers. Unlike traders who profited from them or colonial officials who deployed them as allies, ordinary colonists had little use for Indians. Natives made poor servants and worse slaves; they obstructed settlement; they attracted enemy warriors to the area. Even men who respected Indians and earned a living by trading with them admitted that they made unpleasant neighbors. "We may observe of them as of the fire," wrote the South Carolina trader James Adair after considering the Catawbas' situation on the eve of the American Revolution, " 'it is safe and useful, cherished at proper distance; but if too near us, it becomes dangerous, and will scorch if not consume us.' "

A common fondness for alcohol increased the likelihood of intercultural hostilities. Catawba leaders acknowledged that the Indians "get very Drunk with [liquor] this is the Very Cause that they oftentimes Commit those Crimes that is offensive to You and us." Colonists were equally prone to bouts of drunkenness. In the 1760s the itinerant Anglican minister, Charles Woodmason, was shocked to find the citizens of one South Carolina upcountry community "continually drunk." More appalling still, after attending church services "one half of them got drunk before they went home." Indians sometimes suffered at the hands of intoxicated farmers. In 1760 a Catawba woman was murdered when she happened by a tavern shortly after four of its patrons "swore they would kill the first Indian they should meet with."

Even when sober, natives and newcomers found many reasons to quarrel. Catawbas were outraged if colonists built farms on the Indians' doorstep or tramped across ancient burial grounds. Planters, ignorant of (or indifferent to) native rules of hospitality, considered Indians who requested food nothing more than beggars and angrily drove them away. Other disputes arose when the Nation's young men went looking for trouble. As hunting, warfare, and other traditional avenues for achieving status narrowed, Catawba youths transferred older patterns of behavior into a new arena by raiding nearby farms and hunting cattle or horses.

Contrasting images of the piedmont landscape quite unintentionally generated still more friction. Colonists determined to tame what they considered a wilderness were in fact erasing a native signature on the land and scrawling their own. Bridges, buildings, fences, roads, crops, and other "improvements" made the area comfortable and familiar to colonists but uncomfortable and unfamiliar to Indians. "The Country side wear[s] a New face," proclaimed Woodmason proudly; to the original inhabitants, it was a grim face indeed. "His Land was spoiled," one Catawba headman told British officials in 1763. "They have spoiled him 100 Miles every way." Under these circumstances, even a settler with no wish to fight Indians met opposition to his fences, his outbuildings, his very presence. Similarly, a Catawba on a routine foray into traditional hunting territories had his weapon destroyed, his goods confiscated, his life threatened by men with different notions of the proper use of the land.

To make matters worse, the importance both cultures attached to personal independence hampered efforts by authorities on either side to resolve conflicts. Piedmont settlers along the border between the Carolinas were "people of desperate fortune," a frightened North Carolina official reported after visiting the area. "[N]o officer of Justice from either Province dare meddle with them." Woodmason, who spent even more time in the region, came to the same conclusion. "We are without any Law, or Order," he complained; the inhabitants' "Impudence is so very high, as to be past bearing." Catawba leaders could have sympathized. Headmen informed colonists that the Nation's people "are oftentimes Cautioned from . . . ill Doings altho' to no purpose for we Cannot be present at all times to Look after them." "What they have done I could not prevent," one chief explained.

Unruly, angry, intoxicated—Catawbas and Carolinians were constantly at odds during the middle decades of the eighteenth century. Planters who considered Indians "proud and deveilish" were themselves accused by natives of being "very bad and quarrelsome." Warriors made a habit of "going into the Settlements, robbing and stealing where ever they get an Opportunity." Complaints generally brought no satisfaction—"they laugh and makes their Game of it, and says it is what they will"—leading some settlers to "whip [Indians] about the head, beat and abuse them." "The white People . . . and the Cuttahbaws, are Continually at variance," a visitor to the Nation fretted in June 1759, "and Dayly New Animositys Doth a rise Between them which In my Humble oppion will be of Bad Consequence In a Short time, Both Partys Being obstinate."

The litany of intercultural crimes committed by each side disguised a fundamental shift in the balance of physical and cultural power. In the early years of colonization of the interior the least disturbance by Indians sent scattered planters into a panic. Soon, however, Catawbas were few, colonists many, and it was the natives who now live in fear. "[T]he white men [who] Lives Near the Neation is Contenuely asembleing and goes In the [Indian] towns In Bodys . . . ," worried another observer during the tense summer of 1759. "[T]he[y] tretton the[y] will Kill all the Cattabues."

The Indians would have to find some way to get along with these unpleasant neighbors if the Nation was to survive. As Catawba population fell below five hundred after the smallpox epidemic of 1759 and the number of colonists continued to climb, natives gradually came to recognize the futility of violent resistance. During the last decades of the eighteenth century they drew on years of experience in dealing with Europeans at a distance and sought to overturn the common conviction that Indian neighbors were frightening and useless.

This process was not the result of some clever plan; Catawbas had no strategy for survival. A headman could warn them that "the White people were now seated all round them and by that means had them entirely in their power." He could not command them to submit peacefully to the invasion of their homeland. The Nation's continued existence required countless individual decisions, made in a host of diverse circumstances, to complain rather than retaliate, to accept a subordinate place in a land that once was theirs. Few of the choices made survive in the record. But it is clear that, like the response to disease and to technology, the adaptation to white settlement was both painful and prolonged.

Catawbas took one of the first steps along the road to accommodation in the early 1760s, when they used their influence with colonial officials to acquire a reservation encompassing the heart of their ancient territories. This grant gave the Indians a land base, grounded in Anglo-American law, that prevented farmers from shouldering them aside. Equally important, Catawbas now had a commodity to exchange with nearby settlers. These men wanted land, the natives had plenty, and shortly before the Revolution the Nation was renting tracts to planters for cash, livestock, and manufactured goods.

Important as it was, land was not the only item Catawbas began trading to their neighbors. Some Indians put their skills as hunters and woodsmen to a different use, picking up stray horses and escaped slaves for a reward. Others bartered their pottery, baskets, and table mats. Still others traveled through the upcountry, demonstrating their prowess with the bow and arrow before appreciative audiences. The exchange of these goods and services for European merchandise marked an important adjustment to the settlers' arrival. In the past, natives had acquired essential items by trading peltry and slaves or requesting gifts from representatives of the Crown. But piedmont planters frowned on hunting and warfare, while provincial authorities—finding Catawbas less useful as the Nation's population declined and the French threat disappeared—discouraged formal visits and handed out fewer presents. Hence the Indians had to develop new avenues of exchange that would enable them to obtain goods in ways less objectionable to their neighbors. Pots, baskets, and acres proved harmless substitutes for earlier methods of earning an income.

Quite apart from its economic benefits, trade had a profound impact on the character of Catawba-settler relations. Through countless repetitions of the same simple procedure at homesteads scattered across the Carolinas, a new form of intercourse arose, based not on suspicion and an expectation of conflict but on trust and a measure of friendship. When a farmer looked out his window and saw Indians approaching, his reaction more commonly became to pick up money or a jug of whiskey rather than a musket or an axe. The natives now appeared, the settler knew, not to plunder or kill but to peddle their wares or collect their rents.

The development of new trade forms could not bury all of the differences between Catawba and colonist overnight. But in the latter half of the eighteenth century the beleaguered Indians learned to rely on peaceful means of resolving intercultural conflicts that did arise. Drawing a sharp distinction between "the good men that have rented Lands from us" and "the bad People [who] has frequently imposed upon us," Catawbas called on the former to protect the Nation from the latter. In 1771 they met with the prominent Camden storekeeper, Joseph Kershaw, to request that he "represent us when [we are] a grieved." After the Revolution the position became more formal. Catawbas informed the South Carolina government that, being "destitute of a man to take care of, and assist us in our affairs," they had chosen one Robert Patten "to take charge of our affairs, and to act and do for us."

Neither Patten nor any other intermediary could have protected the Nation had it not joined the patriot side during the Revolutionary War. Though one scholar has termed the Indians' contribution to the cause "rather negligible," they fought in battles throughout the southeast and supplied rebel forces with food from time to time. These actions made the Catawbas heroes and laid a foundation for their popular renown as staunch patriots. In 1781 their old friend Kershaw told Catawba leaders how he welcomed the end of "this Long and Bloody War, in which You have taken so Noble a part and have fought and Bled with your white Brothers of America." Grateful Carolinians would not soon forget the Nation's service. Shortly after the Civil War an elderly settler whose father had served with the Indians in the Revolution echoed Kershaw's sentiments, recalling that "his father never communicated much to him [about the Catawbas], except that all the tribe . . . served the entire war . . . and fought most heroically."

Catawbas rose even higher in their neighbors' esteem when they began calling their chiefs "General" instead of "King" and stressed that these men were elected by the people. The change reflected little if any real shift in the Nation's political forms, but it delighted the victorious Revolutionaries. In 1794 the Charleston *City Gazette* reported that during the war "King" Frow had abdicated and the Indians chose "General" New River in his stead. "What a pity," the paper concluded, "certain people on a certain island have not as good optics as the Catawbas!" In the same year the citizens of Camden celebrated the anniversary of the fall of the Bastille by raising their glasses to toast "King Prow [*sic*]—may all kings who will not follow his example follow that of Louis XVI." Like tales of Indian patriots, the story proved durable. Nearly a century after the Revolution one nearby planter wrote that "the Catawbas, emulating the examples of their white brethren, threw off regal government."

The Indians' new image as republicans and patriots, added to their trade with whites and their willingness to resolve conflicts peacefully, brought settlers to view Catawbas in a different light. By 1800 the natives were no longer violent and dangerous strangers but what one visitor termed an "inoffensive" people and one group of planters called "harmless and friendly" neighbors. They had become traders of pottery but not deerskins, experts with a bow and arrow but not hunters, ferocious warriors against runaway slaves or tories but not against settlers. In these ways Catawbas could be distinctively Indian yet reassuringly harmless at the same time.

The Nation's separate identity rested on such obvious aboriginal traits. But its survival ultimately depended on a more general conformity with the surrounding society. During the nineteenth century both settlers and Indians owned or rented land. Both spoke proudly of their Revolutionary heritage and their republican forms of government. Both drank to excess. Even the fact that Catawbas were not Christians failed to differentiate them sharply from nearby white settlements, where, one visitor noted n 1822, "little attention is paid to the sabbath, or religeon."

In retrospect it is clear that these similarities were as superficial as they were essential. For all the changes generated by contacts with vital Euro-American and Afro-American cultures, the Nation was never torn loose from its cultural moorings. Well after the Revolution, Indians maintained a distinctive way of life rich in tradition and meaningful to those it embraced. Ceremonies conducted by headmen and folk tales told by relatives continued to transmit traditional values and skills from one generation to the next. Catawba children grew up speaking the native language, making bows and arrows or pottery, and otherwise following patterns of belief and behavior derived from the past. The Indians' physical appearance and the meandering paths that set Catawba settlements off from neighboring communities served to reinforce this cultural isolation.

The natives' utter indifference to missionary efforts after 1800 testified to the enduring power of established ways. Several clergymen stopped at the reservation in the first years of the nineteenth century; some stayed a year or two; none enjoyed any success. As one white South Carolinian noted in 1826, Catawbas were "Indians still." Outward conformity made it easier for them to blend into the changed landscape. Beneath the surface lay a more complex story.

Those few outsiders who tried to piece together that story generally found it difficult to learn much from the Indians. A people shrewd enough to discard the title of "King" was shrewd enough to understand that some things were better left unsaid and unseen. Catawbas kept their Indian names, and sometimes their language, a secret from prying visitors. They echoed the racist attitudes of their white neighbors and even owned a few slaves, all the time trading with blacks and hiring them to work in the Nation, where the laborers "enjoyed considerable freedom" among the natives. Like Afro-Americans on the plantation who adopted a happy, childlike demeanor to placate suspicious whites, Indians on the reservation learned that a "harmless and friendly" posture revealing little of life in the Nation was best suited to conditions in post-Revolutionary South Carolina.

Success in clinging to their cultural identity and at least a fraction of their ancient lands cannot obscure the cost Catawba peoples paid. From the time the first European arrived, the deck was stacked against them. They played the hand dealt them well enough to survive, but they could never win. An incident that took place at the end of the eighteenth century helps shed light on the consequences of compromise. When the Catawba headman, General New River, accidentally injured the horse he had borrowed from a nearby planter named Thomas Spratt, Spratt responded by "banging old New River with a pole all over the yard." This episode provided the settler with a colorful tale for his grandchildren; its effect on New River and his descendants can only be imagined. Catawbas did succeed in the sense that they adjusted to a hostile and different world, becoming trusted friends instead of feared enemies. Had they been any less successful they would not have survived the eighteenth century. But poverty and oppression have plagued the Nation from New River's day to our own. For a people who had once been proprietors of the piedmont, the pain of learning new rules was very great, the price of success very high.

On that August day in 1608 when Amoroleck feared the loss of his world, John Smith assured him that the English "came to them in peace, and to seeke their loves." Events soon proved Amoroleck right and his captor wrong. Over the course of the next three centuries not only Amoroleck and other piedmont Indians but natives throughout North America had their world stolen and another put in its place. Though this occurred at different times and in different ways, no Indians escaped the explosive mixture of deadly bacteria, material riches, and alien peoples that was the invasion of America. Those in the southern piedmont who survived the onslaught were ensconced in their new world by the end of the eighteenth century. Population levels stabilized as the Catawba peoples developed immunities to once-lethal diseases. Rents, sales of pottery, and other economic activities proved adequate to support the Nation at a stable (if low) level of material life. Finally, the Indians' image as "inoffensive" neighbors gave them a place in South Carolina society and continues to sustain them today.

Vast differences separated Catawbas and other natives from their colonial contemporaries. Europeans were the colonizers, Africans the enslaved, Indians the dispossessed: from these distinct positions came distinct histories. Yet once we acknowledge the differences, instructive similarities remain that help to integrate natives more thoroughly into the story of early America. By carving a niche for themselves in response to drastically different conditions, the peoples who composed the Catawba Nation shared in the most fundamental of American experiences. Like Afro-Americans, these Indians were compelled to accept a subordinate position in American life yet did not altogether lose their cultural integrity. Like settlers of the Chesapeake, aboriginal inhabitants of the uplands adjusted to appalling mortality rates and wrestled with the difficult task of "living with death." Like inhabitants of the Middle Colonies, piedmont groups learned to cope with unprecedented ethnic diversity by balancing the pull of traditional loyalties with the demands of a new social order. Like Puritans in New England, Catawbas found that a new world did not arrive all at once and that localism, self-sufficiency, and the power of old ways were only gradually eroded by conditions in colonial America. More hints of a comparable heritage could be added to this list, but by now it should be clear that Indians belong on the colonial stage as important actors in the unfolding American drama rather than bit players, props, or spectators. For they, too, lived in a new world.

◈ *F U R T H E R   R E A D I N G*

James Axtell, *After Columbus: Essays in the Ethnohistory of Colonial North America* (1989)
———, *Beyond 1492: Encounters in Colonial North America* (1992)
———, *Natives and Newcomers: The Cultural Origins of North America* (2000)
Colin G. Calloway, *New Worlds for All: Indians, Europeans, and the Remaking of Early America* (1997)

Alfred Crosby, *The Columbian Exchange: Biological and Cultural Consequences of 1492* (1972)

———, *Ecological Imperialism: The Biological Expansion of Europe, 900–1900* (1986)

———, "Virgin Soil Epidemics as a Factor in Aboriginal Depopulation in America," *William and Mary Quarterly* 33 (1976), 289–299

William M. Denevan, *The Native Population of the Americas in 1492* (1976)

Henry F. Dobyns, *Their Number Become Thinned: Native American Population Dynamics in Eastern North America* (1983)

Kathryn E. Holland-Braund, *Deerskins and Duffels: Creek Indian Trade With Anglo-America, 1685–1815* (1993)

Jonathan H. C. King, *First Peoples, First Contacts: Native Peoples of North America* (1999)

Peter C. Mancall, *Deadly Medicine: Indians and Alcohol in Early America* (1995)

David E. Stannard, *American Holocaust: The Conquest of the New World* (1992)

Ian K. Steele, *Warpaths: Invasions of North America* (1994)

Margaret Connell Szasz, ed., *Between Indian and White Worlds: The Cultural Broker* (1994)

Bruce G. Trigger, *The Children of Aataentsic: A History of the Huron People to 1660* (1972)

Richard White, T*he Roots of Dependency: Subsistence, Environment, and Social Change among the Choctaws, Pawnees, and Navajos* (1983)

CHAPTER
4

The Southern Borderlands

◈

In the southern borderlands, the country that now comprises the tier of states from California to the Carolinas, Spaniards made the first contacts with Indians. In the sixteenth century, these newcomers proceeded to settle permanently in Florida and New Mexico, and extended their grip to Texas and California in the eighteenth century. In the eighteenth century, France founded small communities from New Orleans to the northern reaches of the Mississippi Valley, a region they called Louisiana. From 1762 until 1800, Spain ruled the vast Louisiana Territory, although French people and customs continued to predominate until the United States purchased it in 1803. Europeans wished to convert Indians to the Christian faith as they appropriated America for themselves. Thus, Spain and France sent Catholic missionaries among the Indians and hoped to convert them to Christianity.

Spain's missionary efforts were part of a comprehensive plan to conquer the Indians and integrate them into Spanish colonial society. While Spaniards regarded their missionary enterprises as a humane, Christian duty that benefited Indians, native people often resented and resisted European efforts to alter American religious traditions. Before the arrival of Europeans, Indians followed many religious traditions. The Pueblo Indians had different beliefs and rituals from the Ojibwa; Chumash and Iroquois Indians likewise led distinctive religious lives. While there was great religious variety among them, on the whole Indians possessed a spiritual life that was quite different from the Christian beliefs of Europeans. Indians were not monotheists. A pantheon of culture heroes, earth creators, magical animals, and spirits populated the Indian religious world. These beings could bring power, sickness, health, disaster, and knowledge to humans. In addition, all living creatures and many inanimate things possessed spiritual power. There were places that were associated with magical force where Indians fasted, prayed, and dreamed for sacred revelations and the power that came with them. Each tribe had its own priests, shamans, doctors, and other spiritual leaders, but ordinary people could also possess power and communicate with the spirit world. In general, Indians' sense of religious well-being was strongly linked to place; each rock, stream, tree, valley, and mountain range had special power and meaning for the human inhabitants.

These beliefs and practices had served Indians well for many centuries. Their observations of prescribed rites, prayer, and respect for tradition brought fertility, abundant crops, health and well-being to Indians most of the time. When rain failed or game was scarce and people suffered, continued faith in age-old beliefs ordinarily brought a return of storm clouds and animals. Thus, the cycle of the seasons, ritual, food, healing ceremonies, and the land itself made religious beliefs palpable to Indians. Missionaries thought that Indian spirituality was merely a manifestation of ignorance. At worst, clergymen concluded that Indians worshiped the devil. In the opinion of these Christians, Native American religions were not only wrong, they were evil and had to be wiped out. During the first centuries of the colonial era, the conquest of America was a contest for spiritual as well as political supremacy.

Indians confronted missionaries with mixed feelings. Some (we will never know how many) willingly converted to the new religion, while others staunchly resisted. And some tribes integrated Christianity into their societies while continuing to practice their ancient religious rituals. This is called religious syncretism, and the Pueblo Indians are perhaps the best known example of this practice. The road to syncretism could be rocky in the southern borderlands. Nor did Indians necessarily appreciate the efforts of individual missionaries, as the following documents and essays show.

◈ D O C U M E N T S

In the late summer of 1680, the Pueblo Indians rose against the Spanish colonists of New Mexico and drove them out. The Pueblos had chafed under Spanish rule since 1598 when Don Juan de Oñate founded the first Spanish settlements. The conquest of the Pueblo Indians was harsh. Military, civilian, and religious *españoles* found ways to exploit Pueblo labor and expropriate Pueblo lands. The Spanish regime impoverished the Pueblos, and exotic new diseases, which the Spaniards inadvertently brought to New Mexico, caused the native population to decline. Pueblo rebels were especially keen to kill the missionaries and eliminate all reminders of Christianity. The Pueblo revolt devastated Spanish New Mexico. More than ten years passed before Spanish authorities could reestablish settlements there. Documents 1 and 2 are depositions taken one year after the uprising that provide Pueblo explanations of the revolt's causes and its leaders. Naranjo reveals that Pueblo religious beliefs played an important part in the rebellion, while Juan indicates that discontent was brewing among the Pueblos because the leaders' promises were not being realized. Document 3 shows that some mission Indians in California were also resentful of missionary authority, so much so that they murdered a friar. Document 4, however, shows that some Indians fully accepted Catholic religious teachings. Pablo Tac, a Luiseño Indian reared in a California mission, studied for the priesthood in Rome where he recorded these recollections of mission life.

1. Pedro Naranjo's (Keresan Pueblo) Explanation of the 1680 Pueblo Revolt, 1681

In the . . . plaza de armas on [December 19, 1681], for the prosecution of the judicial proceedings of this case his lordship caused to appear before him an Indian prisoner named Pedro Naranjo, a native of the pueblo of San Felipe, . . . who was captured in the advance and attack upon the pueblo of La Isleta. He makes himself

Pedro Naranjo's (Keresan Pueblo) Explanation of the 1680 Pueblo Revolt, 1681, in Charles W. Hackett, ed., *Revolt of the Pueblo Indians of New Mexico and the Otermín's Attempted Reconquest, 1680–1682*, 2 vols., translated by Charmion C. Shelby (Albuquerque, N. Mex.: University of New Mexico Press, 1942), 2:245–249. Copyright © 1942 University of New Mexico Press. Reprinted by permission of the publisher.

understood very well in the Castilian language and speaks his mother tongue and the Tegua. He took the oath in due legal form in the name of God, our Lord, and a sign of the cross, under charge of which he promised to tell the truth concerning what he knows. . . .

Asked whether he knows the reason or motives which the Indians of this kingdom had for rebelling, forsaking the law of God and obedience to his Majesty, and committing such grave and atrocious crimes, and who were the leaders and principal movers, and by whom and how it was ordered; and why they burned the images, temples, crosses, rosaries, and things of divine worship, committing such atrocities as killing priests, Spaniards, women, and children, the rest that he might know touching the question, he said that since the government of Señor General Hernando Ugarte y la Concha they have planned to rebel on various occasions through conspiracies of the Indian sorcerers, and that although in some pueblos the messages were accepted, in other parts they would not agree to it; and that it is true that during the government of the said señor general seven or eight Indians were hanged for this same cause, whereupon the unrest subsided. Some time thereafter they [the conspirators] sent from the pueblo of Los Taos . . . two deerskins with some pictures on them signifying conspiracy after their manner, in order to convoke the people to a new rebellion, and the said deerskins passed to the province of Moqui [the Hopi pueblos], where they refused to accept them. The pact which they had been forming ceased for the time being, but they always kept in their hearts the desire to carry it out, so as to live as they are living to-day. Finally, in the past years, at the summons of an Indian named Popé who is said to have communication with the devil, it happened that in an estufa [kiva] of the pueblo of Los Taos there appeared to the said Popé three figures of Indians who never came out of the estufa. They gave the said Popé to understand that they were going underground to the lake of Copala. He saw these figures emit fire from all the extremities of their bodies, and that one of them was called Caudi, another Tilini, and the other Tleume; and these three beings spoke to the said Popé, who was in hiding from the secretary, Francisco Xavier, who wished to punish him as a sorcerer. They told him to make a cord of maguey fiber and tie some knots in it which would signify the number of days that they must wait before the rebellion. He said that the cord was passed through all the pueblos of the kingdom so that the ones which agreed to it [the rebellion] might untie one knot in sign of obedience, and by the other knots they would know the days which were lacking; and this was to be done on pain of death to those who refused to agree to it. As a sign of agreement and notice of having concurred in the treason and perfidy they were to send up smoke signals to that effect in each one of the pueblos singly. The said cord was taken from pueblo to pueblo by the swiftest youths under the penalty of death if they revealed the secret. Everything being thus arranged, two days before the time set for its execution, because his lordship had learned of it and had imprisoned two Indian accomplices from the pueblo of Tesuque, it was carried out prematurely that night, because it seemed to them that they were now discovered; and they killed religious, Spaniards, women, and children. This being done, it was proclaimed in all the pueblos that everyone in common should obey the commands of their father whom they did not know, which would be given through El Caydi or El Popé. This was heard by Alonso Catití, who came to the pueblo of this declarant to say that everyone must unite to go to the villa to kill the governor and the Spaniards who had remained with him, and that he who did not obey would, on their return, be beheaded; and in fear of this they agreed to it. Finally the señor governor and those who were with him escaped from the siege, and later this declarant saw that as soon as the Spaniards had left the kingdom an order came from the said Indian, Popé, in which he commanded all the Indians to break the lands and enlarge their cultivated fields, saying that now they were as they had been in ancient times, free from the labor they had performed for the religious and the Spaniards, who could not now be alive. He said that this is the legitimate cause and the reason they had for rebelling, because they had always desired to live as they had when they came out of the lake of Copala. Thus he replies to the question.

Asked for what reason they so blindly burned the images, temples, crosses, and other things of divine worship, he stated that the said Indian, Popé, came down in person, and with him El Saca and El Chato from the pueblo of Los Taos, and other captains and leaders and many people who were in his train, and he ordered in all the pueblos through which he passed that they instantly break up and burn the images of the holy Christ, the Virgin Mary and the other saints, the crosses, and everything pertaining to Christianity, and that they burn the temples, break up the bells, and separate from the wives whom God had given them in marriage and take those whom they desired. In order to take away their baptismal names, the water, and the holy oils, they were to plunge into the rivers and wash themselves with amole, which is a root native to the country, washing even their clothing, with the understanding that there would thus be taken from them the character of the holy sacraments. They did this, and also many other things which he does not recall, given to understand that this mandate had come from the Caydi and the other two who emitted fire from their extremities in the said estufa of Taos, and that they thereby returned to the state of their antiquity, as when they came from the lake of Copala; that this was the better life and the one they desired, because the God of the Spaniards was worth nothing and theirs was very strong, the Spaniards' God being rotten wood. These things were observed and obeyed by all except some who, moved by the zeal of Christians, opposed it, and such persons the said Popé caused to be killed immediately. He saw to it that they at once erected and rebuilt their houses of idolatry which they call estufas, and made very ugly masks in imitation of the devil in order to dance the dance of the cacina [kachina, or spirit]; and he said likewise that the devil had given them to understand that living thus in accordance with the law of their ancestors, they would harvest a great deal of maize, many beans, a great abundance of cotton, calabashes, and very large watermelons and cantaloupes; and that they could erect their houses and enjoy abundant health and leisure. As he has said, the people were very much pleased, living at their ease in this life of their antiquity, which was the chief cause of their falling into such laxity. Following what has already been stated, in order to terrorize them further and cause them to observe the diabolical commands, there came to them a pronouncement from the three demons already described, and from El Popé, to the effect that he who might still keep in his heart a regard for the priests, the governor, and the Spaniards would be known from his unclean face and clothes, and would be punished. And he stated that the said four persons stopped at nothing to have their commands obeyed. Thus he replies to the question. . . .

2. Juan (Tiwa Pueblo) Explains the Pueblo Revolt, 1681

. . . [H]e had brought into his presence another Indian who said his name is Juan, and in his language Vnsuti, that he is a native of the pueblo of Alameda, a widower, and that he did not know his age. Apparently he is more than a hundred years old because he declares that he remembers distinctly, as if it were yesterday, when the Spaniards entered this kingdom, and that when he was baptized he was able to stand on his own feet. His lordship received the oath from him in due legal form before God, our Lord, and a sign of the cross, under charge of which he promised to tell the truth as he might be questioned and might know it, the seriousness of the oath having been explained to him by the said interpreter. Being asked if he knows why he is arrested, he said that he judges it was because some Spaniards caught him in the pueblo of Alameda on the occasion when, finding himself alone and without any relative and having kin among the Spaniards, he had gone in search of them; and that before he arrived the Spaniards caught him and brought him to this camp. He did not hide himself or do anything whatever; rather, he is rejoiced to find himself among Christians, and although he is a prisoner, he is well content. Asked to state truly what he knows or has heard of the discussions and juntas which the rebellious Indians are holding, he says what he has heard in general is that they are saying they must die from hardships of cold and want; that they have gone to the sierras, leaving the sick in caves among the rocks; and that although it is true that many have desired to go down to their pueblos peacefully, because the señor governor and captain-general has sent to find them, and because the Spaniards who went to Cochití also summoned them, granting them the said peace to which many of them agreed so that they might go to the quiet of their houses, the chief captains who governed them took them away from their pueblos, carrying them to the sierras, and being unwilling to agree to anything; and the rest of the people do what they order out of fear. This is what he knows and has heard, and this is why they say that they want to die. He has heard nothing else about this matter. Asked to state and declare truthfully what reasons or motives the natives of this kingdom had for rebelling, he said that he does not know, nor has he heard any reason given. Asked why they killed religious and Spaniards and burned the church and all the houses, which they did after living so long a time among the Spaniards, protected from the enemy Apaches, being Christians and living quietly in their pueblos and under the law of God, he said that to him, he being so old, they never communicated anything; that the most he knew, which is common knowledge, was that when they committed this destruction it was by order of an Indian from San Juan whom he does not know, who came down through all the pueblos in company with the captains and many other people, ordering them to burn the churches, convents, holy crosses, and every object pertaining to Christianity; and that they separate from the wives the religious had given them in marriage and take those whom they wished; and other things that he does not remember. He said that

Juan (Tiwa Pueblo) Explains the Pueblo Revolt, 1681, in Charles Wilson Hackett, ed., *Revolt of the Pueblo Indians of New Mexico and Otermín's Attempted Reconquest, 1680–1682*, 2 vols., translated by Charmion C. Shelby (Albuquerque, N. Mex.: University of New Mexico Press, 1942), 2:344–46. Copyright © 1942 University of New Mexico Press. Reprinted with permission.

this Indian of San Juan told and gave all the people to understand in the pueblos where he went that they should do as he said because they would thereby be assured of harvesting much maize, cotton, and an abundance of all crops, and better ones than ever, and that they would live in great ease. The people have remained very well content and pleased with all this until now, when they have experienced the contrary, and have seen that they deceived them, for as a matter of fact they have had very small harvests, there has been no rain, and everyone is perishing.

3. A Luiseño Recollection of Mission Life, 1835

. . . The Fernandino Father, as he was alone and very accustomed to the usages of the Spanish soldiers, seeing that it would be very difficult for him alone to give orders to that people, and, moreover, people that had left the woods just a few years before, therefore appointed alcaldes from the people themselves that knew how to speak Spanish more than the others and were better than the others in their customs. There were seven of these alcaldes, with rods as a symbol that they could judge the others. The captain dressed like the Spanish, always remaining captain, but not ordering his people about as of old, when they were still gentiles. The chief of the alcaldes was called the general. He knew the name of each one. . . . In the afternoon, the alcaldes gather at the house of the missionary. They bring the news of that day, and if the missionary tells them something that all the people of the country ought to know, they return to the villages shouting, "Tomorrow morning. . . ."

Returning to the villages, each one of the alcaldes wherever he goes cries out what the missionary has told them, in his language, and all the country hears it. "Tomorrow the sowing begins and so the laborers go to the chicken yard and assemble there." And again he goes saying these same words until he reaches his own village to eat something and then to sleep. In the morning you will see the laborers appear in the chicken yard and assemble there according to what they heard last night.

With the laborers goes a Spanish majordomo and others, neophyte alcaldes, to see how the work is done, to hurry them if they are lazy, so that they will soon finish what was ordered, and to punish the guilty or lazy one who leaves his plow and quits the field keeping on with his laziness. They work all day, but not always. At noon they leave work, and then they bring them *posole.* (*Posole* is what the Spaniards of California call maize in hot water.) They eat it with gusto, and they remain sated until afternoon when they return to their villages. The shoemakers work making chairs, leather knapsacks, reins and shoes for the cowboys, neophytes, majordomos and Spanish soldiers, and when they have finished, they bring and deliver them to the missionary to give to the cowboys. The blacksmiths make bridle bits, keys, bosses for bridles, nails for the church and all work for all. . . .

In the Mission of San Luis Rey de Francia the Fernandino Father is like a king. He has his pages, alcaldes, majordomos, musicians, soldiers, gardens, ranchos,

---

A Luiseño Recollection of Mission Life, 1835. This document can be found in Pablo Tac, *Indian Life and Customs at the Mission San Luis Rey: A Record of California Mission Life by Pablo Tac, An Indian Neophyte,* edited by Minna Hewes and Gordon Hewes (San Luis Rey, Calif., 1958), 12–13, 19–21.

livestock, horses by the thousand, cows, bulls by the thousand, oxen, mules, asses, 12,000 lambs, 200 goats, etc. The pages are for him and for the Spanish and Mexican, English and Anglo-American travelers. The alcaldes to help him govern all the people of the Mission of San Luis Rey de Francia. The majordomos are in the distant districts, almost all Spaniards. The musicians of the Mission for the holy days and all the Sundays and holidays of the year, with them the singers, all Indian neophytes. Soldiers so that nobody does injury to Spaniard or to Indian; there are ten of them and they go on horseback. There are five gardens that are for all, very large. The Fernandino Father drinks little, and as almost all the gardens produce wine, he who knows the customs of the neophytes well does not wish to give any wine to any of them, but sells it to the English or Anglo-Americans, not for money, but for clothing for the neophytes, linen for the church, hats, muskets, plates, coffee, tea, sugar and other things. The products of the Mission are butter, tallow, hides, chamois leather, bear skins, wine, white wine, brandy, oil, maize, wheat, beans and also bull horns which the English take by the thousand to Boston.

[Daily life in a mission Indian household begins] when the sun rises and the stars and the moon go down, then the old man of the house wakens everyone and begins with breakfast which is to eat *juinis* heated and meat and tortillas, for we do not have bread. This done, he takes his bow and arrows and leaves the house with vigorous and quick step. (This is if he is going to hunt.) He goes off to the distant woods which are full of bears and hares, deer and thousands of birds. He is here all day, killing as many as he can, following them, hiding himself behind trees, climbing them, and then loaded with hares he returns home happy. But when he needs wood, then he leaves the house in the morning with his tumpline [carrying strap] on his shoulders and his ax, with companions who can help him when the load is very heavy, and in the afternoon he returns home. His old woman staying at home makes the meal. The son, if he is man, works with the men. His daughter stays with the women making shirts, and if these also have sons and daughters, they stay in the mission, the sons at school to learn the alphabet, and if they already know it, to learn the catechism, and if this also, to the choir of singers, and if he was a singer, to work, because all the musical singers work the day of work and Sunday to the choir to sing, but without a book, because the teacher teaches them by memory, holding the book. The daughter joins with the single girls who all spin for blankets for the San Luiseños and for the robe of the Fernandino Father. At twelve o'clock they eat together and leave the old man his share, their cups of clay, their vessels of well-woven fiber which water cannot leak out of, except when it is held before the face of the sun, their frying pans of clay, their grills of wood made for that day, and their pitchers for water also of clay. Seated around the fire they are talking and eating. Too bad for them if at that time they close the door. Then the smoke rising, being much, and the opening which serves as a window being small, it turns below, trying to go out by the door, remains in the middle of the house, and they eat, then speaking, laughing and weeping without wishing to. The meal finished they return to their work. The father leaves his son, the son leaves his sister, the sister the brother, the brother the mother, the mother her husband with cheer, until the afternoon. Before going to bed again they eat what the old woman and old man have made in that time, and then they sleep. . . .

4. A Costanoan Account of the Murder
of a Missionary, 1812

Lorenzo's Narrative: "The Death of Padre Andrés Quintana"

The following story which I shall convey was told to me by my dear father in 1818. He was a neophyte of the Mission of Santa Cruz. He was one of the original founders of that mission. He was an Indian from the rancheria of *Asar* on the *Jarro* coast, up beyond Santa Cruz. He was one of the first neophytes baptized at the founding, being about 20 years of age. He was called Venancio Asar, and was the gardener of the Mission of Santa Cruz.

My father was a witness to the happenings which follow. He was one of the conspirators who planned to kill Father Quintana. When the conspirators were planning to kill Father Quintana, they gathered in the house of Julian the gardener (the one who made the pretense of being ill). The man who worked inside the plaza of the mission, named Donato, was punished by Father Quintana with a whip with wire. With each blow it cut his buttocks. Then the same man, Donato, wanted vengeance. He was the one who organized a gathering of 14 men, among them were the cook and the pages serving the Father. The cook was named Antonio, the eldest page named Lino, the others named Vicente and Miguel Antonio. All of them gathered in the house of Julian to plan how they could avoid the cruel punishments of Father Quintana. One man present, Lino, who was more capable and wiser than the others, said, "The first thing we should do today is to see that the Padre no longer punishes the people in that manner. We aren't animals. He [Quintana] says in his sermons that God does not command these [punishments]—but only examples and doctrine. Tell me now, what shall we do with the Padre? We cannot chase him away, nor accuse him before the judge, because we do not know who commands him to do with us as he does." To this, Andrés, father of Lino the page, answered, "Let's kill the Padre without anyone being aware, not the servants, nor anyone, except us that are here present." (This Lino was pureblooded Indian, but as white as a Spaniard and man of natural abilities.) And then Julian the gardener said, "What shall we do in order to kill him?" His wife responded, "You, who are always getting sick—only this way can it be possible—think if it is good this way." Lino approved the plan and asked that all present also approve it. "In that case, we shall do it tomorrow night." That was Saturday. It should be noted that the Padre wished all the people to gather in the plaza on the following Sunday in order to test the whip that he had made with pieces of wire to see if it was to his liking.

All of the conspirators present at the meeting concurred that it should be done as Lino had recommended.

On the evening of Saturday at about six o'clock [October 12] of 1812, they went to tell the Padre that the gardener was dying. The Indians were already posted between two trees on both sides so that they could grab Father when he passed. The

From Edward D. Castillo, trans. and ed., "The Assassination of Padre Andrés Quintana by the Indians of Mission Santa Cruz in 1812: The Narrative of Lorenzo Asisara," *California History* 68 (Fall 1989), 117–125. Reprinted by permission of the California Historical Society.

Padre arrived at the house of Julian, who pretended to be in agony. The Padre helped him, thinking that he was really sick and about to die. When the Padre was returning to his house, he passed close to where the Indians were posted. They didn't have the courage to grab him and they allowed him to pass. The moribund gardener was behind him, but the Padre arrived at his house. Within an hour the wife of Julian arrived [again] to tell him [the Father] that her husband was dying. With this news the Padre returned to the orchard, the woman following behind crying and lamenting. He saw that the sick man was dying. The Padre took the man's hand in order to take his pulse. He felt the pulse and could find nothing amiss. The pulse showed there was nothing wrong with Julian. Not knowing what it could be, the Padre returned to pray for him. It was night when the Padre left. Julian arose and washed away the sacraments [oil] that he [the Padre] had administered, and he followed behind to join the others and see what his companions had done. Upon arriving at the place where they were stationed, Lino lifted his head and looked in all directions to see if they were coming out to grab the Father. The Father passed and they didn't take him. The Father arrived at his house.

Later, when the Father was at his table dining, the conspirators had already gathered at the house of the alleged sick man to ascertain why they hadn't seized Father Quintana. Julian complained that the Padre had placed herbs on his ears, and because of them, now he was really going to die. Then the wife of Julian said, "Yes, you all did not carry through with your promised plans; I am going to accuse you all, and I will not go back to the house." They all answered her, "All right, now, in this trip go and speak to the Father." The woman again left to fetch Father Quintana, who was at supper. He got up immediately and went where he found the supposedly sick man. This time he took with him three pages, two who walked ahead lighting his way with lanterns and behind him followed his Mayordomo Lino. The other two were Vincente and Miguel Antonio. The Father arrived at the gardener's house and found him unconscious. He couldn't speak. The Father prayed the last orations without administering the oils, and said to the wife, "Now your husband is prepared to live or die. Don't come to look for me again." Then the Father left with his pages to return to his house. Julian followed them. Arriving at the place where the two trees were (since the Father was not paying attention to his surroundings, but only in the path in front of him), Lino grabbed him from behind saying these words, "Stop here, Father, you must speak for a moment." When the other two pages who carried the lanterns turned around and saw the other men come out to attack the Father, they fled with their lanterns. The Father said to Lino, "Oh, my Son, what are you going to do to me?" Lino answered, "Your assassins will tell you."

"What have I done to you children, for which you would kill me?"

"Because you have made a *cuarta de hierro* [a horse whip tipped with iron] . . . ," Andrés answered him. Then the Father retorted, "Oh, children, leave me, so that I can go from here now, at this moment." Andrés asked him why he had made this *cuarta de hierro*. Quintana said that it was only for transgressors. Then someone shouted, "Well, you are in the hands of those evil ones, make your peace with God." Many of those present (seeing the Father in his affliction) cried and pitied his fate, but could do nothing to help him because they were themselves compromised. He pleaded much, promising to leave the mission immediately if they would only let him.

"Now you won't be going to any part of the earth from here, Father, you are going to heaven." This was the last plea of the Father. Some of them, not having been able to lay hands on Father, reprimanded the others because they talked too much, demanding that they kill him immediately. They then covered the Father's mouth with his own cape to strangle him. They had his arms tightly secured. After the Father had been strangled, they took a testicle *[grano de los companonez]* so that it would not be suspected that he had been beaten, and in a moment Padre expired. Then Lino and the others took him to his house and put him in his bed.

When the two little pages, Vincente and Miguel Antonio, arrived at the house, the former wanted to tell the guard, but the other dissuaded him by saying, "No, they, the soldiers, will also kill your mother, father, all of the others and you yourself and me. Let them, the conspirators, do what they want." The two hid themselves. After the Indians had put the Father in his bed, Lino looked for the two pages, and he found them hidden. They undressed the body of Father Quintana and placed him in the bed as if he were going to sleep. All of the conspirators, including Julian's wife, were present. Andrés asked Lino for the keys to the store-room. He handed them over saying, "What do you want?" And they said silver and beads. Among the group there were three Indians from the Santa Clara mission. These proposed that they investigate to see how much money there was. Lino opened the box and showed them the accumulated gold and silver. The three Indians from Santa Clara took as much as they could carry to their mission. (I don't know what they have done with that money.) The others took their portions as they saw fit.

Then they asked for the keys to the convent or the nunnery. Lino gave the keys to the *jayunte,* or barracks of the single men, to one of them in order to free them and gather them together below in the orchard with the unmarried women. They gathered in the orchard so that neither the people in the plaza nor in the rancheria nor in the guard-house would hear them. The single men left and without a sound gathered in the orchard at the same place where the Father was assassinated. There was a man there cautioning them not to make any noise, that they were going to have a good time. After a short time the young unmarried women arrived in order to spend the night there. The young people of both sexes got together and had their pleasure. At midnight Lino, being in the Padre's living room with one of the girls from the single women's dormitory, entered the Father's room in order to see if he was really dead. He found him reviving. He was already on the point of arising. Lino went to look for his accomplices to tell them that the Padre was coming to. The Indians returned and they crushed the Father's other testicle. This last act put an end to the life of Father Quintana. Donato, the one who had been whipped, walked around the room with the plural results of his operation in hand saying, "I shall bury these in the outdoor privy."

Donato told Lino that they should close the treasure chest with these words, "Close the trunk with the colored silver (that is the name that the Indians gave to gold) and let's see where we shall bury it." The eight men carried it down to the orchard and buried it secretly without the others knowing.

At about two o'clock in the morning, the young girls returned to their convent and the single men to their *jayunte* without making any noise. The assassins gathered once more after everything had occurred in order to hear the plans of Lino and Donato. Some wanted to flee, and others asked, "What for? No one except us knows." Lino asked them what they wanted to take to their houses, sugar, *panocha* [a sugar loaf], honey, or any other things, and suggested that they lay down to sleep for a while. Finally everything was ready. Donato proposed to return to where the Father was to check on him. They found him not only lifeless, but completely cold and stiff. Lino then showed them the new whip that the Padre was planning to use for the first time the next day, assuring them that he [Father Quintana] would not use it. He sent them to their houses to rest, remaining in the house with the keys. He asked them to be very careful. He arranged the room and the Bible in the manner in which the Father was accustomed to doing before retiring, telling them that he was not going to toll the bells in the morning until the Mayordomo and Corporal of the guard came and he had talked to them. All went through the orchard very silently.

This same morning (Sunday) the bells should have been rung at about eight o'clock. At that hour the people from the villa de Branciforte began to arrive in order to attend the mass. The Mayordomo, Carlos Castro, saw that the bells were not being rung and went to ask Lino, who was the first assistant to the Father, in order to ask why the Padre had not ordered him [to toll the bells]. Lino was in the outer room feigning innocence and answered the Mayordomo that he couldn't tell him anything about the Father because he was still inside sleeping or praying, and that the Mayordomo should wait until he should speak to him first. The Mayordomo returned home. Soon the Corporal of the guard arrived and Lino told him the same as to the Mayordomo. The Mayordomo returned to join in the conservation. They decided to wait a little while longer. Finally Lino told them that in their presence he would knock on the door of the room, observing, "If he is angry with me, you will stand up for me." And so he did, calling to the Father. As he didn't hear noise inside, the Mayordomo and Corporal asked Lino to knock again, but he refused. They then left, encharging him to call the Father again because the hour was growing late. All of the servants were busy at their jobs as always, in order not to cause any suspicion. The Mayordomo returned after ten o'clock and asked Lino to call the Padre to see what was wrong. Lino, with the keys in his pocket, knocked at the door. Finally the Mayordomo insisted that Lino enter the room, but Lino refused. At this moment, the Corporal, who was old Nazario Galindo, arrived. Lino (although he had the key to the door in his pocket) said, "Well, I am going to see if I can get the door open," and he pretended to look for a key to open the door. He returned with a ring of keys but he didn't find one that opened the lock. The Mayordomo and Corporal left to talk to some men who were there. Later, Lino took the key that opened the door, saying that it was for the kitchen. He opened another door that opened into the plaza (the key opened three doors), and through there he entered. Then he opened the main door from inside in front of which the others waited. Lino came out screaming and crying, and carrying on in an uncontrolled manner and saying that the Padre was dead. They asked him if he was certain and he responded, "As this light that illuminates us. By God, I'm going to toll the bells." The three entered, the Corporal, the Mayordomo, and Lino. He didn't allow anyone else to enter. The Corporal and the Mayordomo and the other people wrote to the other missions and to Monterey to Father Marcelino Marquinez. (This Marquinez was an expert horseman and a good friend.) The poor elderly neophytes, and many other Indians who never suspected that the Father was killed, thought that he had died suddenly. They cried bitterly. Lino was roaring inside the Father's house like a bear.

The Fathers from Santa Clara and from other missions came and they held the Father's funeral, all believing that he had died a natural death, but not before examining the corpse in the entrance room, and had opened the stomach in order to be certain that the Padre had not been poisoned. Officials, sergeants, and many others participated in these acts but nothing was discovered. Finally, by chance, one of those present noted that the testicles were missing, and they were convinced that this had been the cause of death. Through modesty they did not reveal the fact and buried the body with everyone convinced that the death had been a natural one. . . .

◈ *E S S A Y S*

The Pueblo Revolt of 1680 has fascinated historians for generations. Who led the revolt? Why? Independent scholar Dr. Stefanie Beninato reviews the answers that other historians have given and provides her own assessment of the nature of Pueblo leadership. Her analysis shows that anthropological knowledge is critical to understand Indians' motivations. Readers should return to the first three documents to further assess Dr. Beninato's argument. Professor Steven W. Hackel of Oregon State University examines the nature of Indian leadership in the California missions. He finds that missionaries often appointed Indians to leadership positions whom the neophytes (new Christian Indians) already recognized as leaders in native society. While this practice helped to forward the work of the mission, it could also lead to unexpected trouble. Professor Hackel's essay raises important questions about the nature of the California mission experience and makes an interesting comparison with leadership in the Pueblo revolt.

Popé, Pose-yemu, and Naranjo: A New Look at Leadership in the Pueblo Revolt of 1680

STEFANIE BENINATO

Although the Pueblo Revolt of 1680 was one of the most successful rebellions against Spanish authority anywhere in the world, historians have largely ignored its tactical aspects, including the question of native leadership in the revolt. In a controversial article published in 1967, Fray Angelico Chavez, however, looked at the long-ignored role of "hybrid" leaders. Believing that the Pueblos were too passive and too disunited to form the alliance, Chavez postulated that a mulatto of Mexican-Indian ancestry, taking on the role of the god Pose-yemu, secretly directed the revolt from a kiva at Taos. Documentary evidence does support Chavez' assertion that a Naranjo was a leader of the revolt. A cultural analysis, however, undermines his assumption that Naranjo was an adult non-Pueblo or even from the first generation of a Pueblo/non-Pueblo marriage. To take on the revered role of Pose-yemu, the sun god and savior, one would have had to achieve an esteemed status. Given the apprentice-like system within the Pueblo sociopolitical structure, it would be nearly

Stefanie Beninato, "Popé, Pose-yemu, and Naranjo: A New Look at Leadership in the Pueblo Revolt of 1680," *New Mexico Historical Review* 65 (October 1990), 417–435. Reprinted with permission.

impossible for an adult non-Pueblo to achieve this status and very difficult even for for a first generation of a mixed marriage to do so.

The Revolt of 1680 marked the high point in the Pueblos' long struggle against Spanish economic, political, and religious domination. For the eight decades prior to the revolt, tensions had mounted steadily throughout the region as Spanish civil and religious authorities as well as settlers exploited the Pueblo Indians. Respect for Spanish authority was also eroded among the Pueblos by the continuous struggle between church and state in colonial New Spain.

The Pueblo people populated dozens of autonomous villages and spoke several distinct languages. There had been a number of unsuccessful attempts to expel the Spaniards, but there had never been a sufficient degree of unity among the various pueblos. By 1680, however, the situation had reached crisis proportions. Death and devastation, brought on by a long period of drought beginning in 1667 and by disease in the following decade, fertilized the seeds of rebellion already planted in the Pueblo region. The Spaniards forbade kachina dances; they raided kivas and destroyed masks and other ceremonial items. They arrested native leaders and humiliated and even killed them. As the Franciscan missionaries became more and more determined to suppress and abolish the native religions, a unified resistance formed among the priestly elite of the pueblos.

Most historians and writers, using the scattered testimonies in the Antonio de Otermín journals of 1680–1682, point to Popé as the moving force (*"motor"*) behind the revolt. Even though the seminal documents list other leaders, there is nothing in the commentaries accompanying these documents to suggest that scholars seriously entertained the idea that anyone else shared the principal leadership with Popé. For many, Popé has become the symbol of "uncompromising hostility to the conquerors" and the unquestioned leader.

What little is known of this Tewa medicineman from San Juan lends weight to this point of view. Popé was deeply involved in native religion, probably through leadership in one of the moieties or societies of the pueblo. Refusing to take a Christian name, he had long resisted the Spanish religion and struggled with a fierce and bitter energy to keep alive the traditional beliefs and rituals among his people. Popé was one of the many medicinemen whom the Spaniards labeled a troublemaker and kept under constant surveillance because of their continuing defiance in conducting kachina dances and other rituals. In 1675, with the coming of the drought, Popé's religious activities began to take on political colorings. He told the people that the gods were displeased with the people's acceptance of the Spanish religion and that the Spaniards must be made to leave their land. He was among the forty-seven religious leaders that Governor Juan Francisco Treviño arrested and tried for witchcraft in that year in an attempt to control the restlessness of the Pueblo population. Four of the leaders were hanged; the rest were whipped and publicly humiliated before a group of Tewas secured their release. After this, Popé became more determined to drive the Spaniards out of the region. Returning to San Juan for a short time, he began to hold secret organizational meetings. Eventually Popé moved his base of operation to the remote pueblo of Taos, in order to escape Spanish surveillance and the concern of his relatives for themselves. In contemporary sources, Popé was described as a leader who possessed extraordinary talents and the ability to communicate with spiritual beings. Later, he was repeatedly named as the principal leader of the revolt.

In his "Pohé-yemo" article, Chavez asserted that a mulatto named Naranjo from Santa Clara secretly led the revolt, using Popé as his principal spokesperson. He concluded that Naranjo, as the *teniente* of Pose-yemu, was the sole tactical leader of the revolt. His theory challenged the long-held assumption that Popé was the primary leader of the revolt. Like the commentaries, however, Chavez' article failed to address the existence of multiple leadership in Pueblo culture.

Chavez focused on unraveling the mystery of the identity of Pose-yemu's representative ("*teniente*") described by the Indians caught during the first days of the Pueblo Revolt. Chavez first suspected that a real person was the representative of Pose-yemu when he studied the records of a controversy which took place in Santa Fe in 1766 involving the Naranjo family of the Santa Clara/Santa Cruz valley. By tracing back what he believed were five generations of this family, Chavez discovered that not only were the ancestors Negroid, but also that they were accused of having fomented Indian insurrections in the past.

In his Pose-yemu article, Chavez stated that the basic truth about the leadership of the revolt was preserved in the records of the Naranjo family and in the more legendary tradition of *Nuestra Senora de la Macana*. He used certain discrepancies in the mythological elements in Pedro Naranjo's testimony of 1681 to further support his theory.

Chavez relied on three main bodies of documentary evidence to support his thesis: the testimonies given by Indians captured on August 9 and 10, 1680; declarations by Pedro Naranjo and four other Indians in December 1681; and several documents in *AGN Tierras: Civil tomo* 426 relating to the 1766 controversy (and supporting documentation for the genealogy Chavez constructed from this *tomo*).

The two Indian runners caught outside Tesuque on August 9, 1680 stated that there was a letter from a "teniente of Pose-yemu" to the effect that all pueblos should revolt. They described the teniente as being "very tall, black with very large, yellow eyes." The Indians captured on August 10 confirmed that there had been a "mandate of an Indian who lives a long way from this kingdom toward the north from which Montezuma came and who is a teniente of Pose-yemu."

In this first set of testimony, Chavez focused on the use of the word *teniente* to establish the existence of another leader. The term expresses the double function of "taking the place of" and "assuming the person of." Chavez accurately translated the word as representative, which does seem to indicate the existence of a real human being. He also used this first body of evidence as the basis for a physical description of the person. Because of the clear reference to the teniente's black appearance, Chavez postulated that the teniente was Negroid or mulatto.

Chavez also used the testimony given by Pedro Naranjo before Otermín on December 1681 in a rather circumspect way to confirm that another leader was present. Naranjo was the only one of five Indians interrogated at that time to testify that the "command of the father whom they did not know . . . would be given through El Caydi, one of the three spirits or El Popé" and that the mandate came "from Caydi and the two other spirits." Chavez merely stated that even though Naranjo wanted to steer away from the "dangerously close" description of the tall, black representative of Pose-yemu, he was unwilling to let Popé take full credit. Chavez felt that this impression based on circumstantial evidence was further bolstered by Naranjo's leadership role, which presumably gave him more knowledge.

Chavez relied most heavily on the third body of records, that is, the genealogy contained in the documents surrounding the 1766 controversy to establish the identity of this other leader. (He also used supplementary documentation, which he later incorporated into his book on the genealogy of New Mexico families.)

The following is a brief history of the relevant members of the Naranjo family pieced together by Chavez: the original ancestor was a very black mulatto from Puebla, New Spain, named Mateo who was freed at twenty years of age by his master Mateo Montero on the condition that he settle in New Mexico. He served a soldier named Alonso Martin Naranjo and married an Indian woman servant, whom Chavez believed was from New Spain. Mateo was the only male Negroid servant mentioned in the Juan de Oñate papers of 1597–1600.

The second generation included Diego, Pedro, and Domingo. In 1632, Diego was arrested by Capitán Bartolomé Romero for participating in a kachina dance inside a kiva at the Alameda Pueblo. According to Chavez, nothing more was heard of him. Pedro was the eighty-year-old sorcerer caught by Otermín's forces near Isleta. He had been sent from the upper pueblos to teach the "old ways." Domingo, according to Chavez, was identified by Spanish officers of the colonial militia as the forebearer ("*tronco*") of the rebellious Naranjos of Santa Clara. These officers declared that he was a son of a very black Negro ("*Negro atezado*") and an Indian servant ("*india criada*"). Chavez stated that Domingo "cast his lot with the Taos Indians in 1680 and seems to have died by the time of Diego de Vargas's return to Taos in 1692. (It is important to note that Chavez believed that Domingo was the tactical genius of the revolt in his "Pohé-yemu" article; although in an earlier study, he had postulated that Diego was the leader.)

The third generation included Lucas and Joseph, sons of Domingo. Lucas was referred to as "el mulato Naranjo del pueblo de Santa Clara." Chavez believed Lucas was one of the five Indians interrogated by Otermín in December 1681. At that time, Lucas claimed he was a Piro Indian. He participated in the revolt of the Tewas in 1696 and was killed by his brother Joseph, who shifted alliances frequently. Chavez believed that Joseph, too, was one of the four other Indians interrogated with Pedro Naranjo in December 1681. At that time he was referred to only as Joseph and he gave no tribal affiliation. He could, however, speak fluent Castilian. According to Chavez, Joseph went to live at Taos, after escaping from Otermín. Twelve years later, he was sent with another Indian to parley with Diego de Vargas when Vargas approached the deserted Taos Pueblo. At that time, he referred to himself as Josephillo and was called "el espanol" by the Taos Indians because of his language proficiency. Later, Joseph went over to the Spaniards, killing Lucas to expiate his own role as an apostate. This marked Joseph's rise in the Spanish society to become the first Chief War Captain of the Pueblo auxiliaries. In the testimony of 1766, those who claimed to know Joseph described him as a black-complected person using such sobriquets of "*el Negro*" and "*el Mulato*."

In developing the mythological bases for his argument, Chavez examined Pedro Naranjo's testimony in detail to show that this was "no mere Pueblo speaking in Pueblo terms and concepts." Chavez viewed his testimony as an Hispanic-Indian concoction from New Spain grafted onto Pueblo mythology and expressed in terms the Spaniards could understand, e.g. "communication with the devil." He looked at three elements in Naranjo's testimony in detail: his use of the mythological lake of

Copala as an equivalent to the Pueblos' point of emergence, Shipapu; his use of the names of the three guiding spirits in the Taos kiva; and his use of the Pueblo god Pose-yemu. Chavez believed on the whole, that these three mythological elements demonstrated that not only was there a mulatto leader of Mexican-Indian ancestry, but also that he had a grasp of both Spanish and Pueblo psychology. In particular, Chavez asserted that the first two elements established Naranjo's Mexican-Indian ancestry and the third element demonstrated his superior intelligence, which Chavez attributed to his non-Pueblo ancestry.

Pedro Naranjo repeatedly stated that the three spirits in the kiva were going to the lake of Copala. Chavez focused on this to point out that Pedro Naranjo confused Pueblo and Aztec myths. According to Chavez, the word "Copala" had no connection with New Mexico Pueblo mythology. In a very detailed note, Chavez traced the origins of this word and outlined the genesis of the legend. It has a long history of confused associations starting with the "Tale of Seven Cities" told by Amadis of Gaul in the beginning of the sixteenth century. It was associated with the Aztec and Toltec origin myths of the seven caves and later became interchangeable with New Mexico. To show Naranjo's confusion between Copala and Shipapu, Chavez created a composite sketch of the Pueblo emergence myths, using reports by such outstanding ethnologists as Adolph Bandelier, Elsie Clews Parsons and Leslie A. White. According to Chavez' reading of the myths, the ancestors lived underground under the lake; but they emerged through a hole in the ground.

The second element Chavez looked at in the mythology was the connection of the three spirits—especially their names—to Aztec religious lore. Chavez relied heavily on the *Florentine Codex,* which was a compilation by Fray Bernardino de Sahagún in the sixteenth century with an English translation done in the 1950s. It is a series of volumes with the Nahuatl and English texts side-by-side.

El Caudi, Tilini and Tleume were the three fire-emitting gods in the Taos kiva. The names, Chavez said in a note, have the sound and look of Nahuatl (the Aztec language) rather than of any of the Pueblo tongues. More specifically, they suggest the names of two Aztec gods of Fire and War and one of the names of the high priest of Tlascala, i.e. Achcautli.

Chavez concluded that this melange of mythological figures could only have come from Mexican-Indians in general and more specifically, from ones that were familiar with Spanish culture and who were second generation or who had been removed from their original culture.

As for the third element, Chavez merely stated that the myth of Pose-yemu was known in one linguistic form or another in all the pueblos. He believed that the use of the myth as a unifying device showed Naranjo's understanding and knowledge of native mythology's effects on Indian behavior; as a subterfuge, it showed his grasp of Spanish psychology. Naranjo correctly assumed that by becoming Pose-yemu's teniente, his existence as a person would be obscured because the Spaniards looked upon the "ancient ones" as evil spirits.

By concentrating on establishing the ancestry and physical description of Domingo Naranjo, Chavez' theory failed to make use of significant information in the documents. It also ignored certain cultural factors that militate against any adult non-Pueblo being a Pueblo leader at the time of the revolt.

The documentary evidence supports Chavez' assertion of a leadership role for the Naranjo family and of their ancestry. An analysis of the evidence in a cultural framework, however, contradicts the following two elements: that an adult non-Pueblo could assume a leadership position at that time in Pueblo society and that there was a single leader of the revolt. My hypothesis is that the mother of Domingo (and presumably of Diego and Pedro) was a Pueblo Indian and that there was a generation between Domingo and Joseph from which came the teniente of Pose-yemu. (I think it is also possible that Domingo and Diego were the same person.)

An understanding of the religion and social organization of the Pueblos, therefore, is essential in order to evaluate my alternative. The Pueblos' way of life was based on spiritual worship and religious ceremony. Every phase of Pueblo life had its religious aspects. The people saw themselves as inextricably woven into an eternal cycle of life, where the welfare of the individual was indivisible from the welfare of his people. The *caciques,* the religious leaders, were responsible for the total well-being of the entire village. They directed not only spiritual affairs, but also the political and secular activities within the pueblo.

Because of its religious base, therefore, Pueblo society in its religious, political and social aspects tended to be a centralized theocracy with a complicated, and often overlapping, hierarchical system controlled by an elite of older men. There were a number of organizations within the hierarchical structure. Each had its own priest and each priest played a special role in the religious life. In Tewa society, there were moieties, that is, a system of dual leadership. Other pueblos had clans which served similar functions. The top echelon of these theocracies was the managing group or the "keepers of the gateway of the lake" as they are known in Tewa. They dominated the political arena and planned and executed many of the ceremonial rituals. Each cacique had subordinates (called the right and left arms) who implemented decisions. There was also an outside chief, known as the war captain. He served as a defensive military leader and as an internal law enforcement officer. He and his second-in-command would act together in an official capacity when a decision for the whole pueblo had to be rendered by someone. Moreover, there is evidence to suggest that there was interpueblo structural links, especially for religious ceremonies such as initiation.

Membership in the moiety or the clan was a normal part of the growth and development of the Pueblo child; it allowed the child to assume a legal identity in the eyes of the society. In Keres society, clan membership was matrilineal; while in Tewa society, moiety membership generally followed a patrilineal pattern, although there was no rigid adherence to this rule. Young men who showed aptitude and interest were groomed for positions of leadership within the religious and political structure—much like an apprenticeship. It is obvious from the documents of the revolt that offspring of mixed blood marriages, such as Alonso Catiti of Santo Domingo Pueblo and Francisco El Ollita of San Ildefonso, did attain leadership positions in each pueblo's ruling hierarchy. According to Alfonso Ortiz, however, the acceptance of an outsider by marriage into the Pueblo social structure was markedly different from the acceptance of a child of a mixed marriage. The order of prestige given to a marriage to a member of a different Pueblo or to a non-Pueblo depended on the degree of intercultural amicability. For such an outsider to be accepted into the religious hierarchy in the seventeenth century would have been highly unlikely because of Spanish persecution of native religions and the fear of informers. In any event, such a person would have been treated as a child in terms of the initiation process.

Candidates for leadership positions, therefore, were gradually acquainted with the necessary esoteric knowledge through stages of initiation, similar in concept to an apprentice system. Years of training were necessary before such a person became familiar with the enormous amount of ritual and administrative details that these roles required. The ability "to talk like an Indian," that is, the acquisition of an advanced level of esoteric knowledge, necessitated not only membership in a religious society but also an intensive preoccupation with matters of a religious nature. Usually there were not more than three or four men in any pueblo who had acquired this level of knowledge. To achieve an esteemed status, a man had to have above average success in at least a few mandatory roles and to give unstintingly of his time in religious or secular affairs. Members of the priestly hierarchy who achieved esteemed status wielded tremendous power in the pueblo. Not only were they guardians of traditional cultural values, but they also were liaisons between the supernatural and secular worlds. In his study of Santa Clara Pueblo, W. W. Hill found that the attitude toward persons of this status generally was ambivalent: they were praised and feared at the same time.

This discussion of Pueblo culture, therefore, highlights several important elements that form the basis for an ethnographic analysis of the issue of leadership in the Pueblo Revolt: First, the ruling system was autocratic and its members had distinct, but complementary, functions. Moreover, there is some indication that an interlocking of the religious system on an intervillage basis was not foreign to the Pueblos. Participation in the religious system was an incremental learning process defined by initiation rites; a person with an eteemed status signified the achievement of an upper echelon position after a long rise through the hierarchy. Although a Pueblo's status and position are not hereditary, a family's position did influence a child's attitudes and experiences.

These cultural elements, therefore, strongly suggest the following: the need to rise through the religious hierarchy militates against any adult non-Pueblo from becoming a leader of the revolt since the basis for such authority was religious. In addition, there are several instances in the Otermín documents in which Popé and the teniente are described as "greatly feared." This may, in fact, be a watchword indicating an esteemed status—which required a long initiatory process. It would seem, therefore, that such status would not normally be achieved by the offspring of a mixed marriage—and certainly not by an adult non-Pueblo. Finally, the inter-Pueblo ritual experience gives a strong historical basis for discounting the possibility of a single leader and indicates a pattern of shared authority among several pueblos.

The documentary basis of Chavez' theory is narrow and selective in its use of information. Using evidence taken from a few Indians during and immediately after the revolt, Chavez' article focused only on establishing the existence and description of another leader besides Popé. These statements could have been connected to testimonies taken from Spaniards during this period. This would have strengthened the idea that someone other than Popé was the tactical leader by negating the possibility that the Indians' declarations were merely reflections of Popé's interpretation of the gods' message. For instance, the statement of an Indian that Popé "had the mandate of an Indian who lives very far away from this kingdom toward the north . . . who is the representative of Pose-yemu" could have been tied to the report made by Fray Francisco de Ayeta, the *visitador general* of the

Franciscans, to Otermín in which he declared that "other heretics and sectarians" ordered the Indians to wash at the river with herbs to "cleanse themselves of the stain . . . of the holy sacrament of baptism."

This wider use of the documents, however, raises the question of multiple leadership—an issue the article does not address. Besides Ayeta's report, there are other contemporary testimonies that would confirm the historical model of intertribal leadership. Don Pedro Nanboa, a native of the pueblo of Alameda, for example, declared that the "nations of the Teguas, Taos, Percuris, Pecos, and Jemez had long been plotting to overthrow the Spaniards." This implication of multiple leadership was also corroborated in the information given by several Spaniards immediately after the revolt.

Moreover, Chavez' thesis would be strengthened by connecting the impression of another leader in the testimonies made in 1680 with that given by Pedro Naranjo in 1681, who stated that "the command of the father whom they did not known . . . would be given through El Caydi, one of the three spirits or El Popé" and that "the mandate came from Caydi and the other spirits." The article did not note the fact that two of the other Indians interrogated in December 1681 also mentioned other leaders. Juan of Tesuque indicated that Saca of Taos had a leadership role. Joseph, whom Chavez believed was a Naranjo, stated that there were four primary leaders including El Taque from San Juan, whom other sources did not mention. In addition, the article failed to pick up what might be a significant clue as to the identity of the leader and his mulatto ancestry in Pedro's statement that Popé came down in person with El Saca and *El Chato* (my emphasis) from the Pueblo of Taos. In Spanish, *"chato"* means "flatnosed," suggesting negroid features.

Instead of making these connections, however, Chavez' article focused on Pedro Naranjo's testimony (that is the use of certain terms) to show the latter's familiarity with Spanish civil and religious practices in order to establish his ancestry. In terms of the records of the Naranjo family history, Chavez was able to document thoroughly the third to the fifth generation of the family. The interconnections between the first two generations and the later ones, however, were fragmentary. Chavez has worked extensively with these documents in genealogical studies and the basis of many of his interconnections were, by his own admission, "educated guesses."

Most problematic, however, is the role of Domingo himself. In his "Pohéyemo" article, Chavez admitted that the only reference to Domingo in the archives involved his ancestry—the question of which was essential to the 1766 controversy. In his article, Chavez also failed to identify the causes for Domingo's move to Taos or to document clearly his past involvement either with the religious leadership or the resistance movement against the Spaniards. (It is important to note that a single reference to an individual does not necessarily rule out his role as a leader in the revolt since the identity of the religious leaders were often unknown to the Spaniards, especially during the time of Spanish persecution.)

A close reading of the 1766 documents corroborates the interpretation of the cultural factors that form the basic assumptions of my alternative theory concerning the Naranjo genealogy—that is, that Domingo's mother was a Pueblo and that there was a generation between Domingo and Joseph. The records upon which Chavez relied so heavily traced the genealogy of the Naranjo family. In it, Domingo was identified only as the *tronco,* that is, the forebearer, of the rebellious Naranjos and as the offspring of a very black Negro and an Indian woman servant of an original settler of the colony who belonged to the Martínez family. Because of his class, ancestry, and absence from the rolls of either Oñate (1590s) or Vargas (1690s), Domingo could have been nothing more than a high ranking leader (*capitán mayor*) of the Indians. This term indicates a warrior-type role, which would complement Popé's role. It is descriptive, however, and does not indicate a position in the local Spanish military system. The document states that the members of the family became apostates and took part in the revolt after they had been accepted by the Indian rebels. It also indicates that members of the Naranjo family may have been some of the primary movers ("*motores*") of the revolt. There is no indication in the document, however, that Domingo was a leader at the time of the revolt or even that he was alive then; rather it implies that Domingo's generation marked the beginning of this mulatto family's acculturation into Pueblo society. The implication is supported by Diego's role in the kachina dances, Pedro's reputation as sorcerer and Domingo's implied leadership and is explicable only if their mother was a Pueblo Indian. The family's acculturation into Pueblo society ("*familiarzados con los indios*") conforms to the hierarchical structure of that society and supports the assumption that a later generation of this family supplied a leader of the revolt. This leadership role is circumstantially confirmed by Joseph's and Lucas' roles as capitán mayor and *caudillo* respectively and by Pedro's reputation as a sorcerer which implies a role as a religious leader.

In addition to the cultural factors that indicate a missing generation between Domingo and Joseph, there is circumstantial evidence in Chavez' "Pohé-yemo" article that supports this assumption. There is an inconsistency in Chavez' generations. Chavez stated that the Lorenzo boys, who were approximately eighteen and twenty years old, were Diego's grandsons; Joseph, who was twenty, was said to be Domingo's son—even though Domingo and Diego were of the same generation. Moreover, the early maturation of people in the seventeenth century militated against this wide gap of approximately fifty to sixty years between generations.

In terms of the mythological aspects of his theory, Chavez demonstrated the Mexican-Indian ancestry of Domingo by concentrating on the Aztec and Spanish elements in Pedro Naranjo's testimony. In particular, Chavez focused on Naranjo's use of the lake of Copala and the names of the three gods in the kiva to show his familiarity with Spanish and Aztec culture. This point seems well taken. As Chavez has shown, both elements have strong links to Spanish and/or Mexican lore. The names of the gods are very similar to those of two of the Aztec gods of fire and war and that of the high priest of Tlascala, Achcautli. The only comparable name of a Pueblo god is the Tewa god Tinini Povi (Olivella Flower Shell Youth) for the spirit Tilini. This god appears to be an unlikely identity for a person to assume who is seeking power. Although Ortiz calls him a revered god, he appears to be a Mercury-like figure. He definitely lacks the powerful and universal significance of Pose-yemu.

I think that Chavez' argument that Naranjo's use of the lake of Copala showed confusion with the Pueblos' origin myths, however, is unwarranted. First of all, Chavez' interpretation of the Pueblo myths, that is, having the first people emerge from a hole in the ground, seems questionable. Many of the emergence myths are recorded as having the ancestors "come out of the lake." Tewa and Zuñi myths, in particular, clearly state that the people came out of the lake, and in fact, have actual geographic locations for Shipapu. For Tewas, it is natural for the spirits to relate their entrance and exit to a lake, since they believe that lakes and ponds are used exclusively by deities as entrances to the underworld. It is quite possible that Pedro Naranjo was using mythological devices that Spaniards could relate to. The Aztec war gods would create a strong visual image. Like the myth of the lake of Copala, it was an image with which the Spaniards had previous experience. These concepts would have meaning for the Spaniards.

The greatest deficiency in the mythological basis of Chavez' argument was his failure to develop the importance of Pose-yemu in Pueblo culture. Not only was the myth a common one in Pueblo culture, and thus acted as a unifying device; but its functional aspect was highly significant during the time of the revolt, which, in fact, marked a crisis in Pueblo religion and culture. In addition, an analysis of the inter-relations between Pose-yemu and the three Aztec gods show a remarkable under-standing of the interworkings of the mythological elements of these three cultures.

The general outline of the Pose-yemu myth is as follows: Pose-yemu was begot magically by World Man using a piñon nut. As a youth, Pose-yemu was badly treated by his people, even after he was recognized by his father, the Sun, and given a name. Eventually he became a great wizard and the village prospered. He pre-dicted coming events. Pose-yemu left his people and traveled to the south, promis-ing to return at a later date.

Not only is the myth of Pose-yemu known in one linguistic form or another in all the pueblos; but the legend is highly developed, especially among the Rio Grande Tewas. A loose translation of "Pose-yemu" is "he who strews morning dew." The Pueblo people find Pose-yemu rising in the mist of a lake on a warm summer's day, which, at least, indirectly correlates to Pedro Naranjo's testimony on the lake of Copala. Pose-yemu is also known as the sun-youth and is popular as a religious figure and as a culture hero.

Besides the ideological power of this mythological device in the Pueblo Revolt due to its universal appearance in Pueblo religion, the legend contains several im-portant themes relating to Pueblo social structure. Perhaps the most important ones to the offspring of a mixed-blood marriage would be the idea of non-acceptance during youth and that of testing through adversity, which is an important factor in gaining esteem in Pueblo society.

More important than its mythological elements, however, are the functional aspects of Pose-yemu in Pueblo culture. Pose-yemu is a savior. He will "return to restore his people to their proper place" and "rule over them and be father to them all"; in other words, he provided for the general well-being of the pueblo. More important, during the Spanish contact period, Pose-yemu played the role of ritual leader and teacher. He served as an "early warning system" for the preservation of native religious ceremonies. For instance, he ordered kachina dances to be held underground. According to Ralph Emerson Twitchell, representing Pose-yemu was an office of great responsibility. It required an outstanding knowledge of ritual lore, wisdom, and prudence, which would discredit the idea that an adult non-Pueblo or even a child of a mixed marriage could fill this office. As noted before, the taking on of this role of kachina corresponds to the meaning of "teniente" as used in the documents of the Pueblo Revolt. It expresses the double function of "taking the place of" and "assuming the person of" (Pose-yemu, in this case).

Another important factor is the close association of Pose-yemu with the Twin War gods. These three figures share many similar characteristics and many of the same mythological elements; however, the Twin War gods stayed in the pueblos and established institutions. They were the patrons of the Zuni Bow priests, which correspond closely to the Tewa War Society. In earlier times, the head of the Warrior Society and the caciques shared responsibility. If a Naranjo was Pose-yemu, this might point to a role as a leader in the Warrior Society, indicating a fighting function which would not be incompatible with Popé's function as cacique. This interpretation is supported by the designation of both Domingo and Joseph as capitán mayor.

The interrelation of Pose-yemu with the Aztec gods and the interrelation of the role of Pose-yemu's teniente and that of the Caydi strongly bolster Chavez' theory that a mulatto individual of Mexican-Indian ancestry was a leader in the revolt. In the kachina dances, the mask of the sun is used to portray Pose-yemu. The insignia of the Aztec god Tlaltatecuini (the spirit Tilini in the kiva) is the sun, which appears on the god's flag, shield, shoes, and paper vestments. It is also significant that the representatives of these Aztec gods would smear their faces with black pigment during rituals. Although the fact that the Aztec priests painted their faces black may be coincidental, it would certainly heighten the authority of a black mulatto who played the role. With Pose-yemu's connection with the Twin War gods, there is not only a close association of symbols, but also an indirect association of functions (that is, war) among these Aztec and Pueblo gods.

In Pedro Naranjo's testimony, there is a change from the three spirits giving orders to the "commands of the father . . ." being given through "El Caydi or El Popé" to the "mandate being given by Caydi" before he and the other two spirits "return to their state of antiquity." In a note, Chavez suggested that El Caydi is the name of a high priest in Aztec culture. There was a transformation, therefore, from god to high priest.

These similarities associated with the gods and with the roles of Caydi and the teniente suggest a desire for consistency, which is understandable if these mythological figures were represented by a real person who wanted to maintain his authority, and yet, camouflage his identity from Spanish officials. More important, however, Pedro Naranjo's testimony indicates the giving up of the role of kachina and the return to the role of priest. This transition would allow one to hide his identity but to maintain the same role as intermediary between the gods and the people. It also suggests the assumption of a more active role outside the kiva. If the representative of Pose-yemu was a medicineman of war, then he, unlike a cacique, could carry a weapon and fight. This transition also seems to point to the larger role the person played in Pueblo society and to indicate that he was a highly esteemed leader, who had been well integrated into the culture.

In conclusion, I feel that analysis of the mythology, ancestry and other information in the documents in a cultural framework supports Chavez' contention that there was a mulatto who was a tactical leader. By concentrating on establishing genealogical lines instead of analyzing the evidence in the contemporary sources in the context of Pueblo culture, however, Chavez' theory overlooked significant information in the documents as well as certain cultural factors that militate against an adult non-Pueblo from being a Pueblo leader in the revolt. It suggests that such a person would have to be at least from the first generation of a marriage between a Pueblo and non-Pueblo. More probably, it indicates an offspring from the second generation of such a marriage because of the necessity of achieving an esteemed status so one could take on the revered role of Pose-yemu. Moreover, cultural analysis indicates that the concept of a single leader is not viable in the theocratic social structure of the Pueblo world. In addition, the mythological aspects indicate that the teniente of Pose-yemu occupied the position of tactical leader as the head of a warrior society. Such a role was not incompatible with the functions of the caciques.

The Staff of Leadership: Indian Authority in the Missions of Alta California

STEVEN W. HACKEL

In 1769, Spain set out to defend the Pacific Coast against settlement by other European powers by developing a series of colonial outposts that eventually stretched from San Diego to San Francisco. In this region, known to Europeans as Alta California, Spain depended on religious missions more than military fortifications or civilian towns to solidify its control. During the second half of the eighteenth century, missions had declined in importance in the rest of northern New Spain. In 1767, the crown expelled the Jesuits from Spain and its colonies and gradually converted most surviving missions in Arizona, New Mexico, and Texas to parishes overseen by secular priests. But in Alta California, Franciscan missions steadily increased in number and power as the most important centers of interaction between Indians and Spaniards. By 1821, when Spanish rule gave way to Mexican independence, roughly 70,000 Indians had been baptized in the region's twenty missions. Even after more than five decades of demographic disaster brought on by the ravages of disease, mission Indians still outnumbered Spanish settlers and soldiers 21,750 to 3,400; missions outnumbered military garrisons by a ratio of five to one and civilian settlements by six to one.

The Franciscans' strategies to convert and control Indians in Alta California have sparked an intense debate that has recently involved the general public as well as scholars. Public interest has focused on the canonization of Fray Junípero Serra, founding father of the California missions, and more generally on Indian-Spanish relations in those missions. Promoters of the Spanish colonial past portray the Franciscans as saving childlike Indians from savagism; detractors depict the missions as brutal labor camps, committed to cultural genocide. Although participants in this dispute have generated a considerable number of articles and books, the involvement of Indian leaders in the running of the California missions remains largely unexplored. Neither side has sufficiently examined the extent to which the missions depended on the persistence of Indian leadership, nor has either explored how Indian authority was created and legitimated within the missions.

Steven W. Hackel, "The Staff of Leadership: Indian Authority in the Missions of Alta California," in *The William and Mary Quarterly*, 3d Series, 54(2) (April 1997), 347–376.

Most Alta California missions counted between 500 and 1,000 Indian residents, two missionaries, and a military guard of four or five soldiers. Because their numbers were few and their resources limited, Spaniards looked to Indian leaders to help organize and regulate the missions' life and work. To this end, they instituted and directed annual elections in which the mission community chose its own officials, thereby enabling Spanish religious and military authorities to rule Indians through Indians. This system, though hierarchical in form, was flexible in operation. Indian officials not only served the needs of Spanish overlords, but they also protected the interests of the Indian community and, in some cases, ultimately rebelled against the Spanish order.

Recent studies of Indian communities in colonial America have noted the importance of Indian leaders and the challenges of their position. Colonists frequently tried to advance their objectives by co-opting Indian leaders, on whom they attempted to impose European forms of leadership. This practice involved a risk, for Indian leaders could subvert as well as implement colonial objectives. They, too, had much to gain though even more to lose in these encounters, for by participating in European systems of governance, they could foster or hinder their own autonomy as well as that of their communities. Indians, therefore, responded in a variety of ways to imposed forms of governance, and Europeans accommodated those forms to the communities they sought to control. These responses and accommodations are crucial to the ethnohistory of all of colonial America from the sixteenth century through the nineteenth, from New France to New England to New Spain.

After giving an overview of the Indians of Alta California and the colonial strategies of the Spaniards who settled among them, this article analyzes the system of elections and the responsibilities of Indian officials in the missions and identifies patterns of Indian leadership among the men who served as officials. These patterns, which are most visible at Mission San Carlos Borromeo on the Monterey peninsula, reveal a complex interplay of Indian and Spanish priorities. At first, the Spanish system of indirect rule relied on Indians who held power in their own communities before the missions were founded. Later, annual elections promoted new Indian leaders, from whose ranks came men who instigated rebellions against the Franciscans in the 1820s and reorganized Indian communities after the missions collapsed in the 1830s. Thus the Spaniards' use of and dependence on Indian officials reveal a noteworthy paradox of the colonial history of the Americas: indirect rule not only reshaped Indian lives, but it also provided Indians with the means and the personnel to retain control over some aspects of their communities, in some areas long after the collapse of colonial rule.

In California, Spaniards encountered the most linguistically diverse and densely settled native population in all North America. Estimating that 310,000 Indians lived within the boundaries of the present state on the eve of Spanish colonization, scholars have classified these Indians into six culture areas and at least ninety distinct languages. Spanish settlement was concentrated in the coastal region between San Diego and San Francisco, where Indians probably numbered around 60,000 in 1769. As settlement spread north from San Diego, it most directly and immediately affected the Tipai and Ipai around San Diego, the Luiseño to their immediate north, the Gabrielino of Los Angeles, the Chumash of the Santa Barbara region, the Yokuts of the Central Valley, the Salinan, Esselen, the Costanoan of the central coast, and the Miwok, Wappo, and Pomo of the San Francisco Bay area. These classifications simplify a complex mosaic, for Indians encompassed by them lived in semisedentary settlements of 100 to 1,000 people, and language and culture often varied from village to village. Trade, marriage, and ritual connected these communities, but most villages steadfastly maintained autonomy and protected their areas against encroachment.

Despite this great linguistic and cultural diversity, Indians in Alta California pursued a common subsistence strategy. They were hunter-gatherers who used burning, irrigation, and pruning to maximize food sources. Women collected and processed the acorns, seeds, roots, and berries that constituted the mainstay of the diet; men fished and hunted game, birds, and sea mammals. Crafts were also divided by sex: women wove baskets, clothes, and household articles; men made tools and weapons.

Social organization in precontact California is poorly understood, but recent studies suggest that villages—the principal unit of organization—were stratified into a ruling elite, commoners, and an underclass. The elite was treated with respect, awe, and caution by commoners, who had no rank, and the underclass, who had no formal ties to an intact lineage. Social status was ascribed and authority was distributed hierarchically: elite males inherited political, religious, and economic power through their fathers' lines. Access to power and control of ritual knowledge distinguished the elite, who also wore the finest clothes, inhabited the largest houses, and avoided manual labor. The community owned the village land, but the elite determined its use. At the top of the village hierarchy stood a chief, who oversaw the production, allocation, and trade of the community's food and material goods. This was the complex and stratified Indian world Spain sought to control after 1769.

In California, soldiers and friars drew on policies, developed during the Reconquest of the Iberian peninsula and refined through two and a half centuries of colonization in New Spain, that promoted the incorporation of frontier peoples and regions into the expanding Spanish realm. In the Reconquest, the *municipio* (township) emerged as the principal vehicle through which new territories were settled and secured, and in the New World it became the primary form of local political organization. In areas settled by Spain, formal attachment to a municipality was not an option but a legal requirement and one of the preconditions for a productive and civilized life. As early as 1501, Ferdinand and Isabella instructed Nicolás de Ovando, the first royal governor of Hispaniola, to ensure that none of that island's Christian inhabitants "lives outside the communities that are to be made on the said island." Within a few years, the monarchs extended a similar requirement to Indians: in 1503, they ordered Ovando to gather the Indians into towns in order to facilitate their economic integration and religious instruction. This policy of *congregación* became a basic strategy for community organization and social control in virtually all of New Spain, especially after Old World diseases had decimated native populations.

To eighteenth-century Spaniards, the California Indians' small huts and scattered villages were a sure indication of a savage and undisciplined existence. Like their predecessors elsewhere in New Spain, the Franciscans took as their first goal the resettlement of Indians into compact villages. In Alta California, as in Baja

California and Sonora, where Indian settlements were dispersed, missionaries combined coercion and incentives to create new, large, Indian communities. Furthermore, disease reduced the Indian population, undercut the native economy, and prompted Indians to relocate to the missions. As a result, Indians from different villages, who had had only occasional contact in trade or war, began to live, work, and pray together.

Officials in New Spain used the Castilian *cabildo* (town council) as a model for the political organization of these new Indian communities as well as their own. In Spain, most towns were governed by a council composed of six to twelve *regidores* (councilmen). Regidores usually represented the economic interests of the most important families, and they served long tenures, sometimes for life. Two *alcaldes* (judges) served ex officio on the town council, but unlike regidores, who were their social superiors, they rotated off the cabildo after a single year in office. A *corregidor,* a crown-appointed outsider who represented both the town and the central government, presided over the cabildo. True to this model, most Spanish towns in the Americas were administered by a cabildo composed of four to eight regidores, two elected alcaldes, and various minor officials, all governing in concert with an *adelantado* or a governor. These New World cabildos, whose members were usually *encomenderos* or Spaniards with aristocratic pretensions, had authority over the basics of urban life: they drafted ordinances, punished wrongdoing, and regulated the local economy.

As conquered peoples, Indians rarely served on Spanish cabildos, but they retained a measure of control over their communities through annually elected cabildos of their own. Known collectively as the "Republic of Indians," these councils by the late seventeenth century were regulated by the *Recopilación de leyes de los reynos de las Indias,* which prescribed the frequency of elections and the number of officials. Most Indian cabildos in New Spain were composed of a governor, several regidores and alcaldes, and various lesser officials, in numbers proportional to the population of the settlement.

In establishing Indian cabildos in New Spain, Spaniards accommodated and to a certain extent institutionalized Indian forms of social and political organization. In central Mexico, newly appointed Indian governors continued the roles of preconquest dynastic rulers: they had judicial and financial responsibilities and oversaw the use of land. These governors, who were assigned to assist in the collection of tribute, marshal military support for the Spaniards, and promote the spread of Catholicism, retained or increased their sizable landholdings and the economic advantages they derived from them. Although their participation in the collection of taxes and in the exploitative *encomienda* (royal grant of Indian tribute and labor) and *repartimiento* (forced labor draft) led to frequent disputes between them and their communities, Indian governors could limit the Spaniards' demands through litigation. The responsibilities of Indian alcaldes and regidores in central Mexico also blended Indian leadership responsibilities with Castilian political forms. These officials collected tribute and organized labor, handled local land deals, oversaw the apprehension of criminals, supported the local church, and, through litigation, tried to protect the interests of the community.

In addition to the governor, alcaldes, and regidores, most Indian cabildos had a religious official known as a *fiscal.* Because there were so few missionaries in New

Spain, *fiscales* frequently held wide-ranging responsibilities. Elected or appointed annually, they managed local church finances, rang bells for mass, and gathered parishioners for religious celebrations. At a minimum, fiscales were "church constables" who punished villagers for violating Catholic teachings, but usually they were full members of the cabildo; most had previously served as regidores or alcaldes. All together, the officials of the cabildo formed an elite that controlled many of the most important aspects of Indian community life in New Spain.

As the seventeenth century drew to a close, Spanish settlement in northern New Spain took different forms than in central Mexico. *Presidios* (military garrisons) and missions became the primary means for extending Spanish control into the region and for protecting the silver mines and the roads linking them to central Mexico. In Nueva Galicia, Nueva Vizcaya, Baja California, and Sonora, many factors limited the full elaboration of Indian cabildos: the loose organization of Indian settlements, the resistance of many Indians to Spanish intrusion, the waning of the encomienda and repartimiento, and the priorities of the Jesuit and Franciscan missionaries who oversaw the appointment and election of Indian officials. In these northern areas, although Indian officials rarely sat on full-blown cabildos, they nevertheless held a wide range of offices. Most of the Indian communities in these regions were based on a mission, and many of these offices were tied to the mission church. Thus, as Spaniards advanced into the far reaches of northern New Spain during the eighteenth century, they adapted the cabildo as a model for the political organization of new communities.

In December 1778, after a decade of Franciscan activity in Alta California and the founding of eight missions, Felipe de Neve, military and civil governor of California, ordered the Franciscans to allow the Indians in the oldest missions to elect their own alcaldes and regidores. Neve based his order on historical precedent and his interpretation of the *Recopilación*. Missions San Diego (1769) and San Carlos Borromeo (1770) were to proceed with the election of two alcaldes and two regidores; smaller, more recently founded missions, such as San Antonio (1771), San Gabriel (1771), and San Luis Obispo (1772), were to elect one alcalde and one regidor. On election, each official was to report to the nearest military garrison, where the commander would install him in office in the name of the king. The presidial commander would then give the official the certificate he needed to exercise his powers; alcaldes also received a large wooden staff of leadership that symbolized their authority.

Despite the acceptance of Indian officials in missions elsewhere in New Spain, the Franciscans in Alta California bitterly opposed the elections. The ensuing conflict between Neve and the friars emerged not from Franciscan objections to indirect rule but from suspicions between secular and religious officials in New Spain that deepened during the late eighteenth century. Although Roman Catholicism was the official religion of Spain, church and state officials held opposing views about the origin of civil authority, and each claimed ultimate jurisdiction over Indians. Royal jurists increasingly insisted that the king was the vicar of Christ and that the power to oversee the church and instruct Indians therefore resided, first and foremost, with the king and his representatives. Clerics and canon lawyers maintained that the king was a vicar of the pope and that the church was therefore the principal protector and instructor of Indians. These disputes intensified under the Bourbon ascendancy.

They became urgent after Spain's defeat in the Seven Years' War, when Charles III (1759–1788) and his ministers set out to bolster royal authority by curtailing the powers of the Catholic church and strengthening the economy of New Spain.

True to the spirit of the Bourbon reforms, the first military and civil administrators of Alta California brought to their posts an official hostility to religious orders in general and missions in particular, which they saw as impediments to the transformation of Indians into useful subjects of the king. In 1767, just two years before the Franciscans founded the first mission in Alta California, Charles III expelled the Jesuits from New Spain because he feared they would use their wealth and independence to obstruct his secular reforms. Gaspar de Portolá, who commanded the first overland expedition to Alta California, oversaw the Jesuits' removal from Baja California, and Neve himself directed their expulsion from the mining center of Zacatecas. At the same time, it was the crown's need to conserve troops and limit expenditures, not an enthusiasm for missionary orders, that led royal emissary José de Gálvez to enlist the mendicant Franciscan order to pacify the Indians of Alta California.

As governor of Alta California, Neve implemented the national policy of assimilating Indians into the conquerors' political system. In Neve's words: "With the elections and the appointment of a new Republic, the will of His Majesty will be fulfilled in this region, and under our direction, in the course of time, He will obtain in these Indians useful vassals for our religion and state." Neve and his successors believed that extending to Indians the rudiments of Spanish municipal government would teach them a civics lesson that was at least equal in importance to the Franciscans' catechism.

The governor's inclusive political vision was challenged by the Franciscans' restrictive religious agenda. The friars wanted absolute control over the missions and the Indians who lived in them, and they believed that Indians so recently subjugated to the church and the crown could not possibly be ready for a measure of self-government, no matter how elementary its form. Moreover, they did not want the Indians to understand that the Spanish governor had civil and judicial authority over Indians, and the Franciscans feared that Indian officials would use their status to pursue their own goals. The Franciscans formally based their opposition to Indian elections on a legal technicality. The *Recopilación* specified that in each Indian town and *reducción* Indians were to elect officials and that *curas* (local priests) should supervise these elections. The Franciscans argued that they themselves were apostolic missionaries, not parish priests; therefore, the *Recopilación* did not apply, and the governor's order had no foundation in law.

At San Diego, where in 1775 the Tipai and Ipai had signaled their rejection of Spanish authority by destroying the mission and killing one Franciscan and two Spaniards, the governor's insistence in 1779 on elections in the rebuilt mission prompted the Franciscans to threaten resignation. Fray Junípero Serra called on the governor to suspend the elections in all the designated missions. The conflict came to a climax just before mass on Palm Sunday in 1779 when Governor Neve and Father Serra exchanged bitter words. Later that evening, overcome with agitation and unable to rest, Serra cried out: "¿Qué es esto Señor?" ("What is the meaning of it, Lord?") Serra was calmed by a voice from within that repeated one of Christ's admonitions to the Apostles: "Be prudent as serpents and simple as

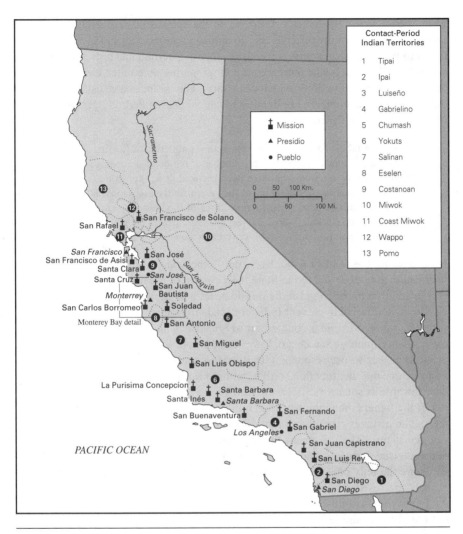

Map 4.1   Contact-Period Indian Territories with Spanish Settlements in Alta California.

doves." Reassured, Serra decided to go along with the governor's orders but only in ways that would not "cause the least change among the Indians or in the mode of governing" that the Franciscans had established. Serra believed that, with God's help, he could join the simplicity of the dove with the cunning of the serpent and thus outmaneuver the governor and prevent the elections from decreasing Franciscan authority. After the early 1780s, elections of Indian officials usually occurred annually in the largest and oldest missions.

As Serra intended, the Franciscans quickly gained a large degree of control over the elections. Even though Neve sought to extend the crown's power into the missions, the Franciscans convinced him that only with their guidance would Indians and Spaniards profit from the elections. At several of the missions, according to Serra, Indian officials had committed crimes or behaved arrogantly, as if they were "gentlemen." By January 1780, when the second annual elections were to take place, several of the officials had abandoned their missions, while others were too ill to vote. Consistent with Spanish law, Neve specified that only former Indian officials could vote, but he increased the missionaries' role in the elections, telling them to supply "direction" when necessary. The Franciscans usually supplied direction by controlling the nomination of candidates, as Pedro Fages, Neve's successor as governor, described:

> It has been established that each mission at the completion of [its first] five years must elect one or two alcaldes and the same number of regidores according to the number of individuals in the mission who have been reduced. They are to make these appointments successively, at the beginning of the year, with the assistance and intervention of the respective missionaries, who propose three of the least unqualified. A plurality of votes decides the elected, [whose names] are submitted to the governor, who approves or disapproves them according to his criteria, in the name of His Majesty.

By narrowing the field of candidates, the Franciscans guaranteed the election of men whom they expected to facilitate their control of the mission.

In addition to securing for the missionaries a large measure of control over the elections, Serra tried to prevent Indian officials from learning that the military constituted a powerful secular counterpart to Franciscan authority. Serra instructed his trusted subordinate at San Diego, Fray Fermín Francisco de Lasuén, to speak to the presidio officer whose responsibility it was to confirm the Indians in office: "Ask him to carry out this function so that, without failing in the slightest degree in his duty toward his superior officer, the Indians may not be given a less exalted opinion of the fathers than they have had until now." Furthermore, Serra preferred that the Indian officials remain ignorant of the responsibilities with which the military charged them. "The document that is used in conferring these offices on them," Serra advised Lasuén, "may be as powerful as they wish, provided Your Reverences are the only ones to receive it and read it." Even after these precautions, the Franciscans resisted sending newly elected Indians to the presidios for installation. An inquiry in the mid-1790s by Governor Diego de Borica revealed that none of the current presidio commanders had ever been called on to give Indians their oaths of office.

The Indian cabildos elected in the California missions—like those in the missions of Sonora, Texas, and New Mexico—had fewer officials, smaller responsibilities, and less autonomy than those in the Indian *pueblos* and parishes of central Mexico at the same time. Rarely did a California mission have more than two alcaldes and two regidores. Nor was an Indian governor appointed. Throughout the missions of northern New Spain, the duties of ecclesiastical and civil Indian officials overlapped, but in Alta California, perhaps to a greater extent than elsewhere in the Spanish borderlands, Indian alcaldes and regidores served as assistants to the missionaries, much like the fiscales of central Mexico.

The subordination of Indian officials to the Franciscans was noted in 1787 by Governor Fages: "Although these authorities are granted some powers, they are necessarily dependent on the missionaries, without whose direction they would not be able to exercise them." Franciscans treated Indian officials with the same heavy-handed paternalism that characterized all their interactions with Indians. Officials were subject to corporal punishment at Franciscan hands, and they were not permitted to bring charges against the missionaries. This disability set them apart from their counterparts in central Mexico, who frequently used legal channels to claim that their curates manipulated elections, misappropriated communal funds, and imposed excessive labor demands. In New Spain, to be left without the right to seek protection or redress through the law rendered one virtually defenseless.

Under Franciscan supervision, Indian officials in California nevertheless had wide-ranging authority over other mission Indians. According to the *Recopilación,* they were charged with ensuring that Indians attended mass and remained sober. They were to "keep guard" around the mission village at night and to "lead the people to prayer and to work." Pablo Tac, a Luiseño who in 1832 at age ten was taken from California to Europe by a Franciscan, was one of a handful of California Indians who provided a description of the responsibilities of the Indian officials. According to the narrative Tac wrote while studying Latin in Rome, one of the alcaldes' main functions was to speak for the Franciscans: "In the afternoon, the alcaldes gather at the house of the missionary. They bring the news of that day, and if the missionary tells them something that all the people of the country ought to know, they return to the villages . . . [and] each one of the alcaldes wherever he goes cries out what the missionary has told them, in his language, and all the country hears it." Given the alcaldes' roles in conveying Franciscan directives to the missions' Indians, Tac's statement that Indian officials "knew how to speak Spanish more than the others" comes as no surprise.

The Franciscans, emphasizing religious indoctrination, used catechisms to ready Indians for baptism and confessional manuals to prepare them for penance and communion. Whether Indian officials helped translate these handbooks into local languages is not clear, but the records show that they were among the few Indians who participated in the sacraments of baptism and marriage as godparents and witnesses. On these occasions, the Franciscans relied on Indian officials to translate Catholic rites into terms that were comprehensible to their people. We do not know the content of these unrecorded translations, but in trying to explain Catholic rituals, officials may well have invoked concepts that gave the rituals an Indian meaning.

Never content simply to instruct Indians, the Franciscans tried to control their lives, especially their sexual behavior. To that end, most missions had single-sex dormitories for the unmarried, and Indian officials were charged with keeping unmarried men and women from having illicit contact. In 1797, Mission Santa Cruz even had one alcalde for men and another for women. In this area of responsibility, many alcaldes showed more regard for the desires of other Indians than for the demands of the Franciscans. In 1821, Modesto, an alcalde at Mission San Juan Bautista, took advantage of the illness of one of the friars and "delivered" the single women to the men. He was quickly suspended from office and replaced by Francisco Sevilla, a former alcalde who had "taken good care of the single women."

Franciscans also attempted to remake the Indians' daily routines, primarily through a rigid labor regime; here, too, Indian officials often played a crucial role. Tac recounted how alcaldes circulated through the villages telling people when and where to report for work: "Tomorrow the sowing begins and so the laborers go to the chicken yard and assemble there." When their calls went unheeded, officials punished those who they or the Franciscans believed were shirking. In 1797, Claudio, an Indian baptized at Mission San Francisco who later absconded, declared that one of the reasons he had run away was that the alcalde Valeriano "made him go to work" when he was sick. Homobono, who also fled, declared that Valeriano "hit him with a heavy cane for having gone to look for mussels at the beach," an outing that most likely took him away from his work at the mission. Not all Indian officials could be counted on to enforce the Franciscans' labor regime. In 1814, the *padres* at Mission San Francisco lamented that, when they asked the alcaldes to supervise work in and around the mission, "not infrequently the alcaldes and the men spend their time in play and remain away [from the mission] for another day despite the fact that their task is an urgent one."

Franciscans also looked to Indian officials to administer a share of the corporal punishment they considered necessary for the Indians' souls. Foreign visitors and Anglo-American immigrants emphasized that Indians "did a great deal of chastisement, both by and without [Franciscan] orders." Frederick Beechey, an English sea captain who visited Mission San Francisco in 1826, claimed that officials used goads to keep fellow Indians kneeling during mass, for "goads were better adapted to this purpose than the whips, as they would reach a long way, and inflict a sharp puncture without making a noise." Hugo Reid, a Scot who married an Indian from Mission San Gabriel, later wrote that alcaldes carried "a wand to denote their authority, and what was more terrible, an immense scourge of raw hide, about ten feet in length, plaited to the thickness of an ordinary man's wrist!" Although these may well exaggerations motivated by religious and national differences, Indian complaints substantiate the basic claim of alcalde violence in the mission. However severe, corporal punishments by Indian officials did not take the place of beatings dealt directly by the Franciscans. Viewing themselves as the spiritual fathers of the Indians, Franciscans maintained that it was their responsibility to chastise them; they flogged Indians for repeatedly running away, for practicing native religious beliefs, and for performing a host of other acts considered disrespectful or sinful. When Indians remained incorrigible after several floggings, the friars sent them to the presidio for more beatings and hard labor.

In addition to being the intelligible voice and strong arm of the Franciscans, Indian officials were meant to be the military's eyes and ears at the missions. Military officials expected Indian alcaldes to investigate and report crimes that occurred at the missions. When a man at Mission San Juan Capistrano killed his wife, it was Bruno, the mission alcalde, who heard the murderer's first admission of guilt and carried the news to Spanish officials. Indian officials, however, rarely cooperated as readily as Bruno; in fact, alcaldes exposed very few of the crimes committed at the missions. In 1808, after several Indians at Mission San José brawled and fled the mission, an alcalde failed to notify the Spanish authorities, a dereliction of duty that led the governor to brand him a criminal accomplice. More often than not, when Indian officials were called on to explain murders or robberies at their missions, their testimony proved unremarkable, merely echoing accounts offered by others.

Some actions of Indian officials, such as administering punishment, may have had no precedent in pre-mission village leadership, but many of their duties and responsibilities resembled those of earlier native leaders. Village leaders oversaw the production of the community's food while remaining exempt from basic manual labor; similarly, alcaldes participated in the productive life of the mission as coordinators, not laborers. Village captains made crucial decisions concerning the distribution of food; alcaldes, too, decided how to allocate the mission's food resources. In 1786, for example, Franciscans at Mission Santa Clara discussed the distribution of the mission's harvest with the Indian leaders:

> We called together the principal [Indian] leaders at the mission and we said to them: . . . The soldiers are suffering much from hunger. They have no corn, no wheat, no beans. They are asking us to sell them some of these things. . . . If we do sell, there will not be enough on hand to support you until the time of the wheat harvest. If you wish to go away for some weeks to gather nuts, it will be possible to sell them some corn, and there will be that much extra to spend on clothes. You may consult with your own people if you wish.
>
> In less than an hour they returned to say that they would choose life in the open, for the pinole was already getting ripe.

Indian village captains reportedly led their people in battle, a responsibility subsequently held by alcaldes when the Franciscans and presidio commanders experimented with using armed parties of Indian auxiliaries to defend the missions from foreign attack.

The alcaldes' perquisites of office resembled the advantages that had distinguished village captains from the rest of the Indian community. The elite had constituted a self-perpetuating oligarchy; similarly, in the early years of the elections, only Indian officials cast votes for their successors. Village captains, like Indian officials, were supported by the labor of the community. Both sets of leaders wore distinctive clothing and lived in special houses. And according to Julio César, an Indian baptized at Mission San Luis Rey, alcaldes were among the few Indians allowed to ride horseback, a privileged act in Spanish California. Despite these advantages, Indian officials—like village captains—enjoyed only a slight material advantage over their people, and that advantage was never secure, dependent as all Indians were on a fragile mission economy.

As intermediaries between cultures, Indian officials were often caught between the conflicting demands of the Indian community and the Franciscans. Indians such as Homobono and Claudio at San Francisco—and surely others who do not appear in the historical record—resisted the labor regime the alcaldes reinforced and so resented the alcaldes' use of their authority that they left the missions. Conversely, officials' conformity to Indian expectations often invited Franciscan condemnation. Baltazar, one of the first alcaldes at San Carlos Borromeo, ran afoul of Serra when he fathered a child by his wife's sister. Serra's god demanded that his people be monogamous, whereas Indians expected their leaders to be polygamous. The Indian community probably saw Baltazar's sororal polygyny as an emblem of his status; the Franciscans considered it proof of his depravity. They hounded him out of the mission, branded him a deserter, and tried to sever his connection to his people. Serra then accused Baltazar of "sending messages to the people here, meeting personally with those who leave here with permission, and thereby trying to swell the numbers of his band from the mountains by new desertions of the natives of this mission."

Resistance by some alcaldes, such as Modesto and Baltazar, to Franciscan notions of marriage and sexuality and acquiescence by others, such as Francisco Sevilla and Valeriano, to their directives suggest the ambiguities of the alcalde's role and rule. Even though their behavior at times appeared unpredictable—even unacceptable—to Indians or Spaniards, Indian officials occupied a privileged space in the Spanish system as interpreters, mediators, and enforcers of the new colonial order. The influence of Indian officials within the Indian community, however, depended not only on the authority Spaniards invested in them but also on the legitimacy these men brought to their leadership positions. Based on kinship and lineage networks, this legitimacy, in turn, helps explain the ability of Spanish officials to orchestrate social, religious, economic, and political change within native communities and the ability of native officials on occasion to keep such initiatives at bay.

The historical record speaks far more directly about what Indian officials did than about who they were—an imbalance that is mirrored in the scholarship. Fortunately, records created by colonial administrators allow investigation of the place of Indian leaders in the complex web of kinship and lineage that defined the Indian community. Franciscans notified presidio commanders of election results and occasionally mentioned Indian officials in baptismal, marriage, and burial records. By combining these reports—fragmentary as they are—with information on family relations, village affiliations, and vital statistics contained in sacramental registers, we can sketch a composite portrait of the mission staff of leadership.

Mission San Carlos Borromeo presents the most complete materials for a case study. Its sacramental registers are intact and thorough, and more reports of its annual elections have survived than for any other California mission. Established in June 1770 as the second mission in Alta California and the first on the central coast, San Carlos Borromeo served as the early residence of the father president, who set policy for the region. Located about three miles from the Monterey presidio, the headquarters of the region's governor, Mission San Carlos was overseen by Franciscans until its secularization by the Mexican government in 1834. The record keeping of the Franciscans and the efficiency of the microcomputer enable one to identify and situate within the native community forty-six alcaldes and regidores who served at San Carlos Borromeo from 1779 to 1831, probably about half the officials during those five decades. References by Franciscans at San Carlos Borromeo to fiscales cease at roughly the same time that elections for alcaldes and regidores begin. The Franciscans may have continued to appoint fiscales, but in all likelihood they relied on alcaldes and regidores instead.

Typically diverse, the Indian community at the mission comprised Indians from the Costanoan and Esselen linguistic families who came from at least ten different villages. At the time the mission was founded, the population of the Monterey region seems to have numbered around 2,800. In almost every year, because disease was endemic, the Franciscans recorded more burials than births; only the baptisms of Indians from the surrounding area allowed the mission's population to reach a peak of around 875 in the mid-1790s. The mission population subsequently declined, and after 1808, when the friars recorded the baptisms of the last Indians they recruited from the surrounding area, went into free fall. Disease continued to take a heavy toll, and by 1825, the mission had only about 300 Indians.

At San Carlos Borromeo, Indian officials were always baptized men who were married or widowed. They were usually older and had been baptized earlier than other men from their villages. Thirteen out of fourteen, for example, who served

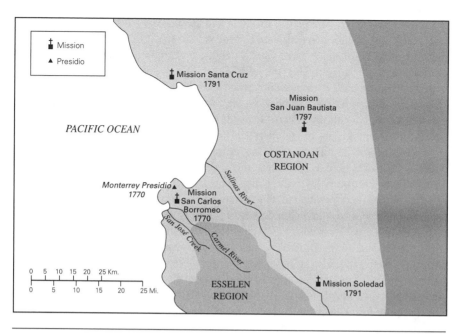

Map 4.2   Monterey Bay Area. Contact-Period Indian Territories with Spanish Settlements.

during the period 1779–1798 fit this pattern. Of those who served in 1792, Hilario José was one of the first adult Esselen men baptized, Atanasio José was older and had been in the mission longer than most Costanoan men, and Sancio Francisco and Nicomedes were older than most of the men from their communities.

During the mission's early recruiting years, Indian officials were likely to have been village captains or their close associates. For example, the sacramental registers identify Sancio Francisco and Abrahan—officials in the 1790s—as former village leaders. The baptismal record of Nicomedes, also an official in the 1790s, describes him as the "principal confidant" of the village captain Aristeo José. Later, the mission community tended to produce its own leadership. After the early 1790s, fewer captains came to the mission; those who did were not elected to leadership positions. As the mission population matured, it developed a cadre of men who spoke Spanish and were familiar with the Franciscan regime—qualifications that supplanted previous experience as village captains.

In native California, political leadership customarily descended from father to son. This practice carried over to San Carlos Borromeo, although it was disrupted by persistently high mortality. Of the thirty-seven baptized sons of village captains identified in the mission's records, only eight lived to their mid-thirties. Four of these gained positions of responsibility, three as officials, one as an interpreter. The high death rate among the young made it very hard for elite families to maintain a direct line of influence. Yet the son of a village leader who lived to adulthood had a far better chance of becoming a mission official than others his age. Officials who did not have blood ties to former village captains were frequently related to other leading Indians: two were the sons of officials, three pairs were brothers, ten pairs were brothers-in-law, and eleven officials had close ties to mission interpreters. In addition, many alcaldes were related by marriage to soldiers. For example, Atanasio José, an alcalde for many years, had a daughter whose first and second husbands were soldiers at the Monterey presidio. Other officials were related to privileged Indians from Baja California who worked closely with the Franciscans during the first years of the mission. Extended leadership families such as these suggest that in the face of high death rates, marriage provided a means for surviving members of powerful Indian families to maintain leadership status in the mission.

Spanish laws regulating cabildos promoted turnover in officeholding, but at San Carlos Borromeo, as elsewhere in New Spain, these laws proved ineffective, because they conflicted with the native practice of long-term rule and the Spanish desire to support cooperative local leaders. A common strategy to assure continuity of leadership was to rotate alcaldes and regidores in office each year. At Mission San Carlos, Oresio Antonio was regidor in 1810, 1812, and 1814 and alcalde in 1811, 1813, and 1815. Other officials sat out a year or two and then returned to office. As the rotational system suggests, differences between the responsibilities of alcaldes and of regidores faded over time. Important and cooperative Indians, provided they could stay alive, were thus never far from office; some served continuously for up to six years, and others rotated in and out over more than fifteen years.

Indian officials reflected the ethnic and linguistic diversity of the mission community, as the mission's two language families and four largest village groups could each frequently claim one of the officials. After 1776, when Esselen villagers first came to the mission, San Carlos was composed of both Costanoan- and Esselen-speakers, the former enjoying numerical superiority over the latter throughout the mission's life. The Franciscans carefully noted the village affiliation of all Indians at baptism and monitored the changing composition of the population. If late eighteenth-century guidelines for the Franciscan missionaries at Mission Nuestra Señora de la Purísima Concepción in San Antonio, Texas, are typical of Franciscan electoral management in northern New Spain—and there is no reason to suppose otherwise—the Franciscans at San Carlos Borromeo worked hard to ensure that officials were drawn from the mission's largest groups. The San Antonio instructions, probably written in 1787 or 1788 by Fray José García, urged the missionaries to "remind" voters that the positions of governor and alcalde alternated annually between the most populous groups at the mission, the Pajalache and the Tacame. This correlation between the ethnic and linguistic composition of officials and that of the mission population reflected the needs of Spaniards and Indians alike. Franciscans and governors would have found it difficult to incorporate and control the Indians without assistance from native leaders who could effectively communicate with the mission's most populous groups, and powerful Indian groups might have rebelled had they been excluded from positions of authority.

Not until 1810, when twenty-six-year-old Teopisto José became regidor did a mission-born Indian serve as an official at San Carlos Borromeo. The policy of drawing the officials from the mission's different village and linguistic groups helps to explain why so few—only seven—were born in the mission. Indian officials were usually in their late twenties or early thirties when first elected. Thus Indians born in the 1770s at the mission could not have served until the mid-1790s, and yet they did not dominate the leadership positions when they reached maturity.

Rather, the representation of different village groups, some of which did not come to the mission until the mid-1780s, took precedence over the selection of the individuals who, having spent their entire lives in the mission, might have been the most acculturated to Spanish ways and loyal to Franciscan wishes. Even after 1810, Indians born at the mission filled only one quarter of the leadership positions; those baptized before age ten took only slightly more than half.

Beginning in 1810, repercussions from the Mexican independence movement shook the hybrid system of indirect and representative rule in the missions of Alta California. Economic and political support for the frontier missions evaporated during the Mexican struggle, and, after Mexico won independence in 1821, the new federal government attempted to expel Spanish missionaries, whose loyalty it doubted, and challenged the missions as anachronistic relics of Spanish rule and impediments to economic growth. Municipal electoral reforms that were instituted elsewhere in Mexico after 1810 did not directly affect the missions. While politicians at the national level debated the form that the new government would take, Indians contested political authority in the missions, as they, too, tried to clarify who had the right to rule.

During the 1820s, soldiers and settlers increasingly relied on the missions for food and Indian laborers. The missions themselves continued to be unhealthy, and labor demands on Indians increased, just as Franciscan authority was weakening. At several missions, these circumstances prompted Indian officials to reject the colonial order altogether and lead their people out of the missions. Had the officials been given the right to bring charges against the missionaries, they might have used that legal leverage to improve conditions in the disintegrating missions. Had they been in a better position to profit personally from the missions' economic system, they might have been more loyal. But in Alta California at this time, many Indian officials found little to gain by preserving the Franciscans' collapsing regime.

Lacking both an institutional means to reform the system from within and a significant personal stake in its survival, Indian officials at several missions turned their authority against the Spanish system. In 1824, Andrés, an alcalde at Mission Santa Barbara, joined forces with Indians at Missions Santa Inés and La Purísima to lead the largest of the Indian uprisings in Mexican California. In 1827, Narciso and two other officials persuaded 400 Indians to flee San José; another alcalde, Estanislao, joined the resistance the following year; and a fifth San José official, Victor, was later implicated and punished. These insurgencies dealt hard blows to the missions even though soldiers eventually put them down. Such rebellions did not merely demonstrate the dissatisfaction of Indians with the Franciscan regime. Taken collectively, they laid bare the dependence of the Spanish colonial system on Indian authority, for they showed how Indian officials frequently held the fate of the mission in their hands.

At San Carlos Borromeo during the 1820s, worsening economic conditions and declining Franciscan control did not lead to overt rebellion; instead, they prompted a scramble among Indians for authority in the crumbling mission. No longer a source of conflict solely between Franciscans and soldiers, political control of the mission was openly negotiated and disputed among the Indians, some of whom held power while others wanted it. As disease, disaffection, and flight greatly reduced the pool of Indians most likely by lineage to assume the staff of leadership, Indian elections began to create rather than merely reinforce Indian political authority, and the elections themselves became vulnerable to contestation. When the Franciscan-brokered electoral system failed, one group of Costanoan Indians came to control the vast majority of leadership positions. Their political dominance in the decade 1822–1831 finally provoked open dispute and formal appeals for the intervention of Mexican secular authorities.

The time, day, and place of the contested election of 1831 show how far Indians at San Carlos Borromeo had transformed and made their own a practice that Spaniards had originally considered an emblem of Spanish civility. Held on Saturday after mass under the watchful eyes of the Franciscans, Indian elections in the 1780s and 1790s had been thoroughly infused with Catholic meaning and Franciscan authority. As time passed, however, elections combined Indian culture and Spanish procedures. By 1831, the annual election was no longer fixed to the Catholic schedule of worship; rather, it occurred on Saturday evening, a time when Indians gathered for their own diversions and discussions. Furthermore, elections did not take place in or near the church but in the ritual space of an Indian *temescal* or sweatbath, a place sheltered from Franciscan oversight. In addition to the return to an Indian ceremonial site, this election also reveals continuities in the way mission Indians recognized and achieved leadership early and late in the mission period, for, in conformity with an earlier pattern, two of the Indians elected, Domicio and Romano, were sons of a village captain.

Although this election of Indian officials linked to earlier authority systems demonstrates a continuity with pre-mission times, the dispute afterward signals that some Indians at the mission had grown accustomed to the representative system that the Franciscans had overseen. In January 1831, four Indians asked that the recent election be invalidated because it had not occurred at the proper time and place and because the winners did not represent the different village groups in the mission. The Indians' letter to Antonio Buelna, magistrate at the Monterey presidio, stated their principal objections to the recently elected officials: "Domicio is the half-brother of Romano, and the first cousin of Francisco. Francisco is the brother-in-law of Agricio, and furthermore, Agricio is a distant relative of Domicio; they are one people." The protesters proposed a return to the system of drawing officials from the mission's different groups, arguing that "it be made a condition that each direction or tribe will elect only one [official]." Their awareness of the winners' shared family ties and their assertion of diversity in the mission underscore the extent to which mission Indians continued to derive their identities from their places of origin decades after their ancestral villages were incorporated into the mission. Furthermore, the protestors implicitly accepted the annual elections as a means of generating and legitimating Indian authority: their letter denounced the procedures of one election, not the practice of electing officials annually.

During the 1830s, national and provincial political leaders transferred control of the missions to secular administrators and parceled out the bulk of mission lands and resources to local soldiers and settlers. Some former missions continued as secular communities; most fell in ruins after the exodus of Indians to their ancestral homelands or the emerging pueblos. In all of these places—former missions,

Mexican towns, and regions beyond state control—vestiges of the Indian-Spanish political system survived: Indian officials continued to lead their communities in the face of growing economic, political, and demographic challenges.

Two Indian officials, José Jesús of Mission San José, a recently baptized Miwok, and Romano of San Carlos Borromeo, baptized three decades earlier, took divergent paths after the missions were secularized; José Jesús cut his ties to Mexican California while Romano became more entrenched in its political system. Their experiences suggest that former mission officials were among the few Indians who had the skills to negotiate two cultures during this period of accelerating change. José Jesús returned to the Central Valley, where he led a group of Indians who stole livestock from Mexican ranchers. In 1845, he was briefly engaged by John Sutter—whose fame in the Gold Rush still awaited him—to catch horse thieves. Two years later, Sutter enlisted him again to form an Indian brigade for the California Battalion in action against Mexican resistance to the United States regime. In 1848, to prove his friendship to the new government, José Jesús offered the San José magistrate Indian laborers whom he and his men had captured in the surrounding hills. Never far removed from important events, during the Gold Rush José Jesús also supplied Indian laborers to Charles Weber, the founder of Stockton.

Like José Jesús, Romano participated in many of the central transformations of California. Born the son of a village captain and baptized as an infant in 1799, he served as an official at San Carlos Borromeo in 1830 and 1831, the year of the disputed election. Romano lived through epidemics at the mission and made an effective adjustment to life in Mexican California. In 1835, a year after the secularization of Mission San Carlos, he served as alcalde for the Indian community living at the site of the former mission. And in 1844, the Monterey municipal government appointed him *Juez de Campo* for this community, called San Carlos by the 1840s. Romano's duties as *juez* (judge) are unknown, but his appointment demonstrates a continuity of leadership from pre-mission times. Few Indians in Alta California had the linguistic and cultural skills, much less the good fortune, to survive such remarkable changes. Fewer still have had their stories told. But the experience of Indians like José Jesús and Romano testify to the ability and creativity of California Indians who did adjust to life in a rapid changing world.

To most Indians in Alta California, Spaniards brought disease, cultural dislocation, and an early grave; to some, they also provided political opportunity. The prominence of individuals like Baltazar, Andrés, José Jesús, and Romano and the coherence of the groups they led suggest that the political system the Spaniards relied on to control the missions—and the Indians' ability to shape that system to their needs—fostered the preservation and creation of Indian authority. Indians who held legitimate authority among their people frequently served as officials, and the composition of the Indian cabildos reflected the divisions of village groups in the missions. When officials did not reflect the community, disgruntled or excluded Indians sought redress from Spanish authorities. For the most part, Indian officials cooperated with the Spanish, but a personal crisis or the declining welfare of their communities could incite them to reject the colonial system and replace Spanish authority with their own. When Indian officials contradicted or challenged Spanish authorities, they courted dismissal. Still, it was never in the interest of Spaniards to replace uncooperative officials with Indians whose legitimacy was not recognized by their own people. Nor was it in their interest to level the distinctions of rank among Indians. To have done so would have provoked opposition from the Indians who could most effectively assist in controlling the missions.

Doubtless, there were Indian officials in the missions of Alta California whose malleability rather than their kinship or lineage recommended them to the Franciscans. But for the most part the alcalde system depended on the extent to which native villages, leadership, and traditions were incorporated into the missions. The authority of Indian officials in colonial California originated from more than brute force, Franciscan missionaries, or the Spanish state. It was carried over from native villages, legitimated and re-created in annual mission elections, and ultimately strengthened by the extent to which the staff of Indian leadership remained embedded in a network of shifting family relations that defined Indian communities throughout the colonial period.

◈ F U R T H E R   R E A D I N G

Gary Clayton Anderson, *The Indian Southwest, 1580–1830: Ethnogenesis and Reinvention* (1999)

James Axtell, *The Indians' New South: Cultural Change in the Colonial Southeast* (1997)

Henry Warner Bowden, *American Indians and Christian Missions* (1981)

Edward D. Castillo, "Gender Status and Decline, Resistance, and Accommodation Among Female Neophytes in the Missions of California: A San Gabriel Case Study," *American Indian Culture and Research Journal* 18 (no. 1, 1994), 67–94

Sherburne F. Cook, *The Conflict between the California Indian and White Civilization* (1976)

Rupert Costo and Jeannette Henry Costo, eds., *The Missions of California: A Legacy of Genocide* (1987)

Harry W. Crosby, *Antigua California: Mission and Colony on the Peninsular Frontier, 1697–1768* (1994)

Charles R. Cutter, *The Protector de Indios in Colonial New Mexico, 1659–1821* (1986)

William C. Foster, *Spanish Expeditions into Texas, 1689–1768* (1995)

Patricia Galloway, *Choctaw Genesis, 1500–1700* (1996)

Frederic, W. Gleach, *Powhatan's World and Colonial Virginia: A Conflict of Cultures* (1997)

Ramón Gutiérrez, *When Jesus Came the Corn Mothers Went Away: Marriage, Sexuality and Power in New Mexico, 1500–1846* (1991)

Steven W. Hackel, "The Staff of Leadership: Indian Authority in the Missions of Alta California," *William and Mary Quarterly* 54 (1997), 347–376

Thomas D. Hall, *Social Change in the Southwest, 1350–1880* (1989)

Charles M. Hudson and Carmen Chaves Tesser, eds., *The Forgotten Centuries: Indians and Europeans in the American South, 1521–1704* (1994)

Albert L. Hurtado, *Intimate Frontier: Sex, Gender, and Culture in Old California* (1999)

———, "Sexuality in California's Franciscan Missions: Cultural Perceptions and Sad Realities," *California History* 71 (1992): 371–385

Robert H. Jackson, *Indian Population Decline: The Missions of Northwestern New Spain, 1687–1840* (1994)

——— and Edward Castillo, *Indians, Franciscans, and Spanish Colonization: The Impact of the Mission System on California Indians* (1995)

Elizabeth A. John, *Storms Brewed in Other Men's Worlds: The Confrontation of Indians, Spanish, and French in the Southwest, 1540–1795* (1975)

Thomas W. Kavanaugh, *Comanche Political History: An Ethnohistorical Perspective, 1706–1875* (1996)

John L. Kessell, *Kiva, Cross and Crown: The Pecos Indians and New Mexico* (1979)

Andrew K. Knaut, *The Pueblo Revolt of 1680: Conquest and Resistance in Seventeenth-Century New Mexico* (1995)

Jerald T. Milanich, *Florida Indians and the Invasion from Europe* (1995)

Theda Perdue, *Cherokee Women: Gender and Culture Change, 1700–1835* (1998)

Edward H. Spicer, *Cycles of Conquest: The Impact of Spain, Mexico, and the United States on the Indians of the Southwest, 1533–1960* (1962)

David Hurst Thomas, ed., *Columbian Consequences,* 3 vols. (1989–1991)

Stephen Trimble, *The People: Indians of the American Southwest* (1993)

Fredrika J. Tuete and Andrew R. L. Cayton, eds., *Contact Points: American Frontiers from the Mohawk Valley to the Mississippi, 1750–1830* (1998)

Daniel H. Usner, Jr., *Indians, Settlers, and Slaves in a Frontier Exchange Economy: The Lower Mississippi Valley Before 1783* (1992)

David J. Weber, *The Spanish Frontier in North America* (1992)

The Northern Borderlands

◈

The northern borderlands stretched across the broad forest lands of North America and included the northern tier of states from the mid–Atlantic region to the arctic. Here, the English and the French were the principal colonial actors. The French and the British were interested in converting Indians to Christianity in their colonial precincts, although neither nation devoted as much energy to this pursuit as did the Spanish. Nevertheless, British Protestant missionaries worked among the Indians in the British colonies, and Catholic priests labored in Canada.

The fur trade was one of the most distinctive features of the French and British colonies in the northern borderlands, and was an important aspect of European colonial expansion generally. Beaver, otter, and other animal pelts lured entrepreneurs because of their beauty, warmth, and value in European markets. Eventually, the beaver came to dominate the trade because its unique fur made a durable and handsome felt for hats. In addition, deer hides, buffalo robes, and other animal skins became articles of Indian-white commerce throughout the Americas. Lively trade in these items characterized Indian-white relations in much of the present United States and Canada. Often, Indians trapped and traded fur-bearing animals to white merchants, but the richness of fur resources also attracted independent white trappers, traders, and large commercial trapping concerns such as the Hudson's Bay Company and North West Company in Canada, John Jacob Astor's American Fur Company in the United States, and a host of lesser enterprises. Representatives of these outfits often lived among Indians and married native women, a practice that was known as the custom of the country. Such marriages provided kinship relations, which smoothed trade with Indians and gave the white husband protection of the tribe. But the fur trade was not an altogether peaceful enterprise. It caused conflict between Indians and whites who encroached on tribal territory. National states vied for colonial supremacy, and tribes quarreled as they expanded their hunting grounds. The commercial demands of the fur trade caused the rapid depletion of fur resources as trapping extinguished the most valuable species, and intertribal warfare erupted as Indians looked for country that still had animals in commercial quantities. The trade brought a period of prosperity to some tribes, but it also caused dependence on Europeans for guns, traps, and other manufactured items that were necessary to the trade. It also created a taste for various trade goods and the adulterated but powerful alcoholic beverages that polluted tribal society. Thus, the fur business fostered commerce and expansion for Europe and the United States, while it generated a cycle of trade, violence, dependence, and poverty for American Indians.

British missionaries succeeded in converting some Indians to Protestant Christianity in New England, but they were constantly on the alert for backsliders as they made the rounds of their native parishioners. Document 1 presents the views of a New England missionary, Joseph Fish, who was convinced that Indian souls could be saved but who was scandalized at the "lewdness" of his native parishioners. Samson Occom, a Mohegan man, narrates his life in Document 2. Occom relates how he became a Christian and gives special attention to achieving literacy. Document 3 shows that Christien LeClerq, a Micmac man, was critical of French innovations in Canada. Indians were happier and more healthy before the French arrived, he argued. In Document 4, a Frenchman describes Indian women on the upper Missouri River. Polygamy, easy divorce, and seemingly lax sexual mores shocked some Europeans, but also formed a social basis for intimate relations with fur traders. Document 5 shows that the purchase of Indian slave women was a part of the fur trade society. While many fur traders married Indian women according to native customs, the demand for women was so great that some whites resorted to purchasing slave women for wives.

1. Joseph Fish Preaches to the Narragansett Indians, 1768

June 20. 1768 . . . Found the School kept us as Usual, and more Schollars, of late, attending: about 15 Children, pretty Steadily come to School. Nothing Materially differing in Indians Circumstances Since last there: but Mr. Deake's Situation very difficult and distressing, on Account of his Debts. Tells me he Owes about £20-£Money, and all of it, to divers persons, now due, by Notes of hand or Obligations on Demand. His Creditors Patience no longer to be expected. Two Notes already committed to hands of Authority, to be heard. He expects a *Writ* or Two, before this Week is out: And can't See Any Way to avoid being taken out of his Business; which must break up the School. The Consequence he Apprehends will be, That the Indians, From their great Regard to Mr. *Greaves* N. Londo., Will Make Application to *Him,* or to the *Church* of England for a Schoolmaster and *Support.* On Consulting his Case, I promised him to write the Commissioners in his Behalf.

A[t] about Two, Preachd at Indian Meeting house, to 20 Indians, (They having heard that I would not Come today, and Numbers of them, through Carelessness, having forgot the Lecture.) From Matth: 22–39. *Thou Shalt love thy Neighbour as Thy Self*—A grace and Duty much Wanting and greatly Neglected Among these Indians. In the Fore part of My Discourse, Indians Seemd Sleepy and Careless— Digressed and rousd them, by Awakening Touches. Towards the Close of my Discourse, A Molatto (Ammon,) a Lusty Man, having for Some time discovered Something Singular in his Countenance, fell into great distress, manifested by Crying out bitterly, which continued through the Remainder of Sermon. Finishd off with a fervent Prayer, trembling as he Spoke. Found upon Speaking to him after Sermon, that the Word reachd his Conscience, Wakd up a Sense of his Guilt, in late evil Conduct, having been long reputed a Christian, but of late Years or Months,

William S. Simmons and Cheryl L. Simmons, eds., "Joseph Fish Preaches to the Narragansett Indians, 1768," in *Old Light on Separate Ways: The Narragansett Diary of Joseph Fish,* 42–45. Copyright © 1982 by the University Press of New England. Reprinted by permission.

walkd unbecoming his Profession. Several other Indians, manifested Some deep Impressions from the *Word.*

After Lecture, Visited Two Families. Wm. Sachem (of the Sachems Party and his Uncle,) who never heard me preach Save once. Found him Serious and Attentive, while I talkd to him on the Affairs of his Soul. Has got a hope of Grace, in Former times but for Years past lives poorly. I endeavour to Awake him to a Sense of his Duty and Danger. Here found about a Dozen Indians, Men and Women, who had been *Hoeing* for Will. I gave *Them* an Exhortation, and proceeded to find *Toby.*

The Indians commonly Fence their Fields with thick *Hedges*—No *Barrs,* I was obligd to break through their Hedges, with my Horse, and repair them, Well as I could. After travelling through the Thickets, many times no path, and passing deep valleys and Steep Hills, over Which I could but just climb, with my Horse in hand, for near 3/4 hour, (Mr. Deake in company my Guide) I found Sqr. *Tobys* (as Calld,) living much retird and then Alone. He's the Oldest Indian Man, in the Tribe. In his 86th Year. Entirely (or Near it) *blind.* Reckoned (not without good reason,) a pious Man. Talkd familiarly of *Death* and *Heaven.* Said he longd to go Home to his Fathers house, which he hopd for, in a little time. Twas now Night. Took leave of the Old Man. . . .

Tuesday, June 21. Returnd to the Indian houses, in the Morning. Visitted Four Indian Families. Discoursed with a Christian Indian Woman, (*Henry Harrys* Wife,) Under Soul Trouble, declining Health and many Afflictions. Her Daughter (a Widow) A bed with a Bastard Child—I endeavourd to awake the poor thoughtless, unconcernd Creature to a Sense of her Guilt and Danger. Calld at [?*Sachs*] Daughters—Dropped a Word of encouragement to a poor Creature in Travail.

Visited old Robins. His Daughter an Impudent Secure, Lewd person—Two Bastard Children with her. I endeavourd to Alarm her Conscience, by Shewing the certain Destruction of *Fornicators* etc.

Visited John *Shattock,* And, among other things, Reprovd him for not reading the *Bible* (as he Says he Can read it Well,) in his Family daily. Owns he has not read it for a long time. I endeavourd to Convince him of his Sinfull neglect, and excite him to his Duty. Left the Indians between Ten and Eleven o'Clock, and returnd home by post Road. . . .

Monday July 18. 1768 . . . Very hot and I much unwell; but reachd the School house about *One.* The School kept up, and about the Number of Schollars as before (15, or more). Mr. Deake Somewhat relievd of the pressures mentiond in Journal of last Visit. He approved of my Proposal to Commissioners for advancing half a years pay—Said twould much relieve him.

Many people at the Indian Meeting, Yesterday (Lords day,) English and Indians. Numbers behavd very wickedly, in time of the Indians Worship. In the day time or Evening Some of Them got drunk and Two Squaws fell upon another Squaw, that was heavy with Child, and beat, kickd and abusd her, So that her Life was much doubted of.

Preachd at Indian Meeting house to 30 Indians, Chiefly Women and young persons, from Matth. 5.4. Nothing Special Appeard in the Audience.

After Lecture Visited Samel. *Niles,* (about 1 1/2 Mile North East from Meeting house) intending, to have Spent the Remainder of the Day and Next Day Forenoon, in Visiting Indians: but Mr. Deake and Niles told me there was (likely,) Scarce An Indian to be found at home; As the Busy Season calld them Abroad. So thought it pity to Spend my time, in Visiting Empty Houses. Concluded to deferr my intended Visits to the Next Journey. . . .

2. Samson Occom (Mohegan) Gives a Short Narrative of His Life, 1768

From my Birth till I received the Christian Religion

I was Born a Heathen and Brought up In Heathenism, till I was between 16 & 17 years of age, at a Place Calld Mohegan, in New London, Connecticut, in New England. My Parents Livd a wandering life, for did all the Indians at Mohegan, they Chiefly Depended upon Hunting, Fishing, & Fowling for their Living and had no Connection with the English, excepting to Traffic with them in their small Trifles; and they Strictly maintained and followed their Heathenish Ways, Customs & Religion, though there was Some Preaching among them. Once a Fortnight, in ye Summer Season, a Minister from New London used to come up, and the Indians to attend; not that they regarded the Christian Religion, but they had Blankets given to them every Fall of the Year and for these things they would attend and there was a Sort of School kept, when I was quite young, but I believe there never was one that ever Learnt to read any thing,—and when I was about 10 Years of age there was a man who went about among the Indian Wigwams, and wherever he Could find the Indian Children, would make them read; but the Children Used to take Care to keep out of his way;—and he used to Catch me Some times and make me Say over my Letters; and I believe I learnt Some of them. But this was Soon over too; and all this Time there was not one amongst us, that made a Profession of Christianity— — Neither did we Cultivate our Land, nor kept any Sort of Creatures except Dogs, which we used in Hunting; and we Dwelt in Wigwams. These are a Sort of Tents, Covered with Matts, made of Flags. And to this Time we were unaquainted with the English Tongue in general though there were a few, who understood a little of it.

From the Time of our Reformation till I left Mr. Wheelocks

When I was 16 years of age, we heard a Strange Rumor among the English, that there were Extraordinary Ministers Preaching from Place to Place and a Strange Concern among the White People. This was in the Spring of the Year. But we Saw nothing of these things, till Some Time in the Summer, when Some Ministers began to visit us and Preach the Word of God; and the Common People all Came frequently and ex-horted us to the things of God, which it pleased the Lord, as I humbly hope, to Bless and accompany with Divine Influence to the Conviction and Saving Conversion of a Number of us; amongst whom I was one that was Imprest with the things we had

---

Samson Occom (Mohegan) Gives a Short Narrative of His Life, 1768. This document can be found type-script in Baker Library Special Collections, Dartmouth College, Hanover, N.H. It can also be found in Colin Calloway, ed., *The World Turned Upside Down: Indian Voices from Early America* (Boston: Bedford Books, 1994), 55–61.

heard. These Preachers did not only come to us, but we frequently went to their meetings and Churches. After I was awakened & converted, I went to all the meetings, I could come at; & Continued under Trouble of Mind about 6 months; at which time I began to Learn the English Letters; got me a Primer, and used to go to my English Neighbours frequently for Assistance in Reading, but went to no School. And when I was 17 years of age, I had, as I trust, a Discovery of the way of Salvation through Jesus Christ, and was enabl'd to put my trust in him alone for Life & Salvation. From this Time the Distress and Burden of my mind was removed, and I found Serenity and Pleasure of Soul, in Serving God. By this time I just began to Read in the New Testament without Spelling,—and I had a Stronger Desire Still to Learn to read the Word of God, and at the Same Time had an uncommon Pity and Compassion to my Poor Brethren According to the Flesh. I used to wish I was capable of Instructing my poor Kindred. I used to think, if I Could once Learn to Read I would Instruct the poor Children in Reading,—and used frequently to talk with our Indians Concerning Religion. This continued till I was in my 19th year: by this Time I Could Read a little in the Bible. At this Time my Poor Mother was going to Lebanon, and having had Some Knowledge of Mr. Wheelock and hearing he had a Number of English youth under his Tuition, I had a great Inclination to go to him and be with him a week or a Fortnight, and Desired my Mother to Ask Mr. Wheelock whether he would take me a little while to Instruct me in Reading. Mother did so; and when She Came Back, She Said Mr. Wheelock wanted to See me as Soon as possible. So I went up, thinking I Should be back again in a Few Days; when I got up there, he received me With kindness and Compassion and in Stead of Staying a Fortnight or 3 Weeks, I Spent 4 Years with him.—After I had been with him Some Time, he began to acquaint his Friends of my being with him, and of his Intentions of Educating me, and my Circumstances. And the good People began to give Some Assistance to Mr. Wheelock, and gave me Some old and Some New Clothes. Then he represented the Case to the Honorable Commissioners at Boston, who were Commission'd by the Honorable Society in London for Propagating the gospel among the Indians in New England and parts adjacent, and they allowed him 60 £ in old Tender, which was about 6 £ Sterling, and they Continu'd it 2 or 3 years, I can't tell exactly.—While I was at Mr. Wheelock's, I was very weakly and my Health much impaired, and at the End of 4 Years, I over Strained my Eyes to such a Degree, I Could not peruse my Studies any Longer; and out of these 4 years I Lost Just about one year;—And was obliged to quit my Studies.

3. Christien LeClerq (Micmac) Responds to the French, 1677

I am greatly astonished that the French have so little cleverness, as they seem to exhibit in the matter of which thou hast just told me on their behalf, in the effort to persuade us to convert our poles, our barks, and our wigwams into those houses of stone and of wood which are tall and lofty, according to their account, as these trees.

Christien LeClerq (Micmac) Responds to the French, 1677. This document can be found in William F. Ganong, trans. and ed., *New Relation of Gaspesia, with the Customs and Religion of the Gaspesian Indians,* by Christien LeClerq (Toronto: Chaplain Society, 1910), 104–106. It can also be found in Colin Calloway, ed., *The World Turned Upside Down: Indian Voices from Early America* (Boston: Bedford Books, 1994), 50–52.

Very well! But why now, . . . do men of five to six feet in height need houses which are sixty to eighty? For, in fact, as thou knowest very well thyself, Patriarch—do we not find in our own all the conveniences and the advantages that you have with yours, such as reposing, drinking, sleeping, eating, and amusing ourselves with our friends when we wish? This is not all, . . . my brother, hast thou as much ingenuity and cleverness as the Indians, who carry their houses and their wigwams with them so that they may lodge wheresoever they please, independently of any seignior whatsoever? Thou art not as bold nor as stout as we, because when thou goest on a voyage thou canst not carry upon thy shoulders thy buildings and thy edifices. Therefore it is necessary that thou preparest as many lodgings as thou makest changes of residence, or else thou lodgest in a hired house which does not belong to thee. As for us, we find ourselves secure from all these inconveniences, and we can always say, more truly than thou, that we are at home everywhere, because we set up our wigwams with ease wheresoever we go, and without asking permission of anybody. Thou reproachest us, very inappropriately, that our country is a little hell in contrast with France, which thou comparest to a terrestrial paradise, inasmuch as it yields thee, so thou sayest, every kind of provision in abundance. Thou sayest of us also that we are the most miserable and most unhappy of all men, living without religion, without manners, without honour, without social order, and, in a word, without any rules, like the beasts in our woods and our forests, lacking bread, wine, and a thousand other comforts which thou hast in superfluity in Europe. Well, my brother, if thou dost not yet know the real feelings which our Indians have towards thy country and towards all thy nation, it is proper that I inform thee at once. I beg thee now to believe that, all miserable as we seem in thine eyes, we consider ourselves nevertheless much happier than thou in this, that we are very content with the little that we have; and believe also once for all, I pray, that thou deceivest thyself greatly if thou thinkest to persuade us that thy country is better than ours. For if France, as thou sayest, is a little terrestrial paradise, art thou sensible to leave it? And why abandon wives, children, relatives, and friends? Why risk thy life and thy property every year, and why venture thyself with such risk, in any season whatsoever, to the storms and tempests of the sea in order to come to a strange and barbarous country which thou considerest the poorest and least fortunate of the world? Besides, since we are wholly convinced of the contrary, we scarcely take the trouble to go to France, because we fear, with good reason, lest we find little satisfaction there, seeing, in our own experience, that those who are natives thereof leave it every year in order to enrich themselves on our shores. We believe, further, that you are also incomparably poorer than we, and that you are only simple journeymen, valets, servants, and slaves, all masters and grand captains though you may appear, seeing that you glory in our old rags and in our miserable suits of beaver which can no longer be of use to us, and that you find among us, in the fishery for cod which you make in these parts, the wherewithal to comfort your misery and the poverty which oppresses you. As to us, we find all our riches and all our conveniences among ourselves, without trouble and without exposing our lives to the dangers in which you find yourselves constantly through your long voyages. And, whilst feeling compassion for you in the sweetness of our repose, we wonder at the anxieties and cares which you give yourselves night and day in order to load your ship. We see also that all your people live, as a rule, only upon cod which you catch among us. It is everlastingly nothing but cod—cod in the morning, cod at midday, cod at evening, and always cod, until things come to such a pass that if you wish some good morsels, it is at our expense; and you are obliged to have recourse to the Indians, whom you despise so much, and to beg them to go a-hunting that you may be regaled. Now tell me this one little thing, if thou hast any sense: Which of these two is the wisest and happiest—he who labours without ceasing and only obtains, and that with great trouble, enough to live on, or he who rests in comfort and finds all that he needs in the pleasure of hunting and fishing? It is true, . . . that we have not always had the use of bread and of wine which your France produces; but, in fact, before the arrival of the French in these parts, did not the Gaspesians live much longer than now? And if we have not any longer among us any of those old men of a hundred and thirty to forty years, it is only because we are gradually adopting your manner of living, for experience is making it very plain than those of us live longest who, despising your bread, your wine, and your brandy, are content with their natural food of beaver, of moose, of waterfowl, and fish, in accord with the custom of our ancestors and of all the Gaspesian nation. Learn now, my brother, once for all, because I must open to thee my heart: there is no Indian who does not consider himself infinitely more happy and more powerful than the French.

4. J. B. Truteau's Description of Indian Women on the Upper Missouri, 1794

. . . They have a singular kind of polygamy among them. If a man take a woman to wife who has several younger sisters, it is common for him to marry them all in succession, as fast as they become old enough. I have seen several who had as many as six wives, and all these sisters.

A young Indian seldom however lives long with his first wife. This is so much the case, that by the time he is thirty years old, he has perhaps cohabited with ten different women, and abandoned them. After that age, they usually grow more permanent in their attachments. The men generally are allowed the liberty of divorcing their wives when they please, and of marrying again. The women have not the freedom of doing this until after they have been deserted by their first husband. Then they have full range and power to act as they please. Accordingly these woman take new husbands as often as their curiosity or convenience prompt them. After a woman becomes more advanced in life, she attaches herself to some one man and he is commonly that one by whom she has had the greatest number of children. If a man quits a woman by whom he has had a number of children, he only takes away his arms with him; but the horses and other things remain with the wife.

When a young woman has lost her husband by wars or otherwise, and there are surviving brothers of the husband, one of them marries the widow, or rather has the right to do so. It must be observed, however, that this takes place only among the savages who value themselves most highly in keeping up an observance of their ancient customs. The Indians to whom we relate the circumstances of our marriages,

J. B. Truteau's Description of Indian Women on the Upper Missouri, 1794. This document can be found in A. P. Nasatir, ed., *Before Lewis and Clark: Documents Illustrating the History of the Missouri, 1785–1804,* 2 vols. (Lincoln, Nebr.: University of Nebraska Press, 1990), I:257–259.

are wholly at a loss to comprehend how white men, possessing so much under-standing and knowledge, should be so blind as not to see that marriage is a source of pain and torment to them; they look upon it as a monstrous thing for a man and woman to be so indissolubly bound together as never to get loose. In short, talk to them as we please, they remain unalterably persuaded that white men are the slaves of women. There are few Indian females who are constant and faithful to their hus-bands, but are much given to intrigue and incontinence. This is however not equally the case with all the nations; for among some of them, the women are more reserved and chaste.

The Panis, Mandanes, Ricaras and Bigbellies, are somewhat more than ordinar-ily indifferent as to their women.—No such sentiment as jealousy ever enters their breasts. They give this reason for it, that when a man dies he cannot carry women with him to the regions of the dead; and that they who quarrel, fight, and kill each other about the possession of a woman, are fools or mad-men. They are so firmly convinced of this, that many of them take a pride in treating some of the consider-able men among them with their youngest and handsomest women. So true is this, that husbands, fathers and brothers, are importunate with the white men who visit them, to make free with their wives, daughters and sisters, particularly those who are most youthful and pretty; and in consideration thereof accept a few baubles or toys. Indeed both the girls and married women are so loose in their conduct, that they seem to be a sort of common stock; and are so easy and accessible that there are few among them whose favours cannot be bought with a little vermillion or blue rib-bon. This kind of commerce is carried on to a great length by our young Canadian traders. The consequence of these libertine manners is the venereal disease. This is very frequent among them; but the Indians cure it by decoction [concoction] of cer-tain roots. I have seen some that were rotten with it, cured in six months.

When menstruation happens, the woman goes out of the hut, makes a fire by herself, and cooks her food alone. No person takes any of her fire on any account, not even to light a pipe with, for fear of bringing some misfortune upon himself. Their war-mats and Physic-bags are at these times carried out of the house, and suspended from the end of a pole in the open air, until the operation is over. While the women are in this situation they are very careful not to enter any cabin where there is a sick or wounded person; lest the patient's recovery should be retarded. When a woman finds herself with child, she receives the embraces of her husband no longer, but abstains from them entirely until thirty days after her delivery. There are, as may be supposed, exceptions to this: but such women are considered as behaving foolishly, and endangering both the lives of mother and child. When a pregnant woman finds her labour approaching, she withdraws to the hut built for the lying-in business, at all places where they have a stationary settlement: some old women follow her and give her all the help they can. But parturition is effected without the aid of a midwife; for they bring forth their young ones with a facility of which our civilized ladies have little idea. The term of their confinement seldom lasts more than two days. And if the party should find it necessary to march, the woman's lying-in never detains them half a day. For the mother, as soon as the child is born and swaddled, travels with the assistance of some of her friends, the whole day's journey to the place of encampment. And the next day after the infant is brought into the world, she plunges and washes it in water, both winter and summer. Then she wraps it in a piece of Bison-skin and ties its back to a plank about three feet long. The women nurse their children themselves, and as they never wean them, they suck as long as they please.

5. James Sutherland Notes Canadian Traders Who Wish to Buy an Indian Slave, 1797

Dear Sir

By the arrival of M^r De Murier and men the 16th Ins^t from your place, I was favoured with yours of the 20th of Dec. ^{br} last, and although personally unknown to me, as a Country man I was pleased to hear of your wellfare.

It is not my business to enquire into the causes of your exposing yourself to such dangers and difficulties which from hearsay attends your situateion [?], it is sufficient for me to suppose that your future views doubtless are adequate to your present hardships.

The Canadians, having lost their Horses the first or 2d night from the Missourie obliged them to leave their property behind, which they now return for, two of my men out of curiosity accompanys them to see the Mandan Villages and to try if they can purchase a Slave girl, they bring with them no goods of any consequence—I send by them 6 lbs. of Flour, two cakes of chocolate, and a little sugar as a small present, supposing you to be none [run?] out of such articles I am only sorry I have not any thing more worthy of your acceptance as my stock is near out, but hope you will take the will for the deed—all the news from this quarter you can hear from our men, a little from you would be very acceptable such as when you expect the gentlemen from below to your post, what your future Intentions are with regards to exploring further up the River &, if your agent general be the same Mr James Makay who was formerly a trader here in Red River. These perhaps you will say are tedious enquiries, but I suppose a gentleman of your abilitys can have no objection to any communication which does not immediately concern the Companys affairs in so remote a country I remain with Respect

Dear Sir
Your Obedient H^{ble} Servant
James Sutherland [rubric]

◈ *E S S A Y S*

The fur trade persisted in North America for centuries. It was the object of European colonial and American national policies as well as private business ventures. For many tribes the trade became a crucial part of their economy and culture. Once they were reliant on trade goods Indians had little choice but to continue down the commercial road to dependence. Professor Sylvia Van Kirk of the University of Toronto suggests

---

James Sutherland Notes Canadian Traders Who Wish to Buy an Indian Slave, 1797. This document can be found in A. P. Nasatir, ed., *Before Lewis and Clark: Documents Illustrating the History of the Missouri, 1785–1804*, 2 vols. (Lincoln, Nebr.: University of Nebraska Press, 1990), II:501.

that too little attention has been given to the role of Indian women in fur trade society. She examines the importance of interracial marriage *a la fa du pays,* after the custom of the country. Professor Jean M. O'Brien of the University of Minnesota examines the changing conditions of life for Indian women in colonial New England. English law, religion, and social customs dispossessed native people, made them economically marginal, and reordered Indian gender roles. These changes weakened Indian families and in some cases set homeless women completely adrift in New England. How does the use of gender as a category of analysis change our understanding of Indian history? What does this new perspective on Indian women say about Indian men?

The Role of Native American Women in the Fur Trade Society of Western Canada, 1670–1830

SYLVIA VAN KIRK

In essence the history of the early Canadian West is the history of the fur trade. For nearly 200 years, from the founding of the Hudson's Bay Company in 1670 until the transfer of Rupert's Land to the newly created dominion of Canada in 1870, the fur trade was the dominant force in shaping the history of what are today Canada's four western provinces.

This long and unified experience gave rise in western Canada to a frontier society that seems to me to be unique in the realm of interracial contact. Canada's western history has been characterized by relatively little violent conflict between Indian and white. I would like to suggest that there were two major reasons why this was so. First, by its very nature the Canadian fur trade was predicated on a mutual exchange and dependency between Indian and white. "The only good Indian" was certainly not "a dead Indian," for it was the Indian who provided both the fur pelts and the market for European goods. New research has revealed that not just Indian men but also Indian women played an active role in promoting the fur trade. Although the men were the hunters of beaver and large game animals, the women were responsible for trapping smaller fur-bearing animals, especially the marten whose pelt was highly prized. The notable cases of Indian women emerging as diplomats and peacemakers also indicate that they were anxious to maintain the flow of European goods, such as kettles, cloth, knives, needles and axes, that helped to alleviate their onerous work role.

The second factor in promoting harmonious relations was the remarkably wide extent of intermarriage between incoming traders and Indian women, especially among the Cree, the Ojibwa, and the Chipewyan. Indian wives proved indispensable helpmates to the officers and men of both the British-based Hudson's Bay Company and its Canadian rival, the North West Company. Such interracial unions were, in fact, the basis for a fur trade society and were sanctioned by an indigenous rite known as marriage *à la façon du pays.*

The development of marriage *à la façon du pays* underscores the complex and changing interaction between the traders and the host Indian societies. In the

Sylvia Van Kirk, "The Role of Native American Women in the Fur Trade Society of Western Canada, 1670–1830," *Frontiers* 7, no. 3 (1984), 9–13. Reprinted with permission.

initial phase of contact, many Indian bands actively encouraged the formation of marital alliances between their women and the traders. The Indians viewed marriage in an integrated social and economic context: marital alliances created reciprocal social ties that served to consolidate their economic relationships with the incoming strangers. Thus, through marriage, many a trader was drawn into the Indian kinship circle. In return for giving the traders sexual and domestic rights to their women, the Indians expected reciprocal privileges such as free access to the posts and provisions.

The Indian attitude soon impressed upon the traders that marriage alliances were an important means of ensuring good will and cementing trade relations with new bands or tribes. The North West Company, a conglomerate of partnerships that began extensive trading into the West in the 1770s, had learned from its French predecessors of the benefits to be gained from intermarriage, and it officially sanctioned such unions for all ranks, from *bourgeois* (officer) down to *engagé* (laborer). The Hudson's Bay Company, on the other hand, was much slower to appreciate the realities of life in Rupert's Land (the name given to the chartered territory of the Hudson's Bay Company encompassing the vast drainage basin of Hudson Bay). Official policy formulated in faraway London forbade any intimacy with the Indians, but officers in the field early began to break the rules. They took the lead in forming unions with women related to prominent Indian leaders, although there was great variation in the extent to which their servants were allowed to form connections with native women.

Apart from the public social benefits, the traders' desire to form unions with Indian women was increased by the absence of white women. Although they did not come as settlers, many of the fur traders spent the better part of their lives in Rupert's Land, and it is a singular fact in the social development of the Canadian West that for well over a century there were no white women. The stability of many of the interracial unions formed in the Indian Country stemmed partly from the fact that an Indian woman provided the only opportunity for a trader to replicate a domestic life with wife and children. Furthermore, although Indian mores differed from those of whites, the traders learned that they trifled with Indian women at their peril. As one old *voyageur* (canoeman) explained, a man could not just dally with any native woman who struck his fancy. There was a great danger of getting his head broken if he attempted to take an Indian girl without her parents' consent.

It is significant that, just as in the trade ceremony, the rituals of marriage *à la façon du pays* conformed more to Indian custom than to European. There were two basic aspects to forming such a union. The first step was to secure the consent of the woman's relations; it also appears that the wishes of the woman herself were respected, for there is ample evidence that Indian women actively sought fur trade husbands. Once consent was secured, a bride price had then to be decided; though it varied considerably among the tribes, it could amount to several hundred dollars' worth of trade goods. After these transactions, the couple were usually ceremoniously conducted to the fort where they were duly recognized as man and wife. In the Canadian West marriage *à la façon du pays* became the norm for Indian-white unions, which were reinforced by mutual interest, tradition, and peer group pressure. Although ultimately "the custom of the country" was to be strongly denounced by the missionaries, it is significant that in 1867, when the legitimacy of the union between Chief Factor William Connolly and his Cree wife was tried before a Canadian court, the judge declared the marriage valid because the wife had been married according to the customs and usages of her own people and because the consent of both parties, the essential element of civilized marriage, had been proved by twenty-eight years of repute, public acknowledgment, and cohabitation as man and wife.

If intermarriage brought the trader commercial and personal benefit, it also provided him with a remarkable economic partner. The Indian wife was possessed of a range of skills and wilderness know-how that would have been quite foreign to a white wife. Although the burdensome work role of the nomadic Indian woman was somewhat alleviated by the move to the fur trade post, the extent to which the traders relied upon native technology kept the women busy.

Perhaps the most important domestic task performed by the women at the fur trade posts was to provide the men with a steady supply of "Indian shoes" or moccasins. The men of both companies generally did not dress in Indian style (the buckskinned mountain man was not part of the Canadian scene), but they universally adopted the moccasin as the most practical footwear for the wilderness. One wonders, for example, how the famed 1789 expedition of Alexander Mackenzie would have fared without the work of the wives of his two French-Canadian *voyageurs*. The women scarcely ever left the canoes, being "continually employ'd making shoes of moose skin as a pair does not last us above one Day." Closely related to her manufacture of moccasins was the Indian woman's role in making snowshoes, without which winter travel was impossible. Although the men usually made the frames, the women prepared the sinews and netted the intricate webbing that provided support.

Indian women also made a vital contribution in the preservation of food, especially in the manufacture of the all-important pemmican, the nutritious staple of the North West Company's canoe brigades. At the posts on the plains, buffalo hunting and pemmican making were an essential part of the yearly routine, each post being required to furnish an annual quota. In accordance with Indian custom, once the hunt was over the women's work began. The women skinned the animals and cut the meat up into thin strips to be dried in the sun or over a slow fire. When the meat was dry, the women pounded it into a thick flaky mass, which was then mixed with melted buffalo fat. This pemmican would keep very well when packed into ninety-pound buffalo-hide sacks, which had been made by the women during the winter. But pemmican was too precious a commodity to form the basic food at the posts themselves. At the more northerly posts the people subsisted mainly on fish, vast quantities of which were split and dried by the women to provide food for the winter. Maintaining adequate food supplies for a post for the winter was a precarious business, and numerous instances can be cited of Indian wives keeping the fur traders alive by their ability to snare small game such as rabbits and partridges. In 1815, for example, the young Nor'Wester George Nelson would probably have starved to death when provisions ran out at his small outpost north of Lake Superior had it not been for the resourcefulness of his Ojibwa wife who during the month of February brought in fifty-eight rabbits and thirty-four partridges. Indian women also added to the diets by collecting berries and wild rice and making maple sugar. The spring trip to the sugar bush provided a welcome release from the monotony of the winter routine, and the men with their families and Indian relatives all enjoyed this annual event.

As in other preindustrial societies, the Indian women's role also extended well beyond domestic maintenance as they assisted in specific fur trade operations. With the adoption of the birchbark canoe, especially by the North West Company, Indian women continued in their traditional role of helping in its manufacturer. It was the women's job to collect annual quotas of spruce roots, which were split fine to sew the seams of the canoes, and also to collect the spruce gum that was used for caulking the seams. The inexperienced and understaffed Hudson's Bay Company also found itself calling upon the labor power of Indian women, who were adept at paddling and steering canoes. Indeed, although the inland explorations of various Hudson's Bay Company men such as Anthony Henday and Samuel Hearne have been glorified as individual exploits, they were, in fact, entirely dependent upon the Indians with whom they traveled, being especially aided by Indian women. "Women," marveled one inlander, "were as useful as men upon Journeys." Henday's journey to the plains in 1754, for example, owed much of its success to his Cree female companion, who not only provided him with a warm winter suit of furs, but also with much timely advice about the plans of the Indians. The Hudson's Bay Company men emphasized to their London superiors that the Indian women's skill at working with fur pelts was also very valuable. In short, they argued that Indian women performed such important economic services at the fur trade posts that they should be considered as "Your Honours Servants." Indian women were indeed an integral part of the fur trade labor force, although, like most women, because their labor was largely unpaid, their contribution has been ignored.

The reliance on native women's skills remained an important aspect of fur trade life, even though by the early nineteenth century there was a notable shift in the social dynamic of fur trade society. By this time, partly because of the destructive competition between rival companies that had flooded the Indian country with alcohol, relations between many Indian bands and the traders deteriorated. In some well-established areas, traders sometimes resorted to coercive measures, and there were cases where their abuse of Indian women became a source of conflict. In this context, except in new areas such as the Pacific Slope, marriage alliances ceased to play the important function they had once had. The decline of Indian-white marriages was also hastened by the fact that fur trade society itself was producing a new pool of marriageable young women—the mixed-blood "daughters of the country." With her dual heritage, the mixed-blood woman possessed the ideal qualifications for a fur trader's wife: acclimatized to life in the West and familiar with Indian ways, she could also make a successful adaptation to white culture.

From their Indian mothers, mixed-blood girls learned the native skills so necessary to the functioning of the trade. As Governor Simpson of the Hudson's Bay Company emphasized in the 1820s, "It is the duty of the Women at the different Posts to do all that is necessary in regard to Needle Work," and the mixed-blood women's beautiful bead work was highly prized. In addition to performing traditional Indian tasks, the women's range of domestic work increased in more European ways. They were responsible for the fort's washing and cleaning; "the Dames" at York Factory, for example, were kept "in Suds, Scrubbing and Scouring," according to one account. As subsistence agriculture was developed around many of the posts, the native women took an active role in planting and harvesting. Chief Factor John Rowand of Fort Edmonton succinctly summarized the economic role of native women in the fur trade when he wrote in the mid-nineteenth century, "The women here work very hard, if it was not so, I do not know how we would get on with the Company work." With her ties to the Indians and familiarity with native customs and language, the mixed-blood wife was also in a position to take over the role of intermediary or liaison previously played by the Indian wife. The daughters of the French-Canadian *voyageurs* were often excellent interpreters; some could speak several Indian languages. The timely intervention of more than one mixed-blood wife was known to have saved the life of a husband who had aroused Indian hostility. Indeed, in his account of fur trade life during the Hudson's Bay Company's monopoly after 1821, Isaac Cowie declared that many of the company's officers owed much of their success in overcoming difficulties and maintaining the Company's influence over the natives to "the wisdom and good counsel of their wives."

In spite of the importance of native connections, many fur trade fathers were most concerned to introduce their mixed-blood daughters to the rudiments of European culture. Since the place of work and home coincided, especially in the long winter months, the traders were able to take an active role in their children's upbringing, and they were encouraged to do so. When the beginnings of formal schooling were introduced at the posts on the Bay in the early 1800s, it was partly because it was felt to be essential that girls, who were very seldom sent overseas, should be given a basic education that would inculcate Christian virtue in them. Increasingly fathers also began to play an instrumental role in promoting the marriage of their daughters to incoming traders as the means to securing their place in fur trade society. In a significant change of policy in 1806, the North West Company acknowledged some responsibility for the fate of its "daughters" when it sanctioned marriage *à la façon du pays* with daughters of white men, but now prohibited it with full-blooded Indian women.

As mixed-blood wives became "the vogue" (to quote a contemporary), it is notable that "the custom of the country" began to evolve more toward European concepts of marriage. Most importantly, such unions were definitely coming to be regarded as unions for life. When Hudson's Bay Company officer J. E. Harriott espoused Elizabeth Pruden, for example, he promised her father, a senior officer, that he would "live with her and treat her as my wife as long as we both lived." It became customary for a couple to exchange brief vows before the officer in charge of the post, and the match was further celebrated by a dram to all hands and a wedding dance. The bride price was replaced by the opposite payment of a dowry, and many fur trade officers were able to dower their daughters quite handsomely. Marriage *à la façon du pays* was further regulated by the Hudson's Bay Company after 1821 with the introduction of marriage contracts, which emphasized the husband's financial obligations and the status of the woman as a legitimate wife.

The social role of the mixed-blood wife, unlike that of the Indian wife, served to cement ties within fur trade society itself. Significantly, in the North West Company there were many marriages that cut across class lines as numerous Scottish *bourgeois* chose their wives from the daughters of the French-Canadian *engagés* who had married extensively among the native people. Among the Hudson's Bay

Company men, it was appreciated that a useful way to enhance one's career was to marry the daughter of a senior officer. Whatever a man's initial motivation, the substantial private fur trade correspondence that has survived from the nineteenth century reveals that many fur traders became devoted family men. Family could be a particular source of interest and consolation in a life that was often hard and monotonous. As Chief Factor James Douglas pointedly summed it up, "There is indeed no living with comfort in this country until a person has forgot the great world and has his tastes and character formed on the current standard of the stage . . . habit makes it familiar to us, softened as it is by the many tender ties which find a way to the heart."

However, the founding of the Selkirk Colony in 1811, the first agrarian settlement in western Canada, was to introduce new elements of white civilization that hastened the decline of an indigenous fur trade society. The chief agents of these changes were the missionaries and the white women. The missionaries, especially the Anglicans who arrived under the auspices of the Hudson's Bay Company in 1820, roundly denounced marriage *à la façon du pays* as immoral and debased. But while they exerted considerable pressure on long cohabiting couples to accept a church marriage, they were not in any way champions of miscegenation. In fact, this attack upon fur trade custom had a detrimental effect upon the position of native women. Incoming traders, now feeling free to ignore the marital obligations implicit in "the custom of the country," increasingly looked upon native women as objects for temporary sexual gratification. The women, on the other hand, found themselves being judged according to strict British standards of female propriety. It was they, not the white men, who were to be held responsible for the perpetuation of immorality because of their supposedly promiscuous Indian heritage. The double standard tinged with racism had arrived with a vengeance.

Both racial prejudice and class distinctions were augmented by the arrival of British women in Rupert's Land. The old fabric of fur trade society was severely rent in 1830 when Governor Simpson and another prominent Hudson's Bay Company officer returned from furlough, having wed genteel British ladies. The appearance of such "flowers of civilization" provoked unflattering comparisons with native women; as one officer observed, "This influx of white faces has cast a still deeper shade over the faces of our Brunettes in the eyes of many." In Red River especially, a white wife became a status symbol; witness the speed with which several retired Hudson's Bay Company factors married English schoolmistresses after the demise of their native wives. To their credit, many Company officers remained loyal to their native families, but they became painfully anxious to turn their daughters into young Victorian ladies, hoping that with accomplishments and connections the stigma of their mixed blood would not prevent them from remaining among the social elite. Thus, in the 1830s a boarding school was established in Red River for the children of Company officers; the girls' education was supervised by the missionary's wife, and more than one graduate was praised for being "quite English in her Manner." In numerous cases, these highly acculturated young women were able to secure advantageous matches with incoming white men, but to some extent only because white ladies did not in fact adapt successfully to fur trade life. It had been predicted that "the lovely, tender exotics" (as they were dubbed) would languish in the harsh fur trade environment, and indeed they did, partly because they had no useful social or economic role to play. As a result, mixed marriages continued to be a feature of western Canadian society until well into the mid-nineteenth century, but it was not an enduring legacy. Indian and mixed-blood women, like their male counterparts, were quickly shunted aside with the development of the agrarian frontier after 1870. The vital role native women had played in the opening of the Canadian West was either demeaned or forgotten.

Changing Conditions of Life for Indian Women in Eighteenth-Century New England

JEAN M. O'BRIEN (Ojibwe)

In 1624, Edward Winslow, Governor of Plymouth colony, observed about Native Americans that "[t]he women live a most slavish life; they carry all their burdens, set and dress their corn, gather it in, and seek out for much of their food, beat and make ready the corn to eat and have all household care lying upon them." Winslow's use of the term "slavish" in this passage is instructive. The portrayal of the Native American woman as "squaw drudge" who toiled endlessly for her "lazie husband" was both a common English analysis of Native American division of labor in the northeastern woodlands and a commentary upon English expectations about gender roles. Observers viewed Indian women as "slaves" because, unlike English women, they performed virtually all of the agricultural labor in their societies. In fact, most labor the English would have regarded as male work was performed by Indian women.

The "squaw drudge" permeated early observations of Native Americans in the northeast. Two centuries later, different kinds of images of Indian women could be found in local accounts. Consider the following: "The last Indian here was 'Hannah Shiner,' a full-blood who lived with 'Old Toney,' a noble-souled mulatto man . . . Hannah was kind-hearted, a faithful friend, a sharp enemy, a judge of herbs, a weaver of baskets, and a lover of rum." This description, taken from a nineteenth-century history of Medford, Massachusetts, reflects not just the passage of time but also the extent to which relations, roles, and expectations had changed on both sides of a sustained cultural encounter.

The juxtaposition of these two fundamentally different portrayals reveals crucial changes in the circumstances of Indian women in New England. Four key structural changes differentiate the historical eras from which the images come. First, Indian societies that were "tribal" and politically independent prior to intensive colonization became effectively "detribalized" and politically encompassed by the late seventeenth century. By this time, most Indian individuals and families were incorporated into English communities, mostly in small clusters that rendered Indians virtually invisible within the context of the now-dominant New English society. Second, the prosperity of Indian societies, based on diversified agricultural economies and intensive use of seasonally available plant and game resources, was undermined as the English gained possession of nearly all Indian land by the end of the seventeenth century. The central element of the Indian economy was thus eliminated, requiring fundamental changes that resulted in the recasting of Native gender roles. Third, Indian societies that stressed communal values, sharing, and reciprocity were thrust into a market economy with the advent of colonization. Immersion in the market left Indians at the mercy of English legal institutions and affected the shape of Native social welfare practices. And fourth, Indians were quickly rendered a minority population within their own homelands by the astounding success of the English demographic regime, which was coupled with Indian struggles caused by imported diseases and military encounters. These structural changes compelled Indians to see the landscape in a different way, requiring them to make massive adjustments, and eliciting myriad and contradictory responses.

As they successfully dispossessed and displaced Indians, the heirs of English colonialism seized the power to define the rules governing the social order, and they constructed surviving New England Indians as peculiar and marginal. Local historians underscored the "disappearance" of the Indian population by singling out individuals such as Hannah Shiner as representing the "last survivor" of their "tribe." Even so, historians used their representations of Indians as peculiar and marginal, as hopelessly "other," to continue to constitute and affirm an English identity. They presented Indians such as Hannah Shiner as the complement to "Englishness," thereby reminding themselves of the persistent difference between Indian survivors and themselves. But more than just reinforcing the difference between Indians and themselves, the ways in which they used this binary operated to emphasize English dominance.

The English colonial regime imposed a different landscape, one requiring Indians to transform their relationship to the land. Gender figured prominently in this transformation. The English aimed to "divorce" Indians from their possession of the land in order to establish themselves and English culture in their place. New England Indians' agricultural, hunting, fishing, and gathering economy was interpreted as wasteful, and the sedentary agriculture pursued by English men was seen as the only proper pursuit for Native men. Yet even as they pursued the larger project of English colonialism (replacing Indians and Indian ways of using the land with English people using the land in English ways), colonists also aimed to convert surviving Indians to English culture. As they separated Indians from possession of virtually all their land, colonists also sought to "divorce" Indian women from their role as agriculturalists, replacing them with male Indians working drastically reduced plots of land to the exclusion of hunting and other older economic pursuits. From the perspective of the English, "divorce" from the land would fulfill the biblical directive to "subdue the earth and multiply" by bringing land into agricultural production to sustain a growing English Christian population. And it would also place Indian women and men in a "proper" relationship to the land. In the most crucial sense, however, the English failed to "divorce" either Indian women or Indian men from the land. Although in narrow legal terms, the English succeeded in imposing their own rules for possessing the land, New England Indians did not monolithically embrace English gender ways. They remained crucially connected to the land that sustained their kinship and visiting networks and their own sense of proper place.

In addressing the transformations accompanying the cultural conflicts between Indians and English colonists, I will focus on the issue of "gendered division of labor" rather than on the important problem of lineality in the northeastern woodlands, which also involved different conceptions of how gender ought to operate. Use of the dichotomous construction of matrilineal/patrilineal obscures much diversity in the ordering of families, reckoning of descent, ordering of power relations, and much more. Because of the paucity of early sources that provide detailed information on social organization, combined with the early occurrence of devastating epidemics throughout the region, there is much we will never know about the "precontact" shape of social organization in the northeastern woodlands. Indian peoples in early New England were concerned overwhelmingly with resisting and surviving English incursions, and the disruptions of epidemics that accompanied early contact certainly must have obscured their previous shape at least to some extent. About all that is evident is that, by the eighteenth century, patrilineal naming practices predominated among Indians; whether this was the case because it had always been so, or because the English imposed these forms on Indians in bureaucratic transactions, is not so clear.

About a gendered division of labor, much more seems to be apparent. Most scholars agree that women performed most agricultural labor (except growing tobacco), built and transported bark or mat wigwams from place to place, manufactured baskets and pottery, gathered shellfish and wild foodstuff, processed hides, made clothing, and raised children. Men also made some household tools and were the principal woodworkers, making canoes and fortifications, for example.

By 1700, Native American groups in New England had a long history of encounters with Europeans. Indians reeled from the impact of imported epidemic diseases, with many groups suffering demographic declines on the order of 90 percent. Military conquest followed quickly on the heels of the epidemiological disasters. The last major war in southeastern New England ended in 1676, terminating the political independence of those Native groups who had hitherto avoided encompassment by the English. These events effectively ended the autonomy of Indian groups in that region and rendered many aspects of the aboriginal economy obsolete through massive displacement and dispossession. Under the cumulative impact of the colonial experience, a great many New England Indians found themselves landless, a diasporic population vulnerable to the institutions of English colonialism.

Missionary sponsorship had secured land bases for several Indian groups in the seventeenth century as part of English efforts to transform Indian cultures. Here, the English expected Indians to alter their gender roles in conformity with English cultural prerogatives. Indian groups were allowed to retain small plots of land provided they would express responsiveness to missionary messages about cultural change. The English expected Indians to erect compact, English-style towns in order to fix them in particular places, directed men to forego hunting in favor of agricultural duties, and trained women in "household skills," especially spinning and weaving. Indians were encouraged to adopt English work habits, individual ownership of land, English tastes in material culture, and values structured by a market economy. Some Indians experimented with cultural transformations along these lines, but success in the market economy did not follow so easily. Many Indians were landless at the beginning of the eighteenth century, and, as their land was transformed into a commodity, Indian landowners continued to lose land. Many were encompassed within the flourishing English settlements, finding niches in colonial economies, performing agricultural and nonagricultural labor.

Although some Indians steadfastly resisted English influences on their life-ways, and others struggled within the market economy, still others borrowed exten-sively from English culture as a means of accommodating to English colonialism. In some senses, Jacob and Leah Chalcom symbolized Indian transformation as conceptualized by the English. Chalcom purchased land, established an English-style farm, and built a frame house in Natick, Massachusetts, an important mission town established seventeen miles southwest of Boston. He was involved actively in the local land market, buying and selling small parcels from time to time as he strove to upgrade his farm. The cultural priorities of this family are visible in their childrearing practices. The Chalcom children were literate, and the daughters were given dowries upon their marriages to local Indian men. After his death, Chalcom's estate included a thirty-acre homelot and "Buildings thereon," plus other lands, an assortment of household goods and husbandry tools, a horse, a cow, and books. After debts against his estate were discharged, fifty-two acres of land remained to be divided among his heirs.

The women in Chalcom's family had made corresponding changes in their life-ways, including their separation from agricultural tasks. Leah Chalcom and her widowed daughters, Esther Sooduck and Hepzibeth Peegun, inherited land from their husband and father respectively. Finding themselves without husbands, they pondered what to do with their inheritance. In 1759 they petitioned the Massachu-setts General Court to sell their forty-six acres, arguing that "as your Petitioners [have been] brought up to Household business, [we are] incapable of improving said lands." They requested that their lands be sold and the money be put out to earn in-terest for their income and support, a strategy adopted by a number of women. The implication here is quite clear: These women were no longer farmers and were thus unable to "improve" the land except insofar as it represented a monetary resource. The mother and daughters recognized that English financial strategies could sustain them and prolong the nurturing functions of land from which they were effectively torn loose. Putting money "at interest" constituted one strategy for women who had maintained clear "legal" connections to the land. Their decision not to use the land for gardening, as English women often did, in part reflected their perception that if they chose to keep the land it would "speedily be exhausted by frequent Law-Suits."

The "Household business" to which Leah Chalcom and her daughters referred reflects the efforts of English missionaries to realign Native American gender roles. Biblical imperatives motivated missionaries who aimed to train Indian women in English skills for structuring a household, and to integrate Indian families into the market economy. In 1648, missionary John Eliot wrote that: "[t]he women are desirous to learn to spin, and I have procured Wheels for sundry of them, and they can spin pretty well. They begin to grow industrious, and find something to sell at Market all the yeer long[.] Some Indian women continued to pursue these tasks that missionaries had pushed so vigorously in the early years of intensive English-Indian contact. Fifteen percent of inventories of Indian estates from Natick filed between

1741 and 1763 listed spinning wheels. Ruth Thomas, who died in 1758, was described in her probate docket as a weaver; Esther Freeborn and Hannah Lawrence, sisters who both left wills, were described as spinsters.

Esther Sooduck, also a weaver, died in 1778. Her probate documents vividly evoke the kinds of changes Indian women confronted even though very few accumulated and held onto material goods as successfully as Esther had. Her house, described as "much out of repair," nonetheless contained an impressive array of furnishings and sat upon thirty acres of land. Included among her belongings were a bed and bedstead, a chest, a trunk, a rug, a table and two chairs, plus knives, forks, and pewter. She read her two old Bibles with "speticals." She owned two spinning wheels, as well as baskets and "Baskets Stuf." Apparently merged in her economic pursuits were English skills (spinning and weaving) and Native American artisanal production (basket-making).

Native American women displayed transformations in their work habits, material life, aesthetic emphases, and even their physical appearance. Hannah Lawrence owned several articles of clothing when she died in the 1770s, including several gowns and aprons (one of them linen) as well as quilted petticoats and a pair of shoes with buckles. Cloth replaced animal skins, petticoats and gowns were substituted for skirts and leggings. These accommodations were rooted in more than a century of profound cultural change. And in many ways, they represent an *up*rooting, a broken connection: English-style clothing signified the distance women had moved from their former way of life. Eighteenth-century economic adaptations no longer produced the materials for older ways of clothing production, and adopting English styles probably reflected not just this reality but also newer Indian tastes.

There were many ways in which Native American women in eighteenth-century New England *were* divorced from the land: the colonial experience reoriented their relationship to the land in tangible and not so tangible ways. English ideals for cultural change aimed to realign the Indians' gendered economy and make room for English people to subdue the land in English ways. For Indian women, this meant a stark separation: once the principal producers of the crucial agricultural element of subsistence economies, women were expected to sever the vital connection they had to the soil as its principal cultivators and nurturers. Though the English who wanted to accomplish these changes may not have noticed, their models for transformation went well beyond a simple shift in the gendered organization of labor. On the practical level, knowledge and skills were altered drastically, and the content of material life was dramatically recast. On the ideological level, less visible reverberations can only be imagined in individual and corporate identity, belief systems, and other deeply rooted cultural values. The tensions accompanying these transformations can be glimpsed in one possible explanation for the ultimate failure of Indian men as farmers in a market economy, which suggests that their reluctance to tend crops stemmed from their view that these "effeminate" pursuits properly remained women's work. In refusing English gender ideals, many Indian men resisted this foundational concept of English colonialism.

Leah Chalcom, Esther Sooduck, Hannah Lawrence—all of these women came from one kind of Indian community. They all lived in Indian-dominated towns, their land ownership sanctioned by the English, who conferred "possession" of these reduced plots of land according to English legal principals. At least in this nominal sense, they were beneficiaries of missionary endeavors. Although they were relatively successful in emulating English ways, as the eighteenth century unfolded, the slow but steady dispossession of Indian landowners allowed fewer Indians to replicate earlier successes. Other Indians were uprooted utterly almost from the beginning of their contact with the English. They adjusted to English invasion differently, mapping out alternative kinds of lifeways. After the 1660s, for example:

> The remnant of the Pocumtuck Confederacy, adopting in part the English costume, had gathered about the English in the valley towns . . . Here they lived a vagabond life, eking out, as they could, a miserable existence on the outskirts of civilization . . . So hampered, their stock of venison or beaver, with which to traffic for English comforts, was small, and the baskets and birch brooms made by the squaws ill supplied their place.

This is a stark outline of the principal difficulties Indians faced in making the transition to landlessness within a society emphasizing the market. With the possibilities for hunting gone, and no land—what remained? Production of Indian crafts constituted one possibility for women, who remained important in the economy and maintained this earlier economic role, which was possible even when landless. In their artisanal production, women continued to cultivate the specialized knowledge required to gather materials for fashioning baskets and other crafts. Their craftwork represented a revealing accommodation to dispossession: reaping basket stuff did not require "possession" of the land. At the same time, in marketing Indian goods, they earned an income and reinforced their "Indianness" in the popular perception.

Craft production by Indian women constituted one of the crucial threads that ran through the seventeenth, eighteenth, and nineteenth centuries in New England. Indian women in the eighteenth century were engaged especially in basket making as an economic activity, but other artisanal skills were added as well. In 1764, Abigail Moheag attested that she was "64 years of Age and . . . a widow [for] more than fifteen years and hath . . . by her Industry in the business of making Brooms Baskets and horse Collars; Supported her Self till about two years ago She was taken sick." The inventory from Hannah Speen's estate listed "baskets and barkes, brombs and brombsticks." Craftwork, including the production of "new" items like horse collars, moved from the periphery of women's economic activities to the center as Indian women became enmeshed in the market and were no longer engaged in farming. For some women, craft production was fundamentally redefined. No longer one activity in an integrated economy, performed seasonally and for purposes largely internal to the household, artisanal activities became specialized and divorced from seasonal rhythms, and a principal means to get a living.

Wage labor constituted another possibility for Indian women. It remains unclear just what kind of work Indian women were doing, or what it was they received in return. In 1755, the circumstances of some Indian women at Mattakeset were such that "at present they live among White People, and work with them for a living." The formula in these kinds of situations may have involved the contribution of unskilled and unspecialized labor, perhaps domestic work, in exchange for small wages or even some degree of basic sustenance. The existence of small clusters of Indians in virtually every Massachusetts town suggests that the lives of English colonists and Indians were intertwined in ways we are only beginning to understand.

Disruption of Native societies extended to every sphere, requiring their constant adjustment. Marginal individuals, that is, those with few relatives or friends, Indian or non-Indian, and little in the way of economic resources, suffered the most. Prior to Indian enmeshment in the market, caretaking and nursing constituted central kinship obligations. During the eighteenth century, as kinship networks thinned, families became fractured, and involvement in the market made prosperity precarious at best. Individuals could no longer count on thick networks of relatives to care for them when they were in need of shelter, sustenance, or support. Nursing and caretaking became commodified and unreliable. Even when an intact family was in place, taking on caretaking obligations in this changed context could spell the economic ruin of a precariously established family. These developments represented the cumulative effect of generations of demographic decline, military conquest, economic disruption, and cultural transformation. Abigail Speen reported to the General Court in 1747 that she had

> by Reason of her great age & infirmities . . . been long and still is Unable to do anything to Support herself, & so having cast herself on Mr. Joseph Graves of Sd Natick [an Englishman;] She has been kind entertained & Supported at his House now for near two years, & has nothing to recompense Sd Graves with nor to procure for her the Necessaries of Life for the time present & to come.

This woman had land, and she liquidated the remainder of her estate in order to pay Graves. No doubt he realized that his "investment" was secured by that plot of land she owned in Natick. This replacement of Indian kinship obligations with market-driven social welfare occurred throughout New England and accounted for much dispossession of Indian peoples who might otherwise face legal proceedings for debts they accumulated.

Just as Abigail Speen cast herself on Joseph Graves, Indian women cast themselves upon other Indian women, too. What differed in the eighteenth century was that these women were not necessarily relatives, and that nursing or caretaking was often given in exchange for monetary compensation. The administrators of the estate of Elizabeth Paugenit, for example, allowed nearly two pounds to Hannah Awassamug "for nursing." Sarah Wamsquan was cared for by Eunice Spywood, among others. Englishman John Jones petitioned the General Court in 1770, setting forth Sarah's dire circumstances and begging: "let something be done that Shall Speedily relieve the poor person that has her—or they will perish together." Town authorities did not always countenance such arrangements. In 1765, when "Sarah Short a molatto woman Last from Wrentham [was] Taken in by Esther Sodeck," Natick selectmen feared she would become a town charge and warned her that she should leave the town.

Banding together just to survive, these women struggled within a radically changing world. Often their situation was complicated by the dramatic transformations accompanying their dispossession, which stretched Indian communities thinly across the landscape to form a network of small clusters of families throughout southeastern New England. One response was to move constantly in search of a niche. As landlessness accelerated throughout the eighteenth century, a pattern of Indian vagrancy emerged: this pattern, accepted by the dominant society as natural, was also an accommodation strategy. Indian women, especially, were described as wandering from place to place, a characteristic that was associated in the pubic mind particularly with Indians. An Englishman of Dorchester petitioned the General Court in 1753 as follows:

> An Indian Woman called Mercy Amerquit, I think Born Somewhere about Cape-Cod, but had no settled Dwellingplace any where, . . . Strolled about from one Town & Place to another, & sometimes she wrought for persons that wanted her work[. She] came to my House . . . and desired liberty to tarry a little while, and your Petr condescended, expecting that she would go some other place in a little time (as their manner is) and what work she did for your Petr she was paid for as she earned it.

It is clear from this passage that English observers expected Indians to "wander." Their semisedentary lifeways had always been regarded most simplistically as nomadism. In the eighteenth century this translated into constant movement, "from one Town & Place to another . . . as their manner is." In this case, an arrangement seems to have been negotiated that involved Mercy Amerquit performing labor for wages as well as for her temporary residence with the narrator. He expected her to "go [to] some other place in a little time," and the arrangement was regarded as rather unexceptional. The only reason this relationship was documented at all was because Amerquit died while in the petitioner's residence and he sought to recover money he expended for her burial.

The story of Mercy Amerquit was by no means unique. An Englishman from Roxbury reported to the General Court about sixty-year-old Hannah Comsett, who became ill at his house: "She informs that her Mother was born at Barnstable, she at Scituate, and that for 30 years past she has been [strolling] about from Town to Town getting her living where she could but never lived During that time the space of one year at any Town at any time." Though Hannah Comsett's mobility seems rather astounding, there are so many similar stories available that it is certain it was not an aberration.

The mechanisms behind Indian vagrancy were complex. Prior to the arrival of the English, Indian societies in New England reaped abundance from economies that depended upon knowledge about and extensive use of resources and a semi-sedentary lifeway. Scheduled mobility lay at the center of this system. In the eighteenth century, Indian migrations may have been scheduled, but if so, they were motivated by very different priorities since they could no longer rely on movements governed by independently composed Indian communities to and from places that "belonged" to them in the strict legal sense. Probably kinship ties and some knowledge of labor markets entered into movements, but for women like Mercy and Hannah, there seemed to be nothing particularly patterned about their shifting about. Perhaps it was setting about to track the occasional charitable English colonist that spurred on the solitary and needy Indian women, from whom a different kind of resource might be procured. One important element that differentiated earlier migratory practices from new patterns was their largely individual nature; this new "vagrancy" drew upon older patterns and places, but was not necessarily kin-group sponsored movement with planned, deliberate ends in mind. At the heart of the problem lay landlessness, whether it had resulted from military conquest in the seventeenth century or from failure in the market economy in the eighteenth. "Divorced" from the land initially when their economic role was redefined along

English lines, a much more literal separation had been accomplished for most by the middle of the eighteenth century.

The situation of these women hints at two recurrent themes regarding Indian women in eighteenth-century New England. First, transiency is graphically described in a manner consistent with the emerging problem of landless poverty in New England more generally. The "wandering Indian" had much in common with the "strolling poor," although the fact that the English categorically distinguished between the two offers testimony for their separatist views about race. The problem of Indian women seems to have been compounded, however. The extent to which these are stories of women alone, or mostly alone, is the second theme and it is most striking.

Where were the men? The evidence suggests that, despite the missionary model of settled agriculture performed by men within nuclear families on family farms, transiency also remained characteristic even of landowning Indian men. Most Indian landowners lost what they had over time, and the tendency for Indian men to enter service in two areas (military service and the emerging whaling industry) contributed to a grossly distorted sort of transiency. As a result of their participation in these activities, Indian men were absent for extended periods of time, engaged in dangerous pursuits that seriously jeopardized their lives and well-being and compromised their ability to function effectively within the English-dominated society. Whaling, in fact, fostered the same sort of debt peonage that proved so devastating in fur trade relationships. These orientations contributed to uncertainty and instability for Indian families and also reduced the number of Indian men available as desirable spouses. Interpretations of the involvement of Indian men in the military and labor at sea have stressed the continuity in skills and culturally determined priorities they offered them. But some men also abandoned their families to escape their predicaments; evidence may be found in scattered narratives of Indian men "absconding" as difficult circumstances evolved into insurmountable economic and legal problems. Such was the case for Eunice Spywood's husband, who "Some Years Ago Absconded and left her in very distressing Circumstances, and he . . . never returned."

An important cumulative effect of English colonialism was to reconfigure the relationships among Indian mobility, a gendered division of labor, and household structures. The semisedentary Indian economy entailed a gendered mobility that assumed that women and men would be apart for periods of time: Men departed central villages for hunting and fishing, leaving women to tend crops and gather wild plant resources near their villages, for example. But these periods of separation were scheduled, part of the seasonal rhythm of life, and as such they rendered neither women nor men helpless. Newer patterns of male mobility (such as participation in the whaling industry and the military) that drew upon older Indian lifeways frequently left women alone to experience harsher circumstances than before, when kin-based social welfare and flexible marriages had provided them with the means to alleviate their wants. At least for women like Mercy Amerquit and Hannah Comsett, mobility was circumscribed by virtue of their being separated from men. And whereas whaling and military service may have reformulated earlier patterns of Indian male mobility, allowing men to resist the redefinition of gender in economic and social roles, the wives of these men—women like Eunice Spywood—

were defined as "responsibilities" in new ways and experienced far greater hardship as a result of their men's flight. The English nuclear family model thus reconfigured kin responsibilities and marriage, leaving Indian women newly vulnerable to "divorce" in dramatically different ways.

Whatever the underlying motivations, Indians of both sexes experienced hardship as a direct result of participation of Indian men in military service, especially. The social and demographic impact of the Seven Years' War on Indian enclaves in New England was enormous. In 1756, a cluster of Indians at Mattakesett in Pembroke, Massachusetts, pleaded to the General Court "that Several of us [have] in the late Warrs, lost our husbands & Sons, & Some of our Sons [are] yet in Sd Service, & that some of us are old, blind, & bed rid & helpless poor Creatures, Many of us [are] old Women & want help." Indians of Eastham and Harwich in Barnstable County, Massachusetts, complained that many of their men "Have Died in ye Service & left their Squa & Children in Distressing Circumstances." In 1761 Ezra Stiles reported that in Portsmouth, Rhode Island, "4 Ind. Boys [had] enlisted in the service . . . only one Boy more in Town, & he [is] about 10 y. old. I can't find . . . any Ind. Men in Town, . . . but several Squaws, perhaps 8 or 10." At Milford, Connecticut, there were twenty male Indians in 1755, at the beginning of the Seven Years' War, but in 1761 "not one: but 3 or 4 Squaws."

Even when they did return, many Indian men were rendered incapable of working to support themselves or their families as a result of war-related disabilities. Thomas Awassamug complained to the Massachusetts General Court in 1761 that "he having been engaged . . . as a Soldier . . . for more than thirty years past, has indured inexpressible hardships, and fatigues and thereby brought on him the Gout, and many other ailments . . . And [he has] no means of support." Awassamug sought to stir compassion by describing in detail his "deplorable Circumstances," and to clarify his own relationship with the colony by reminding the magistrates that he had "jeopardized his life in so many . . . very dangerous Enterprizes against those of his nation who remain Savage, and in behalf of his friends, the English." The General Court allowed a small sum to be paid out of the public treasury for his temporary relief.

No comprehensive evidence is available to investigate the precise dynamics of demographic change for Indians in eighteenth-century New England. Several censuses gathered by Stiles in his journeys through the region are suggestive, however. In addition to his more random observations, Stiles compiled detailed lists of residents by household from three Indian communities he visited in 1761 and 1762. In these communities, widows constituted heads of households in proportions ranging from 29 percent (Mashantucket Pequot in Groton, Connecticut) to 52 percent (the "Potenummekuk" Indians in Eastham and Nauset, Massachusetts). These figures suggest that the tribulations outlined above were not idle and unconnected complaints.

One solution to the apparently growing problem of unbalanced sex ratios and insufficient numbers of Indian men was for Indian women to find spouses among free or enslaved African Americans, who occupied similarly marginal positions in New England. The dynamics of intermarriage between Indians and African Americans are difficult to map precisely from the surviving documentary record. Impressionistic evidence does exist. Stiles observed in 1761 that "At Grafton

[Massachusetts] . . . I saw the Burying place & Graves of 60 or more Indians. Now not a Male Ind. in the Town, & perh. 5 Squaws who marry Negroes." A nineteenth-century history of Needham, Massachusetts, noted that there was "a colony of negroes, with more or less Indian blood, dwelling along the south shore of Bullard's Pond (Lake Waban)." Clearly, intermarriage did occur, as yet another kind of accommodation on the part of Indian women, representing an important demographic shift for Native populations of the northeast.

Equating "Indianness" with "blood quantum" (the perceived importance of "pure" blood lines) in rigid ways, English observers failed to understand the demographic and cultural changes that were reconfiguring "race" in New England. Intermarriage, which blurred the picture for those who looked for racial "purity," helped the Native population of New England to survive the devastating consequences of English colonization. Most colonists who noticed Indians just lamented what they saw as an inevitable process of extinction. Some vaguely grasped the complex process of vagrancy and intermarriage that was so central to eighteenth-century accommodations, even if their cultural blinders rendered them incapable of analyzing the changes. In 1797, the minister at Natick observed that

> It is difficult to ascertain the complete number of those that are now here, or that belong to this place, as they are so frequently shifting their place of residence, and are intermarried with blacks, and some with whites; and the various shades between these, and those that are descended from them, make it almost impossible to come to any determination about them.

Indians became, like other groups displaced by the colonizing impulse of the English, a diasporic population defined by the complex transformations and dislocations brought about by English colonialism. In the end, the migratory pattern and complexities of intermarriage created an erroneous impression in the minds of English observers that the Native population was simply and inevitably melting away.

In truth, monumental Indian adjustments spanned the entire colonial period and stretched into the nineteenth century. Both precontact Native American societies in the northeast and early modern European societies were organized according to particular expectations about gender roles. In New England, Indian women were responsible for most agricultural tasks, for gathering wild foods, building houses, most craft production, and childrearing. Men were warriors, diplomats, hunters, and fishermen, and they aided women in agricultural production by clearing fields. This way of organizing society came into direct conflict with English expectations, and the ability to maintain an economy that perfectly reflected older Native gender roles ran into the hard realities of changing circumstances. The loss of political independence and the massive displacement of Indians within their homelands brought tremendous changes that affected Indian women and men in different ways. Hunting and fishing became marginal, diplomacy became obsolete, and military involvement was transformed into economic activity. Agriculture was enormously altered in technique and organization: it became predominantly if not exclusively a male activity for Indian landowners, and it became a diminishing element of the Indian economy as Indians continued to lose land throughout the eighteenth century.

Although English expectations for change within Indian culture (encapsulated most fully in missionary platforms) called for altering the gendered Indian division of labor, the English did not fully succeed in "divorcing" Indian women (or men) from the land. Even though they quite successfully dispossessed Indians, Indians remained in the homelands that continued to sustain their kin, community, and sense of place. Indian women and men found creative solutions for resisting displacement and surviving as Indian people in a milieu theoretically designed to erase their difference completely.

How does all of this connect to Hannah Shiner? The manner in which she is portrayed in the nineteenth-century account that I began with, compared to how she might have been characterized in the seventeenth century, speaks volumes. This Indian woman is not described generically, as most Indian women were when regarded as members of a tribal unit, but as an individual with an Anglicized name. Her categorization as an Indian is based on the observer's judgment of her (pure) genealogy. And her husband is seen as a "mulatto," a mate who probably could trace some African American heritage. Hannah Shiner was assigned several traits, including two ("judge of herbs" and "weaver of baskets") that were associated in the public imagination with "Indianness," and especially with Indian women. They also suggest trades, or means of support, that had always been female activities. Hannah Shiner symbolizes the tumultuous changes experienced by Native peoples in seventeenth- and eighteenth-century New England. Indian peoples survived the catastrophe of English colonization, and they resisted the erasure of their Indianness. Men and women experienced the fundamental transformations in their lifeways differently. "Divorced" from the land in some respects but, crucially, not in others, many women displayed the characteristics that are visible in this brief description of Hannah Shiner. Apparently accepted and incorporated as an individual member of the community of Medford, Massachusetts, Hannah Shiner represents a particular kind of transformation, though not of the sort English missionaries had in mind. "Marginal" and a bit "exotic," she was portrayed as a bit of "local color," a tangible tie to what seemed to be (but was not) an increasingly distant Indian past. Her configuration by a local historian as such was precisely what Anglo-Americans needed for her to continue to represent the "otherness" necessary for the ongoing construction of their own difference.

◈ *F U R T H E R   R E A D I N G*

Karen Anderson, *Chain Her by One Foot: The Subjugation of Native Women in Seventeenth-Century New France* (1991)
James Axtell, *The European and the Indian: Essays in the Ethnohistory of Colonial North America* (1981)
———, *The Invasion Within: The Contest of Cultures in Colonial North America* (1985)
———, *The Rise and Fall of the Powhatan Empire: Indians in Seventeenth-Century Virginia* (1995)
———, *White Indians of Colonial America* (1991)
Theodore Binnema, "Old Swan, Big Man, and the Siksika Bands, 1794–1815," *Canadian Historical Review* 77 (March 1996), 1–32
Nancy Bonvillain, "The Iroquois and the Jesuits: Strategies of Influence and Resistance," *American Indian Culture and Research Journal* 10:1 (1986), 29–42
Henry Warner Bowden, *American Indians and Christian Missions* (1981)
Kathleen J. Bragdon, *Native Peoples of Southern New England, 1500–1650* (1996)

Jennifer S. H. Brown, *Strangers in Blood: Fur Trade Company Families in Indian Country* (1980)

Colin G. Calloway, ed., *After King Philip's War: Presence and Persistence in Indian New England* (1997)

Carol Cooper, "Native Women of the Northern Pacific Coast: An Historical Perspective, 1830–1900," *Journal of Canadian Studies* 27 (Winter, 1993), 44–75

William Cronon, *Changes in the Land: Indians, Colonists, and the Ecology of New England* (1983)

Denys Delâge, *Bitter Feast: Amerindians and Europeans in Northeastern North America, 1600–1664* (1993)

Carol Devins, "Separate Confrontations: Gender as a Factor in Indian Adaptation to European Colonization in New France," *American Quarterly* 38 (1986): 461–480

Olive P. Dickason, *Canada's First Nations: A History of Founding Peoples from Earliest Times* (1992)

W. J. Eccles, "The Fur Trade and Eighteenth-Century Imperialism," *William and Mary Quarterly* 40 (1983), 341–362

R. David Edmunds and Joseph L. Peyser, *The Fox Wars: The Mesquakie Challenge to New France* (1993)

John C. Ewers, *Indian Life on the Upper Missouri* (1968)

———, "The Influence of the Fur Trade upon Indians of the Northern Plains," in Malvina Bolus, ed., *People and Pelts: Selected Papers of the Second North American Fur Trade Conference* (1972), 1–26

William N. Fenton, *The Great Law and the Longhouse: A Political History of the Iroquois Confederacy* (1998)

Alexandra Harmon, *Indians in the Making: Ethnic Relations and Indian Identities Around Puget Sound* (1998)

Ted C. Hinckley, *The Canoe Rocks: Alaska's Tlingit and the Euroamerican Frontier, 1800–1912* (1996)

Cornelius J. Jaenen, *Friend and Foe: Aspects of French-Amerindian Cultural Contact in the Sixteenth and Seventeenth Centuries* (1976)

Francis Jennings, *The Ambiguous Iroquois Empire: The Convenant Chain Confederation of Indian Tribes with English Colonies from Its beginnings to the Lancaster Treaty of 1774* (1984)

———, *Empire of Fortune: Crowns, Colonies, and Tribes in the Seven Years' War in America* (1988)

———, *The Invasion of America: Indians, Colonialism, and the Cant of Conquest* (1975)

Ruth Landes, *Ojibwa Woman* (1971)

Eleanor Leacock, "Montagnais Women and the Jesuit Program for Colonization," in Mona Etienne and Eleanor Leacock, eds., *Women and Colonization: Anthropological Perspectives* (1980)

Calvin Martin, *Keepers of the Game: Indian-Animal Relationships and the Fur Trade* (1978)

James Merrell, *The Indians' New World: Catawbas and Their Neighbors from European Contact through the Era of Removal* (1989)

Montana, the Magazine of Western History, 43 (Winter 1993) (special fur trade issue)

Roger L. Nichols, *Indians in the United States and Canada: A Comparative History* (1998)

Jean M. O'Brien, *Dispossession by Degrees: Indian Land and Identity in Natick, Massachusetts, 1650–1790* (1997)

Laura L. Peters, *Into the American Woods: Negotiators on the Pennsylvania Frontier* (1999)

———, *The Ojibwa of Western Canada, 1780–1870* (1994)

Jacqueline Peterson and Jennifer S. H. Brown, eds., *The New Peoples: Being and Becoming Métis in North America* (1985)

Arthur J. Ray, *Indians in the Fur Trade: Their Role as Trappers, Hunters, and Middlemen in the Lands Southwest of Hudson's Bay, 1660–1870* (1974)

——— and Donald Freeman, *"Give Us Good Measure": An Economic Analysis of Relations Between the Indians and the Hudson's Bay Company Before 1763* (1978)

Daniel Richter, *The Ordeal of the Longhouse: The Peoples of the Iroquois League in the Era of European Colonization* (1992)

James P. Ronda, "The Sillery Experiment: A Jesuit-Indian Village in New France, 1637–1663," *American Indian Culture and Research Journal* 3 (1979), 1–18

Neal Salisbury, *Manitou and Providence: Indians, Europeans, and the Making of New England, 1500–1643* (1982)

William R. Swagerty, "Marriage and Settlement Patterns of Rocky Mountain Trappers and Traders," *Western Historical Quarterly* 11 (1980): 159–180

Sylvia Van Kirk, *Many Tender Ties: Women in Fur-Trade Society, 1670–1870* (1980)

———, "Women and the Fur Trade," *The Beaver* 303 (no. 3) (1972), 4–21

Alden T. Vaughan, *New England Frontier: Puritans and Indians, 1620–1675* (1995)

Anthony F. C. Wallace, *The Death and Rebirth of the Seneca* (1970)

Bruce White, "Encounters with the Spirits: Ojibwa and Dakota Theories about the French and Their Merchandise," *Ethnohistory* 41 (July 1994), 369–405

Richard White, *The Middle Ground: Indians, Empires and Republics in the Great Lakes Region, 1650–1815* (1991)

W. Raymond Wood and Thomas D. Thiessen, eds., *Early Fur Trade on the Northern Plains: Canadian Traders Among the Mandan and Hidatsa Indians, 1738–1818* (1985)

Bobby Wright, "'For the Children of the Infidels'?: American Indian Education in the Colonial Colleges," *American Indian Culture and Research Journal* 12:3 (1988), 1–14

CHAPTER
6

New Nations, New Boundaries: American Revolution in Indian Country

◈

The era of the American Revolution and its aftermath was a period of rapid change and adjustment for Indian tribes. In the 1760s, the government in London attempted to limit the expansion of whites into Indian country. The royal officials who proposed this measure knew that expansion caused friction that all too often erupted into frontier warfare. Colonists expected the crown to assist them in these wilderness conflicts, and the royal government preferred to avoid the trouble and expense of fighting in America. The Indian war of 1763, sometimes named after the Ottawa leader Pontiac, provided abundant evidence that British concerns were well founded. The proclamation of 1763 established a boundary between white settlements and Indian country beyond the crest of the Appalachian Mountains. Colonists regarded the Proclamation Line as an unwarranted intrusion, and it became one of the many grievances against the British government that led to the Revolution.

During the Revolution, tribes were faced with a serious problem of diplomacy. Should they side with the Americans, the British, or remain neutral? Tribesmen tried all three paths, although most Indians sided with the British because that course seemed most likely to protect Indian interests. Indians paid a heavy price for fighting with the losing side, as the United States forced them to sign treaties that stripped them of land. Even the Oneidas, who sided with the Americans, lost their homelands, despite U.S. promises that they would be permitted to return after the war. Instead, New York state and private speculators dispossessed these loyal Indian allies. After the Revolution, the new United States government assumed responsibility for Indian affairs. The United States faced essentially the same problem that British authorities had wrestled with in 1763: how to promote orderly westward expansion while minimizing Indian and white conflicts. Once powerful eastern tribes, like those of the Iroquois confederacy, found that their power was broken. Some Indian groups were surrounded by white settlements and had to adjust to these new circumstances. Still others tried to reestablish their independence in the

Ohio River Valley. It is one of the ironies of American history that a Revolution fought in the name of independence limited the freedom of American Indians.

⬧ D O C U M E N T S

In 1776, Congress was concerned that the Iroquois confederation might join the British and fight against revolutionary forces. In the summer, a delegation of Iroquois leaders went to Philadelphia and received presents and a message from Congress urging the Indians to spurn British advances and to remain neutral (Document 1). Similar messages were given to other tribes, but often they went unheeded as Indians began to fight on the British side. The Cherokees under the leadership of Dragging Canoe joined the Mohawks and others and went to war against the new American nation. By the spring of 1777, American forces had made the Cherokees suffer for their alliance with the British, and most were ready to make peace. Colonel Nathaniel Gist, who had a Cherokee wife, sent messages to the Cherokees offering peace. Document 2 is one of Gist's proffers of peace, but it included a threat if the Indians did not agree to stop fighting. Even Dragging Canoe was forced to make peace, and he put the best face on it in Document 3. In Document 4, Mary Jemison, a white woman, provides an account of the hardships that the Revolution brought to Indian country. Jemison had been captured by the Senecas, but they eventually adopted her into the tribe, and she married an Indian. For most Indians, the peace brought dispossession, especially for those who fought with the British. Document 5, the Treaty of Fort Stanwyx, required Iroquois tribes to give up land and hand over hostages to the Americans until American prisoners were relinquished.

1. Speech of Congress to Visiting Iroquois Delegation, 1776

[June 11, 1776]

The presents being provided for the Indians, they were called in, and the speech agreed to, was delivered as follows:

BROTHERS,

We hope the friendship that is between us and you will be firm, and continue as long as the sun shall shine, and the waters run; that we and you may be as one people, and have but one heart, and be kind to one another like brethren.

BROTHERS,

The king of Great Britain, hearkening to the evil counsel of some of his foolish young men, is angry with us, because we will not let him take away from us our land, and all that we have, and give it to them, and because we will not do everything that he bids us; and hath hindered his people from bringing goods to us; but, we have made provision for getting such a quantity of them, that we hope we shall be able to supply your wants as formerly.

Speech of Congress to Visiting Iroquois Delegation, 1776. This document can be found in Colin Calloway, ed., *Early American Indian Documents: Treaties and Laws, 1607–1789*, vol. 18, *Revolution and Confederation* (Bethesda, Md.: University Publications of America, 1994), 39.

BROTHERS,

We shall order all our warriors and young men not to hurt your or any of your kindred, and we hope you will not suffer any of your young men to join with our enemies, or to do any wrong to us, that nothing may happen to make any quarrel between us.

BROTHERS,

We desire you to accept a few necessaries, which we present you with, as tokens of our good will towards you.

The presents being delivered, the Indians begged leave to give a name to the president; the same being granted, the Onondago chief gave the president the name of Karanduawn, or the Great Tree, by which name he informed him the president will be known among the Six nations.

|| After which the Indians took their leave and withdrew. ||

2. Nathaniel Gist of Virginia Addresses the Cherokee Chiefs, 1777

[March 28, 1777]

Brothers, Occunastotah, Raven, Dragging Canoe, and old Tassel.

When I parted with you I promised to be back before cold Weather was done, and according to your desire, have spoke to the great Warriours of the American states for Peace for you, and now send by your own People some of the Talks they gave me and have several more good Talks to give when you come to this Place to treat. I also now send you two strings of Wampum that was delivered me by the Delawares and Shawnees, for the Cherokees, desiring that they would no more listen to the Lying bad Talks carried you by some of their foolish People and the Mingoes.

You know all, particularly the Dragging Canoe, that what I advised last year, before you went to War, was for your good, and would have saved the Lives of many of your People, and saved your Towns from being destroyed. Now I tell you again, this Year, it will be much worse than last, unless you now make Peace, when the good Time is come As it is the last offer of Peace you will get from Virginia. So dont blame me when hard time comes again among you. As I have now told you the Truth, advised you for your good, and now offer to shake hands with all my Brothers the Cherokees in behalf of Virginia. The Bearer hereof or Runner sent from you with a white Flag, must come to me here in twenty days, that I may know whether you are coming for Peace or not; they shall be kindly treated and kept from harm.

Great Island Fort 28 March 1777

Nathal. Gist.

Nathaniel Gist of Virginia Addresses the Cherokee Chiefs, 1777. This document can be found in Colin Calloway, ed., *Early American Indian Documents: Treaties, and Laws, 1607–1789,* vol. 18, *Revolution and Confederation* (Bethesda, Md., University Publications of America, 1994), 216.

3. Dragging Canoe (Cherokee) Replies to Colonel Gist, 1777

[April 1777]

At a Treaty held at this place last April the Commissioners sent a Talk by Col. Gist to the Dragging Canoe who returned Colo. Gist the following answer.

Brother

Though your messenger is not come to me yet I have heard your Talks and hold them fast as long as I live, for they have opened my Eyes and made me see clear, that Cameron and Stewart have been telling me lies, when we had any Talks with the Virginians he was always mad with us, and told us that all that the Virginians wanted was to get our Land and kill us, and that he had often told us we would not hear him till the Virginians would come and kill us all. Now Brother I plainly see that he made me quarrel with the greatest friends that we ever had, who took pity on us even in the greatest distress, when my old men, women and children is perishing for something to live on, this makes it more plain to me that he cared not how many of us were killed on both sides so that we were dead, killed in Battle, or perrished with hunger, any way so we were dead.

Brother, I heard you were taken prisoner and confined, my heart was sorry as tho you had been my born Brother, when I thought of their bad treatment to you I expected never to see you. I thought they had killed you or sent you away as that I should never see you more. That made my heart very cross and I went to war more for revenge for you than any other reason. But now Brother I am sorry for it, since I see that the great being above has sent you back to save me and my people. Now Brother the great Warrior and your beloved men are sitting together, I am determined that I nor my people shall never spoil their good talks while I live, when I am dead there will be annother man to take my place.

Brother I am going to see the man that told me all those lieing Talks and return him his meddle and Beds and tell him for the future to keep all his lieing talks to himself. He sends me word that he is coming from Mobile with a great many Scotsmen and intends to offer you a peace; if you wont accept it he intends to kill and force you to it. Brother I shall make no stop on the road, but shall be back soon and come straight to you and tell you all the news. If I should not come in soon pray excuse me to the beloved men as you are better acquainted with me than they are, and you can talk better than I can, and you know Brother I will not do anything that will make you ashamed of me among your people.

Dragging Canoe (Cherokee) Replies to Colonel Gist, 1777. This document can be found in Colin Calloway, ed., *Early American Indian Documents: Treaties, and Laws, 1607–1789*, vol. 18, *Revolution and Confederation* (Bethesda, Md., University Publications of America, 1994), 217–218.

4. Mary Jemison's (Seneca) Memory of the Revolution, 1775–1779

Thus, at peace amongst themselves, and with the neighboring whites, though there were none at that time very near, our Indians lived quietly and peaceably at home, till a little before the breaking out of the revolutionary war, when they were sent for, together with the Chiefs and members of the Six Nations generally, by the people of the States, to go to the German Flats, and there hold a general council, in order that the people of the states might ascertain, in good season, who they should esteem and treat as enemies, and who as friends, in the great war which was then upon the point of breaking out between them and the King of England.

Our Indians obeyed the call, and the council was holden, at which the pipe of peace was smoked, and a treaty made, in which the Six Nations solemnly agreed that if a war should eventually break out, they would not take up arms on either side; but that they would observe a strict neutrality. With that the people of the states were satisfied, as they had not asked their assistance, nor did not wish it. The Indians returned to their homes well pleased that they could live on neutral ground, surrounded by the din of war, without being engaged in it.

About a year passed off, and we, as usual, were enjoying ourselves in the employments of peaceable times, when a messenger arrived from the British Commissioners, requesting all the Indians of our tribe to attend a general council which was soon to be held at Oswego. The council convened, and being opened, the British Commissioners informed the Chiefs that the object of calling a council of the Six Nations, was, to engage their assistance in subduing the rebels, the people of the states, who had risen up against the good King, their master, and were about to rob him of a great part of his possessions and wealth, and added that they would amply reward them for all their services.

The Chiefs then arose, and informed the Commissioners of the nature and extent of the treaty which they had entered into with the people of the states, the year before, and that they should not violate it by taking up the hatchet against them.

The Commissioners continued their entreaties without success, till they addressed their avarice, by telling our people that the people of the states were few in number, and easily subdued; and that on the account of their disobedience to the King, they justly merited all the punishment that it was possible for white men and Indians to inflict upon them; and added, that the King was rich and powerful, both in money and subjects: That his rum was as plenty as the water in lake Ontario: that his men were as numerous as the sands upon the lake shore:—and that the Indians, if they would assist in the war, and persevere in their friendship to the King, till it was closed, should never want for money or goods. Upon this the Chiefs concluded a treaty with the British Commissioners, in which they agreed to take up arms against the rebels, and continue in the service of his Majesty till they were subdued,

Mary Jemison's (Seneca) Memory of the Revolution, 1775–1779. This document can be found in James Seaver, ed., *The Narrative of the Life of Mary Jemison.* Copyright © 1824.

in consideration of certain conditions which were stipulated in the treaty to be performed by the British government and its agents.

As soon as the treaty was finished, the Commissioners made a present to each Indian of a suit of clothes, a brass kettle, a gun and tomahawk, a scalping knife, a quantity of powder and lead, a piece of gold, and promised a bounty on every scalp that should be brought in. Thus richly clad and equipped, they returned home, after an absence of about two weeks, full of the fire of war, and anxious to encounter their enemies. Many of the kettles which the Indians received at that time are now in use on the Genesee Flats. . . .

Previous to the battle at Fort Stanwix, the British sent for the Indians to come and see them whip the rebels; and, at the same time stated that they did not wish to have them fight, but wanted to have them just sit down, smoke their pipes, and look on. Our Indians went, to a man; but contrary to their expectation, instead of smoking and looking on, they were obliged to fight for their lives, and in the end of the battle were completely beaten, with a great loss in killed and wounded. Our Indians alone had thirty-six killed, and a great number wounded. Our town exhibited a scene of real sorrow and distress, when our warriors returned and recounted their misfortunes, and stated the real loss they had sustained in the engagement. The mourning was excessive, and was expressed by the most doleful yells, shrieks, and howlings, and by inimitable gesticulations.

During the revolution, my house was the home of Col's Butler and Brandt, whenever they chanced to come into our neighborhood as they passed to and from Fort Niagara, which was the seat of their military operations. Many and many a night I have pounded samp for them from sun-set till sun-rise, and furnished them with necessary provision and clean clothing for their journey. . . .

At that time I had three children who went with me on foot, one who rode on horse back, and one whom I carried on my back.

Our corn was good that year; a part of which we had gathered and secured for winter.

In one or two days after the skirmish at Connissius lake, Sullivan and his army arrived at Genesee river, where they destroyed every article of the food kind that they could lay their hands on. A part of our corn they burnt, and threw the remainder into the river. They burnt our houses, killed what few cattle and horses they could find, destroyed our fruit trees, and left nothing but the bare soil and timber. But the Indians had eloped and were not to be found.

Having crossed and recrossed the river, and finished the work of destruction, the army marched off to the east. Our Indians saw them move off, but suspecting that it was Sullivan's intention to watch our return, and then to take us by surprise, resolved that the main body of our tribe should hunt where we then were, till Sullivan had gone so far that there would be no danger of his returning to molest us.

This being agreed to, we hunted continually till the Indians concluded that there could be no risk in our once more taking possession of our lands. Accordingly we all returned; but what were our feelings when we found that there was not a mouthful of any kind of sustenance left, not even enough to keep a child one day from perishing with hunger.

The weather by this time had become cold and stormy; and as we were destitute of houses and food too, I immediately resolved to take my children and look out for myself, without delay. With this intention I took two of my little ones on my back, bade the other three follow, and the same night arrived on the Gardow flats, where I have ever since resided. . . .

. . . The snow fell about five feet deep, and remained so for a long time, and the weather was extremely cold; so much so indeed, that almost all the game upon which the Indians depended for subsistence, perished, and reduced them almost to a state of starvation through that and three or four succeeding years. When the snow melted in the spring, deer were found dead upon the ground in vast numbers; and other animals, of every description, perished from the cold also, and were found dead, in multitudes. Many of our people barely escaped with their lives, and some actually died of hunger and freezing.

5. Treaty of Fort Stanwix, 1784

Articles

Concluded at Fort Stanwix, on the twenty-second day of October, one thousand seven hundred and eighty-four, between Oliver Wolcott, Richard Butler, and Arthur Lee, Commissioners Plenipotentiary from the United States, in Congress assembled, on the one Part, and the Sachems and Warriors of the Six Nations, on the other.

The United States of America give peace to the Senecas, Mohawks, Onondagas and Cayugas, and receive them into their protection upon the following conditions:

Article I.　Six hostages shall be immediately delivered to the commissioners by the said nations, to remain in possession of the United States, till all the prisoners, white and black, which were taken by the said Senecas, Mohawks, Onondagas and Cayugas, or by any of them, in the late war, from among the people of the United States, shall be delivered up.

Article II.　The Oneida and Tuscarora nations shall be secured in the possession of the lands on which they are settled.

Article III.　A line shall be drawn, beginning at the mouth of a creek about four miles east of Niagara, called Oyonwayea, or Johnston's Landing-Place, upon the lake named by the Indians Oswego, and by us Ontario; from thence southerly in a direction always four miles east of the carrying-path, between Lake Erie and Ontario, to the mouth of Tehoseroron or Buffaloe Creek on Lake Erie; thence south to the north boundary of the state of Pennsylvania; thence west to the end of the said north boundary; thence south along the west boundary of the said state, to the river

Treaty of Fort Stanwix, 1784. This document can be found in Wilcomb E. Washington, comp., *The American Indian and the United States: A Documentary History,* 4 volumes (Westport, Conn.: Greenwood Press, 1973), IV: 2267–2271.

Ohio; the said line from the mouth of the Oyonwayea to the Ohio, shall be the western boundary of the lands of the Six Nations, so that the Six Nations shall and do yield to the United States, all claims to the country west of the said boundary, and then they shall be secured in the peaceful possession of the lands they inhabit east and north of the same, reserving only six miles square round the fort of Oswego, to the United States, for the support of the same.

Article IV. The Commissioners of the United States, in consideration of the present circumstances of the Six Nations, and in execution of the humane and liberal views of the United States upon the signing of the above articles, will order goods to be delivered to the said Six Nations for their use and comfort.

Oliver Wolcott	*Oneidas.*
Richard Butler,	Otyadonenghti,
Arthur Lee.	Dagaheari.
Mohawks.	*Cayuga.*
Onogwendahonji,	Oraghgoanendagen.
Towighnatogon.	
	Tuscarora.
Onondagas.	Ononghsawenghti,
Oheadarighton,	Tharondawagen.
Kendarindgon.	
	Seneca Abeal.
	Kayenthoghke.
Senecas.	
Tayagonendagighti,	
Tehonwaeaghriyagi.	

Witnesses: Sam. Jo. Atlee, Wm. Maclay, Fras. Johnston, Pennsylvania Commissioners. Aaron Hill, Alexander Campbell, Saml. Kirkland. Miss'y. James Dean, Saml. Montgomery, Derick Lane, Capt. John Mercer, Lieut. William Pennington, Lieut. Mahlon Ford, Ensign. Hugh Peebles.

◈ *E S S A Y S*

The Revolution was a watershed event for Indians as well as whites in North America. By the Peace of Paris, the United States replaced England as the sovereign power within the new nation's borders, which stretched to the Mississippi River. Significant as it was, this political change did not have an immediate impact, especially in the country west of the Appalachians. Nor did the British immediately lose influence in the Great Lakes region that bordered Canada. Dartmouth College professor Colin Calloway's essay shows that the aftermath of the Revolution was just as costly for Indians as the War for Independence had been. In the second essay, Ruth Wallis Herndon of the University of Toledo and Ella Wilcox Sekatau from the Narragansett Tribe show that for the Narragansetts revolutionary changes were less dramatic and bloody, but just as far-reaching.

In the late eighteenth century, Rhode Island officials erased the Narragansetts from the record and ceased to recognize them as a people, despite the continuing presence of these resourceful native people in their midst.

The Aftermath of the Revolution in Indian Country

COLIN CALLOWAY

For all the devastation the American Revolution brought to Indian country, Indians remained a force to be reckoned with at the war's end. In reading the reports of American invasions of Indian country, it is easy to assume, as did some American commanders, that burning Indian villages and destroying crops constituted a knockout blow. But burning homes, razing fields, and killing noncombatants does not necessarily destroy people's will to fight or even their ability to win. Geoffrey Parker's observation about the resilience of peasant communities victimized by European wars—"as in Vietnam, what was easily burnt could also be easily rebuilt"—sometimes held true for Indian communities during the Revolution. Many survived the destruction of their villages. George Rogers Clark recognized the limitations of the American search-and-destroy missions, and an officer on Sullivan's campaign agreed that burning crops and villages was not the same as killing Indians: "The nests are destroyed but the birds are still on the wing." A British officer reviewing the American campaigns against the Iroquois and the Cherokees agreed that such a system of warfare was "shocking to humanity," and as sound military strategy was "at best but problematical." The Indians in the West were holding their own in 1782. The real disaster of the American Revolution for Indian peoples lay in its outcome.

Speaking on a war belt in council with the British in Detroit in December 1781, the Delaware war chief Buckongahelas declared that his warriors had been making blood "fly" on the American frontier for five years. The next year, 1782 the last of the war, witnessed even bloodier conflict. Indians routed American forces at Blue Licks and Sandusky. Americans slaughtered Moravian Delawares at Gnadenhütten and burned Shawnee villages. Delawares ritually tortured Colonel William Crawford and, as atrocities mounted, they and the Shawnees pushed "their retaliation to great length by putting all their prisoners to death."

Then the British and Americans made peace. The Peace of Paris recognized the independence of the thirteen colonies and transferred to the new United States all land east of the Mississippi, south of the Great Lakes, and north of the Floridas. Wyandot chiefs, who had heard rumors of peace, told Major De Peyster "we hope your children [i.e., the Indians] will be remembered in the Treaty," but the peace terms made no mention of the Indian people who had fought and died in the Revolution and who inhabited the territory to be transferred. The Peace of Paris brought a temporary lull in hostilities, but it brought no peace to Indian country. Rather, by ending open conflict between non-Indian powers, it deprived Indians of allies and

Colin Calloway, "The Aftermath of the Revolution in Indian Country," in *The American Revolution in Indian Country* (Cambridge, U.K.: Cambridge University Press, 1995), 272–291. Reprinted with the permission of Cambridge University Press.

diplomatic opportunities as they continued their struggle for independence against Americans who claimed their lands as the fruits of victory.

If a speech that John Heckewelder attributed to Captain Pipe is accurately dated and recorded, Indians were apprehensive of British betrayal even as they carried war to the Americans in 1781. "Think not that I lack *sufficient sense to convince me,*" the Delaware chief told Major De Peyster at Detroit, "that altho' You *now* pretend to keep up a perpetual enmity to the Long Knives (American People), you may, e'er long, conclude a Peace with them!" The British, he said, had set him on their enemy like a hunter setting his dogs on his quarry, but he suspected that if he glanced back, "I shall probably see my Father shaking hands with the Long Knives." Pipe's worst fears were now realized. As news of the peace terms filtered into Indian country, Indian speakers in council after council expressed their anger and disbelief that their British allies had betrayed them and handed their lands over to their American and Spanish enemies. The head warrior of the Eufalees refused to believe that the English would abandon the Indians; another Creek chief dismissed reports of the treaty as "a Virginia Lie." The Iroquois were "thunderstruck" when they heard that British diplomats had sold them out to the Americans without so much as a reference to the tribes. Little Turkey of the Overhill Cherokees concluded, "The peacemakers and our Enemies have talked away our Lands at a Rum Drinking." Okaegige of the Flint River Seminoles reminded the British that the Indians took up the hatchet for the king "at a time we could scarce distinguish our Friends from our Foes," and asked if the king now intended to sell them into slavery. Fine Bones, speaking for his Cowetas and other Upper Creeks, said they could not now turn around and take the Spaniards and Virginians by the hand; if the English intended to evacuate, the Indians would accompany them.

Alexander McGillivray told the British he could no longer keep his people in the dark. After nine years of faithful service, "at the Close of it to find ourselves & Country betrayed to our Enemies & divided between the Spaniards & Americans is Cruel & Ungenerous." The Indians had done nothing to permit the king to give away their lands, "unless . . . Spilling our blood in the Service of his Nation can be deemed so." The Indians had been "most Shamefully deserted." Turning to the Spaniards, McGillivray reiterated that Britain had no right to give up what it did not own, and that the Creeks as a free nation had the right to choose what allies they thought most appropriate. "The protection of a great Monarch is to be preferred to that of a distracted Republic," he said, courting Governor Estevan Miró, but making it clear he would turn to the Americans for trade if necessary. Spanish officials referred patronizingly to McGillivray as "nuestro mestizo," but McGillivray deftly pursued Creek, not Spanish, interests in the decade after the Revolution.

Many southern Indians—"having made all the world their Enemies by their attachment to us"—expressed their determination to evacuate along with the British rather than stay and come to terms with the Americans and Spaniards, but the British discouraged them. William Augustus Bowles, masquerading as a Creek chief in London eight years later, summed up the situation: "The British Soldier, when he left the shore of America, on the proclamation of peace, had peace indeed, and returned to a Country where Peace could be enjoyed; But to the Creek & Cherokee Indians was left, to drain to the dregs the remainder of the bitter cup of

War, unassisted & alone." McGillivray asked the British army at least to leave the Creeks military stores so that they could defend themselves against the Americans.

Indian people farther from the center of revolutionary conflict felt the betrayal equally hard. The Chippewa chief, Matchekwis, visited Michilimackinac in September 1784, and when Captain Daniel Robertson refused his requests for presents, the Indian

> abused me in a very particular manner, as all our great men below, saying we were all Lyers, Impostures &c. that had encouraged him and others to go to Canada &c. to fight and loose their Brothers and Children, now despise them, and let them starve, and that they, the Indians ought to chasse us and our connections out of the country.

British officers and Indian agents scrambled to save face and reconcile the Indians to "this unfortunate event," fearing that their former allies might with good reason turn and vent their rage on the people who had betrayed them. British traders prepared to leave Indian villages even as British officers stressed the need to maintain the usual supplies to the Indians although the war was over. Sir John Johnson's speech to the Iroquois, in which he naively or cynically reassured them that he could not believe the United States intended to deprive them of their land on pretext of having conquered it, was relayed to other tribes. The Indians were advised to bear their losses with fortitude, forget what was past, and look forward to the blessings of peace. Not too sure themselves about the peaceful intentions of the new republic, and determined to protect their interests among the Indians, the British resolved to hold on to the frontier posts that were supposed to be handed over to the United States "with all convenient speed" under the peace terms. Retention of these posts, which stretched from Lake Champlain to Michilimackinac, conveyed the impression that the British were on hand to support the tribes in continuing resistance to the United States, even though Britain carefully avoided renewed war with the United States. Spain operated a similar policy to check American expansion in the south: Spanish officials encouraged McGillivray "by word of mouth" and did their best to "help the Indians without the Americans being able to prove that we have done so."

Meanwhile, Americans made the most of British perfidy. They told the Shawnees that Britain had cast them aside "like Bastards." Virginian emissary John Dodge told the Chickasaws that the English had been forced to withdraw from the country and "their Poor foolish Indians which refused to make Peace with us, is miserable on the Earth, Crying & begging for mercy Every Day." General Philip Schuyler told the Six Nations Indians that the British deceived them if they told them they were included in the peace; "the treaty does not contain a single stipulation for the Indians, they are not even so much as mentioned." At the beginning of the war, Schuyler said, he had asked the Six Nations to sit still and they had not listened. Now, like the Loyalists, they had forfeited their lands. "We are now Masters of this Island, and can dispose of the Lands as we think proper or most convenient to ourselves," the general declared. Six Nations delegates listened in bewilderment. From what he heard from his messengers, Joseph Brant thought Schuyler "as Saucy as [the] very devil," and thought the Iroquois delegates behaved shamefully. "After our friends the English left us in the lurch, still our own chiefs should make the matter worse," he wrote to Major Robert Mathews. "I do assure you I begin to prepare my death song for vexation will lead one to rashness."

The peace signed in Paris did little to change things in the backcountry world inhabited by Indians and American frontiersmen. Frontier vendettas continued and old scores remained unsettled. Some people on the eastern seaboard were appalled by the massacre of the Moravian Delawares in 1782, but William Irvne, commanding at Fort Pitt, knew that people who lived closer to the Indians and had lost relatives in the war felt very differently. He warned his wife to keep her opinions about the massacre to herself, as he would: "No man knows whether I approve or disapprove of killing the Moravians." The Indianhating that produced and sanctioned the Moravian massacre paid no regard to words of peace exchanged in Paris and made real peace impossible in Indian country. Commander De Peyster at Detroit warned his superiors in the fall of 1782 that the backcountry settlers would continue to make war on the Delawares, Shawnees, and Wyandots even after Britain and her revolted colonists made peace. Allan MacLean at Niagara feared that while he was busy preventing the Indians from going to war in the spring of 1783, the rebels "were preparing to cut the throats of the Indians.

Nor were all Indian people eager to embrace the peace. Warriors with relatives to avenge paid little attention to formal peace terms worked out by men far from the bloodletting. A Potawatomi, singing the war song, told Major De Peyster he was eager for action in 1781 because "you see me here in mourning and I am ashamed to remain so." Another asked De Peyster "for means to enable him to revenge himself" for the loss of his kinsman. John Montour, a mixed-blood Delaware who flits in and out of the records, "was one of Seven Brothers, all of them reckoned able good Warriors at the Commencement of the Rebellion, five of them have been Since killed in the service." While the war drew to a close and the British tried to keep their allies at peace, John and his surviving brother were out in Indian country, anxious for revenge. In November 1782, they came into Fort Niagara with four scalps and three young female prisoners, saying they knew nothing about the suspension of hostilities.

The end of the Revolution produced a new phase of conflict between Indians and Americans in the Ohio country. Murders, horse thefts, raids, and counterraids continued with little abatement. "While empires and states went about making peace," explains Richard White, "the villages continued to act on their own." Like the British after 1763, American policymakers could no more control their citizens than Indian chiefs could control their young men. A flood of backcountry settlers invaded Indian country, broke down what remained of the "middle ground" arrangements of coexistence that had been built up over generations, and knocked the heart out of federal attempts to regulate the frontier. Many of these people, reported a congressional committee, had no more desire for peace with the Indians than the British had for peace between Indians and Americans. As revolutionary violence gave way to postwar peace and a future of prosperity in some other areas of the country, vengeance and strife continued to be a way of life and of getting things done in Indian country, even in relations between whites. Tension between frontier settlers and eastern elites resulted in western demands for autonomy, separatist movements, violent confrontations, and the breakdown of normal means of redress.

During the war, American soldiers had returned from expeditions into Indian country with stories of the rich lands awaiting them once independence was won. With the Peace of Paris under their belts, Americans now set about taking over Indian lands as the spoils of victory. Peace initiated a new era of land speculation and unleashed a new land rush into Indian country. Between 1783 and 1790, the white population of Pennsylvania's three western counties grew by 87 percent; by the end of the century, western Pennsylvania's population had jumped from around thirty-three thousand to ninety-five thousand. Governor Benjamin Harrison of Virginia confessed to Governor Alexander Martin of North Carolina that he was "shocked when I reflect on the unbounded thirst of our people after Lands that they cannot cultivate, and the means they use to possess themselves of those that belong to others." Frenchman Francois Jean de Chastellux, traveling in North America as the war wound down, predicted that an inevitable consequence of the peace for the Indians "must be their total destruction, or their exclusion at least from all the country within the lakes." A delegation of 260 Iroquois, Shawnee, Cherokee, Chickasaw, Choctaw, and "Loup" Indians visiting the Spanish governor of Saint Louis in the summer of 1784 already felt the effects of the American victory:

> The Americans, a great deal more ambitious and numerous than the English, put us out of our lands, forming therein great settlements, extending themselves like a plague of locusts in the territories of the Ohio River which we inhabit. They treat us as their cruelest enemies are treated, so that today hunger and the impetuous torrent of war which they impose upon us with other terrible calamities, have brought our villages to a struggle with death.

Faced with an empty treasury and no means of replenishing it except by selling off Indian lands, the United States government focused its attention on the Old Northwest, where individual states relinquished their claims to western lands to the national government. A congressional committee, reporting in October 1783, noted that the Indian tribes of the northwest and the Ohio Valley seriously desired peace, but cautioned that "they are not in a temper to relinquish their territorial claims, without further struggles." Nevertheless, the report continued, the Indians were the aggressors in the recent war. They had ignored American warnings to remain neutral and "had wantonly desolated our villages and destroyed our citizens." The United States had been obliged, at great expense, to carry the war into Indian country "to stop the progress of their outrages." The Indians should make atonement and pay compensation, "and they possess no other means to do this act of justice than by compliance with the proposed boundaries." Rather than continue a costly war, the report recommended that the United States make peace with the tribes and negotiate boundaries that could then be renegotiated as Indians retired west before the inevitable press of settlement.

Acting on the assumption of Indian war guilt and eager for the spoils of victory, American commissioners demanded lands from the Iroquois at Fort Stanwix in 1784; from the Delawares, Wyandots, and their neighbors at Fort McIntosh in 1785; and from the Shawnees at Fort Finney in 1786. They brushed aside Indian objections in arrogant confidence that Indian lands were theirs for the taking by right of conquest. In 1775, Congress had instructed its treaty commissioners to "speak and act in such a manner as they shall think most likely to obtain the friendship or at least the neutrality of the Indians." Times had changed. James Duane, chairman of the Committee on Indian Affairs in the Continental Congress and mayor of New York City from 1784 to 1789, urged the United States not to continue the British practice of cultivating relations with the Indians as if they were nations of equal standing. The Six Nations should be treated as dependents of the State of New York. They should adopt American diplomatic protocol, not vice versa. Unless the United States seized the opportunity to implement this new hardline approach, said Duane, "this Revolution in my Eyes will have lost more than half its' [*sic*] Value." American treaty commissioners followed Duane's advice and dispensed with wampum belts and elaborate speeches. "In their place," writes James Merrell, they "substituted blunt talk and a habit of driving each article home by pointing a finger at the assembled natives." Moreover, the federal government was just one player in the competition, as individual states, land companies, and speculators scrambled for Indian lands.

Iroquois delegates at Fort Stanwix tried to argue for the Ohio River as the boundary to Indian lands, but the American commissioners would have none of it. "You are a subdued people," they lectured the delegates. "We are at peace with all but *you; you* now stand out *alone* against our *whole* force." Lest the Indians miss the point, American troops backed up the commissioners. At Fort McIntosh, when chiefs of the Wyandots, Chippewas, Delawares, and Ottawas said they regarded the lands transferred by Britain to the United States as still rightfully belonging to them, the American commissioners answered them "in a high tone," and reminded them they were a defeated people. At Fort Finney, when Shawnees balked at the American terms and refused to provide hostages, one of the American commissioners picked up the wampum belt they gave him, "dashed it on the table," and told them to accept the terms or face the consequences.

Indian representation at these treaties was partial at best, and the Americans exploited and aggravated intratribal divisions. Six Nations delegates who returned home from Fort Stanwix were denounced by their own people, and the Six Nations in council at Buffalo Creek refused to ratify a treaty made under such duress. Western Indians were furious at the Six Nations for making a treaty without consulting them. In 1785, the Seneca chief Cornplanter delivered up his copy of the articles of peace concluded at Fort Stanwix, saying they had become "burdensome." Chiefs who made cessions lost face with their people. Captain Pipe, who lost his place to other Delaware war captains in 1782, tried to regain standing by acting as a mediating chief rather than a warrior, and signed the Treaty of Fort McIntosh, which only cost him more support. Nevertheless, chiefs had little choice but to make land cessions. Their ability to act as chiefs by backing up their words with the distribution of gifts to their followers had long made them dependent on outsiders. The British had provided them with gifts as allies seeking their support, but the Americans demanded land in return for the few gifts they offered. Some chiefs signed treaties knowing that others would do so if they refused.

"If ever a peace failed to pacify, it was the peace of 1783," observed historian Arthur Whitaker in reference to the South. The end of the Revolution marked the beginning of years of turmoil as the region became an arena of competing national, state, and tribal interests, international intrigues, land speculation, and personal ambitions. The principal result of the war in the southern backcountry was to transfer control of a vast frontier from the Indians and their British allies and associates to the Whigs and the new men who emerged to lead them in the course of the Revolution. Until the southern states yielded their claims to western lands, the federal government had no lands to sell in the South and simply hoped to prevent full-scale Indian war. North Carolina did not cede its western land claims to Congress until 1789; Georgia not until 1802. These states, plus the "state" of Franklin, made their own treaties with the Indians, generally refused to cooperate with the federal government in its attempts to implement a coherent Indian policy in the region, and sometimes tried to sabotage federal treaty-making efforts. Meanwhile, the aggressions of Carolinian and Georgian backcountry settlers threatened to embroil the whole frontier in conflict. The United States negotiated the Treaties of Hopewell, with the Cherokees in late 1785 and with the Choctaws and Chickasaws in January 1786. The treaties confirmed tribal boundaries but did little to preserve them. Cherokee leaders appealed for assistance to Patrick Henry of Virginia in 1789: "We are so Distrest by the No. Carolina People that it seems Like we sho'ld soon become no People. They have got all our Land from us. We have hardly as much as we can stand on, and they seem to want that little worse than the Rest."

The Creeks emerged from the Revolution with their lands relatively intact, but Georgia demanded all the lands between the Oconee and Ocmulgee rivers as war damages. At the Treaty of Augusta in November 1783, a handful of compliant Creek chiefs, primarily from the neutral and pro-American groups in the nation, led by Hopoithle Mico (the Tame King) of Tallassee and Cussita Mico (the Fat King) of Cussita ceded roughly eight hundred square miles to Georgia. McGillivray and the rest of the Creeks condemned the treaty, and in June 1784 signed the Treaty of Pensacola, placing themselves under Spanish protection. The Creeks entered the postrevolutionary era further divided into bitter factions. Factionalism had helped them avoid exclusive dependence on one ally throughout much of the eighteenth century and had secured them multiple outlets for trade. But as European allies began to fall away after the Revolution, McGillivray recognized that without Spanish support, "we may be forced to purchase a Shameful peace & barter our Country for a precarious Security." Now factionalism became dangerously dysfunctional, and the conflict between McGillivray and Hopoithle Mico augured the civil strife of 1813.

Treaties made over the opposition of the majority of the tribes left boundaries in dispute. Indians punished intruders whom the United States government failed to keep off their lands, and settlers retaliated. Even where there was no conflict, the fiction that all Indians had fought for the British in the Revolution justified massive dispossession of Native Americans in the early republic, whatever their role in the war. Catawbas derived maximum mileage from their revolutionary services, and by wrapping themselves in the flag used their record of service in the patriot cause "to carve a niche for themselves in the social landscape of the Carolina piedmont." However, they were an exception. Whereas other revolutionary veterans were granted land bounties, Indian veterans lost land. The Mashantucket Pequots served and suffered in the patriot cause, but in 1785 they were complaining to the government of Connecticut that "our Tribe find ourselves Interrupted in the Possession of our Lands by your People round about Cutting & Destroying our Timber & Crowding their Improvements in upon our Lands." Neighboring Mohegans found that both "white strangers & foreign Indians" encroached on their land and sold their timber from under them in defiance of state laws. In Massachusetts, Indians had fought and bled alongside the colonists in their struggle for liberty, but in 1788 the state reinstituted its guardian system for Indians, and deprived Mashpee of its right of self-government by establishing an all-white board of overseers. The Penobscots and Passamaquoddies found their Maine hunting territories invaded by their former allies. Passamaquoddies appealed for justice to Congress, "that we may Enjoy our Privileges which we have been fighting for as other Americans," but Congress dismissed John Allan from his role as superintendent of eastern Indians, and Massachusetts resumed its pursuit of Indian lands in Maine. The state stripped the Penobscots and Passamaquoddies of most of their land in a series of post-Revolution treaties. New England Indians who had moved to Oneida country only to be driven back by the war, and "who for their Fidelity and Attachment to the American Cause, have suffered the Loss of all things," petitioned the Connecticut Assembly for relief at the war's end.

The Oneidas had suffered mightily in the American cause during the war. General Philip Schuyler had assured them during the Revolution that "sooner should a fond mother forget her only son than we shall forget you." Once they had helped the Americans win independence, the Oneidas would "then partake of every Blessing we enjoy and united with a free people your Liberty and prosperity will be safe." But the Oneidas fared little better than their New England friends or their Cayuga and Seneca relatives in the postrevolutionary land grabbing conducted by the federal government, New York State, and individual land companies. Schuyler interceded on their behalf, and Congress guaranteed the territorial integrity of their Oneida and Tuscarora allies at the Treaty of Fort Stanwix, a guarantee the United States confirmed at Fort Harmar in 1789, and at Canandaigua and Oneida in 1794. But paper commitments gave little protection. In 1794, the government absolved its obligations to the Oneidas with an award of $5,000, an annuity of $4,500, and promises to build a sawmill, a gristmill, and a church. The State of New York meanwhile negotiated a string of treaties, illegal under the Indian Trade and Non-Intercourse Act of 1790, that by 1838 had robbed the Oneidas of their entire homeland. The bitter divisions the Revolution produced within the Oneidas were "not yet forgotten" by 1796.

As many Revolutionary War veterans, often illiterate, signed away their land grants for a pittance to more powerful and prosperous citizens of the new nation, so too Indian veterans, who had fought to win the United States's independence, often found themselves reduced to selling off land simply to survive. Simon Joy Jay, or Choychoy, a Mohegan who was wounded in the Revolution, "fighting for the Country," had to sell his land to support himself in old age and infirmity. The widow of Indian Daniel Cyrus, a white woman named Sarah, who lost two sons in the war, likewise had to sell her land to support herself in old age. Abenaki Indian patriots in Vermont fell on equally hard times.

The widows of men from Mashpee who had given their lives in the struggle for independence were forced to look outside their communities for husbands. By 1793, Indian towns like Mashpee included not only Africans and Anglo-Americans, but also Germans who had served in the war as mercenaries and had since married into the community and were raising families.

Many Indian peoples clung to their ancestral lands, even where those lands had been in the middle of war zones. Some Mohawk families returned and remained in their Fort Hunter and Canajoharie homes until the 1790s. But most Mohawks found new homes at Grand River or the Bay of Quinté. The peace that ended the Revolution did not end the vast movement of people that scattered Loyalists and African Americans across the globe and displaced Indian populations throughout North America. The war's end found Indian refugees at Niagara, Schenectady, Detroit, Saint Louis, Saint Augustine, and Pensacola, and the peace continued to dislocate thousands of Indians. Indian peoples pressured by Anglo-American expansion continued, as they had in the past and would in the future, to seek refuge in Canada. The Moravians established a new Delaware mission village at Moraviantown on the Thames River. Indian Loyalists moved to new homes at Grand River and the Bay of Quinté in Ontario rather than return to homelands engulfed by the Americans. By the end of the Revolution, Shawnees who remained in Ohio were crowded into the northwestern reaches of their territory. In time they joined other Indians in creating a multitribal, multivillage world centered on the Glaize. There some two thousand people lived around three Shawnee towns, two Delaware towns, a Miami town, and British-French trading communities, along with some Nanticokes, Mingoes, and Chickamauga Cherokees. Stockbridge Indians, unable to secure relief from their former allies after the Revolution, joined other Christian Indians from New England in moving to lands set aside for them by the Oneidas in New York, joining "People of many Nations" at New Stockbridge. Hundreds of refugee Indians drifted west of the Mississippi and requested permission to settle in Spanish territory. Abenaki Indians, dispersed by previous wars from northern New England into the Ohio Valley, turned up in Arkansas and Missouri in the decade after the Revolution, testimony to the continuing dislocation of Indian communities that the conflict occasioned in eastern North America. The migrations of Indian peoples across the Mississippi generated repercussions on the plains and threatened to disturb "the tranquility of the Interior Provinces of New Spain."

For American Indians, the new republic was still very much a revolutionary world in which their struggles continued with little abatement. For many Indian peoples, the Revolution was one phase of a "Twenty Years' War" that continued at least until the Treaty of Greenville in 1795. Before it was over, a whole generation had grown up knowing little but war. The Indians' war of independence went on until 1795, 1815, and beyond, and it took many forms, as Indians mounted "spirited resistance" and "sacred revolts." Confronted with renewed pressures and aggressions, spurred on by the murder of mediation chiefs like Moluntha and Old Tassel, and encouraged by the presence of Britons and Spaniards waiting in the wings for the experiment in republicanism to fail, many of the tribes renewed their confederacies. Shawnees, Chickamaugas, and Creeks carried war belts throughout the eastern woodlands; Indian ambassadors traveled from Detroit to Saint Augustine and back, urging united resistance. Warriors from a host of tribes continued a war of independence that was multitribal in character. In a council held at the mouth of the Detroit River in November and December 1786, delegates from the Five Nations, as well as Hurons, Delawares, Shawnees, Ottawas, Chippewas,

Potawatomis, Miamis, Cherokees, and Wabash allies, sent a speech to the United States from the "United Indian Nations," declaring invalid all treaties made without the unanimous consent of the tribes. Led by capable chiefs who had risen to prominence during the Revolution—Joseph Brant, Little Turtle, Buckongahelas, Blue Jacket, Dragging Canoe, and McGillivray—revived Indian confederacies continued the wars for their lands and cultures into the 1790s and exposed the American theory of conquest for the fiction it was.

Americans in the new republic, like their British and Spanish rivals, were often hard-pressed to keep up with the political changes the Revolution generated in Indian country, as new communities emerged, new power blocs developed, and new players called different tunes. "Tribes" ceased to be the functioning unit of Indian politics and diplomacy, if they ever had been. Young warriors continued the war from multitribal communities. "Banditti of several tribes find asylum in the Lower Towns of the Cherokees," Arthur Campbell reported to George Washington; Cherokees removed to new homes with the Creeks, a nation that "seems always to have been the receptacle for all distressed Tribes," said the Cherokee Turtle at Home, who had joined the Chickamauga resistance and had spent so much time in Shawnee country that he spoke Shawnee fluently.

Not until the mid-1790s did the Indian war for independence as waged by these warriors come to an end. General Josiah Harmar and General Arthur St. Clair met with defeat and disaster in their campaigns against the northwestern confederacy. Only in 1794 did the Americans inflict a telling victory on the tribes at Fallen Timbers and get at the extensive cornfields on the Auglaize and Maumee rivers, which had sustained the Indian war effort for years. Anthony Wayne described this as "the grand emporium of the hostile Indians of the West," and claimed he had never seen "such immense fields of corn, in any part of America, from Canada to Florida." Defeated in battle and abandoned by the British, the Indians could only watch as Wayne's troops put the area to the torch. A dozen years after the end of the Revolution, the American strategy of burning Indian food supplies finally ended the Indians' war for independence. Before the war, said Little Turtle to the French scientist Constantin-Francois de Volney several years later, "We raised corn like the whites. But now we are poor hunted deer." Cherokees had voiced similar sentiments after the Revolution and the devastation of their crops: "We are now like wolves, ranging about the woods to get something to eat."

By 1795 the war for Ohio was lost. Little Turtle and others who had been on the forefront of resistance joined the old chiefs in making peace at the Treaty of Greenville, and ceded most of Ohio to the United States. That same year, the Treaty of San Lorenzo effectively deprived southern Indians of Spanish support in their resistance to American expansion.

In the Northwest Ordinance of 1787, the United States had committed itself to expansion while simultaneously treating Indian people with "the utmost good faith." Men like Henry Knox and Thomas Jefferson wrestled with the dilemma of how to take Indian lands and still act with "justice and humanity." With their victory finally secured and Indians no longer a major military threat, Americans finally resolved the dilemma inherent in their belief that United States Indian policy could combine "expansion with honor." Since too much land encouraged idleness and presented an obstacle to "civilization," and Indian people could survive in the new nation only by becoming "civilized," the United States would deprive them of their lands for their own good. Not surprisingly, the good intentions of a few men became lost amid the pressure to rid the Indians of their lands.

Burned villages and crops, murdered chiefs, divided councils and civil wars, migrations, towns and forts choked with refugees, economic disruption, breaking of ancient traditions, losses in battle and to disease and hunger, betrayal to their enemies, all made the American Revolution one of the darkest periods in American Indian history. The emergence of the independent United States as the ultimate victor from a long contest of imperial powers reduced Indians to further dependence and pushed them into further dark ages. Two Mohegans, Henry Quaduaquid and Robert Ashpo, petitioning the Connecticut Assembly for relief in 1789, expressed the sentiments and experiences of many Native Americans as the new nation came into being: "The Times are Exceedingly Altr'd, Yea the Times have turn'd everything Upside down." Seneca communities, in Anthony Wallace's words, became "slums in the wilderness," characterized by poverty, loss of confidence in traditional certainties, social pathology, violence, alcoholism, witch fear, and disunity. Cherokees, reeling from the shock of defeat and dispossession, seemed to have lost their place in the world, and the very fabric of their society seemed to be crumbling around them.

And yet, in the kaleidoscopic, "all-change" world of the revolutionary era, there were exceptions and variations. Despite new colors on the map of Florida, political change in Seminole country reflected not new dependence on a foreign power so much as increasing independence from the parent Creek confederacy. While Alexander McGillivray continued traditional Creek policies of playing off competing nations with considerable skill, the Seminoles emerged by the new century as a new player and an unknown quantity in the Indian and international diplomacy of the southeast. Many Indian communities succumbed and some disappeared in the new world produced during the Revolution, but others were in process of formation and asserting their separate identity.

Like the Shawnees who built and rebuilt Chillicothe, Indians adjusted and endured. Contrary to predictions of extinction and assumptions of stasis, Indian communities survived, changed, and were reborn. The Revolutionary War destroyed many Indian communities, but new, increasingly multiethnic, communities—at Niagara, Grand River, Chickamauga, and the Glaize—grew out of the turmoil and played a leading role in the Indian history of the new republic. The black years following the Revolution saw powerful forces of social and religious rejuvenation in Handsome Lake's Longhouse religion among the Iroquois, far-reaching stirrings of cultural assertiveness, political movements like the northwestern Indian confederacy of the 1780s and 1790s, a renascence in Cherokee country, and pan-Indian unity under the leadership of Tecumseh and the Shawnee Prophet in the early years of the new century.

The American Revolution was a disaster for most American Indians, and the turmoil it generated in Indian country continued long after 1783. But by the end of the eighteenth century, Indian peoples had had plenty of experience suffering and surviving disasters. They responded to this one as they had to others and set about rebuilding what they could of their world. But now they were rebuilding on quicksand, for the new America had no room for Indians and their world.

The Right to a Name: The Narragansett People and Rhode Island Officials in the Revolutionary Era

RUTH WALLIS HERNDON AND
ELLA WILCOX SEKATAU (Narragansett)

In 1675, in the heat of a regional war with native peoples, New England colonists killed hundreds of the Narragansett, uninvolved in the war at that point, in an unprovoked attack on one of their winter camps located in the Great Swamp in South Kingstown, Rhode Island. Two hundred years later, in 1880, the Rhode Island state legislature, without federal approval, declared the Narragansett people "extinct" and illegally took away the tribal status of people who still called themselves by that name.

In the centuries between these notorious events, generations of the Narragansett faced the choice of staying on their native land, surrounded by non-Indians, or migrating to western land less settled by Europeans. Many of these native people, deeply alienated by the religious beliefs and cultural practices of the Europeans, left, mainly for Massachusetts, New York, and Wisconsin. Others stayed on ancestral lands; oral history tells us that they continued their tribal affairs and government, held frequent meetings, kept track of their heritage and lineage, and kept alive the religion, language, and customs of the people.

Preserving Narragansett culture on Narragansett land was an arduous task initially. Within the first decades of English colonization, Narragansett leaders realized what were the goals of these newly arrived people. The colonists' attitudes toward land clashed radically with the practices of native people. Traditional ways of gardening and hunting proved impossible for the Narragansett after English settlers had altered the ecosystem by dividing the land into private tracts for individual use; by prosecuting trespassers; by cutting down forests, constructing fences, and otherwise helping to extinguish game; and by introducing free-ranging livestock. The Rhode Island government's protective act to set apart sixty-four square miles of land as a Narragansett reservation in 1709 signaled that native people could no longer move freely over their ancestral territory and observe the cultural practice of having summer and permanent residences in different places. During the eighteenth century, moreover, the reserved area shrank as non-Narragansett people acquired tracts through sale, theft, and gifts.

The Narragansett living on the reservation could not always avoid contact with Rhode Island colonists; some were pulled into the European American world by the economic necessity of working as day laborers in nearby towns. Others left the reservation and drifted away, physically and spiritually, from the paths of the elders. Some converted to Christianity. Some married non-Indians and merged into the cultures of European and African Americans. Some, prisoners at the end of the 1675–76 conflict or trapped in debt to Rhode Islanders, became bound servants to and thus members of English households. Oral tradition tells us that many native

Ruth Wallis Herndon and Ella Wilcox Sekatau, "The Right to a Name: The Narragansett People and Rhode Island Officials in the Revolutionary Era." *Ethnohistory* 44(3) (Summer 1997), 434–455. Copyright © 1997, American Society for Ethnohistory. All rights reserved. Reprinted by permission of Duke University Press.

family and clan names disappeared as local officials attached English names to Narragansett people who were indebted or bound to colonists.

So things seemed to outsiders. But tribal history passed down orally from generation to generation informs us that hardship and oppression strengthened the resolve of many Narragansett to maintain traditional ways. The majority of the Narragansett on or around the reservation did not convert to Christianity, and those who did usually moved away from Rhode Island. Many native people whom outsiders counted as converts were actually struggling to coexist with the English. These Narragansett presented themselves in ways that won the approval of outside observers and authorities, but in their own confines they continued to practice the cultural ways of the ancients. Not until the illegal detribalization of 1880 did true conversions begin in some Narragansett families.

Historians have studied the general outline of Narragansett history, although not often from the native point of view, from 1675 to 1880, but little has been written about the details of relationships between native people and Rhode Islanders during those two centuries. This essay analyzes interactions between the Narragansett people and local Rhode Island officials in the latter half of the eighteenth century, a fifty-year period midway between the Great Swamp massacre and illegal detribalization. We investigate how the officials viewed the Narragansett and how the Narragansett viewed the officials.

By "Narragansett" we mean native people who lived on ancestral Narragansett land in what is now called Rhode Island. In the view of some tribal members, Narragansett tribal boundaries encompassed all of what is now Rhode Island and much more land inhabited by all the subtribal divisions and tribute tribes dwelling in what became parts of Massachusetts, Connecticut, New Hampshire, Vermont, and a small area of southeastern Maine. Since the written records rarely refer to the "Narragansett"—only to "Indians" or "mustees"—it is impossible to be sure that every native person in the record was indeed of the Narragansett except where the name coincides with tribal genealogies. Some native people in the documents may have been members of neighboring tribes. But since fourteen of the towns under study were established directly on Narragansett land and the fifteenth (Warren) bordered it, we assume that the majority of native people in the record were of Narragansett heritage.

We also include in this study people described in the record as "mustees." Rhode Island town records provide ample evidence that local officials used this term to refer to people of native ancestry. For example, town clerks described as "mustee" the children of "Indian" women Elizabeth Broadfoot, Moll Pero, Deborah Anthony, and Lydia Rodman. Contemporaries recognized "mustee" people as native, at least in part; so do we.

Native people lived among colonists in every Rhode Island town in the eighteenth century, when local officials thought of themselves as "fathers of the towns." Just as they ruled over their own households, so these leaders headed a civic "family" as well. Theoretically, all of a town's inhabitants came under their patriarchal authority, and thus Narragansett people living away from the reservation had to deal with them from time to time.

Even the Narragansett living on the reservation and under tribal government could not avoid contact with town magistrates. Colonial officials had long tried to have a say in how the Narragansett governed themselves, a habit that local officials also adopted. During the late 1700s, when the sachemship was replaced by the Indian council that formerly had governed the Narragansett people under the sachem's leadership since time immemorial, officials from Charlestown, which completely surrounded the shrinking Narragansett reservation, sometimes attempted to influence tribal affairs. Town records show that tribal council members and town councilmen met and talked on a number of occasions, but always at the convenience of the latter.

How did Narragansett people and local officials view each other? Town leaders dealt with the Narragansett most often as "the poor," in need of official oversight, and thus reinforced the dispossessed and demeaned status of Indians. Further, and just as hurtful to native people in the long run, town officials stopped identifying native people as "Indian" in the written record and began designating them as "Negro" or "black," thus committing a form of documentary genocide against them. Yet Narragansett people often maintained a sense of their own identity, understood that the English system of government sometimes conflicted with their interests, and at times manipulated that system to their advantage.

Our argument rests upon two kinds of sources: the oral history of the Narragansett people and the written records of fifteen Rhode Island towns. Ella Sekatau is the source of Narragansett oral history. She has been learning Narragansett history, language, religion, and medicine from her parents, grandparents, and tribal elders since her birth, when she was charged with the responsibility of ensuring her people's continuity. Further, she has acted in official capacities for the Narragansett people since the 1970s, when the tribal governing body appointed her as an ethnohistorian and the tribe approved her as a medicine woman (a responsibility inherited through her father's line). Like the majority of present-day Narragansett, she traces her genealogy to the sachems of the sixteenth and early seventeenth centuries. During the intervening centuries Narragansett elders have trained young people to maintain the tribe's unwritten history through oral tradition. Now in her late sixties, Sekatau trains young people of the tribe and educates outsiders about Narragansett history through presentations in classrooms and other public forums. In this essay, we use the terms *oral history* and *oral tradition* to refer to the knowledge that she embodies, passed down to her and through her to others.

Ruth Herndon has investigated the archival sources; town meeting minutes, town council minutes, vital statistics, and probate documents for Charlestown, Cumberland, East Greenwich, Exeter, Glocester, Hopkinton, Jamestown, Middletown, New Shoreham, Providence, Richmond, South Kingstown, Tiverton, Warren, and Warwick. The population of these towns, which constituted about half of Rhode Island's population in 1770, fairly represents the wealth, age, economic orientation, and geographic location of the colony's thirty late-eighteenth-century towns.

Both oral and archival sources have their problems. Narrators have probably introduced some changes in the oral history entrusted from one Narragansett memory to another over two hundred years, but the documentary sources also reflect mediation, since town clerks served as gatekeepers who decided what material should be included in the historical record and in what form. Internal evidence from rough drafts and final copies of town records reveals that clerks edited out of the official version any matters and any people they considered "unimportant."

We need both sources to reconstruct the relations between Narragansett people and Rhode Island leaders in the eighteenth century, and we find the oral history of the Narragansett people particularly important as a corrective to the archival sources. Narragansett oral traditional and unwritten laws and lore challenge the records of the official gatekeepers in many respects, and they challenge us to hear voices long ignored and suppressed. Since native people were half of the equation in interactions between Indians and English colonists, we had better take the word of the former as seriously as we have taken that of the latter.

Narragansett People as "the Poor of the Town"

Narragansett people who lived away from the reserved lands and among colonists were legal inhabitants of the towns where they were born. As such, they had certain obligations (e.g., paying taxes) and certain rights (e.g., access to poor relief). But tax revenues were rare, and no native people appear in the probate records as owners of lavish estates. Most Narragansett existed on the economic margins of colonial society. Stripped of their ancestral lands, they were seen as people without property in a society that measured worth by ownership of real estate.

Narragansett people seldom participated in English-style private landowner-ship in the eighteenth century. A few wrote wills that disposed of their property in accordance with colonial probate law. In 1781, for example, Narragansett man James Niles left a will that satisfied the Charlestown council acting as a court of probate on his estate. In 1788 Joseph Cozens, also of Charlestown, left his "Lands" to his daughters Sarah and Mary, stipulating that the property "be Equally Divided between them in Quantity & Quality." But Cozens combined English and Narra-gansett customs: he appointed a non-Indian as his sole executor, but in his will he appealed to "my indian Brethren" to see that his daughters "have [the Land] & Enjoy it according to our Indian custom."

If wills were rare, guardianships were nonexistent. In eighteenth-century Rhode Island, local officials routinely placed minor children under guardianship when their fathers died, ensuring that adults experienced in such matters would manage the property until the children reached adulthood. But of 1,504 guardian-ships enacted by local Rhode Island officials between 1750 and 1800, none was on behalf of a child identified as an Indian. Apparently, local officials did not extend the protection of guardianship to Narragansett people with property.

From the official point of view, this was only logical. Most native people accu-mulated only meager estates. When Thomas Bartlet of Hopkinton died in 1759, his outstanding debts totaled almost £174; not surprisingly, the officials who inven-toried his estate valued his possessions at little more than £174, leaving a mere 8s. 5d. for his heirs. When Betty Sawnos died of smallpox in Exeter in 1760, an inven-tory of her property revealed only some clothing and a pair of shoes. When Tent Anthony was rendered helpless by a stroke in 1767, the Jamestown town leaders inventoried her goods before taking control of her estate; they valued her posses-sions at less than £24—about $3.00 in silver.

What officials saw as a lack of property may simply have been evidence of a traditional native life unencumbered by material objects. Oral tradition tells us that ownership and accumulation of goods, in personal property and also in real estate, were foreign concepts to the Narragansett. To this day, members of the tribe have "give-away celebrations" to avoid building up large amounts of material things.

Narragansett people who wrote wills very likely did not attach the same significance to them that Rhode Island officials did; instead they intended that their children should enjoy and use an area as long as they treated it with respect and honor, in accordance with traditional Narragansett belief (still adhered to by the tribe). Human beings do not own the Earth Mother; she owns them.

From the viewpoint of Rhode Island officials, however, a lack of property meant vulnerability to debt and bondage. A number of native people appear in the records as someone else's "property" by virtue of bound service. In 1764, when Capt. Benjamin Sheffield of Jamestown died, he left behind, among his chattels, "an Indian Woman Slave called Philis." Five years later Jamestown officials inventoried Robert Hull's estate, which included "1 Mustee boy named Tavin," a slave valued at £23. In a not untypical labor contract, Alice Arnold bound herself to Dr. Jabez Bowen of Providence for five years to work off a debt of £150; she had no property at all to offer in payment.

People without property and separated from the native community of support needed public assistance in times of crisis, when town leaders most frequently interacted with them. In New England, poor relief was administered locally; town officials arranged for the support of aged, ill, or helpless inhabitants, including native people. When Hannah Broadfoot of East Greenwich became too old and blind to care for herself, her town provided "all Nessarys [*sic*] of Life at the Cheapest Lay." Rose Davids, "a blind squaw," was supported by Tiverton. When Eunice Yocake was "badly hurt" and "in a helpless Condition," South Kingstown councilmen ordered the overseer to "go immediately & take proper Care of sd. Indian in order that She may not suffer."

For native people, poor relief often came too late. Jamestown did not see to Sarah Fitten's needs prior to her death in 1751, although it did pay for her coffin and burial. In the winter of 1767–68 the Tiverton councilmen reimbursed the inhabitants who had cared for two native women during their final illnesses—and then buried them. When Dorcas Fry died in East Greenwich in 1780, the town underwrote the cost of burying her "in a Decent Manner."

As these examples suggest, women dominate the records of poor relief granted to native people, in part because local officials encountered more native women than native men. Oral tradition relates that women lived among colonists more often than men did; they moved more easily between the two worlds. Narragansett men, in contrast, were reluctant to be identified by officials; they adopted aliases and took to the woods, unwilling to risk servitude. Anecdotal evidence in the archival sources suggests that Indian men suffered higher mortality because of their involvement in military and maritime occupations, and Narragansett oral history tells us that women always outnumbered men; until recently, female babies survived more often than male babies. It is not surprising, then, that native women appear in the records more often than native men, especially as they approach old age.

There may be more behind the poor relief figures. The overrepresentation of women suggests also that native women were more likely than native men to draw official attention. Local leaders, steeped in traditions of male responsibility, probably were more disposed to "see" needy women than needy men. Conversely, women familiar with the conventions of patriarchal hierarchies probably were more apt than men to seek assistance from authorities. In any case, local officials opened the town treasury to native women far more often than to native men.

Native children seldom appear as recipients of poor relief, for a very good reason: most needy children were bound out as indentured servants to colonial masters. This was a common practice in eighteenth-century New England; town "fathers," acting in the stead of natural parents, placed poor and/or orphaned children of all races in more prosperous households under contracts that obligated the children to live with and work for their masters until adulthood. Town officials did not hesitate to remove a child from birth parents and thus break up a family; they considered it better to take the child from an "improper" situation than to support its family with poor relief. This practice saved the town the cost of raising the child on welfare, and some "respectable" family gained the labor of another household member.

If the master fulfilled the contract, the servant child received more than "suitable" food, clothing, and shelter; at the end of the term of indenture, the young adult was equipped with a rudimentary education (reading and writing) and training in some marketable skill. Job Smith contracted to teach Peter Norton, "a Poor Mustee Boy," the cooper's trade, but he also promised that Norton would learn to read, write, and "keep common Book Accounts." Town leaders expected indentured servitude to prepare poor children for independent adulthood. Whether or not masters always fulfilled their obligations to the children is another question. Oral history tells us that many native people emerged from indenture without literacy skills.

From the child's point of view, indentured servitude was only as good as the master or mistress. Bonds of real affection and support formed between the servant and the master's family in some cases. In other cases, servitude was only slightly disguised slavery; the town records document servants "absconding" from their masters and masters being charged with abusing their servants.

Native children appear frequently in the public indentures of the towns under review for the latter half of the eighteenth century: ninety-eight contracts name a child identified as "Indian" or "mustee" (see Table 1). Boys were indentured twice as often as girls, but both boys and girls could expect a dozen or more years of servitude. The children averaged eight years old at the beginning of the contracts, but some were considerably younger. One Indian boy named John entered bound service when he was "4 years 4 months & 6 days old"; another, also named John, was only twenty-one months old. Both youngsters were obligated until they were twenty-four

---

Table 1. Public indentures of children in Rhode Island, 1750–1800

	NATIVE		ALL	
Total indentures	98		712	
Indentures of girls	30	(30.6%)	227	(31.9%)
Indentures of boys	64	(65.3%)	461	(64.7%)
Child's sex unknown	4	(4.1%)	24	(3.4%)
Average age at contract	8.0		7.6	
Average age at freedom, male	21.7		21.0 (whites)	
Average age at freedom, female	19.1		18.0 (whites)	

years old, but the average "freedom" age for native children was about twenty-two years for boys and nineteen years for girls, higher than for white children.

By placing poor children as bound servants and supplying care for helpless adults, local officials met their obligation to the needy members of their town family. But public charity did not cover everyone; towns were required to support only their own legal inhabitants. Local officials invested considerable time in determining the legal settlement of "transient" residents; if transients ever needed public assistance, town leaders would compel them, by means of "warnout order" or "removal order," to return to their hometowns, where they were entitled to poor relief. Since transient people often had lived within a town for years, being warned out meant the loss of homes, jobs, and neighbors and the total disruption of their lives. Sarah Greene had lived in Providence "for 24 Years past" and Deborah Church for "near Twenty-five Years" when the councilmen ordered these two native women back to the towns where they had been indentured servants in their youth.

For warned-out transients, the trip back to a "hometown" emphasized their powerlessness. Those who were too ill or weak to leave on their own were "removed" by the town sergeant or his constables. At the end of this unwelcome journey, other town officials took over the management of their lives. The Providence town sergeant was ordered to take transient Isabel Hope to South Kingstown "by the most direct way" and to put her in the care of the overseers of the poor there. Primus Thompson, a sailor crippled by a wharf accident in Jamestown, was carried by horse and sled across the frozen Rhode Island countryside to Westerly, where the overseer of the poor boarded him out. When Warwick and Jamestown councilmen squabbled over which town had responsibility for Mary Pisquish, the poor woman was transported several times between the homes of the overseers in the two towns.

Women were the targets of most of the warnout orders issued to native people. Town leaders throughout Rhode Island kept a close eye on transient women unrepresented by men. Women who did not live in patriarchal households as daughters, wives, and mothers seemed "out of place" to the town fathers, for they did not have male heads present to govern them. Narragansett women especially fell into this trap, since native traditions of household formation did not emphasize the nuclear unit that the English expected. Oral history tells us that native women often migrated between two worlds; they lived for a time in the woods with their mates and other native people; then they moved into Rhode Island towns for another space of time. Such independent women stirred fears of disorder in town officials wedded to their own customs and prompted their close attention.

Indian men contributed to this "problem" (as town leaders saw it) by supporting their families through work as sailors and soldiers, which meant being absent for long periods of time. Such jobs accommodated traditional male roles more easily than others. Unlike most European men, native men were not farmers; archival sources and oral tradition tell us that many Narragansett men provided for their families by hunting and fishing, which required travel and separations. Although Narragansett families had flourished under this way of life for centuries, Rhode Island town leaders believed that absent husbands and fathers left their families vulnerable. Consequently, councilmen stayed alert to what they considered poverty or trouble in these households and were quick to warn out native women to their hometowns. The Jamestown councilmen had become anxious to move Mary

Pisquish because she was "lame & uncapable of supporting herself." Mary Carder, with two small children but no husband present, stirred the Providence councilmen to order this small family removed to Warwick "as soon as may be."

Charlestown councilmen presented a sharp contrast to most local Rhode Island leaders, who stayed busy ordering transient families out of towns where they had settled, placing grieving children as servants among strangers, and supporting elderly people in their last days as boarders in households they did not choose. Charlestown leaders kept their distance from needy Narragansett people, whom they considered the responsibility of tribal members. Only once did these officials act on behalf of a suffering native person—"a Cripple and unable to support himself"—and their action was limited to identifying this man as "one of the Tribe of Indians called Ninegretts Tribe" and notifying the Indian council to take care of him. One other time the councilmen complained that the Narragansett tribe "doth neglect to Support their Poor," suggesting that these leaders were aware of need among native people but were determined to avoid this obligation.

This curious lack of official oversight in Charlestown extended to public indentures of native children; there are none in the town records. This leaves the impression that Charlestown had no Indian inhabitants, that all native people in its vicinity belonged to the reservation tribe on adjoining land. But not so. At one council meeting, Charlestown leaders referred to the Narragansett as the "Tribe of Indians belonging to this Town," and during the 1777 census of men for military fitness, Charlestown officials counted sixty-six "Indians" among the town's adult male inhabitants. Charlestown leaders did not hesitate to claim native men willing to enlist as soldiers and their possessiveness became pronounced when recruits were hard to find in the last years of the Revolutionary War. Then, Charlestown officials took offense because surrounding towns enlisted "several Indians that were Inhabitants of this Town" and complained that the other towns "had no right to inlist them until this Town had inlisted their full Quota." In times of crisis, it seems, local leaders viewed native men as a labor pool for jobs that colonists would not undertake.

Charlestown leaders ignored or recognized native people as official convenience dictated. When native people needed aid, the authorities were blind to their presence, but when townspeople needed bodies to perform dangerous or tedious manual labor, official vision was miraculously restored. In each case, town leaders solved their problems to their own advantage and to the disadvantage of the Narragansett, thus sending a clear message that Indians were disposable people.

Writing the Narragansett off the Record

In October 1793 a Rhode Island physician named John Aldrich brought suit against Narragansett man John Hammer before the Hopkinton justices of the peace. Aldrich wanted payment from Hammer (a matter of three and one-half shillings) for medical care provided the year before. The official warrant for Hammer's arrest described him as a "Black Man" and a "Husbandman," but neither description was accurate. When Hammer appeared before Justice Abram Coon, he asked for a reduction of the charge because of the error in racial designation: "[Hammer] pleads that he is Not [a black man] but that he is an Indian man." When the judge overruled this objection, Hammer pleaded instead that the charge should be reduced because

"Husbandman" was an incorrect description of his livelihood. The judge overruled this second objection as well, and all subsequent paperwork for the case referred to Hammer as both "Black man" and "Husbandman."

John Hammer's remarkable objections reveal that he understood the judicial system sufficiently well to counter the original suit with complaints about the mechanics of his case. Equally remarkable is the struggle revealed in the court papers between a Narragansett man and a European American man over the right to determine a person's racial designation in official documents. The magistrate did not dispute Hammer's identity as an Indian; Aldrich's book account, presented to the court as evidence, detailed his professional services to "John Hammer Indian." But in the magistrate's eyes, Hammer's identity as an Indian did not clash with his official designation as a "Black Man." Coon, who heard Hammer's protests, persisted in retaining the original description of Hammer in the arrest warrant drawn up by Justice David Nichols. To Coon and Nichols, Hammer had been described adequately by a term that signified non-European skin in a general way.

By registering his protest before a magistrate, Hammer forced the record keepers to document a new weapon that local leaders wielded against the Narragansett a century after the Great Swamp massacre. The native people in southern New England had been drastically reduced by war, disease, and outmigration; now those who remained struggled to exist on paper and to retain the rights of freedom, landownership, and state revenues that paper documents alone secured in the European American system.

The Hopkinton justices' decision to describe Hammer as a "Black Man" was no fluke; it was part of a pattern traceable throughout the official documents of Rhode Island's towns. Between 1750 and 1800 "Indians" disappeared from these records. Individual native people were still named in the pages, of course; officials simply called them something besides "Indian."

Early on Rhode Island leaders exhibited their reluctance to acknowledge the name of the people who had welcomed Europeans to this part of North America: the town records contain only rare references to "Narragansett." After the war of 1675–76 colonists found even more reason to rely on general terms such as *Indian* and *natives,* since Narragansett people sometimes intermarried with neighboring tribes. But in the late 1700s official record keepers made an even greater leap in racial designations. By 1800 the town records contain only scattered references to "Indians"; instead, "Negroes" and "blacks" fill the pages.

This redesignation of subjugated people had antecedents on the other side of the Atlantic. The first European slave dealers to the west coast of Africa often erased the heritage of the native people they purchased there and sold elsewhere. Seldom did the European sellers or buyers know what kingdoms, states, tribes, or villages these men, women, and children left behind. The Europeans lumped them all together under the umbrella designation *Negro,* which means "black" in Portuguese and Spanish. In eighteenth-century Rhode Island, local leaders stretched this designation to cover not only the people among them who had been torn from their African homeland but also the Narragansett among them who had been pushed off their native land.

New England officials made liberal use of the term *mustee* as a first step in transforming "Indians" into "Negroes." In the latter half of the eighteenth century town clerks used *mustee* most frequently to describe children bound out in indentures. Where clerks record the parentage of these children, it is always the mother who is identified as Indian. But what of the father? The use of *mustee* indicates that officials considered the child to have a non-Indian father, even though no details about the father are provided. The implications of this designation are enormous. In the tribes of southern New England a child was a member of the mother's clan and tribe, regardless of who the father was. But in the colonial world, inheritance came through the father. By denying "mustee" children an "Indian" father, officials prepared the ground for denying these children any rights they might later claim as descendants of Narragansett or other native fathers.

Thus officials transformed Indians into "mustees" and then into "Negroes" and "blacks." The labels are applied so haphazardly in the record that the changes are easy to overlook. They would have passed undetected if we had assumed that a clerk used the same racial designation each time he referred to a particular individual. But he did not. The East Greenwich town clerk described Benjamin Austin as an "Indian" in 1767 but as "a Malatoo Fellow" in 1768. Sarah Hill was an "Indian or Mustee Woman" to the Providence clerk in 1784, but he recast her as a "Negro" in 1791. Harriet (given no last name) was first described as "an Indian" by the Jamestown clerk in 1788 and five months later as "a Molato girl." Mary Carder appears as an "Indian" in the Warwick town records in 1775 but as a "Negro" in 1784. From 1780 on a certain ambiguity appears in the record as clerks replace their previously clear descriptions of native people with unclear ones. In Providence, Susannah Tripp was "a Molatto or Indian Woman," Eber Hopkins "a Mustee or Mulatto Man," and an unnamed stranger "a Negro, Indian or Molatto Woman." In East Greenwich, Dorcas Fry was "an Indian or Negro Woman," and in Warwick three-year-old Lucy Spywood was "a molatto, or Mustee Child."

Although specific examples provide the clearest evidence of the shift in racial designations, there are other ways to document it. One is to trace the racial designations of people warned out of Rhode Island towns between 1750 and 1800. People identified as "Indian" constituted 2.5 percent of this group; however, over two-thirds of these warnouts occurred before 1776. Thereafter the number of "Indians" dropped off sharply, and only two persons warned out after 1787 were described as "Indian" or "mustee." Warnout statistics for "Negro," "mulatto," and "black" people show the opposite trend. Those so identified accounted for about 10 percent of all warnout orders, the great majority of them after 1775 (see Table 2).

The same trend occurs in public indentures. Of all indentures binding out minors, 14 percent were for children identified as "Indian" or "mustee." But the great majority, 78 percent, were arranged between 1750 and 1775. The number of contracts affecting native children dwindled after the mid-1770s, and none were recorded after 1795. The opposite is true for children identified as "Negro," "mulatto," or "black." Only a handful of contracts for them were recorded before 1776; then the number surged, reaching a peak in the 1790s (see Table 3).

That "Indians" pepper the town records before the Revolution and "Negroes" and "blacks" afterward strikes us as suspect. Of course, unusual forces were at work during the Revolutionary era. The increase in African American transients may be due in part to an increase in mobility, thanks to manumission fervor during the war and gradual emancipation laws of the 1780s. The increase in African American

Table 2.   Warnouts of non-European people from Rhode Island towns, 1750–1800

	NATIVE	AFRICAN AMERICAN
Warnouts	48	184
1750–75	33 (68.8%)	22 (12.0%)
1776–1800	15 (31.2%)	162 (88.0%)

Note: Between 1750 and 1800, 1,913 people were warned out. Of that total, 48 (2.5 percent) were designated Indian and 184 (9.6 percent) were designated African American.

indentures may reflect a change in European American tactics of controlling black labor by indentured servitude rather than by slavery. But those dynamics cannot explain the *disappearance* of native people from the ranks of transients and indentured children. The evidence points to the deliberate redesignation of native people as Negro or black as officials replaced cultural description with physical description.

Narragansett Identity

The Narragansett were keenly aware of the pressure to lose their Indianness. Then, and for generations afterward, oral history tells us, they expressed hatred for the terms *mulatto* and *mustee,* which implied the loss of tribal distinctiveness. Some grew to hate white people for grouping Indians and Africans together without regard for their heritage, and some grew to hate the latter as well, for being the group that the Narragansett were conflated with. That hatred surfaced at "crying rocks" and unmarked graves, where some native mothers abandoned babies fathered by non-Indians. Traditionally, the Narragansett had used these sites to abandon babies born with physical disabilities. After contact with Europeans and Africans, some Narragansett considered children fathered by non-Indians imperfect and rejected them instead of incorporating them into the tribe. Other women found a less grim alternative by abandoning children in the care of non-Indians. Now and then colonial householders complained that native women had "left" them little children and disappeared. Ironically, the complainers were willing to take care of the children as long as officials enacted indentures that bound the youngsters until adulthood. The children that Narragansett mothers grieved over thus became a labor supply for the colonists.

A strong Narragansett identity sometimes surfaced in the town records, occasionally in phrases that the Narragansett used to describe their native heritage. Delight Robbins informed the Providence councilmen that her father was "one of the Native Inhabitants of the said Charlestown." Mary Fowler told the South Kingstown officials that "her Mother was one of the Tribe of the Indians in Charlestown." She also followed native customs: she had lived with James Fowler "for about thirty Years & had Ten Children by him," but she had not married him "in the Manner white People are married in these parts." Similarly, her daughter Mary Champlin had lived with John Champlin for eleven years and had six children by him "but never was Married to him according to the form Used by the

Table 3. Public indentures of non-European children in Rhode Island, 1750–1800

	NATIVE	AFRICAN AMERICAN
Total contracts	98	74
1750–75	76 (77.6%)	15 (20.3%)
1776–1800	22 (22.4%)	59 (79.7%)

White People in these parts." (These women had very likely married their spouses in traditional native ceremonies. Such weddings were and still are accepted as valid under federal law.)

Native people not only identified themselves and each other but sought each other's company. Some families stayed together well after their children reached maturity. Mary Fowler and Mary Champlin (and their children) were living together in South Kingstown when they were questioned by the councilmen. Sarah Gardner, a mother of twelve, kept her family together against formidable odds. In 1762 the South Kingstown council ordered her to bind out her children to various masters when it seemed to them that she could not support them all. Later Gardner managed to gather together her scattered offspring; when she left South Kingstown for Providence in 1767, she had six of her children with her. In 1780, when she was warned out of Providence, four of her adult daughters were still living with her; in 1787, when she was warned out again, her household included three adult daughters and a grandson.

The Narragansett also took in and cared for other native people in distress. Jack Marsh, an elderly Narragansett man living in Jamestown, housed and tended "an Indian Squaw" until she died; he then arranged the details of her burial. In another case, an Indian woman named only Freelove received payment from the town of Warren for supplying room and board to Phebe Wood, a native woman who was one of the town's poor. The Jamestown council acknowledged the cohesiveness of native people when they decided that the best way to care for Mary Mew, an elderly and lame Indian woman, was "to put her into some Indian Family."

The records also suggest that native people sought each other out for times of relaxation and celebration. Homes whose householders had liquor licenses often served as gathering places. In 1753 Christopher Fowler was accused of "Entertaining Indeons, Negros &c" in his tavern. In 1760 Joshua Gardner obtained a tavern license on the condition "that he Entertain no Indian or Black people on ye day Calld Fair day at his House on any pretence whatever." The Rhode Island General Assembly had long been distressed at the tendency of native and black servants to patronize taverns and had passed legislation in 1704 and again in 1750 to restrict their activities. This legislation made it an offense to sell liquor "to any Indian, Mulatto or Negro Servant or Slave" or to entertain such a person in one's home without the master's consent; it also forbade any Indian or black servant to be out and about after 9 P.M. without the master's consent. Colony and town records suggest that the Narragansett, both bound and free, knew where they might enjoy each other's company and often did.

As evidence of their cultural heritage, some Narragansett living among non-Indians chose traditional dwellings. South Kingstown's local leaders were aware of "ye wigwam [of] Jo Robinson in Point Judeth"; others caught the attention of town leaders, who feared that they would be unable to survive winter weather unless they moved into English-style houses.

Given these links to their people and their past, it is not surprising that the Narragansett living among non-Indians rarely thought of themselves as "belonging" to a particular Rhode Island town. Oral tradition tells us that the Narragansett moved from winter residence to summer residence and back again, in accordance with the seasons. In addition, they often traveled to home clans and familiar places for celebrations and long-term visits. They moved and lived where they wished; there is little evidence that they felt rooted in the settled, ordered communities that English people valued.

Narragansett habits of travel and long-term visiting clashed with European concepts of "belonging" to a particular place. Local Rhode Island officials, alert to the presence of "strangers" within their jurisdictions and uneasy about the large numbers who congregated for native celebrations, sometimes tried to break up gatherings by warning out the participants who were not legal inhabitants. When confronted by the town sergeant with order in hand, oral tradition tells us, many Narragansett quietly melted into the woods; several days later they returned and resumed the visit or celebration. Local officials, for their part, complained about transients who returned persistently, despite repeated warnouts. Native people appear regularly in warnout orders, but these orders probably netted only a fraction of the native people actually moving around the region.

Because European regulations interfered with their traditional customs, native people seldom obtained settlement certificates as they traveled from one place to another. The settlement certificate was the "passport" that poor people needed to reside for more than a week in a town where they did not have a legal settlement by virtue of birth or bound service; that certificate promised that the bearer's hometown would pay the costs of support and transportation if the need arose. Of the 919 settlement certificates granted by town councils between 1750 and 1800, only 10 (1.1 percent) were issued to people identified as Indians. To judge from the warnout orders, native people moved about in greater numbers than the settlement certificates indicate, but they ignored the regulations associated with legal settlement, a concept that had little resonance for native people adrift on occupied ancestral lands.

Occasionally, town leaders made the Narragansett people aware of those regulations in a way that could not be ignored. Cato Gardner moved from South Kingstown to Jamestown without a certificate, and in time the Jamestown council demanded that he leave or get a certificate. Gardner disregarded this first warning, but a second citation some months late was delivered so forcefully that he made the trip back to South Kingstown to get a certificate from the council. Martha Bristol dodged the Jamestown town council for five years, but after receiving her fourth warnout, she obtained a settlement certificate from the New Shoreham council to avoid further harassment in Jamestown. Bristol, Gardner, and other native people complied with regulations only when they could not avoid them. By doing so, they signaled their unconcern about pleasing the non-Indian "fathers" of the town family; they had another agenda, derived from their own and their families' needs.

Narragansett People Maneuvering through the System

Just as Bristol and Gardner learned to keep local authorities at bay over the issues of certificates, some Narragansett learned to maneuver through a system heavy with regulations. The record is rich with instances of Indians beating officials at their own game. It is tempting to think of native people relating such "trickster tales" to delighted audiences at home and in taverns, encouraging those who labored daily to make European Americans even more prosperous.

Old Toby Smith, Young Toby Smith, and Moses (no last name) figured out how to avoid paying taxes. As inhabitants of Rhode Island towns, native people who owned real estate were subject to paying taxes, just as the colonists were. In Middletown the assessors included these three men on the rate list for a town tax due in March 1757. But the men failed to pay the six pounds they owed, even after repeated visits from the tax collector and a two-month extension. The collector finally reported to the councilmen "that he Cannot get the Rates" from the Indians, and the council covered the sum out of the town treasury. It was not unusual for towns to write off uncollected taxes as "bad rates" from time to time, when the collector advised that certain cases were not worth pursuing. Moses and the Smiths somehow convinced the collector that theirs was such a case; perhaps by pleading, spinning a tale, or temporarily moving away, they beat the system.

Simeon Matthews got out of both a tax assessment and a guardianship. The Charlestown town council had put him under guardianship "on account of his being a common Drunkard." The idea was to keep him from purchasing liquor by assigning a guardian who would control his ward's money and property. At the same time, perhaps to underscore the town's authority, the tax assessors levied a tax on him. Matthews promptly petitioned the General Assembly, arguing that he was a member of the Narragansett tribe and therefore not under Charlestown's jurisdiction. The General Assembly agreed. The tax was canceled, and the Charlestown officials dismissed Matthews's guardian, noting that "it is not the Duty of this Council to appoint Guardians to the Indian Tribe."

Marcy Scooner used persistence and skill in hiding to beat the warnout system. In 1759 the Jamestown councilmen warned her out to North Kingstown, the hometown where she did not wish to live. She soon returned to Jamestown and continued to live there until the council caught wind of her presence and warned her out again in 1763. And again in 1766. Each time, the councilmen ordered the town sergeant to whip Scooner publicly to deter her from returning. But she was so adept at hiding that the councilmen had to extend the usual time granted the sergeant to find and whip a miscreant. For seven years Scooner dodged the council and the sergeant, coming and going as she pleased. After 1766, she disappears from the record. Perhaps she died. Perhaps she changed her name. Perhaps she found a more congenial place to live and moved on. In any case, she provided a fine example of how to frustrate authority.

One young Indian boy (unnamed in the record) figured out how to escape indentured servitude without flight and the dangers of capture and persecution. In 1780, this young servant of Capt. Samuel Babcock enlisted in the Continental Army as part of Hopkinton's quota in the most recent draft. Upset about this defection, Babcock disputed the validity of his enlistment, claiming that his "apprentice" was under sixteen, the lawful age of enlistment, and that he had "a Right to detain him." The town's voters, who met to break this impasse, overruled Babcock's objection and accepted the enlistment of the young man, choosing to believe that he was of legal age. Three weeks later, Babcock produced the indenture papers, which "proved" that the Indian apprentice was underage, but it was too late; Hopkinton's latest soldier had already gone to muster. The record contains no explanation of where the servitude contract had been when Babcock so vigorously objected to the boy's enlistment.

Narragansett people living among European Americans were not helpless against local officials and the systems they constructed to keep order in their towns. Native people understood these systems and could maneuver around them. The evidence is there in the very records kept by the officials who tried to govern their lives. Assuredly, some Indians lived and died among non-Indians without fighting back, but people like John Hammer, Simeon Matthews, and Marcy Scooner dot the record in sufficient numbers to remind us that the war did not end in the Great Swamp.

Conclusion

At the heart of our study of Indian-European relations in Rhode Island is the phenomenon of local leaders erasing native people from the written record by redesignating them as "Negro." By 1793, when John Hammer vainly argued his case before a local justice, authorities clearly considered "Indians" to be "black." A major shift had occurred in official thought about native people in the latter part of the 1700s. Those leaders certainly knew the difference between Indian and African peoples; in earlier days they had not hesitated to make the distinction. But as European Americans drew lines between themselves and person of color, they lumped all non-Europeans together as the other.

What prompted this particular expression of racism during the Revolutionary era? Social upheaval, economic depression, and political nation making are all possible answers. Most obvious, perhaps, is the tension in race relations occasioned by the end of slavery in New England. In their revolutionary fervor, many masters voluntarily freed their slaves during or soon after the war. Then, in 1784, gradual emancipation became a legal reality in Rhode Island; it signaled the eventual freeing of young adult slaves beginning in the early 1800s. During and after the Revolution a growing number of former slaves from the farms and plantations of southern Rhode Island swelled the ranks of free African Americans seeking employment on the docks and in domestic service in the commercial centers of the state. Joanne Melish has shown that emancipation upset the carefully ordered world of European Americans in Rhode Island. No longer did all (or even most) people of color fit neatly into the category of "slave," with all the subservience and control that implied. Faced with free black people in growing numbers, European Americans directed at "blacks" the attitudes they had had toward "slaves." They replaced old regulations designed to control slaves with new ones designed to control free blacks; racism bloomed in a political environment that encouraged emancipation.

European Americans swept up the Narragansett in their effort to control people of color. Indians had already been associated with people of African descent by their shared status as others in a world governed by Europeans, by their bondage in European households, and by their unions that produced children who were both Indian and African. In the racially charged atmosphere of the late 1700s European American bigotry affected the Narragansett just as it did Africans and others of a darker color.

Narragansett land provided another catalyst. The Narragansett had been stripped of most of their land by the 1780s, but even the remnants looked appealing to European American farmers who were faced with economic depression, exhausted soil, and unprofitable harvests, and whose restless sons were ready to migrate westward. But there was a more fundamental problem. Some European Americans must have considered the possibility that the Narragansett would seek to regain what had been tribal territory. The way to forestall them was to deny the existence of people with any claim to the land. New Shoreham voters tolled that bell in 1780. Noting that "the native Indians [are] extinct in [this] Town," they passed a law taking over the reserved Indian lands, which were to be sold to augment the town treasury. By writing Indians out of the record, local leaders helped ensure that native people would not regain land in their towns.

European American leaders were right to be concerned. When the United States was born, native peoples on tribal land came under the authority of Congress, not the state legislatures. Article 9 of the Articles of Confederation, ratified in 1781, gave Congress "the sole and exclusive right and power of . . . regulating the trade and managing all affairs with the Indians, not members of any of the States." The federal Constitution, ratified by the required nine states in 1788 (Rhode Island, the last of the original thirteen states to ratify it, did so, reluctantly, in 1790), granted Congress the right to "regulate Commerce" with all the Indian tribes. Since state and local leaders could not be sure how the federal government would treat native people, it made sense to them to prevent unwelcome interference by making those people disappear.

We can never know exactly why Rhode Island officials wiped native people from the written record in the late eighteenth century. The full answer, including a burgeoning racial ideology that would divide the nation into white and nonwhite peoples, is probably as complicated as the explanation for the Rhode Island state government's resistance to Narragansett economic development in the late twentieth century. Nevertheless, the Narragansett survived in the flesh, keeping their identity and tribal history intact.

◈ *F U R T H E R   R E A D I N G*

Colin G. Calloway, *The American Revolution in Indian Country: Crisis and Diversity in Native American Communities* (1995)

————, ed., *The World Turned Upside Down: Indian Voices from Early America* (1994)

Gregory Dowd, *A Spirited Resistance: The North American Indian Struggle for Unity, 1745–1815* (1992)

Barbara Graymont, *The Iroquois in the American Revolution* (1972)

William T. Hagan, *Longhouse Diplomacy and Frontier Warfare: The Iroquois Confederacy in the American Revolution* (n.d.)

Tom Hatley, *The Dividing Paths: Cherokees and South Carolinians through the Era of Revolution* (1993)

Francis Jennings, "The Indians' Revolution," in Alfred Young, ed., *The American Revolution: Explorations in the History of American Radicalism* (1976)

Bruce E. Johansen, *Forgotten Founders: How the American Indian Helped Shape Democracy* (1982)

Peter C. Mancall, "The Revolutionary War and the Indians of the Upper Susquehanna Valley," *American Indian Culture and Research Journal* 12 (1) (1988), 39–57

James H. O'Donnell, III, *Southern Indians in the American Revolution* (1973)

Jack M. Sosin, *The Revolutionary Frontier, 1763–1783* (1967)

Domestic Dependent Nations:
Indians in the New Republic

◈

The title for this chapter comes from Justice John Marshall's famous U.S. Supreme Court decision in Cherokee Nation v. Georgia *(1831) declaring that the Cherokees were a "domestic dependent" nation rather than a foreign state. Marshall's phrase delineated the anomalous status of Indians in the new nation. In the early nineteenth century, white Americans advanced rapidly westward beyond the Appalachians. Expansion put new pressure on western tribes and in the East created islands of Indian territory within states. In some cases, as with the Cherokees in Georgia, Indians made every effort to accommodate to white society, but this was not enough for white Georgians who demanded that the federal government remove Indians. Cherokees and their white supporters argued that the federal government should support the Indians in the peaceful possession of their homeland. This debate came to a head during the presidency of Andrew Jackson, who sided with the state of Georgia. The federal government then moved the Cherokees west to Indian Territory in present-day Oklahoma. Several thousand Cherokees died on the road to their new homes, and the Cherokees fittingly remember this experience as the "Trail of Tears." The Cherokee experience foreshadowed the fate of many other Indians who left ancestral homelands for a new home in the West. Historians have argued about the merits of Indian removal ever since.*

Cherokee removal was the most famous and defining Indian experience in the first decades of the nineteenth century, but it did not begin to describe the variety of Indian social and political conditions in that era. The Indians of the Old Northwest under the leadership of the Shawnee chief Tecumseh mounted a serious military threat and sided with the British during the War of 1812. U.S. troops eventually killed Tecumseh, and his followers either settled for peace and reservation lands in the West or fled to Canada. Still other tribes saw no reason to alter their way of life or to leave their homelands. In 1803, the United States had purchased the Louisiana Territory, which included a vast region to the headwaters of the Missouri River. Many of the Indians there were involved in the fur trade and lived according to the customs of the country that had evolved for two centuries. Still other tribes lived independently on the Plains as horse-mounted buffalo hunters who did not think of themselves as "domestic dependent nations."

◈ D O C U M E N T S

The United States had constitutional authority to govern Indian affairs, although states would contest this fact from time to time. Even under the Articles of Confederation, the national government asserted its primacy in Indian affairs, and in Document 1, the Northwest Ordinance, Congress declared that it would always show the "utmost good faith" toward the Indians. In times of war, good will was in short supply. Document 2 is Miami Chief Little Turtle's statement at the Treaty of Greenville negotiations in 1795. Little Turtle, who had just lost a war with the United States, hoped that this treaty would provide lasting peace and security, but in truth he was at the mercy of the victors. The Indians he spoke for had to trade land for peace, as Little Turtle's speech shows. The cession of lands to the United States was perhaps the most divisive issue within tribes. Document 3 is a statement by the famous Shawnee leader Tecumseh, who argued against the principle of giving up land by treaty, unless by unanimous consent of the tribe. Indian removal was a hotly debated issue among Indians and whites. Land-hungry whites, of course, made no bones about their desire for Indian lands and paid little attention to the legal and moral niceties. Other whites held reasoned and principled positions on both sides of the argument. Nor were Indians unanimous in their opinions about removal. Many were intransigent opponents, but others concluded that they would not be secure until they moved away from white influence. In Document 4, Commissioner of Indian Affairs Thomas L. McKenney briefly summarizes the problem in 1828. In 1829, President Andrew Jackson set forth a rationale and basic plan for Indian removal, which became a basic principle of his administration of Indian affairs. In Document 5, Speckled Snake, a Cherokee, ridiculed Jackson's declarations of sympathy for the Indians. Document 6 is the opinion of Cherokee newspaper editor Elias Boudinot. Boudinot, who was educated in New England schools and married a white woman, at first opposed removal but finally believed it was necessary to save the Cherokee nation. Nevertheless, many Cherokees remained firmly opposed. After the Cherokees had moved to their new home, opponents of removal killed Boudinot and other Indians who had signed the removal treaty. The Cherokee debate over removal was a world away from the Indians on the upper Missouri. In Document 7, the fur trader Pierre Chardon confides to his journal some intimate domestic arrangements with Indian women. His statements show how casual matters of sex and marriage could be among fur traders. Friederich Kurz, a Swiss artist who lived among Indians on the Missouri River, provides a more romantic vision of Indian-white relationships in Document 8, although it is tinged with disappointment.

1. Northwest Ordinance, 1787

Article III

Religion, morality, and knowledge, being necessary to good government and the happiness of mankind, schools and the means of education shall forever be encouraged. The utmost good faith shall always be observed toward the Indians; their lands and property shall never be taken from them without their consent; and, in their property, rights, and liberty, they never shall be invaded or disturbed, unless in just and lawful wars authorized by Congress; but laws founded in justice and

---

From Francis N. Thorpe, ed., *Federal and State Constitutions: Colonial Charters and Other Organic Laws of the States, Territories, and Colonies, Now or Heretofore Forming the United States of America,* vol. 2 (Washington, D.C.: U.S. Government Printing Office, 1909), 957–964.

humanity shall, from time to time, be made, for preventing wrongs being done to them and for preserving peace and friendship with them.

2. Little Turtle (Miami) on the Treaty of Greenville, 1795

Elder Brother [U.S. negotiator], and all you present: I am going to say a few words, in the name of Pottawatamies, Weas and Kickapoos. It is well known to you all, that people are appointed on those occasions, to speak the sentiments of others; therefore am I appointed for those three nations.

Elder Brother: You told your younger brothers, when we first assembled, that peace was your object; you swore your interpreters before us, to the faithful discharge of their duty, and told them the Great Spirit would punish them, did they not perform it. You told us, that it was not you, but the President of the Fifteen Fires [states] of the United States, who spoke to us; that, whatever he should say, should be firm and lasting; that it was impossible he should say what was not true. Rest assured, that your younger brothers, the Miamis, Ottawas, Chippewas, Pottawatamies, Shawnees, Weas, Kickapoos, Piankeshaws, and Kaskaskias, are well pleased with your words, and are persuaded of their sincerity. You have told us to consider of the boundaries you showed us; your younger brothers have done so, and now proceed to give you their answer.

Elder Brother: Your younger brothers do not wish to hide their sentiments from you. I wish to be the same with those of the Wyandottes and Delawares; you have told us that most of the reservations you proposed to us belonged to our fathers, the French and the British. Permit your younger brothers to make a few observations on this subject.

Elder Brother: We wish you to listen with attention to our words. You have told your younger brothers that the British imposed falsehoods on us when they said the United States wished to take our lands from us, and that the United States had no such designs. You pointed out to us the boundary line, which crossed a little below Loromie's Store and struck Fort Recovery and runs from thence to the Ohio, opposite the mouth of the Kentucky River.

Elder Brother: You have told us to speak our minds freely, and we now do it. This line takes in the greater and best part of your brothers' hunting ground. Therefore, your younger brothers are of the opinion you take too much of their lands away and confine the hunting of our young men within the limits too contracted. Your brothers, the Miamis, the proprietors of those lands, and all your younger brothers present, wish you to run the lines as you mentioned to Fort Recovery and to continue it along the road; from thence to Fort Hamilton, on the great Miami River. This is what your brothers request you to do, and you may rest assured of the free navigation of that river, from thence to its mouth, forever.

Brother: Here is the road we wish to be the boundary between us. What lies to the east we wish to be yours; that to the west, we would desire to be ours.

Elder Brother: In speaking of the reservations, you say they are designed for the same purpose as those for which our fathers, the French and English, occupied them. Your younger brothers now wish to make some observations on them.

From W. C. Vanderwerth, *Indian Oratory: Famous Speeches by Noted Indian Chieftains* (Norman: University of Oklahoma Press, 1971), 56–59. Copyright © 1971 by the University of Oklahoma Press, Norman.

Elder Brother: Listen to me with attention. You told us you discovered on the Great Miami traces of an old fort. It was not a French fort, brother; it was a fort built by me. You perceived another at Loromies. 'Tis true a Frenchman once lived there for a year or two. The Miami villages were occupied as you remarked, but it was unknown to your younger brothers until you told them that we had sold the land there to the French or English. I was much surprised to hear you say that it was my forefathers had set the example to other Indians in selling their lands. I will inform you in what manner the French and English occupied those places.

Elder Brother: These people were seen by our forefathers first at Detroit. Afterwards we saw then at the Miami village—that glorious gate, which your younger brothers had the happiness to own, and through which all the good words of our chiefs had to pass, from the north to the south, and from the east to the west, Brothers, these people never told us they wished to purchase our lands from us.

Elder Brother: I now give you the true sentiment of your younger brothers the Miamis, with respect to the reservation at the Miami villages. We thank you for kindly contracting the limits you at first proposed. We wish you to take this six miles square on the side of the river where your fort now stands, as your younger brothers wish to inhabit that beloved spot again. You shall cut hay for your cattle wherever you please, and you shall never require in vain the assistance of your younger brothers at that place.

Elder Brother: The next place you pointed to was the Little River, and said you wanted two miles square at that place. This is a request that our fathers, the French or British, never made us. It was always ours. This carrying place [portage] has heretofore proved in a great degree the subsistence of your younger brothers. That place has brought us in the course of one day the amount of one hundred dollars. Let us both own this place and enjoy in common the advantages it affords. You told us at Chicago the French possessed a fort. We have never heard of it. We thank you for the trade you promised to open in our country, and permit us to remark that we wish our former traders may be continued and mixed with yours.

Elder Brother: On the subject of hostages, I have only to observe that I trust all my brothers present are of my opinion with regard to peace and our future happiness. I expect to be with you every day when you settle on your reservations, and it will be impossible for me or my people to withhold from you a single prisoner. Therefore, we don't know why any of us should remain here. These are the sentiments of your younger brothers present, on these particulars.

3. Tecumseh (Shawnee) Speaks Out Against Land Cessions, 1810

. . . It is true I am a Shawnee. My forefathers were warriors. Their son is a warrior. From them I only take my existence; from my tribe I take nothing. I am the maker of my own fortune; and oh! that I could make that of my red people, and of my country, as great as the conceptions of my mind, when I think of the Spirit that

From Samuel Gardner Drake, *Biography and History of the Indians of North America* (Boston: Antiquarian Institute, 1837), 5:21–22.

rules the universe. I would not then come to Governor Harrison, to ask him to tear the treaty, and to obliterate the landmark; but I would say to him, Sir, you have liberty to return to your own country. The being within, communing with the past ages, tells me, that once, nor until lately, there was no white man on this continent. That it then all belonged to red men, children of the same parents, placed on it by the Great Spirit that made them, to keep it, to traverse it, to enjoy its production, and to fill it with the same race. Once a happy race. Since made miserable by the white people, who are never contented, but always encroaching. The way, and the only way to check and stop this evil, is, for all the red men to unite in claiming a common and equal right in the land, as it was at first, and should be yet; for it never was divided, but belongs to all, for the use of each. That no part has a right to sell, even to each other, much less to strangers; those who want all, and will not do with less. The white people have no right to take the land from the Indians, because they had it first; it is theirs. They may sell, but all must join. Any sale not made by all is not valid. The late sale is bad. It was made by a part only. Part do not know how to sell. It requires all to make a bargain for all. All red men have equal rights to the unoccupied land. The right of occupancy is as good in one place as in another. There cannot be two occupations in the same place. The first excludes all others. It is not so in hunting or travelling; for there the same ground will serve many, as they may follow each other all day; but the camp is stationary, and that is occupancy. It belongs to the first who sits down on his blanket or skins, which he has thrown upon the ground, and till he leaves it no other has a right.

4. Indian Commissioner Thomas L. McKenney Explains Removal, 1828

. . . I forbear also to remark, except briefly, upon measures of general policy in regard to our Indians. The subject is growing in interest every day, and is surpassed only by the extreme delicacy of their situation, and of our relations with them. I refer especially to those whose territory is embraced by the limits of States. Every feeling of sympathy for their lot should be kept alive, and fostered; and no measures taken that could compromit [compromise] the humanity and justice of the nation; and none, I am sure, will be. But the question occurs—*What are humanity and justice in reference to this unfortunate race?* Are these found to lie in a policy that would leave them to linger out a wretched and degraded existence, within districts of country already surrounded and pressed upon by a population whose anxiety and efforts to get rid of them are not less restless and persevering, than is that law of nature immutable, which has decreed, that, under such circumstances, if continued in, *they must perish?* Or does it not rather consist in withdrawing them from this certain destruction, and placing them, though even at this late hour, in a situation where, by the adoption of a suitable system for their security, preservation, and improvement, and at no matter what cost, they may be saved and blest? What *the means* are which are best fitted to realize such a triumph of humanity, I leave to be determined upon by those who are more competent than I am to decide. But that

---

From *Annual Report of the Commissioner of Indian Affairs, 1828.*

something must be done, and done soon, to save these people, if saved at all, it requires no very deep research into the history of the past, or knowledge of their present condition, embracing especially their relation to the States, to see.

5. Speckled Snake's (Cherokee) Reply to President Jackson, 1830

Brothers! We have heard the talk of our great father; it is very kind. He says he loves his red children. *Brothers!* When the white man first came to these shores, the Muscogees gave him land, and kindled him a fire to make him comfortable; and when the pale faces of the south made war on him, their young men drew the tomahawk, and protected his head from the scalping knife. But when the white man had warmed himself before the Indian's fire, and filled himself with the Indian's hominy, he became very large; he stopped not for the mountain tops, and his feet covered the plains and the valleys. His hands grasped the eastern and the western sea. Then he became our great father. He loved his red children; but said, "You must move a little farther, lest I should, by accident, tread on you." With one foot he pushed the red man over the Oconee [River], and with the other he trampled down the graves of his fathers. But our great father still loved his red children, and he soon made them another talk. He said much; but it all meant nothing, but "move a little farther; you are too near me." I heard a great many talks from our great father, and they all begun and ended the same, *Brothers!* When he made us a talk on a former occasion, he said, "Get a little farther; go beyond the Oconee and the Oakmulgee [River]; there is a pleasant country." He also said, "It shall be yours forever." Now he says, "The land you live on is not yours; go beyond the Mississippi; there is game; there you may remain while the grass grows or the water runs." *Brothers!* Will not our great father come there also? He loves his red children, and his tongue is not forked.

6. Cherokee Editor Elias Boudinot Opposes Removal, 1828

. . . Our last Washington papers contain a debate which took place in the house of representatives, on the resolution, recommended by the Committee on Indian Affairs, published in the second Number of our paper. It appears that the advocates of this new system of civilizing the Indians are very strenuous in maintaining the novel opinion, that it is impossible to enlighten the Indians, surrounded as they are by the white population, and that they assuredly will become extinct, unless they are removed. It is a fact which we would not deny, that many tribes have perished away in consequence of white population, but we are yet to be convinced that this will always be the case, in spite of every measure taken to civilize them. We contend that suitable measures to a sufficient extent have never been employed. And

From Speckled Snake's reply to Jackson, in Charles Moquin and Charles Van Doren, eds., *Great Documents in American Indian History* (New York: Praeger, 1973), 149–150.

From Theda Perdue, ed., *Cherokee Editor: The Writings of Elias Boudinot* (Knoxville: University of Tennessee Press, 1983), 95–96.

how dare these men make an assertion without sufficient evidence? What proof have they that the system which they are now recommending, will succeed? Where have we an example in the whole history of man, of a Nation or tribe, removing in a body, from a land of civil and religious means, to a perfect wilderness, *in order to be civilized.* We are fearful these men are building castles in the air, whose fall will crush those poor Indians who may be so blinded as to make the experiment. We are sorry to see that some of the advocates of this system speak so disrespectfully, if not contemptuously, of the present measures of improvement, now in successful operation among most of the Indians in the United Sates—the only measures too, which have been crowded with success, and bid fair to meliorate the condition of the Aborigines. . . .

7. Pierre Chardon on Sex and Marriage with Indians on the Upper Missouri River, 1836–1839

Aug. 30, 1836 "Committed fortification [*sic*] to day and got a Whipping from my beloved—Wife—, for my trouble—Oh poor Me—"

Sept. 16, 1836 "The Saons left here early this Morning for their Camp—Sent with them a Yancton woman that I bought from the Gros-Ventres, . . ."

April 24, 1837 "My Childrens Mother died this day at 11 OClock—Sent her down in a canoe to be entered at Fort Pierre, in the Lands of her Parents—Pressed Packs 15—Trade going on slow—"

May 10, 1837 "Two Yancton squaws (Prisoners) that were taken at the Massacre last winter, Made their escape last Night it is rumored that I am the cause of their elopement—"

March 24, 1838 "Garreau turned his Wife off for infidelity, poor thing—"

May 18, 1838 "Separated from My dear Ree Wife, after a Mariage of one Year—"

June 15, 1838 "haveing lived for two Months a single life, and could not stand it any longer, I concluded to day, to buy myself a Wife, a young Virgin of 15—which cost $ 150—"

June 25, 1838 "after and [*sic*] absence of 39 Days My Absent Wife thought that she fared better at the Fort, made her appearance, after a few reproaches on both sides, harmony was restored."

June 29, 1838 "the few remaining Mandans that were liveing with the Rees all started up to remain with the Gros Ventres, as they can not agree with the Rees, as the latter are continually stealing their women's—"

July 13, 1838 "Great rejoicing at the Village, Scalps flying in all directions, Men Women and Children—singing, crying and dancing. . . . One of the Prisoners that was taken in the fight of Yesterday (A girl of 12 years) was presented to me today by the one that made her Prisoner." [Rees and Gros Ventres had killed 64 Assiniboines and taken eight women prisoners.]

From Annie Heloise Abel, ed., *Chardon's Journal at Fort Clark, 1834–1839* (Pierre, S.D.: Department of History, State of South Dakota, 1932), 80, 96, 111, 164, 165, 170, 175, 180, 181.

Sept 3, 1838 "found all Well, except my beloved Ree wife, who has deserted my bed & board. . . ."

Nov. 17, 1838 "Gave a good Whipping to my young Wife, the first since our Union, as I am united to one, that I stole from my Friend, J. Halsey, on my visit to Fort Pierre last summer—"

January 2, 1839 "One of the wives of the Fort eloped this morning, a young Ree damsel of 16, regretted by us all."

8. Friederich Kurz Gives a Romantic View of Indian-White Love, 1849

"One evening, when the wilderness was irresistibly beautiful, I wandered in the forest, paid some visits, listened to the enamored lads as they made love to the girls with their flutes or made signals by blowing through their clenched fists. I, too, had a trysting place with the dainty little Niukogra near a hollow tree on the bank of the Missouri, whose waters refreshed the entire region. Several small herds of the most noble wild animals came there to graze, happily unconscious of their woeful fate.

"The moon never shone so brilliantly, the trees never seemed so huge, nor life so romantic as that spot. I sat there for a long time with the dear little wanton on the trunk of a fallen tree, under the spell of the moon, mirrored in the stream before us, and of her languishing eyes. I asked many questions but wrote nothing down. We sat until late into the night, then went into the tent, wrapped ourselves in a cloak or blanket, and those who could fell asleep."

In January 1850 Kirutsche offered Witthae in marriage to Kurz. Kurz would get about 2,000 acres of Iowa land. Kirutsche wanted Kurz to go into the stone business with him. Kirutsche complained that his lazy relatives took advantage of his industry, always begging for food. With Kurz as his partner, Kirutsche could avoid some of these responsibilities by hiding behind Kurz. Kurz agreed, and the marriage went well until the Iowas moved away, and Witthae became sad. Finally, she left without a word. Her mother assured Kurz that she would return, but she did not. "'If she does not wish to come of her own accord, she may remain at home,' I told her mother. Wuotschime was very much grieved. I held to my resolve. That was the end of my romantic dream of love and marriage with an Indian. Brief joy!" With that, Kurz moved further up the Missouri.

◈ E S S A Y S

The conditions of Indian life depended upon the many variables that were in play in the early nineteenth century. One of the most important variables was proximity to white settlements. In the first essay, Daniel Usner of Cornell University shows that in the southern states Choctaws, Creeks, and other tribes lived amid agricultural expansion,

From J. N. B. Hewitt, ed., *Journal of Rudolph Friederich Kurz* (Bureau of American Ethnology Bulletin No. 115. Washington, D.C.: Government Printing Office, 1937), 49–50.

cotton plantations, and slavery. They adjusted their lives accordingly. Historical circumstances also played an important part. The second essay by Tanis Thorne of the University of California, Irvine, describes life on the Missouri River where many years of fur trade marriages had created a substantial community of Indian and mixed-blood people. Among these people, kinship provided a stabilizing influence, even as mixed marriages and other fur-trade influences tended to disrupt the tribes. Together, these essays investigate the range of options for Indians who lived among whites. Were there other possibilities that the essays do not mention?

American Indians on the Cotton Frontier

DANIEL H. USNER, JR.

... By 1793, when use of Whitney's patented gin began to spread across the southern hinterland, the region between the Chattahoochee and the Mississippi Rivers was still very much Indian country. The Indian population in that area numbered at least 30,000 individuals, most of whom lived in the more than one hundred villages that constituted the Creek, Choctaw, and Chickasaw nations. Within the same territory were only about 2,500 whites and 2,000 blacks, mostly concentrated in settlements along the lower Tombigbee River and around the Natchez banks of the Mississippi. In order to counteract the United States' claims to territory and its demands for navigating the Mississippi River, Spanish officials made serious efforts during the 1790s to attract American settlers to Louisiana. A generous land policy offered immigrants sizable grants of free land in proportion to the size of their families and the number of their laborers. Larger diplomatic considerations, however, compelled Spain in the Treat of San Lorenzo, 1795, to cede to the United States all lands east of the Mississippi River and above the thirty-first parallel. In 1798 the United States Congress organized that cession into the Mississippi Territory, which was by the turn of the century occupied by nearly 5,000 whites, 3,500 black slaves, and 200 free blacks, in addition still to more than 30,000 Indians.

Indian nations not only comprised the majority of the new territory's population in 1798 but held title, guaranteed by treaties with both Spain and the United States, to most of its land. Indian policy, therefore, was an integral priority in the United States government's territorial organization of Mississippi. The United States entered the nineteenth century with four major goals in Indian affairs. The first goal of establishing and maintaining alliances with tribes required, in compliance with Indian customs, a well-regulated, steady trade relationship. In the Mississippi Territory the task was especially difficult because Spain, which had developed strong political and commercial ties with the tribes of the area, possessed adjacent territories—Louisiana until 1803 and Florida until 1819. To enforce a second policy goal, the maintenance of peace and order among Indian peoples and between them and American citizens, United States agents in the Mississippi Territory entered a highly volatile world shaped by two decades of Anglo-American encroachment into Indian country and of intertribal struggle over diminishing resources. As reported by [Governor] Winthrop

Daniel H. Usner, Jr., "American Indians on the Cotton Frontier," *Journal of American History,* September 1985, 297–317. Reprinted with permission.

Sargent in 1799, the Choctaws already felt "that their Country once affording abundance had become desolate by the hands of a People who knew them not but to increas their Wretchedness." Partially to diffuse resentment among Indians over such conditions and to make them more tractable, the government also pursued a third goal of reforming Indian societies by teaching "the Arts of husbandry, and domestic manufactures" and encouraging, as Secretary of War Henry Dearborn further suggested to Choctaw agent Silas Dinsmoor, "the growth of Cotton as well as Grain." Finally and most importantly, the goal of acquiring land cessions from Indian nations shaped policy in the Mississippi Territory. "[T]he time will come when a cession of land may be necessary to us and not injurious to them," Secretary of State Timothy Pickering informed Sargent. Suggesting how bribery might work as a means toward effecting that end, he mentioned that when the time came "the grant of an annuity should be the consideration."

An important instrument for implementing all of those goals was the establishment of government trading posts among the many tribes of the eastern woodlands and midwestern prairies. The first two having been legislated into existence by Congress in 1795, those stores or trade factories provided Indians with fixed exchange rates and ample supplies of merchandise and thereby facilitated regulation of Indian trade. . . .

. . . While the literature on United States trade houses has tended to emphasize losses incurred by the government, the impact of a deteriorating trade position upon Indian livelihood evidenced at the factories has remained poorly understood.

At a time when prices for deerskins were dropping in Europe and when supplies of game were diminishing in the southeastern woodlands, the economic position of Indians was further exacerbated by the fiscal tightening exerted by their private and public trading partners. Through most of the eighteenth century, colonial officials and merchants had followed Indian trade protocol, which included the practices of offering presents, smoking the calumet [peace pipe], and sharing food. By the end of the century, however, the United States began to discourage outright gift giving and, through its trade houses, to replace what had been political obligations with accountable debts. Influential leaders and intermediary traders still received extra merchandise for their peltry, but each advance was now carefully recorded in the debt column of the tribe's account book. In the Mississippi Territory the results of that practice materialized first among the Creeks in the Treaty of Fort Wilkinson, 1802. Of the $25,000 received by the tribe for a cession of land between the Oconee and Ocmulgee rivers, $10,000 went "to satisfy certain debts due from Indians and white persons of the Creek country to the factory of the United States."

After sending the Creek treaty to Congress, President Thomas Jefferson turned his attention to that portion of Chickasaw territory "of first importance to us" and evaluated several means through which the Untied States "may advance towards our object." One means was to encourage plow agriculture, which would reduce the acreage of farmland needed by Indians; another was to nourish their allegiance "by every act of justice & of favor which we can possibly render them." But a third approach involved selectively extending credit to draw the Chickasaws into debt. Jefferson realized it would be beneficial "to establish among them a factory or factories for furnishing them with all the necessaries and comforts they may wish (spirituous liquors excepted), encouraging these and especially their leading men, to run in debt for these beyond their individual means of paying; and whenever in that situation, they will always cede lands to rid themselves of debt" . . .

. . . Choctaw, Creek, and Chickasaw treaties made during the first decade of the Mississippi Territory's existence reflected the entanglement of Indian villagers in the region within a chronic cycle of trade indebtedness and land cessions, a cycle that would steadily weaken their power and eventually culminate in removal. By 1822 the Choctaw nation, for example, ceded nearly thirteen million acres of land but still owed approximately thirteen thousand dollars to the United States trade house. The transfer of Indian land to the United States was, as the Choctaw and Chickasaw treaties of 1805 explicitly illustrate, further accelerated by cooperation between the federal government and merchant companies—a lesson that would not be lost on future administrators of Indian affairs.

Indian inhabitants of the Mississippi Territory responded to their deteriorating economic position in a variety of ways, evincing a resourceful adaptability among Native Americans too often neglected by historians. Beginning in the late eighteenth century, numerous Choctaw families and even some Creek villagers migrated across the Mississippi River and settled in the still-plentiful hunting grounds of the Ouachita, Red, and Atchafalaya river basins. As government trade-house records reveal, those who remained in their homelands continued to produce, although at a diminishing rate, deerskins and other furs. Still hoping to perpetuate their tradition exchange economy through adaptation, Indian men and women provided an array of other goods and services to the trade stores. During the five years from 1809 through 1813, the Choctaw factory received $22,877 worth of raw deerskins (44,232 skins), $4,109 worth of dressed deerskins, raccoon, lynx, and other miscellaneous pelts, $1,749 worth of beeswax (7,958 pounds), $145 worth of tallow (1,161 pounds), $249 worth of corn (443 barrels), and $24 worth of snakeroot (96 pounds). Indians occasionally sold their labor to the trade house in exchange for merchandise, working as boat hands, messengers, and boatbuilders. In January 1809, for example, the Choctaw factor "Bartered with an Indian" two yards of strouds valued at $3.50 for a "Canoe" (pirogue) that he gave to the trade house.

Many Indians became seasonal laborers or itinerant peddlers around the towns and plantations of the Mississippi Territory. As early as 1808 Choctaw women picked cotton during the harvest season for cloth, blankets, utensils, and even cash wages. John A. Watkins first became acquainted with the Choctaws in 1813–1814, "as they came into Jefferson Co. in the fall and winter in large numbers, the women to pick cotton, the men to hunt in the Louisiana swamps." From bark-covered huts that were always left open on the south side, hunters pursued deer and bear across the Mississippi while women worked in the cotton fields east of the river. Those seasonally mobile camps of Choctaw families—the cotton economy's first migrant labor force—also sold dressed deerskins, bear oil, and venison at landings along the Mississippi or took those and other products to Natchez, where according to Watkins "they were usually exchanged for blankets, stroud & calico supplemented by a jug of whiskey."

To maintain an economic base within their diminishing tribal domains, the Indian peoples also changed their farming and settlement patterns. Many Creeks, Choctaws, and Chickasaws had been raising livestock for some time, but at the opening of the nineteenth century that activity became a more important means of livelihood. As more grazing land was needed and as immigrants and travelers created a demand for foodstuffs, Indian villages began to spread outward from their previously more compact centers. The process was most visible among the Upper Creeks, many of whom settled on the outskirts of their towns as they became more attentive to cattle, hogs, and horses. The inhabitants of Hoithlewalli, for example, formed new settlements with fenced-in fields along the small tributaries of the Oakfuskee Creek, once reserved by the town for bear hunting and now providing "delightful range for stock." Choctaw and Chickasaw farmers also homesteaded outward from their villages during the early territorial period. Traveling from Natchez to the Chickasaw nation in the summer of 1805, Dr. Rush Nutt observed some Choctaws "building log houses & cultivating the earth in corn, cotton & other garden vegetables." Farther along the Natchez Trace—at Chukasalaya, Estockshish, and Bear Creek—he found Chickasaws establishing supply stations for travelers, raising "plenty of hogs & cattle," and farming grain cops. Chickasaw families were also settling westward in the Yazoo delta in order to use better range for their horses, cattle, and hogs.

The Indian trade economy that had grown around the exchange of deerskins for European manufactures was not impervious to accommodating the cotton economy, although the latter did threaten to displace the former entirely. During the eighteenth century Indians in the Lower Mississippi Valley had adopted European and African food crops, developed their own herds of livestock, and traded those and other items to colonists. In keeping with that pattern of adaptation, Indian villagers in the Mississippi Territory began to grow their own cotton for the export market. Traders Abram Mordecai and John and William Price established cotton gins at "Weathersford's racetrack" and "the Boat Yard," both along the Alabama River, where they purchased cotton produced by Creek farmers. Chickasaw chiefs inquired as an early as 1803 whether the United States factory at Chickasaw Bluffs would accept their cotton for cash.

But even though the cotton economy began to replace the deerskin trade economy, Indian communities in the Mississippi Territory continued to create economic niches for some settlers and slaves. Before the region became an United States territory, many French and English traders had established their deerskin commerce in particular villages by marrying Indian women. Into the nineteenth century many of their offspring continued to play prominent roles in the regional economy and were joined by American newcomers licensed by the territorial government. As transportation on roads through Indian country increased, some of those traders even opened facilities that provided food and lodging to travelers. In addition to the actual traders who dealt directly with Indian villagers, Indian commerce employed black as well as white laborers at several different tasks: transporting products by packhorses or by boats, helping to preserve and to pack the deerskins, and doing construction work on the facilities. At both private trade firms and government factories, settlers worked for wages, and slaves were hired out by their owners. The experience among Indians gained by some black slaves, particularly those owned by whites and Indians engaged in trade, was evident to early territorial witnesses by the presence of blacks in settlements and villages who could interpret between the various Indian languages and English.

Obstacles to landownership and uncertainties of cotton production during the territorial years challenged settlers in Mississippi to find means of livelihood that resembled the Indian mixture of hunting, farming, and herding. That adaptation by whites to the cotton frontier, more than the production of cotton itself, brought them face to face with local Indians. Before the United States even began to survey land in the Mississippi Territory, an estimated two thousand settlers had already squatted on unused lands. . . .

. . . As the territory entered the second decade of the nineteenth century, mounting hostility from the Creek Indians and impeding war against Great Britain deepened uncertainty and instability, pushed down the value of cotton . . . and slowed the sale of public lands. In one petition sent to Congress by inhabitants of the Mississippi Territory, the trap that cotton already set for the South—an economy highly sensitive to the price of a single commodity—was clearly defined: "Confiding as we have done on the measures of Government which were intended to restore foreign intercourse, and which held out the probability of success, we have continued to cultivate the article of cotton, to the growth of which our soil is so propitious, and omitted all or most other pursuits calculated to command money."

Under those circumstances, squatting on the periphery of private landholdings and Indian villages or on federal lands and then raising livestock to sell to planters, townspeople, and newcomers became a pervasive means to economic security. Already familiar with open grazing in the backwoods of Georgia and the Carolinas, many settlers in Mississippi's promising pine forests acquired cattle, horses, and hogs from Indians. Some bought the animals; others sequestered strays. In time, a family of squatters might earn enough from its own herding to purchase title to the land, or, if not, the mobility of livestock eased their relocation to another tract when threatened with eviction. Meanwhile, competition over grazing lands and ambiguity between trading and rustling heightened antagonism in their relations with Indians. Symbiotically, the success of some farmers in producing cotton and buying slaves—by creating a growing market for food—allowed those who were unable or unwilling to grow the staple a distinct avenue to economic security and social autonomy. From that process, among others, emerged the yeoman farmers of the nineteenth-century South, whose intermittent participation in the cotton economy through livestock trade buffered them from the risks of cotton agriculture and yet perpetuated their hopes of becoming slave-owning cotton farmers themselves.

By the second decade of the nineteenth century, the Mississippi Territory was fast becoming a cotton export region. Within a decade the non-Indian population had surpassed the number of Indians, increasing nearly fivefold to more than 23,000 settlers and 17,000 slaves. Although most white settlers still contended with obstacles to land acquisition and relied on multiple means of subsistence, planters who already possessed land or who could afford to purchase some in the private market committed more slaves to the production of more cotton. As one such individual described the process, "Here you will ask, what do they want with so many Negroes, the answer is, to make more Money—again, you will ask what do they want with so much Money, the answer is to buy more Negroes. . . . A Man's merit in this country, is estimated, according to the number of Negroes he works in the field."

The influx of Afro-American slaves into the territory affected the economic life of the Indians as deeply and equivocally as did white migration. More vulnerable to territorial laws than were Indians, Afro-Americans also struggled to preserve some economic autonomy and resilience within the narrowing interstices of a slave-labor, cotton economy. By trading among themselves and with Indians and whites—in foodstuffs, home manufactures, and even forbidden horses—slaves tried to secure for themselves what has been lately called an "internal economy," distinct from but tied to the larger regional system of staple agriculture. But legislation and slave patrols discouraged forms of economic exchange and social interaction that had previously brought blacks and Indians together—for example, in weekend marketing on the streets of Natchez. Meanwhile, some individuals within the Indian nations—principally members of mixed-blood, trade families—were themselves becoming owners of black slaves and planters of cotton. Although those developments eventually generated greater racial separation and stratification between southern Indians and blacks, they were too nascent before 1820 to close all channels of interethnic communication.

Throughout the colonial period slaves had perceived Indian country as potential refuge from bondage, and the increasing presence there of blacks owned by tribal members during territorial years may have even encouraged some runaways to take advantage of the confusion accompanying the movement of slaves to and from Indian jurisdictions. Cases of slaves being arrested by Untied States Indian agents for "want of a passport" and disputes over ownership of slaves who "ran away or were stolen" suggest that the blacks involved were playing an active role in creating their uncertain status within Indian country. Whether as slaves or as runaways, blacks who interacted closely with Indians during the early nineteenth century contributed to the formation of multiracial families and even of scattered communities across the South. One such community, whose members became known as "Cajuns of Alabama," grew rapidly during the territorial period along the west bank of the Mobile River; another group known as "Freejacks" took shape on the Tchefuncte River in Louisiana, along the Natchez-to-New Orleans road.

Given the potential for increasing ties with blacks, Indians found their own activities and mobility being curtailed by the Mississippi territorial government's efforts to reinforce the institution of slavery. In addition to federal laws requiring licenses and prohibiting alcohol in Indian trade, which were enforced by all territorial governors, Governor Sargent issued an ordinance in May 1880 to strengthen control jointly over commerce with Indians and slaves in Mississippi. The mere sight of an Indian or slave carrying into a house or store "any article which may be supposed for sale, or any bottle, jug or other thing in which liquor may be conveyed" was sufficient evidence for convicting the storekeeper or housekeeper. An initial law requiring slaves who participated in the Natchez marketplace to carry permits issued by their owners was extended over the entire territory in 1805 to declare that "no person whatsoever shall buy, sell, or receive of, to or from a slave, any commodity whatsoever without the leave or consent of the master, owner or overseer of such slave, expressive of the article so permitted to be bought, sold or bartered." Guilty persons would pay to slave owners four times the value of the item exchanged, the slave would receive ten lashes, and owners who allowed a slave "to go at large and trade as a freeman" had to pay a fine of fifty dollars. A statute enacted in 1810 further increased the risk of independent marketing to slaves by making it lawful for any citizen to apprehend a slave suspected of carrying goods without written consent.

The exchange of two items in particular—cotton and horses—threatened the property of planters and received special attention from lawmakers. In the spring of 1800, slaves were prohibited from the "raising and Vending of Cotton" and from "holding property in horses." Although some owners apparently permitted those activities, both the need to prevent theft of those valuable products and the desire to limit avenues of financial independence activated a comprehensive prohibition against possession of cotton and horses by slaves. To reduce the chances of petty rustling by black and Indian herdsmen, an act of March 4, 1803, prescribed that "no person whosoever shall send or permit any slave or Indian to go into any of the woods or ranges in the territory, to brand or mark any horse, mare, colt, mule, ass, cattle, hog, sheep, under any pretense whatsoever; unless the slave be in company, and under the direction of some reputable white person."

In southern folklore and history, Natchez and the road linking it with Nashville became legendary for crime and violence during the early nineteenth century. As the oldest and largest town in the territory (until Mobile was annexed in 1813), Natchez resembled urban places in other frontier or colonial regions in its very real function as a nexus of underground exchange activity and of volatile ethnic contact. "Ebriety [drunkenness] of Indians and Negroes on Sundays," complained Sargent on arriving in Natchez, made it "a most Abominable place"—a message that signaled his and subsequent governors' commitment to reversing customary trends. The seasonal encampment of one hundred or so Choctaw families around Natchez, where they bartered for ammunition and other supplies for hunting trips, had become a familiar part of the cultural landscape before the end of the eighteenth century. Under United States territorial control, however, officials and propertied residents loathed what they saw as pilfering, loitering, and carousing; thus they discouraged Indians from visiting the area. In 1807 Gov. Robert Williams even tried, with little effect, to require that Indians leaving their tribal lands carry passports to be issued at the discretion of government agents.

Incidents of drunken affrays and robberies among Choctaws, blacks, and whites, of violent and often fatal assaults committed against Indians, and of Indian thefts of livestock and crops were too numerous and various to describe here, but they all involved a confrontation between two different systems of justice. Much of the aggravation and theft perpetuated by Indians represented a form of banditry committed to protest against and compensate for the abandonment of protocol and respect by the growing American population. Because Choctaws traveling to hunt or to trade, for example, encountered more and more settlers unwilling or unable to share some corn or meat with them, as had traditionally been the case, they would simply take what was available from a field or pasture. Whenever an Indian was killed by a white or black assailant, an acute clash between tribal and territorial laws ensued. Although officials often expressed concern over the Indians' "Spirit of Retaliation," territorial courts rarely convicted and punished white men who murdered Indians on the pretense that guilt was difficult to prove in such crimes. Meanwhile, Indians followed their own rules of retributive justice, which required the kin of a victim to avenge his death by killing either the guilty person or some surrogate. As those of other United States territories, the early government of Mississippi tried, with great difficulty, to replace tribal systems of law and order with its own codes of trial and punishment. But in some cases of homicide against Indians, officials compromised by paying merchandise to relatives in compensation for their loss. In January 1809, for example, the Choctaw agent gave two hundred dollars' worth of strouds, blankets, and ammunition to the uncle and brother of an Indian killed the previous summer by William Bates. Bates reimbursed the agency in August. A revealing case of territorial conflict with Indian jurisdiction occurred in 1810, when two young Choctaws who executed another Choctaw under blood law outside the tribal boundary were arrested and imprisoned at Fort Stoddert. Fearful of "unpleasant consequences," Gov. David Holmes pardoned them but urged Judge Harry Toulmin "that they should be made sensible that they have been guilty of an infraction of our laws and that in future such conduct will not be tolerated."

Behind all of the legislative and police action directed against slaves and Indians reigned a deep anxiety over black insurrection, Indian warfare, and even combined rebellion by the two groups. News of the Gabriel Prosser revolt that was barely averted in Virginia drove Sargent to address a circular letter of November 16, 1800, to slave owners in the Mississippi Territory, exhorting "the utmost Vigilance" toward all slaves. Recent assaults on two overseers were evidence enough that greater attention to the slave laws had to be given by "all good Citizens." Fear that the increasing in-migration of slaves would introduce experienced insurgents from other slave regions nearly produced in the territorial legislation a law that would have prohibited the importation of "Male Slaves, above the age of Sixteen."

The self-conscious endeavor by white Mississippians to establish slavery safely in the midst of a large Indian population elicited from their officials an obsessive concern with well-organized and trained militias, adequate weaponry, and a responsive federal army—all overtly effective means of controlling subjugated ethnic groups. Although military officials repeatedly assured the government that the army and the militia were prepared to quell any outbreak of Indian or black hostility, the very prospect of having to mobilize against rebellion in one part of the territory heightened the fear of exposing another part to concurrent attack. In January 1811 hundreds of slaves in the adjacent territory of Louisiana turned their hoes and axes against planters outside New Orleans. Their march toward the city was quickly and violently stopped by troops of the United States Army's Southern Division, led by the cotton planter Gen. Wade Hampton. That revolt, which resulted in the brutal and speedy killing of nearly one hundred blacks in Louisiana, intensified apprehension the Mississippi Territory over thinly stretched defenses against both external and internal enemies. The declaration of war against Great Britain in 1812 then brought fear of racial war on different fronts to a climax. In a letter to General Wilkinson concerning possible withdrawal of troops from the territory for action elsewhere, Governor Holmes recited his faith in the friendship of the Choctaws but warned that "knowledge of our defenceless state . . . may tempt them to commit aggressions." Regarding blacks, Holmes continued, "Of the slaves, who compose so large a portion of our population I entertain much stronger apprehensions. Scarcely a day passes without my receiving some information relative to the designs of those people to insurrect."

The Creek War of 1813–1814, waged in the eastern valleys of the Mississippi Territory, has recently received skillful attention in regard to both its wide context of international affairs and its internal dimension of tribal politics. But the function of the military conflict in expanding the cotton economy and in enforcing concommitant racial control is not yet fully appreciated. As already indicated, the territorialization of Mississippi imposed multiple pressures upon Indian societies. In the

Creek nation, those pressures provoked increasing rebelliousness from a large segment of its population. Persistent demands by the Forbes company and the United States government that trade debts be paid through cessions of land severely tested the patience of Creek villagers. Indian leaders contested debts that were accounted to the nation but that actually had been incurred by individuals whose tribal status they did not recognize. When the company tried to add interest to their account, the Creeks grew angrier, insisting that "there was no word for it in their language" and accusing their old trade partner of wanting "to tear the very flesh off their backs."

Further aggravating those issues, settlers were sprawling from the Tennessee and Tombigbee-Alabama valleys, and territorial militiamen were making frequent border patrols into Creek country. The government's program of reforming, or "civilizing," Indian societies, which was aggressively implemented among the Lower Creeks by agent Hawkins, undermined the ability of the Creek nation to respond effectively to such pressures by expediting the emergence of a new class of assimilated Creek citizens who were themselves becoming cotton planters and slave owners. The tour of the rising Shawnee leader, Tecumseh, among the southern tribes during the summer and fall of 1811 injected into the already fractionalized Creek nation a surge of religious nativism and political militance, which took hold most strongly among the angry young men of the Upper Creek towns. In the summer of 1812, the tribal council ordered the execution of a group of Red Sticks, as the rebels were called, who were accused of killing settlers in Tennessee on their return from the town in Indiana where Tecumseh and his brother, the "Shawnee Prophet," resided. And in November it agreed to pay some $22,000 of debts owed the Forbes company by turning over to the firm each year the tribe's annuities from the United States. Those two explosive developments helped bring civil war to the Creek people by 1813.

United States intervention against the rebellious Creeks came swiftly and forcefully, making the Mississippi Territory the theater of one of the nation's bloodiest and most costly Indian wars. In July 1813 a party of Red Sticks, carrying ammunition and other supplies from Pensacola, was attacked by a joint force of territorial militiamen and Lower Creek adversaries. In retaliation Creek rebels attacked Fort Mims at the confluence of the Alabama and the Tombigbee rivers. On August 30, 1813, approximately 250 of the men, women, and children who had sought refuge inside the fort were killed during a siege that lasted five hours. News of the "massacre," which included reports that black slaves had joined the Red Sticks, threw the Mississippi Territory and adjacent states into an alarm that speedily mobilized soldiers and citizens into action.

The invasion of Upper Creek country by four separate armies of militiamen and federal troops proved to be a painful experience for Indians and non-Indians. Red Stick fighters and their families managed to evade United States soldiers and their Indian allies, who in turn resorted to burning abandoned villages to the ground. After suffering ten months of sickness, hunger, desertion, and severe discipline, the invasionary armies backed the Creek rebels into a bend of the Tallapoosa River. On March 27, 1814, approximately 1,000 Red Sticks stood up against a combined force of 1,400 whites, 500 Cherokees, and 100 Lower Creeks in the Battle of Horseshoe Bend, losing by the end of the day approximately 800 tribesmen killed. Having led personally the western Tennessee volunteers and provided much of the strategy in the Creek War, Andrew Jackson—a merchant, planter, and land speculator long interested in the Mississippi Territory—received command of the United States Army's Seventh Military District and proceeded to impose a peace treaty on the Creek nation. The beleaguered Creek leaders who signed the Treaty of Fort Jackson on August 9, 1814, agreed to cede fourteen million acres of land—more than one-half of present-day Alabama—even though most of them were Lower Creeks who had not rebelled against the United States.

The military subjugation of the Creek Indians greatly accelerated the transformation of the ethnic relations already underway in the Mississippi Territory. Indian trade in deerskins and other frontier commodities would never recover in the Deep South, forcing most Indian villagers to become marginal participants in the emerging cotton economy while allowing some to accumulate their own property in cotton lands and Negro slaves. Although banditry and violence would continue to serve many Indians in Mississippi and Alabama as means of resistance, the Creek War demonstrated the futility and danger of military confrontation and drove surviving militants out of the territory and into Florida. The Creek land cession that resulted from their defeat drastically contracted the area of Indian country and intensified the physical isolation of Indian villages from other inhabitants. Furthermore, the sudden availability of so much land to settlers, coinciding with the post-Napoleonic expansion of the demand for cotton in Europe, set in motion the great wave of public land sales and immigration that guaranteed the dominance of cotton agriculture over the territory's political offspring—the states of Mississippi and Alabama.

The "Alabama Fever," as the postwar boom in land sales and cotton production was called, revived the conflict between immigrant settlers and land speculators. As the average price of public land in the Creek cession rose above five dollars per acre by 1818, crowds of angry squatters assembled at land auctions to push for registration of their claims at the minimum price. Hostility toward large purchasers was tempered, however, by the heady climb of cotton prices above thirty cents per pound. Eager to produce for such an export market, small farmers and wealthy planters alike borrowed more and more money in order to purchase both land and labor. In 1817, the year in which Alabama became a separate territory and Mississippi acquired statehood, cotton annually exported from the region exceeded seventeen million pounds. The fragile financial basis of the expansion, though, soon reached its braking point. Just as Alabama was becoming a state, cotton prices plummeted in the panic of 1819 well below twenty cents per pound and stranded Alabamians with a land debt of eleven million dollars. But the cotton-export economy had already taken hold of land and labor across the South. Following a short period of contraction and adjustment, white Mississippians and Alabamians proceeded to import more slaves from eastern states and to expand cotton production across more land, of course borrowing more money to finance both.

Development of a cotton economy drastically altered the economic relations of Indian peoples with citizens and slaves in the Mississippi Territory. The United States government, through its own trade houses and with cooperation from private companies, pressured Indian tribes into making repeated cessions of land. In the concomitant transfer of public land into private market, the federal government allowed speculation by land companies and made ownership difficult for early nineteenth-century migrants. Settlers coped with that obstacle and with the uncertainty of cotton production through means of livelihood similar to those of neighboring Indians. Territorial laws meanwhile restricted the economic activities of slaves and limited their interaction with free individuals, confining them more to the production of cotton for their owners. The Creek War, more than any other action, accelerated the physical confinement of Indians into ethnic enclaves. By 1820 an American Indian population of more than 30,000 persons was surrounded by 42,000 whites and 33,000 blacks in the state of Mississippi and by another 85,000 whites and 42,000 blacks in Alabama.

While a new socioeconomic order originated from those processes, the strategies used to mitigate or to avert them created undercurrents of resistance that have been only slowly and inadequately uncovered by historians. The different economic adaptations selected variantly by Indian inhabitants of the Mississippi Territory greatly influenced impending struggles over removal, with some committed to commercial agriculture becoming the most staunch defenders of tribal homelands. Slaves in Mississippi and Alabama, meanwhile, continued to take economic initiative in defiance of their owners' economic interests, maintaining a market in self-produced and pilfered goods reminiscent of earlier exchange with Indians and settlers. Although they had greater freedom of choice, nonslaveholding whites also struggled to secure a safe, albeit uneasy, relationship with the cotton export market. Becoming endemic to life in the nineteenth-century South, those widespread attempts to minimize dependence on the expanding cotton economy made the conquest of peoples and places by King Cotton more tenuous and complex than perhaps the participants themselves believed it to be. Old Carothers McCaslin bought the land, as portended by William Faulkner, "with white man's money from the wild men whose grandfathers without guns hunted it, and tamed and ordered or believed he had tamed and ordered it for the reason that the human beings he held in bondage and in the power of life and death had removed the forest from it and in their sweat scratched the surface of it to a depth of perhaps fourteen inches in order to grow something out of it which had not been there before and which could be translated back into the money he who believed he had bought it had had to pay to get it and hold it."

Multiple Marriages, Many Relations

Fur Trade Families on the Missouri River

TANIS THORNE

The range of familial relationships among French-Creole and Central Siouan peoples in the 1820s, 1830s, and 1840s is so broad as to seemingly defy categorization. Intelligent outside observers such as Paul Wilhelm, Amos Stoddard, and the Jesuit and Protestant missionaries, found much to criticize in the French-Indian "half-breeds," but they also acknowledged there was a surprisingly diverse range in morality, character, and cultural leanings among them. Many mixed-bloods were

From Tanis Thorne, *The Many Hands of My Relations: French and Indians on the Lower Missouri* (Columbia: University of Missouri Press, 1996), 160–176. Reprinted by permission of the University of Missouri Press. Copyright © 1996 by the Curators of the University of Missouri.

born of casual sexual encounters and transient relationships. Mothers and their small children were callously abandoned by the fathers, and children were sometimes orphaned or were victims of neglect. Some ordinarily decent men had children by Indian women whom they abandoned when moving on to employment in different regions; examples are François Chouteau and François Chardon. Years later, Chardon tried in vain to locate his French-Osage child. Other relationships were long-lasting and harmonious. Some French-Indians were raised by the Central Siouans and knew no other identity except as Indians. Other had little or no contact with their Indian mothers or kin. There was a wide range of experiences for mixed couples and their French-Indian children.

Without question, there was sexual license at the lower Missouri trading posts in the 1820s and 1830s. Multiple unions of both men and women can be interpreted as clear indicators of the breakdown of the strict moral codes of both the Central Siouans and the French Catholics. Traditional morals plummeted, especially when people were under the influence of alcohol. Judged by Christian as well as native ethical standards, the sexual conduct of many of the French traders and trappers was morally reprehensible and irresponsible. Catholic codes of sexual conduct clearly had little power over a majority of westering Frenchmen, who departed from strict rules of sexual chastity and marital monogamy. An English visitor in 1833 described the French as "grossly licentious and profligate," stating that they had wives in every tribe with which they traded. Traders could be charged with using Indian women to advance their careers, just as Indian men could be indicted for using their sisters and daughters to advance their interests. Having multiple alliances with women in different tribes was good business, and it was a convenience as well. For example, Benito Vasquez, Jr., cousin and brother-in-law to the Papin brothers—Pierre Mellicour, Alexander LaForce, and Pierre Didier Papin—had three children by an Ioway woman and another by the sister of an Otoe chief, in addition to his numerous children by his Creole wife in St. Louis. "LaForce" Papin had four children by the sister of Pawnee Whiteman Chief, a daughter by an Otoe woman, and a son by an Omaha. The Shawnee mixed-blood William Rogers had children by each of his Omaha, Otoe, and Kansa wives.

In addition to having multiple relationships with Indian women, often simultaneously, it was not uncommon for a trader or trapper to have a white wife in St. Louis to whom he had been married by vows in the Catholic Church. Individuals who had white and Indian wives simultaneously included Joseph Robidoux, Manuel Lisa, Peter Sarpy, "LaForce" Papin, P. D. Papin, Benito Vasquez, and A. A., A. P., and Liquest Chouteau (the Papin brothers' first cousins)—to name only a few of the more prominent individuals in the trade. Manual Lisa, J. P. Cabanné, Peter Sarpy, and others brought their white wives to their trading posts, which was a source of anguish and embarrassment to the native wives. A few traders polygamously married Indian sisters (such as Bill Williams marrying Osage sisters), or two brothers married sisters, or brothers or business partners shared the same Indian woman. Wa-ko-tah-kende, a Yankton woman from the chiefly lineage of Little Crow, had five children by three trading partners—Menard, Picotte, and Chenie—from 1831 to 1842. Late in life, she married an Anglo-American.

Just as fur-trade fathers were likely to have multiple marriages, full-blood and mixed-blood women frequently had more that one spouse. The Pawnee mother of

LaForce Papin's children and the Ponca mother of Joseph and Frank La Flesche remarried full-blood men of their own or different tribes after separating from their French husbands, as did the Omaha woman, Mitain, and the Osage, Marie Pawhushan. Separations were not always the result of male abandonment, but were sometimes due to female initiative. Some Indian women severed ties over differences in child rearing, while others found their husbands' constant absences on voyages or trading expeditions too much to bear. Still others could not endure the rigors and dangers of traveling with husbands into territory of alien tribes. For these reasons women remarried men in their own tribes with relief. Their own kin groups provided the security and comfort they desired. Cultural and kinship ties among French Creoles on the one hand, and among Indian people on the other, frequently proved to be stronger and more enduring that marital bonds. The French man preferred to live with his kin, speaking French, and enjoying cultural practices familiar to him, while the native woman preferred her own kind. These social conflicts, often accompanied by irreconcilable views about the educational and religious training of French-Indian children, separated husbands and wives.

Nonetheless, there were many instances of faithful relationships that lasted until the death of one of the partners, for example, the Drips and Fontenelle couples. Other relationships, though not strictly monogamous, were enduring. Some examples include Sarpy's union with Nicomi, A. P. Chouteau's relationship with Rosalie Lambert, P. M. Papin's relationship with Sophie Mongraine, and Edward Chouteau's union with Rosalie Capitaine. Peter Sarpy provided a life estate for Nicomi in his will. Papin left his sizable estate in Bates County, Missouri, to his son Edward (one-quarter Indian) by Sophie Mongraine. Edward Chouteau, though he retired from the Indian country and married a white woman, provided for his children by his French-Osage wife in his will. Manuel Lisa charged the executor of his will with providing for the education of his two children by Mitain and left each child $2,000.

It was not unusual for fur traders to honor the Indian women they were allied to by Indian custom, though it was more rare to seal these bonds in the Catholic Church. Ambitious men hoping to win influence sought marriages within families of the hereditary elite. Some of these women carried tattoos on their foreheads as an emblem of their rank. Their children inherited high status from their Indian mothers. The imperious Nicomi, daughter of an Ioway chief and a woman of the Otoe-Omaha nobility, hardly fits the stereotype of the passive squaw, sold by male relatives for a horse or handful of trinkets. On one occasion, she decided to display her resolve: "Sarpy had refused her some blankets and calico she wanted. Madame Nekoma marched into the store, with that look on her face that bade the clerks stand aside, and grabbing several bolts of calico, she made for the Missouri river and heaved them in, declaring, in Indian, she would clear the store out in the same way. Before she got her second load to the bank Sarpy gave in and [told the clerk] to let her have anything she wanted."

Nicomi was a status-conscious, full-blood woman, who resisted being separated from her daughter, and who resented the implication that she was unfit to rear her properly. Nicomi had a very strong sense of her own consequence and authority and had a great deal of pride in her Central Siouan cultural heritage. She imparted to her daughter and granddaughters a pride and awareness of the responsibilities of their rank, and she adhered to traditional Indian customs in their training. Another

Indian woman who bore herself with regal bearing was the Osage wife of American Fur Company trader Giraud. Men who married such women were marrying up, rather than down, in the social scale.

European and Anglo-American travelers in the Indian country were bewildered by the deferential treatment accorded trader's wives. The personal pride these women occasionally displayed did not conform to these travelers' preconceived notions of the inferiority of Indians to whites and women to men. The Washington Irving party, which toured the West in the 1830s, was dismayed by the marked absence of servility on the part of the persons of Negro and Indian blood at A. P. Chouteau's trading post. Irving and his companions were astounded by the arrogance of Antoine Lambert, a French-Osage, just as Tixier on another tour was baffled by Baptiste Mongraine's presumption that the high birth of his daughter, Prairie Rose, made her a suitable match for a white man of his stature. Irving perhaps exaggerated when he said of A. P. Chouteau's post on the Grand Saline where French-Indians reposed: "In these establishments, the world is turned upside down: the slave is the master, the master the slave." Outsiders found that the Indian and the bicultural ranking system of the fur trade were quite different from the way they imagined it to be.

Monogamous, lifelong unions were definitely not the prevalent pattern. The mobility and ambitions of traders, trappers, and boatmen, combined with native customs that tolerated polygyny and remarriages for incompatible couples, encouraged multiple unions for both men and women. One consequence was that mixed-blood children were very rarely reared in family settings in which both parents were a continuous presence and guiding force. Extended family networks took the place of biological parents in acculturating children. Second, the frequency of remarriages of both mothers and fathers of mixed-bloods resulted in a wide and complex network of family ties among French, mixed-bloods, and full-bloods. There was also a marked increase in native people forming unions with persons from other tribes that produced children. It thus became a common experience for French-Indian children born after 1815 to have half-siblings in St. Louis, in other tribes, or within their mothers' tribes.

Child-rearing Practices

Mixed-bloods, even those born to the same set of parents, were reared in a perplexing variety of familial settings. No doubt a predominant experience was for the French-Indian children to be raised in the environs of trading posts, near the villages of their mother's people. They were thus exposed to a number of French Creoles and other mixed-bloods who frequented the posts, as well as having occasion to reside with their mother's kin as well. Among the Omaha and Kansa, a husband was expected to join the wife's household and materially contribute to her family. There are numerous examples where Omaha women openly resisted having their children taken from them to be educated. This was perhaps a violation of cultural norms in more matricentered horticultural tribes. Mitain never saw her young daughter, Rosalie, again after the child was taken to St. Louis, so Omaha women learned from her tragedy that the separation from young children could be permanent. When Michel Barada wanted to have his many children by Tag-a-lee-ha, an Omaha woman, taken to St. Louis to be baptized and educated in the care of Creole relations, Tag-a-lee-ha was adamantly opposed according to family traditions: "I don't want them to leave my people." Despite the opposition, some of the French-Omaha Baradas were educated and baptized in St. Louis and vicinity, and were reared among their kinfolk there. Antoine Barada, a legendary voyageur known for his strength, was raised by his Omaha kin, but was taken at age seven to St. Charles and reared by relatives there and trained as a stonemason. As in the Osage country, mixed-blood women were desirable sexual partners for chief traders. Two of the teenage Barada sisters became mothers of children by trading post commanders. Mary Barada contracted a liaison with Jean Pierre Cabanné (or his brother Frank), though he was twice her age. Their son, Antoine, was raised in St. Louis and became a riverboat engineer. Mary Barada afterwards married Edward Loise, a French-Osage, employed by the American Fur Company at Council Bluffs. Another French-Omaha Barada had a child, John, by Joshua Pilcher. By some reports, John was taken under the care of Chief Big Elk after the death of the mother; other reports indicate he was taken to St. Louis and raised by the French.

Documented cases of mixed-blood children being raised exclusively by their Indian kin are relatively rare. To move back and forth between Indian and French relatives, as many of the French-Osages appear to have done, was a surprisingly common childhood experience for many biracial persons born between 1800 and 1830. A benefit was that these children became bilingual and bicultural. Lucien Fontenelle and Rising Sun's children, for example, stayed close to their mother's people during their early years. Occasionally they traveled as a family with their father on his western ventures, as did the Drips family. Fontenelle sent the older boys to school in St. Louis; Logan, the eldest, was later employed as the Omaha interpreter. Lucien Fontenelle's premature death in 1842, an apparent suicide resulting from financial stress and alcoholism, kept him from realizing his ambitions for a large, well-stocked plantation south of Bellevue and high status for his children. In 1844, the Fontenelle boys were learning trades as Fort Leavenworth at the Indian Manual Labor School: Albert was 18, Tecumseh, 13, and Henry, 10. Albert was trained as a striker for a blacksmith; Henry learned the wagon-maker's trade.

Logan Fontenelle's contemporary, Joseph La Flesche (born in the early 1820s), was the son of a Ponca mother and a trapper-trader father. (It is possible, though unlikely, that the father was "Lafleche," the son of "Baptiste of Gonvil," enumerated in the 1825 Kaw treaty as a beneficiary of the "half-breed" tract.) Joseph had a half-brother among the Ponca. His mother did not like the father's long absences and eventually remarried a Ponca man. Joseph's Ponca uncle raised him and another orphan, Omaha-Ponca Wajepa, but when Joseph grew older and became more useful, the father took him on trading trips, and he learned through his apprenticeship the Pawnee, Ioway, and Omaha languages. Both Logan Fontenelle and Joseph La Flesche worked for Sarpy at his Bellevue post in their early manhoods. Joseph La Flesche married Mary Gale in 1846, and Logan married an Omaha woman in 1843. Henry Fontenelle, Logan's younger brother, married Emily Papin, daughter of LaForce Papin and the sister of Pawnee Whiteman Chief. Emily Papin had grown up among the Pawnee and Omaha and did not know for many years that she had a white father. She attended a missionary school in her teens.

Childhood upbringings like those of Emily Papin, Joseph La Flesche, Mary Gale, and the Fontenelle and Drips siblings are suggestive of the range of experiences of the more privileged French-Indians born of high-ranking native women and entrepreneurial French men. Both Indian and French kin were influential in their upbringing. The children of these unions were educated to the best of their relatives' ability with the expectation that they would enjoy continuity in their family's position of status. Many such fortunate mixed-blood children found nurture, acceptance, and training from a range of extended kin. The mixed-blood issue of short-term relationships also invariably carried their father's names and their mother's status as a badge of their identity; by the norms of the fur-trade society, they were "legitimate," too. Mixed-blood children knew who their parents were. A half-million-dollar probate case decided by the Missouri Supreme Court in 1872 tested the legitimacy of the "country" marriage of trader William Gilliss to Kahketoquoa, daughter of Piankashaw chief Leharsh in the 1820s. Although the testimony confirmed Gilliss's use of Indian women for short-term sexual gratification and political advantage, the court nonetheless confirmed the legitimacy of the marriage in Indian eyes and awarded Kahketoquoa's descendants by Gilliss a share in the estate.

One pervasive pattern seems to be that children received some formal "white" education or training. French fathers drew older children away from their Indian kin to attend missionary schools or to be raised by foster mothers in French bicultural society. For the French fathers of mixed-bloods, having their children baptized, educated, and Christianized at the mission schools was a demonstration of their concern for their moral development, as well as a sign of their children's rank, respectability, and suitability to marry non-Indians. Mixed-bloods who had received education and religious training at missionary establishments were more likely to marry whites or Christianized mixed-bloods from their own or other tribes whom they met in school. For example, Harmony Mission mixed-bloods Elizabeth Rogers and Susan Larine found husbands there in the early 1830s.

Berenice Menard Chouteau was at odds with the Catholic Church on some issues, but she did try to bring Christian influences to the Kawsmouth. Whether she and other French-Creole women at the Kawsmouth actively sought this responsibility, or whether it was foisted upon them, they were frequently entrusted with the upbringing of mixed-blood children, schooling them in religion and the conventions of white society. Although she had ten children of her own, Berenice also cared for French-Indian and mulatto children. One of these was Josephine Gonville, the daughter of Louis Gonville and the niece of Kansa Chief White Plume, who was married in her home in 1840 to Joseph Pepin. (The Sac-Fox Gonvilles and Pepins were both originally from Cahokia and had family ties that drew them together at the Kawsmouth.) Another was Elizabeth Datcherute, a Kaw "half-breed" reservee, daughter of mulatto Baptiste Datcherute and a Kaw woman; Elizabeth married an Illinois minister. Another Kawsmouth woman who served as a step-mother to mixed-blood children was Julie Roy Lessert, daughter of Louis Roy (hero of the Côte Sans Dessein battle against the Sac-Fox), and granddaughter of André Roy. Born in 1812 at the Côte, Julie Roy relocated with her family to a fifty-seven-acre parcel at the Kawsmouth after her father was remarried to a Capitaine, kin to the French-Osage Capitaine at Flat Rock Creek. Julie Roy married the Kaw interpreter, Clement Lessert, some time before 1830, and raised his French-Kaw daughter, Adele, though the natural mother was still alive. Adele married a devout Catholic, Moyse Bellemaire, in 1841. (Adele's brother, Clement, was an interpreter and guide for John C. Frémont). Julie Roy also cared for Charles Curtis, son of a white man and a "half-breed" Kaw allottee. (Charles Curtis became the Vice President of the United States under Herbert Hoover.) Still another foster mother was Andrew Drips's second wife, Creole Louise Geroux. Lucien Fontenelle had hoped to have his French-Omaha daughter Susan raised by his aristocratic Creole sister in Louisiana, but when the aunt peremptorily refused, Susan was sent to stay with the Drips family for polishing.

Sending mixed-blood children to be educated at mission schools or entrusting them to the care of foster mothers was a pronounced pattern on the lower Missouri River in the first half of the nineteenth century. Those who could afford it either sent their children to Catholic schools in St. Louis (the Sacred Heart seminary) or Marysville, Kansas. The Marysville school opened in 1849 with fifty-seven boarders and ten day scholars. Susan Bordeaux Bettelyoun, a French-Oglala-Brulé Sioux, recalled that "Most of the mixed-blood children taken to Marysville never knew any other home but the mission."

As Protestant and Catholic missionaries persistently ministered to the French-Indians along the Missouri River in the 1820s, 1830s, and 1840s, the chasm gradually widened between the full- and mixed-blood population. Although the missionaries' initial efforts were disappointing, over time their sustained efforts further accentuated cultural, economic, and religious differences between the full- and mixed-blood Osage. After 1820, the growing number of French and French-Indians in the Osage country from which to choose eligible mates encouraged Christianized mixed-bloods to intermarry with other Christianized mixed-bloods or whites, rather than with full-bloods. One missionary had a dangerous scrape with a Yankton warrior in the 1850s, because the Indian was convinced that by baptism the mixed-blood woman he wished to marry "became a white woman and that she would not be let marry him." Louis Burns, an expert on Osage history and culture, wrote that "Between 1675 and 1800, the predominate pattern was Euro men marrying Indian women. Mixed-blood men often married Indian women in this same period. After 1820, the pattern was established of intermarriage among and within the mixed-blood sub-culture."

Conclusion: Patrilineality and Rank

Catholic Church records of baptisms and marriages made by traveling missionaries along the lower Missouri River in the 1820s, 1830s, and 1840s, combined with fur company documents and government records of "half-breed" tracts, suggest a predominant pattern of unions between wintering partners (and their lower ranking employees) and Central Siouan women of local villages producing mixed-blood issue. As a composite population, mixed-bloods appear to have been cared for in their early years by their natural mothers in the Indian villages or trading post communities. Multiple marriages for both mothers and fathers were typical. Mixed-blood children were often temporarily sent to foster mothers or missionary schools as they grew older; sons frequently followed in their father's footsteps occupationally. Most mothers and fathers of mixed-bloods, though cultural values conflicted, acted responsibly as parents; they trained and educated their children, arranged good marriages, and in general provided for their well-being and prepared them for future success and happiness. Those who could afford it provided seminary education for female children, promoting marriages with either white men or their mixed-blood peers. Boys' bilingualism and occupational continuity with fathers encouraged them to marry full-bloods or mixed-bloods.

Such impressions from reconstructed family genealogies is supported by statistical data drawn from the "half-breed" reserve tracts. These data attest that it was more likely for first- and second-generation French-Indians to be drawn into the world of their French fathers through patrilineal family forms, and hence into the customs, religion and other cultural influences of bicultural French society. Unlike the Kaw and Osage treaties of 1825, which specifically enumerated individuals (38 Osages and 23 Kansas), granting them each one section of land in specific riverfront locations, the Great Nemaha Treaty of 1830 did not specify the names of the reservees. In 1841, a survey was made that identified a total of 121 eligible claimants: 50 Ioway, 47 Omaha, 21 Otoe, and 3 Sioux. The author of the report attempted to ascertain the current residences of these individuals for a possible sale of the reserve. He found them to be "widely dispersed." The Ioway, Omaha, and Otoe mixed-blood children were twice as likely to be raised at trading posts, military establishments, or French-Creole villages downriver than within tribal societies and thus were subject to strong detribalizing influences.

A similar tendency toward detribalization and geographic dispersal due to fathers' roles in upbringing can be found in the comparable evidence from the Sac-Fox and the Kansa "half-breed" reserves. When agent Thomas Forsyth compiled a list of the Sac-Fox mixed-blood claimants in 1830, six years after the treaty, ten were then living at Prairie du Chien, one at Florissant (attending the Sacred Heart Academy), one at St. Charles, five at Cahokia, and four in St. Louis. A petition made to the House of Representatives in 1829 by the Sac-Fox claimants stated that while some of the reservees live among the Indians, others "reside with and are raised and educated in the habits, manners and customs of the whites. [Many] have received good and some a very liberal education and are in all respects identified with the white population." An investigator trying to locate the Kansa mixed-bloods in the 1850s found it very difficult to ascertain their locations. Multiple marriages and geographic mobility made the identification and location of beneficiaries of the original reservees extremely difficult only twenty years after the treaty.

Similar problems confounded administrators in 1859 when another Great Nemaha list was compiled. The number of beneficiaries had grown to 461 mixed-bloods: 200 Yankton, 99 Otoe, 70 Omaha, 78 Ioway, and 14 Santee. Only a few reservees were born before the 1830 treaty, and about two-thirds of the Great Nemaha claimants were born after 1839. If the Yankton mixed-bloods are deleted from the sample, 51 percent of the claimants were second-generation with at least one "half-blood" parent, and 10 percent were third-generation. Twenty percent of the Ioway claimants, 7 percent of the Otoe, and 4 percent of the Omaha claimants were third-generation mixed-bloods with a smaller blood quantum. Based upon percentages drawn from a sample of 396 Nemaha claimants about whom information regarding ancestry is available, 32 percent were quarter-blood, 16 percent were half, 32 percent were three-quarter, and 8 percent were third generation. If the Omaha, Otoe, and Ioway alone are considered: 35 percent were quarter-blood, 38 percent were half (second generation unions of persons with half-blood quantum marrying others with half-blood quantum), and 17 percent were three-quarter-blood quantum.

These statistics show that there was a peak time period for cross-cultural alliances and the birth of French-Indian children, coinciding with competitive trade conditions. Children born of French-Creole/Canadian fathers and full-blood mothers were twice as likely to marry whites or other "half-breeds." From the available information, it appears that female mixed-bloods tended to marry whites (usually French Canadians or Creoles) more than male mixed-bloods tended to marry white women. Mixed-blood men frequently married full-bloods of their own tribes, were polygynous, and sired large families.

The data from the Great Nemaha Half-Breed Tract allotment records, collaborated by comparable information from the Osage and Kaw "half-breed" reserves, repudiate the stereotype of the isolated, alienated "breed" abandoned by an irresponsible father and scorned by both whites and Indians. Instead of an only child, it is more common to find two, three, or four mixed-blood siblings by the same parents. There were polygynous marriages and multiple marriages for both fathers and mothers, and having half-siblings was quite common. Having no full- or half-siblings was atypical. Frenchmen did enjoy much sexual freedom, but their purported "licentiousness," opportunism, and victimization of Indian women have been overdrawn by historians promulgating the myth of male anarchy on the frontier.

As both the Central Siouan and French-Creole peoples subscribed to patrilineal forms of kinship organization, the tendency for "half-breeds" to identify themselves with their father's French kinfolk appears to be a natural consequence. Because of this, the mixed-bloods were generally drawn into residential proximity, habits of dress, lifeways, and other shared symbolic indicators of identity (like language and baptism in the Catholic Church). Patrilineality and patrilocality, continuity in occupations as go-betweens, biculturalism passed from generation to generation, and endogamous marriages among mixed-bloods of different tribes— all of these served to distinguish the culture of the French-Indians from that of the full-blood peoples. Over time the pronounced patrilineal leanings, combined with the efforts of missionaries and government policy-makers who attempted to residentially segregate and unify mixed-bloods in Christian agricultural colonies, tended to widen the breach between Central Siouan full- and mixed-bloods.

Compared to the biracial families of Hudson's Bay and Montreal-based Northwest Company traders analyzed by Jennifer S. H. Brown, the lower Missouri River French-and-Central-Siouan mixed-bloods were subject to similar "centrifugal" forces of fragmentation—working against the formation of Central Siouan people as a distinct category and community of persons—as well as "centripetal" forces towards cohesion and *métissage*. However, the demographic, residential, economic, and political patterns among the Central Siouan mixed-bloods most closely resembles those of the Northwest Company (and also those of the French trading families of the Great Lakes in the 1600s and 1700s studied by Jacqueline Peterson) where patrilineal patterns of residency and continuity in fur-trading occupations brought mixed-bloods together in small, semi-endogamous settlements. Moreover, U.S. government policy encouraged métis community development by at least nominally supporting the creation of mixed-blood land bases and promoting identification with a "half-breed" identity.

Although the early 1800s were a time of rapid change for Central Siouan and French peoples, the social world that mixed-bloods inherited had a degree of continuity. The French and Central Sioux shared two basic premises of social organization: patrilineality and marriages between individuals of equal rank. Children knew who their parents were and knew their places within ranking systems to which both Indians and the French subscribed and both sought to preserve. Marriages were contracted between persons of comparable status in such a way as to allow families to perpetuate their status; there was a precarious social stability maintained by merchant-traders' (or ambitious clerks') marriages into chiefly families. Simply put, the traders were enriched while the chiefly lineages maintained their political authority.

◈ *F U R T H E R   R E A D I N G*

W. David Baird, *Peter Pitchlynn: Chief of the Choctaws* (1972)

Robert F. Berkhofer, Jr., *Salvation and the Savage: An Analysis of Protestant Missions and American Indian Response, 1787–1862* (1965)

James Taylor Carson, *Searching for the Bright Path: The Mississippi Choctaw from Prehistory to Removal* (1999)

Michelle Daniel, "From Blood Feud to Jury System: The Metamorphosis of Cherokee Law from 1750 to 1840," *American Indian Quarterly* 11 (1987), 97–125

Angie Debo, *The Rise and Fall of the Choctaw Republic,* 2nd ed. (1961)

Arthur H. DeRosier, Jr., *The Removal of the Choctaw Indians* (1970)

Arrell Morgan Gibson, *The Chickasaws* (1971)

———, ed., *America's Exiles: Indian Colonization in Oklahoma* (1976)

Michael D. Green, *The Politics of Removal: Creek Government and Society in Crisis* (1982)

Laurence M. Hauptman, *Oneida Indian Journey: From New York to Wisconsin, 1784–1860* (1999)

Reginald Horsman, *Expansion and American Indian Policy, 1783–1812* (1967)

———, *The Origins of Indian Removal* (1970)

Clara Sue Kidwell, "Choctaws and Missionaries in Mississippi Before 1830," *American Indian Culture and Research Journal* 11, no. 2 (1987), 51–72

———, *Choctaws and Missionaries in Mississippi, 1818–1918* (1995)

William G. McLoughlin, "Thomas Jefferson and the Beginning of Cherokee Nationalism, 1806–1809," *William and Mary Quarterly* 32 (1975), 547–580

———, *Cherokees and Missionaries, 1789–1839* (1984)

Frank L. Owsley, Jr., *Struggle for the Gulf Borderlands: The Creek War and the Battle of New Orleans, 1812–1815* (1981)

Joyce B. Phillips and Paul G. Phillips, *The Brainerd Journal: A Mission to the Cherokees, 1817–1823* (1998)

Francis Paul Prucha, *American Indian Policy in the Formative Years: The Indian Trade and Intercourse Acts, 1790–1834* (1962)

———, *American Indian Treaties: The History of a Political Anomaly* (1994)

James P. Ronda, *Astoria and Empire* (1990)

———, *Lewis and Clark Among the Indians* (1984)

Ronald N. Satz, *American Indian Policy in the Jacksonian Era* (1975)

Bernard W. Sheehan, *Seeds of Extinction: Jeffersonian Philanthropy and the American Indian* (1973)

John Sugden, *Tecumseh: A Life* (1998)

Robert A. Trennert, Jr., *Indian Traders on the Middle Border: The House of Ewing, 1827–1854* (1981)

Daniel H. Usner, Jr., *American Indians in the Lower Mississippi Valley: Social and Economic Histories* (1998)

Anthony F. C. Wallace, *Jefferson and the Indians: The Tragic Fate of the First Americans* (1999)

Thurman Wilkins, *Cherokee Tragedy; The Story of the Ridge Family and the Decimation of a People,* 2nd rev. ed. (1986)

J. Leitch Wright, Jr., *Britain and the American Frontier, 1783–1815* (1975)

———, *The Only Land They Knew: The Tragic Story of the American Indians in the Old South* (1981)

Mary C. Wright, "Economic Development and Native American Women in the Early Nineteenth Century," *American Quarterly* 33 (1981), 525–535

Mary E. Young, "Indian Removal and Land Allotment: The Civilized Tribes and Jacksonian Justice," *American Historical Review* 64 (1958), 31–45

CHAPTER
8

The Trans-Mississippi West
Before 1860

◈

The Plains warrior on his pony, galloping across the prairie with flowing war bonnet and lance is the image that most people call up when they think about Indians. Sioux, Cheyenne, Arapaho, Comanche and other peoples relied on the vast bison herds that spread over the plains. They erected buffalo-skin tipis wherever the hunting was good and moved on when the game retreated. In the popular imagination, this roving existence came to be associated with all Indians, and the conception of the Indian as a hunter/warrior/nomad was a stereotype that justified the dispossession of all native people. This stereotyped image, however, obscured the realities of Plains Indian life and history. The selections in this chapter will show that Plains tribes were far more complex than the image suggests. The history of these people provides a fresh insight into American westward expansion.

Even though there were more Indians in California than in any other area of comparable size north of Mexico, these native people are not well known to the average American. Most of them lived in small communities (sometimes called rancherías) *and lived by hunting and collecting plant foods. There was a gendered division of labor: men brought in game and fish, and women gathered nuts and acorns, and dug for tubers with digging sticks. Whites who saw these women at work derisively called California and Great Basin Indians "diggers," a slur against Indian gender roles as well as race. Spanish and Mexican settlements were limited to the Pacific Coast south of the San Francisco Bay area. The Anglos who settled in Mexican California clustered around John A. Sutter's Fort in the Sacramento Valley. The Treaty of Guadalupe Hidalgo ended the Mexican War and transferred California and the Great Basin to the United States in 1848. More importantly, in January 1848 Sutter's workers found gold in the Sierra Nevada foothills and set off a frenzied, worldwide rush for the precious metal. Tens of thousands of gold seekers stampeded into California. These men had little regard for Indian life or property. This huge influx of miners changed the conditions of life of California Indians forever.*

In the eighteenth and nineteenth centuries, some Plains Indian tribes enlarged the areas that they controlled. The Comanches seemed to expand their hunting and commercial territory at will. Document 1 is a Spanish account of the destruction of the San Saba mission in Texas in 1758. Sergeant Flores thought that the Comanche force was the largest and best armed he had seen in thirty years of experience. In Document 2 a Spanish official suspects that "foreign political agents" instigated the Comanches. These documents show how important trade was to the Comanches, who obtained firearms from the French. Trade enriched Indians, but it could cause problems, too. The white demand for buffalo robes led some tribespeople to hunt bison exclusively for their hides. In Document 3, the Pawnee chief Sharitarish explained this practice and its consequences to President James Monroe in 1822. Conditions in California were radically different from those on the Plains. In the early years of the Gold Rush, Indians outnumbered whites. In many areas they remained an important part of the California labor force. In 1850, the California State Legislature passed a law that provided for the indenture of Indians, which is reproduced in Document 4. This law consigned some California Indians to a life of servitude to white masters. Document 5 is an Indian description of the Gold Rush by William Joseph, a Nisenan Indian. Document 6 is an Indian agent's bleak report on Indian conditions in the California Mother Lode region.

1. Joseph Antonio Flores Describes the Comanche Destruction of the San Saba Mission in Texas, 1758

. . . The Sergeant was asked then why he had not tried to reach the Mission by some other route, instead of the one occupied by the hostile Indians. He said: There is a canyon between the hillsides and the river, and his party was caught in it when the enemy opened fire. The squadron became disorganized, and only one soldier, Joseph Vázquez, was able to slip through the barbarians to the shelter of the woods along the river bank, and he made his way as best he could by unobstructed paths. The witness declared that he and his soldiers would have put up a stronger resistance if the enemy had been armed only with bows and arrows, for the Spaniards were accustomed to fighting Indians armed with less powerful weapons [than muskets] and were able to protect themselves against arrows by means of their leather jerkins and shields, but they were helpless against the accurate musket fire of the Indian barbarians. The Sergeant expressed regret that there was no force in the Presidio able to prevail against a strong body of the enemy equipped with the same weapons as ours, and very cunning and treacherous besides.

He was asked whether, in his 30 years in the King's service, in the presidios and on the frontiers, he had ever before seen so many hostile Indians equipped with firearms and so skilled in their use as those he encountered on his way to the Mission. He replied that he had never seen or heard of hostile Indians attacking our forces in such numbers and so fully armed. Formerly the barbarians had fought

From Leslie Byrd Simpson, ed., *The San Saba Papers: A Documentary Account of the Founding and Destruction of the San Saba Mission* (San Francisco: John Howell Books, 1959), 52–53.

with arrows, pikes, hatchets, and similar weapons, against which the officers and soldiers of the presidios had held the advantage and had won many victories: at the Presidio of San Antonio del Río Grande, for example, and elsewhere. At the same time our forces had endured much suffering and many deaths at the hands of the savage barbarians, who did not spare the lives of the religious, or those of the women and children. Nor did they spare the buildings and workshops, which they burned to the ground.

2. A Spanish Official Gives an Analysis of Comanche Power, 1758

. . . [T]he new Presidio of San Luis, as well as the Mission under its protection, was attacked by 2,000 Comanche Indians and other allied nations, equipped with fire-arms and apparently instigated by [French] foreign political agents. They have in fact destroyed the Mission, with the lamentable murder of the Reverend Father President, two other Missionaries, two of the soldiers of the guard, and four others whom Colonel Don Diego Ortiz Parrilla had sent to their relief. The rest then retreated.

This occurrence, your Excellency, besides the sorrow that such a disaster must bring us, ought to make us cautious on many points, for the Comanche Nation is warlike and well instructed in the use of firearms through frequent communication with the French. The San Sabá River, moreover, flows through the very middle of the Apache Nation, which is as unfriendly to the Spaniards as it is unfaithful and treacherous, and false to its promises. The Governor [of Coahuila], having learned by experience, has made this clear. Another circumstance (which deserves the closest attention) is that the invaders are directed by foreign political agents.

3. Chief Sharitarish Foretells the End of the Pawnee Way of Life, 1822

My Great Father:—I have travelled a great distance to see you—I have seen you and my heart rejoices. I have heard your words—they have entered one ear and shall not escape the other, and I will carry them to my people as pure as they came from your mouth.

My Great Father— . . . If I am here now and have seen your people, your houses, your vessels on the big lake, and a great many wonderful things far beyond my comprehension, which appear to have been made by the Great Spirit and placed in your hands, I am indebted to my Father [Major Benjamin O'Fallon] here, who invited me from home, under whose wings I have been protected . . . but there is still another Great Father to whom I am much indebted—it is the Father of us all. . . . The Great Spirit made us all—he made my skin red, and yours white; he placed us on this earth, and intended that we should live differently from each other.

From Leslie Byrd Simpson, ed., *The San Saba Papers: A Documentary Account of the Founding and Destruction of the San Saba Mission* (San Francisco: John Howell Books, 1959), 32–33.

From James Buchanan, *Sketches of the History, Manners, and Customs of the North American Indians* (New York: W. Borradaile, 1824), 38–42.

He made the whites to cultivate the earth, and feed on domestic animals; but he made us, red skins, to rove through the uncultivated woods and plains; to feed on wild animals; and to dress with their skins. He also intended that we should go to war—to take scalps—steal horses from and triumph over our enemies—cultivate peace at home, and promote the happiness of each other.

My Great Father:—Some of your good chiefs, as they are called [missionaries], have proposed to send some of their good people among us to change our habits, to make us work and live like the white people. . . . You love your country—you love your people—you love the manner in which they live, and you think your people brave. I am like you, my Great Father, I love my country—I love my people—I love the manner in which we live, and think myself and warriors brave. Spare me then, my Father; let me enjoy my country, and I will trade skins with your people. I have grown up, and lived thus long without work—I am in hopes you will suffer me to die without it. We have plenty of buffalo, beaver, deer, and other wild animals—we have an abundance of horses—we have everything we want—we have plenty of land, if you will keep your people off of it. . . .

There was a time when we did not know the whites—our wants were then fewer than they are now. They were always within our control—we had then seen nothing which we could not get. Before our intercourse with the whites, who have caused such a destruction in our game, we could lie down to sleep, and when we awoke we would find the buffalo feeding around our camp—but now we are killing them for their skins, and feeding the wolves with their flesh, to make our children cry over their bones.

Here, my Great Father, is a pipe which I present you, as I am accustomed to present pipes to all the red skins in peace with us. It is filled with such tobacco as we were accustomed to smoke before we knew the white people. It is pleasant, and the spontaneous growth of the most remote parts of our country. I know that the robes, leggings, moccasins, bear claws, etc., are of little value to you, but we wish you to have them deposited and preserved in some conspicuous part of your lodge, so that when we are gone and the sod turned over our bones, if our children should visit this place, as we do now, they may see and recognize with pleasure the deposits of their fathers; and reflect on the times that are past.

4. A California Law for the Government and Protection of the Indians, 1850

The People of the State of California, represented in Senate and Assembly, do enact as follows:

1. Justices of the Peace shall have jurisdiction in all cases of complaints by, for, or against Indians, in their respective Townships in this State.

2. Persons and proprietors of land on which Indians are residing, shall permit such Indians peaceably to reside on such lands, unmolested in the pursuit of their usual avocations for the maintenance of themselves and families: *Provided,* the

A California Law for the Government and Protection of the Indians, 1850. This document can be found in Statutes of California, 1850.

white person or proprietor in possession of lands may apply to a Justice of the Peace in the Township where the Indians reside, to set off to such Indians a certain amount of land, and, on such application, the Justice shall set off a sufficient amount of land for the necessary wants of such Indians, including the site of their village or residence, if they so prefer it; and in no case shall such selection be made to the prejudice of such Indians, nor shall they be forced to abandon their homes or villages where they have resided for a number of years; and either party feeling themselves aggrieved, can appeal to the County Court from the decision of the Justice: and then divided, a record shall be made of the lands so set off in the Court so dividing them, and the Indians shall be permitted to remain thereon until otherwise provided for.

3. Any person having or hereafter obtaining a minor Indian, male or female, from the parents or relations of such Indian minor, and wishing to keep it, such person shall go before a Justice of the Peace in his Township, with the parents or friends of the child, and if the Justice of the Peace becomes satisfied that no compulsory means have been used to obtain the child from its parents or friends, shall enter on record, in a book kept for that purpose, the sex and probable age of the child, and shall give to such person a certificate, authorizing him or her to have the care, custody, control, and earnings of such minor, until he or she obtains the age of majority. Every male Indian shall be deemed to have attained his majority at eighteen, and the female at fifteen years.

4. Any person having a minor Indian in his care, as described in the foregoing Section of this Act, who shall neglect to clothe and suitably feed such minor Indian, or shall inhumanly treat him or her, on conviction thereof shall be subject to a fine not less than ten dollars, at the discretion of a Court or Jury; and the Justice of the Peace, in his discretion, may place the minor Indian in the care of some other person, giving him the same rights and liabilities that the former master of said minor was entitled and subject to.

5. Any person wishing to hire an Indian, shall go before a Justice of the Peace with the Indian, and make such contract as the Justice may approve, and the Justice shall file such contract in writing in his office, and all contracts so made shall be binding between the parties; but no contract between a white man and an Indian, for labor, shall otherwise be obligatory on the part of an Indian.

6. Complaints may be made before a Justice of the Peace, by white persons or Indians; but in no case shall a white man be convicted of any offence upon the testimony of an Indian.

7. If any person forcibly conveys any Indian from his home, or compels him to work, or perform any service against his will, in this State, except as provided in this Act, he or they shall, on conviction, be fined in any sum not less than fifty dollars, at the discretion of the Court or jury.

8. It shall be the duty of the Justices of the Peace, once in six months in every year, to make a full and correct statement to the Court of Sessions of their county, of all moneys received for fines imposed on Indians, and all fees allowed for services rendered under the provisions of this Act; and said Justices shall pay over to the County Treasurer of their respective counties, all money they may have received for fines and not appropriated, or fees for services rendered under this Act; and the Treasurer shall keep a correct statement of all money so received, which shall be

termed the "Indian Fund" of the county. The Treasurer shall pay out any money of said funds in his hands, on a certificate of a Justice of the Peace of his county, for fees and expenditures incurred in carrying out the provisions of this law.

9. It shall be the duty of Justices of the Peace, in their respective townships, as well as all other peace officers in this State, to instruct the Indians in their neighborhood in the laws which relate to them, giving them such advice as they may deem necessary and proper; and if any tribe or village of Indians refuse or neglect to obey the laws, the Justice of the Peace may punish the guilty chiefs or principal men by reprimand or fine, or otherwise reasonably chastise them.

10. If any person or persons shall set the prairie on fire, or refuse to use proper exertions to extinguish the fire when the prairies are burning, such person or persons shall be subject to fine or punishment, as a Court may adjudge proper.

11. If any Indian shall commit an unlawful offence against a white person, such person shall not inflict punishment for such offence, but may, without process, take the Indian before a Justice of the Peace, and on conviction, the Indian shall be punished according to the provisions of this Act.

12. In all cases of trial between a white man and an Indian, either party may require a jury.

13. Justices may require the chiefs and influential men of any village to apprehend and bring before them or him any Indian charged or suspected of an offence.

14. When an Indian is convicted of an offence before a Justice of the Peace punishable by fine, any white person may, by consent of the Justice, give bond for said Indian, conditioned for the payment of said fine and costs, and in such case the Indian shall be compelled to work for the person so bailing, until he has discharged or cancelled the fine assessed against him: *Provided,* the person bailing shall treat the Indian humanely, and clothe and feed him properly; the allowance given for such labor shall be fixed by the Court, when the bond is taken.

15. If any person in this State shall sell, give, or furnish to any Indian, male or female, any intoxicating liquors (except when administered in sickness), for good cause shown, he, she, or they so offending shall, on conviction thereof, be fined not less than twenty dollars for each offence, or be imprisoned not less than five days, or fined and imprisoned, as the Court may determine.

16. An Indian convicted of stealing horses, mules, cattle, or any valuable thing, shall be subject to receive any number of lashes not exceeding twenty-five, or shall be subject to a fine not exceeding two hundred dollars, at the discretion of the Court or Jury.

17. When an Indian is sentenced to be whipped, the Justice may appoint a white man, or an Indian at his discretion, to execute the sentence in his presence, and shall not permit unnecessary cruelty in the execution of the sentence.

18. All fines, forfeitures, penalties recovered under or by this Act, shall be paid into the treasury of the county, to the credit of the Indian Fund as provided in Section Eight.

19. All white persons making application to a Justice of the Peace, for confirmation of a contract with or in relation to an Indian, shall pay the fee, which shall not exceed two dollars for each contract determined and filed as provided in this Act, and for all other services, such fees as are allowed for similar services under other law of this State. *Provided,* the application fee for hiring Indians, or keeping

minors, and fees and expenses for setting off lands to Indians, shall be paid by the white person applying.

20. Any Indian able to work and support himself in some honest calling, not having wherewithal to maintain himself, who shall be found loitering and strolling about, or frequenting public places where liquors are sold, begging, or leading an immoral or profligate course of life, shall be liable to be arrested on the complaint of any resident citizen of the county, and brought before any Justice of the Peace of the proper county, Mayor or Recorder of any incorporated town or city, who shall examine said accused Indian, and hear the testimony in relation thereto, and if said Justice, Mayor or Recorder shall be satisfied that he is a vagrant, as above set forth, he shall make out a warrant under his hand and seal, authorizing and requiring the officer having him in charge or custody, to hire out such vagrant within twenty-four hours to the best bidder, by public notice given as he shall direct, for the highest price that can be had, for any term not exceeding four months; and such vagrant shall be subject to and governed by the provisions of this Act, regulating guardians and minors, during the time which he has been so hired. The money received for his hire, shall, after deducting the costs, and the necessary expense for clothing for said Indian, which may have been purchased by his employer, be, if he be without a family, paid into the County Treasury, to the credit of the Indian fund. But if he have a family, the same shall be appropriated for their use and benefit: *Provided,* that any such vagrant, when arrested, and before judgment, may relieve himself by giving to such Justice, Mayor, or Recorder, a bond, with good security, conditioned that he will, for the next twelve months, conduct himself with good behavior, and betake to some honest employment for support.

5. William Joseph (Nisenan) Describes the Gold Rush, c. 1849

Long ago the Indians had a camp on the north side of the oke·m mountain, the white people call that Mt. Oakum. The bluff by the river at the north side of that, (they) call that pu·lak' Bluff, and the white people call that Buck's Bar, in that river Indians and white men prospected for gold.

On the west side of Mt. Oakum two white men had their home in a small log cabin. From there they used to go to work at the river every day. The door of their house being left open, an Indian boy who was hunting around, felt hungry and went to that house to eat. When he had finished eating he saw two buckskin sacks full of gold, and silver money on that table. He took (it), put (it) in his pocket, and went off with (it).

When the two men came home from work they missed the gold and the money. They followed that Indian's tracks. They tracked (him) to the Indian's camp. They saw (him) playing cards and putting down sackfuls of gold. The white men took

From Hans Jorgen Uldall and William Shipley, *Nisenan Texts and Dictionary,* vol. 46 of the *University of California Publications in Linguistics* (Berkeley: University of California Press, 1966), 177–181. Copyright © 1966 The Regents of the University of California.

him right there. They took back all the money. But they took him all the same to a little valley on the west side of Mt. Oakum.

The white men gathered. From there, afterwards, they summoned all the Indian chiefs. They kept him there all day, waiting for one chief. When it was about three o'clock, they put a rope around (his) neck.

At length, that chief arrived. The Indians said, "(They) are waiting for you, they are going to hang the boy, go and prevent (it)!"

That chief went in the center (of the group of people). He talked, speaking white language, "Captain he says, Lowas he says, Hemas he says, 'Hang him up!'" he said.

(The white people) said to the mule, "Get up!" (The mule) pulled (him) up by the rope and hanged (him). All the Indians hollered and cried. When (he) was dead, (they) let (him) back down. They gave (him) to the Indians. The Indians took the body along and burned (it).

After that the Indians did not burgle or steal anything belonging to white people, "That is the way (they) will treat us if they catch (us)," they said. When the chiefs made speeches they said, "Do not take anything from (them), do not steal from (them), (they) will treat you that way if they catch (you)! Those white men are different men, they are not our relatives," they said, "(They) will hang you without mercy!" they said. All the chiefs preached that. They talked about that at every big time [celebration]. The Indians were very much afraid of the whites in the early days. That is what was done, the whites were bad in the old days, those who prospected for gold. Those who have come now brought women along, white women, those ones were good, they gave us all kinds of food when we went to their houses. That was bad whites in the early days, those who prospected for gold. Those who came next were good whites, married people, that was how it was in the old days.

About a year after that hanging (an Indian boy) found gold in a creek while he was hunting a deer, he killed the deer near that. He looked around for a tree to hang it on. He saw this gold. He took the deer along instead of hanging it up. When he brought (it) in to camp he told his relatives, "There is a lot of this gold, let us go tomorrow!" he said.

That morning at dawn they went, only the men, they left the women. They all brought a lot of gold. They took (it) to town to exchange (it), five or six times to that town, the same fellows.

The white men talked about (it), "Those Indians bring in a lot of gold from somewhere," said the storekeeper. Those white men talked about (it), those who worked on that river. "Let us watch those Indians, where is it they are always going?" they said. They saw those fellows go, the white men tracked (them) that way. From the hills they watched them at work. When the sun was in the west the Indians went back from work. (The white men) went past them in the opposite direction and found the gold.

The whites gathered and went there. When the Indians tried to go to work they found the whites there. They sneaked away, "That is those fellows, those who hanged that boy!" they said. That way those white men stole their prospecting place. The whites name that Indian Digging. The white men made a small town there and a ditch, and then they placer-mined with a lot of water and went twenty feet into the mountain.

This is over now, even the town is dead now, only one keeps a store there, a Chinaman. That is still called Indian Digging. That is what they did long ago, those fellows are dead and gone, there is not one of the Indians alive now. That is that.

6. An Indian Agent Views Conditions in the California Mines, 1854

Nevada City. Dec. 16, 1854

In accordance with your request, I have proceeded to obtain from the best information possible the number of Indians in Nevada and adjoining Counties, the names & number of their respective tribes, Their present condition and means of living, and herewith have the honor to report to you the result of my examinations. . . .

In order the more satisfactorily to ascertain their numbers & condition, I have been compelled to visit the most of their camps, and the counties of Yuba, Sierra Nevada, and Placer, in person and altho' my Estimates may not be strickly correct, yet they may be relied upon to be as near as correct as the nature of the circumstances will permit. The difficulty of ascertaining their exact number arises from the fact that they are frequently changing their camps from one section of their respective domain to another and sub-dividing their camps so as to be more convenient to the towns & ranches of the Whites. The great number of deaths which have in the last few years occured among them have tended to mislead many as to their real numbers at present. It will be seen by reference to this report that death has reduced their numbers in these counties more than half in the last 4 years. The cause of this mortality has been attributed to different causes. Some allege that it is the result of the change of their mode of living, being now compelled to live on entirely different food to what they were formally accustomed. Again it is said it is caused by adopting the Customs of the Americans in wearing clothes, that habitual use of ardent spirits which some traders have very improperly and illegally sold to them. These are some of the causes which have tended to swell the list of mortality among them, but the greatest number of deaths has been caused by that great Indian Scourge the Small Pox. This disease has in some instances entirely extinguished some of the smaller tribes, there being so few left by the disease that they have abandoned their camp and joined their neighboring tribes.

At this time there is none of this disease among them. Yet I find many of the Indians sick in the camps, I have visited and evidences of Mourning in almost every family. The disease with which they seem to be complaining most of this time, is a kind of slow feever which I think is the result of eating excessive quantities of spoiled meat, offal picked up by them about the various butcher pens which are to be found all over the mining country. With this refuse flesh they fill themselves, and perhaps it will be another week before they will get another meal, this creates diseases. Near the Emigrant road, and in the foothills many of the emigrant

An Indian Agent Describes Conditions of the California Mines, 1854. This document can be found in the Office of Indian Affairs, Letters Received, California Superintendency, RG 75, U.S. National Archives, Washington, D.C.

Stock die, diseased & the Indians driven by pinching hunger have lived upon these carcasses. In one tribe I visited 7 had died from this cause, (as was supposed) in the two weeks preceeding my visit. . . .

"Their present condition" is worse in my opinion than when the country was first settled by the Whites. They arrange their camps for the Winter more carelessly than formerly. Their manner of building huts now is to set up a few old sticks about ten feet in length & about eight feet apart at the base and fastened at the top by vines or withes. On this conical shaped frame they throw . . . brush and cover that either with old pieces of canvas obtained from deserted tents, or set up the bark of the pine against it making a kind of shelter from the rain of the winter season. An Apurture is left in the hut about two feet wide and three feet high through which the family and dogs crawl into them. They build a fire in the center around which they sit and sleep apparently comfortable. I am informed that prior to the settlement of the country by the Whites, they covered most of their huts with dirt, thus making them a perfect shelter and quite warm and comfortable in the winter.

Ten or twelve of these huts compose one camp they are generally crowded close together leaving the chiefs or sub-chiefs hut in the center.

They subsist chiefly upon Flour & Beef. They purchase it in the towns & at the ranches near which they camp with the gold dust they obtain by panning arround in the gold mines.

Sometimes a Miner will permit them to take a pan of dirt from his claim from which they get some gold. They scrape up the dirt about the end of the sluice boxes which sometimes pays them very well. On the rivers they obtain gold by scraping out the crevasses that has been abandoned by the Whites. The mining is done almost exclusively by the Squaws. I have known a company of four or five Squaws to obtain as much as $8. in one day. With this they purchase flour & beef & most generally of the worst that there is in Market.—Meat that can not be sold to others is sold to them.

The men are very indolent spending their time mostly laying about camp. Formerly they exercised more in search of game. Now there is no game since the settlements of the Whites. The Deer which were in the greatest abundance around their camps are now entirely driven off or killed. The Hares & Quail are mostly destroyed by the White man, and now the country is entirely without game up on which the Indian can at all subsist. They hunt but little therefore, and seldom kill anything but a few squirrels. They have nothing to [do]. When their Squaws fail to bring them enough to eat they will go arround the ranches in the country & kitchens in towns & beg something to eat. In the counties I have visited all the streams are mining streams & the water is constantly muddy which drives all the fish out.

Prior to 1849 in one weeks fishing on the Yuba & its tributaries in the fall season the Warriors would kill enough fish to last them through the Winter. These were dried & packed in their huts to be used when wanted in the Winter. At present there are no fish in the streams. A few Warriors visited the shoals in the Yuba near Col. Brofitts ranch this past fall for the purpose of fishing, but I am informed that they could eat them as fast as they caught them. This source of subsistence is entirely destroyed. Another great source of suffering among the Indians arises from the singular, & to the Indian unaccountable fact that the crop of acorns have failed completely for the last three years. The acorns formerly furnished them an abundant supply of Bread & that without any trouble to them. They think this is very strange & wonder much Why the Oaks bear no more. The present season a few acorns are to be found in the foot hills in Yuba County. Not one has been seen in Nevada & Sierra Counties.

◈ *E S S A Y S*

The spread of European colonization, trade, firearms, and the horse set in motion forces that altered Plains Indian life. Tribes adopted the horse, increased their reliance on the buffalo, and contended with each other for the best hunting grounds. Plains tribes also sought commercial advantages based on their control of hunting grounds and trade networks. In the first essay Pekka Hämäläinen, doctoral candidate at the University of Helsinki, argues that the Comanches operated a major trade center in the Upper Arkansas River Basin. In his view, Comanche trading was the justification for the expansion of Comanche territory. Perhaps Comanche raiding should be viewed as a kind of trade war. The second essay illustrates that not all western Indians were masters of their own destinies in this period. California during the Gold Rush offers a stark contrast to the Comanche experiences. The Gold Rush (1848–1860) was so chaotic that sorting out its impacts on Indians is a difficult matter. While Indians died at astonishing rates, some seemed to be able to find ways to accommodate to startling new and dangerous conditions. Albert L. Hurtado, professor of history in the University of Oklahoma and coeditor of this volume, examines several California regions and argues that Indians had different experiences according to time, place, and historical circumstances. His essay depicts a world where Indians had little room to maneuver and where Anglo-Americans used brutal means to dominate the native population.

The Western Comanche Trade Center
Rethinking the Plains Indian Trade System

PEKKA HÄMÄLÄINEN

Few works in Plains Indian scholarship have been as influential as John C. Ewers's 1954 portrayal of the Upper Missouri River trade center. In a compelling, tightly argued essay entitled "Indian Trade of the Upper Missouri before Lewis and Clark," Ewers demonstrated that in the eighteenth- and early nineteenth-centuries Mandans, Hidatsas, and Arikaras operated a thriving trade center at their earth lodge villages along the banks of the Upper Missouri River. This trade center was a great gathering point for peoples and goods alike. The corn, horses, manufactured goods, and luxuries of the villagers attracted both Indians and Euro-Americans from all directions, creating one of the busiest trading hubs in Native North America. Since its publication, Ewers's classic article has inspired a plethora of studies, which have further elaborated on his model of a Missouri River-centered trade system. Perhaps

From Pekka Hämäläinen, "The Western Comanche Trade Center: Rethinking the Plains Indian Trade System," *Western Historical Quarterly,* vol. 29 (Winter 1998), 485–513. Copyright by Western History Association. Reprinted by permission.

the greatest contribution of these works is the insight that the Upper Missouri villagers were not only a major trading locale within the Plains region, but also a focal point in an extraordinarily complex Native American trade network that stretched from the Great Lakes in the East to the Pacific Ocean in the West.

Our enduring intellectual fascination with Mandan, Hidatsa, and Arikara commerce has greatly deepened our understanding of the dynamics of Plains Indian trade, but the focus on this system has also created problems. The elaborate Upper Missouri trade has captured the scholarly imagination so completely that the other Plains regions have received only meager coverage. There has been particularly little interest toward the eighteenth- and nineteenth-century Southern Plains hunters—Comanches, Kiowas, and Plains Apaches. Scholars have identified active trading points among Caddos, Wichitas, and other eastern horticulturists of the Southern Plains, and while the hunters appear in these studies as trading allies, the primary attention has clearly been on the villagers. A more balanced picture can be found from the recent studies on Plains-Pueblo interaction, but these works have concentrated solely on the precontact and early contact periods before 1700. Ignored as an object of specific studies, the eighteenth- and nineteenth-century southwestern Plains have been viewed as a mere hinterland for the adjacent, more sophisticated trade centers. Almost without exception, the Comanches, Kiowas, and Plains Apaches have been depicted as secluded and unspecified groups, whose only function was to procure commodities, mainly horses and bison products, for the bustling Mandan, Hidatsa, and Arikara markets, and to provide an outlet for the surplus goods of the Upper Missouri that villagers channeled to the south. On a map, a single arrow extending from the Upper Missouri villages to the southwestern Plains has usually sufficed to describe the hunters' participation in the Plains trade system.

Enveloped in the myth of independent, self-sufficient bison hunters and horse raiders, the Comanches, Kiowas, and Plains Apaches form a largely unwritten chapter of Plains Indian economic history. It has been only in the last few years that scholars have begun to fill in the details. Pivotal in this trend have been recent Comanche studies, which show that these people, especially Western Comanches who lived near New Mexico on the western flank of Comanchería, were much more active traders than has previously been thought. However, what kind of role the Comanches played in the Plains Indians trade system is still largely unclear. This essay attempts to answer that question by taking the new Comanche studies a step further: Western Comanches were not only active traders, but also operated a major trade center. This center existed from the 1740s to about 1830 on the Upper Arkansas River Valley and was the nexus point of an extensive trade network that stretched from the Rio Grande to the Mississippi River and from central Texas to the Missouri River. Describing the evolution, structure, and eventual collapse of this previously unrecognized trade center should dispel the traditional conceptualization of the Plains trade system that relegates to the southwestern Plains a mere backup role. Or, to put it another way, the Western Comanche center is the missing piece that allows us to abolish the old bias toward the Northern Plains and to form a picture of the Plains trade system that is more balanced geographically and more accurate and richer historically.

Before entering the Euro-American historical consciousness as the horse-mounted rulers of the Southern Plains, Comanches were members of the Eastern

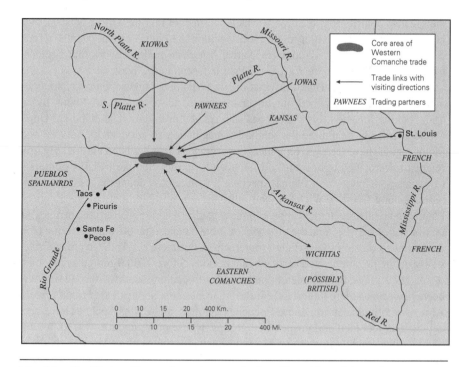

Map 8.1   The Western Comanche trade center in the mid- and late-eighteenth century.

Shoshone people who hunted bison on foot along the northwestern margins of the Plains. Having left their traditional homelands in present-day Nevada, Utah, and Idaho around 1500, the Shoshones flourished as Plains hunters until the late seventeenth century, when a Siouan expansion from the east forced them to retreat to the Great Basin. While migrating toward the mountain deserts, the Shoshones apparently intersected the northward expanding horse frontier, which had been launched during the Pueblo Revolt in 1680, when the fleeing Spanish colonists left behind most of their livestock. Horse technology opened unforeseen hunting possibilities on the bison-rich Plains, thus encouraging some Shoshones to reenter the grasslands. This time taking a more southern route across the mountain ranges, these Shoshone bands moved onto the southwestern Plains around 1700. The southern route brought the Shoshones in contact with the Utes, who named them *komantcia,* and when the Spanish encountered them in 1706, they followed the Ute practice and called them Comanches.

When the Shoshone-Comanches reentered the Plains they were the aggressors. In 1700, most of the western shortgrass Plains were the domain of various Apache bands, which in the preceding centuries had gradually migrated southward from the Subarctic. The two groups were immediately drawn into intense warfare for the region's natural resources, markets, and trade routes. Even though the southwestern Plains encompassed a huge expanse, both groups depended on relatively small areas, the river valleys, for their survival. The Comanches needed the water, grass, cottonwoods, and shelter of the valleys for their growing horse herds, and the Apaches needed the same micro-environments for their mixed hunting and farming economy. The Comanches also tried to replace the Apaches as the preferred trading allies of New Mexico. This would have allowed them to monopolize the access to Spanish manufactured goods and Pueblo garden products that were an indispensable addition to their high protein and high fat, bison-based diet. Another allurement of the New Mexican markets was that Taos, Pecos, and other eastern Pueblos were attached to a complex Native trade network that covered most of the Southwest and thus provided access to distant luxuries, such as exotic pottery. On the broadest level, the wars can be seen as a rivalry over the crucial trading location between the Pueblos in the west and the Southern Plains villages in the east. East-west trade routes along the major waterways of the Southern Plains date back at least to the last centuries of the first millennium. Later, around the mid-fifteenth century, an elaborate exchange system with two geographically differentiated branches emerged between the Pueblos and the southeastern Plains. In the north, Apaches trafficked in meat, hides, and corn along the Arkansas River, while farther south, a semi-nomadic community called Jumanos built a flourishing trading culture along the Red, Brazos, and Colorado Rivers. The more numerous Apaches gradually replaced the Jumano middlemen, seizing total control of the east-west routes by 1700. But the dominance of the Apache traders was short-lived. As the Jumanos faded away, Comanche contenders emerged, touching off yet another chapter in the struggle over the lucrative Southern Plains trade.

Comanche-Apache rivalry continued into the nineteenth century, but all-out warring lasted only a few decades. The Apaches' semi-sedentary way of life made them vulnerable to Comanche cavalry attacks and guerrilla warfare. The well-mounted and mobile Comanches were also able to acquire firearms from French traders, while the Apaches' only access to European markets was through the Spanish, who refused to sell guns to Indians. Militarily beaten and economically marginalized, most Apache bands abandoned the Plains and fled westward to the Sangre de Cristo Mountains. By the early 1730s, Comanches controlled most of the major river valleys of the southwestern Plains as well as the trade with New Mexico. The stage was also open for them to seize the highly desired trading niche between the commercial and population clusters of the Southwest and southeastern Plains.

However, if the Comanches had expected their victory to yield immediate prosperity, their hopes soon vanished. The hard-won monopoly of New Mexico markets proved to be a disappointment. The Comanches traded rather extensively with the Pueblos, bartering hides, dried meat, and tallow for corn, beans, squash, tobacco, and pottery, but trade with the Spanish, who redirected much of Pueblo commerce into their own hands, was a constant source of frustration. The Spanish did trade axes, knives, hoes, bridles, horses, and mules for bison products, deerskins, Apache and Pawnee slaves, and salt, but the volume of the trade did not meet Comanche expectations. (The Comanches obtained salt, a highly demanded commodity, from the Salinas area in present-day New Mexico.) It is important to note that the problem had more to do with the limitations of Spanish supply than the magnitude of Comanche demands; the Comanches had relatively finite needs— they obeyed the nomadic maxim that favors mobility over material accumulation.

The Spanish failure to supply the Comanches stemmed from several factors, the principal of which was New Mexico's marginal position in the Spanish overseas empire. Lacking exploitable natural resources, New Mexico was regarded essentially as a buffer colony that served to protect the empire's more vital southern areas from foreign invasion. It received limited financial support from the Crown and consequently suffered from chronic economic stagnation and shortages of goods. These problems were aggravated by Spain's mercantilistic trade laws, which protected Spain's own manufacturers by forcing the colonies to rely on the mother country for their supply of manufactured commodities. The effects of these laws on New Mexico were disastrous. Remote from the sea, the colony had to ship its goods from Mexico City along a circuitous and extremely costly land route. New Mexican merchants also suffered from the bureaucratic inflexibility of the Spanish administrative system. In 1501, in order to guarantee the continuity of Spain's military hegemony in the Americas, the Crown had forbidden the distribution of firearms among Indians. Fearful of losing the Comanche trade to French gun traders, Spanish officials petitioned frequently for an exemption from the law, but the rigid bureaucracy did not react until the late 1780s. Similarly, the sale of livestock was also restricted by laws, again preventing New Mexicans from meeting Comanche demand. In the 1750s, for example, New Mexican governors repeatedly forbade the sale of mares, studs, and donkeys to Indians, thereby trying to prevent them from raising surplus animals for exchange with the French.

To compensate for their unfavorable trading position with New Mexico, the Comanches began to raid the colony for the goods they could not acquire by trade. This proved to be a perfect solution to their dilemma, for they could still carry on a limited exchange with the New Mexicans, whose options were restricted by a delicate play-off situation: the Spanish could not punish Comanche raiders by cutting off their trade completely, because that would have left the door wide open for French traders—and French colonialism—to filter in from the Mississippi Valley. Consequently, from about the late 1730s to the late 1770s, a peculiar pattern of alternating trade and warfare dominated Comanche-New Mexican relations. Governor Thomas Vélez Cachupín's notations at Taos in 1750 summarize the situation well:

> [T]he trade that the French are developing with the Cumanches [*sic*] . . . will result in most serious injury to this province. Although the Cumanche nation carries on a like trade with us, coming to the pueblo of Taos, where they hold their fairs and trade in furs and in Indian slaves whom they take from various nations in their wars, and in horses, mares, mules, knives, large knives [*belduques*], and other trifles, always, whenever the occasion offers for stealing horses or attacking the pueblos of Pecos and Galisteo, they do not fail to take advantage of it.

Also in reaction to the insufficiency of the New Mexican trade, the Comanches began to form other commercial ties, thereby initiating a process that eventually established them as the dominant trading group on the Southern Plains. The first logical step in this direction was to seek contact with French traders and unlicensed *coureurs de bois,* who in the early eighteenth century began to inch their way up the Arkansas River from their infant colonies in the Lower Mississippi Valley and the Illinois Country. Although the primary motive of the French was to open trade with New Mexico, which they erroneously imagined was rich in silver, they were also eager to trade with the Indians, whose products fueled their domestic consumption and external commerce. The first tentative Comanche-French contacts occurred in the 1720s, but it took more decades before Louisiana's slowly growing economy reached a level that allowed large-scale trading operations in the West. A final barrier to the trade was removed in the late 1740s, when the French unlocked the Upper Arkansas commerce by mediating an alliance between the Comanches and Wichitas. Vélez, writing in 1754, provides one of the best accounts of the evolution, structure, and geography of Comanche-French trade:

> Along the banks [of the Arkansas River] the French come to trade with the Jumanos tribe [Wichitas] living there, whom they favor and work toward subduing. Through them they have begun to have trade with the Comanches, friends of the Jumanos, who live like nomads along the banks of [the Arkansas] and other nearby rivers . . . French trade with the Comanches is confined to the barter of rifles, gunpowder, bullets, pistols, sabers, coarse cloth of all colors, and other inexpensive merchanise [*sic*], for skins of deer and other animals, horses, mules, burros, and a few Indian captives whom the Comanches have taken as prisoners from other tribes with whom they are at war.

Meanwhile, the Comanches also forged commercial ties with the various horticultural groups to the east and northeast. Such trade offered considerable benefits for both groups. Reflecting their proximity to New Mexican ranches, the Comanches had quantities of horses and mules to sell, while the horticulturists had traded with the French since the early eighteenth century and consequently had sizable surpluses of guns and other manufactured products. The two groups could also engage in a complementary exchange of subsistence goods: the horticulturists could use hides, dried meat, and fat to supplement their diets and trade with the French, while the Comanches needed corn, beans, squash, and fruit to eliminate the chronic carbohydrate deficiency from their diets. The trade in subsistence goods must have become increasingly important for the Comanches during the eighteenth century as their fluctuating relations with the Spanish prevented them from maintaining stable interaction with the Pueblos, their traditional suppliers of garden products.

These mutual benefits laid the foundation for a rapid expansion of the Comanche trade network. This expansion began in the late 1740s, when the Comanches entered into an alliance with the Wichitas, who lived along the Lower Arkansas River and consisted of four subgroups: Taovayas, Tawakonis, Iscanis, and Wichita proper. The Wichitas formed the cornerstone of the Comanche trade system. They were the main importers of garden produce and tobacco to the Comanches, and they were the primary exporters of Comanche horses, mules, and products of the hunt. The Wichitas also served as middlemen between the Comanches and French, channeling horses, mules, bison products, and Apache slaves to the east and guns and other manufactured goods to the west. This lucrative tripartite trade continued to thrive even after Osage pressure forced the Wichitas to relocate to the Red River in the late 1750s.

The momentum of the Wichita accord also carried the Comanches into an alliance with the Pawnees, the Wichitas' close relatives, by the early 1750s. Trade with the Pawnees, who controlled an extensive territory from a core area of villages along the Loup and Platte Rivers, was an important addition to the Comanche commercial system. It provided the Comanches access to the guns and other manufactured goods the Pawnees acquired from their Arikara and Wichita relatives and French traders. The peace also decreased Pawnee horse raids, which had plagued the Comanches since the 1720s, although it did not make the new allies entirely immune to mutual aggressions. As with most Plains Indians, the Comanches and Pawnees viewed occasional raids on trading allies as a sanctioned way to rectify periodic imbalances in resource distribution.

During the latter part of the eighteenth century, the Comanches also managed to extend their trade zone among the Kansas, who lived near the junction of the Missouri and Kansas Rivers and who were engaged in the burgeoning fur trade the Spanish and French were developing from St. Louis and Louisiana. The French-Spanish pathfinder Pedro Vial wrote in 1785 that the Comanches received guns and ammunition from "Canses [Kansas], Guahes, and Guitavoiratas, who live in the north, and who are supplied by the traders, who come from Nueva Horleans and Yliones [Illinois], and who enter among them via the Rio del Misuri [Missouri]." In return for manufactured goods and agricultural products, the Comanches supplied the Kansas with horses, mules, and "buffalo hides, with and without hair, which they process and tan very well."

Guahes and Guitavoiratas, the two other groups mentioned by Vial besides the Kansas, provide further clues to the evolution of the Comanche trade network. Guahes apparently means Iowas, who occupied villages and cultivated crops on the stretch between the Missouri and Des Moines Rivers, and Guitavoiratas is a translation of the Cheyenne name for Kiowas, who resided south of the Black Hills in the mid-eighteenth century. Unfortunately, like the Kansa connection, the beginnings of the Comanche-Iowa and Comanche-Kiowa ties are lost to history.

While the majority of Comanches were carving out a trade empire in the east and north, a part of the nation migrated in the 1740s and 1750s southeastward to Texas, where they put down new roots and began to raid Spanish horse ranches. The result was a division of the Comanches into two distinct branches, which Spanish officials labeled as Eastern (Texas) and Western (New Mexican) Comanches. The eastern division consisted mainly of Kotsotekas (*kuhtsutƱhka,* "buffalo eaters") who resided around the middle Red River Valley, while the more diverse western branch included Yamparikas (*yampatƱhka,* "root eaters"), Jupes (*hupenƱƱ,* "timber peoples"), and Kotsotekas who occupied a core region extending from the Upper Canadian Valley north of the Arkansas River. Although distinct units, the two branches continued to interact, as Domingo Cabello y Robles, governor of Texas, reported in 1786: "[T]he Eastern Cumans [Comanches] take the horses which they acquire in their wars and pillages to the rancherías of the Western Cumanches, who are known by the name Yambaricas, and barter them for guns, powder, bullets, lances, cloth, pots, knives, etc., which the Western Indians acquire from the Canse [Kansas] . . . and Aguaés [Pawnees]."

This account is significant for several reasons. First of all, Cabello makes a clear distinction between the economic orientation of the divisions: he associates the Western Comanches more with trading and the Eastern Comanches more with raiding. Although overgeneralized—the eastern bands traded quite actively with the Wichitas and Euro-Americans—Cabello's distinction is valid in the sense that the Western Comanches qualify better as specialized traders. The Eastern Comanche commercial system never became as extensive as that of their western relatives, for they focused increasingly on raiding the wealthy but poorly protected Spanish ranches and missions in Texas and Northern Mexico. Cabello's account also shows that the two Comanche divisions had an established trade relationship, in which the western bands bartered a portion of their manufactured goods for the eastern bands' horses and mules. This trade channel was critical to the Western Comanches, who needed large numbers of animals to stock their trade with Wichitas, Pawnees, Kansas, Kiowas, Iowas, and French. The need for horses became even more acute in the 1760s, when the Western Comanches began to supply animals to the New Mexicans, the very same people they had stripped of horses through their incessant raids.

An often overlooked aspect of the Southern Plains trade system is the involvement of British traders. When the Treaty of Paris in 1763 established the Lower Mississippi Valley as a boundary between Spain and England, the British immediately secured their control of the eastern bank by lining it with a string of military and trading posts. During the following years, these posts became centers for a sizable British contraband trade to the Southern Plains. Although most British traders focused their activities among the eastern horticulturists, some pushed toward western Comanchería, probably using the Wichita villages as their base. Because of its illegal nature, this trade is poorly documented in the historical record, but the reports of panic-stricken Spanish officials shed some light on it. In 1772, for example, Athanese de Mézières, lieutenant governor of Natchitoches, demanded that countermeasures be taken to block the threatening British commercial expansion among the Western Comanches. In a similar vein, Viceroy Antonio María de Bucareli lamented in 1772 that the Comanches, along with most Southern Plains groups, had obtained such quantities of British guns that they had begun to abandon their traditional weapons. In return for their firearms, the British probably received typical Western Comanche exports—horses, mules, and products of the hunt—as well as precious intelligence concerning the military conditions in Spain's northern frontier.

The Western Comanches were, therefore, consummate traders, who controlled an extensive commercial network on the Southern Plains. More than this, however, they also operated a trade center that was very similar to the other well-known major centers of Native North America. To sustain this argument it is necessary to define exactly what is meant by a major trade center. Although no systematic theoretical treatment of the concept in the Native North American context is available, most scholars agree that a major trade center meets most or all of the following criteria: 1) the center serves an extensive hinterland by being an axis of several trade routes, some of which involve long-distance trade; 2) commodities moving through the center are varied and preferably include both durable and non-durable goods; 3) the volume of commodities moving through the center is considerable; 4) the center is capable of producing surplus commodities for exchange; 5) the center serves as a collecting and redistribution point of commodities; and 6) the center has a precise geographical location.

The Western Comanche case fits this profile almost perfectly. To begin with, the Western Comanche traders were the main axis of a complex and multifaceted commercial network that spanned several environmental zones, linking together numerous groups and embracing a vast hinterland. Further, a great variety of both durable and non-durable commodities passed through their hands: guns, powder, ammunition, knives, axes, kettles, bridles, textiles, horses, mules, slaves, salt, bison products, deerskins, tobacco, corn, beans, squash, fruit, and other agricultural products.

Although lack of significant quantities of data prevents a detailed analysis of the amount of goods moving through the Western Comanche center, fragmented sources indicate that the volume was substantial. Several observers noted in the eighteenth century that the Western Comanches were remarkably well supplied with manufactured products through their numerous trade contacts. For instance, Pedro Fermín de Mendinueta, governor of New Mexico, reported in 1768 that a Wichita trading party had brought 17 horseloads of guns to the Western Comanches. Moreover, their trade with the Wichitas received a considerable boost in 1771, when the Spanish agreed to pay the Taovayas artificially high prices for their products if they stopped trading with the British. The increased wealth allowed the Taovayas to expand their commerce with the Western Comanches even further. This was also discerned by Fray Francisco Atanasio Domínguez, who was astonished by the Western Comanches' wealth and trading power at the 1776 Taos fair. He noted that "they sell buffalo hides 'white elkskins,' horses, mules, buffalo meat, pagan Indians . . . good guns, pistols, powder, balls, tobacco, hatchets, and some vessels of yellow tin" and explained, "They acquire these articles, from the guns to the vessels, from the Jumanas Indians." A rare glimpse at the extent of the French trade is provided by a Spanish report from 1748, which relates that 33 French traders visited the Western Comanches and bartered large quantities of muskets for mules.

When not interrupted by raiding, the Western Comanche-New Mexican trade was quite voluminous too. In 1774, for example, 60 Western Comanche households came to Taos and traded 140 horses, more than two per family. But horses were not the only staple exchanged in great quantities. The high demand for labor in the silver districts of Nueva Vizcaya and the *Recopilación* of 1681, which obliged Spanish to ransom Indian captives enslaved by other Native groups, stimulated the slave trade. When visiting the Taos fair in 1750, Fray Andrés Varo noticed that the Spanish "gathered everything possible for trade and barter [with Western Comanches] . . . for deer and buffalo hides, and, what is saddest, in exchange for Indian slaves, men and women, small and large, a great multitude of both sexes, for they are gold and silver and the richest treasure for the governors." So crucial were the Western Comanches' goods to the local New Mexican economy that regardless their unrelenting raiding in the 1740s, Spanish officials decided in 1748 that they could not afford to deny their access to Taos fairs.

However, to understand the true significance of the Western Comanche trade, the questions of culture and meaning must also be considered. The value of trade goods is not a given; it is culturally determined, and when goods cross ethnic boundaries, culture intervenes and attaches new meanings to them. To Western Comanches, as to many other Native peoples of North America, the value of many Euro-American goods was less utilitarian than supernatural and symbolic; paints were not just simple mixtures of oil, water, and dye, but powerful symbols that helped the Western Comanches perform ceremonies, and medals were not just pieces of cheap silver, but important tokens of chiefly authority. This notion has far-reaching implications when estimating the extent of Western Comanche trade. Although an exchange of a few containers of paint may not seem to add much to the volume of exchange from an Euro-American perspective, it may have been a major transaction for Western Comanches, as they were purchasing something that was laden with symbolic value. A telling manifestation of the power of beads, mirrors, medals, and other non-utilitarian trade goods is that a large portion of them accompanied their owners to graves and the afterlife. It is, of course, impossible to give any exact measure to this non-material element of the Western Comanche trade, but it would be equally impossible to understand that trade without acknowledging its existence.

One of the most compelling factors supporting the view that the Western Comanches ran a major trade center is their massive surplus production. They were famous for their skillfully tanned bison and deer hides, but horses were clearly their primary export product. They were first reported to have large herds in 1740, and by the late 1770s and 1780s they had between two and one-half to three horses per capita. This number attests to the existence of a substantial surplus economy since hunting and transportation needs on the Plains required only a maximum of one horse per person. To understand just how heavily the Western Comanches were committed to surplus production, one has to realize that their horse wealth was not based exclusively on their access to the New Mexican ranches. Instead, they adopted an elaborate horse production system, which featured advanced herding strategies, extensive use of Indian and New Mexican captives as herders, and a dispersed settlement pattern that was geared to the demands of horse foraging rather than bison hunting. Through its vast capacity, this production system functioned as an engine that allowed the Western Comanches to build and operate their complex and far-flung trade network.

The Western Comanches also played an important redistributive role in the Plains commercial system. Besides purchasing horses from the Eastern Comanches with manufactured goods, they also passed on guns, powder, ammunition, and tools to New Mexicans, who suffered from a chronic shortage of manufactured items. The first reference to such trade is from 1760, and by 1776 it had become established enough to be based on a specified exchange rate, as Fray Domínguez pointed out: "If they sell a pistol, its price is a bridle." What makes these redistribution activities significant is that they contradict so strikingly the conventional view of the Southern Plains hunters as mere consumers of the manufactured goods that adjacent trade centers channeled to the interior. Like the Mandan, Hidatsa, and Arikara villages, whose status as a pivotal trade center was enhanced greatly by their strategic location at the intersection point of the expanding gun and horse frontiers, the Western Comanches too could profit from their position between the sources of these goods. Like their northern counterparts, the Western Comanches ran a major redistribution point, which absorbed and sent out various commodities to all directions.

The only difficulty in identifying the Western Comanches as operators of an important trade center is that their mobile lifestyle makes it difficult to visualize a geographically fixed center. A closer look reveals, however, that despite their migratory way of life, their trading activities were geographically focused. In his detailed discussion on Comanche foreign policies, Thomas W. Kavanagh has distinguished between two contrasting and spatially distinct Western Comanche strategies. The southern groups, primarily Kotsotekas living east of Pecos, specialized in raiding and were often hostile toward Europeans, while the Yamparika, Jupe, and Kotsoteka bands ranging northeast of Taos usually welcomed foreign traders. Kavanagh's analysis places the nucleus of Western Comanche commercial activities in the vicinity of the Upper Arkansas Basin, a view that is supported by direct evidence pertaining to Western Comanche trade. The eighteenth-century historical record contains several references to traders visiting the Western Comanches on the Upper Arkansas Valley. One of the most telling accounts comes from the Spaniard Felipe de Sandoval. While traveling to New Mexico in 1749, Sandoval encountered a huge Western Comanche trade fair of more than four hundred tipis on the Big Timbers of the Arkansas, a thick growth of cottonwood stretching from the Purgatoire River to the present-day Colorado-Kansas border, and the favorite campsite of the Western Comanches. During his sojourn at the camp, Sandoval witnessed visits from other Comanche, French, Wichita, and even German traders, who stayed several days among their hosts bartering firearms, powder, ammunition, hatchets, and glass beads for horses, slaves, and robes.

Situating the trade center on the Upper Arkansas River was founded on compelling strategic logic. The valley was separated from New Mexico only by the relatively passable Sangre de Cristo Range, and it was easily accessible to the Pawnees, Kansas, Iowas, and Kiowas from the north and northeast and to the Wichitas, French, British, and Eastern Comanches from the east and southeast. This central location freed the Western Comanches from the arduous and often treacherous task of traveling after the trade and allowed them to focus their commercial activities at their own camps. The French, who considered the Arkansas artery the key to the Southern Plains trade, frequented Western Comanche camps, but others came too. Cabello noted that the Eastern Comanches took horses to Western Comanche camps, and Sandoval observed that the surrounding Western Comanche bands "came to this [Upper Arkansas] rancheria from several others which I did not see." José Francisco Ruíz, a knowledgeable Mexican frontier official, wrote in 1828 that the Pawnees went to trade with the Comanches, but the Comanches never visited them. Although there is no direct evidence, it is almost certain that this pattern dates back to the eighteenth century. Before 1800, the Pawnees traveled to the western shortgrass Plains to hunt bison twice a year and to Santa Fe to trade about once every three years, and it is likely that they conducted most of their trade with the Western Comanches during those hunting and trading expeditions. It is also probable that the Kansas and Iowas visited Western Comanche camps during their regular hunting excursions to the western Plains and Upper Arkansas country. Facilitating the Pawnee, Kansa, and Iowa trade journeys was an intricate web of established Indian trails that led from the Republican and Kansas Rivers to the Great Bend of the Arkansas, almost at the doorsteps of the Western Comanches.

The Western Comanches made trade journeys only to New Mexico and the Wichita villages, and even these routes were active in two directions. Although the New Mexican law strictly forbade trade expeditions among the Western Comanches, they do appear in the historical record. In 1746, for example, the ongoing traffic prompted Governor Joachín Codallos y Rabal to make unlicensed trade excursions from Taos to Western Comanche country punishable by death. Further, in 1768, five Spaniards and a Pueblo Indian were killed under unknown circumstances during a trade venture among the Western Comanches. There is also evidence that the increasingly equestrian and mobile Wichitas were more frequent visitors to Western Comanche camps than previously has been supposed.

The historical and archeological evidence does not allow locating specific sites of the Western Comanche trade center on the Upper Arkansas Basin. One reason

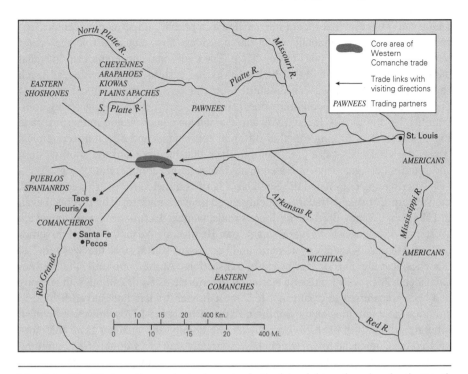

Map 8.2   The Western Comanche trade center in the late-eighteenth and early nineteenth centuries.

for this is that the late eighteenth- and nineteenth-century Comanches have received little attention from archeologists, who have focused their efforts on earlier periods and other areas. Moreover, the temporary camps of the nomadic Western Comanches do not yield enough diagnostic artifacts for systematic spatial analysis of their economic and commercial activities. On the other hand, even if the problem of evidence could be eliminated, it still would be impossible to determine an exact location. Although the Big Timbers was its focal point, the center constantly shifted up, down, and across the Arkansas corridor as the Western Comanches moved from one source of game, grass, and timber to another. This does not mean, however, that the Western Comanches did not operate a genuine trade center. Like the great Shoshone rendezvous on the Great Basin or the Dakota rendezvous on the James River, the Western Comanche center is best conceptualized, to use William R. Swagerty's terminology, as a significant impermanent center, a shifting trading point within a confined geographical region. This places the Western Comanche center below primary permanent centers, but above minor trading points, tertiary centers, and local trade hubs in Swagerty's finely-grained scale.

Because of their temporary nature, Swagerty ranked the Shoshone and Dakota rendezvous as secondary centers in order to distinguish them from the primary permanent centers in the Southwest, Pacific Northwest, and on the Upper Missouri. The Western Comanche center does not necessarily fit into this category, however. The fact that the center was more stable than the seasonal Shoshone and Dakota rendezvous suggests that it could be labeled as a primary impermanent center. This becomes even more emphatic when one considers how crucial a role the center played in the Southern Plains trade system. The traditional conceptualization is that the system revolved around the Pueblo towns and eastern farming villages, which can be viewed as gateway communities, crucial passage points into and out of distinct ecological and economic zones. However, between the two gateway communities lay the ideally located Western Comanche center, where numerous trade routes intersected, linking together different ecosystems and different economies. It was the vital nucleus, a great central place that incorporated the southwestern and southeastern gateways into a compact interregional commercial system.

After having dominated the Southern Plains commerce for over three decades, the Western Comanche traders suddenly faced a severe reversal. The reversal began in 1779, when Spain, tired of continuous raids, launched a full-scale war against the Western Comanches. For several years Juan Bautista de Anza, the gifted governor of New Mexico, waged a systematic and successful war against the Western Comanches, leaving no room for peaceful transactions. At the same time, the Western Comanches' ties with Louisiana started to deteriorate as well. Although the colony had been transferred to Spain in 1762, most French traders had stayed behind to continue their activities on the Southern Plains. During the 1770s, however, Spanish officials gradually took full control over the colony and enacted laws that suppressed the Comanche trade, which they accurately saw as a stimulus for continuing horse raids in New Mexico and Texas. Moreover, to protect Upper Louisiana against British encroachments from Canada and American expansion from the Ohio River Valley, Spanish officials redirected the colony's commercial power toward the strategically crucial Northern Plains. Finally, British traders were eliminated from the Southern Plains after 1779, when Spain joined the thirteen rebelling colonies against England and seized the eastern side of the Lower Mississippi River, thus making it difficult for British traders to slip into the Southern Plains. This situation was ratified in 1783 by the Treaty of Paris, which expelled England from the southeastern corner of North America. Although the Spanish granted a monopoly over the Indian trade in the Floridas to a Scottish company, they were careful not to allow the company to extend its operations across the Mississippi River onto the Southern Plains, which were regarded as a buffer zone for Northern New Spain.

As the Western Comanches' ties with colonial powers were quickly loosened, their relations with their Native trading allies began to unravel as well. Exchange with the Kansas and Iowas, whose trading power was impaired by overhunting and Osage expansion, seems to have faded in the late eighteenth century, for there is no trace of such trade in the nineteenth-century historical record. Interaction with the Kiowas was disrupted by hostilities, which were sparked by Kiowa and Plains Apache expansion toward Western Comanche territory in the late eighteenth century. But the most serious setback was an erosion of the Wichita alliance, which reflected a general decline of the Wichita trading culture. The downfall of Wichita traders began when Spain rechanneled the bulk of Louisiana's commercial resources to the Northern Plains, but an even more serious blow was their virtual elimination from the Mississippi Valley trade by the formidable Osages. The Western Comanches-Wichita trade did not end completely, but contacts were sporadic at best and strained by violence as the Comanches attempted to steal what they could not get through trade.

By the late eighteenth century, then, the Western Comanche trade center had become virtually paralyzed. Of earlier contacts, only the Pawnees and Eastern Comanches remained, while the ties with the other allies had been either badly frayed or completely cut off. To make matters worse, the Southern Plains were swept in 1780–1781 by a devastating smallpox epidemic, which killed thousands, further slowing the already sluggish pulse of the Western Comanche trading economy. The Western Comanche community curled inward to regroup itself economically and socially. However, this hiatus lasted only a short time. As the old trade contacts melted away, new ones were already being forged, and within a few years the Western Comanche trade center was as busy as ever.

This swing of the pendulum was triggered by the famous Comanche-Spanish accord in 1786. In this peace initiative, the Western Comanches and the Spanish agreed to refrain from all hostilities and to develop commercial relations with each other. For their part, the Spanish promised to establish regular trade fairs, to distribute presents to peaceful chiefs, and to regulate the fairs so that the shrewd New Mexican traders could not exploit their Native clients. In return, the Western Comanches agreed to stop raiding, to trade only with New Mexico, and to accompany Spain on joint military expeditions against the Apaches. These agreements gave rise to a thriving trade. Nine fairs were held at Taos, Pecos, and Picurís in 1787 alone, and during the following decades the Spanish sponsored regular fairs at the eastern Pueblos.

On the other hand, the peace also opened the southwestern Plains to New Mexican traders, who soon challenged the Pueblo fairs as the main link between the Western Comanches and the colony. Trade on the Plains became an official part of New Mexico's frontier policy in the late 1780s, when the Spanish, Pueblos, and *génizaros* (detribalized Plains Indians) were allowed to take their trade out to the grasslands. These traders, commonly known as Comancheros, made several annual visits to the Plains, bartering metal goods, fabrics, tobacco, and beads for Western Comanche horses, mules, bison hides, dried meat, tallow, deerskins, and captives. Reflecting their waning interaction with the Pueblo farmers, the Western Comanches also bought large amounts of bread, flour, corn meal, sugar, and other foodstuffs from the Comancheros. The fragmented record suggests a brisk exchange. In 1814, for example, two Comancheros reported to have bartered 46 blankets, about five hundred pounds of provisions, and large quantities of tobacco for about 20 horses and mules and six hundred to eight hundred pounds of meat and lard. Perhaps the most striking feature of the New Mexican-Comanche trade was, however, the gun trade, which was legalized in 1786. Viceroy Bernando de Gálvez, the architect of the policy, justified the sale of guns by arguing that it would weaken the Indians' military force because the muzzle-loading musket was a less effective weapon than the bow, which "is always ready for use." Moreover, to ensure this, Gálvez specified that guns should have long barrels, to "make them awkward for long rides on horseback, resulting in continual damages and repeated need for mending or replacement." Nonetheless, the Western Comanches were eager to buy even these inferior guns because they did kill effectively in inter-tribal wars and thus made precious commodities in inter-tribal trade.

As to the geography of the trade, it was formerly believed that the Comancheros depended on chance meetings with their Native clients, but recent studies suggest that they relied more on fixed rendezvous. Significantly, one of the most important of these gatherings was held at the confluence of the Arkansas and Pur-gatoire Rivers, at the western edge of the Big Timbers of the Arkansas. When the members of the Stephen H. Long expedition explored the Upper Arkansas River in 1820, they found a well-marked Spanish trail leading from the valley toward Taos via the Purgatoire corridor.

At the same time the Western Comanches were enjoying their revitalized trade with New Mexico, they also managed to reactivate their eastern trade contacts. Enticed by the commercial vacuum left by French and British traders, the Americans began to infiltrate the Southern Plains in the 1790s from their bases at the Lower Mississippi watershed and Kentucky. The first recorded Western Comanche-American contact took place in 1796, when a group of Americans built a block-house among the Yamparikas. Spurred by the Louisiana Purchase and the opening of the Santa Fe Trail in 1821, the trickle of American traders gradually grew into a stream, and during the first third of the century several American trading parties visited the Upper Arkansas and Western Comanche countries. The dynamics of the American trade closely resembled those of the Comanchero trade: Americans took manufactured goods and foodstuffs among the Western Comanches and received in return horses, mules, and bison products. The only major difference was the ab-sence of trade in captives, which played an important part in the Comanchero trade. Although the Comanche-American trade clearly violated the Comanche-Spanish treaty, there was little the Spanish could do. As was the case during the earlier Spanish-French competition, their options were limited by the dynamics of colonial rivalry: coercing the Western Comanches by cutting commercial ties with them would have only meant losing them permanently to the American orbit. Once again, the Western Comanches had managed to turn their strategic position be-tween two colonial spheres into a commercial success.

A major chapter in the renaissance of the Western Comanche commerce was the revival of northern contacts. Between about 1790 and 1806, possibly through several truces, the Western Comanches, Kiowas, and Plains Apaches gradually forged a lasting peace. The three groups established a joint occupancy of the southwestern Plains, which involved a distinct geographical division of labor: the Western Comanches traded to the south, west, and east from their Upper Arkansas core area, while the Kiowas and Plains Apaches traded with the Mandans and Hidatsas to the north. Moreover, the three groups also traded with each other, taking advantage of variations in their resource domains: the experienced Western Comanche herders could offer more horses and mules, but the Kiowas and Plains Apaches had better access to the handy, high-quality British guns through their Upper Missouri contacts.

The ethnic composition of this northern trade branch changed in the early nineteenth century, when Cheyennes and Arapahoes, driven from their homelands near the Black Hills by the Lakotas, displaced the Kiowas and Plains Apaches as intermediaries between the Western Comanches and the Upper Missouri villages. This change seems to have taken place sometime in the 1810s, because by the opening of the next decade the Cheyennes and Arapahoes were making regular trade journeys among the Western Comanches. In 1820, the Long expedition heard of a hybrid Western Comanche, Kiowa, Plains Apache, Eastern Shoshone, Cheyenne, and Arapaho camp on the Upper Arkansas. A year later, on the Big

Timbers of the Arkansas, the Jacob Fowler expedition came across an enormous Western Comanche-dominated trade assembly, which hosted about five hundred Kiowa, Plains Apache, Eastern Shoshone, Cheyenne, and Arapaho households as well as Indian traders from Taos. If anything, this change was favorable for the Western Comanches. The Cheyennes were highly effective as middlemen and in all probability provided a more reliable access to the Upper Missouri markets than the Kiowas and Plains Apaches.

Already bustling with renewed trading activity, the Western Comanche trade center received a further boost when the Eastern Shoshones established a trade relationship with their relatives. It has been argued that the Comanche-Shoshone trade dates back to the late eighteenth century, but decisive proof of this does not exist until the early 1820s, when Fowler and Edwin James, the botanist of the Long expedition, listed the Eastern Shoshones among the many groups who attended the Upper Arkansas fairs. The Eastern Shoshones were apparently drawn to the Arkansas Valley by the Western Comanches' gun supply. In 1805, Lewis and Clark found the Eastern Shoshones in a desperate need for firearms, as they had been cut off from the Canadian fur trade by Blackfeet. In exchange for guns, the Eastern Shoshones probably offered horses, for they were known as highly successful herders.

Besides incorporating new groups into their commercial system, the Western Comanches also continued to trade with some of their traditional allies. Although often interrupted by raiding and violence, the trade connection with Pawnees endured, as Ruíz noticed in 1828: "The Comanches trade horses for guns and ammunition with other Indians, who in turn secure them from the United States of North America. The Aguaje [Skidi Pawnee] Indians of New Mexico sell guns made in Great Britain which are preferred by the Comanches." The French scientist Jean Louis Berlandier remarked that the Comanches were, in the late 1820s, "abundantly supplied with firearms" through the Pawnee trade. Yet the most important of the old, persisting trade contacts was the one with the Eastern Comanches. As before, the Western Comanches exchanged manufactured products for the horses and mules the Eastern Comanches stole from Texas. Spanish officials tried to stop the raids by extending the New Mexican peace to Texas, but to little avail. In fact, instead of serving as an example for the eastern bands, the Comanche-Spanish accord in New Mexico encouraged their raiding, because they could now sell large numbers of animals to New Mexico through the Western Comanches. The Spanish were fully aware of this connection, but they feared that closing the New Mexican horse markets might jeopardize the New Mexican peace. Ever keen to manipulate the complexities of the postcontact geopolitics, the Comanches continued their raiding and trading endeavors, creating an intricate flow of commodities that guaranteed for both their divisions an ample supply of necessities.

So, as the eighteenth century drew to a close, the Western Comanches once again operated a major trade center, which fanned out to all directions to involve numerous groups. This new system differed from the earlier one in several ways. The volume of the trade was higher, reflecting matured and more regular trade links. Although the Western Comanches had engaged in systematic trade before, their commerce with Comancheros, Americans, and central Plains middleman tribes was even more institutionalized. The type of commodities moving through the center changed too. Trade in subsistence goods decreased, and horses and manufactured products became the primary items of trade. This shift can be attributed to a decline in trade with Pueblo and Wichita farmers, emergence of horse markets in the Northern Plains, and an increased southward flow of guns and other Euro-American goods through Cheyenne middlemen. Manufactured products poured in also from New Mexico, which was enjoying the blessings of Spain's Bourbon reforms—increased financial support from the Crown, refined administration, and resultant economic revitalization. Clearly, the Western Comanches were becoming dependent on Euro-American merchandise and technology.

Yet another, more internal, change was that the Upper Arkansas center became increasingly a Yamparika and Jupe enterprise. Around the turn of the century, the Kotsotekas and some Yamparika bands gradually severed their ties to the Upper Arkansas country and established their core region on the Upper Canadian, Red, and Brazos Rivers. There, they forged a new trade system, which revolved around Santa Fe and Pecos fairs and Comanchero rendezvous. This left the Arkansas commerce to the Jupes and remaining Yamparikas, who now dominated the Comanche trade. Although the southern bands enjoyed quite a lucrative trade with the New Mexicans, the multifaceted Arkansas center was still clearly the focal point of Comanche—and Southern Plains—commerce.

Finally, the Western Comanches focused their commercial activities on their own camps almost exclusively, thereby etching their trade center in the cultural landscape of the Southern Plains even more firmly. Kiowas, Plains Apaches, Cheyennes, Arapahoes, Pawnees, Eastern Comanches, Eastern Shoshones, Comancheros, and Americans all gathered in the late eighteenth and early nineteenth centuries at the Yamparika and Jupe camps on the Upper Arkansas. The Yamparikas and Jupes made regular trade journeys only to the Taos, and even these visits became more infrequent as the Comancheros moved the trade from the Rio Grande Valley to the Plains. Although the Western Comanches were still nomadic bison hunters and as mobile as ever, their favorite campsites on the Upper Arkansas functioned as remarkably stable trading places. They spent the long winter months in the shelter of the Big Timbers and they often hunted and camped in the valley or its vicinity during other seasons, making it easy for their trading partners to find them on almost a year-round basis. Consequently, there was no contradiction in being both mobile hunters and operators of a geographically fixed trade center. Although the two activities required dissimilar settlement patterns, they were bound together by the central position of the Upper Arkansas Valley in the Western Comanche universe.

The trading success of the Western Comanches stemmed largely from their strategic location at the confluence of several highly contrasting ecological and economic zones. They occupied a superb hunting niche between two major agricultural spheres, the Southwest and southeastern Plains, which allowed them to engage in mutual exchanges in two directions. Furthermore, the mild winters and abundant shortgrasses made the southwestern Plains the most favorable region of the Plains for horse herding and put the Western Comanches in a strong trading position over other Plains tribes and Euro-Americans. On the other hand, many of their trading allies either came from or lived near colonial centers and consequently had better access to manufactured goods. Such marked differences in resource availability generally promote exchange and inter-dependence, but they can also foster hostilities by encouraging groups to level out the imbalances by force. This was especially true on the Plains, where fluctuating climatic and political conditions often caused short-term difficulties for Indians in producing enough surplus goods to maintain their trade at a desired level. When such difficulties arose, Plains groups recurrently relied on raiding to acquire the goods they needed. The Western Comanche trade system was no exception: Pawnees often stole horses from Western Comanches, who in turn raided Pawnees for slaves, Spanish for horses, and Pueblos for corn.

Due to this delicate balance between trading and raiding, the Western Comanches used a variety of social, ritual, and political mechanisms to maintain or reestablish peaceful relations within their trade network. The most famous of these sustaining mechanisms was the calumet ceremony, which created intersocial cohesion by establishing fictive kinship bonds between prominent members of two parties. The ceremony involved reciprocal gift-giving, ritual feasting, and dancing, and it climaxed with the handing of the calumet from the father to his adopted son. Although there are no direct references to the use of the calumet among the Western Comanches, it is almost certain that they were familiar with the ceremony, for all their key trading partners practiced it. A less formal variation of the calumet ceremony was the "peace of the market," a method that allows societies to engage in trade despite ongoing warfare between them. This strategy played a central role in structuring Western Comanche-Spanish interaction before the 1780s, when the relations vacillated between war and peace. The two groups regularly arranged a peace for a few days to allow trade to take place. After the fairs, the Comanches consistently resumed their raids, apparently at no surprise to the Spanish.

Yet another key institution that helped maintain stable intergroup relations was gift-giving. To establish or reaffirm friendship, the Western Comanches exchanged presents—usually such luxury items as tobacco, paints, and special clothing—with all their trading partners. Gifts not only bound strangers together in fictive kin relations, but also stimulated trade, for the Native cultural code obliged relatives to supply each other's needs. Thus, when American traders left for the Southern Plains to buy horses and bison products from the Comanches, they equipped themselves with large amounts of goods to be distributed before the actual trade. The most revealing example of the crucial importance of gifts comes, however, from New Mexico, where Spanish officials spent thousands of pesos annually to maintain peaceful relations with the Western Comanches.

To ease communication within their multifaceted and linguistically diverse trade system, the Western Comanches promoted the use of their own language among their trading allies. They seem to have been highly successful in this. By the late eighteenth century, they could conduct most of their commerce with the New Mexicans in their own language, and as their trading power continued to grow, Comanche became the Southern Plains Indians' other universal language along with the sign language. In a word, Comanche may have well been to the Southern Plains what the famous Chinook jargon was to the Pacific Northwest: a trade lingua franca. On the other hand, to further smooth interaction, the Comanches adopted many Euro-American, particularly Spanish, terms for key trade items. For example, the Comanche word for an iron bar is *póro,* which is a derivation from a Spanish word *barra.* Other telling examples include *pijura* (*frijole;* bean) and *supereyos* (*sombrero;* hat).

The efforts of Western Comanche chiefs also helped stabilize the trade system. It was the chiefs, particularly the political leaders, *paraibos,* who decided when, where, and how trading took place, what was exchanged, and at what prices. This chiefly control supported the trade system in several ways. By confining the exchange to their own tipis, chiefs provided a safe trading environment for visitors and thereby guaranteed the continuity of trade relations. Their control over price negotiations largely eliminated Euro-American attempts to push up their prices, which in turn could have undermined Western Comanche trading power. By regulating the commodity flows, chiefs also managed to curtail the distribution of alcohol, thus minimizing drinking-related social problems and the subsequent decline of commercial drive. Perhaps most importantly, chiefs acted as a filter against Euro-American attempts to turn the trade into a tool for political manipulation. For example, while seemingly yielding to colonists' attempts to elevate powerful but loyal Native leaders who could enforce trade agreements, Western Comanche chiefs seldom coerced those agreements, because they wanted to keep their followers' trading and raiding options open. Chiefs maintained their control over trade well into the nineteenth century, and in this way were a major factor behind Western Comanche commercial success.

This discussion of the sustaining mechanisms is important not only because it sheds light on the inner operations of the Southern Plains trade system, but because it reinforces the argument that the Western Comanches were a major trading group. They were astute traders who controlled a complex trade system through an active and skillful use of various social, ritual, and political mechanisms. In fact, the Western Comanches can be fittingly portrayed as specialized traders, who not only produced, collected, and redistributed commodities, but also nurtured a mature trading culture, complete with effective communication systems and elaborate trade etiquette.

This trading culture, together with an advantageous geographical location, allowed the Western Comanches to dominate the Southern Plains trade for almost a century. Despite massive geopolitical changes, diseases, and depopulation, their trade center flourished until about 1830, when a complex set of international, regional, and local changes finally resulted in its decline. Like its emergence, the disintegration of the Western Comanche center was a gradual process. The first trading connection to dissolve was the important northern one, which linked the Western Comanches to the Upper Missouri center via Cheyenne and Arapaho middlemen. Pushed by the Lakotas and drawn by the lush southern horse pastures, the Cheyennes and Arapahoes began in the late 1820s to gravitate toward the Arkansas Valley, which became in the 1830s a scene of bitter fighting between them and a Western Comanche, Kiowa, and Plains Apache alliance. The Western Comanche trade network shrank further when their New Mexican connection crumbled. The catalyst here was Mexico's acute financial troubles, which prevented the new republic from maintaining comparable commercial ties Spain had forged with the Western Comanches between 1786 and 1821. As New Mexico lost its commercial value, it once again became a target for raiding, and from the late 1820s on, war rather than trade dominated the Western Comanche-New Mexican relations.

The most serious blow to the Western Comanche traders was, however, the establishment of Bent's Fort on the Upper Arkansas River in the early 1830s. Boasting an annual trade of 15,000 hides and large quantities of horses, the lucrative post simultaneously opened new commercial opportunities for the Western Comanches and replaced them as the paramount traders of the Southern Plains. In the 1830s and 1840s, Southern Plains tribes, Santa Fe traders, and New Mexicans no longer gathered at Western Comanche camps but at Bent's Fort, which, in a sense, was an American sequel to the once flourishing Western Comanche trade center. The displacement of the Western Comanches was a calculated move by the Bent brothers, who were fully aware of the Big Timbers' history as a major commercial point.

Outmaneuvered by the Bents, the Western Comanche traders were relegated to secondary importance. They traded sporadically with the Osages in the 1830s and 1840s, and the Comancheros visited them until the 1870s, but Bent's Fort had put an end to their role as major traders. Edged out from commercial supremacy, the Western Comanches began to rely increasingly on raiding, inextricably linking themselves with that activity in the minds of the encroaching Americans as well as later historians.

The tumultuous 1830s also witnessed the collapse of the other Native trade centers of the Plains. The combined effects of smallpox and expansion of American fur companies up the Missouri River terminated the Mandan, Hidatsa, and Arikara villages as a major trade center. Similarly, increasing Osage aggression and the removal of tribes from the eastern United States in the 1830s delivered a fatal blow to the crumbling Wichita trading culture. The disintegration of the Western Comanche trade center should thus be seen as a part of the general collapse of the Plains Indians trade system. By the 1830s, there were no major Native trade centers left on the Plains, and for the next three or four decades commerce on the Great Plains was dominated by large Euro-American fur companies and their capitalistic production systems, which utilized the Indians only as a source of cheap labor in the expanding world economy.

Indian and White Households on the California Frontier, 1860

ALBERT L. HURTADO

In 1851 Major John Bidwell, a prominent Butte County farmer, commented on Indian affairs in gold rush California. In comparison with conditions in eastern states, he emphasized, California's settlers had not only to contend with Indians on the frontier, but they were "all *among* us, *around* us, *with* us—hardly a farm house—a kitchen without them." According to Bidwell, when a farmer needed laborers he told the Indians to "go into his fields," and in return he fed and clothed them. He thought the Indian farm workers looked up to an employer with "a kind of filial obedience to his commands" and expected from him "a kind of parental protection." The earnest farmer contrasted his description of agrarian paternalism with the activities of "malicious and brutal vagabonds" who roamed the country

From Albert L. Hurtado, "Hardly a Farm House—a Kitchen Without Them: Indian and White Households on the California Borderland Frontier in 1860," in *Western Historical Quarterly*, Vol. 13 (July 1982), 245–270. Copyright by Western History Association. Reprinted by permission.

murdering Indians. Such depredations caused native people to retaliate in kind "thereby exposing the industrious and well disposed miner to dangers and death." In these desperate times, Bidwell believed, Indians were "sure to cling around and shelter themselves under the protection of him who treats them best."

Bidwell's remarks evoke a strikingly different picture of Indian and white relations than the one conveyed by the usual Anglo-American frontier stereotypes. Instead of resisting the whites, restricting settlement, and impeding development, California's Indians worked obediently in the whites' fields and houses in return for food and shelter. The relationship that Bidwell described was in part the product of nearly a century of Hispanic colonization, with traditions of Indian and white relations far different from Anglo-American practices. Herbert E. Bolton [a prominent historian] compared these different customs and noted that in Anglo-America "the only good Indians were dead Indians," while in Hispanic America Indians were assimilated and exploited. Moreover, Bolton believed that California and other parts of the Spanish Borderlands were "the meeting place and fusing place of two streams of European civilization," each with substantially different histories with regard to the Indian.

The fusing of Anglo and Hispanic traditions was not a smooth process in gold rush California, especially for Indians. Some Anglos adopted Hispanic labor practices as a convenient expedient, while others sought to drive Native Americans out of the work force where Indians could expect to find little protection. The federal government established a stopgap, temporary reservation system that ministered to only a fraction of the Indian population. Ineffectual federal administration enabled the state government to take a powerful role in Indian affairs. Although the state constitution outlawed slavery, the legislature passed chapter 133, "an act for the government and protection of the Indians," that provided for the indenture of loitering and orphaned Indians, regulated their employment, and defined a special class of crimes and punishment for them. Some students of California history have referred to this law as a form of legalized slavery. Certainly it resembled the "black codes" adopted by slave states as a means to control free blacks and bondsmen alike. Simultaneously, the state government subsidized scores of military campaigns aimed at Indian communities considered threatening to white settlement. In fact, these expeditions often killed Indians indiscriminately.

To describe this situation as chaotic hardly does it justice. The gold rush proved to be a catastrophe for the Indians. By 1860 the native population had fallen from perhaps 300,000 to about 32,000. According to Sherburne F. Cook, the preeminent demographer of California Indians, native numbers continued to fall until about 1900, when they reached a population nadir of between 20,000 and 25,000. Cook postulated that Indian demographic decline was due to starvation, homicide, and a "palpable fall in the birth rate concerning which we have little factual knowledge."

Cook's lack of knowledge about the declining birthrate is not surprising. Like other poor working people, the California Indians left no well-documented record of their daily lives. But using techniques derived from social history and demography, it is possible to find evidence that gives a fuller understanding of the gold rush's effect upon native survival. This evidence shows how Indians were useful to white society in the 1850s and provides insights into the ways that Anglo and Hispanic traditions merged on the Spanish Borderland frontier. At the same time, it furnishes a fresh perspective for Native American history, for the California experience is a case study of the process of Indian integration with white society in the mid-nineteenth century. Amidst the turbulent disorders of a unique age, native Californians became the mudsills of Victorian society in the American West.

The 1860 federal census offers a starting point for this reexamination, since it contains a wealth of information on Indian people at the household level. The Constitution and the census law of 1850 empowered United States marshals to enumerate the population in 1860. Under this authorization federal officers enumerated Indians to determine political apportionment and taxation. The census takers received two cents for each person they counted, thus giving them an incentive to do a thorough job.

In 1860 the census takers enumerated 17,798 Indians in California, by far the highest state Indian population. Excluded were reservation Indians, those in flight or rebellion, and those "retaining their tribal character," who were estimated to number 13,540. The manuscript census includes such demographic data as name, age, sex, and usually occupation for nearly 18,000 Indians. Often marital status is indicated or can be inferred from circumstantial evidence. In addition, all this data was organized on the basis of each dwelling visited by the census officer, thus making possible an analysis of the household. Moreover, since the enumerated Indians frequently lived in close association with whites, the manuscript census provides a close-up view of their relations with one another.

The census indicated several general demographic characteristics of the California population that must be taken into account in any study of Indian people in 1860. The state contained 379,994 persons, 70 percent of whom were males and 60 percent of whom were white males. Overall, the population was young—nearly 60 percent were under thirty. Of the four racial categories identified in the census—white, colored, Indian, and Asian—all showed exceedingly low female-to-male rations. Such ratios usually mean that a population will not be able to reproduce itself unless new females of child-bearing age can be acquired elsewhere by migration or by intermarriage with other groups.

Like the white population, the enumerated Indians were mostly young males (see Table 1). Theoretically, this Indian population was the soundest reproductive group because it had the highest female-to-male ratio. Statistically, however, Indian women bore fewer live children and raised fewer of them to maturity than their white counterparts. The published census reveals that the Indian population was not distributed uniformly throughout the state. Fresno County had the highest reported population with 3,294, while Sierra and Yolo counties reported no Indian residents. Likewise, sex and age ratios varied from county to county. The differing regional population patterns displayed in Table 1 assume a larger significance when viewed through the microscope of household analysis.

For comparative purposes this study subdivides California into five areas with differing settlement histories: the Southern, Central Coast, Sacramento Valley, San Joaquin Valley, and Northern regions. To analyze Indian households I reviewed the unpublished manuscript censuses for precincts that illustrate demographic patterns consistent with those in the published census. I have categorized households in which Indians are found according to five types: No Family, Simple Family, Simple Family Plus Others, Extended Family, and Multiple Family. Household types are

Table 1 Regional Indian Population by Age and Sex

| | AGE AND SEX | | | | | | | | | | | | TOTALS | | |
| | 0–14 | | | 15–39 | | | 40–59 | | | 60+ | | | | | |
REGION	% M	% F	F/M	% M	% F	F/M	% M	% F	F/M	% M	% F	F/M	N M	N F	TOTAL
1	16.92	14.27	.84	26.58	23.41	.88	7.86	5.23	.67	3.40	2.34	.69	4640	3834	8474
2	19.84	13.94	.70	31.10	17.04	.55	7.42	3.39	.46	4.66	2.61	.56	1690	992	2682
3	13.04	7.42	.57	47.68	25.11	.53	4.72	1.20	.25	0.82			884	450	1334
4	14.01	14.26	1.02	39.58	17.08	.43	8.60	2.37	.28	3.12	0.98	0.31	3059	1625	4684
5	24.36	19.39	.80	22.28	28.37	1.27	3.37	1.92	.57	0.32			314	310	624

Regions 1–5 are the Southern, Central Coast, Sacramento Valley, San Joaquin Valley, and Northern regions respectively.
% M = the percentage of males in the regional population.
% F = the percentage of females in the regional population.
F/M = the ratio of females to males.
[N = the number of Indians in each category.]

compared with data about ethnicity of the household head, as identified by the census takers. For the purposes of this study there are only three kinds of ethnic households: Indian, Non-Indian, and Mixed. Indian households were headed by Indians, although people of other backgrounds may have lived there. Conversely, Non-Indian households were headed by non-Indians and may have included other ethnic representatives. A Mixed household was headed by a conjugal couple, one of whom was an Indian. The correlation of ethnicity and family structure shows wide variations in patterns of Indian household life by their historical origins.

The Southern region was originally the home of Indians whom anthropologists associate with the southern California culture area near the coast and Great Basin culture area further inland. These people, like other California Indians, divided their labor between the sexes, with men hunting and fishing and women gathering plant foods. Parents often arranged the marriage of their children, a practice that reflected the economic and social utility of the unions. Most couples lived in single family households near the husband's parents. Generally speaking, only chiefs, shamans, or other powerful men had more than one wife.

The Indians in the Southern region were the first California native people to experience Hispanic colonization. Beginning in 1769 Spanish soldiers and missionaries founded a series of twenty-three missions, four military presidios, and three pueblos. With two centuries of frontier experience, Franciscan missionaries sought to convert the native people to Catholicism and place them on the lowest rungs of the Spanish social ladder as farmers and laborers. The neophytes, as the native converts were called, formed the labor pool for the mission system, the primary economic institution of the colony. The mission profoundly affected the neophyte and adjacent Indian populations; they died at a rapid rate, thus requiring the recruitment of new converts from the interior valleys. Still the demographic decline continued, undercutting the missions' source of labor and causing their decay as the economic mainstay for Spanish California. After 1821 the success of the Mexican Revolution led to the secularization of the missions, the distribution of their vast property holdings, and the dispersal of the neophytes. Some of the Franciscan-trained natives returned to their homes in the interior, while others found work in the Mexican settlements or on large land-grant ranchos that replaced the missions as the dominant institution in the province. Under Mexico, Indians remained California's basic labor force. For Indians, eighty years of relations with Hispanic people led to a statewide demographic decline from an estimated 300,000 to about 150,000, due principally to disease.

After the United States acquired California, the native population decline was exacerbated by the gold rush, even outside the mining regions. The discovery of gold led to a great influx of non-Indian people who soon outnumbered the native people. In the Southern region, Los Angeles grew rapidly and became an important, albeit a slow-moving, regional trading center. The new immigrants displaced many of the old Mexican landholders, but the Indians remained as house servants and field hands. Their subservient position was institutionalized to a certain extent by the enforcement of chapter 133, which provided for the arrest and indenture of loitering and intoxicated Indians. Local authorities added another legal feature— every week in Los Angeles Indian prisoners were "auctioned off to the highest bidder for private service." At week's end the rancheros paid these coerced Indian workers partly with liquor, helping to assure enough intoxicated Indians for the next auction and a steady supply of labor. Under the threat of arrest and auction, Indians competed fiercely for a limited number of steady jobs as house servants at wages reportedly from fifty cents to one dollar per day.

The sample household analysis of Los Angeles Indians illustrates the results of these local social and economic conditions (see Table 2). More than half of the Indians lived in Non-Indian households, and most of them lived in No-Family quarters on nearby ranchos with other male workers. Nearly 20 percent of the Indians were household servants in Non-Indian homes. About 30 percent of the sample Indian population lived in Indian-headed households, but less than half of them lived in dwellings with identifiable conjugal couples. There were almost as many Indians living in Mixed households as there were in Indian-headed families.

Examples from the manuscript census provide additional insights into the nature of Los Angeles Indians' town and country life. Typically, Indian household servants lived in the homes of people who were at least moderately well to do. Twenty-five-year-old Indian servant Maria, for example, lived in the house of Polish merchant David Solomon, his wife, and their three children. Solomon owned $1,000 in real and $4,000 in personal property. Maria, no doubt, assisted Mrs. Solomon with domestic chores and the many tasks associated with raising three children, all of whom were less than five years old. Indian men as well as women worked as domestics, and occasionally an Indian couple served in a household, but this was rare.

Some of the large landholders on the town's outskirts kept large houses filled with family, friends, and employees. Abel Stearns, a Massachusetts man who became one of the wealthiest southern Californians, lived with his wife and nineteen unrelated people, including Juan and Antonio, Indian laborers. One of Stearns's neighbors, Mexican Californian Julian Chaves, was a person of more modest means, but he kept eight Indian servants, including six males in their twenties. The former American fur trapper William Wolfskill, according to the manuscript census, kept more Indians on his rancho than any of his Los Angeles counterparts. Altogether there were thirty-seven Indians living on Wolfskill's property, including eleven male farm workers, eight washerwomen, a servant, and their children. Wolfskill's rancho was an exception; most ranchos kept only a few workers, except during peak seasons of the year.

Compared with other regions, Los Angeles Indians married non-Indians fairly often (see Tables 2–6). There were twenty-two households with Mixed couples— about 14 percent of the households sampled. Los Angeles Indian women had spouses from Mexico, Kentucky, and elsewhere. The estates of their non-Indian spouses varied greatly, from moderate wealth to apparent pauperism.

George Harwood Phillips has recently described the history of Los Angeles Indians as a dual process of "economic integration" and "social disintegration." Phillips writes that Indian society disintegrated as a result of a limited and essentially exploitative economic role and that the disintegrative process was indicated by Indian drunkenness, vice, and violence, "which in turn led to a drastic population reduction." A main contributor to the decrease in Indian numbers was disease that, in Phillips's view, took its toll among the weakened natives. Beyond the immediate impact of disease, as the analysis of Los Angeles households shows, comparatively

Table 2   Los Angeles County Indian and White Sample Households

	ETHNICITY											
	NON-INDIAN			INDIAN			MIXED			TOTAL		
HOUSEHOLD TYPE	C	N	%	C	N	%	C	N	%	C	N	%
No family	52	125	26.77	16	75	16.06	6	15	3.21	68	200	42.83
Simple family				4	15	3.21	13	42	8.99	10	30	6.42
Simple family plus others	51	93	19.91	2	8	1.71				66	143	30.62
Extended family	1	7	1.50							1	7	1.50
Multiple family	6	35	7.49	2	45	9.64	3	7	1.50	11	87	18.63
Total	110	260	55.67	24	143	30.62	22	64	13.70	156	467	100.00

C = the number of households with Indian members.
N = the number of Indians in each category.
% = the percentage of the sample Indian population in each category.

few Indians lived in situations in which reproduction and child rearing were feasible. In short, the Los Angeles social order that integrated most Indians into Non-Indian and No Family households substantially contributed to the overall demographic decline. Social disorder, at least as contemporary whites defined it, may have been an ancillary symptom of Los Angeles' socioeconomic conditions.

The 1860 household patterns of Los Angeles Indians were extreme by comparison with households in other parts of Hispanic California. The divergency of living conditions is illustrated in the Central Coast region. In anthropological terminology, the Central Coast Indians belonged to the Central California culture area. Like their southern neighbors, these people were basically monogamous and patrilocal, although anthropologists have reported occasional polygyny. With Spanish settlement in the eighteenth century, Central Coast Indians entered the Franciscan missions, where they suffered the usual consequences of disease and demographic reduction. During the 1820s and 1830s, mission secularization dispersed the Indians to the surrounding ranchos and urban settlements, where they worked as herdsmen and servants. By the time of the gold rush, the Central Coast Indians were gaining social acceptance in the Mexican community. Increasingly, people of undiluted Indian ancestry were recorded in local records as *vecinos* and *vecinas* (citizens) rather than *indigenas* (Indians).

In 1860 the Indian population of the Central Coast region was only about one-third as large as that in the Southern region (see Table 1). The Central Coast Indians were mostly young males, although the age and sex ratios were not so radically deformed as those in other parts of California. The ratio of females of child-bearing age to males shows there was an important deficit of potentially fertile women in the Indian population.

The town of Monterey and its surrounding ranchos provide a household population sample that sheds additional light on the historical demography of the region. The correlation of household types and ethnicity indicates that a majority of Monterey's Indians lived in Indian households (see Table 3). Most of the remainder lived in Non-Indian households, while a small segment of the sample were residents of Mixed households. By household type, Indians were distributed about equally among No Family, Simple Family, and Simple Family Plus Others households. The largest correlative Indian group was living in Simple Families, while the next largest number of Indians lived in Non-Indian Simple Families Plus Others. About 32 percent of the population sample lived in Indian and Non-Indian No Families.

The Monterey census indicates that Indians played economic roles similar to those in southern California. Most of the men were unskilled laborers working on white ranchos, while women labored as domestics in the homes of affluent whites. The Indian women in these homes were usually between the ages of fifteen and forty, although servants as young as eight were recorded. The Indian domestic staff in the David Spence home offers an example. Spence, a wealthy merchant and landowner, lived with his wife, their son and daughter-in-law, and two grandchildren. The Spences kept three female Indians to serve them, aged twenty-five, twelve, and eight. The Spence home was not unlike those of Spence's landed Mexican contemporaries—the Garcias, the Sepulvedas, and the de la Torres. In Monterey's genteel Anglo and Mexican society, for those households classified as Simple Family Plus Others, Indian servants were the others.

Table 3 Monterey County Indian and White Sample Households

					ETHNICITY								
HOUSEHOLD TYPE	NON-INDIAN			INDIAN			MIXED			TOTAL		
	C	N	%	C	N	%	C	N	%	C	N	%
No family	14	16	11.94	8	27	20.15				22	43	32.09
Simple family				8	37	27.61	3	6	4.48	11	43	32.09
Simple family plus others	18	36	26.87	1	5	3.73	1	4	2.99	20	45	33.58
Extended family	1	3	2.24							1	3	2.24
Multiple family												
Total	33	55	41.04	17	69	51.49	4	10	7.46	54	134	100.00

C = the number of households with Indian members.
N = the number of Indians in each category.
% = the percentage of the sample Indian population in each category.

Monterey Indian Simple Family and No Family households differed in their social composition, but they were similar in other respects. Both households were composed of working people variously identified as laborers and servants. In some cases the census takers even identified children as servants. For example, in the Indian Simple Family household apparently associated with the rancho of County Treasurer Thomas Day, the Indian parents as well as their children, ages eleven, four, and one, were identified as farm servants. In the mind of the census taker, as this classification implies, Indian occupational status was to some extent hereditary.

The Indian and white household structure in Monterey was the result of several generations of Hispanic colonization and tradition. Like Los Angeles, Monterey's Indians were integrated into the social and economic structure, but they had an additional measure of control over their lives because they headed most of their own households. Still, the deficit of potential Indian mothers and the relative lack of identifiable conjugal couples meant that the Monterey population could not easily sustain itself. Moreover, while Monterey Indians lived in relative peace, they also lived in poverty. None of them reported any real or personal property to the enumerators. As in Los Angeles, Indians in Monterey comprised a part of the working class whose reproductive future was in doubt.

Until the 1840s, permanent settlement in California was confined to a fairly narrow strip of land near the coast. The great interior spaces—the central valleys and the sierras—remained in the hands of native people who were troubled only by the incursions of a few Hispanic exploring expeditions. The natives of this region have also been classified within the Central California culture area, and like their western neighbors, they were principally monogamous and patrilocal, with polygyny reserved for the privileged few.

The first important intrusions in the Sacramento Valley region began in 1827 when American, and subsequently Hudson's Bay Company, fur trappers began to exploit this territory. In 1833 the Hudson's Bay brigade brought a virulent form of malaria to the region, already the habitat of the anopheles mosquito. The insect quickly spread the malaria among the Indians, and it is estimated that twenty thousand native people died in the lowlands of the Great Central Valley in a few summer months. Severely weakened by this epidemic, the valley Indians could not successfully resist the first permanent non-Indian settler, John A. Sutter, who used Indian workers after 1839 to built New Helvetia, a fortified frontier enterprise near the confluence of the American and Sacramento rivers.

By the time of the Mexican War, Sutter and other newcomers controlled most of the Sacramento Valley and the Indians in it. But for native people the worst was yet to come. Sutter's Indian and white workers discovered gold on the American River in January of 1848. During the first season of gold mining, the experienced California settlers maintained the usual white employer–Indian employee relationship, with native workers digging and panning gold for non-Indians. By the end of 1848 there arrived a huge influx of miners who were unfamiliar with the established place of Indian laborers in California. These latecomers drove most Indian people out of the mines, attacking and murdering the native work force, leaving only a remnant population in the mining districts.

In the 1860 census only a handful of Indians were enumerated in the mining counties of the Sierra foothills, but modest populations were recorded in the bordering Sacramento Valley agricultural counties. More than 60 percent of the male Indians were under forty, about twice the number of their female cohorts. Proportionately, there were more Indian women of child-bearing age in the Sacramento Valley than in any other region except the Northern, but they produced fewer children. Indians over forty were downright rare, accounting for less than 7 percent of the population (see Table 1).

Reasons for these disparities are found in the household structure of Indians in Butte County (see Table 4). More than 70 percent of the Butte Indians lived in Indian No Family households, and most of them were male workers. The remaining Indians were about equally divided between Non-Indian No Family and Simple Family Plus Others households as workers and servants. Three Indians lived in Mixed households. Most remarkably, in the 1860 Butte census there were no identifiable Indian conjugal couples.

The Indian living arrangements on Bidwell's Rancho Chico illustrate the kind of household that dominated Indian life in Butte County. Bidwell kept fifty-two Indians on his rancho, and fifty-one of them lived in Indian No Family households. They lived in four dwellings and were segregated by sex. Thirty-nine male herders, gardeners, and farm laborers lived in three households. Eleven women day laborers lived in a separate dwelling headed by a male named Yummarine, who was designated chief. Ten of the women were in their prime child-bearing years, between the ages of sixteen and thirty-one, yet there were no children listed in the census. Given the segregated living conditions, the absence of children was not surprising. In 1860 the Indians at Rancho Chico were there to work, not to raise families or sustain tribal population.

The Butte County ranchos with Indian households like those on Rancho Chico were all large operations. Bidwell owned $52,000 in real estate and $56,640 in personal property. Former Pennsylvanian J. A. Keefer employed twelve young Indian men and four young women. He owned $3,800 worth of land and had personal property valued at $10,000. Similarly, R. W. Durham claimed $8,000 in real estate and personal property worth $2,000 and employed twenty-one male Indians, all except one in their twenties.

As in Monterey, most of the Butte County Indians who lived in Non-Indian Simple Family Plus Others were servants, but unlike their coastal counterparts, most were young males. On the whole, Butte servants lived in modest homes of white couples with some money, although there were occasional servants in impoverished households.

On the whole, Butte County contrasted sharply with Monterey and Los Angeles in its demographic composition. The Sacramento Valley Indian population seemed precariously based on one generation, with a sharp deficit of women of child-bearing age, although the whole Butte native population may have been more broadly based than the census shows. In the margin of the manuscript census an officer wrote, "16 Indians in Rancheria unemployed," implying that Indians who did not work were not enumerated. If there were other unenumerated Indian communities in the county, they cannot be identified. To have stable family lives, Indian people would have to establish them outside the social and economic realm of 1860 Butte County ranchos, where the sexes were segregated and marriage and child rearing were discouraged.

Table 4   Butte County Indian and White Sample Households

	ETHNICITY											
	NON-INDIAN			INDIAN			MIXED			TOTAL		
HOUSEHOLD TYPE	C	N	%	C	N	%	C	N	%	C	N	%
No family	11	15	12.61	6	85	71.43				17	100	84.03
Simple family							2	3	2.52	2	3	2.52
Simple family plus others	10	16	13.45							10	16	13.45
Extended family												
Multiple family												
Total	21	31	26.05	6	85	71.43	2	3	2.52	29	119	100.00

C = the number of households with Indian members.
N = the number of Indians in each category.
% = the percentage of the sample Indian population in each category.

In 1860 living conditions for Indians in California's Great Central Valley were by no means uniform. At the southern end of the valley, in the San Joaquin region, Indian household structure contrasted sharply with the Butte County sample. The San Joaquin region Indians were also associated with the Central California culture area with mainly monogamous marriage customs, but their historical experience was markedly different. While no permanent non-Indian settlers reached their area until the late 1840s, the Franciscan missionaries had progressively recruited neophytes from the San Joaquin Valley as the coastal population died out. Some of the interior Indian neophytes fled the missions to return to their old homes, and frequently they took mission and rancho horses with them. By 1819 Indians from the valley were raiding the mission herds regularly. It was said that even the San Joaquin women and children rode horseback. One observer claimed that the Indians of that region held regular horse fairs. Periodically, the Spanish and Mexican authorities sent armed expeditions to the San Joaquin Valley to capture runaway neophytes and reclaim stolen horses, but they were never able to quell Indian livestock raiding. While Mexicans and Indians rode east and west, American and Hudson's Bay trappers marched north and south, trapping and trading for furs. Indians continued to hold sway even after the 1833 malaria epidemic swept thousands of them away. Sutter occasionally sent his Indian troops south to suppress livestock raiding, but there were no permanent non-Indian settlements in this region until after the gold rush brought thousands of whites into the area.

The gold rush had an uneven impact upon the San Joaquin region's Indian population. San Joaquin, Mariposa, Merced, and Stanislaus counties were virtually depopulated, but according to the 1860 census, Fresno County had 3,294 Indian people, the largest Indian population in the state, and adjacent Tulare County had 1,340 Indians. In Fresno County the Indians remained a substantial majority, since there were only 999 whites and 312 other non-Indians in the county.

The concentration of Indians in Fresno County was due in some measure to the presence of the Fresno River Farm, an Office of Indian Affairs subagency that operated until 1861. The farm was the home of several Indian groups who tilled the soil under white supervision. To augment the farm's produce, some of the agency Indians worked on local ranchos. Even Indians who lived in the mountains relied to some extent on the Fresno River Farm. For example, the Mono Indians worked for white settlers during planting and harvest times, mined gold in the winter and spring, and gathered "the natural products of the mountains," a federal subagent reported. In addition, the Mono Indians received some food and clothing from the subagency. With all these sources of supply, the federal official believed, the Monos had "been able to provide themselves with a comfortable living for Indians." The Fresno River Farm was also a refuge for Indians who were driven off their land by whites.

The Fresno County household sample reveals another distinctive pattern. Almost 90 percent of the Fresno Indians lived in Indian households; more than 50 percent of the sample population lived in dwellings containing identifiable conjugal couples. Fewer Indians lived in all kinds of Non-Indian homes than in any other region, and less than 1 percent lived in Mixed households (see Table 5).

Not only did Fresno's native people live in Indian households, they lived in their own communities. One of these communities contained 286 Indians in thirty-seven households. The census officer recorded a forty-year-old man named Wuemekana as

Table 5 Fresno County Indian and White Sample Households

Household Type	Ethnicity											
	Non-Indian			Indian			Mixed			Total		
	C	N	%	C	N	%	C	N	%	C	N	%
No family	15	43	8.88	28	169	34.92				43	212	43.80
Simple family				11	58	11.98	2	2	0.41	13	60	12.40
Simple family plus others	9	10	2.07	20	147	30.37	1	2	0.41	30	159	32.85
Extended family												
Multiple family				5	53	10.95				5	53	10.95
Total	24	53	10.95	64	427	88.22	3	4	0.82	91	484	100.00

C = the number of households with Indian members.

N = the number of Indians in each category.

% = the percentage of the sample Indian population in each category.

chief of the community. Wuemekana lived with his wife and three children, a sixty-year-old servant, the servant's wife, and their four children, plus a forty-year-old woman. No other household listed a servant in this entire large community. Except for Wuemekana's servant, the census taker indicated no non-Indian occupations but occasionally noted that a man was a "brave," which apparently indicated a different status, at least in the mind of the white officer. In other communities the census taker found a "Great War Chief," a woman "fortuneteller," and several Indian "doctors."

Native people defined their own household and social relationships within Fresno County's Indian communities, even though they worked periodically for white ranchers. Outside the Indian communities the patterns in Non-Indian No Families were similar to those found in Butte. Young Indian men lived with whites as servants. Most of the Non-Indian household heads appeared to be men of moderate means or better, with sufficient capital to afford a servant.

Although, as previously stated, Fresno County Indians remained the local majority population and many of them retained some control over their community and household lives, they were somewhat reliant on the white economy and federal assistance for survival. Far from being autonomous native societies in Indian country, the Fresno Indians were a dependent and declining refugee population with a deficiency of women of child-bearing age.

The last example of Indian household life comes from the Northern region, formerly the territory of the northwestern, northeastern, and a small part of the central California culture areas. Polygyny seems to have been more frequent in the two northern culture areas than it was in other parts of California, but like the others, most societies were patrilocal. As in other California native societies, marriage served economic and social functions that extended beyond the conjugal family and affected their larger kin groups.

Hispanic colonization had no direct effect on these people; they first encountered whites when fur trade began in the late 1820s. The Hudson's Bay Company established friendly relations with the northern Indians, who insured safe passage from Oregon to California, but the fur trade caused hostility between some tribes. The Modoc Indians, for example, raided neighboring tribes for slaves they traded in Oregon for horses and other goods. These raids continued until the gold rush, when as elsewhere in northern California, the first permanent non-Indian settlers arrived. Only poor mines, located in rugged country, were found in the Northern region, so the area attracted comparatively few miners. Furthermore, some Indian groups strove to keep the whites out of their territory. There was armed conflict in mining districts everywhere in the state, but in the northern mines there was almost uninterrupted warfare between 1850 and 1865. State volunteers and federal troops frequently killed Indians indiscriminately, drove off the survivors, or took them to reservations and indentured them under the provisions of chapter 133. In short, worse conditions for Indians can hardly be imagined than those found in this country in 1860.

As might be anticipated, federal census takers enumerated fewer Indians in the Northern region than in any other area in the state. But the small Indian population in the 1860 census presents a unique demographic picture (see Table 1). There were nearly as many Indian women as men in the total population, and there were more women of child-bearing age than their male cohorts. Children under fourteen formed more than 40 percent of the Indian population; nearly 95 percent of the enumerated native people were under forty.

The Trinity County household sample is likewise unique (see Table 6). Nearly three-quarters of the enumerated people lived in Mixed Simple Family and Multiple Family households. All of the conjugal couples consisted of white males and Indian females. Their racially mixed offspring—sometimes recorded as half-breeds by the census takers—were counted as Indians. Typically, the husbands of these unions were landless farmers and miners with little or no personal property. Most of the males were between twenty and forty years of age, but their spouses were very young, usually between the ages of thirteen and twenty.

The emotional depth of these unions is difficult to judge, and it is not unreasonable to suspect that many of them were alliances of male convenience. Still, the manuscript census indicates that about half of the white partners conferred their last names on their spouses and children. Two families from the manuscript census offer illustrations of this point. David Peters, a landless Pennsylvania blacksmith with $190 worth of personal property, headed a Trinity Mixed household. Peters was thirty, and his Indian wife, Ellen Peters, was eighteen. They had a two-month-old infant son named Samuel Peters. On the other hand, J. Stewart, a propertyless miner from Maine, lived with an Indian woman, Mary Jane, and her two-year-old daughter, Mary Ann. Peters seems to have married Ellen and legitimized—at least for the census taker—his young son. Stewart apparently did not seek to formalize his relationship with Mary Jane or her daughter.

Conjugal coupling did not necessarily indicate conjugal bliss nor a humane attitude on the part of the white men who lived with Indian women. A white army officer remarked upon the casual brutality that erupted in one Mixed household in 1862. A frontiersman had lived in the Northern region with an Indian woman for years when without warning the man beat "his own child's brains out against a tree and kill[ed] the squaw, its mother" because he had no other way of getting rid of them, and "to keep them from falling into another person's hand." These intimate murders convey the terrible possibilities of a Mixed household in the war-torn and remote Northern region.

The Trinity County Indian and white social arrangements were distinct from those in other regions in the state. There was no place for Indian households within the compass of white society. Indian labor was important specifically in the context of the family, where women performed the wifely duties of housework and child rearing. The Trinity Indians who lived in Non-Indian households had a place in arrangements that resembled those in Butte and Fresno counties. Young Indian men lived in white households as servants, acting, in a sense, as surrogate wives—cooking, cleaning, and serving for white men.

The regional patterns of Indian and white household life found in the 1860 census illustrate the variety of the native experience in the decade following the gold rush. In regions with Hispanic traditions, individual Indians and families were integrated into the large society as rancho workers and servants in middle- and upper-class homes. Out of the direct path of the gold rush and in areas with substantial Hispanic populations, Anglos in Los Angeles and Monterey counties seemed to conform to the social patterns that were evident among their Hispanic neighbors. In contrast, Butte County ranchers used Indians as workers but rigidly segregated

Table 6   Trinity County Indian and White Sample Households

		ETHNICITY													
	NON-INDIAN			INDIAN			MIXED			TOTAL		
HOUSEHOLD TYPE	C	N	%	C	N	%	C	N	%	C	N	%
No family	9	12	15.19	1	1	1.27				10	13	16.46
Simple family							18	35	44.30	18	35	44.30
Simple family plus others	8	9	11.39				8	16	20.25	16	25	31.65
Extended family												
Multiple family							2	6	7.59	2	6	7.59
Total	17	21	26.85	1	1	1.27	28	57	72.15	46	79	100.00

C = the number of households with Indian members.
N = the number of Indians in each category.
% = the percentage of the sample Indian population in each category.

Indian households by sex. In this Anglo-dominated region, white settlers valued Indian labor, but the Indian family had no role to play in Butte society. To the south in Fresno County, Indians were the majority and maintained their own communities with households that they defined. Nevertheless, Indians in Fresno County relied on whites for seasonal work on farms and livestock ranchos. In Trinity County, Indians filled the usual servant's role in Non-Indian households, but more of them lived in Mixed homes as the spouses and children of white men. These different patterns mark the range of household life for Indians who were permitted to live in white society.

Despite the regional variations in households, two trends can be seen throughout California. Except for the Northern region, there were fewer women of childbearing age than their male cohorts. Even in the north, a significant number of potentially fertile Indian women lived with white men, thus creating a shortage of women available to Indian men. The scarcity of potential mothers was a severe problem for California's Indian population, already under stress and in rapid, prolonged decline. The second trend apparent in the manuscript census was the movement of a large proportion of Indians into living situations that were not conducive to reproduction. This movement explains in part the fall in the birthrate noted by Cook some years ago. To our understanding of Indian death and survival we may now add the limited effects of household arrangements that discouraged Indian marriage and child rearing. Economic and social integration created conditions that permitted individual Indians to survive but also contributed to an overall decline in native numbers.

A better knowledge of Indian and white household arrangements raises an old and troubling problem that extends beyond California's borders. Given the economic and social possibilities of nineteenth-century America, was integration into white society a better alternative for Indians than segregation or even armed resistance? In Anglo and Hispanic California, the transformation of native Californians from a racial and cultural majority into a working-class minority contributed to their drastic, tragic population decline. Bolton's two streams of European civilization rushed together in California and nearly obliterated native people on the northwestern flank of the Spanish Borderlands frontier. More research is needed to understand the broad range of social and demographic questions implicit in this study. We are fortunate that such questions are only academic for us. California Indians faced them directly. Somehow they quietly persisted, living in a land radically transformed during the course of a single lifetime. For them, the 1860 census charts the landscape of survival and demographic decline.

◈ *F U R T H E R   R E A D I N G*

Gary C. Anderson, "Early Dakota Migration and Intertribal War: A Revision," *Western Historical Quarterly* 11 (1980), 17–36

———, *Kinsmen of Another Kind: Dakota–White Relations in the Upper Mississippi Valley, 1500–1862* (1984)

Lynn R. Bailey, *Indian Slave Trade in the Southwest* (1966)

Donald J. Berthrong, *The Southern Cheyennes* (1963)

Judith A. Boughter, *Betraying the Omaha Nation, 1790–1916* (1998)

Robert Boyd, "Commentary on Early Contact-Era Smallpox in the Pacific Northwest," *Ethnohistory 43* (Spring 1996), 307–328

John C. Ewers, "Intertribal Warfare as the Precursor of Indian–White Warfare on the Northern Great Plains," *Western Historical Quarterly* 6 (1975), 397–410

George Bird Grinnell, *The Cheyenne Indians: Their History and Ways of Life,* 2 vols. (1924)

Albert L. Hurtado, *Indian Survival on the California Frontier* (1988)

George E. Hyde, *Red Cloud's Folk: A History of the Oglala Sioux Indians* (1957)

Alvin M. Josephy, *The Nez Perce Indians and the Opening of the West* (1965)

Charles L. Kenner, *A History of New Mexican–Plains Indian Relations* (1969)

John J. Killoren, *"Come, Blackrobe": De Smet and the Indian Tragedy* (1995)

Brigham Madsen, *The Lemhi: Sacajawea's People* (1980)

———, *The Northern Shoshoni* (1980)

Warren Metcalf, "A Precarious Balance: The Northern Utes and the Black Hawk War," *Utah Historical Quarterly* 57, no. 1 (1989), 24–35

Roy W. Meyer, *The Village Indians of the Upper Missouri: The Mandans, Hidatsas, and Arikaras* (1977)

Christopher Miller, *Prophetic Worlds: Indians and Whites on the Columbia Plateau* (1985)

John Alton Peterson, *Utah's Black Hawk War* (1998)

George Harwood Phillips, *Chiefs and Challengers: Indian Resistance and Cooperation in Southern California* (1975)

———, *Indians and Indian Agents: The Origins of the Reservation System in California, 1849–1852* (1997)

———, *Indians and Intruders in Central California, 1769–1849* (1993)

James J. Rawls, *Indians of California: The Changing Image* (1984)

Robert H. Ruby and John A. Brown, *Indian Slavery in the Pacific Northwest* (1993)

Allen P. Slickpoo, *Noon nee-me-poo (We the Nez Perce): Culture and History of the Nez Perces* (1973)

Theodore Stern, *Chiefs and Change in the Oregon Country: Indian Relations at Fort Nez Percés, 1818–1855* (1996)

William F. Strobridge, *Regulars in the Redwoods: The U.S. Army in Northern California, 1852–1861* (1994)

John E. Sunder, *The Fur Trade on the Upper Missouri, 1840–1865* (1965)

Robert A. Trennert, Jr., *Alternative to Extinction: Federal Indian Policy and the Beginnings of the Reservation System, 1846–1851* (1975)

William E. Unrau, *The Kansa Indians: A History of the Wind People, 1673–1873* (1971)

Elizabeth Vibert, *Trader's Tales: Narratives of Cultural Encounters in the Columbia Plateau, 1807–1846* (1997)

Elliott West, *The Contested Plains: Indians, Goldseekers, and the Rush to Colorado* (1998)

David J. Wishart, *An Unspeakable Sadness: The Dispossession of the Nebraska Indians* (1994)

CHAPTER 9

Indian Perspectives on the Civil War

◈

Historians often view the American Civil War as a conflict in which brother fought brother. For some Indians embroiled in the fighting, this was figuratively, if not literally true, as tribes fractured along longstanding divisions as well as over the question of slavery. Just as many Indians thought that Britain was more likely to safeguard Indian independence than the United States, some tribes thought that their freedom would be more secure under the Confederacy. Ironically, this was especially true among the tribes that southern states had forced the federal government to remove to Indian Territory in present-day Oklahoma. The Cherokees, Chickasaws, Choctaws, and Creeks held slaves, and this fact figured importantly in their decision to side with the Confederate States of America, although tribesmen were divided on the issue. Elsewhere, the issues of the Civil War were not important to Indians, but the disruptions that the war caused meant that the United States could not effectively administer reservations or protect the frontier. Still other Indians, especially in the eastern states, enlisted in the Union Army to fight as scouts and regulars. The Union victory meant that tribes that sided with the Confederacy would suffer losses of land as well as the destruction of property that the war entailed.

◈ D O C U M E N T S

In 1862, the Dakota Sioux living in Minnesota were in a desperate condition. The reservation agent had not adequately supplied them with food and other necessities, while greedy traders exploited the impoverished Dakotas. In Document 1, Wabasha, a Dakota leader, explains how traders took advantage of his people and finally provoked war. In Indian Territory, the Cherokees were divided on the issue of fighting with the Confederacy or the Union. The Cherokee Stand Watie, who became Brigadier General in the Confederate army, was the most prominent Indian military leader to emerge during the war. Document 2 is a letter from his wife Sarah, who urged her husband to watch over their son Saladin, and another relative named Charles.

Document 3 is Stand Watie's reply to Sarah. While these letters show how intensely personal the fighting was (some of the enemy were mentioned by name), they are also remarkable because they are so similar to the letters of thousands of white soldiers and their wives. Document 4 is the conscription law that the Chickasaw nation passed pursuant to their treaty with the Confederate States of America. Document 5 is the Chickasaw governor's proclamation calling on able-bodied men to volunteer for military service. Document 6 is U.S. Commissioner of Indian Affairs Dennis N. Cooley's account of a council with the tribes that had signed treaties with the Confederacy. In addition to making new treaties, the Indians were also compelled to cede territory to the United States.

1. Wabasha (Dakota) Explains How Nefarious Trading Practices Caused the 1862 Minnesota War, 1868

I went to Washington the first time as I have stated above [1837]. I went again a second time [1858] before [after?] our removal to Red Wood. I went for this purpose; I had then sold our lands from east to west, from sunrise to sunset; I went to secure a reservation for my people. The Great Father put a garrison of soldiers near our country at Red Wood [Fort Ridgely], and before going to Washington I collected the chief men of the tribe and took them to the fort; some of them failed to come. I spent half a day in hunting them up, and getting their signatures to a letter that they wished to write to the President [Franklin Pierce]. The soldiers were put there to take good care of us and see that we were not interfered with by the whites. I told the commandant at the fort that I wished him to write a nice letter for us. I told him that I had always been brought up as an Indian, had worn a blanket and feather, painted my face and carried a gun. I wished him now to write to the Great Father that I had determined to leave off these things. I said write that I am determined to leave the war path, and to leave off drinking whisky, and give up plundering and thieving, and I want you to give me your ways. I know that your ways are good, and that your people obtain land and hold it, they plant corn and raise domestic animals. I wish you to give my people land where we may do the same. If we are left without a country, we will be obliged to go out on the plains. We would be in danger of perishing by cold and starvation; and then there are other tribes that live there that are likely to make war on us. I wish, therefore, the Great Father to give us land on the Minnesota River, and to help us to live like whites. I took this letter and carried it to Washington. After a few days I had an interview with the President. He shook hands with me, and told me to tell him all that I wanted. I said, my Father, all that I wish is written in this letter, and I handed him the letter. (Little Crow and Little Six were the only chiefs that did not sign the letter.) A few days afterwards, I was called to the Interior Department to attend to our business. I was told that our request had been granted, and that a reservation

From *Papers Relating to Talks and Councils Held with the Indians in Dakota and Montana Territories in the Years 1866–1869* (Washington, D.C.: Government Printing Office, 1910), 90–91. This document can also be found in Gary Clayton Anderson and Alan R. Woolworth, eds., *Through Dakota Eyes: Narrative Accounts of the Minnesota Indian War of 1862* (St. Paul: Minnesota Historical Society Press, 1988), 28–31.

had been appropriated for us at Red Wood on the Minnesota River, and that each head of a family should have assigned to him 100 acres of land; 80 of prairie and 20 of timber. When I saw our Great Father, I spoke to him about what was my chief desire, which was to have land. The traders were constantly following me for other purposes, and opposing me bitterly; but I paid no attention to them—I shut my ears against them. I only desired to get a title to lands and fix my people so that they could live. I made a treaty at this time, and lands were given to us at Red Wood, on both sides of the Minnesota River. I went home, and lived upon the land, and built houses there. The Great Father told me, before leaving, that he wished us to be well off, but that the whites would endeavor to get this land from us, and that the traders were like rats; that they would use all their endeavors to steal our substance, and that if we were wise, we would never sign a paper for anyone. If we did so, he said, we would never see 10 cents for all our property. I remembered the words of our Great Father and I knew that they were true. I was, consequently, always afraid of the traders.

Two years after this, when we had gathered our corn, we all went out on the fall hunt for furs. After we had been out some time the traders, the most active of whom was Mr. [Nathan?] Myrick, sent out for the chief to come in to sign papers for him in reference to selling the land on the north side of the Minnesota River [1858]. I refused to go in. The others, I am told, went home and signed some papers and received for doing so, horses, guns, blankets, and other articles. They told me this after I came home. I always refused to sign papers for the traders, and they therefore hated me. By the result of this paper signed without my consent or knowledge, the traders obtained possession of all the money coming from the sale of the land on the north side of the Minnesota River, and also half of our annuity for the year 1862. When this became known to the young men of the tribe, they felt very angry. The tribe then assembled a council of soldiers near Wakutes' house, and invite me to attend. I did attend. In that council it was determined that they would not submit to having half of their annuity taken from them, and it was ordered that all Indians should draw their annuity in full from the disbursing officer, and refuse to pay the credits to the traders for that year. I made a speech in council and told the Indians that I thought it was proper that they should obtain their whole annuities and refuse to pay the traders, and that I did not want the half-breeds to be admitted to our councils; that they had always been the tools of the traders, and aided them to deceive the Indians. After this council I thought about this matter a great deal, but heard nothing about it further until early one morning, as I was making a fire, an Indian on horseback rode up to my house and said that the Indians were fighting the traders. I asked him the cause of this sudden outbreak. He said that some of Little Six's band had killed some whites in the big woods and had come back determined to kill all the traders, and that fighting had already commenced. I got on my horse and rode up to the store. I saw that the traders were already killed. I then went to Mr. [Philander] Prescott's house; he was an Indian farmer and a half breed. I told him to write me a letter to the fort, for that I would have no part in this matter. I was determined to fly to the whites. Mr. Prescott was very much frightened and did not write the letter well. I then went home and sent word to Wa ku ta [Wakute] and Hu sha sha [Red Legs], who had not yet heard of the outbreak. I then wished to go to the fort, but found it impossible for I was afraid of the Indians.

2. Letter from Sarah C. Watie (Cherokee) to Her Husband, Stand Watie, During the Civil War, 1863

My dear half

I have just got home from Rusk and found Grady here and a letter from you dated the 27th of April it gave me a great deal of pleasure to know that you still have time to write and cast a thought on home and home folks Mr. Kelly and W. Fields will start as soon as I finish my letter. I have not had a chance to write you a long letter since you left. Grady tells me that Charles and Saladin have killed a prisiner write and tell me who it was and how it was, tell my boys to always show mercy as they expect to find God merciful to them. I do hate to hear such things it almost runs me crazy to hear such things I find myself almost dead sometimes thinking about it. I am afraid that Saladin never will value human life as he ought. If you should ever catch William Ross dont have him killed I know how bad his mother would feel but keep him till the war is over. I know they all deserve death but I do feel for his old mother and then I want them to know that you do not want to kill them just to get them out of your way. I want them to know you are not afraid of there influence. Always do as near right as you can. I feel sorry that you have such a bad chance and so much to do be careful of yourself. We have not a bit of water here we almost starve for water. Old man Martin is sick I have not seen him since you left. he started the next day after you left and went to some house some fourteen miles of. I expect he will die. He has the consumption. Sister Nancy I do not think will live through the summer she wants me to go and stay with her while she lives. She cant walk across the house tell Major Bradley to hunt me up and I will take care of him if I go to Rusk for the summer. I will get me a house in Bellview so the children can go to school it (is) impossible for (me) to stay here I will get some one to stay and take care of our corn it will do to fatten our horses you must write every chance and direct it to Lanagin and let him mail it to Rusk Bellview, it looks like I cant live and not hear from you. You must write and tell me when it will be safe to come. I sent the bay horse the black was to poor to go. I will bring him. you can either send that back or keep him till I come. I can sell him for six hundred here I have not time to say good by, yours

S. C. Watie.

Write soon.

3. Letter from Stand Watie (Cherokee) to His Wife, Sarah C. Watie, 1863

My dear Sarah:

I have not heard from you since your letter brought in by Anderson. When Medlock went away I was out on a scout. I went to Tahlequah and Park Hill. Took Dannie Hicks and John Ross. Would not allow them killed because you said Wm.

From Edward E. Dale, ed., "Some Letters of General Stand Watie," *Chronicles of Oklahoma* 1 (1921–23), 30–59.

From Edward E. Dale, ed., "Some Letters of General Stand Watie," *Chronicles of Oklahoma* 1 (1921–23), 30–59.

Ross must not be killed on old Mrs. Jack Ross's account. Killed a few Pins in Tahlequah. They had been holding council. I had the old council house set on fire and burnt down, also John Ross's house. Poor Andy Nave was killed. He refused to surrender and was shot by Dick Fields. I felt sorry as he used to be quite friendly towards me before the war, but it could not be helped. I would great deal rather have taken him prisoner Since my return I have been sick but now good deal better. Another scout has since been made to Tahlequah under Battles. He returned today. They found some negro soldiers at Park Hill, killed two and two white men. They brought in some of Ross's negroes.

There is a grand council of the different (tribes) to be held at Armstrong Academy on the 16th. Would like to attend but cant leave the command. Since Steele's and Cooper's retreat from Fort Smith I have been placed in command of the Indian troops (all) but Choctaws.

When I first sat down to write I thought I would send you a long letter but I am annoyed almost to death by people calling on me on business of various kinds, this and that,

I will send you pork enough to do you in a few days. I have concluded to have the hogs killed here and the meat hauled to you. You need not try to buy any. I can get it here.

A few days ago I received a letter from Sally Paschal. She said she had written to us and received no answer. Thinks perhaps we were displeased with her about something. I am sorry we did not write, it seemed to me you did. I will write to her soon. Let me hear from you often and let me know how you are all doing. Whenever the troops go into winter quarters I will go home to you. I have not been as well this fall as I used to. I cant get rid of this bad cough. Saladin is well. He is going to start in the morning with a party under Mose Fry on a scout to Fort Smith. Fry is not dead but is now a Major. He commands a battalion. I will write soon again.

Love to the little ones and everybody else.

> Your husband
> Stand Watie

4. Act of Conscription, Chickasaw Nation, 1864

First. *Be it enacted by the Legislature of the Chickasaw Nation,* That from and after the passage of this act the Governor be, and he is hereby, required to issue his proclamation calling upon all able bodied free male citizens of this nation to volunteer in the service of the Confederate States.

Second. *Be it further enacted,* That should not the people respond to the call of the Governor for volunteers for the C. S. service in one month from the passage of this act, all able-bodied free male citizens of this nation between the ages of eighteen and forty-five years of age shall be conscripted according to the conscript act of the Confederate States.

From Act of Conscription, Chickasaw Nation, 1864. Horace Pratt Collection, Western History Collection, University of Oklahoma, Norman. Also in *The War of the Rebellion, Series 1,* vol. 53, pt. 1 (Washington, D.C., 1898), 1024–1025.

Third. *Be it further enacted,* That the lieutenant-colonel commanding the Chickasaw Battalion shall have power, and he is hereby authorized, to appoint enrolling officers, whose duty it shall be to enroll all able-bodied free male citizens, as specified in the second section of this act, according to the conscription act of the Confederate States.

Fourth. *Be it further enacted,* That no free male citizen of this nation between the ages specified in the second section of this act shall be allowed to enlist in any Caddo, Comanche, or Osage company now in the service of the Confederate States.

Passed the House October 11, 1864.

> WM. McLISH,
> Speaker of the House.

Attest:

> S. S. GAMBLE,
> Clerk of the House.

Passed the Senate with the amendment October 11, 1864.

> EDMUND PERRY,
> President pro tempore of the Senate.

Attest:

> B. F. PERRY,
> Clerk of the Senate.

Approved October 11, 1864.

> HORACE PRATT,
> Governor of the Chickasaw Nation.
> ALEX. RENNIE,
> National Secretary.

Be it enacted by the Legislature of the Chickasaw Nation, That from and after the passage of this act all civil officers of this nation shall be exempt from military duty.

Second. *Be it further enacted,* That all judges, clerks, sheriffs, and constables of this nation shall be exempt from military duty, provided, however, that in case of threatened invasion of our country all shall respond to the call of the Governor.

Passed the Senate October 8, 1864.

> WM. KEMP,
> President of the Senate.

Attest:

> B. F. PERRY,
> Secretary Senate.

Passed the House October 8, 1864.

> WM. McLISH,
> Speaker of the House.

Attest:

> S. S. GAMBLE,
> Clerk of the House.

Approved October 8, 1864.

HORACE PRATT,
Governor of the Chickasaw Nation.
ALEX. RENNIE,
National Secretary.

5. Proclamation Ordering Conscription in the Chickasaw Nation, 1864

Whereas, the necessities of the times, our treaty stipulations with the Confederate States of America, and a call from the President of the Confederate States require the Chickasaw Nation to furnish troops for the C. S. service, according to the fifty-first article of the treaty made at North Fork, C. N., July 12, 1861, between the Confederate States of America and the Choctaw and Chickasaw Nation, to co-operate with our allied Indian forces now in the field for the defense of our country; and

Whereas, the Legislature of the Chickasaw Nation did, on the 11th day of October, 1864, pass an act of conscription, to take effect within thirty days from the passage of that act.

Now, therefore, I, Horace Pratt, Governor of the Chickasaw Nation, do issue this my proclamation, in accordance with the first section of that act, calling upon all able-bodied free male citizens to volunteer in the service of the Confederate States and fill up the ranks of the First Chickasaw Regiment before the 12th day of November next, and thereby avoid conscription and raise the honor of the Chickasaw Nation, as on the 12th day of November the conscription act goes into effect. And I am justified in stating, for the information of all concerned, that efforts are being made by the proper officers to furnish the soldiers with good and comfortable clothing, as well as tents and other articles necessary, as soon as possible.

HORACE PRATT,
Governor Chickasaw Nation.
ALEXANDER RENNIE,
National Secretary.

Tishomingo, October 12, 1864.

6. Commissioner of Indian Affairs Dennis N. Cooley on the Consequences of the Civil War, 1865

. . . The council assembled at Fort Smith, September 8, and delegates were present in the course of the sittings (though not all in attendance at first) representing the Creeks, Choctaws, Chickasaws, Cherokees, Seminoles, Osages, Senecas, Shawnees, Quapaws, Wyandotts, Wichitas, and Comanches. Immediately upon the opening of

---

From Proclamation Ordering Conscription in the Chickasaw Nation, 1864. Horace Pratt Collection, Western History Collection, University of Oklahoma, Norman. Also in *The War of the Rebellion, Series 1,* vol. 53, pt. 1 (Washington, D.C., 1898), 1025–1026.

Commissioner of Indian Affairs Dennis N. Cooley on the Consequences of the Civil War, 1865. This document can be found in the *Annual Report of the Commissioner of Indian Affairs, 1865.*

proceedings, the tribes were informed generally of the object for which the commission had come to them; that they for the most part, as tribes, had, by violating their treaties—by making treaties with the so-called Confederate States, forfeited all *rights* under them, and must be considered as at the mercy of the government; but that there was every disposition to treat them leniently, and above all a determination to recognize in a signal manner the loyalty of those who had fought upon the side of the government, and endured great sufferings on its behalf. On the next day the delegates were informed that the commissioners were empowered to enter into treaties with the several tribes, upon the basis of the following propositions:

1st. That each tribe must enter into a treaty for permanent peace and amity among themselves, each other as tribes, and with the United States.

2d. The tribes settled in the "Indian country" to bind themselves, at the call of the United States authorities, to assist in compelling the wild tribes of the plains to keep the peace.

3d. Slavery to be abolished, and measures to be taken to incorporate the slaves into the tribes, with their rights guaranteed.

4th. A general stipulation as to final abolition of slavery.

5th. A part of the Indian country to be set apart, to be purchased for the use of such Indians, from Kansas or elsewhere, as the government may desire to colonize therein.

6th. That the policy of the government to unite all the Indian tribes of this region into one consolidated government should be accepted.

7th. That no white persons, except government employees, or officers or employees of internal improvement companies authorized by government, will be permitted to reside in the country, unless incorporated with the several nations.

Printed copies of the address of the commissioners involving the above propositions were placed in the hands of the agents, and of members of the tribes, many of whom were educated men.

On the third day the delegates from the loyal Chickasaws, Choctaws, Senecas, Osages, and Cherokees, principally occupied the time with replies to the address and propositions of the commissioners, the object being partly to express a willingness to accept those propositions, with some modifications, if they had been clothed with sufficient power by their people, but chiefly in explanation of the manner in which their nations became involved with the late confederacy. The address of the Cherokees was especially noteworthy, inasmuch as they attempted to charge the causes of their secession upon the United States, as having violated its treaty obligations, in failing to give the tribe protection, so that it was *compelled* to enter into relations with the confederacy. The next day the loyal Seminoles expressed their willingness to accede to the policy of the government, and to make peace with those of their people who had aided the rebellion. The president of the commission then read a reply to the address of the loyal Cherokees above referred to, showing, from original and official documents, that, *as a tribe,* by the action of their constituted authorities, John Ross being then, as at the time of the council, their head, they had, at the very opening of the rebellion, entered into alliance with it, and raised troops for it, and urged the other tribes to go with them, and that they could not now, under the facts proven, deny their original participation in the rebellion. (The documents establishing the bad faith of John Ross had but recently come into possession of the department. They are very interesting, and taken in connexion with his course at Fort Smith in keeping aloof from the council, but exercising his powerful influence to prevent an amicable settlement with the hitherto disloyal part of the nation, will be found fully to justify the course taken by the commission in refusing to recognize him in any manner as chief of the Cherokees.)

The loyal Creeks on this day presented their address of explanation, setting forth the manner in which their nation, by the unauthorized action of its chief, entered into treaty relations with the confederacy, and the terrible sufferings which the loyal Creeks endured in battle and on the march to Kansas seeking protection from the United States, and asking "to be considered not guilty."

It being certain that no final treaties could be now concluded with the tribes represented, for the reason that, until the differences between the loyal and disloyal portions were healed, there could be no satisfactory representation of most of them, it was determined to prepare for signature by the commission, and by the delegates representing all factions and opinions, a preliminary treaty, pledging anew, on behalf of the Indians, allegiance to the United States, and repudiating all treaties with other parties; and on the part of the United States agreeing to reestablish peace and friendship with them. . . .

Friendly relations were established between the members of the various tribes hitherto at variance, except in the case of the Cherokees. The ancient feuds among this people are remembered still, and the Ross, Ridge, and Boudinot difficulties have never been healed.* This portion of the nation was ably represented in council by Boudinot and others, and having learned from the action of those representing the loyal party that if they came back it must be as beggars and outlaws, asked the protection and good offices of the commission. Efforts were then made on the part of the commission to effect a reconciliation, but all that could be brought about was a promise upon the part of those representing the loyal party to present the question to their council, which is now in session, and I entertain the hope that soon I shall be able to furnish you a report of their proceedings, in which they offer fair and honorable terms of adjustment. If, however, I should be disappointed in this reasonable expectation, I trust the government will take the matter in hand, and, by a just and equitable division of their property, make a final settlement of all their difficulties.

When the majority of this nation returned to their allegiance to the government, in 1863, action was taken by their council, under direction of John Ross, confiscating the property of those who still continued in the service of the confederacy, thus cutting off about five thousand five hundred of the nation, leaving them homeless and houseless. This destitute portion of the tribe are still refugees on the Red river, suffering from the want of every necessary of life, and existing only upon the charity of the humane people of northeastern Texas. The department has, however, sent a special agent to look into the wants of these refugees, and must rely upon Congress for the necessary means to relieve their necessities. . . .

---

*Major Ridge and Elias Boudinot had opposed Ross and had agreed to the treaty that forced most of the Cherokees on the Trail of Tears. Ridge and Boudinot were killed in Indian territory because of their signing of this treaty.

◈ *E S S A Y S*

The Civil War presented a difficult challenge to leaders in Indian Territory. They had to contend with the political division of the United States as well as the political and social divisions of their own nations. Nowhere was this more complicated than in the Cherokee nation, as Professor Ari Kelman of the University of Denver demonstrates in his essay on John Ross, principal chief of the Cherokees. Ross's decision to side with the Confederacy in 1861 was based on what he perceived as the best interests of the Cherokees rather than on deeply held convictions about the nature of the federal union or slavery. The second essay, by University of Oklahoma professor Gary Clayton Anderson, demonstrates how complicated was the Dakota situation when the Minnesota uprising occurred in 1862. The Dakotas would learn with dismay that they were too closely tied to white traders, technology, and the reservation economy to easily abandon them. If it was impossible to return to the old life of hunting and gathering, what then? These essays show how complicated were Indian decisions to fight and how problematic the outcomes of fighting were. On the other hand, one challenge to Indian leadership was how to avoid fighting when insults, injuries, and desperation were piled so high.

Deadly Currents

John Ross's Decision of 1861

ARI KELMAN

On August 21, 1861, John Ross, the principal chief of the Cherokee Nation, stood before a gathering of approximately 4,000 Cherokees; the tribe faced a situation so grave that almost all of the eligible tribal electorate attended the meeting. The secession of the southern states left the Cherokees with Confederate neighbors to the east and south, and Union neighbors to the north, all of whom demanded to know which side the nations of Indian Territory would choose as allies in the coming war.

In the spring and early summer of 1861 Ross counseled neutrality, not just for the Cherokees, but for all the tribes of Indian Territory. As the summer drew to a close, Ross, subjected to tremendous pressures from inside and outside the Cherokee Nation, realized the impossibility of that stance. Facing his assembled people, he expounded on the validity of both the Union and Confederate causes. He acknowledged the importance of the Cherokees' treaty with the federal government in whose hands lay the tribe's trust funds. The tribe's policy of neutrality seemed successful to that point, but Ross addressed his greatest concern, the unity of the Cherokee Nation, with the following words:

> The great object with me has been to have the Cherokee people harmonious and united in the full and free exercise and enjoyment of all of their rights of person and property. Union is strength, dissension is weakness, misery ruin! In time of peace together! in time of war, if war must come, fight together.

From Ari Kelman, "Deadly Currents: John Ross's Decision of 1861," *Chronicles of Oklahoma* 73 (Spring 1995), 80–103. Copyright © 1995. Reprinted by permission from *The Chronicles of Oklahoma* (Oklahoma City: Oklahoma Historical Society, 1995).

His speech contained no surprises and nothing indicated what was to follow. Ross concluded:

> The permanent disruption of the United States into two governments is now probable. The State [Arkansas] on our border and the Indian nations about us have severed their connection from the United States and joined the Confederate States. Our general interest is inseparable from theirs and it is not desirable that we should stand alone. The preservation of our rights and of our existence are above every other consideration.
>
> And in view of all the circumstances of our situation I say to you frankly, that, in my opinion, the time has now arrived when you should signify your consent for the authorization of the Nation to adopt preliminary steps for an alliance with the Confederate States upon terms honorable and advantageous to the Cherokee Nation.

Three days later Ross wrote to Confederate general Benjamin McCulloch asking for protection from possible "movements against the Cherokee people upon their Northern border." He enclosed a copy of his address and noted his willingness to negotiate a treaty between the Cherokees and the Confederate government. Less than one year later Ross changed his position again, assuring President Abraham Lincoln that the Cherokee Nation had always been faithful to the Union. What caused Ross to alter his stance on neutrality? Why did he recommend a Confederate alliance and later rejoin the Union?

Despite some sympathy for elements of both the northern and southern positions, Ross was neither a Union nor a Confederate man; rather he sought a path leading to tribal unity and sovereignty. Maintenance of his personal power, he believed, was integral to achieving those ends. Ross did not make his decisions in a political or historical vacuum. As leader of the Cherokee Nation, he lived and ruled amid deadly currents.

The factors that influenced Ross's decision in 1861 included internal tribal conflict whose roots lay in four intertwined situations—the thirty-year-old conflict over removal; the often strained relationship between mixed- and full blood members of the tribe; the debate between Cherokee slaveholders and non-slaveholders; and the conflict between traditionalists and non-traditionalists over language and custom. Ross dealt with each of those conflicts by seeking solutions that would preserve the unity of his tribe. He faced a difficult situation as whites consistently exacerbated and exploited those conflicts by employing divide and conquer tactics in their relations with the Cherokees. In his dealings with whites, particularly the federal government, Ross demanded that his people be treated as a sovereign nation. Thus an exploration of Cherokee-white relationships, particularly between the tribe and the federal government, yields a more complete understanding of Ross's decision-making process in 1861.

During the Indian removal debate that took place in the 1830s, powerful factions within the Cherokee Nation became disenchanted with Ross's hardline stance opposing removal and began actively criticizing his sometimes autocratic leadership. The events surrounding removal forever recast the Cherokee Nation, undermining tribal peace and replacing it with factionalism that threatened Ross's vision of unity for his people. In 1861 as the Civil War enveloped the Cherokees, old factional wounds, dating back to removal, reopened in Indian Territory and Ross sought an effective remedy in neutrality. When neutrality failed to cool the fever of factionalism, Ross was forced to choose sides in a conflict he believed would yield only sorrow for the Cherokee Nation. Surrounded by tribal conflict, Ross grappled with his choices.

The roots of Cherokee factionalism lie in Washington and Georgia in 1832. In that year, Stand Watie, one of the key members of a growing anti-Ross faction in the Cherokee Nation, acted as editor of the bilingual Cherokee newspaper, *The Cherokee Phoenix,* in lieu of his brother, Elias Boudinot. Boudinot and John Ridge comprised part of a Cherokee delegation to the federal government negotiating the issue of removal. In a letter to Watie, Ridge suggested that *The Cherokee Phoenix* be used as a forum for expressing views undercutting Ross's authority, that is, urging the Cherokees to accept removal. Ridge, along with his father Major Ridge, Boudinot, and Watie became the leading figures in what would be called the "Treaty Party" after they went against Ross's wishes by signing the Treaty of New Echota. According to that treaty the Cherokees agreed to cede land east of the Mississippi River for land in Indian Territory. The Cherokee Council never ratified the treaty, thus under Cherokee law it was an illegal document. Despite the existence of a petition of protest signed by more than 13,000 Cherokees, the United States Senate ratified the treaty in May, 1836, leading to decades of strife within the Cherokee Nation, and profoundly influencing John Ross's decision of 1861.

The events surrounding removal nourished Ross's nascent political consciousness and eroded his faith in the federal government. Ross looked on as the government supported Georgia's land grab and ignored past treaties with the Cherokees. President Andrew Jackson's failure to honor the United States Supreme Court's decision in *Worcester* v. *Georgia* illustrated a profound disrespect for the law of the land when it fell on the side of Cherokee sovereignty. In the years leading up to removal, the growth of pro-treaty sentiment among the Ridge-Watie-Boudinot faction provided the federal government with a powerful tool in the Cherokee Nation. Ross suspected that collusion between the tribal factions and the federal government led to the Treaty of New Echota. In a protest to the Senate, Ross screamed of Georgia's insidious actions and the role of the federal government in fostering the growth of Cherokee factionalism:

> A system was devised and prosecuted to force them to emigrate, by rendering them unhappy where they were. This was the original design, but it was soon found profit was to be had, by keeping up a division among the Cherokees, and protracting their difficulties, and with this view the party of which the Delegation have before spoken, soon threw itself under the wing of the government agents.

In the removal period, the Supreme Court was the only one of the three branches of the federal government in which Ross had confidence. However, the government failed to enforce Chief Justice John Marshall's decisions. While Ross's interaction with the Jackson administration particularly disheartened him, his relationship with the legislative branch suffered as well. His appeal to Congress in the spring of 1835 centered on the removal issue, but an unfavorable response led Ross to contemplate moving the Cherokees from the United States. Ross's faith in Congress reached its nadir with the Senate's acceptance of the Treaty of New Echota. Because it was negotiated by an unauthorized minority faction within the tribe, Ross believed the treaty utterly spurious.

From 1832 to 1838 the federal government undercut Ross's tribal authority and ignored his authority as principal chief. From Andrew Jackson's threats to hold Ross responsible for the murder of a pro-removal Cherokee, to the government's decision to negotiate a final removal treaty with Ross's rivals, the federal government treated Ross as an obstacle rather than an ally.

Factionalism followed the Cherokees to Indian Territory, and the Treaty Party's antipathy for Ross and his followers did not abate. The contentious issue of tribal government and the brutal murder of three leaders of the Treaty Party divided the Cherokees anew. In his old opponents from the Treaty Party as well as their new allies from the Old Settlers (Cherokees who had voluntarily moved west prior to 1836), Ross faced a substantial threat that plagued him until the eve of the Civil War. Prominent leaders of the Treaty Party had arrived in Indian Territory as early as the spring of 1837. Once there they reunited with 3,000 members of the Old Settlers. The 2,000 new immigrants from the Treaty Party accepted the Old Settlers' loosely organized system of government and Ross found himself facing two factions united in a challenge to his authority.

When the body of 13,000 Cherokees arrived in 1839, tribal government became a hotly contested issue. John Ross wanted to continue in his role as chief of a reunited Cherokee Nation, while the leaders of the Old Settlers suggested separate governments. On June 10, 1839, Ross addressed the General Council of the Cherokee Nation. He did not insist that the Cherokee Constitution of 1828 be adopted for the nation in Indian Territory. Rather, he pointedly referred to the fact that the "late emigrants . . . constitute a large majority." Only a unified nation, he believed, could successfully negotiate with whites. He assured the assembled Cherokees, "[T]here is no intention nor desire on the part of their representatives to propose or require any thing, but what may be strictly equitable & just and satisfactory to the people." Ross concluded, "[A] House divided against itself can not stand." Three days later Ross wrote to John Brown, John Looney, and John Rogers, the chiefs of the Old Settlers, saying he hoped all Cherokees could reunite under a new constitution. The Brown and Ross groups agreed to meet to discuss their differences at the Illinois Camp Ground on July 1, 1839.

Much to Ross's dismay, his supporters, as well as his opponents, erected obstacles blocking the road to unity. Another effort to discuss tribal unity at the General Council on June 10 failed. A group of conspirators, perhaps holding the Treaty Party responsible for the failure to achieve unity or perhaps enforcing the "death penalty for signing land cession treaties," executed three key members of the Treaty Party on June 22. The killers murdered John Ridge and Elias Boudinot in their homes and gunned down Major Ridge near the Arkansas River. With the deaths of his uncle (Major Ridge), cousin (John Ridge), and brother (Boudinot), Stand Watie vowed vengeance on the killers and on John Ross whom he held responsible. When Ross heard the news of the murders and learned of Watie's reaction, he surrounded his house with members of his constituency to protect himself from Watie's armed mob. General Matthew Arbuckle, stationed in Missouri, and alarmed at what he perceived to be near anarchy in the Cherokee Nation, suggested that the various factions meet at Fort Gibson to work out their differences. Ross declined; he feared that the journey would be too dangerous.

The brutal executions of the leaders of the Treaty Party left Ross in a state of shock and dismay as violent factionalism placed the tribe further than ever from unity. Although the conspirators supported Ross, it appears likely that the chief knew nothing of their plans. Ross was further devastated when on June 28 the chiefs of the Old Settlers told him they believed the scheduled July 1 meeting was "irregular." They feared Ross wanted to pass laws benefiting the new eastern immigrants, and suggested meeting at Fort Gibson where "both parties shall be equally represented; and that the said convention shall have power to remodel the government for the Cherokee Nation."

Ross ignored the invitation to Fort Gibson and presided over the scheduled meeting at the Illinois Camp Ground on July 1 instead. The result was the Act of Union, ratified primarily by Ross's supporters, and a new Cherokee Constitution similar to the one used by the Eastern Cherokees. Most leaders of the Old Settlers, determined to maintain their power in government, avoided the meeting as a protest over its legitimacy; some attended, however, and signed the Act of Union. Ross viewed the new Act of Union and Constitution as hopeful documents.

Ross moved quickly to consolidate his perceived advantage in the aftermath of the meeting. First he wrote to Arbuckle, who still hoped that representatives of the Ross Party, the Old Settlers, and the Treaty Party would meet at Fort Gibson. Ross assured Arbuckle no threat of a Cherokee civil war existed, and he wanted only unity for the tribe. On September 12, 1839, Ross addressed the new National Council believing he had succeeded in reuniting the Cherokees, and had legitimized the new constitution by including representatives of the Old Settlers in the new government. However, the Old Settlers and their allies in the Treaty Party bitterly denounced the new government, a move backed by the United States Army and federal government. Once again meddling from outside the tribe heightened tensions within the Cherokee Nation.

While Ross savored his accomplishments, the new Cherokee Constitution and Act of Union infuriated members of the Old Settlers who had boycotted the Illinois Camp Ground meeting. The Treaty Party also remained at odds with Ross and both factions enjoyed the support of the federal government. Andrew Jackson answered an appeal from Watie in a letter dated October 5, 1839, in which he expressed sympathy for Watie's plight in light of Ross's "tyranny." He assured Watie he would write a letter to President Martin Van Buren expressing his views. Van Buren's government, no doubt influenced by Jackson, undercut Ross's authority when Arbuckle demanded the Cherokees turn over the parties responsible for the Ridge-Boudinot murders. United States courts did not have jurisdiction over Cherokee territory, Ross reminded Arbuckle. On July 19 Arbuckle authorized the arming of the Missouri State Militia, ostensibly to allay fears in the white population resulting from the disputes in the Cherokee Nation. Ross, upset by what he viewed as white incursion into Cherokee affairs, assured Arbuckle that he was overreacting and that there was no threat of civil war. He implied that Arbuckle relied on untrustworthy and inflammatory sources for his information about the affairs of the Cherokees. Arbuckle also took up the cause of the dissatisfied Old Settlers who had not attended the Illinois Camp Ground meeting. Ross countered by stating that representatives of the Old Settlers, including one of their chiefs, John Looney, were present at the meeting and had signed the Act of Union and the constitution. Ross erroneously believed the affairs of the tribe were in order, and he left for Washington as head of another delegation.

After arriving in Washington Ross's confidence in tribal stability diminished as familiar sources undermined his authority. At a general assembly of the Cherokee

Nation called by Cherokee agent Montford Stokes on January 15, 1840, the Act of Union and the new Cherokee Constitution were ratified. The disgruntled Old Settlers met in February of that year and decided not to recognize Ross as chief. They sought and received Arbuckle's sanction for their actions. The federal government also chose not to recognize the Act of Union nor Ross as chief. At the same time a separate delegation in the capital made up of members of the Treaty Party jeopardized Ross's work in Washington. In a letter to Secretary of War Joel Poinsett, Ross worried about possible mistreatment because Poinsett believed he was involved in the murders of the Ridges and Boudinot. On February 28 the Ross delegation addressed Congress in an effort to illustrate the validity of the Act of Union and the new constitution. In April the delegation addressed the House Committee of Indian Affairs with much the same message. In the end Ross's trip to Washington proved fruitless, and he returned to Indian Territory to face new problems at home. The chasm between the Ross and Treaty parties yawned wider than ever and the dispute with the Old Settlers represented one more threat to the Cherokee Nation. Only the results of the January general assembly and a June meeting during which the Old Settlers and the Ross faction recognized the Act of Union offered Ross any hope for tribal unity in the future.

In late summer, 1841, Ross prepared to head another delegation to Washington. He worried that a return home, once again with no good news, would further undermine the tribe's trust in him and possibly consolidate his rivals' growing support. Ross appealed to Secretary of War John Bell on August 26, asking Bell to provide him with something tangible and positive to tell the tribe. On September 20 President John Tyler wrote to Ross regarding the Treaty of New Echota. Tyler believed negotiating a new treaty to replace the fraudulent one "would be satisfactory and just to the Cherokees and just to both parties." Ross could not contain his elation when he addressed the National Council on November 29, 1841. He praised the "brief administration" of William H. Harrison and President Tyler's promises. Ross was bitterly disappointed when his optimism proved premature. Like Chief Justice Marshall's decisions, Tyler's promise came to naught. For Ross that served as one more example of the federal government's dishonest dealings with the Cherokees. However, the betrayal was not immediately apparent and Ross, at least momentarily, believed he had an ally in Washington.

Ross's optimism seemed to affect the disparate groups within the Cherokee Nation during a period marked by relative calm. However, when Stand Watie, one of the last surviving members of the original Treaty Party's leaders, killed James Foreman on May 14, 1842, it brought the Cherokee Nation to the brink of civil war. Foreman was one of the men accused of the murder of Watie's uncle, Major Ridge. A white pro-Watie Arkansas court tried and acquitted Watie on the grounds of self-defense. Soon after, on August 8, 1843, three of Ross's supporters, acting in their capacity as election workers, were attacked; one, Isaac Bushyhead, was murdered. The tides of factionalism had not receded completely and would affect the Ross delegation's affairs in Washington the following year.

The presence of multiple Cherokee groups undermined all appearances of unity in Washington in 1844, and once again jeopardized Ross's ongoing quest to secure sovereignty and unity for his people. The Treaty Party and the Old Settlers, both intent on dividing the Cherokees, each had representatives in the capital. Ross attempted to diminish the importance of the other bodies in a letter dated May 14, 1844, to Secretary of War William Wilkins. He wrote, "We have not been delegated to represent a party, but the whole Cherokee people." Wilkins responded that neither he nor President John Tyler were satisfied that Ross's delegation represented the consensus voice of the Cherokees. He referred to "oppression upon two classes of your nation—the 'Treaty Party' and the 'Arkansas or Western Cherokee.'" Wilkins intended to send a "commission of officers" to the Cherokee Nation to determine the "true and exact extent of the discontent and spirit of hostility which prevails amongst your people." That proved to be a devastating blow for Ross who had grown increasingly optimistic after his interaction with President Tyler. Due to the political climate, Ross believed his delegation's presence in Washington would accomplish little, and he left the capital at the end of the summer.

Ross knew the commission appointed by Wilkins could badly damage his authority and he was wary of its report. He also felt betrayed as the federal government again demonstrated its willingness to interfere even at the risk of tribal unity. Thus Ross was surprised and elated when the federal commission, composed of Roger Jones, Roger Mason, and Cherokee agent Pierce Mason Butler, indicated in its report of January, 1845, that the members believed many of the complaints coming from Indian Territory existed only because Washington lent a sympathetic ear. The commissioners also recommended against splitting the nation. That substantiated the opinion Ross expressed to Wilkins in Washington the previous summer. Ross had implored then:

> It is with communities as with individuals that when they know that their destinies are united forever many small causes of strife are passed over and reconciled—but where separation is easy the happiness of all parties is too often sacrificed to temporary excitement and momentary passion.

Despite Ross's opinion and the commissioners' suggestions, tribal factionalism exploded into bloodshed and terrorism in late 1845. The burning of John Meigs's house (Ross's son-in-law) preceded the murders of James Starr, a proponent of removal, and Thomas Watie, Stand Watie's brother. Stand Watie, confronted with the murder of another family member, gathered a group of men at Old Fort Wayne for his own protection. George Lowrey, acting as principal chief during Ross's absence, wrote to Watie that the "combination of so many armed men at 'Old Fort Wayne' is a subject of general and just complaint." While the Cherokee Nation remained mired in a state of guerrilla warfare, Ross appealed to the new president, James Polk, as a member of yet another delegation to Washington. Delegations representing the Treaty Party and Old Settlers competed with Ross's group in Washington. Ross's opponents again argued in favor of dividing the Cherokee Nation to avoid further bloodshed. President Polk and the commissioner of Indian affairs supported their view and reported their opinion to Congress. With tribal unity in the balance, the various factions met in Washington and agreed to a treaty addressing the concerns of each group—a unified nation for the Ross party; a share of the per capita payment from the federal government for the Old Settlers; amnesty and monetary reparations to compensate for their suffering for the Treaty Party. In signing the treaty Ross illustrated his commitment to tribal unity by reluctantly accepting the validity of the Treaty of New Echota after more than fifteen years of trumpeting its fallaciousness.

The treaty of 1846 marked the beginning of an extended period of calm in the Cherokee Nation. But repercussions from the dislocation of removal, continued tribal conflict, and poor relations with the federal government would all play a role in John Ross's decision of 1861. Internal peace resulting from the treaty of 1846 held until the approach of the American Civil War, when recurring themes of con-. flict resurfaced and new divisions among the Cherokees emerged. Finally, the issue of slavery profoundly impacted John Ross's choice in the coming conflict.

Following passage of the Kansas-Nebraska Act in 1854, Kansas Territory, just north of the Cherokees, fractured over the issue of slavery. "Bleeding Kansas" exported the debate over slavery and open warfare across the border into the Cherokee Nation as slavery became an increasingly contentious topic. While most Cherokee full bloods did not own slaves, Ross owned more than fifty slaves by 1860 and, like most Cherokee slaveholders, was of mixed ancestry (he was one-eighth Cherokee). However, Ross's loyal constituency consisted largely of full bloods. In his annual message of October 6, 1856, Ross affirmed slavery's protected place within the Cherokee Nation, but acknowledged growing trouble between slaveholders and abolitionist missionaries in Indian Territory. In his reports to Congress in 1854 and 1855, Cherokee agent George Butler also referred to the controversy. Pro-slavery Cherokees often accused the Northern Baptist missionaries Evan and John Jones of stirring up abolitionist sentiment. The Joneses did encourage slaveholding members of their congregation to free their slaves or leave the church. In his study of slavery in the Cherokee Nation, Rudi Halliburton argued that Ross's relationship with the Jones family led him to veto an 1855 pro-slavery bill, but the National Council subsequently passed it over his veto. The bill made it illegal for missionaries and teachers in the Cherokee public schools to espouse abolitionist beliefs. Despite that official censure, however, Evan and John Jones continued to play a key role in the slavery debate among the Cherokees.

The slavery issue divided the Cherokee Nation into opposing camps. The formation of a secret pro-slavery organization called the Knights of the Golden Circle in 1855, and the creation of the opposing Keetoowah Society (commonly known as "Pins" because of the crossed pins members wore on their shirts) in 1856, illustrated the depth of the controversy. The Knights' constitution stipulated that all members had to be supporters of slavery. Article 6 stated:

> The Captain or in case of his refusal, the Lieutenant has power to compel each and every member of their encampment to turn out and assist in capturing and punishing any and all abolitionists in their minds who are interfering with slavery.

Wealthier mixed-bloods with secessionist leanings filled out the Knights' membership (the organization was also called the Southern Rights Party). In contrast Unionist full bloods were more often the members of the Keetoowah Society. In his collection of Cherokee myths, ethnologist James Mooney noted that Cherokees banded together in the Keetoowah Society in response to the presence of secret societies among the mixed-bloods. He looked to class issues as a foundation of the society, noting that the non-slaveholding full blood Keetoowahs were poorer than their mixed-blood counterparts who gathered together in the "Blue Lodge and other secret secessionist organizations." The Keetoowah Constitution and its amendments, written between April, 1859, and January, 1866, stipulated that membership was limited to full bloods (defined as those Cherokees who were uneducated or did not speak English). It also provided that revealing Keetoowah business was punishable by death. Other provisions included protocols for accepting new members, paying dues, and caring for sick members. The Keetoowah Constitution contained two elements critical to understanding Ross's decisions of 1861 and 1862. First, the constitution bemoaned the loss of tribal unity and offered adherence to Cherokee laws and loyalty to the government as the remedy for tribal factionalism. Second, amendments passed on September 20, 1860, read in part, "in the division between North and South, we should not take sides with either."

The Keetoowah Constitution blamed mixed-bloods and their secret societies for the difficulties facing the tribe. Mixed-blood leaders believed the same of the Keetoowahs, feared their numbers, their support of Ross, and their apparent alliance with the Jones family. Stephen Foreman, a slaveholder, prominent member of the Treaty Party, and later a supporter of the Confederacy, reflected on the Keetoowahs in 1862. He thought the Pins hated him solely because he was a "Watie man. . . . They themselves had drawn the distinction between themselves and the half-breeds, and being a half-breed, I naturally fell on the Watie side." Foreman argued that the goals of the Pins included controlling the government and abolishing slavery, and he believed the Joneses founded the Keetoowah organization.

The link between the Keetoowahs and the Jones family echoes frequently in the literature on the subject. Mooney, writing in 1890, pointed to John Jones as the founder of the Pins. D. J. MacGowan in his 1866 article, "Indian Secret Societies," wrote, "The Pin organization originated among the members of the [Northern] Baptist congregation at Peavine, Going-snake district, in the Cherokee Nation." The conflict between the Keetoowahs and the Knights encompassed divisions between rich and poor, slaveholder and abolitionist, full blood and mixed-blood, and the Ross Party and the Treaty. The secret societies founded during that period simply provided a new forum for the expression of old conflicts.

Once again interference from whites exacerbated and manipulated fractious intertribal conflicts. On January 29, 1861, Ross received a letter from Henry M. Rector, the governor of Arkansas, in which Rector attempted to sway Ross to the side of the South by evoking fears of abolition he claimed would necessarily follow a treaty with the North. Ross responded to Rector's letter in late February. He expressed Cherokee sympathy for the Southern cause, prayed for peace, and finally noted the importance of the treaties with the federal government. Ross also dealt with pressure from white secessionists working within his tribe. Both Elias Rector and R. J. Cowart, the federal superintendent of Indian affairs and the Cherokee agent respectively, were pro-slavery and secessionists. Cowart and Rector believed the Joneses led the Pins and viewed their abolitionist activity as subversive and dangerous. In the summer of 1860 they exerted their influence to quell the work of the "secret societies" under the Joneses. A. B. Greenwood, the commissioner of Indian affairs, instructed Rector to have Cowart:

> institute inquiry as to the existence of this secret organization, its objects and purposes; who are the counselors and advisors of this movement, and proceed at once to break it up. . . . If in his investigation he should be satisfied that any white persons residing in the Nation are in any way connected with this organization he will notify such person or persons forthwith to leave the Nation.

The pressure on Ross mounted after Arkansas's secession. He received letters from private Arkansas citizens and J. R. Kannady, the commander of Fort Smith, demanding to know which side of the coming conflict the Cherokees would choose.

Kannady wrote of the importance of slavery to the Cherokees, noting that Indian Territory was "salubrious and fertile and possesses the highest capacity for future progress and development by the application of Slave Labor." On May 17 Ross answered Kannady much as he had answered Rector months earlier. He acknowledged friendship with the people of Arkansas, but remained neutral, citing the Cherokees' treaties with the federal government. Ross was prescient when he wrote:

> Our interests all center in peace. We do not wish to forfeit our rights or to incur the hostility of any people and least of all the people of Arkansas, with whom our relations are so numerous & intimate. We do not wish our soil to become the battle ground between the states and our homes to be rendered desolate and miserable by the horrors of a civil war. If such a war should not be averted yet by some unforeseen agency but shall occur my own position will be to take no part in it whatever and to urge the like course upon the Cherokee people by whom in my opinion it will be adopted.

In May, 1861, the Confederate government commissioned Albert Pike, a Massachusetts-born lawyer living in Arkansas, as special agent to the tribes of Indian Territory, and authorized him to engage the tribes in an alliance with the Confederacy. Because of legal work he had done for the tribes, Pike knew about the divisions in the Cherokee Nation and planned to exploit them in his negotiations. The other Confederate commissioner to Indian Territory, General Benjamin McCulloch, wrote Ross on June 12, 1861. His position of neutrality would be respected, McCulloch assured Ross, unless "good cause" demanded otherwise. He asked that "those of your people that are in favor of joining the Confederacy must be allowed to organize into military companies as home guards." David Hubbard, the Confederate commissioner of Indians affairs, applied additional pressure by attempting to undermine Ross's trust in the federal government. On June 17, 1861, Ross wrote to both men. His letter to Hubbard echoed past sentiments that he had no reason not to believe the Cherokees would be well treated by the Confederate government, but he would not make war on the forces of the North. Ross denied McCulloch's request to allow Cherokees to form companies of "home guards" to defend Indian Territory from Northern invasion. Such companies would violate his policy of neutrality and risk the internal security of the Cherokee Nation. Ross feared, once again with incredible foresight, the companies would "soon become efficient instruments in stirring up domestic strife and creating internal difficulties among the Cherokee people." On July 1, Ross wrote to Pike and enclosed a copy of his letter to Hubbard reiterating his neutral position.

Pike was not the only secessionist who viewed the disaffected factions within the Cherokee Nation as potential southern allies. On May 18, 1861, A. M. Wilson and J. W. Washbourne, private citizens of Fayetteville, Arkansas, wrote to Stand Watie assuring him of their support in the event that he could raise a company of 200 men. They promised to arm Watie's men and used the threat of Union-imposed abolition to spur his efforts. Those events seriously threatened Ross's vision of tribal unity as Watie and his followers were more than willing to unseat Ross by coup d'état, if given the necessary Confederate support. On July 12, long before Ross agreed to treat with the Confederacy, and despite his letter to McCulloch that he would not sanction "home guards," the Confederate army mustered in Stand Watie as a colonel along with a regiment of his men. Also in July, pro-Confederate Cherokees attempted to raise the Confederate flag over the Cherokee capital in Tahlequah. Ross addressed the intertribal conflict in a letter to John Drew. A relative and supporter of Ross, Drew would soon be called on to command one of the two Confederate Cherokee regiments with Watie commanding the other. Ross expressed dismay over renewed Cherokee factionalism, sensed the precarious nature of his position, and implored:

> There is no reason why we should split up & become involved in internal strife and violence on account of the political condition of the states. We should really have nothing to do with them, but remain quiet and observe those relations of peace & friendship towards all the People of the States imposed by our treaties. By this means alone can we avoid every cause for hostility from either section of the Country and upon this policy we ought all to be able to attend to our ordinary affairs and avoid all causes of strife among ourselves.

Confederate victories at first Bull Run on July 21 and Wilson's Creek on August 10 further increased pressure on Ross by demonstrating to the Cherokees the South's apparent military superiority. In addition, the federal government began transferring troops stationed in the West, leaving the Cherokees unprotected. At the same time Pike signed treaties with the Cherokees' neighbors—Creeks on July 10, Choctaws and Chickasaws on July 12, Seminoles on August 1, and some of the Plains tribes on August 12. After Ross's August 21 address to his people, members of the Treaty Party recommended that Watie negotiate a treaty with Pike before Ross was able to. They wrote:

> The Pins already have more power in their hands than we can bear & if in addition to this they acquire more by being the treaty making power, you know our destiny will be inalterably sealed. It seems we should guard against this. Now is the time for us to strike, or we will be completely frustrated.

Ross's speech of August 21 was understandable in light of the circumstances. He faced an armed contingent of opponents within the tribe, hostile neighbors, the withdrawal of federal troops, and his dream of a unified neutral Indian bloc destroyed. As he had in 1845 Ross willingly made great sacrifices to preserve unity within his tribe when he met with Albert Pike and signed a treaty on October 7, 1861. The treaty seemed attractive; it guaranteed the Cherokees authority over their lands, self-government, jurisdiction over the physical boundaries and persons within Cherokee territory, approval of governmental agents, a representative in the Confederate Congress, and a $500,000 financial guarantee for the sale of the Cherokee Neutral Lands. Additionally the treaty addressed several of Ross's concerns. It seemed the best hope for maintaining unity; it guaranteed the Cherokees their land; it dealt with the Neutral Lands (a thorn in Ross's side for some time); and it made tribal sovereignty explicit. But Ross must have realized that he had capitulated for none of those reasons. Rather, Ross allied with the Confederacy due only to pressures beyond his control, the same pressures that had weighed on him for more than thirty years.

Immediately after the August 21 meeting, Ross made provisions for raising a regiment of men composed largely of full bloods and Pins to be commanded by John Drew. McCulloch viewed the regiment as inferior to Watie's troops. In a strange echo of the federal government's policy during the Polk administration, which ignored the issue of tribal unity, he recommended that Watie be allowed to expand his force and that the two regiments be kept separate. Thus, at the start of the war two distinct regiments of Indian soldiers existed—one led by Watie, leader of the Treaty Party, and the other led by Drew, a supporter of Ross. Ross's relatives and supporters made up most of Drew's regimental officer corps. Although unified under the Confederate flag, the Cherokees remained divided, so much so that Watie's nephew, E. C. Boudinot, asked his uncle to allow him to serve in Watie's regiment as an officer because "John Ross and you are rivals, he has appointed his nephew [W. P. Ross] Lt. Col. intent on keeping a foothold in the military organization."

Drew's troops performed poorly during the Civil War because many of the full blood soldiers fought unwillingly. On December 8, 1861, over 400 members of Drew's force deserted at the Battle of Caving Banks to join the followers of Opothleyahola, the Chief of the Upper Creeks, who remained faithful to the Union. Opothleyahola and his followers fled from Indian Territory toward Kansas where they hoped to find sanctuary from the Confederate element of their tribe. Historian John Bartlett Meserve noted, "The Civil War wrought havoc among the Creeks in the Indian Territory, opening old tribal wounds and fanning the flames, the smoldering embers of their ancient tribal antagonisms." His words describe the Cherokees' situation as well, which may partially explain Ross's sympathy for Opothleyahola's plight. Prior to the war, Ross had urged the Creeks to remain united and neutral. When that failed, he stayed involved in Creek affairs, acting as mediator between the tribal factions. When war appeared inevitable, Ross remained firm in his belief that a conflict between whites should not scuttle peace among the Indian tribes.

The desertion of Drew's men at Caving Banks indicated the level of division between Drew's and Watie's men. Already separated purposely by the Confederate leadership, the regiments soon slipped into open conflict. In the aftermath of the Caving Banks debacle, Stand Watie's nephew, Charles Webber, killed a member of John Drew's regiment. The murdered man had prevented the raising of the Confederate flag in Tahlequah the previous summer, and Watie described him as "hostile to southern people and their institutions." Another of Drew's troops, Arch Snail, also was killed after he deserted at Caving Banks. Watie had no remorse over his death and implied Drew's and Ross's indignation over the event was hypocritical. Ross wrote to Albert Pike expressing outrage and fear over what he described as "reckless and unprincipled persons belonging to Watie's Regiment who are under no subordination or restraint of their leaders in domineering over and trampling up the rights of peaceable and unoffending citizens." Ross watched as the foundation of his alliance with the Confederacy disintegrated. As the full blood troops under Drew did not believe in the Confederate cause, they continued to desert, leaving Ross with neither a strong power base nor unity for his people.

As divisions among tribal factions exploded into violence, the Confederate government, much as the federal government had in the past, ignored crucial stipulations in their treaty with the Cherokees, further shaking Ross's crumbling commitment to the Confederacy. The Indian regiments stood mostly inactive until the Battle of Pea Ridge on March 7 and 8, 1862. Despite promises from Pike during treaty negotiations that the Indian regiments would be used only to protect their land, the Battle of Pea Ridge took place outside Indian Territory. The Union victory at Pea Ridge eroded Ross's faith in the military superiority of the South. In the aftermath of Pea Ridge, Confederate troop withdrawal from the Cherokee Nation left Indian Territory largely unprotected, a source of great irritation to Ross who worried about the Cherokee treasury and tribal documents. In answer to Ross's complaints, Pike assigned Drew's force the task of protecting Indian Territory. That comforted Ross, despite the meager size of Drew's force after massive desertions and furloughs. On May 10, 1861, a disgruntled Ross wrote to Jefferson Davis stressing Cherokee loyalty, but complaining that the Confederacy inadequately armed Indian soldiers and failed to protect Indian Territory. By June Ross openly expressed feelings of betrayal at the hands of the Confederate government.

By mid-summer, as Ross grew increasingly disenchanted with the Confederacy, Union forces in Kansas under the command of Colonel William Weer prepared for an assault on Indian Territory. Weer, who contacted Keetoowah Cherokees loyal to the Union, believed Ross was a Union man as well. On June 26 Weer communicated his presence to Ross and assured him that he believed he knew Ross's true loyalty. The Union forces faced little opposition and quickly advanced into Indian Territory. On July 7 Weer asked to meet with Ross. Ross responded negatively, citing his treaty with the Confederacy as binding. While those interchanges took place, large groups of Cherokee soldiers continued to cross the lines into the Union camp, and on July 12 Albert Pike resigned his post. Pike believed the Confederates had mistreated the Indians and used him as a scapegoat. He cited political intrigue as his motivation for stepping down. Two days later a contingent of Union troops occupied the Cherokee capitol at Tahlequah and prepared to contact Ross. The captain in charge also believed that Ross held Union sympathies. On July 15 the Union force placed Ross under arrest.

Union troops took Ross to Kansas and then to Washington to meet with President Abraham Lincoln. Union general James Blunt of Kansas sent the president a letter vouching for Ross's credibility. On September 16, 1862, Ross wrote to President Lincoln, invoking the federal government's treaty obligations to the Cherokees and maintaining the Cherokees had negotiated their treaty with the Confederacy under duress. He noted:

> [N]o other alternative was left them, surrounded by the Power and influences that they were and that they had no opportunity freely to express their views and assume their true positions until the advance into their Country of the Indian Expedition during the last summer. . . . The advance of the Indian Expedition gave the Cherokee People an opportunity to manifest their views by taking far as possible a prompt and decided stand in favor of their relations with the U States Government.

A variety of external pressures impacted on Ross's decision to return to the Union. The continuation of factional strife imperiled tribal unity. The conflicts between the members of the Drew and Watie forces illustrated the tenuous nature of the alliance between the Ross Party and Treaty Party. Their relationship exploded almost immediately after Ross's capture. On August 21, 1862, Stand Watie's supporters elected him principal chief. The Confederacy's negligence in fulfilling treaty obligations to the Cherokees also influenced Ross's return to the Union.

Many scholars have argued that Ross told the truth when he assured Lincoln that he was a Union man throughout. Support for that argument lies in the letters of

Evan Jones, William Weer, and James Blunt. Annie Heloise Abel's excellent three-volume account of Indian activity in the Civil War also supports this argument. While his position as a slaveholder coupled with his distrust of the federal government offer support for the view that Ross's true sympathies lay with the Confederacy, few have argued that position. Of his contemporaries, Confederate colonel James McIntosh believed Ross strongly supported the Confederacy, but his view is in the minority. A third possibility—that Ross supported neither the North nor the South, but chose his allies based on his desire for tribal unity, sovereignty, and the related issue of maintaining his personal power—is compelling. John Ross believed neither in the Union nor the Confederacy, but rather in the advancement of the Cherokee people and in his own ability to lead his tribe intact and sovereign. Prior to the Civil War he counseled neutrality because he did not want to become embroiled in what he saw as a white man's conflict. He preferred to wait out the war and negotiate with the victor. Ultimately, recurrent tribal factionalism and external pressures destroyed Ross's dream.

Finally, military considerations and experience with past betrayals at the hands of whites also influenced Ross. The recall of federal troops from the West to supplement the Union's battered eastern forces in the spring of 1861 left Indian Territory unprotected. By abandoning their western posts, the federal government failed to maintain a presence in Indian Territory, to inspire confidence in neutral parties, and to live up to its treaty obligations. When the Union abandoned Indian Territory, the Confederacy sent representatives to negotiate treaties with the tribes. Ross's belief in unity—in his tribe, and with all of the tribes of Indian Territory—left him little choice when the Creeks, Choctaws, Chickasaws, and Seminoles all signed treaties with the Confederacy. The Confederate Indians, Watie's force of secessionist Cherokees, and the presence of Arkansas and a divided Missouri left the Cherokees with secessionist neighbors on three borders and internally.

John Ross, isolated in a sea of Confederate support, threatened by factionalism within his tribe, and victimized by the federal government, had few attractive options when making his decision in 1861. Sometime after his fateful address of August 21, 1861, Ross said:

> We are in the position of a man standing alone upon a low, naked spot of ground, with the water rising rapidly all around him. He sees the danger but does not know what to do. If he remains where he is, his only alternative is to be swept away and perish. The tide carries by him in its mad course, a drifting log; it perchance, comes within reach of him. By refusing it he is a doomed man. By seizing hold of it he has a chance for his life.

Ross's decision to accept an alliance with the secessionists did not result from a genuine belief in their cause, nor from a desire to maintain the institution of slavery, but rather arose out of pressures present for much of his career. The same factors compelled Ross's return to the Union.

John Ross was not a secessionist, but the history of his people made certain that his ties to the Union were not overly strong. In August, 1861, his goals were tribal unity and sovereignty. Ross feared that the Civil War offered little opportunity for advancing the position of the Cherokees, and thus he acted from a defensive posture throughout the war. Ross's early belief in neutrality represented what he believed to be the ideal scenario, one in which the tribes of Indian Territory remained aloof while white men fought out their differences. It can be argued that the combination of a Confederate policy of divide and conquer, Union government negligence, and intertribal conflict undermined Ross's vision as it had at New Echota thirty years earlier. John Ross was neither a unionist nor a secessionist. Throughout his tenure as chief, his vision of a unified and sovereign Cherokee Nation dominated his political consciousness.

Dakota Sioux Uprising, 1862

GARY CLAYTON ANDERSON

The history of the Sioux Outbreak is a story of two engagements—one between Indians and whites, the second the futile struggle of militant Dakota leaders to reestablish cultural cohesiveness. Many detailed accounts of the first have been written, several of which carefully document the terrible carnage inflicted upon Minnesota's white settlement by the Sioux. In all, nearly five hundred whites lost their lives in the fray, four-fifths of them noncombatants. Since so many narratives of the destruction exist, there is little need to do more than briefly outline the fighting. Events within the Dakota community, on the other hand, offer a final illustration of how dramatic social, political, and economic change had been in the later 1850s, the degree of polarization that had occurred as a result of these changes, and the means the [Dakota] soldiers' lodge would employ to reverse this cultural deterioration.

Tragically for the hostiles, they would soon discover that the social, political, and economic bonds that tied their people to Euroamericans were not as easy to dispose of as they had initially supposed. While some Sioux warriors blamed whites for their troubles, other Dakota men and women disagreed with them or thought war was an extreme, immoral response. Individual kinship bonds among whites, mixed-bloods, and Indians, though strained in the later 1850s, still remained. In addition, the Dakota people were simply not accustomed to fighting the kind of sustained campaign that would be necessary to gain advantages in western Minnesota, especially when many of their soldiers had once viewed individual whites as human beings and allies. The truth was that the eastern Sioux had moved too far along the road: revitalization, or a reversal of the culture change that had become commonplace by the later 1850s, was an unattainable goal.

The elusiveness of this primary goal seemed unimportant during the first few days of fighting. Such necessary items as guns, ammunition, and food were readily obtained from plundered white farms and traders' stores. The question of what would be done once these supplies ran out never came up. Thus from the start the eastern Sioux warrior and his family lived on bread and beef and fought with shotguns and rifles. It was impossible to return to a traditional hunter-gatherer life or to fight whites with bows and arrows.

From Gary Clayton Anderson, "Dakota Sioux Uprising, 1862," in *Kinsmen of Another Kind: Dakota-White Relations in the Upper Mississippi Valley, 1650–1862* (Lincoln, Nebr.: University of Nebraska Press, 1984), 261–280. Reprinted by permission of the University of Nebraska Press. Copyright © 1984 by the University of Nebraska Press.

Still, Dakota soldiers did believe that some social revitalization could occur. Most agreed that farmer Indians had failed to reinforce kinship ties; almost immediately after starting the war, members of the soldiers' lodges forced farmers to demonstrate allegiance to the cause, threatening most with death. Second, while soldiers recognized that for years the tribal council had failed to act as a political forum, they turned the soldiers' lodges into a political body that served as a medium to discuss the future of the war. Although historians have suggested that Little Crow acted as the leader of the outbreak, nothing could be further from the truth. The lodge made decisions by consensus. Ironically, farmers who opposed the war slowly gained access to the new "tribal" council and used it as a forum for their own views. However, farmer opposition formed rather late in the fighting; initial successes made resistance unpopular.

News regarding the Dakota assault at the lower agency reached Fort Ridgely by midmorning 18 August. Captain John S. Marsh, a seasoned commander, immediately assembled a platoon and started toward the agency. Dakota warriors ambushed the command, killing interpreter Peter Quinn and about two dozen men. Marsh, who underestimated the seriousness of the trouble, later drowned while attempting to withdraw his troops from the engagement. With the exception of the handful of soldiers who quickly returned to the fort under Lieutenant Timothy J. Sheehan, no military units existed in the west to stop the vengeful Sioux from sweeping down the Minnesota valley.

The hostile elements in the Dakota camps, buttressed by the victory over Marsh, quickly launched a campaign against Minnesota's white settlements. Marauding parties first attacked the German farmers living just north of New Ulm and east of the lower agency, then carried their assault into the Big Woods. When the rampages were over, no fewer than twenty-three western Minnesota counties had been evacuated. Large-scale battles followed at New Ulm on 19 and 23 August and at Fort Ridgely on the afternoons of August 20 and 22. The struggle at New Ulm on the twenty-third was carried into the streets of the town. Houses were burned so the Sioux could not use them for cover. The fighting was every bit as vicious as the clashes then occurring in the eastern United States. Despite suffering considerable losses at New Ulm, white settlers and the army held out at both the town and the fort, though at times it appeared that both would fall. During the week of intense fighting, the state organized its own offensive, placing militia under the command of Colonel Henry Hastings Sibley, the former Minnesota fur trader. This force of several hundred men relieved Fort Ridgely on 27 August, ending any possibility of a major Indian victory.

The easternmost Sioux, especially the Mdewakantons and Wahpekutes, had little chance of winning a prolonged war with the United States. They were less prepared for fighting than their western relatives, and they lacked mobility. Even more ominous was the indecisiveness of native leaders, who could not agree on how to proceed. Some wanted to limit the fighting to military objectives, engaging and defeating American armies. Indeed, had the soldiers' lodge followed up the victory over Marsh with an immediate attack on the fort, Sheehan's small garrison no doubt would have fallen. Unfortunately for the hostiles, many warriors wasted time plundering and killing in the settlements, while whites fled to the fort for protection. Once the orgy of killing in the settlements had ended—by the afternoon of 19 August—the Mdewakanton soldiers' lodge faced yet another difficulty: members had to sustain support for an increasingly unpopular war effort in the face of growing opposition from Indian farmers. Almost from the beginning it became clear that the extensive ties that had linked the native farming communities to whites made a unified Dakota front impossible.

Intratribal strife over past interethnic ties surfaced within minutes of the first attack at the lower agency. As the fighting commenced, many Dakota people did their best to save friends and kinsmen, many of whom were white. Most often, farmer Indians who did not support the war were involved in this, but even many of the Dakota soldiers who were actively fighting made exceptions, saving whites from death at the hands of their fellow tribesmen. For example, on the first day Little Crow and his head soldier, Wakinyantawa, saved the lives of trader George Spencer and Charles Blair, Joseph R. Brown's white son-in-law. According to one account, Wakinyantawa had a unique relationship with Spencer, based upon "a species of freemasonry." Spencer's kinship ties obviously averted his death, since all the other traders, including Myrick, Lynd, and several less important clerks, were killed at their stores.

In most cases, those saved from the tomahawk had demonstrated friendship with certain Sioux people and attained some degree of fictive kinship ties. The experience of Helen M. Tarble illustrates the role of these interlinking ties. A settler's wife, Tarble had moved into the German community across from the lower agency at Beaver Creek four years before the outbreak. She spent many hours thereafter with an old shaman, believed to be Parent Hawk, who showed her many of the medical secrets of his trade. She, in turn, fed the man and his friends. When Dakota warriors overtook the Tarbles and several of their fleeing neighbors on 18 August, Mrs. Tarble talked to them in Dakota, pleading for the lives of the party. Although the Sioux men saved her and her children, they purposefully killed eleven others, among whom were the wife and children of a settler named Henderson. As Tarble noted, the Indians "seemed especially enraged against her [Mrs. Henderson]. I have since believed that they were instigated in their feeling by the old medicine man . . . who took revenge for the insults and abuse which Mr. Henderson had heaped upon him." One Henderson girl, only two and a half, was beaten to death and another was hacked to pieces. Their helpless mother was burned to death while lying ill on an old mattress. The Dakota warriors responsible for the killings were quick to assure Mrs. Tarble that she need not fear for her life, and even in captivity she was allowed to do as she pleased.

Other whites benefited in similar ways because of fictive kinship ties. The wife of the physician at the upper agency, Sarah F. Wakefield, found that the generous assistance her husband had given to various Indian patients proved invaluable after her capture. Taken to Little Crow's camp on the afternoon of 18 August Wakefield found Indian women and children competing among themselves to "spread down carpets for me to sit on . . . they prepared my supper, and tried in every way possible to make me comfortable."

Some reservation employees received warning to flee on 18 August. Among them were Joseph Reynolds and his wife, owners of a boardinghouse and government schoolteachers; John Narin, a government carpenter; Samuel Hinman, missionary at the lower agency; and old Philander Prescott. With the exception of Prescott, all were saved while other whites around them were being slaughtered.

Prescott probably would have survived had he stayed indoors as he was told. Reynolds and his wife were convinced to leave by no other than young Shakopee, later thought to be one of the most active Dakota participants in the killing of white civilians. The saving of whites provoked discord within the Dakota camp; their fate as captives prompted even more intense squabbling.

While a few whites benefited from past generosity, the kinship ties fostered by mixed-bloods made them practically immune to the assaults of Dakota soldiers. Killing mixed-bloods would have invited retribution from full-blood kinsmen. In an exhaustive study of the war, Marion Satterlee found only one mixed-blood who had been killed by hostile parties. Yet many mixed-bloods clearly functioned in a white world and in some respects were hated by traditional Dakota people as much as were the Germans. This was surely the case with Louis Brisbois and his wife, who, according to one account, had mistreated Dakota men and women when they came to their house seeking aid. Just as the couple were to be killed for their social indiscretion, some whites distracted the warriors, and Brisbois and his wife escaped.

Despite threats and assaults, many mixed-bloods attempted to help white friends. Joseph La Framboise and Narcisse Freniere, for example, warned traders and government workers at the upper agency. Most escaped without harm. Missionaries likewise were protected by their flocks, many of whom were mixed-bloods. Both the Riggs and the Williamson families stayed near the upper agency for some time after news of the war had reached them. When it became clear they could not safely remain, they received food and horses from friendly Indians and mixed-bloods and escaped onto the prairies east of Yellow Medicine.

Perhaps the most illustrative use of kinship connection by mixed-bloods came during the capture of Mrs. Joseph R. Brown, a Sisseton woman who was the wife of the former agent, her eleven children, and nearly a dozen white settlers. The Brown party had fled from a farm near Yellow Medicine the day after the killing started at the lower agency. Unfortunately, while moving south they came upon a party led by Cut Nose, Dowanniye, and young Shakopee. Fearful of a frightful slaughter, Mrs. Brown "stood up in the wagon, waved her shawl and cried in a loud voice, in the Dakota language, that she was a Sisseton and relative of Wannatan, Scarlet Plume, Sweet Corn, Ah-kee-pah [Joseph Akipa Renville], and the friend of Standing Buffalo." She demanded protection for her family and the whites with them.

The tactic worked, and the Dakota warriors, spattered with blood from earlier killings, escorted the Brown party to Little Crow's camp. Even so, along the way they taunted the whites who had been saved by Mrs. Brown's actions. Shakopee was particularly troublesome, shaking his tomahawk at a German settler and at one of Mrs. Brown's white sons-in-law, all the while shouting, "The Dutch [Germans] have made me so angry, I will butcher them alive." Once at Little Crow's village, all members of the party received good treatment, and several whites were freed. Shortly thereafter, full-blood relatives came and took charge of the Browns, removing them to Yellow Medicine.

Unfortunately, most whites on the upper Minnesota had made no attempt to develop kinship bonds with the nearby Sioux. This was true of some government employees, but more particularly so of the Germans, who generally received no quarter in the war. Men, women, and children were indiscriminately slaughtered or, in some cases, taken captive. Most often the chance to live as a captive depended upon the mood of the war party. In the case of Dr. John Humphrey and his wife and two children the Sioux manifested no compassion. Humphrey, physician at the lower agency, was an unbending man with a strong penchant for preaching "Christian doctrine." Dakota warriors trapped him and his family in a cabin not far from Fort Ridgely and massacred them. The same fate befell fifty or so German settlers living just north of New Ulm. Virtually all of them—men, women, and children—were slaughtered, because most had been responsible for forcing the eviction of the lower Sioux from this region back in 1855. Mass killings likewise occurred in the Beaver Creek settlements, regions that the Sioux felt had been wrongly occupied in 1858. So few people survived in these areas that there are no reliable accounts of the carnage.

Although numerous stories about these killings quickly surfaced in the Minnesota newspapers, there is some question about their trustworthiness. Clearly some Sioux warriors used knives and hatchets to mutilate their victims. Traditionally, Dakota men had scalped, decapitated, and disfigured the bodies of enemies. Women occasionally were stripped of clothes, a practice meant to offend their menfolk rather than to gratify sexual deviance. The extent to which mutilation occurred in 1862 is still somewhat clouded, however. Dr. Jared W. Daniels, who accompanied the burial party to the lower agency, denied that bodies had been disfigured; yet reliable sources too numerous to list contradict him. Several eyewitnesses attest that Sioux warriors frequently disrobed female corpses. One badly wounded woman, thought to be dead, was stripped at night while still conscious. Clearly Dakota warriors had come to view whites as enemies in the traditional sense, unworthy to be treated as human beings. On the other hand, such actions lent credence to charges by whites that the Dakotas deserved no better fate than extermination.

Undoubtedly the most serious charge levied by newspapers was rape, or the "fate worse than death." Some white women were saved from the tomahawk with the intent of incorporating them into the tribes as wives, a practice occasionally applied in intertribal war. But there were strong taboos against rape by a war party; the Sioux believed it would displease native spirits. Accordingly, far fewer women were assaulted than the Minnesota press implied. The evidence shows that members of Sleepy Eyes's village did sexually abuse two women sometime after taking them captive near Lake Shetek. Testimony also indicates that two other women were raped while prisoners in the Mdewakanton camp, both giving sworn statements to the fact.

Once captured women reached the Indian camp, however, they fell under the protection of tribal institutions, such as the family, designed to prevent abuse. Mary Schwandt, a German teenager, was adopted by Snana, and once she was part of the kinship group no harm came to her. Ćaska, a friendly Indian, protected Sarah Wakefield, even claiming to have taken her as a wife in order to stop other men from bothering her. Rumors of this relationship spread among other white captives, and the army later executed Ćaska despite Mrs. Wakefield's courageous defense of his actions. She undoubtedly realized that her futile attempt to save Ćaska's life would result in her condemnation by every white person in Minnesota. Another female captive reported that native matrons slept on each side of her to prevent abuse. Clearly Sioux men felt that once in camp taboos against the assault of white women ended. Indeed, it was not uncommon for men to waylay women of their own tribe while out gathering wood or fetching water. For this reason farmer Indians did their best to gain control of female captives and keep them out of sight.

On the evening of 18 August the white captives reached Little Crow's village, which quickly became the nucleus of the hostile movement. There they discovered a celebration in progress. "We saw papooses of all sizes robed in rich laces and bedecked in many fantastic styles," Mrs. N. D. White later reported. For the first time in months there was an abundance of fresh meat from slaughtered oxen, flour, dried fruit, tea, and coffee. Ransacked trunks were strewn over the ground, and sunbonnets and jewelry graced Sioux women. A few Indians smashed clocks to get the gears, which they used for earrings. Captives, mixed-bloods, and farmer Indians alike were told to discard their white clothes and don Indian dress. Mixed-bloods ran frantically about the camp searching for breechcloths, leggings, native dresses, and skins and cloth for tepees. Those living in houses were forced to abandon them, and the soldiers burned many homes. Warriors were doing their best to force a rebirth of Sioux life-style amid the confusion of continuous dancing, singing, beating of drums, and departure and return of war parties.

The celebrations lasted only a short while, however, and as soon as it became obvious that Fort Ridgely and New Ulm would not be overrun the Indian soldiers decided to withdraw north. The Indian train that left the lower agency on 26 August extended over five miles of Minnesota prairie. Soldiers struggled to maintain order, but as one reporter noted, the caravan soon resembled "the confusion of Babel." Stopping for a day at Rice Creek, the assemblage finally reached Yellow Medicine River, or the upper agency, on the twenty-eighth.

While near the upper agency, the soldiers organized two war parties, one heading east toward the Big Woods and the second south, supposedly to attack New Ulm. This latter camp soon discovered a reinforced burial detail of two companies of troops surveying the ruins of the lower agency. Under the joint command of Joseph R. Brown and Captain Joseph Anderson, the military patrol camped for the evening near Beaver Creek on Birch Coulee. Little care was taken to select a defensive camp, since Colonel Sibley had sent scouts nearly to Yellow Medicine River the previous day and they had failed to see any hostile Indians. But at dawn on 2 September the Indians, following various leaders, quietly surrounded the troops and attacked. The battle of Birch Coulee lasted through most of the day, with the white soldiers suffering heavy losses. In all, the Sioux killed twenty troopers and wounded upward of sixty. Every horse in the command save one—eighty-seven in all—fell to Sioux bullets. Fortunately Colonel Sibley arrived on 3 September with a relief column to save the exhausted and nearly defeated militia.

In the aftermath of the Birch Coulee debacle, Sibley adopted a cautious course in dealing with the eastern Sioux, aware that a like disaster could befall his poorly equipped army of twelve hundred men. He seemed especially concerned about the determination with which the Sioux fought; most whites had generally believed Dakota warriors would never fight a pitched battle, and traditional Indian warfare almost precluded it. Obviously the hostile Indians had adopted many of the military techniques of their white opponents, assaulting positions in force. Hopeful of averting such a struggle, Sibley left a note at the Birch Coulee battlefield calling on the supposed leader of the hostiles, Little Crow, to explain why he had opted for war. Sibley hoped to negotiate a release of the prisoners in the main Sioux camp and possibly to convince the hostiles to surrender without further bloodshed. To obtain better information on Indian movements, he also enlisted at least one full-blooded Dakota scout, John Otherday, who offered to serve Sibley's army on 4 September. Sibley increasingly sought assistance from friendly Indians throughout the campaign that followed, a recruiting pattern that formed the basis for a permanent organization of Sioux scouts.

Meanwhile, strong factional divisions surfaced at the main Mdewakanton-Wakpekute camp on Yellow Medicine River. The trouble began on 28 August, before the Birch Coulee battle, when Mdewakantons attempted to convince Sissetons and Wahpetons, who had stayed near the upper agency, to join them. Instead a large number of Sissetons and Wahpetons under the leadership of Gabriel Renville, Joseph Akipa Renville, Solomon Two Stars, Henok Mahpiyadenape, the Sisseton Cloud Man, Iron Walker, and Paul Mazakutemani spoke against the war, demanding to know why the Mdewakantons and Wahpekutes had brought such a disaster upon themselves. Fearful of reprisals, the men above then formed a soldiers' lodge of their own. Its organization came none too soon, since on 29 August about three hundred Mdewakanton-Wahpekute warriors surrounded the Sisseton-Wahpeton camp and threatened to kill those men who refused to join them. But upon seeing the main lodge of the soldier group in the center of the Sisseton-Wahpeton village the hostile warriors withdrew, knowing it meant the upper Sioux intended to resist them militarily. A long dialogue followed in which farmers, mixed-bloods, and nonhostile elements tried their best to negotiate an end to the rebellion, presenting their arguments both individually and in what one observer described as a "big council."

One important council discussion got under way sometime between 29 and 31 August. Paul Mazakutemani spoke for those Indians professing friendship toward whites, and various soldiers represented the hostile Mdewakanton camp. As in most council debates during this period, Little Crow played only a minor role. More than a thousand Indians were present as Mazakutemani asked the soldiers why they had started the war. He complained that it was begun "without a council being called." Furthermore, he could not understand how warriors could make war on women and children, and he told the Mdewakanton soldiers to give up their captives and fight Sibley's soldiers. But the vast majority of soldiers present refused to accept his logic, prompting him to make several more attempts to convince the Mdewakantons of their folly. Finally, on 6 September he gathered large quantities of food and invited the Mdewakantons to a feast in the Sisseton-Wahpeton village, a ploy traditionally used to create a sense of obligation. This time the Mdewakanton soldiers strongly warned him against bringing up the subject of the captives again, one soldier declaring: "The Mdewakantons are *men*, and as long as one of them lives they will not stop pointing their guns at the Americans."

Despite initial diplomatic failures, a new series of discussions commenced after Little Crow received Sibley's message on 4 September. Even though the previous councils had demonstrated that the soldiers' lodge was running the war rather than Little Crow, the chief was able to convince lodge members that the query should be answered. Little Crow selected two mixed-bloods, Tom Robinson and Thomas A. Robertson, to deliver his message to Colonel Sibley on 8 September. In the reply Little Crow attempted to justify the war, citing the government's failure to distribute annuities and the traders' stinginess as primary causes for discontent. Little Crow also reminded Sibley that the hostiles had many prisoners and asked the colonel to pass along his explanation to Alexander Ramsey, now governor of the state of Minnesota.

Sibley found little encouraging in the note, but the information he received from the mixed-blood messengers proved fruitful. He learned from them that the white captives were being reasonably well treated, that considerable numbers of Mdewakantons—mostly farmers—had been forced to participate in the battles, and that many Sissetons and Wahpetons remained steadfastly opposed to the war. Sibley remained hopeful that the captives could be saved, and he instructed Robinson and Robertson to tell Little Crow that he wanted the Indians to surrender them.

After the two messengers arrived back at Yellow Medicine River, the soldiers' lodge ordered a further retreat north to Lac qui Parle. It seems likely that Robinson and Robertson not only had given the Mdewakanton soldiers Sibley's message but had also reported on the large number of troops now near Fort Ridgely. The march north began early on 9 September, the Sissetons and Wahpetons joining in with the Mdewakantons and Wahpekutes, making a train five miles long. Toward evening the lead elements were within fourteen miles of Lac qui Parle when the Wahpeton Red Iron met them at the head of 150 Sisseton and Wahpeton warriors. Red Iron was still a farmer and still friendly to whites despite his confinement by Ramsey in 1852. He now told the Mdewakantons to proceed no further: "You commenced the Outbreak, and must do the fighting in your country. We do not want you here to excite our young men." Standing Buffalo, a major chief from Lake Traverse, joined Red Iron a few days later in condemning the war. Although elements of the Lake Traverse Sissetons had joined the Mdewakanton and Wahpekute camp and some of their young men had even harassed the garrison at Fort Abercrombie north of Lake Traverse, the defection of the main leaders to the peace party seriously hampered the hostile cause.

Even before the upper Sissetons made known their disapproval of the war, however, factions within the main Mdewakanton-Wahpekute camp began suing for peace. Little Crow even joined the effort, writing Sibley on 12 September that the hostiles had failed to obtain the support of the Sissetons and Wahpetons and closing with an interesting plea: "I want to know from you as a friend what way that I can make peace for my people." Little Crow was trying to use his past fictive ties with Sibley to help extricate his people from the war. Robinson and Robertson again delivered the message, giving Sibley more information about the situation near Lac qui Parle. They told him of the extreme divisions among the Dakotas, even within the Mdewakanton camp. Little Crow's life had been threatened, presumably for raising the issue of peace. Robinson and Robertson also carried a private note from Wabasha, Taopi, the principal farmer at the lower agency, and a dozen others— mostly farmers—who said that they had favored peace all along and had not partici- pated in the murder of the whites. They noted that the Mdewakanton soldiers had carefully guarded them and even used threats to keep them in line. While again de- manding the captives from Little Crow, Sibley told Robinson and Robertson to have the friendly Sioux separate themselves from the main hostile group. On 14 Septem- ber many of those who opposed the war left the Mdewakanton-Wahpekute camp. Robinson and Robertson had given these people the distinct impression that Sioux warriors who had not killed civilians would be well treated by Sibley.

Over the next week, tensions reached extreme levels in the two Indian camps, which were separated by only a mile. Squabbles especially erupted over the cap- tives, who were slowly being removed, a few at a time, to the friendly camp. "Raids" of a sort also occurred, with hostile Indians descending upon the friendly camp and destroying tepees and goods. This sort of destruction was characteristic of warriors, who felt their kinsmen had failed to demonstrate loyalty. Fighting was miraculously averted. The struggles reached a climax on 22 September when news arrived that Sibley's force had reached Wood Lake, just south of the upper agency. The colonel had been prodded by authorities in the east to do something to punish the Sioux and save the captives. He had finally decided to force the issue.

In the Mdewakanton camp, the soldiers' lodge ordered every able-bodied man to prepare for war, forcing Indians friendly to whites to join them. Rewards were offered to those who could procure the scalps of Sibley, Brown, or any of the better-known whites. In all, 738 warriors left the camps below Lac qui Parle on the afternoon of the twenty-second, but only about 300 engaged Sibley the next morning at Wood Lake. Large numbers of Indians who went to the battleground could not be prodded into fighting. Losses during the engagement that followed were minimal on both sides, Sibley losing only four men and the Sioux sixteen. The unwillingness of many Indians to participate doomed the assault from the start. Tired and discouraged, the main body of Dakota men returned to their old camp below Lac qui Parle on the evening of 23 September, now aware that they must either surrender or flee out onto the western prairies.

Back in camp, the hostiles learned that the friendly Indians had removed most of the remaining white captives to Red Iron's village and were prepared to defend them with their lives. They had dug rifle pits in the floors of the tents and organized a perimeter guard. Sibley learned of the removal of the captives to the friendly camp on the twenty-third from A. J. Campbell, a mixed-blood, who carried the message to Wood Lake. Many members of the Mdewakanton soldiers' lodge wanted to overrun the friendly camp, yet the lodge had steadily been losing power, and Little Crow strongly advised against hurting the captives, arguing that it would only enrage the white soldiers. Little Crow now urged those who had taken part in the war to divide up and flee.

Before leaving, Little Crow called on A. J. Campbell, a relative who had played a major role in organizing the friendly camp, to come and feast with him. Campbell went, not knowing what to expect. The meeting that followed illustrates the tragedy of the entire Sioux Outbreak. When Campbell arrived in Little Crow's lodge, the chief greeted him as "cousin," then asked if there was anything he could do for him before leaving for the west. Campbell asked him to surrender to Sibley, whereupon Little Crow laughed and said, "Sibley would like to put the rope around my neck, but he won't get the chance." Little Crow then agreed to do what he could to have any captives still held by hostile warriors—there were perhaps a dozen—turned over to Campbell, and the two parted, still friends and relatives despite the different roles they had taken in the war.

Several hundred hostiles did follow Little Crow onto the plains west of Lac qui Parle, leaving the friendly Indians in charge of ninety-four white captives. The mixed-bloods who were held against their will totaled 162. For unexplained reasons, Sibley waited until 26 September to march on the friendly village, now called Camp Release, and claim the unfortunate captives. It was a joyous day for most, though the two dozen or so white women fretted over their appearance. All were dressed in "squaw suits," and Sibley had nothing better for them to wear. The only mission remaining for the army was to capture and punish those responsible for the war—no small order, since Sibley's soldiers lacked horses and the supplies necessary to operate on the plains.

The hostile Indians seemed reluctant to escape out onto the plains. Most were Mdewakantons or, to a lesser degree, Wahpekutes, who had always lived in the woodlands. They viewed the plains as a forbidding place where food would be difficult to find. A few moved in with relatives at Camp Release, hoping that Robinson and Robertson had spoken the truth about Sibley's intentions and no doubt convinced that their kinship ties with nonhostile Indians could afford them protection from punishment. Indeed, this camp grew from 150 lodges on the twenty-third to nearly 250 by the twenty-sixth, and more Dakotas kept moving in after the army arrived, usually at night.

Sibley soon realized that he might persuade many hostiles to surrender if it appeared that he had forgiven the farmer groups and did not intend to punish them. His early promise to Robinson and Robertson to punish only those directly involved in killing civilians was clearly understood by the Sioux. In addition, on 24 September he wrote both to members of the friendly camp and to the upper Sissetons, assuring them that they had nothing to fear if they had not been involved in the murder of civilians. Nonetheless, as the friendly camp grew in number, Sibley ordered the formation of a military tribunal to gather evidence against all those present. He made no move to take large numbers of prisoners, however, securing only sixteen men. Other Dakota men were even allowed to keep their weapons, a move that encouraged still more to surrender.

During the two weeks that followed, Camp Release slowly increased to more than a thousand people. Some men who returned to it had been deeply implicated in the fighting; others were tied to the killing of civilians. Finally, on 11 October, when Sibley was convinced that he had "three-fourths of those primarily concerned in the Outbreak," he surrounded Camp Release and arrested more than 100 men. He apprehended others over the next few days, including a large number of warriors who had been sent back to Yellow Medicine to dig potatoes. By 17 October Sibley had close to 400 prisoners, only 68 of whom were deemed to have been "friendly" throughout the entire war. Their dependents totaled another 1,400 people. Perhaps 200 hostile Mdewakanton warriors were still at large on the plains.

For those in custody, trials moved at a fast pace. By 21 October, 120 had been judged guilty, 40 cases being determined on one day alone. At this point Sibley moved the prisoners and their dependents south, building log jails along the way to accommodate the guilty men. The last case was determined at Fort Ridgely on 4 November. In all, the military commission condemned 303 Dakota men. While the government debated their eventual fate, they were moved to a stockade near Mankato. En route a mob attacked the chained men in New Ulm, killing two prisoners. A second assault by civilians was narrowly averted on 9 December.

The ents of the prisoners, 1,658 people, were marched to St. Paul on 9 November. The government built a walled enclosure for them below Fort Snelling to keep angry whites from abusing them. Protection was necessary, since the caravan of old men, women, and children had been attacked by enraged whites while passing through Henderson, Minnesota, and further abuse occurred when the party reached St. Paul. Washington officials, aware that these people could no longer stay in Minnesota, selected Crow Creek on the Missouri as a new home for them, and they were moved west in the spring. More or less uninhabited, Crow Creek was a dreadfully barren place where many eastern Sioux Indians later perished.

All along, Sibley had wanted to execute en masse the men judged guilty. Even the missionary Riggs, who acted as military chaplain for Sibley and as occasional interpreter during the trials, reluctantly concurred, noting that "the great majority of those who are condemned should be executed." Yet President Abraham Lincoln, warned by Bishop Henry Benjamin Whipple and others of the haste with which the trials had been conducted, demanded to see the proceedings of the military commission. What he saw undoubtedly disturbed him. Only two cases showed credible evidence of rape, though congressmen from Minnesota had informed Lincoln that nearly all of the condemned had sexually abused white women. Most trials contained only a paragraph or two of testimony, frequently only a man's admission that he had been present at one of the major battles and had fired a gun. The military court had agreed to condemn any Indian who admitted to firing either at the fort or at New Ulm. Time and again men who had not sided with the hostiles testified that although they had charged their guns with powder and fired them, they had not used balls, thus harming no one. Evidence also frequently demonstrated that members of the soldiers' lodge had to threaten reluctant Sioux men—mostly farmers—to make them participate in the fighting.

Lincoln finally agreed to execute 39 men, partly to satisfy the thirst for revenge in Minnesota and partly because circumstantial evidence indicated that these men had been party to the killing of civilians. On 26 December, 38 were hanged in Mankato, one man in the group receiving a reprieve. The springing of the trap by a white man who had lost most of his family symbolically ended the Sioux Outbreak in Minnesota.

Federal officials removed the remaining 250 male prisoners to Davenport, Iowa, where they served sentences of one to three years. Those who survived the internment—nearly one-half died of disease—eventually joined their families at Crow Creek. In 1866 the government allowed the Crow Creek remnants of the once-powerful eastern Sioux to settle at Santee, Nebraska, where their descendants have a reservation today.

Despite their freedom, the 500 or so people who followed Little Crow and 2,800 Sissetons and Wahpetons who continued to roam north of Lake Traverse suffered nearly as much as the main body of Indians who surrendered. Forced out onto the prairies late in the fall, many perished during the winter. Buffalo had all but disappeared from the lands east of the Missouri River. Both Little Crow's group and the Sissetons and Wahpetons sought aid in Canada, partly out of desperation and partly because of lingering memories of kinship bonds that had once existed between the Sioux and English agents representing the crown. Others joined western Sioux bands and fought alongside Red Cloud, Sitting Bull, and Crazy Horse. Little Crow resorted to raiding the Minnesota frontier, where he was killed by a farmer while picking berries. Upon learning the identity of the corpse, white boys desecrated the body. It was an inglorious end for the once important chief who had tried hard to maintain the ways of the past as well as live peaceably alongside whites. A handful of his followers stayed behind in Canada, where they eventually received a small reservation. By the late 1860s many Sissetons and

Wahpetons were being resettled on reservations in northeastern South Dakota and central North Dakota.

Overall, the uprising of 1862 was a terrible tragedy. Hundreds of whites and Indians lost their lives, most of whom had neither started nor condoned the conflict. Although the Dakota men who started the war had hoped it would lead to a rejuvenated society, the fighting accentuated the split in eastern Sioux camps so that it threatened the very fabric of Dakota existence. The reliance on kinship systems to provide identity in one's descent group and tribe, loyalty to native culture, and assistance in time of trouble seemed on the point of dissolution. Yet Sioux warriors did not openly fight among themselves in 1862, and when differences over the war could not be resolved the hostiles fled to the plains, leaving the friendly camp unmolested. Indeed, some protagonists such as Little Crow and A. J. Campbell could even part friends.

Even so, it is important to remember that the antagonisms the outbreak unveiled were historical exceptions in the chronicle of early Dakota-white contact. The ethnic relations that evolved on the upper Mississippi River after 1650 by and large were characterized by peaceful trade, the creation of strong kinship bonds, and fruitful negotiation. Although these relations underwent change as traders came and went and after the federal government built Fort Snelling, the age was one in which individuals like Le Sueur, Dickson, Taliaferro, and even Sibley met, smoked, and worked out their differences with their Dakota kinsmen Sacred Born, Wabasha, Running Walker, and Little Crow. Differing world views seemed compatible, even complementary, for nearly two centuries. Relations with Euroamericans had brought the Dakotas time-saving items that made life easier as well as new and powerful allies. If ever the eastern Sioux had a golden age, it was this period.

But, as they always do, the golden age came to an end, and the era passed when the game no longer could support villages, white pioneers began to invade Sioux lands, and acculturation programs sought to destroy native culture. Even with such pressures, Dakota people continued to trust their white kinsmen and believed the "Great Father" would always assist them. This lingering faith no doubt explains why so many Mdewakantons who had participated in the war decided to stay near Camp Release and be captured by Sibley. One can only marvel at the patience of the eastern Sioux and their commitment to whites.

Thus, when we remember the Minnesota Sioux we should not recall simply the horrors of those days in late August. The outbreak was begun by a minority of Sioux warriors who were unable to unify their people behind a policy of violence even after initial successes at the lower agency and Birch Coulee gave the leaders of the movement reason to be optimistic. Furthermore, we should not assume that those Indians who counseled peace were unpatriotic or were weaklings who became cultural traitors in exchange for annuities. As is often true in history, the opposing groups both had worthy convictions that must be considered in the context of the time.

Finally, we should also remember that, though early whites willingly assimilated aspects of the Dakota world view, the tendency to do so decreased as the potential for economic exploitation and the need to manipulate Sioux institutions declined. Herein lies the tragedy of this interethnic relationship: successful and peaceful patterns, so well established in the past, were abandoned as whites succumbed to the immensely strong urge to impose the cultural conformity that dominated the American frontier experience. This illiberal attitude brought violence to the land and to people who generally had been committed to living in peace with their white neighbors.

◈ *F U R T H E R   R E A D I N G*

Annie H. Abel, *The American Indians and the End of the Confederacy, 1863–1866* (1993) (reprint of 1925 edition)

W. David Baird, ed., *A Creek Warrior for the Confederacy: The Autobiography of Chief G. W. Grayson* (1988)

Frank Cunningham, *General Stand Watie's Confederate Indians* (1998) (reprint of 1959 edition)

Kenny A. Franks, "The Confederate States and the Five Civilized Tribes: A Breakdown of Relations," *Journal of the West* 12 (July 1973), 439–454

Arrell M. Gibson, "Native Americans and the Civil War," *American Indian Quarterly* 9 (Fall 1985), 385–410

William H. Graves, "Indian Soldiers for the Gray Army: Confederate Recruitment in Indian Territory," *Chronicles of Oklahoma* 60 (Summer 1991), 134–145

Douglas Hale, "Texas Units in the Civil War," *Chronicles of Oklahoma* 68 (Fall 1990), 228–265

Laurence M. Hauptman, *Between Two Fires: American Indians in the Civil War* (1995)

———, "The Implementation of the Confederate Treaties with the Five Civilized Tribes," *Chronicles of Oklahoma* 51 (Spring 1973), 21–33

———, *The Iroquois in the Civil War: From Battlefield to Reservation* (1993)

———, ed., *A Seneca Indian in the Union Army: The Civil War Letters of Sergeant Isaac Newton Parker, 1861–1865* (1995)

Wilfred Knight, *Red Fox, Stand Watie and the Confederate Indian Nations During the Civil War Years in Indian Territory* (1988)

Jane F. Lancaster, *Removal Aftershock: The Seminoles' Struggle to Survive in the West, 1836–1866* (1994)

John C. Nielson, "Indian Masters, Black Slaves: An Oral History of the Civil War in Indian Territory," *Panhandle-Plains Historical Review* 65 (July 1992), 42–54

Christine Schultz White and Benton R. White, *Now the Wolf Has Come: The Creek Nation in the Civil War* (1996)

Resistance and Transition,

1865–1886

◈

After the conclusion of the Civil War, national attention focused on westward expansion. The Homestead Act, passed in 1862, beckoned thousands of Americans and attracted immigrants to the United States. Completion of the first transcontinental railroad in 1868 also signaled that the next generation would be marked by unprecedented pressures on Native lands. Not all Indians resisted militarily, but all Native communities faced questions about their ways of life. In this era, many would be removed from their homelands, and others would see their land holdings reduced or would be forced to share their lands with other Indian nations. The Plains and the Southwest gained prominence from the resistance of leaders like Crazy Horse and Geronimo, but as the case of the Nez Perce illustrated, warfare was hardly limited to those regions.

As early as 1871, Congress declared that no more treaties would be signed; agreements would still be negotiated, but the change in nomenclature signified that times had changed. With Geronimo's final surrender in 1886 at Skeleton Canyon, Arizona, just north of the boundary between Arizona and the state of Sonora in Mexico, an era truly had come to an end. Could the federal government have made other choices or achieved other results? Why might some Native communities have fought and others chosen different tactics?

◈ *D O C U M E N T S*

These documents present Indian perspectives on a turbulent and often tragic era. Allen P. Slickpoo, a Nez Perce historian, provides his view of the famous war of 1877 in Document 1. He notes that other historians have not always given proper attention or credit to his people. In Document 2, James Harris Guy (Chickasaw) offers a plaintive comment on not only the increasing pressure on his people's land base in what would become the state of Oklahoma but on the general dilemma confronting Indian nations. After Indians were confined to reservations, their children were forced to attend federal and mission schools. Students responded in a variety of ways to these schools, some of which were located near their homes, but others of which were hundreds or even thousands of miles away. Richard Henry Pratt's Carlisle Indian Industrial School in Pennsylvania furnished a model for many of these institutions, especially up to the first years of the twentieth century. Luther Standing Bear's decision to go east to Carlisle is recorded here in Document 3, an excerpt from his book, *Land of the Spotted Eagle*. In Document 4, three Apaches—Ace Daklugie, Charlie Smith, and Jasper Kanseah— present oral historical testimony about their remarkable counterpart, Geronimo. Their words were recorded by Eve Ball, a long-time non-Indian resident of New Mexico who had gained the confidence and respect of her neighbors.

1. Allen P. Slickpoo (Nez Perce) Reviews the Nez Perce War (1877), recorded 1973

The Nez Perce War of 1877 resulted from many years of frustration, mistreatment, and broken promises. However, the act that made it all explode was the opening of the Wallowa Valley to white settlers, and the subsequent effort to make Chief Joseph and his band move onto the reservation from the Wallowa Country.

After 1875, as more and more settlers came into the Wallowa Valley, there was an increasing amount of trouble between them and the Indians. Each group felt that it had a right to be there and that the other did not. Frequent clashes, including the killing of an Indian in July 1876 led to consultations, councils, and visits by Monteith [Indian federal agent to the Nez Perce], military authorities, and a special commission. The series of councils which began on May 3, 1877, resulted in an agreement whereby the Indians were to gather their stock and move to the reservation. The chiefs selected land for their new homes and were given thirty days to move.

Monteith and General Howard have been criticized for demanding that our ancestors move onto the reservation in thirty days. Our people felt that they needed at least six months to round up their stock, and that the thirty-day limit was an injustice for which no legitimate excuse has even been offered. Indeed, now that the chiefs had agreed to move and had selected their lands, such haste does not seem to have been necessary. Consequently, Monteith must share the blame for whatever effect this had on the opening of hostilities. The manner in which the war started, however, suggests that the thirty-day ultimatum was not the principal cause of the war.

In mid-June, the people were ready to cross the boundaries of the reservation. At the time the White Bird Band was performing a tel-lik-leen ceremony, a ceremony in which the warriors, both young and old, ride in a circular fashion about the village. Traditionally, the men would show their battle trophies and relate their experiences in battle.

One elderly warrior named Ha-khauts Il-pilhp (Red Grizzly Bear), who was on the sidelines, told three young men as they passed him, "What are you doing this ceremony for, what bravery have you done, when your 'mother and father' have just been killed on the Wel-kil-khit (Horseshoe Bend of the Salmon River, near Slate Creek)?"

From Allen P. Slickpoo, *Noon-Nee-Me-Poo: We, the Nez Perce* (Lapwai, Idaho: Nez Perce Tribe, 1973), 183–194.

He was referring here to the killing of an elderly man and his wife by some whites. The old couple had come on the whites' homestead and when told to leave because the country was no longer theirs, had misunderstood and instead stood still and smiled to show their friendly intentions. This insulted one of the whites who drew his gun and shot both of them out in the garden. The news of this murder had traveled fast and had already reached the village at Lah-ma-ta (White Bird).

Upon hearing this the three young men, named Way-ly-tits, Sop-sis-il-pilhp, and Wah-tsum-yose became angry and determined to get revenge. Wah-ly-tits was particularly angry because his father had been killed in 1875 by a white man named Larry Ott who had managed to escape punishment.

The three set out immediately for the settlements located on the Salmon River. The first white to be killed was a man who had treated the Indians badly. Then two more men who had incited the hatred of the Indians were also killed. The three then went back to the village to get reinforcements. In spite of the fact that the chiefs were opposed to war and continued violence, sixteen other young men joined the first three. A few became drunk after capturing some whiskey, and the killings, which had begun as reprisals, became a free-for-all. The settlers became alarmed and the military moved, not to capture the murderers, but to attack Indian villages, and the war was on. . . .

The news of the deaths on the prairie spread instantly. The whites began to talk of war and the Nez Perces in the area began to move away so that they would not be caught in the crossfire or be blamed for the murders. The Nez Perces at Lapwai told General Howard, the commander of the U.S. Army in that part of Idaho, that the raids were ones of revenge and not a declaration of war. However, Howard chose to believe white informants who said that the Indians were beginning an uprising and he began to act as if he were at war with the Nez Perce nation.

Howard first decided to quickly take the Indians at Whitebird village where the whole disturbance had started and sent a force of ninety-nine soldiers under a Captain Perry to accomplish that task. Perry, however, commanding largely raw recruits, chose to fight after a thirty-six hour forced march and lost the battle. Against a force of sixty to sixty-five Indian braves, many of whom were armed only with bows and arrows, he lost thirty-four soldiers with four wounded. He also lost many horses and rifles which the Indians confiscated.

When Howard heard of this defeat, he sent for reinforcements and when these men arrived about a week later, set out in pursuit of the Indian forces with a view to forcing their defeat and subsequent removal to the reservation. Then a long pursuit began which lasted over a three-month period and was marked by battles and skirmishes.

The first of these battles after Whitebird was at Cottonwood where a whole detachment of soldiers was ambushed and killed. The battle of the Clearwater was next. Howard had been following the Nez Perces for two weeks unable to even come close enough to them to know how many there were. They finally came across the main body of the Nez Perces by chance on a ridge near Stites, Idaho, now called Battle Ridge, and began the battle. Howard began on the offensive, but quickly dug in when the Nez Perces began to resist. Lines were held for some thirty hours. After a time our forces decided to retreat and plan their next move. Many of the younger men wanted to travel to the Plains and join forces with other tribes. They believed that once they were out of Howard's area, he would no longer pursue them, and since they also believed that the quarrel was entirely with Howard and not with the United States government, they felt once they were in the Buffalo Country the fighting would be over. Many of the other men, including Joseph, were against this move and wanted to stay and fight in Idaho. The first group prevailed, however, and it was decided to move to the Buffalo country. . . .

Once the decision to go to the Buffalo country was made, our people left Kamiah, where they had gone after the battle of the Clearwater, and started up the Lolo Trail, a traditional path to the Plains. Howard planned to proceed to Missoula via an easier road, but had to wait in Kamiah for replacements to calm the frightened settlers. The Nez Perces, therefore, got a good start before Howard could begin to move. When our people arrived at "Fort Misery" near Kamiah, they had to cross the river near the First Presbyterian Church. Here refuge was refused for fear of the church's becoming involved. Flags and white clothes were displayed for the soldiers to see.

Once the Nez Perces arrived at Travelers Rest in Lolo Pass they felt they had outdistanced General Howard and so could proceed with more ease toward the Plains. They then held several conferences with the aim of deciding where they were to go and by which route. The Nez Perces at a later date did get through to the Sioux, but they learned that the Sioux were not interested in helping them but only in keeping out of range of the U.S. Army. They were also very short of food and did not think they could support more people. However, after the Battle at Bear Paw, White Bird and his band did manage to find refuge in Canada.

It was finally decided at Lolo Summit that they would proceed in a southerly direction to the Ross Hole Country, on to the headwaters of the Jefferson, then south to Yellowstone National Park. From there they would go to the Shoshone River of Wyoming, which was the home of their good friends, the Crow.

They proceeded on to Big Hole and here were surprised by a Colonel Gibbon who attacked their camp at dawn and in a fierce charge completely overrode one section of the camp. Children, women, young and old, everyone in sight was killed by the charging soldiers. In the other part of the camp those who were not hurt by the main charge attacked and soon had Gibbon and his men on the defensive. While this was going on Joseph was able to move the rest of the camp; the warriors followed soon after and the Nez Perces were able to escape capture again.

General Howard had not given up and doggedly followed the Nez Perces on their flight. After many more weeks of moving northward marred by small skirmishes here and there, the Nez Perces, convinced by now that they had left General Howard behind, stopped to camp and lay in supplies in that region of Montana known as the Bear Paws. Here General Miles caught up with him and after a prolonged battle where the soldiers were at an advantage partly because they had a twelve-pound cannon, the Nez Perces surrendered. In a speech that has become famous, Joseph handed his rifle to General Miles and said:

> Tell General Howard I know what is in his heart. What he told me before, I have in my heart. I am tired of fighting. Our chiefs are killed. Looking Glass is dead. Tulhulhutsut is dead. The old men are all dead. It is the young men who say yes or no. He who led the young men is dead. It is cold and we have no blankets. The little children are freezing to death. My people, some of them, have run away to the hills and have no blankets,

no food; no one knows where they are—perhaps freezing to death. I want to have time to look for my children and see how many of them I can find. Maybe I shall find them among the dead. Hear me, my chiefs. I am tried; my heart is sick and sad. From where the sun now stands I will fight no more, forever.

And so another chapter in the history of a proud and brave people came to an end.

It is interesting to note that many blamed Joseph and Looking Glass for letting the people take their time as if they were not at war. Ho-toe-toe, who had been in command, was removed because he was a half-breed and the full-bloods resented his leadership. Evidently neither Joseph nor Looking Glass realized that Gibbon was moving in from the south. Later, in speaking of the flight and battle, Joseph said, "I knew that I had made a mistake by not crossing into the country of the Red Coats [Royal Canadian Mounted Police], also in not keeping the country scouted in my rear." However, Joseph did not speak of the other things which helped to defeat him and which must have made his heart sad and heavy. One was that along the whole line of flight, the whites were helped again and again by other Indians, even the Crow who were friends of the Nez Perces. For instance, the first wave of General Miles' forces were Cheyenne scouts, and a few days prior to the battle at Bear Paw, the Nez Perces had a running battle with Colonel Sturgis and a group of River Crow. It may seem strange that another tribe would aid the whites to defeat their brothers. Perhaps they did this because of the material rewards promised by the U.S. Army. Then too, Nez Perce horses were highly prized throughout the northwest and many other Indians joined in with the hope of getting many horses.

During the Nez Perce War, many of the battles were referred to as skirmishes by the government. This terminology has also been used by many historians and writers who insist on calling important battles skirmishes. Many of these encounters were full-fledged battles, as the troops who fought in them well know. Battles such as the battle of Cottonwood, of the Clearwater, at Fort Misery, near the Kamiah Valley, at the Clearwater River crossing, and on the Lolo Trail, just to mention a few, were certainly more than skirmishes. In many of these battles, the soldiers under their trained commanders did not come off too well. Many times our warriors were able to hold off vastly superior forces, and often demonstrated a knowledge of classical military strategy. General Howard dared not mention these encounters for his own protection and often tried to write them off by calling them skirmishes. We know them for what they were however, full-scale battles.

2. James Harris Guy (Chickasaw), "The White Man Wants the Indians' Home," 1878

The White man wants the Indians' home,
    He envies them their land;
And with the sweetest words he comes
    To get it, if he can.

From Daniel F. Littlefield, Jr., and James W. Parins, eds., *Native American Writing in the Southeast: an Anthology, 1875–1935* (Oxford: University Press of Mississippi, 1995), 10–11.

And if we will not give our lands,
  And plainly tell him so,
He then goes back, calls up his claim,
  And says, "let's make them go."

The question in the Indians' mind
  Is, where are we to go?
No other country can we find;
  'Tis filled up with our foe.

We do not want one foot of land
  The white man calls his own;
We ask of nothing at his hands,
  Save to be left alone.

3. Luther Standing Bear (Lakota) Recalls His Experiences at the Carlisle Indian Industrial School, 1879

. . . At the age of eleven years, ancestral life for me and my people was most abruptly ended without regard for our wishes, comforts, or rights in the matter. At once I was thrust into an alien world, into an environment as different from the one into which I had been born as it is possible to imagine, to remake myself, if I could, into the likeness of the invader.

By 1879, my people were no longer free, but were subjects confined on reservations under the rule of agents. One day there came to the agency a party of white people from the East. Their presence aroused considerable excitement when it became known that these people were school teachers who wanted some Indian boys and girls to take away with them to train as were white boys and girls.

Now, father was a "blanket Indian," but he was wise. He listened to the white strangers, their offers and promises that if they took his son they would care well for him, teach him how to read and write, and how to wear white man's clothes. But to father all this was just "sweet talk," and I know that it was with great misgivings that he left the decision to me and asked if I cared to go with these people. I, of course, shared with the rest of my tribe a distrust of the white people, so I know that for all my dear father's anxiety he was proud to hear me say "Yes." That meant that I was brave.

I could think of no reason why white people wanted Indian boys and girls except to kill them, and not having the remotest idea of what a school was, I thought we were going East to die. But so well had courage and bravery been trained into us that it became a part of our unconscious thinking and acting, and personal life was nothing when it came time to do something for the tribe. Even in our play and games we voluntarily put ourselves to various tests in the effort to grow brave and fearless, for it was most discrediting to be called *can'l wanka,* or a coward. Accordingly there were few cowards, most Lakota men preferring to die in the performance of some act of bravery than to die of old age. Thus, in giving myself up to go East I was proving to my father that he was honored with a brave son. In my decision to go, I gave up many things dear to the heart of a little Indian boy, and one of the things over which my child mind grieved was the thought of saying good-bye to my pony. I rode him as far as I could on the journey, which was to the Missouri River, where we took the boat. There we parted from our parents, and it was a heart-breaking scene, women and children weeping. Some of the children changed their minds and were unable to go on the boat, but for many who did go it was a final parting.

On our way to school we saw many white people, more than we ever dreamed existed, and the manner in which they acted when they saw us quite indicated their opinion of us. It was only about three years after the Custer battle, and the general opinion was that the Plains people merely infested the earth as nuisances, and our being there simply evidenced misjudgment on the part of Wakan Tanka [the Creator in the Lakota religion]. Whenever our train stopped at the railway stations, it was met by great numbers of white people who came to gaze upon the little Indian "savages." The little ones sat quietly at the car windows looking at the people who swarmed on the platform. Some of the children wrapped themselves in their blankets, covering all but their eyes. At one place we were taken off the train and marched a distance down the street to a restaurant. We walked down the street between two rows of uniformed men whom we called soldiers, though I suppose they were policemen. This must have been done to protect us, for it was surely known that we boys and girls could do no harm. Back of the rows of uniformed men stood the white people craning their necks, talking, laughing, and making a great noise. They yelled and tried to mimic us by what they thought were war-whoops. We did not like this, and some of the children were naturally very much frightened. I remember how I tried to crowd into the protecting midst of the jostling boys and girls. But we were all trying to be brave, yet going to what we thought would end in death at the hands of the white people whom we knew had no love for us. Back on the train the older boys sang brave songs in an effort to keep up their spirits and ours too. In my mind I often recall that scene—eighty-odd blanketed boys and girls marching down the street surrounded by a jeering, unsympathetic people whose only emotions were those of hate and fear; the conquerors looking upon the conquered. And no more understanding us than if we had suddenly been dropped from the moon.

At last at Carlisle the transforming, the "civilizing" process began. It began with clothes. Never, no matter what our philosophy or spiritual quality, could we be civilized while wearing the moccasin and blanket. The task before us was not only that of accepting new ideas and adopting new manners, but actual physical changes and discomfort had to be borne uncomplainingly until the body adjusted itself to new tastes and habits. Our accustomed dress was taken and replaced with clothing that felt cumbersome and awkward. Against trousers and handkerchiefs we had a distinct feeling—they were unsanitary and the trousers kept us from breathing well. High collars, stiff-bosomed shirts, and suspenders fully three inches in width were uncomfortable, while leather boots caused actual suffering. We longed to go barefoot, but were told that dew on the grass would give us colds. That was a new warning for us, for our mothers had never told us to beware of colds, and I remember as a child coming into the tipi with moccasins full of snow. Unconcernedly I would take them off my feet, pour out the snow, and put them on my feet again without any thought of sickness, for in that time colds, catarrh, bronchitis, and *la grippe* were unknown. But we were soon to know them. Then, red flannel undergarments were given us for winter wear, and for me, at least, discomfort grew into actual torture. I used to endure it as long as possible, then run upstairs and quickly take off the flannel garments and hide them. When inspection time came, I ran and put them on again, for I knew that if I were found disobeying the orders of the school I should be punished. My niece once asked me what it was that I disliked the most during those first bewildering days, and I said, "red flannel." Not knowing what I meant, she laughed, but I still remember those horrid, sticky garments which we had to wear next to the skin, and I still squirm and itch when I think of them. Of course, our hair was cut, and then there was much disapproval. But that was part of the transformation process and in some mysterious way long hair stood in the path of our development. For all the grumbling among the bigger boys, we soon had our heads shaven. How strange I felt! Involuntarily, time and time again, my hands went to my head, and that night it was a long time before I went to sleep. If we did not learn much at first, it will not be wondered at, I think. Everything was queer, and it took a few months to get adjusted to the new surroundings.

Almost immediately our names were changed to those in common use in the English language. Instead of translating our names into English and calling Zinkcaziwin, Yellow Bird, and Wanbli K'leska, Spotted Eagle, which in itself would have been educational, we were just John, Henry, or Maggie, as the case might be. I was told to take a pointer and select a name for myself from the list written on the blackboard. I did, and since one was just as good as another, and as I could not distinguish any difference in them, I placed the pointer on the name Luther. I then learned to call myself by that name and got used to hearing others call me by it, too. By the time we had been forbidden to speak our mother tongue, which is the rule in all boarding-schools. This rule is uncalled for, and today is not only robbing the Indian, but America of a rich heritage. The language of a people is part of their history. Today we should be perpetuating history instead of destroying it, and this can only be effectively done by allowing and encouraging the young to keep it alive. A language unused, embalmed, and reposing only in a book, is a dead language. Only the people themselves, and never the scholars, can nourish it into life.

Of all the changes we were forced to make, that of diet was doubtless the most injurious, for it was immediate and drastic. White bread we had for the first meal and thereafter, as well as coffee and sugar. Had we been allowed our own simple diet of meat, either boiled with soup or dried, and fruit, with perhaps a few vegetables, we should have thrived. But the change in clothing, housing, food and confinement combined with lonesomeness was too much, and in three years nearly one half of the children from the Plains were dead and through with all earthly schools. In the graveyard at Carlisle most of the graves are those of little ones. . . .

4. Ace Daklugie, Charlie Smith, and Jasper Kanseah (Chiricahua Apaches) Remember Geronimo, n. d.

[Ace] Daklugie

Not until after the death of my father, Juh, did Geronimo become very prominent. After that he just took over. He was a Bedonkohe and never was elected to the chieftainship. Naiche was chief, but he was very young—too young for the leadership. It took a man to lead the Chiricahua. Geronimo was of middle age, a well-known fighter and superb leader, and he was also a Medicine Man. No White Eyes seem to understand the importance of that in controlling Apaches. Naiche was not a Medicine Man; so he needed Geronimo as Geronimo needed *him*. It was a good combination. Geronimo saw that Naiche was accorded the respect and recognition due a chief and that he always occupied the seat of honor; but Geronimo planned the strategy, with Naiche's help, and made the decisions. Of course, had Juh or Geronimo been chief, nobody could have usurped their prerogatives. But don't forget that not being a Medicine Man was a great handicap to Naiche.

Several years after our capture, and after I returned from school, I lived in Geronimo's village and was his confidant and interpreter. I accompanied him everywhere he went. When he took pneumonia at Fort Sill and was sent to the hospital, Eugene Chihuahua sat beside him during the day and I at night. And he died with his hand in mine. Even in his delirium, he talked of those seventeen men who had eluded five thousand men of the army of the United States for many years; and eluded not only them, but also twenty-five hundred Mexican soldiers—seventy-five hundred men, well armed, well trained, and well equipped against seventeen whom they regarded as naked savages. The odds were only five hundred to one against Geronimo, but still they could not whip him nor could they capture him.

But I am Geronimo's nephew and there are people who might think that I am biased. Go see Charlie Smith. As a child he and his mother were captured by Geronimo's band. Charlie was with Geronimo and Naiche about a year, I think, before going to Florida.

Charlie Smith

. . . I'll never forget that winter. Geronimo would line the boys up on the bank, have us build a fire and undress by it, and then make us plunge into the stream, breaking the ice as we went. The first time he did this, I thought that the ordeal would be over when he let us get out of the water. But no—time after time we warmed ourselves by the fire and returned to the icy water. There were times when I just hated him. Geronimo would stand there on the bank, with a stick in his hand. What for, I don't know; I never saw him strike anybody. But we knew he might and that was enough. Nobody defied Geronimo.

Was I present during the fighting? Geronimo had the women and children along, and of course they saw what happened. If pursued, he, as did all Apaches,

From *Indeh: An Apache Odyssey*, by Eve Ball, 101–105. New edition copyright © 1988 by the University of Oklahoma Press, Norman.

tried to protect them by sending them ahead; but ordinarily, when fighting occurred, it was because he laid an ambush, and every one of the band was there. Some of the women were very good shots—good fighters, too. Lozen, sister of Victorio, was called The Woman Warrior; and though she may not have had as much strength as one of the men she was as good a shot as any of them.

When actually on the warpath the Apaches were under very strict rules. Even words for common things were different. Women would go with their husbands, but they could not live together. No unmarried woman was permitted to go with them. Lozen? No, she was not married; she never married. But to us she was as a Holy Woman and she was regarded and treated as one. White Painted Woman herself was not more respected. And she was brave! Geronimo sent her on missions to the military officers to arrange for meetings with him, or to carry messages.

When Geronimo crossed the border into New Mexico or Arizona, it was usually to get ammunition. I do not think that he wanted to kill, but there were cases when he had no choice. If he were seen by a civilian, it meant that he would be reported to the military and they'd be after us. So there was nothing to do but kill the civilian and his entire family. It was terrible to see little children killed. I do not like to talk of it. I do not like to think of it. But the soldiers killed our women and children, too. Don't forget that. There were times that I hated Geronimo for that, too; but when I got older, I knew that he had no choice.

Stealing horses was fun. I was not quite old enough to get in on that, and how I envied those who were! It was usually the boys, too, who shot the fire-arrows to set houses ablaze. I never saw that done but twice, though. I did see many, many people killed. I wish I could forget it. Even babies were killed; and I love babies.

But Geronimo was fighting not only to avenge his murdered mother, wife, and children, but for his people and his tribe. Later there were Apaches who were bitter against Geronimo, saying that it was his fault that they were sent to Florida and were prisoners of war for twenty-seven years. Well, if they'd had the fighting spirit of Geronimo, they need not have been sent. The big difference was that he had the courage to keep on and they were quitters. Some of them have "gone white" and blame Geronimo for everything. I don't respect them. They were cowards. I won't name them. I am ashamed that they are Apaches.

And don't forget that Geronimo knew that it was hopeless. But that did not stop him. I admire him for that. He was a great leader of men, and it ill becomes the cowardly to find fault with a man who was trying to keep them free. And don't forget that he was fighting against enormous odds, or that nobody ever captured him.

Jasper Kanseah (nephew of Geronimo)

My father died before I was born, and my mother died when they drove us like cattle from Cochise's reservation to San Carlos. I had nobody but my grandmother and she had to walk. I was little, and when I couldn't keep up she carried me. She told me that Geronimo was my uncle, but I didn't remember him till he came to San Carlos. When he came my grandmother had already gone to the Happy Place, and I had nobody. But Indian women were good to me, and even when they were hungry they gave me some of the food their own children needed. We never went hungry till we got to San Carlos; and there we almost died because there was no food.

I think that I was eleven when my uncle, Geronimo, came and took me with him. And he gave me to Yahnosha to be his orderly and learn to be a warrior. I stayed with Yahnosha and cooked his food, and got his horse and fed and watered it; and I never spoke unless somebody asked me a question. And I ate what was left. No matter what happened, I didn't complain. And even when I talked I had to say it differently. (On the warpath we don't talk as we do most of the time, but differently.) I had to think what Yahnosha wanted next and then get it for him before he told me. But I was proud to be taught by a great warrior and I tried to do everything right.

I knew Geronimo and I knew that he was the victim of liars. He was lied about by many of his own people for whom he was fighting. He was betrayed by them. He was betrayed by Miles. I am not sure but that he was betrayed by Crook, though some think not. But I know that he was lied to by Miles. That man did not do what he promised. Geronimo was a really great fighting man, and Miles was a coward. Everything he needed for his troops was provided for him and them, but Geronimo had to obtain food for his men, and for their women and children. When they were hungry, Geronimo got food. When they were cold he provided blankets and clothing. When they were afoot, he stole horses. When they had no bullets, he got ammunition. He was a good man. I think that you have desperados among you White Eyes today that are much worse men and are more cruel than Geronimo.

◈ E S S A Y S

David D. Smits, a professor of history at the College of New Jersey, contributes the first essay. Here he considers the employment of Indian scouts and allies by the frontier army. Smits concludes that Indian scouts, allies, and auxiliaries played an essential role in many of the campaigns against Indian peoples. Why would Indians decide to aid these efforts against other Indians? In the second essay, Tracy Neal Leavelle, a doctoral student in American Indian history at Arizona State University, demonstrates that this era did not mean exactly the same things to all Native communities. The residents of the Grande Ronde reservation in Oregon showed their commitment to make necessary changes and adaptations in order to try to make their surroundings as productive and meaningful as possible. Why do some Indian nations receive more attention than others during this time period?

Indian Scouts and Indian Allies in the Frontier Army

DAVID D. SMITS

This essay will examine the frontier army's rationale for relying on "friendly" Indians, the effects of such reliance on the so-called hostiles, the opposition from tribal chiefs, Indian Bureau officials, and even many army commanders to the enlistment of "friendlies," the exigencies of guerrilla warfare that forced commanders to make

From David D. Smits, "Fighting Fire with Fire: The Frontier Army's Use of Indian Scouts and Allies in the Trans-Mississippi Campaigns, 1860–1890," *American Indian Culture and Research Journal,* vol. 22, no. 1 (1998), 73–116. Reprinted by permission of the American Indian Studies Center, UCLA. Copyright © Regents of the University of California.

use of Indians, the hazardous nature of military service for the "red bluecoats," the multifarious uses of the army's Indian scouts, and the relations between such scouts and their white comrades-in-arms. . . .

High-ranking military commanders offered several reasons, beyond the Indians' proficiency as trailers, for enlisting them in the frontier army. John M. Schofield, one of the Union's most distinguished Civil War generals and, after [Philip] Sheridan, the army's commanding general, believed that service in the army reduced the discontent so common among young Indian men on reservations. . . .

General [George] Crook was the officer most responsible for convincing the army's high command of the psychological value of employing the hostiles' own tribal members against them. . . . The employment of Indians—especially those belonging to the hostiles' own tribe—would destroy the troublemakers' morale. Hence, as early as the spring of 1867, an outmaneuvered General Winfield Scott Hancock wrote to [William Tecumseh] Sherman requesting permission to enlist two hundred to three hundred Indian scouts because he believed it would "demoralize" the recalcitrant Sioux and Cheyennes.

Although Indian voices seldom found their way into the historical record, sufficient fragmentary evidence exists to suggest that the army's efforts to demoralize its Indian foes by employing their own tribesmen were quite effective. Captain John G. Bourke, a member of Crook's staff, recounted that on November 25, 1876, Colonel Ranald MacKenzie, accompanied by Sioux and Cheyenne scouts enlisted at Red Cloud agency after Crook had confiscated their horses, struck the Cheyenne village of Dull Knife and Little Wolf in the Bighorn Mountains. In utter exasperation Dull Knife called out to MacKenzie's Indian scouts: "Go home—you have no business here; we can whip the white soldiers alone, but can't fight you too." MacKenzie had at his disposal about four hundred Indian allies, including Arapahos, Bannocks, Pawnees, and Shoshones, in addition to his Sioux and Cheyennes, and they bore the brunt of the fighting that day.

It is apparent that the "hostiles" ordinarily disdained the white soldiers' fighting abilities, but had a wholesome respect for the army's Indians allies. Wooden Leg, a Northern Cheyenne who fought against Custer at the Little Bighorn, recalled that in that fight the hostile Indians called out to the Seventh Cavalrymen: "You are only boys. You ought not be fighting. We whipped you on the Rosebud. You should have brought more Crows or Shoshones with you to do your fighting."

Not surprisingly, given white Americans' ambivalent attitudes toward Indians, some military officers themselves opposed the army's reliance on Indian confederates. One reason for this opposition was that such opponents doubted that Indians could ever renounce their Indian allegiances and become completely loyal to the United States Army. After Geronimo's escape from the army in March 1886, for instance, Sheridan angrily wired Crook, commander of the Department of Arizona: "It seems strange that Geronimo and party could have escaped without the knowledge of the [Apache] scouts." To the distrustful Sheridan, Crook responded: "There can be no question that the scouts were thoroughly loyal, and would have prevented the hostiles leaving had it been possible."

Two days after Crook's response he was relieved of his Arizona command. His replacement was Brigadier General Nelson A. Miles, who promptly discharged most of the Apache scouts on the assumption that they were disloyal. . . .

An attempt to determine the validity of the prevailing objections to utilizing Indians seems appropriate. The place to begin is with the pervasive fear that "the red bluecoats" would prove disloyal. The simple truth is that the Indian scouts, allies, and auxiliaries who rendered assistance to the army were overwhelmingly loyal. To be sure, there was the notorious 1881 Cibicue mutiny, in which twenty-three of the army's White Mountain Apache scouts under the influence of a shaman named Nakaidoklini actually turned on their white comrades in the Sixth Cavalry, who had the revered shaman in their custody.

Of course, this unfortunate incident confirmed the castigators' worst fear, but it stands as the sole instance of serious Indian disloyalty. The vast majority of Apache scouts were scrupulously loyal to the army. Lieutenant Britton Davis, commander of a company of such scouts in the Geronimo campaign, had unwavering trust in his charges. Davis' confidence was justified, for, as he recalled, of more than five hundred Apaches enlisted as scouts during that campaign, only three had deserted. Given the contrast with the regular army's appalling desertion rate of about one-third in the years between 1867 and 1891, there is no justification for censuring the army's Indian comrades-in-arms. . . .

No incident better exemplifies the army's callous disloyalty to dutiful Indian allies than its imprisonment of the Apache scouts who had made possible the final capture of Geronimo and his renegades in 1886. James Kaywaykla, a Warm Springs Apache with firsthand experiences in the relevant events, bitterly recounted how the victorious Miles had ordered his Apache scouts "round up with the hostiles and forced to share their imprisonment. Many had served the cavalry faithfully and incurred the contempt of their own people to aid the White Eyes. And for this they were made prisoners of war for twenty-seven years!" Among the Apache scouts whose reward was imprisonment in Florida were Martine and Kayitah, the individuals most responsible for Geronimo's final surrender. For the loyal Apache scouts, their long confinement was truly a nightmare. Eugene Chihuahua, son of the Chiricahua Apache chief of the same surname, voiced the contempt that the imprisoned "hostiles" had for the Apache scouts who "had betrayed their people." In the son's words: ". . . the only consolation we got for those terrible twenty-seven years as prisoners of war is that the scouts, too, were prisoners. And we made it miserable for them."

For all the other Apache scouts who served in the southwestern United States and Mexico, army service was extraordinarily hazardous. They might have been killed by renegade Apaches, by Mexicans who hated them, or by American civilians who shared these feelings. Furthermore, the Indian scouts, allies, and auxiliaries were often endangered because of the soldiers' genuine difficulties in distinguishing the hostiles from the so-called friendlies. The army's friendlies faced such dangers on all fronts. Frank Grouard observed that during the Battle of the Rosebud, "it was very hard to keep the soldiers from firing into our [Indian] allies after the troops became engaged with the Sioux, mistaking the Crows and Shoshones for the enemy."

At other times, friendlies were in danger simply because of the soldiers' reluctance to trust any Indian or because frustrated soldiers were unable to find and engage the real hostiles. Thus, in 1866 Black Horse, Red Arm, Little Moon, and several other Cheyenne chiefs, hoping for peace with the Americans, promised Colonel Henry B. Carrington, commander of Fort Phil Kearny, one hundred of their young men to help the army fight Red Cloud's Oglalas (Sioux) in the Powder River country. Carrington had no authority to enlist the Cheyennes and did not accept the offer; he preferred to use the Pawnees and Winnebagos who had served him well in 1865. Nonetheless, the Cheyenne peace chiefs honored their pledges of friendship. Then in September 1866 a band of eight friendly Cheyenne men, including several peace chiefs, and a Cheyenne woman made their way to Fort Phil Kearny for provisions. Carrington supplied them with bacon and coffee and told them to camp on an island near the post. While the Cheyenne band was camped there a rumor spread among the troops that several members of the band had been with a war party that had earlier killed two soldiers. About ninety vengeful armed troopers advanced on the Cheyenne camp, intent on annihilating the occupants. Fortunately Carrington was warned of his troopers' plans and arrived in the nick of time with revolver in hand to prevent a massacre of the peaceful Indians. Margaret Irvin Carrington, the colonel's wife, recorded in her journal that the soldiers involved "were restored to their barracks with only admonition and caution as to future conduct." In this case, friendly Indians nearly lost their lives because of the soldiers' unwillingness to trust their loyalty. . . .

There can be no doubt that the frontier army's Indian scouts, allies, and auxiliaries frequently gave preferential treatment to hostiles who belonged to their own tribes or who were their traditional tribal friends, but such treatment was never offered at the expense of the army's mission in the far West. The army's friendlies fulfilled their assignments remarkably well—far better than the regular troops themselves could have—as their hostile Indian kinsmen routinely admitted. In keeping with this reality, the battle-scarred old Nana recalled with pleasure his time spent in Juh's hideout in the mountains of northern Mexico. When the Warm Springs Apache James Kaywaykla asked Nana if anyone could find Juh's stronghold, Nana replied: "Only the [Apache] scouts, the accursed scouts."

The army's heavy dependence on Indians, despite fears that such dependence reflected unfavorably upon the soldiers, indicates just how indispensable they were to the success of the military's agenda. Even the initially skeptical Miles learned from firsthand experience that his troops needed Indian assistance to be effective. In March 1875 Miles reported on his military operations in Indian Territory during the Red River War. Among his recommendations to the army's assistant adjutant general was to discontinue the use of cavalry for scouting. Miles had become convinced that "desultory scouting, often made without positive design and with less result, has a tiresome, exhaustive and injurious influence upon the Cavalry." Miles had learned that "friendly Indians or daring scouts can be more economically employed to discover the hostile camps, trails or movements of Indians." The cavalry should be saved "for the direct march, resistless dash and rapid pursuit for which that arm of the service is so well adapted." Peace could be maintained on the Staked Plains by enlisting "under good officers" a "small force of friendly Navajo Indians" to the west and "the same of Pawnee or Tonkaways" on the east.

In the autumn of 1877 Miles' troops, with the aid of his Cheyenne scouts, caught the fleeing Nez Perce before they could cross the Canadian border. In the ensuing Battle of Bear Paw Mountain, Miles positioned his Cheyenne scouts on the line encircling the Nez Perce camp "where the most desperate fighting was going on." Writing years afterward, Miles recalled that Hump had killed two Nez

Perce with his own hands, and was severely wounded. The Cheyenne scouts, Miles wrote, "had maintained their position with remarkable fortitude and discharged all the duties required of them during the five days siege." Miles was so grateful to his Cheyennes for their "gallant service" that he rewarded each of them with five ponies captured from the Nez Perce herd. Rather than reflecting badly on the army as Miles had once feared its reliance on friendlies would, his Cheyenne scouts had helped to ensure the success of his mission. Such successes were bound to enhance the frontier army's reputation—and, of course, his own. While in command of the Department of the Missouri in 1885, Miles stated in his annual report that he favored the employment of "a number of Indians in the army as scouts, guides, and trailers." He based his recommendation on his "personal observation that they were endowed with many of the qualities which would make them useful." Besides "having found them of great value in numerous ways," Miles had never known one "to be unfaithful to a trust."

Some of the "numerous ways" in which Miles and other army commanders found friendly Indians "of great value" ought to be listed. Besides scouting for and guiding troops and civilians, the most common and important duties of such Indians include the following: interpreting and translating; carrying dispatches and mail; serving as "secret service" agents (i.e., spying and acting as provocateurs); trailing; "peace-talking" (i.e., encouraging surrender); hunting; providing escorts for hunting parties of prominent men, for paymasters, for scientific expeditions, and for visitors to Indian country; patrolling the railroad lines; guarding railroad construction crews and surveyors; identifying unknown Indians; engaging in combat with hostiles (either independently or together with troops); performing guard duty at picket stations and military posts; helping to keep order on the reservations when Indian police were unable to handle disturbances; chasing army deserters; and more. The Indian scouts continued to prove useful to the Bureau of Indian Affairs long after the Indian wars had ended. In 1909, for example, Indian scouts on the Fort Sill Reservation were actually converted to truant officers.

No frontier army commander had more pride in his regiment than the flamboyant and vainglorious Lieutenant Colonel George A. Custer. The reckless public idol was completely in character when he boasted that he "could whip all Indians on the Continent with the Seventh Cavalry." But Custer enjoyed no success whatever as an Indian fighter until his thirteen Osage Indian scouts, Little Beaver and Hard Rope prominent among them, led the Seventh Cavalry to Black Kettle's winter camp on the Washita River in late November of 1868. There Custer won his first victory as an Indian fighter in the Battle of the Washita. Thereafter, Custer took Arikara and Santee Sioux scouts on his expedition to the Black Hills in 1874. He needed them, he said, "for their knowledge of the country and their watchfulness in camp in detecting the presence of hostile Indians near camp." High praise for the Arikaras came from the geologist, Professor A. B. Donaldson, who accompanied the expedition. "As scouts they are invaluable," Donaldson stated. "They have scouted the whole country over in advance of our marching column. If any hostile Sioux had been anywhere in front of us or on our flanks, these ubiquitous and cunning scouts would certainly have found them out. Where they scour the country no ambush could be successfully laid."

Custer's fondness for Bloody Knife, an Arikara, typified the amicable feelings that many soldiers had for Indian scouts and other friendlies. Thus, the white Crow scout Thomas Leforge commented that in 1876 Colonel John Gibbon's soldiers "chummed and joked" with their Crow scouts and gave them nicknames like "Kelly" and "Skookum." Captain Charles King, who commanded Crow scouts under Crook in the 1876 Bighorn and Yellowstone campaigns, was patronizing toward his charges, but regarded them as "affably disposed." King contended that Crook's troops had "no especial difficulty in fraternizing" with the Crows . . . .

The value of Indian scouts as mediators between hostile Indians and the frontier army was powerfully demonstrated in the final stages of the so-called Sioux Uprising of 1890 to 1891. The year before the Ghost Dance reached the Dakota Sioux, Lieutenant Casey had been authorized to train Northern Cheyennes as regular soldiers at Fort Keogh in Montana. But the fifty-six Cheyenne scouts trained ultimately proved more useful to the army because of their powers of persuasion than because of their military prowess. "Casey's Scouts" were not participants in the tragic events known as the Wounded Knee Massacre. But they personally saw the corpses of the Sioux victims, mostly women and children, and they condemned the conduct of the Seventh Cavalrymen responsible for the deaths. After the massacre Casey's scouts communicated daily with the remaining Ghost Dancers, led by the defiant Oglala, Kicking Bear. As the scouts drummed home the idea that continued resistance was futile, growing numbers defected from Kicking Bear's camp. Finally, on January 16, 1891, Kicking Bear himself surrendered to General Miles at the Pine Ridge agency, ending the Sioux Uprising.

In 1877 the frontier army's Indian scouts and friendlies were critically important to several military commanders who attempted to get the great Oglala war leader Crazy Horse to surrender. These attempts involved the use of Indians who were Crazy Horse's traditional enemies and allies, as well as his relatives and fellow tribesmen. Late in 1876 Miles sent Indian runners from Fort Keogh to try to persuade Crazy Horse to surrender. On December 16, 1876, with his followers hungry, sick, demoralized, and dwindling in numbers, Crazy Horse was moving down the Tongue River toward Fort Keogh to accept the inevitable. The Oglala leader had sent a peace delegation of five headmen toward the post to learn Miles' terms. But Miles' Crow scouts, hunting in the nearby hills, spotted the Sioux delegation before the soldiers did. The Crows charged the delegates, killed all five, scalped the dead, and went whooping in triumph back to the post. Miles was furious with his Crows for depriving him of the honor of capturing Crazy Horse. He punished them by taking away their horses and sending the animals along with a gift of tobacco and a sincere apology to Crazy Horse. The Oglala leader refused the gifts and went back to the Powder River country to spend the rest of the winter.

From his headquarters at Camp Robinson General Crook was also anxious to win the honor of bringing Crazy Horse in. Crook sent the Brulé chief Spotted Tail, an uncle of Crazy Horse, to the Powder River camp of the Oglala. Spotted Tail did not find his nephew, but did learn from Crazy Horse's father that the Powder River camp of about four hundred lodges of Cheyennes and Oglala planned to go into the Red Cloud agency as soon as weather permitted. Crook was delighted with the news.

When the Oglala chief Red Cloud learned that his rival Spotted Tail, then chief of all the Sioux at the Red Cloud agency, was being credited with persuading Crazy Horse to surrender, he was both angry and jealous. Lieutenant Clark, the military head of the Red Cloud agency was also jealous of a rival, namely Crook.

Both Clark and Red Cloud hoped to win the honor of bringing Crazy Horse in. So Clark sent Red Cloud to Crazy Horse's camp with agency rations, gifts, and instructions to escort the recalcitrants in. Late in April of 1877, Red Cloud found Crazy Horse with over five hundred followers moving slowly toward the agency. Historian Stephen Ambrose accurately summed up the situation when he wrote: "Spotted Tail had stolen Crazy Horse from Miles for Crook; now Red Cloud was to steal Crazy Horse from Spotted Tail for Clark." On May 6, 1877, Crazy Horse surrendered for the first and last time to Lieutenant Clark.

That the army's control over a Sioux faction—Crook had sixty Sioux scouts with him in his winter campaign of 1876 to 1877—helped persuade Crazy Horse's band to give up is evident from the remark of former Commissioner of Indian Affairs George W. Manypenny. As Manypenny recalled, High Bear, one of Crazy Horse's followers, stated at the time of the band's surrender: "You sent for us to come in, and we knew that some of our people were with you, and we did not wish to fight them, and so we came." The day after Crazy Horse's capitulation, Miles first used the Cheyennes as scouts in an expedition up the Rosebud that crushed Lame Deer's band of Miniconjou Sioux. Lame Deer's defeat marked the end of the Great Sioux War.

One of the most intriguing issues relating to the frontier army's use of Indian scouts, allies, and auxiliaries is the question of why Indians lent their services to an institution whose mission was the conquest of America's aboriginal inhabitants. Undoubtedly, each Indian had his own reasons for choosing to assist the frontier army. It is evident from anecdotal evidence, however, that many eagerly lent assistance to the army in order to strike a blow at their traditional intertribal enemies. As historian Thomas W. Dunlay states:

> Historical emphasis on Indian-white conflict tends to obscure the fact that Indians interacted long before white contact became significant. Intertribal conflicts and alliances had an importance often more immediate than any problems or pressures created by whites. For many Indians an alliance with the army offered hope of turning the tables on a powerful enemy who represented an immediate and obvious menace.

Rush Roberts, whose Pawnee name was Ahrekahrard, interviewed when he was ninety-five years old, recalled that he had enlisted in North's famous battalion of Pawnee scouts "because the Sioux and Cheyennes were our enemies and I had this chance to operate against them."

As for those Indians whom the army used against their own people, it should be recognized that such scouts and auxiliaries normally believed that by assisting the army they could actually serve their kin. James J. Cook, an army scout himself, recognized that Indian scouts "employed to lead soldiers against their own parents and relatives" were *not* "traitors to their own people." Instead, they were, as Cook saw it, "generally" men "endowed with sense enough to see that there was absolutely no use in the Indians fighting against the white soldiers." The scouts wisely realized that the whites were too numerous and that "there could be out one ending—the Indian would be exterminated."

The two Chiricahua Apache scouts Martine and Kayitah are cases in point. In 1886, hoping to see Apache resistance come to an end, they volunteered both to seek out Geronimo's renegades in Mexico and to induce them to talk with Miles about surrender. Both aims were accomplished. The daring scouts found Geronimo and succeeded in persuading him to surrender for the final time.

Indian scouts also hoped that in the frontier army's campaigns against their own people, situations would arise in which they could be of assistance to their relatives and friends. Such situations often occurred. Jason Betzinez, a cousin and lifelong associate of Geronimo, recounted that in early September of 1877 the principal Warm Springs Apache chiefs Victorio and Loco led a band of 310 of their tribe and some Chiricahuas in a break from their confinement on Arizona's San Carlos Reservation. Soon soldiers and Apache scouts from neighboring Fort Thomas were on their trail. The pursuers overtook and captured several families whom they returned to the hated San Carlos. But, as the nearly one-hundred-year-old Betzinez remembered, the Apache scouts empathized with the fugitives and permitted most of them to return to the more congenial Warm Springs Reservation without further molestation.

Indian scouts often found themselves in situations where they could restrain the army's harshness or where they could selectively enforce the soldiers' orders to the benefit of their Indian relatives and friends. Scouts also found that army service enabled them to be helpful to their own people in a variety of other ways. James Kaywaykla, a Warm Springs Apache whose stepfather, Kaytennae, was a scout for the frontier army, offered additional reasons why Indians enlisted even when the army was campaigning against their own people. Kaywaykla remarked that when his stepfather was asked why he had joined the scouts, he [Kaytennae] explained that he had learned English well enough to "see to it that the interpreters did not twist the meaning of the messages they conveyed to the cavalry," and that army service also enabled him to "check on the scouts" themselves.

Undoubtedly, Indians also enlisted because the army provided one of the few opportunities for gainful employment available to reservation and off-reservation Indians. Most Indians lived a hand-to-mouth existence without such work. Soldier, an Arikara scout stationed at Fort Stevenson, admitted that "the sight of the green paper money" in his hands made his heart leap with happiness. After their discharge from the army the Indian scouts received pensions. In 1931 Wooden Leg claimed that he and a few other Northern Cheyennes who had served as army scouts were the rich men of their tribe because of these pensions. Owing to his service as a scout at Fort Keogh, Wooden Leg subsequently received pension money each month. In his words: "For a while it was twenty dollars monthly. Then it was increased to thirty dollars. Now [1931] it is forty dollars. As I grow older it will be further increased." As late as 1967, John Stands In Timber, a Northern Cheyenne whose grandfather was killed in the Battle of the Little Bighorn, knew two Cheyenne widows who were still drawing pensions because of their husbands' service as army scouts.

Furthermore, the scouts' families were entitled to other fringe benefits. John Rope, a Western Apache who enlisted on the San Carlos Reservation, was delighted because his spouse as well as the other scouts' wives were each allowed to draw out five dollars' worth of supplies monthly from the commissary at Fort Thomas. Chris, a Mescalero Apache whose father joined a company of scouts which twice overlook Geronimo's renegades, remembered that the government gave the scouts' families tools and fences that enabled his father to become a small farmer.

Another economic incentive for enlistment or lending assistance to the army was the hope to gain plunder, especially horses, from the defeated hostiles, or for that matter from whites. In 1877 General Howard made use of about twenty Bannock scouts in his efforts to overtake Chief Joseph's runaway Nez Perce. Howard had great difficulty in controlling the Bannocks, who helped themselves to forty horses belonging to whites along the route of their march. The angry Howard imprisoned his Bannocks in a guarded tent until all of the horses had been returned to their rightful owners. The army also asked the Crows to help run down Chief Joseph's fugitives. But the Crows had been longtime friends of the Nez Perce and were unwilling to shed their blood. Leforge recounted that although the army's Crow scouts "affected to array themselves against the Nez Perces," in reality "their warlike operations were restricted to the capture of ponies."

The Crow chiefs informed Lieutenant Gustavus Doane that one of their major reasons for assisting the army in its campaign against the Sioux and Cheyenne in 1877 was to adopt and assimilate any captive women and children. The Crow desire to maintain their population at a critical mass by adopting enemy captives exemplifies the complexity of Indian motives for assisting the frontier army.

Army service also afforded Indian men, many of whom took great pride in their personal courage and martial skills, an opportunity and the means to demonstrate their valor and military prowess. Normally their arms were taken from them at the time they took up residence on a reservation. James Kaywaykla was keenly aware of the importance to a warrior of being singled out by the army for his fighting ability and also of having a rifle. In Kaywaykla's words: "Ours was a race of fighting men—war was our occupation. A rifle was our most cherished possession. And though the scouts were permitted to have only five bullets at a time, and had to account for each one fired, a weapon is a weapon. And, believe me, there was not a man who did not envy the scout his rifle." Service with the army thus enabled many an Indian scout to regain his self-esteem.

Eugene Chihuahua, a Chiricahua Apache whose father, Chihuahua, signed on as a scout at Fort Apache, echoed Kaywaykla's sentiments in stating that one reason his father had enlisted was to obtain a rifle and ammunition. But in the son's mind the paramount motive for his father's enlistment was that he "could leave his wife and children and know that they would be protected." Chihuahua also enlisted, according to his son, because he "didn't like living on a reservation."

It is apparent that many Indians shared Chihuahua's aversion to reservation life. One reason that Kaywaykla enrolled as a scout for Crook was because it was, in his words, "a relief from the dreary, monotonous existence of the reservation." Grinnell affirmed that four hundred Pawnee males eagerly hoped to enlist under Frank North in 1876 because of the harsh realities of their lives on the reservation. "Each man," said Grinnell, "at any cost, sought to get away from the suffering of his present life; from the fever that made him quake, the chill that caused him to shiver, and above all from the deadly monotony of the reservation life."

It is also evident that some Indians hoped that by supporting the frontier army they would ingratiate themselves with the power that would ultimately prevail and determine their fates. Kaywaykla lamented that Chato, a Chiricahua, enlisted as a scout because he "invariably allied himself with what he thought would be the winning side," so as to reap the spoils of victory. No Indian better understood the benefits that his people had derived from aligning themselves with the whites than the great Crow chief and army scout Plenty Coups. He was later overjoyed that his people had early realized that the white men "were strong, without number in their own country, and that there was no good in fighting them." As Plenty Coups saw it, the Crow chiefs' decision to help the whites was reached,

> not because we loved the white man who was already crowding other tribes into our country, or because we hated the Sioux, Cheyenne, and Arapahoe, but because we plainly saw that this cause was the only one which might save our beautiful country for us. When I think back my heart sings because we acted as we did. It was the only way open to us.

No treatment of Indian motives for rendering assistance to the frontier army would be complete without the recognition of a crucial but generally ignored historical fact: The frontier army often employed coercion to obtain compliance from the so-called friendlies. To be sure, some friendlies longed for a return to the warrior's life, and there were many instances when Indians were more than willing to help the army defeat old tribal enemies, along with the previously mentioned motives that encouraged voluntary enlistments. But army commanders also commonly relied on intimidation, compulsion, the offer of bribes, and on the abject dependence of reservation Indians to acquire their services. The army's strong-arm tactics are not surprising. Commissioned and noncommissioned officers generally sought to win unquestioning obedience to orders by instilling in white private soldiers fear of the punishments for disobedience. No Indian would have been considered deserving of less drastic measures to obtain compliance. . . .

The frontier army's conquest of the Sioux and Cheyennes on the northern Plains was largely the result of the important contributions of its Indian allies. Colonel Dodge, who participated in the final campaigns, claimed that the "hostiles" were conquered because of Crook's "genius, courage, and persistency." Crook had "dared, in spite of the wails of the humanitarians, to adopt the Roman method, and fight fire with fire." Dodge pointed out that Crook had enlisted three hundred "friendly" Indians, who, "acting in conjunction with the troops, so beleaguered the hostile savages, that their combination was soon broken up." Because the Sioux and Cheyenne reservations had been removed from the Indian Bureau's grip and placed under the control of the War Department, Crook was able to seize the opportunity to recruit Indian warriors and scouts. George Hyde, often called "the dean of Indian historians," argued that Crook "had practically forced the Sioux to serve as scouts."

The reformer, George Manypenny, contended that Crook had deceived the Indians at the Red Cloud and Spotted Tail agencies into believing that they were enlisting to campaign against the so-called Northern Indians (usually a term applied to the non-agency bands), not against their own people. Historian Mari Sandoz maintained that Crook's subordinate, MacKenzie, failed to tell his Cheyenne scouts that they were on their way to attack their relatives in Dull Knife's camp on the Powder River late in November 1876. Upon learning en route of their true quarry, the scouts strongly objected. Crook and MacKenzie quieted their Cheyennes, wrote Sandoz, "with the promise to work for a good agency for all the Cheyennes." Having received this promise, the Cheyenne scouts led the soldiers, together with the Pawnee battalion, to Dull Knife's village and helped destroy it. Then to their anguish the defeated Northern Cheyennes were sent to new homes in Indian Territory. There they died in alarming numbers during the winter of 1877 to 1878. Finally, in September 1878, chiefs Dull Knife and Little Wolf fled northward with about three hundred desperate followers. After dividing in Nebraska, Little Wolf's adherents managed to elude the troops during the winter of 1878 to 1879. By late March 1879, largely because of the efforts of Miles' Cheyenne scouts under Two Moon, Little Wolf's band was forced to give up. The able-bodied men in the band were enlisted as army scouts. One of those Cheyenne scouts later told Grinnell: "My friend, I was a prisoner of war for four years, and all the time was fighting for the man [Miles] who had captured me."

That unknown Cheyenne scout accurately characterized his own status as well as that of hundreds of other Indian scouts, allies, and auxiliaries. They were prisoners of war pure and simple. Occasionally, soldiers in the frontier army acknowledged that disagreeable truth. Lieutenant Clark, himself a commander of Indian scouts, referred to the nearly five hundred Cheyennes located at or near Fort Keogh in the early 1880s as "prisoners of war." Most army officers preferred to view such Indian friendlies as willing volunteers who served the army of their own accord, by their free choice, and without compulsion or obligation. Such was by no means the case. Perhaps the army officers' prevailing illusion helps to explain why Sheridan declined to approve Lieutenant Richard Henry Pratt's recommendation to enlist as scouts fifty or sixty Indian prisoners confined in the damp recesses of Fort Marion in St. Augustine, Florida.

In conclusion, it should be stated that Indian scouts, allies, and auxiliaries were unquestionably essential supplements of the frontier army in its struggles against hostile Indians in the late nineteenth century. Richard Irving Dodge was categorically correct when he declared that the army's Indians were "invaluable, indeed indispensable to success against Indians." Unfortunately for the frontier army, its commanders were slow to realize the vital importance of their Indian associates. Initially, proud military commanders thought that the dependence on large numbers of Indian allies would suggest that the army had grave deficiencies. Some commanders also considered the friendlies deficient in soldierly attributes, uncontrollable, and liable to commit atrocities. Furthermore, there were often genuine doubts about the true loyalties of the so-called friendlies. In the end, however, hard necessities compelled the frontier army to rely heavily upon Indian scouts, allies, and auxiliaries.

They performed beyond the army's highest expectations, routinely exceeding the achievements of white regular soldiers. Lieutenant Britton Davis, for instance, called attention to the deficiencies of regular troops that stood in stark contrast to the abilities of the Apache scouts who ran down Geronimo's renegades in their hideouts in Mexico's Sonoran mountains:

> . . . we found that to wear the hostiles down with regular troops was impossible. Without Apache scouts they [the soldiers] could not follow the trails; nor had they the endurance to keep up with the scouts in these mountains where the scouts had been born and bred. They were only a hindrance to rapid movement where rapid movement was essential to success. As well match Londoners against the Alpine Swiss.

"We Will Make It Our Own Place"

Agriculture and Adaptation at the Grand Ronde Reservation, 1856–1887

TRACY NEAL LEAVELLE

"The Americans will never leave us alone. Let us not concern our hearts. . . . We will take [Grand Ronde]. . . . [W]e will make it our own place." These words represent a dramatic decision and transformative vision that emerged in the Native communities of western Oregon in the 1850s. A member of the Tualatin band of Kalapuyans, perhaps Peter Kinai, recalled them for linguist Albert S. Gatschet in 1877. Gatschet's informant related an episode in which the respected Tualatin elder Ki-a-kuts consulted the Tualatins during their treaty negotiations with Joel Palmer in 1855. Ki-a-kuts asked the other members of the band if they wanted to trade their land around Wappato Lake for a portion of the Grand Ronde Valley. Despite reluctance to abandon their native lands, they resolved to accept the new, hopefully more secure home and transform their lives. The year following the treaty council, the Tualatins and other Indians from throughout western Oregon commenced the long project to make Grand Ronde their own.

Between 1856, when the first Indians settled at the Grand Ronde Reservation, and 1887, when the Dawes Act initiated a comprehensive program of allotment, Grand Ronde residents formed a new cultural homeland. They created a reservation culture that looked ahead to a modern Indian future while also relying on the strength of past traditions. In the 1850s the Native peoples of western Oregon's interior valleys recognized that they lived in an age that would not allow them to follow easily in the paths of their ancestors. They traded their vast lands and a life of gathering and hunting for a valley haven and the opportunity to make new lives. In facing the chaos of beginning this endeavor and making the transition to reservation life, the Indians of Grand Ronde demonstrated creativity, flexibility, and initiative. They selectively adapted their culture to meet the physical, social, political, and emotional demands of their situation. They actively pursued an agricultural life and accepted Christianity, yet they also hesitated to send their children to agency schools and continued to seek the advice and the healing powers of Indian doctors. Contrary to the commonly held view that hunter-gatherers resisted incorporation of agriculture into their lives, the Indians at Grand Ronde made agriculture the foundation for an independence that allowed them to mold a new Indian culture and identity that gave meaning to the reservation experience.

Reservations have often been perceived as places of decline and dependence, as sites where Indian peoples confronted an incomplete assimilation within a larger society that abused or ignored them. Critics observe that economic development and Indian agriculture on most reservations have never been adequate. They note

Tracy Neal Leavelle, "We Will Make It Our Own Place: Agriculture and Adaptation at the Grande Ronde Reservation, 1856–1887," *American Indian Quarterly,* vol. 22, no. 4 (Fall 1998), 433–456. Reprinted by permission of the University of Nebraska Press. Copyright © 1999 by the University of Nebraska Press.

that residents often have been dependent on an inconsistent and unfeeling government for support. In the late nineteenth and early twentieth centuries, reservation agents and Indian Office inspectors blamed persistent traditional cultural attitudes among their Indian wards for these failures. Furthermore, historians of the early reservation period have frequently portrayed the reservation experience as destructive, lamenting the loss of Native cultural traditions and the dearth of appropriate and meaningful replacements. The Navajos of the late nineteenth century, who maintained a relative independence through the expansion of stockraising, are a prominent exception to this pattern. Generally, however, it is easier to recall the dramatic decimation of California's Indian communities, Big Foot lying dead in the snow at Wounded Knee, the racist assumptions of assimilationist government programs, and the tragic loss of Native lands throughout the country. Although bleak images have a foundation in the difficult and challenging realities of reservation life during the last century and a half, Indians turned these prisons into homelands, important "places where a native identity could be maintained and passed on to new generations."

In recent years, historians of the reservation era increasingly have tried to counter the simplistic image of defeated and despondent Indians by emphasizing the adaptability of Indian communities. These scholars reject crude acculturation and persistence models as unrealistically static interpretive frameworks that reduce Native peoples to passive objects of government policies and victims of changing social and economic conditions. Highlighting the new strategies, symbols, and identities created and employed in making the transition to reservation life paints a more subtle, three-dimensional portrait that restores agency to Indian individuals and communities. The story of Grand Ronde offers a particularly vivid example of people drawing from a deep well of cultural creativity to assert some control over their destinies in a time of limited options and difficult choices.

On 19 January 1856, twenty Luckiamute Indians arrived in the Grand Ronde Valley, at the headwaters of the South Yamhill River, to settle on just over 60,000 acres of land reserved for the exclusive use of the Indians of western Oregon. Coming in a difficult winter season of dampness and cold, they found only unprepared and overwhelmed government agents to greet them and canvas tents for shelter. Two weeks later some three hundred Upper Umpquas and Yoncalla Kalapuyans ended their long trek to Grand Ronde from the river valleys of southern Oregon. At the end of March, 395 Rogue River Indians from numerous bands stumbled into the reservation after a month-long journey of over 250 miles. During the next several months, armed escorts drove hundreds more Indians to the reservation. The violence of the Rogue River Wars that flared in the interior and coastal valleys of southwestern Oregon between 1853 and 1856 had defeated many Indians. Others, like the Kalapuyan bands that held on to scattered plots of land in their native Willamette Valley, had to make way for the thousands of incoming immigrants who coveted their rich lands. In June 1857, after many of the coastal Indians and most of the Rogue River Indians moved west to the recently formed Coast Reservation, a census listed the Indian population of Grand Ronde as close to twelve hundred.

The people who settled the reserve shared many cultural traits and traditions. The Indians of western Oregon were gathering and hunting peoples who relied on a variety of food resources to meet subsistence needs. From the spring through the fall, families and bands lived in transitory camps. Women, children, and probably older men harvested food staples such as camas and wappato roots, acorns and berries, while men fished and hunted. In the winter months, bands settled in villages for annual ceremonies and a period of social visiting. The villages, consisting primarily of patrilocal extended families, formed the basic unit of political organization. Gradations in wealth and prestige between chiefs, commoners, and slaves marked social distinctions within the societies. Wealthy men and village leaders owned slaves and could have more than one wife. The Indians of western Oregon also shared similar beliefs in the guardian-spirit powers available to shamans and, sometimes, to other individuals. Exchange, intermarriage, and intermittent cooperation fostered connections between the many Indian groups of western Oregon.

The bands that arrived at Grand Ronde were culturally and socially familiar to each other, but variations in these broad cultural patterns and in historical experience gave each band a unique heritage. The mix of subsistence items, the content and form of religious beliefs and winter ceremonies, and the emphasis on wealth gradations varied from band to band. The many languages spoken by the Grand Ronde bands represented the most dramatic element of cultural diversity on the reservation. The settlers of Grand Ronde spoke many mutually unintelligible languages. The Kalapuyan bands alone spoke three different Kalapuyan languages. As for other bands, the Clackamas of the lower Willamette Valley spoke Upper Chinookan, the Upper Umpquas were Athapaskan, and the Cow Creeks and Rogue Rivers of southern Oregon utilized Takelman dialects. The Molalas of the western Cascades spoke yet another tongue, and people of mixed French and Indian ancestry often used Canadian French. In western Oregon and at Grand Ronde people relied on Chinook jargon, the lingua franca of the region, to cope with this linguistic diversity. Consequently, shared cultural practices and attitudes and the common reservation experience helped the Indians of Grand Ronde overcome the challenges of this diversity to forge an Indian identity rooted in the place and the history of their valley home.

Joel Palmer, who in 1853 became Superintendent of Indian Affairs for the Territory of Oregon, directed the removal of Indians to the Grand Ronde Reservation. Palmer faced the difficult task of halting the conflicts between Indians and White settlers in the territory. He concluded that separating the antagonists represented the only hope for peace in the fertile valleys and resource-rich mountains of western Oregon. Moreover, he believed that separation and confinement on reservations offered Indians their only chance for survival as well as the opportunity to ascend to a better, more "civilized" life. Between 1853 and 1855, Palmer worked incessantly to negotiate treaties with the Indians of western Oregon that extinguished their title to the land and opened it for continued American settlement. He signed treaties with the Rogue River Indians, the Cow Creek band of Umpquas, the Umpquas and Yoncalla Kalapuyans, the many Kalapuyan bands of the Willamette Valley, and the Southern Molalas. The territory the Indians ceded included virtually all of Oregon between the main ridges of the Cascades and the Coast Range. On 30 June 1857, President James Buchanan signed an executive order making Grand Ronde the permanent home for these bands.

Reservation policy was well developed in the United States when the Grand Ronde agency opened. Policy makers believed reservations offered a reasonable solution to the problems then plaguing relations between Indians and Whites in the West. Confinement of the Indians reduced and regulated their contact with Whites. Reservation advocates thought a strict separation would reduce tensions and end deadly confrontations. Reservations, it seemed, were the only alternative to the otherwise inevitable extinction of the Indian race. Close containment and control of Indians had the additional benefit of making them available for programs of civilization designed to produce sedentary Christian agriculturalists on the pattern of the idealized yeoman farmer. In this view, reservations were the crucibles of "civilization" out of which new Indian communities and societies would emerge to become part of the expanding Republic.

Agriculture was at the very heart of this government policy of directed culture change well into the twentieth century. The government wanted hunting and gathering peoples like the Indians of western Oregon to give up their seasonal migrations and settle permanently to farm and raise stock on individual plots of land scattered across the reservations. The government expected men to conduct the agricultural labor while women managed the family's domestic economy. Reservation agents intended that Indians learn the value of private property and disciplined labor and hoped that communal ties to clan, band, and tribe would give way to a more individualistic ethos of personal improvement and economic advancement. While their parents worked in field and home, many children attended schools ostensibly designed to reinforce these lessons of modernity. They learned English, other academic basics, and sometimes the skills needed to run an agricultural operation. Teachers worked to suppress Indian languages and other expressions of Native culture and tried to instill in their students the accepted habits of White Christian America.

In the late nineteenth century, with the expansion of the allotment program and the growth of the boarding school movement, these efforts to transform Indians intensified. The ultimate goal was to assimilate them into American society as agricultural producers and citizens and bring about the final breakup of the reservations themselves. The Indian Office followed closely these various comprehensive and complementary policies at Grand Ronde.

In their first years on the reservation, the diverse bands that settled at Grand Ronde faced the numerous challenges of beginning and sustaining agricultural operations. Although preparations for opening the reservation in 1856 were simply inadequate for the large number of Indians who settled there, a much more serious issue for the long term turned out to be the land itself. When Superintendent James W. Nesmith made his 1858 annual report to the Commissioner of Indian Affairs, he complained that "the soil [at Grand Ronde] is a cold, heavy clay, and unproductive. The position is elevated and exposed to violent sea breezes which, at certain seasons, have a deleterious effect upon the growing crops." Unpredictable weather and difficult soil conditions often conspired to reduce yields on Indian farms.

Although some individuals and bands had experimented with stock raising and perhaps with farming before going to Grand Ronde, most, if not all, needed instruction in agricultural techniques. The guidance they received, however, was inconsistent at best. Farmers hired to teach the Indians and to run the agency farm came and went with alarming frequency. The salary was low, the work was difficult, and alternative opportunities were abundant in Oregon. Treaty stipulations that required the agent to employ farmers for the Indians ran out after five years for all bands except the Upper Umpquas, Yoncallas, and Southern Molalas. For these bands the provision for keeping a farmer ended after only ten years.

The lack of proper equipment and sufficient working stock also presented enormous obstacles to efficient subsistence production. In a deposition taken in an 1862 investigation into allegations of incompetence against the reservation agent, several band leaders expressed disappointment at not being supplied with the means to work their land satisfactorily. The grain the Indians managed to raise under these trying conditions often could not even be milled on the reservation. Despite the promises of reservation agents and the expectations of the superintendent, the grist mill was not completed until 1858, and for years thereafter it was constantly in disrepair.

By the late 1860s and early 1870s, however, many people began to enjoy some success in their agricultural endeavors. In September 1869, in response to rumors that they would be removed to make way for Whites, representatives of thirteen bands had a letter written to President Ulysses S. Grant to make "known some of [their] desires, hopes, and fears." In the missive, they told Grant, "We now know how to farm, how to build our houses and barns, how to cook and sew. . . . The land produces well. . . . We have built houses and barns and many of us have made rails and fenced our lands, believing that this was to be our home." Grand Ronde Agent Charles Lafollett predicted that the year's harvest, despite some problems with the weather, would support all but the elderly and the orphaned, who would need government support. He estimated that the Indians had at least eight hundred acres of wheat, five hundred acres of oats, and fifty acres of potatoes and other root vegetables under cultivation.

To supplement the products of farming, the Indians continued many of their traditional subsistence practices. Women and children gathered berries, dug camas and wappato roots, and collected edible seeds and plants, all important items in the pre-reservation diet. The men hunted and fished in the area, taking deer, elk, and small game from the forests and trout and salmon from the mountain streams. In 1862 an agent had allowed the Indians to begin making seasonal fishing excursions to the Salmon River near the coast, and in 1865 they constructed a road to the fishery and made further improvements at the site.

Indians at Grand Ronde complemented such subsistence activities with wage labor in a new seasonal cycle. During the summer months, after the crops were in the ground, hundreds of people obtained passes from the agent and left Grand Ronde for the Willamette Valley to work for White farmers. Men chopped wood and worked in the fields as laborers, an important opportunity to learn and polish agricultural skills while earning cash. Labor was in such short supply in Oregon that they reportedly received fair wages for their work. For their part, women cooked, did laundry and housework, and gathered Native food items. Women also sold handwoven baskets to Whites, made with traditional materials in the patterns and forms their White customers desired.

The money the men and women earned was crucial not only in the short term to help make ends meet from year to year, but also in reaching the long-term goal of establishing successful agricultural operations and nourishing and maintaining a fragile independence. Their harvests did not yet produce the surpluses necessary to generate an income from participation in the market, and the government did not supply many of their basic needs, such as clothes. In a council held in 1871 with Felix R. Brunot, a member of the Board of Indian Commissioners, Joe Hutchings complained that the agents had not done anything for them. He reportedly said, "You see our houses; we worked outside and made money and bought them. . . . Our people go outside and get horses, and they get harness [*sic*], and plow with them." Henry Kilke remarked, "I have a wagon; I bought it. My house I got the same way. My clothes I bought; the Government never gave me any of them. . . . Now we want to know what we will get for our lands [given up in treaties]. We need a grist-mill, harness and horses, and plows and wagons, and that is all we want."

Many of the Indians at the agency also wanted individual allotments. The focus on the disaster that occurred with implementation of the General Allotment or Dawes Act—the widespread alienation of Indian lands and a decline in Indian farming—has obscured the history of allotment prior to 1887. Concentration on the generally poor outcome of the Dawes Act itself has resulted in neglect of Indian perspectives on allotment before and after the destructive act. The loss of Indian land in the twentieth century was as dramatic at Grand Ronde as elsewhere, but these terrible consequences lay beyond the horizon during the reservation's first three decades. For many people at Grand Ronde, allotment appeared to offer stability and some guarantees for their future in a reservation agricultural community. Allotment also seemed to promise eventual acceptance as full citizens of the state and nation.

The treaties with the Kalapuyans and the Umpquas provided for the survey and allotment of reservation land, to be done at the discretion of the U.S. president, in plots from 20 to 120 acres in size. As early in 1860, Agent John F. Miller had assigned small portions of land to individuals in an effort to encourage farming, but the allotment of the reservation as called for in the treaties had yet to begin. In response to the delays, people on the reservation consistently agitated for the full procedure to be carried out. In 1862, in the deposition given in the investigation of the Grand Ronde agent, Tom and John Chamberlin of the Rogue Rivers, Quakata of the Molalas, Peter of the Yamhills, and Ki-a-kuts of the Tualatin band expressed a desire among their people for creating individual allotments. Yet, in 1869, the agent noted that several bands still farmed communally fenced lands. In their letter of the same year to President Grant, Grand Ronde leaders complained, "We have been here a long time and do not know where our lands are, therefore we can not improve them. If our lands had been surveyed . . . we would have known that they were . . . our own land and that we could not be ordered by our Agent to leave them and plow and sow at his pleasure, we would by this time been able to support ourselves."

Government officials, also anxious to implement an allotment program at Grand Ronde, believed it would encourage improvement of lands, further the agricultural program, and move the Indians ever closer to American citizenship. By September 1871, the surveys had finally been completed and only awaited the proper approvals from Washington. A year later, the allotting of lands to individuals commenced under the direction of Agent Peter B. Sinnott. The superintendent of Indian Affairs for Oregon, T. B. Odeneal, was present, and he observed that the Indians were pleased with the program. He further noted that many people would have to build new houses and that most would need to fence their lots. While up to that time their houses had generally been built in clusters according to band, they would in the future be more widely scattered across the valley.

The following year, in 1873, Sinnott reported that the Indians had been so busy constructing houses and barns, putting up fences, and making other improvements that fewer people than usual left the reservation for the now traditional summer work. He gushed, "It is conceded by all who are conversant with Indian affairs who have visited this agency, that the Indians are far in advance of any other tribes of the Pacific coast." Other observers made similar assertions. Perhaps Sinnott was trying to boost his reputation with such a statement, but he had only been on the job for a year and a half and so could not take much of the credit. In any case, the Indians at Grand Ronde had received their allotments and were building what was for them a new kind of community based on the family farm.

Residents also formed other institutions to guide reservation society and to support the transition to a new way of life. In 1869 the leaders who sent the letter to President Grant wrote that the people at Grand Ronde "respect the laws of the whites, as well as our own." In the early 1870s, with the support of the reservation agent, elected leaders of the bands began meeting annually in a legislature, where they gradually put these laws into writing. The preamble to the 1873 legislative record stated that "the laws . . . were enacted for the Government of the Indians, to preserve order, to maintain the laws, and to qualify them for the position which they will have to fill as Citizens of the State of Oregon before many years."

Once they were functioning as a legislative body, the representatives indeed began to make laws that met the needs of their community and that respected their own traditions and standards as well as those of the surrounding White society. They passed laws regulating estate issues and divorce, setting the fines for property crimes, assault, rape, and adultery, and banning the possession of liquor on the reservation. They also instituted an Indian court to hear complaints and to punish those who violated reservation law. The court met the first Monday of every month and on each Saturday for cases demanding immediate action. The court directed jury trials that included prosecuting attorneys, witnesses, a sheriff, and a clerk, and a presiding justice. Justices also made administrative rulings and approved contracts between reservation residents.

The legislature tried as well to promote agriculture on the reservation. In 1873 it voted to hold an annual reservation fair each September "for the encouragement of the people of Grand Ronde Indian Reservation in farming, stock raising and general improvement." Four years later, the legislature set up a fund in the treasury to make short term loans to reservation residents. Some of the fund was held in wheat and oats, ten bushels of which could be borrowed on the promise of returning twelve bushels to the treasury after harvest. Another law passed in the same session set the rules for use of a threshing machine, which anyone could utilize for a percentage of the crop. The machine increased the community's independence by reducing the need to hire the equipment and time of outsiders to process the harvest. Grand Ronde Indians also operated four reapers of their own.

By the late 1870s and early 1880s, the agricultural community at Grand Ronde was maturing. The development of a largely self-sustaining community was necessary because treaty support ended for the Rogue River bands after sixteen years and for the other bands after twenty. Future appropriations would come only at the discretion of a budget-conscious Congress. In 1877 Agent Sinnott reported that the Indians met 90 percent of their subsistence needs through agricultural pursuits, with the remaining 10 percent coming from fishing, hunting, and gathering. According to Sinnott, the government issued no rations. The following year he estimated that the Indians obtained 95 percent of their provisions through farming and again he issued no rations. He reported that farmers had 3,000 acres under cultivation on the reservation and that they owned over 600 horses, 28 mules, 339 head of cattle, and over 400 sheep.

Reservation residents enjoyed displaying this wealth. The Reverend R. W. Summers, who visited the agency on the Fourth of July, 1877, described a bounteous feast and celebration the Indians held. Groups of people entered the festival grounds in processions, wearing "their most gorgeous garments." They invited Summers "to view the tables neatly spread with spotless linen and a lavish display of china & dainties." They informed him that the tables would look even better once the cakes and pies were laid out. A boy of fourteen mounted a wagon and recited the Declaration of Independence before the crowd. Someone then gave a speech that was in some ways an Indian declaration of independence. The orator pointed to the orderly community they had built at Grand Ronde and said they loved their homes and wished to live and die there. They had given up their former possessions for this place and would not, he said, be taken from their homes and moved to some other location to make way for greedy Whites. Like other Indian communities in the United States, the people of Grand Ronde employed the Fourth of July holiday and festivities for their own purposes. In the context of the great American festival, Grand Ronde residents celebrated connections to their new homeland, recognized progress, and looked ahead to the future.

Inspectors from the Indian Office in Washington, on their tours of Western reserves in the early 1880s, noted the transformation of the previous twenty-five years. One commented in 1880 that Grand Ronde was "the first Indian agency yet visited by [him] where *all of the Indians* live in houses, understand the English language and engage with reasonable diligence in civilized pursuits. The first one where all are able to support themselves and want to become citizens." An inspector reported in 1882 that Indians marketed a grain surplus in the nearby towns of Sheridan and Dallas.

Many reservation residents believed, however, that they could still improve their situation considerably. Some were anxious to obtain larger allotments so they could expand their operations, and concern over the permanency of the allotments that they already held continued to irritate them. Agent Sinnott admitted in 1879 that the allotments in severalty were not legally binding on the government. Although he argued that the government had a moral obligation to protect the possessions of the Indians, he concluded that, "if their removal becomes absolutely necessary," they should be compensated for their improvements. Regardless of any promises of compensation, the idea that they could be moved from their new homes without their consent disturbed the Grand Ronde Indians. In 1877 the orator at the Fourth of July festival called on the government to honor its commitment. Ten years later the Indians met with an inspector from the Indian Office and expressed their continuing fears that they would lose their farms.

Agriculture and the possession of land formed the foundation for building a viable and sustainable community at Grand Ronde, but the Indians asserted themselves in other areas as well. While schools were central to the civilizing mission the Office of Indian Affairs promoted, the Indians at Grand Ronde were skeptical consumers of the educational opportunities offered on the reservation. Government officials viewed schools as the most valuable tool for effecting the long-term transformation of Indian cultures that was the ultimate goal of reservation policy. Officials considered adults difficult to change because they often continued to manifest an interest in familiar Native traditions. Children became the focus of the educational project. Agents and teachers especially favored boarding schools in which children would be delivered from the "pernicious" influences of home and family. At boarding schools Indian students could receive a total education that included, in addition to the basics of reading, writing, and arithmetic, intensive practice in the agricultural and domestic arts, as well as the moral instruction deemed so important by those who perceived little of value in Native cultures.

Authorities opened a school within a year of beginning operations at the agency, but the teachers experienced continual frustration. John Ostrander reported that when he took charge of the school in August 1856, there were eighty students who attended irregularly. He complained that "they seemed to think it our sole business to minister to their wants, and that they were doing us a favor by attending school." Further problems erupted in 1857. According to Ostrander, an Indian medicine woman blamed him for a disease infecting the Indians. "The doctress," he explained, "said she distinctly saw the sickness that afflicted the tribes issue from the trumpet which I sounded to announce the hour of school, and settle like a mist upon the camp; and should I continue to sound it, in a few days all the Indians would be in their graves—the camp desolate." He quickly stopped using the trumpet, but over the years, as instructors came and went and schools opened and closed, agency teachers continued to complain about the mixed reception they and their institutions received on the reservation. The Indians of the Grand Ronde community shared with other Indians throughout the United States an ambivalent attitude toward the government's educational project.

In 1874, with religious denominations ascendant in the implementation of Indian policy in the United States, Catholic nuns from a succession of orders took charge of the reservation boarding school, also known as the manual labor school. The Sisters of the Holy Names of Jesus and Mary arrived in 1874 and worked until 1880, when their order recalled them. Sisters from St. Benedict's convent in Minnesota followed with less than a year of service. In 1882 the boarding school came under the direction of the Mount Angel Benedictine Sisters of Oregon.

Agent Sinnott, a Catholic himself, claimed the sisters soon had the school in a prosperous condition. Yet, according to his own statistics, the school was never even close to capacity. In 1879, for example, he recorded a school-age population at Grand Ronde of 180. The boarding school could accommodate fifty students and the day school thirty-five, but only thirty students attended school one month or more during the year, and average attendance was limited to twenty-five. The day school was not even open.

Agents and educators could only convince the Indians at Grand Ronde to send their children to agency schools when it served personal, family, or community interests. Statements at a council held in 1860 to determine whether the Indians preferred the current teacher or wished to bring a Catholic priest to the reservation revealed some of the things they considered important. Of the fourteen Indian leaders present for the conference, six stated they preferred a priest, but five men wanted neither the teacher nor a priest. Louis Nipissing, an Umpqua leader, refused to send his children to school because the Indians had not first been consulted on their needs and desires, but he was interested in securing the services of a priest. Joseph Sanagratti, a leader of a Kalapuyan band and one of the five opposed to maintaining a teacher, suggested, "In place of throwing away our money for schools as we have had, I would rather have the money used for the completion of the Grist Mill." Subsistence concerns and autonomy were simply higher priorities than having their children educated and indoctrinated in government schools.

However, some parents did send their children to school, indicating that they perceived benefits in doing so. Building the reservation community made certain skills quite valuable. Learning to speak, read, and write English and mastering basic math would have been important for the negotiation of the practical matters and bureaucratic challenges of running a farm and living on a reservation. The people who obtained these skills could then act as cultural brokers, as mediators between Indian and White worlds. In the manual labor school boys had the additional opportunity to learn agricultural skills in the school garden. Female students concentrated on the domestic arts. Parents probably sent their children to the schools long enough to learn these valuable skills, but otherwise expected them to contribute to the maintenance of the household. Some parents may also have used the boarding school, where children at least received some clothing and regular meals, as a survival strategy during lean months and years.

In their encounters with Christianity, the Indians at Grand Ronde also displayed skepticism. While many people eventually embraced it to one degree or another, Native traditions continued to hold an important place in reservation lives, and new indigenous religious movements offered further alternatives for spiritual renewal and community life. In 1860 Catholic priest Adrian J. Croquet arrived from Belgium to open a mission at Grand Ronde and stayed for the next thirty-eight years, working tirelessly to build and sustain a Christian Indian community. While itinerant Catholic and Protestant missionaries and interactions with settlers and Indian agents of various denominations exposed the Indians to Christianity, Croquet's arrival marked the beginning of a more intensive encounter with the Christian faith. Croquet, for his part, believed he was engaging in a struggle with two dangerous spiritual foes, the Protestants on the one hand and unbelief and spiritual delusion on the other, with the very souls of Grand Ronde's Indians hanging in the balance. Writing to a friend he said, "Now is the time to take possession of the missions, as the Protestants are on the alert and they may get a foothold before we do. . . . May the Black Robes come, therefore, to preserve the tawny children of the forest from the poison of error that is sure to be spread among them."

Croquet's modest mission station at Grand Ronde clearly attracted many people, but the initial burst of enthusiasm seemed to fade over the next few years. An analysis of Croquet's sacramental register, in which he listed each baptism, marriage, confirmation, and burial, shows that he baptized ninety people at Grand Ronde in his first year and ninety-four in his second. Most were children under the age of sixteen. However, at least twenty-three in the first year and another twenty-three in the second year were people who were near death and received virtually no religious instruction prior to the rite. In the third, fourth, and fifth years, the majority of baptisms were of this type, and the total number of baptisms fell dramatically. Croquet baptized only about 20–25 percent of reservation residents in the first five years of the mission.

In October 1862, Croquet dedicated the first church at Grand Ronde, St. Michael the Archangel. A year later he reported that fifty to sixty people attended Sunday services each week, but he deplored the apparent lack of enthusiasm for his project. By 1866, when he still was not making the progress he hoped for, Croquet complained that a "Catholic missionary has no longer the influence with these Indians that he would have upon still savage tribes; they have come and yet come too much in contact with men who, if not hostile, are at least indifferent to the Catholic religion; and they seem to have contracted a fair dose of these men's religious indifference."

Eventually, however, Croquet's presence and considerable patience seemed to have a major impact. A report for the Board of Indian Commissioners from 1873 indicated that a substantial majority of Indians had become members of the Catholic Church, and attendance at Sunday services had jumped to an average of 250. The arrival of Catholic nuns in 1874 to manage the manual labor school provided another intimate point of contact between the Indians and the Catholic religion. In 1883 the Indians, with assistance from the Catholic Church, constructed a new house of worship for the community. Agent Sinnott felt confident that the church, after over twenty years of labor, was flourishing and that Catholicism had largely supplanted Native beliefs and practices in daily life at Grand Ronde.

Yet Sinnott's successor, J. B. McClane, complained that two large dance houses were hidden in the hills above the valley. Indians from Grand Ronde and from other reservations held ceremonies in them lasting several days. McClane said they had even constructed a boarding house to shelter the participants. These ceremonies may have been related to the revitalization movements that attracted followers at Grand Ronde and at the adjacent Siletz reservation beginning in the 1870s. People from Grand Ronde learned the Ghost Dance in northern California in 1871. This prophetic movement probably influenced the Earth Lodge cult, which first came to the reservation in 1873 and was known locally as the Warm House Dance. Agent McClane, like others before him, tried to prohibit the Indians from participating in these rites and confronted the Indian doctors in an attempt to discredit them. McClane recognized what some people had known for a long time: There was a mix of belief and practice among the Indians, many of whom found meaning and value in traditions both new and old.

In the mid-1870s Reverend Summers conversed with Father Croquet on this subject and recorded that most of the Indians had finally accepted baptism, but that many, especially the older men and women, "mingled with the old religion the comforting assurances of [Catholicism]." Summers also spoke to an Indian man who described the dances and ceremonies held every autumn by men on the reservation at a lodge secluded in the forest. Another resident named two Indian doctors who continued to practice on the reservation. Agency physicians had no trouble drawing patients to Western healing traditions, but Native doctors and traditional healing practices offered an alternative and a supplement that many people found appropriate and useful. Traditional healing arts and Native ceremonialism persisted at least through the first decade of the twentieth century at Grand Ronde.

Living in a reservation community that was both Indian and "modern," the Indians of Grand Ronde carefully evaluated their choices in a search for utility and meaning. Summers visited a house of mourning in the mid-1870s where "a little girl, great grandchild of an ancient patriarch named To-ót-ly, lay on her little white bier, with candles at the head and foot, but dressed in a full suit of native garments[,] not an atom of civilization . . . about her." He asked the mother why the child was dressed in Native clothing, when all the Indians now wore American attire. She reportedly replied, "while they lived on earth it did not matter. They no longer followed their own customs, therefore why cling to their own dress?" She explained that "after death it was different. If her child went to the other world in white people's clothing, they would think she was white, and put her in the pale faces' heaven, and she did not want her little child there. She wanted her to go to the Indian's heaven where she would be with her own people and be happy." This woman could live outwardly as her White neighbors in the Willamette Valley, but, within her, she still nurtured a distinctly Indian self-identity that explained her place in the world, infused her experiences with meaning, and guided her on a path into the future, even beyond death.

By 1887, on the eve of the new government allotment program outlined in the Dawes Act, the people of Grand Ronde had constructed a prosperous community based on an agricultural life. They received very little direct government support and, therefore, had to be largely self-reliant. The lack of government assistance was not the only incentive to develop this quality. The Indians of Grand Ronde, by working within the limitations of the reservation environment to create a sustainable community, cultivated the ability to make institutions work for their interests. They thus achieved a measure of independence.

The process of building such a community encouraged the emergence of a common identity grounded in reservation experiences. Allotment scattered families across the valley on independent homesteads and stretched traditional band affiliations. In 1878, the Indian legislature switched from representation by band to a system based on the division of the valley into three legislative precincts with three representatives each. Intermarriage between bands fostered bonds of kinship, as they had prior to the reservation period, and community celebrations promoted social exchange. Declining use of tribal languages and the general adoption of Chinook jargon as the community's symbolic Indian language further supported a new identity. Moreover, an increasing proportion of residents had been born and raised on the reservation and knew no other way of life. Band affiliation may still have retained importance for some people, but there was a growing sense that they were *from* this place, that it was part of them. The reservation experience transformed the people of many bands into Grand Ronde Indians.

Not everyone responded with the same enthusiasm to the challenges of erecting an agricultural community at Grand Ronde, nor did they achieve the same results. Some people aspired to wealth and prestige and reached for positions of leadership within the community. Social distinctions, important in the pre-reservation period, were significant at Grand Ronde as well. A wealthy and respected man, for instance, could no longer take several wives nor purchase slaves at Grand Ronde, but he could be elected to the legislature or preside over the court. Replacing the slaves at the bottom of the economic ladder were a number of people, primarily the aged and the orphaned, who depended on the government or the charity of neighbors to survive. For these impoverished people, the weakening of traditional band ties and an increase in individualism would not have been welcome developments. A few people, like a small band of Rogue River Indians led by John Chamberlin in 1862, became dissatisfied with reservation life and so missed their native lands that they sought, unsuccessfully, to resettle them. Not even memories of the violence and blood-shed of the 1850s or the presence of numerous White homesteaders kept them from trying to return to their homeland. Some people left the reservation for years to live and work in the farms, villages, and towns of western Oregon.

The people who stayed created a viable community for a new and different world. In the mid-1850s the Native peoples of western Oregon's interior valleys, pressured by American settlers and government agents, faced a chaotic and restrictive situation, but they still had choices. They decided to exchange the troubles of their homelands for the challenges of a long experiment in personal transformation and cultural adaptation. Once settled at the agency, individuals and groups made choices that tended to enhance self-determination and increase independence.

As the Grand Ronde case illustrates, culture can be both conservative and elastic when people confront disorder and the unknown. While culture structures experience and provides the means to interpret it, it also serves as a rich resource for adapting to changing circumstances and unfamiliar environments. The process of selective adaptation at Grand Ronde included both innovation and cultural continuity. On the surface, the Grand Ronde Indians gave up their traditional system of gathering and hunting for the cultivation of wheat, oats, and potatoes. Yet they developed a new yearly cycle that included Native foods as well as an annual migration to the Willamette Valley. They molded institutions, even those that government agents imposed on them, to serve their needs. In many cases, the reservation program of directed culture change only reinforced decisions the Indians had already made themselves. The government and its agents often lagged behind the Indians in response, timing, and vision, actually limiting the ability of the Indians to make desired adjustments to reservation life. In any case, by 1887, the Indians of Grand Ronde had developed a way of life animated and defined as much by their own standards and goals as by the policies and decisions of government agents. Although experiences at Grand Ronde forever altered the Indian societies of western Oregon, Indians also shaped the nature of those changes and maintained a Native identity.

While the Grand Ronde Indians fashioned an agricultural community that generally impressed observers, Indians at other agencies in Oregon and throughout the West frequently struggled without the same success to adapt to reservation life and to meet their needs through agricultural development. A combination of factors, many of which were absent at other Indian reservations, created the conditions that allowed the Grand Ronde Indians to achieve many of their goals. Most importantly, they had arable land. The soil at the agency, while not ideal, could be productive when cultivated with patience and skill. Abundant rainfall in most years made large irrigation works unnecessary. The valley floor contained enough land to support the community during good years. The Grand Ronde Indians managed to retain the land on which they built their dreams until the twentieth century, when they finally faced the loss of land that savaged so many other Indian communities as well. The Indians at Grand Ronde also took advantage of the opportunity to learn agricultural skills alongside White farmers in the Willamette Valley. The cash they earned for their labor purchased needed supplies and implements that the government failed to provide. . . .

. . . Federal allotment policy and pressures from Whites who desired access to rich Grand Ronde land produced severe difficulties in the twentieth century. The loss of land eventually eroded the foundation for independence the people had forged, requiring further adaptations. The Grand Ronde community endures to this day, however, having survived the loss of land and even termination. The story of this reservation community should not be examined as if everything were leading inevitably to these future troubles. In making the transition to reservation life, the people of Grand Ronde created a community strong enough to weather the coming challenges.

When the Grand Ronde resident shared his memories of the 1855 treaty council with the visiting linguist, he explained that his people, the Tualatins, had determined to accept the Grand Ronde Valley in exchange for their native lands. He recalled that the people decided, "[W]e will make it our own place." After thirty years in their reservation home, the inevitable delays and setbacks balanced by numerous accomplishments, the Indians of Grand Ronde had, indeed, made it their own place.

◈ *F U R T H E R   R E A D I N G*

Jean Afton et al., *Cheyenne Dog Soldiers: A Ledgerbook History of Coups and Combat* (1997)

Keith Basso, ed., *Western Apache Raiding and Warfare* (1971)

Robert Begait and Clarence Woodcock, eds., *In the Name of the Salish and Kootenai Nation: The 1855 Hell Gate Treaty and the Origin of the Flathead Indian Reservation* (1996)

Donald Berthrong, *The Southern Cheyennes* (1963)

Tiana Bighorse, *Bighorse the Warrior* (1990)

Martha Royce Blaine, *Pawnee Passage: 1870–1875* (1990)

William Chalfant, *Cheyennes at Dark Water Creek: The Last Fight of the Red River War* (1997)

Angie Debo, *Geronimo: The Man, His Time, His Place* (1976)

Raymond DeMallie, ed., *The Sixth Grandfather* (1984)

Thomas Dunlay, *Wolves for the Blue Soldiers: Indian Scouts and Auxiliaries* (1982)

John Ewers, *The Blackfeet: Raiders of the Northwest Plains* (1958)

Jerome A. Greene, ed., *Lakota and Cheyenne: Indian Views of the Great Sioux War, 1876–1877* (1994)

Bruce A. Hampton, *Children of Grace: The Nez Perce War of 1877* (1994)

Richard G. Hardorff, ed., *Lakota Recollections of the Custer Fight: New Sources of Indian-Military History* (1997)

Alvin M. Josephy, Jr., *The Nez Perce Indians and the Opening of the Northwest* (1965)

Thomas W. Kavanagh, *Comanche Political History: An Ethnohistorical Perspective, 1706–1875* (1996)

Robert W. Larson, *Red Cloud: Warrior-Statesman of the Lakota Sioux* (1997)

William Haas Moore, *Chiefs, Agents, and Soldiers: Conflict on the Navajo Frontier, 1868–1882* (1994)

Peter Nabokov, *Two Leggings: The Making of a Crow Warrior with the U.S. Army* (1967)

Eli R. Paul, ed., *Autobiography of Red Cloud: War Leader of the Oglalas* (1997)

———, ed., *The Nebraska Indian Wars Reader, 1865–1877* (1998)

Peter John Powell, *People of the Sacred Mountain: A History of the Northern Cheyenne Chiefs and Warrior Societies, 1830–1870*, 2 vols. (1969)

Charles E. Rankin, ed., *Legacy: New Perspectives on the Battle of the Little Bighorn* (1996)

David Roberts, *Once They Moved Like the Wind: Cochise, Geronimo, and the Apache Wars* (1993)

Charles M. Robinson III, *A Good Year To Die: The Story of the Great Sioux War* (1995)

Ruth Roessel, ed., *Navajo Stories of the Long Walk Period* (1973)

Henry E. Stamm, IV, *People of the Wind River: The Eastern Shoshones, 1825–1900* (1999)

Edwin R. Sweeney, *Cochise: Chiricahua Apache Chief* (1991)

———, *Mangas Coloradas: Chief of the Chiricahua Apaches* (1998)

Gerald Thompson, *The Army and the Navajo: The Bosque Redondo Reservation Experiment, 1863–1868* (1976)

Robert W. Utley, *The Indian Frontier of the American West, 1846–1890* (1984)

———, *The Lance and the Shield: The Life and Times of Sitting Bull* (1993)

James Welch and Paul Stekler, *Killing Custer: The Battle of the Little Bighorn and the Fate of the Plains Indians* (1994)

Gene Weltfish, *Pawnee Life and Culture* (1965)

David J. Wishart, *An Unspeakable Sadness: The Dispossession of the Nebraska Indians* (1994)

CHAPTER
11

Restrictions and Renewals,
1887–1928

◈

As the Indians were confined on reservations, federal officials and reformers who saw themselves as "friends of the Indian" sought to assimilate native peoples into the larger American society. Private property, Christianity, the English language, and the opportunity to farm or learn a useful trade were considered central to American values and success. The General Allotment Act of 1887, popularly called the Dawes Act, followed the model of the Homestead Act of 1862. The Dawes Act broke up communally held reservation lands and allotted parcels of land to individual families. Any unallotted land could be sold by the government, with the proceeds made available for Indian schools. These schools provided instruction in English and attempted to inculcate white values. Not all reservations were allotted, and not all Indian children attended school, but the overall assimilationist policy during these decades had a major impact in Indian country. The Five Tribes (Cherokee, Chickasaw, Choctaw, Creek, and Seminole) in Indian Territory were exempted from the Dawes Act, but in the 1890s a commission headed by Henry Dawes called for the allotment of their lands and the end of tribal authority. Cherokee delegates, headed by Principal Chief S. H. Mayes, protested against the division of lands and the usurpation of Native authority. They called attention to the impressive institutions established by the Cherokees following their removal to Indian Territory. Even given these and other achievements, the Five Tribes were all forced to submit to allotment; by 1907, the dream of separate statehood had vanished with Indian Territory swallowed by the new state of Oklahoma. Under the rapidly changing circumstances of the period, did federal policymakers have other choices? Was the course they chose the only pragmatic one?

Even with all the difficulties that attended this period, it is important not to portray the era solely in bleak terms. On the national level, Indians created new organizations, including the Native American Church and the Society of American Indians, that offered significant responses to this new age. Within different Indian communities, people faced compelling questions. They made far-reaching decisions about the nature of leadership, the kind of economy that could be developed, and the focus of the education their children should receive. Largely unnoticed, individuals and families weathered the trying period and in many instances built foundations for further revitalization in the years to come.

◈ *D O C U M E N T S*

The General Allotment Act of 1887, also called the Dawes Act after its congressional sponsor, Henry Dawes of Massachusetts, is generally portrayed today as ill advised, although most non-Indians of the nineteenth century thought it a good idea. For those reservations that came under its provisions and were also affected by subsequent policies designed to further reduce Native landholdings, the results usually were disastrous. Indians in the area that later comprised the lower forty-eight states lost two of every three acres that they held prior to 1887. A reading of the Act, which is excerpted in Document 1, gives a firsthand sense of the federal objectives in the era.

Although the Cherokees and the other Five Tribes had been exempted from the provisions of the General Allotment Act, they had only a temporary respite. Non-Indian intruders in Indian Territory continued to demand the division of the tribal estate. In 1893 Congress created a commission, chaired by former senator Henry Dawes, to negotiate with these Indian nations. The Cherokees knew their lands and institutions were imperiled. As Document 2 reveals, they defended themselves with great eloquence. But it would be to no avail. The Dawes Commission soon began to allot Cherokee land.

One of the key questions confronting all Westerners in the early twentieth century concerned the allocation of a precious resource: water. Indians won an important legal victory in 1908, when the U.S. Supreme Court decided that the Gros Ventres and Assiniboines of the Fort Belknap reservation in northern Montana were entitled to sufficient water to allow them to carve out a living on their land. This decision, excerpted in Document 3, became known as the Winters Doctrine, and it embodied the concept that Indians had particular rights to water, regardless of their record of prior use of it.

Another important legal issue of the time revolved around the ritual use of peyote by Indians who had become members of the Native American Church. At congressional hearings in 1918, reprinted in Document 4, ethnologist James Mooney and his associate Francis La Flesche (Omaha) testified in favor of peyote's use by church members. To the present day, the consumption of this substance remains controversial, because peyote is considered a drug. Nevertheless, the Native American church became the most important national Indian religious organization in this century.

Indians participated in the first world war, even though many Native peoples had not yet been accorded full citizenship in the United States. Their distinguished record in the war added more fuel to the fire for universal citizenship. Carlos Montezuma, M.D. (Yavapai) addressed these matters in one of his editorials in his newsletter, *Wassaja*, included here as Document 5.

1. The General Allotment Act (Dawes Act), 1887

An act to provide for the allotment of lands in severalty to Indians on the various reservations, and to extend the protection of the laws of the United States and the Territories over the Indians, and for other purposes.

Be it enacted by the Senate and House of Representatives of the United States of America in Congress assembled, That in all cases where any tribe or band of Indians has been, or shall hereafter be, located upon any reservation created for their use, either by treaty stipulation or by virtue of an act of Congress or executive order setting apart the same for their use, the President of the United States be, and

---

General Allotment Act, February 8, 1887, *U.S. Statutes at Large* 24: 366–391.

he hereby is, authorized, whenever in his opinion any reservation or any part thereof of such Indians is advantageous for agricultural and grazing purposes, to cause said reservation, or any part thereof, to be surveyed, or resurveyed if necessary, and to allot the lands in said reservation in severalty to any Indian located thereon in quantities as follows:

To each head of a family, one-quarter of a section;

To each single person over eighteen years of age, one-eighth of a section;

To each orphan child under eighteen years of age, one-eighth of a section; and

To each other single person under eighteen years now living, or who may be born prior to the date of the order of the President directing an allotment of the lands embraced in any reservation, one-sixteenth of a section: *Provided,* That in case there is not sufficient land in any of said reservations to allot lands to each individual of the classes above named in quantities as above provided, the lands embraced in such reservation or reservations shall be allotted to each individual of each of said classes pro rata in accordance with the provisions of this act: *And provided further,* That where the treaty or act of Congress setting apart such reservation provides for the allotment of lands in severalty in quantities in excess of those herein provided, the President, in making allotments upon such reservation, shall allot the lands to each individual Indian belonging thereon in quantity as specified in such treaty or act: *And provided further,* That when the lands allotted are only valuable for grazing purposes, an additional allotment of such grazing lands, in quantities as above provided, shall be made to each individual.

Sec. 2. That all allotments set apart under the provisions of this act shall be selected by the Indians, heads of families selecting for their minor children, and the agents shall select for each orphan child, and in such manner as to embrace the improvements of the Indians making the selection. Where the improvements of two or more Indians have been made on the same legal subdivision of land, unless they shall otherwise agree, a provisional line may be run dividing said lands between them, and the amount to which each is entitled shall be equalized in the assignment of the remainder of the land to which they are entitled under this act: *Provided,* That if any one entitled to an allotment shall fail to make a selection within four years after the President shall direct that allotments may be made on a particular reservation, the Secretary of the Interior may direct the agent of such tribe or band, if such there be, and if there be no agent, then a special agent appointed for that purpose, to make a selection for such Indian, which election shall be allotted as in cases where selections are made by the Indians, and patents shall issue in like manner.

Sec. 3. That the allotments provided for in this act shall be made by special agents appointed by the President for such purpose, and the agents in charge of the respective reservations on which the allotments are directed to be made, under such rules and regulations as the Secretary of the Interior may from time to time prescribe, and shall be certified by such agents to the Commissioner of Indian Affairs, in duplicate, one copy to be retained in the Indian Office and the other to be transmitted to the Secretary of the Interior for his action, and to be deposited in the General Land Office. . . .

Sec. 5. That upon the approval of the allotments provided for in this act by the Secretary of the Interior, he shall cause patents to issue therefor in the name of the allottees, which patents shall be of the legal effect, and declare that the United States does and will hold the land thus allotted, for the period of twenty-five years, in trust for the sole use and benefit of the Indian to whom such allotment shall have been made, or, in case of his decease, of his heirs according to the laws of the State or Territory where such land is located, and that at the expiration of said period the United States will convey the same by patent to said Indian, of his heirs as aforesaid, in fee, discharged of said trust and free of all charge or incumbrance whatsoever. . . .

Sec. 6. That upon the completion of said allotments and the patenting of the lands to said allottees, each and every member of the respective bands or tribes of Indians to whom allotments have been made shall have the benefit of and be subject to the laws, both civil and criminal, of the State or Territory in which they may reside; and no Territory shall pass or enforce any law denying any such Indian within its jurisdiction the equal protection of the law. And every Indian both within the territorial limits of the United States to whom allotments shall have been made under the provisions of this act, or under any law or treaty, and every Indian born within the territorial limits of the United States who has voluntarily taken up, within said limits, his residence separate and apart from any tribe of Indians therein, and has adopted the habits of civilized life, is hereby declared to be a citizen of the United States, and is entitled to all the rights, privileges, and immunities of such citizens, whether said Indian has been or not, by birth or otherwise, a member of any tribe of Indians within the territorial limits of the United States without in any manner, impairing or otherwise affecting the right of any such Indian to tribal or other property. . . .

Sec. 8. That the provision of this act shall not extend to the territory occupied by the Cherokees, Creeks, Choctaws, Chickasaws, Seminoles, and Osage, Miamies and Peorias, and Sacs and Foxes, in the Indian Territory, nor to any of the reservations of the Seneca Nation of New York Indians in the State of New York, nor to that strip of territory in the State of Nebraska adjoining the Sioux Nation on the south added by executive order. . . .

2. Cherokee Delegates Defend Their Land and Institutions, 1895

To the Senate
And House of Representatives
of the United States Congress:

. . . These are times of imminent danger to those institutions of government and tenure of property that the Cherokees have brought with them from the darkness of time immemorial, modified somewhat by the enlightened influences of your great constitution but distinctive still as Cherokee institutions. The Cherokees are fully alive to the situation, and they know that unless in some way congress shall become acquainted rapidly with their true condition, all that they hold dear of country and

This document can be found in the Cherokee Papers, Oklahoma Historical Society, Oklahoma City, Oklahoma.

people will be swept away by the hands that they have heretofore confidently looked to for protection, and which have in gentleness and friendship been so often extended to them. For some reasons that we cannot explain, the Cherokees have been traduced and grievously misrepresented by persons high in authority, from whom we have had every reason to expect fair statement. It is natural to love the country one lives in, if that country protects life, promotes happiness, and insures equality. When a people are found who are intensely patriotic, it can be taken for granted that their government gives them such assurances. The Cherokees are such a people; there is not upon the face of the earth today a people more thoroughly contented with their condition than the Cherokees. In his humble western home, sequestered from the mad rush one sees in the east, you will find the Cherokee a sober, industrious, religious gentleman, earning his daily bread by honest labor upon the soil, of which he is equal owner with every one else in the nation, irrespective of superior advantage such as wealth, opportunity, or education gives.

He believes in common education; such as is natural with his ideas of common property. Therefore, under the constitution adopted in 1839, we find this provision: "Religion, morality, and knowledge being necessary for good government, the preservation of liberty, and the happiness of mankind, schools, and the means of education, shall forever be encouraged in this nation." Faithful to the idea here expressed, the history of the advancement of the educational interests of the Cherokees for the last fifty years cannot but please the mind and heart of him who loves his fellow-man for the good that he promises. Now, notwithstanding the pall that the civil war threw over the land, the progress of the Cherokee schools and facilities for common education has been marked and rapid. Now, with a population of 40,000 Cherokees, we have over one hundred common schools, running nine months a year, with capable, competent teachers, generally comfortable school houses, where all of necessary appliances, books, etc., are supplied by the Cherokee nation; a male and female college, of brick and stone, at a cost not exceeding each year over $150,000, afford to the youth of both sexes an opportunity of higher education; an orphan asylum of sufficient size to accommodate every orphan of school age in the nation, which has cost over $100,000, have now an attendance of over 2,000 orphans. We have also an asylum for the infirm and unfortunate (a home for these poor stricken people). At the male seminary this year there is over one hundred and eighty young men, at the female seminary over two hundred of our girls. The several missionary societies have not less than fifteen or twenty schools in the various parts of our country, encouraged by generous gifts of land upon the part of the Cherokees. To these earnest Christian workers in our midst we also appeal, in our time of extremity for national existence, to assist us in refuting the false charges made with no other motive, we believe, than to induce congress to withdraw its powerful protection from us, that we might become easy prey of unscrupulous avarice and greed, as the hungry beast devoured his milder companion of the forest. These religious denominations among us, who brought to us the beautiful Christian religion, who witnessed the sowing of its seeds and now behold its plant of vigorous growth in the full bearing of its fruits, can bear us witness of the many false charges of retrogression, immorality, lawlessness, and crime among the Cherokees. We ask, when our enemies traduce us and when grave charges of malfeasance in public offices and trust are hurled at us, that you will require specific proof to accompany the accusation.

Churches are everywhere, organized throughout our land, and their efficient and powerful auxiliaries, the Sabbath schools, are conducted every Sunday in our various churches and school-houses, where the same lesson papers are used that your children study throughout this land and elsewhere. All of this, with the exception of the missionary efforts among us, to which we largely contribute, is done at no expense whatever to the United States, but entirely at the expense of the Cherokees. Is it to be doubted that a people fostering and encouraging such institutions have all the finer sensibilities of education and Christian manhood that will be found among similar communities in the States? Could a nation of irresponsible, corrupt, criminal people produce such conditions? Are these the results of the evil and corruption that the Dawes Commission assert pervade the very atmosphere down there? We earnestly ask that before laying the axe to the root of the tree you yourselves have planted and carefully attended, that you examine the fruits thereof and take not the word of some persons controlled by envy, and in a moment of irritability against us for not blindly following their suggestion, consent to and advise our destruction. We submit that in the nature of things, it would have been impossible for the Dawes commission to have found no good existing in our country, yet not one redeeming word do we find in their report, if there is any. Did they not see us in the worship of the same God they worship? Did they not hear us while with bowed heads we implored the intercession of the Son of God? Then why have they with the black veil of corrupt charges obscured the good that honor would have compelled them to acknowledge if they found it?

In our governmental affairs we have followed in the footsteps of your people; our form of government is as yours, with its three departments, executive, legislative and judicial, where the same authorities govern and the same methods and rules obtain, perhaps somewhat modified, as among you. It may be that at our legislature some of your practices have been adopted, and it may be that some of our methods in the struggle for office may partake of the taint we sometimes hear charged against your legislatures. Walking in your footsteps, it could hardly be expected that, in following the good you practice, some of your evils may not have also left their mark. We pursue some short cuts in office down there sometimes that would hardly receive the approbation of a legislative reformer; but that we are one half as corrupt as the Dawes commission represent us we emphatically deny, neither can we admit that we are to any degree as corrupt as the newspapers assert of your average legislatures. . . .

The Cherokees wish to call your attention to the size of their present country. Within our country as at present bounded there are less than five million acres of land; our population is thirty thousand; the estimate of the number of acres includes river beds, and portions, and all that would be necessary for public travel and commerce. At a glance it will be seen that we have now less than one hundred and sixty acres to the head. The proportion of the arable land to that unfit for cultivation is, by the most liberal estimate, not exceeding one to four, so it will be seen that today the Cherokees have less than forty acres of tillable land to the individual. We invite your close attention to this fact, for not the least among the influences seeking the destruction of our government and the opening of the country is the hope that homes may thereby be obtained for the white people who would come in. It could not be so in the Cherokee nation; we have not now more than will suffice the immediate necessities of our people; nor could we consent to part with any more land whatever without gross injustice to our poor, who depend upon agriculture and stock-raising for subsistence. There is no necessity for a town-site law in the Cherokee nation. The statement by the Dawes commission that towns had been erected, costly business houses and residences built in the Cherokee nation by non citizens is absolutely false with not a single exception. We have half a score or more of beautiful towns in the Cherokee nation, beautifully and symmetrically surveyed, containing many substantial and even fine structures; but all has been done by citizens of the nation, and such buildings are not occupied or owned in any manner by aliens, nor have they any money in them. Our towns have good systems of municipal government, the result of liberal legislation on the part of the national council. A municipal government is run by a mayor and a board of aldermen, and called a town council. The quiet and neatness of our towns commend us to all our visitors. There are no white aliens doing business among us, other than those engaged in farming; we do not, as alleged, invite them into our country; we do not invite or use their money in building our towns; we put every impediment we can in the way of their coming among us; we do not need them in our midst, but we are a hospitable people, our friendship extends beyond the lines of our country, and in our acts of hospitality we sometimes harbor in our midst coming in the guise of friends, who, through motives of envy and covetousness, subsequently advise our undoing. Our country is indeed fair to look upon; to us its lovely valleys, limpid streams, flowing prairies, waving forests, and grand hills are an Eden. There, over fifty years ago, with specious promises of everlasting protection, you planted us, literally driving us from our homes in the mountains of Georgia, Tennessee, and North Carolina. "As long as the grass grows and water runs," wrote General Jackson, "shall the country remain yours." "No state or territorial line shall ever surround you," were the words your minister who induced us to go to that country, and his words are engrafted into the treaty. Now, after the lapse of fifty years, when the bodies of those who made these promises to us have been consigned to the tomb, and their names have taken their places in history, many of them for all time, you, their children, tell us, the children of those with whom they treated, that your parents did not mean all they said, and were only preparing a temporary solution of the questions they were pretending to settle. . . .

S. H. Mayes,
Principal Chief,
and other delegates

3. The U.S. Supreme Court Supports Indian Water Rights: *Winters* v. *United States,* 1908

. . . The case, as we view it, turns on the agreement of May, 1888, resulting in the creation of Fort Belknap Reservation. In the construction of this agreement there are certain elements to be considered that are prominent and significant. The reservation was a part of a very much larger tract which the Indians had the right to occupy

---

This document can be found as part of *Winters* v. *United States,* 207 U.S. 574 (1907).

and use and which was adequate for the habits and wants of a nomadic and uncivilized people. It was the policy of the Government, it was the desire of the Indians, to change those habits and to become a pastoral and civilized people. If they should become such the original tract was too extensive, but a smaller tract would be inadequate without a change of conditions. The lands were arid and, without irrigation, were practically valueless. And yet, it is contended, the means of irrigation were deliberately given up by the Indians and deliberately accepted by the Government. The lands ceded were, it is true, also arid; and some argument may be urged, and is urged, that with their cession there was the cession of the waters, without which they would be valueless, and "civilized communities could not be established thereon." And this, it is further contended, the Indians knew, and yet made no reservation of the waters. We realize that there is a conflict of implications, but that which makes for the retention of the waters is of greater force than that which makes for their cession. The Indians had command of the lands and the waters—command of all their beneficial use, whether kept for hunting, "and grazing roving herds of stock," or turned to agriculture and the arts of civilization. Did they give up all this? Did they reduce the area of their occupation and give up the waters which made it valuable or adequate? And, even regarding the allegation of the answer as true, that there are springs and streams on the reservation flowing about 2,900 inches of water, the inquiries are pertinent. If it were possible to believe affirmative answers, we might also believe that the Indians were awed by the power of the Government or deceived by its negotiators. Neither view is possible. The Government is asserting the rights of the Indians. But extremes need not be taken into account. By a rule of interpretation of agreements and treaties with the Indians, ambiguities occurring will be resolved from the standpoint of the Indians. And the rule should certainly be applied to determine between two inferences, one of which would support the purpose of the agreement and the other impair or defeat it. On account of their relations to the Government, it cannot be supposed that the Indians were alert to exclude by formal words every inference which might militate against or defeat the declared purpose of themselves and the Government, even if it could be supposed that they had the intelligence to foresee the "double sense" which might some time be urged against them.

Another contention of appellants is that if it be conceded that there was a reservation of the waters of Milk River by the agreement of 1888, yet the reservation was repealed by the admission of Montana into the Union, February 22, 1889, c. 180, 25 Stat. 676, "upon an equal footing with the original States." The language of counsel is that "any reservation in the agreement with the Indians, expressed or implied, whereby the waters of Milk River were not to be subject of appropriation by the citizens and inhabitants of said State, was repealed by the act of admission." But to establish the repeal counsel rely substantially upon the same argument that they advance against the intention of the agreement to reserve the waters. The power of the Government to reserve the waters and exempt them from appropriation under the state laws in not denied, and could not be. *The United States* v. *The Rio Grande Ditch & Irrigation Co.,* 174 U.S. 690, 702; *United States* v. *Winans,* 198 U.S. 371. That the Government did reserve them we have decided, and for a use which would be necessarily continued through years. This was done May 1, 1888, and it would be extreme to believe that within a year Congress destroyed the reservation and took from the Indians the consideration of their grant, leaving them a barren waste—took from them the means of continuing their old habits, yet did not leave them the power to change to new ones.

Appellants' argument upon the incidental repeal of the agreement by the admission of Montana into the Union and the power over the waters of Milk River which the State thereby acquired to dispose of them under its laws, is elaborate and able, but our construction of the agreement and its effect make it unnecessary to answer the argument in detail. For the same reason we have not discussed the doctrine of riparian rights urged by the Government.*

4. James Mooney and Francis La Flesch è (Omaha) Testify About Peyote, 1918

Statement of James Mooney, Bureau of American Ethnology

. . . I am one of the ethnologists of the Bureau of American Ethnology. In April I shall have filled 30 years' service in the bureau. A large part of my time has been spent with the tribes of the southern plains, who are particularly devoted to the use of peyote and to the religious rite connected with it. For the most part of the first six years I lived as a member of a family among the Kiowa. In connection with a general study of Indian things among the Kiowa, Commanche, Apache, and associated tribes, and the Cheyenne and Arapaho of Oklahoma, and several other tribes in the other parts of the country, I have made peyote a subject of investigation. It is so closely connected with Indian life in southwestern Oklahoma that any ethnologist going there to make investigations soon has it brought to his attention, and I became interested in it.

I have gotten from the Indians their own story of the origin of the religious rite. You must understand that the use of this plant is not an ordinary habit, but that it is confined almost entirely and strictly to the religious ceremony, excepting that it is frequently employed also for medicinal purposes. It is not an ordinary habit in the way that a man takes to drinking whisky. There are certain times, seasons, and reasons for the use of it. I studied the ceremony first as a scientific observer with the Kiowa, and later in pursuance of a special investigation of the subject. I visited a number of other tribes, among them the Mexican tribes of the Sierra Madre, and as far south as the City of Mexico. Besides what I know of the use of peyote among the tribes in western Oklahoma, I know in a less degree of its use among the tribes in Mexico, from whom those to the north have obtained their knowledge of it.

Peyote grows in the arid regions. It is a small cactus, with a root very much the size and shape of an ordinary long radish, and the part used by the Indians is the sliced-off top, dried to about the size of an ordinary silver quarter or half dollar.

---

*Under the doctrine of riparian rights, the owner of land bordering on a water source such as a river could divert as much water as he or she deemed necessary, regardless of the seniority of property ownership or the needs of others. This system comes from the English tradition and was used in the eastern United States but generally not in the West.

From James Mooney and Francis La Flesch è (Omaha), excerpts from *Hearings on Peyote Before a Subcommittee of the Committee on Indian Affairs in the House of Representatives, on H.R. 2614* (Washington, D.C.: Government Printing Office, 1918), 69–74, 80–83.

Here it is [showing a small boxful of samples of peyote]. It has different Indian names in the various tribes. It is sometimes incorrectly called mescal by the whites, but its proper name is peyote, the Spanish derivative from the old Aztec name. This is the dried top, the blossoming top of a small cactus which grows close to the ground. It grows abundantly about Laredo, Tex., where it is gathered and dried by Mexicans and shipped to the dealers in Oklahoma, who supply the Indian trade. Our tribes, in the ceremonial, eat it dry, using only the top, because, on account of the white blossom center surrounded by circles of white points, they regard it as the vegetable representative of the sun. In Mexico, not only do the Indian tribes use it in the ceremonial way, but the common people of Mexico use it also in a medicinal way. Both Indians and Mexicans slice up the whole plant and make a decoction of it in warm or cold water. What I have here I got myself from a trader, who handled it in western Oklahoma, but I have also dug up the growing plant about Laredo. . . .

The Kiowa story of its origin is that some young men went on the warpath to the south and were gone for so long a time that their friends at home became afraid they would never return. There was a young woman, a sister of one of the war party, who went out to a hill beyond the camp every evening to watch for her brother, in accordance with the Indian custom, and pray for his return. Finally one evening she fell asleep, and a spirit came to her in a dream, telling her that there was something growing out of the ground under her head which would bring her to her brother if used according to the instructions which the spirit then gave her. When she awoke she looked and found a number of peyotes growing. These she gathered and took back to camp, and then, calling the old men together, told them how to prepare everything for the ceremony as the spirit had directed. They set up the tepee and performed the rite, and in the peyote vision they saw where the young man was lying alone, wounded and starving, and they sent out a party and brought him home to his sister. There is always a religious myth in connection with the peyote rite. That is the story the Kiowa tell of how the rite came to them. Each tribe has its own story. The Kiowa say the Comanche knew of it before they did. Both tribes say they got it from the Mescalero and Tonkawa, and probably these got it originally from the tribes near the Mexican border, who in turn had it from the tribes in old Mexico. It has come to the more northern tribes only recently.

You have seen the plant as used. As to their method of using it ceremonially, they have a regular time—Saturday night running into Sunday morning. They set up a special tepee and go into it, after preliminary preparation, about 9 o'clock in the evening. I have seen as many as 30 or more sitting in a circle inside the tepee. They have a drum and rattle. After an opening prayer the leader hands out four peyotes to each man. Each man chews up one peyote after another, making a pellet of each, which he swallows. Then the singing begins. There is one regular song at the beginning, one song at midnight, one song at daylight, and one song at the close, with other songs all through the night as each man chooses, two men singing at a time, one accompanying with the drum and the other with the rattle. The singing goes on through the night, the drum and rattle passing around the circle repeatedly. There is a fire in the center of the tepee and a large sacred peyote on a little crescent-shaped mound behind it. While two men keep up the songs the others are praying or remain in a state of contemplation, looking toward the fire and the sacred peyote. The ceremony goes on in this way through the night. At intervals the worshippers eat more peyotes. At midnight there is a sort of baptismal ceremony, when one man brings in a bucket of spring water, over which the leader recites a prayer, after which they sprinkle themselves with it. The leader stands up while making the prayer. They pray for all their friends and for themselves, as we pray. If there are any sick in camp, they may be brought in to be prayed for. If a woman is sick, her husband brings her in, and they pray for her and give her some of the peyote to eat. She does not prepare it herself, but it is prepared for her. With the peyote-using tribes that I know best, the Kiowa and Comanche, the only occasion on which a woman is present is when she is there to be prayed for as a member of the family of the man who accompanies her. . . .

In the morning the daylight song is the signal for the woman to prepare the food. Later on there is the closing song, and with that the ceremony ends. Special food has been prepared for the worshippers and is eaten before they leave the tepee. Then they go out and sit about chatting with their friends until dinner. Dinner is a family affair. The Indian families come in wagons for miles around as to a church gathering, just as in some parts of the country white families come in wagons to a country church, where they attend a service and afterwards have dinner in the open and sit around until the evening, when they go home. There is nothing at all bad about it, nothing whatever in the nature of an orgy. I can say from experience that there is nothing that the most rigid white man could consider immorality. There is no physical or mental prostration. There is no collapse after it is over. There is only the natural effect of having been up all night with some stimulant that would prevent their feeling fatigue. . . .

Statement of Mr. Francis La Fleschè, Bureau of American Ethnology, An Omaha Indian

. . . I have had numerous opportunities to study the use of the peyote among the Poncas, the Osage, and my own people, the Omahas. I had heard extraordinary stories told about its effects, about the immorality that it produced, and about the promiscuity of the people who used the peyote at their meetings. I expected to find evidence of the truth of these stories.

When I went among the Osage people, some of the leaders of the peyote religion were anxious for me to attend their meetings, and wishing to know what effect this "medicine," as they called it, had upon each individual, I accepted the invitation. I attended a meeting at which the gentleman who has just spoken to you, Mr. Arthur Bonnicastle, was present, and sat with him. At about 6 o'clock in the evening the people entered their "meeting house" and sat is a circle around a fire kindled over some symbolic figures marked in the center of a shallow excavation in the middle of the room. The peyote was passed around, some of it in pellets of the consistency of dough, and some prepared in liquid form. The drum was ceremonially circulated and accompanied by singing. From all that I had heard of the intoxicating effects of the peyote I expected to see the people get gloriously drunk and behave as drunken people do. While I sat waiting to see fighting and some excitement the singing went on and on and I noticed that all gazed at the fire or beyond, at a little mound on top of which lay a single peyote. I said to the man sitting next to me, "What do you expect to see?" He said, "We expect to see the face of Jesus and the face of our dead relatives. We are worshiping God and Jesus, the same God that the white people worship." All night long the singing went on and I sat watching the worshipers. It was about 5 o'clock in the morning when suddenly the singing ceased, the drum and the ceremonial staff were put away, and the leader, beginning at the right of the door, asked each person: "What did you see?" Some replied, "I saw nothing." Others said, "I saw the face of Jesus and it made me happy." Some answered, "I saw the faces of my relatives, and they made me glad." And so on, around the entire circle. I noticed that there were only a few who had been able to see faces, the greater number of the men and women saw nothing. It was explained to me by the leader that these revelations come quickly to those whose thoughts and deeds are pure. To those who are irreverent, they come slowly, although they may come in time. This meeting, as well as others I have been permitted to attend, was as orderly as any religious meeting I have seen in this and other cities. . . .

I do not know about the medicinal qualities of the peyote, whether it can cure consumption or any other disease that the human flesh is subject to, but there is one disease it has cured—the disease of drunkenness.

About 15 years ago, my people passed through an extraordinary experience. White men came among them, generally known as "boot-leggers," to sell whisky and lemon extract. What the whisky was made of I don't know—these "boot-leggers" would sell anything that could produce drunkenness. My people fell into the habit of using this stuff—manufactured by white people—and kept using it until they were in the very depths of degradation. In their drunkenness they attacked men, women, and children. Crimes have been committed that have never been heard of, crimes that have gone unpunished, and white people and Indians alike became afraid to go out at nights on the road for fear of meeting drunken Indians. There came a time when there was a lull in this storm of drunkenness, and after awhile we heard that the peyote religion had been adopted by the Omahas, and there were not as many drunkards as before the introduction of it.

Practically all of those of my people who have adopted the peyote religion do not drink. The peyote plant does much toward destroying the appetite for intoxicants. Moreover, any use of spirituous liquors is forbidden by the teachings of the new religion.

I have a respect for the peyote religion, because it has saved my people from the degradation which was produced by the use of the fiery drinks white people manufacture. . . .

5. Carlos Montezuma (Yavapai) on Indian Service in World War I and the Ongoing Struggle for Freedom and Citizenship, 1919

. . . Brave warriors, you left your humble homes . . . to fight for the principles that throbbed in your hearts, namely, freedom, equality, democracy, humanity and justice. . . .

. . . [Y]ou have demonstrated to the world by taking up arms for your country and standing shoulder to shoulder with your pale face comrades that the Indian race is not helpless and incompetent for freedom and citizenship.

From Carlos Montezuma, "The Duty of Every Indian Soldier Who Entered the War," *Wassaja* (February 1919).

When you entered the war, you have may not have thought of this, but it is a real fact.

Now, what is your duty? Carry on the fight—not as you experienced in the front, but for the freedom and citizenship of your race. What did you fight for? Freedom. . . . Your sacrifice for your country would be a mockery were you to stop this side of freedom of your people. They have not equal rights, they have not democracy, they have not humanity and they have not justice.

. . . You have been loyal to your country. Your country is indebted to you. . . . Your mission, at this hour, is to preach the gospel of truth that your race is ready for freedom and citizenship. . . . You should proclaim this truth everywhere and let it be heard in the hall of Congress. You have fought a good fight for your country, now it is your turn to ask the country to give you what you have helped to win for your race. . . . [S]tand before the world and ask the people of the United States to let your people go free from under the bondage of the Indian Bureau, so that they may enjoy the rights and privileges of citizenship. . . .

❖ E S S A Y S

These essays emphasize key components of the assimilationist policy of these years and Indian responses to the demands of this transitional period. Brenda Child (Red Lake Ojibwe), a professor of American Indian studies at the University of Minnesota, has written a widely acclaimed account, *Boarding School Seasons: American Indian Families, 1900–1940*, from which this first selection is taken. She underlines both the enormous problems posed by the boarding schools for Indian pupils and their families and the strength of Indian families. Child presents damning details of life in these early institutions, drawing from the many letters written between students and their families.

Frederick E. Hoxie, a professor of history at the University of Illinois, has considered the ways in which the Crows adjusted to changing times in *Parading Through History: The Making of the Crow Nation in America*, from which this second essay is excerpted. Hoxie emphasizes the importance of persisting family structures and distinctive social values. Even though the outside world placed ever increasing demands upon them, Crow men and women remained part of a kinship system, with particular expectations and responsibilities. That system made a crucial difference in fostering a continuing community.

Ojibwe Children and Boarding Schools

BRENDA CHILD (Ojibwe)

Boarding school education came to the Ojibwe people, the Anishinaabe, during a turbulent period in their history. The General Allotment Act, passed in 1887, and subsequent legislation had worked to erode the traditional, communal method of tribal landholding in favor of individual ownership on reservations. Few reservations escaped allotment. One notable exception was that of the Red Lake band in

From Brenda Child, *Boarding School Seasons: American Indian Families, 1900–1940* (Lincoln, Nebr.: University of Nebraska Press, 1998), 9–25. Reprinted by permission of the University of Nebraska Press. Copyright © 1998 by the University of Nebraska Press.

Minnesota. As historian William Watts Folwell commented about Red Lake in 1930, "It is still Indian country." For tribes across the United States, as well for many Ojibwes, the results of allotment policies and withdrawal of the protective trust relationship were an often devastating loss of country. Ojibwes in the Upper Midwest, whose seasonal economies were already challenged after being removed to new territories or having their reservation holdings reduced, could ill afford the environmental destruction and dispossession that unfolded in northern Minnesota, Wisconsin, and Michigan after the turn of the century. Land fraud was rampant, and the interests of ecocidal timber companies dominated the political landscape of the woodlands.

By 1920, the once-luxuriant pine trees in the north had been cleared from many reservations. The land base of Ojibwes had declined precipitously, and new Euro-American landowners, beneficiaries of tribal losses, populated the region. Ojibwes were expected to settle down to work as small farmers. This was not a real possibility for many Indians. Lands were so diminished in size that nothing more than a small garden was feasible for most families. Tribes complained that the allotment process itself had been unfair, that high-quality and valuable land had been lost to Indians. Undeniably, remaining reservation lands were frequently far too poor to farm. For example, in Wisconsin during the 1920s, the Lac du Flambeau Reservation was so covered by stumps and brush that the cost per acre of removing the old growth and timber company debris would have exceeded the value of the land. Lac Court Oreilles Ojibwes, who were also left with meager farming land, and the Lac du Flambeau band mostly relied on the traditional economy, tourist work, or off-reservation jobs for support. Red Cliff residents had such poor agricultural lands that most Ojibwes there were forced to labor off the reservation in the fishing and lumber industries.

The story was similar for many Ojibwes in Minnesota. After the devastation of their vast timber lands and the extensive land fraud perpetrated upon the bands congregated at the White Earth Reservation, most residents depended on wage labor or were forced to abandon the reservation entirely due to lack of opportunity. At Leech Lake, 437 allotments had been abruptly transferred from individual trust "for the benefit of the people" of the state when the Minnesota National Forest was created by an act of Congress in 1908. Twenty years later, without intended irony the park was redesigned the Chippewa National Forest.

The increased poverty and landlessness of many Ojibwes both threatened and confirmed the strength of the traditional economy. The seasonal rounds of hunting, fishing, making maple sugar, harvesting fruits and wild rice, this familiar and revered work, remained central to reservation life and Ojibwe identity in the twentieth century. Nett Lake Ojibwes, who were left with a fair amount of swampland after their allotments had been made, still retained ownership of some of the finest wild rice stands in the Great Lakes. Few Nett Lakers were able to maintain adequate gardens, but traditional subsistence activities, tourism, and off-reservation labor maintained the band. Nett Lake also increased its land base slightly in the postallotment period. The people living on the rocky Superior coast at Grand Portage fared somewhat worse. Their reduced reservation was diminished to the extent that by the 1930s, the several hundred band members there owned little more than three acres per person of the original tract that had been reserved for them by treaty in 1854.

As historian Melissa Meyer has argued, if the "government's programs of assimilation had a chance to succeed anywhere, White Earth should have become an experimental showcase" because of its incredibly rich and diverse environment of fishing lakes, rice stands, forests, and fertile farmlands. Historians have documented the corrupt history of the postallotment era at White Earth, a time when the regional pine cartel, Minnesota politicians, the federal government, local banks, and residents mingled interests to defraud conservative Ojibwes of their land and timber. Unfortunately, the corruption and fraud at White Earth was not exclusive to the reservation or even to Minnesota, but instead became part of a larger pattern of tribal dispossession in the nation.

The effects of this immense exploitation of people, land, and resources reverberated in Ojibwe country for many years. Out-migrations from reservation communities, increased participation in wage labor, and a continued degradation of wild-rice stands and other environments contributed to a deterioration of the seasonal economy. As deforestation progressed in the rustic timber and lake country, tourism contributed to tribal incomes in northern Minnesota, Wisconsin, and Michigan. Ojibwes worked at a number of off-reservation odd jobs and many found new sources of income as loggers, millers, and farm workers. Even so, seasonal changes still inspired many Ojibwes to harvest wild rice and blueberries, turn sap into maple syrup, and track deer in fresh snow.

The lives of Ojibwe people in the Upper Midwest were transformed as a result of new land tenure policies and the educational programs designed by the federal government to assure the success of allotment. Ironically, policies and practices of the assimilation years dismantled the economies of self-sufficient people who had for generations successfully educated their children in the cultural knowledge, values, and economic tradition best suited to the integrity of the woodland environment. A new educational agenda from Washington, which mandated forced acculturation away from that source of learning, would create unprecedented sources of stress for Ojibwe families and jar their distinctive cultural foundation.

Throughout most of the boarding school era, Ojibwe families encountered new economic conditions while some migrated to different homes. White Earth, the home of Mississippi, Gull Lake, Pembina, and Otter Tail Pillager bands, never fully realized the plans of Minnesota politicians who hoped to merge all Minnesota Ojibwes, except for those at Red Lake, on a single reservation. Still, migrations to the reservations "peaked in 1891 and again in 1893–1894," causing the population to double "between 1890 and 1920." The reservation was also characterized by ethnic diversity, as Metís families formed a significant community at White Earth. This community, considered among the many people who profited from the exploitation of the reservation, maintained large households with more children than their conservative Ojibwe "cousins."

Conservative families tended to be patrilineal, nuclear, with fewer children, but they identified a greater number of "dependents" in the census of 1910. The census indicated "a rise in the number of extended households" at White Earth after the economic descent precipitated by the land fraud. Widening poverty and landlessness within the community motivated conservatives to incorporate extended family and other tribal members into their households. Reckoning kin in the "Indian way" was often an informal process in a culture that respected cousins as brothers and sisters. The virtues of generosity and flexibility had always served the Ojibwes well.

Poverty, diaspora, and disease were the combined legacies of dispossession at White Earth and other reservations in the United States. In the boarding school era, tuberculosis replaced smallpox as the largest health threat to Indians. It has been estimated that one in every twenty Ojibwes was infected with the deadly disease shortly after the turn of the century. Deaths from pulmonary disease multiplied at White Earth between 1910 and 1920. In 1915, a doctor found 130 cases of it among the 898 Ojibwes he examined on the Bad River Reservation in Wisconsin. Studies conducted during the 1930s still revealed alarmingly high rates of tuberculosis among Indians in Minnesota. The suffering was widespread among Ojibwe communities, as evidenced by the high rates of the disease found at Fond du Lac and Grand Portage. At Nett Lake, an estimated 30 percent of the population was afflicted with tuberculosis. Approximately 15 percent of Minnesota Indians contracted tuberculosis at some point during their lives.

Tuberculosis statistics for Ojibwes were grim, but other communicable diseases also ravaged Ojibwe communities in the early twentieth century, including syphilis, gonorrhea, and trachoma. The Bureau of Indian Affairs, charged with providing medical care for Indians, often placed the blame on American Indians themselves for their poor state of health. The bureau attributed high rates of disease, child morality, and early death to the ignorance of an "immoral," superstitious people who preferred medicine men to government physicians and rejected vaccinations and the concept of cleanliness. The few poorly paid physicians and other health care personnel who served Indians could little alter the crisis in health care that existed on many Ojibwe reservations. Indian people were continually afflicted by diseases, such as trachoma, that were not problems for the majority population in the United States. Communities were particularly vulnerable to epidemic disease, as evidenced by the high death rates during the influenza pandemic of 1918.

During times of crisis, Ojibwe families had historically relied on the generosity of family members and the community at large. When new patterns of homelessness emerged at White Earth and other reservations after the turn of the century, time-honored methods of caring for the needy and adopting parentless children proved inadequate. Disease disrupted family life and other long-standing Native institutions. The ranks of the poor, sick, widowed, and orphaned grew. All too often, husbands, wives, and even older siblings were left with large families to maintain after the death of a spouse or parent. Overcrowding became a common feature of Ojibwe households, and many remaining allotments, some of them held by minor children or vulnerable to tax forfeiture, were secure only temporarily.

During these trying years for American Indians, some promoters of assimilation still looked to boarding school education as a panacea for many social problems, if they lacked the reformist zeal of the previous generation. The idea was conceived decades before that boarding school education, which removed young children from the tribal environment, would "civilize" and prepare Indians for citizenship while providing them with a practical, vocational education. It was widely assumed that vocational education not only suited the "native mentality" but would also help to solve the nation's so-called "Indian problem" by training the growing number of impoverished and landless Indians for wage labor.

Early in the era of forced assimilation, coercion was often used to gather Indian children to the far-away schools. Rations, annuities, and other goods were withheld from parents and guardians who refused to send children to school after a compulsory attendance law for American Indians was passed by Congress in 1891. Boarding schools in the Midwest were seldom located in areas close to Indian communities, making the transition traumatic for children. Visits from parents were rare events in the lives of boarding school students, especially those from very poor families. Assimilationists argued that the task of "civilizing" Indian children would be easier and lapses into tribal ways less likely if students stayed away from their homes and relatives until their education was complete.

Indian parents across the country responded in strikingly similar ways to the residential school concept. For the most part, they proved to be tenacious. They often refused to surrender their children to government authorities, especially the very young, and resisted boarding school education. Stories have filtered out of the Southwest that describe how rural tribal children had to be virtually kidnapped from their parents in order to be taken to the alien schools. In her autobiography, Helen Sekaquaptewa recalled that Hopi children were taught by their parents to play a game similar to "hide and seek" to avoid the police. The most painful story of resistance to assimilation programs and compulsory school attendance laws involved the Hopis in Arizona, who surrendered a group of men to the military rather than voluntarily relinquish their children. The Hopi men served time in federal prison at Alcatraz.

Ojibwe students were often rounded up by the reservation police before being sent to boarding school. Nina King of Red Lake recalled being removed after police came to her home. Certainly coercion was a popular method used to recruit early boarding school pupils, and in 1907 Commissioner of Indian Affairs Francis Leupp still endorsed the use of force in bringing children to school when families would not cooperate with voluntary measures.

Historian Frederick Hoxie has shown that the enthusiasm of reformers for boarding school education waned considerably after the turn of the century in favor of reservation day schools. Reformers and policy-makers began to doubt that full assimilation for Indians was possible. Boarding schools of this era imparted low expectations, and the goal of Indian education became to provide students with primary skills or channel them into a limited number of vocational trades. As expectations diminished, boarding school attendance remained a common experience for American Indians through the 1930s. More children attended day schools, but unfortunately, the bureaucracy was slow to respond to the new trend of reservation-based education. Euro-American reformers lost their initial enthusiasm for the transforming power of Indian education, and budget cuts undermined plans for vocational training. Non-Indian officials and teachers maintained a consistent level of disdain for tribal institutions and languages until a new wave of reformers led by John Collier infiltrated Indian education. Hoxie has suggested twentieth-century boarding schools became "an empty remnant of the reformers' original design." For most Indian students, government boarding schools provided them with a minimal education and a minimum of care.

Like other tribal people in the United States, Ojibwes were primarily educated in off-reservation schools in the late nineteenth and early twentieth centuries, and a still-significant number of children were in residential schools in 1940. A survey conducted at Red Lake in the late 1920s indicated that over 40 percent of the adult residents who had received formal education had been to one of the off-reservation government schools. By 1930, attending Flandreau, Wahpeton, or another school had become an arrangement common for people in the Red Lake community. . . .

Ojibwe families, known for strong kinship ties, only reluctantly sent their children to distant boarding schools even when persuaded it was for their best interest. Although most parents preferred to have their children remain at home or be educated on the reservation when that was an option, it is also evident that a great many Ojibwe families decided based on sheer hardship to send their children away to boarding school. The presence of so much disease on reservations widowed women and men before their time, and, ironically, many Indians began to use the boarding school as a refuge for their children during a family crisis.

There are many examples in the government archives of letters from families in distress who sought help from boarding school officials. When a Wisconsin Ojibwe father who had been recently widowed wrote to the superintendent of Flandreau in South Dakota, he described an unfortunate but all-too-common situation for American Indians living on early-twentieth-century reservations.

> I have lost my wife and left me with six children. . . . I would like to ask you to send these little folks over to you two or three years so I can get along. It is hard for me [to] stay here alone home because children not used home alone when mother gone. When I am going working out it hard for them . . . and this all I ask you if you have a place for them.

Under these sad circumstances, it is not difficult to imagine why a father would ask to place his six children in a residential school, even though it may have meant a separation of several years.

While facing a similar crisis, another father turned to Flandreau's superintendent for help in February 1924, just a week after the death of his wife.

> I am writing you to see if you can do me a favor by taking my daughter in your school it would be a big favor to me as my wife died Feb. 4th and have no way of taking care of the girl we cant stay at home as it is very lonesome for her. . . . Therefore I am asking you this favor, to turn my daughter over in your care.

Indian women were sometimes faced with the predicament of having to relinquish custody of their children to government boarding schools. Again, the death of a spouse was often the compelling factor. When a woman found it impossible to support a large family after the death of a husband, she could be reassured by the idea that clothing, a regular diet, and a stable place to live would be provided for her children. As one woman confided to her granddaughter at Flandreau, she thought the girl would have "better eats" at school than if she were to live at home.

Writing from a reservation in South Dakota, a Lakota woman described the many hardships she suffered after the death of her husband, who left her as the sole caretaker of seven children. The mother, Mrs. Bad Moccasin, wrote the superintendent of the school at Flandreau, where her son and daughter were students:

> I am always glad to hear from my children saying they are improving in their studies and that they sure are taking interest in it. That's what I want them to do is to take interest in their studies so they can learn and try to make man and woman out of themselves as those children have lost their father when they were little, and I have brought them up the best I can.

Due to her own illness, Mrs. Bad Moccasin was no longer able to earn a living for her large family but hoped her children would be someday able to support themselves as well as their younger siblings. She wanted her children to be educated and learn a trade at school. Indian families viewed government boarding schools as the only alternative for their children, one of the few opportunities for young people from rural areas to be educated and develop skills for future employment.

A six-year-old White Earth Ojibwe boy, Wallace, was first sent away to boarding school when his widowed mother was not able to care for him or his five siblings, aged three to seventeen. At the time Wallace entered Flandreau as a teenager, his application form said he had "no fixed home other than [the] Wahpeton Indian School" in North Dakota. Wallace did not return to White Earth; instead he lived his entire childhood and adolescence in government boarding schools.

When Wallace turned nineteen, he entered the army and was sent to Fort Snelling in Saint Paul, Minnesota. In a postcard to the Flandreau school from its longtime student, Wallace, a veteran of government institutions cheerily wrote, "I'll be in uniform by the time you receive this card. Ft. Snelling is a nice place. Lots of freedom, good food (best in U.S.) and two cities to visit." In his message, Wallace fondly referred to his alma mater as "My Shangri-la." That boarding schools proved to be a haven for some children, like Wallace, stands as a somber testimony to the poor quality of reservation life for Ojibwe families in the early twentieth century.

There are many signs that the fabric of Ojibwe community life persisted only under great stress during the boarding school era. For generations, Ojibwe families and other tribal people had traditionally made room for parentless children in their households. Orphans were treated with kindness, and little distinction was made between "natural" children and those adopted. Often, adoptees were blood relatives who simply went to live with a grandparent or aunt and uncle after a parent died. But as family life suffered during the early reservation, postallotment, and Great Depression years, traditional methods of absorbing orphaned children into the extended kinship group were not always possible. For a society that regarded caring for relatives as a virtue, with tender devotion to both the young and the elderly, this was a troubling sign.

When Ojibwe families could no longer maintain traditional methods of adopting orphans, more children were sent away from Indian communities to live and be reared in government boarding schools. Reservations like White Earth in northern Minnesota, devastated by allotment and plundering timber companies greedy to gain title to Indian lands, were unable to provide homes for all their deserving children. When a little White Earth boy, Clifford, described by a social worker as a "half starved undernourished child" was sent to the Pipestone boarding school in Minnesota after the death of his father, a note on his application read, "The boy is absolutely homeless with no relatives to care for him."

Orphaned children often applied to government boarding schools as family networks failed. A young Lac du Flambeau Ojibwe boy, Woodrow, went to Flandreau after numerous family members died, leaving him and a sister orphaned. Because his natural mother died when the boy was small, he already resided with foster parents on the reservation. After the death of his foster father, Woodrow explained that his mother "can't afford to pay board tuition or transportation to and from Ashland the nearest school."

Ojibwe family life was complex and blighted with instability on early-twentieth-century reservations. Children, left alone after the death of parents, were frequently shuttled from one home to another on the reservation as those families met with death or hardship, too. When Bernice, a young Ojibwe girl from Reserve, Wisconsin, applied to boarding school at Flandreau, it was because her shattered family could find no alternative.

Bernice's mother had died in 1924 of tuberculosis. Her father had remarried, giving Bernice a stepmother and eventually two younger siblings. When her stepmother died in 1929 of pneumonia, Bernice and two half-brothers went to live with their maternal grandmother, since their father was unemployed. The grandmother had also taken in the children of two of her recently widowed sons. At the time of Bernice's application to Flandreau, her younger brother, Antoine, a second-grader, was found to have an active case of pulmonary tuberculosis. Though Bernice had been a good student at the local school in Hayward, Wisconsin, achieving above average scores in science, history, arithmetic, English, and music, she stopped attending classes during the winter months because she lacked proper cold-weather clothing. By the time she entered Flandreau as a ninth-grader, Bernice reportedly did not "have a place that she [could] actually call her home nor [had] her living conditions been satisfactory." By going to school in South Dakota, Bernice hoped to attend classes regularly and to study home economics.

Mrs. Mary Twobirds, a Bad River Ojibwe woman from the community at Odanah, Wisconsin, sent several of her grandchildren to Flandreau beginning in the 1920s. Described as a "very intelligent old lady" by the local agent on the reservation, Mrs. Twobirds had raised six of her grandchildren after the death of her daughter, the children's mother. She frequently counseled her grandchildren about the importance of an education and reminded them that she would not always be able to provide for them. Mrs. Twobirds explained: "I am the guardian of these poor children since there mother died. I took care of them. I'm there grandmother and I've worked hard to raise these children on my own. Sent them to school here, our school here only goes as far as 8th grade."

A determined woman, Mrs. Twobirds bought a second-hand car to retrieve her grandchildren during the summer vacation. While driving from northern Wisconsin to South Dakota, they even "tipped over once, on a certain curve." Mrs. Twobirds lived twelve miles from the nearest high school in Ashland, Wisconsin, and daily transportation back and forth from school was problematic for the family, particularly during the northern Wisconsin winters. For the Twobirds grandchildren, Flandreau represented an opportunity for them to complete their schooling. . . .

A surprising number of students, older and orphaned, were not being cared for by adults at all when they enrolled in boarding school. In 1913, Joseph High Elk of Eagle Butte, South Dakota, asked to enter Flandreau after having taken "care of myself since I was old enough to work." Years later, when a teenage Menominee, David, enrolled at Flandreau in 1936, the agent at Keshena, Wisconsin, reported that he was "without parents [and] has no home." The hard-working Menominee boy had been trying to support himself while he attended a local high school. The agent wrote that David had "used practically all of his money paying for board and lodging while attending a nearby high school, and we have decided that he can no longer afford to pay such expenses."

Alphonse Caswell, one of many former Flandreau students from Red Lake, decided to go away to school after his parents died. Alphonse planned to learn a trade and then return home to Red Lake to care for his younger brother and sister, Louis and Priscilla, who resided with relatives. As a young man, Alphonse strongly felt responsible for his younger siblings and assumed the roles of his late parents. By the time of his graduation, Alphonse was described as "an exacting workman, capable of thinking for himself," and with "a pleasing personality." As it turned out, Alphonse's time at Flandreau greatly influenced his later life. After graduation he married a young woman from White Earth, Ethelbert Branchaud, whom he had met while she attended the Pipestone boarding school, just a few miles away from Flandreau. Later, Alphonse's younger sister Priscilla went to Flandreau. Flandreau was undergoing change in the 1930s, developing into a more sympathetic institution, and Alphonse successfully kept his family together with some help from the school. The Caswells remained a close and loving family. . . .

Some Ojibwes tried to make a living on the reservations, whereas others decided to make their way in the cities. In the 1920s, it was not unusual for the growing number of urban Ojibwe parents, especially women, to enroll their children in boarding schools. These women, often single mothers, had left reservations like White Earth, and migrated to urban centers in order to find work to support their families. Once in the city, women generally could find work only at low-paying, menial jobs. In cities like Minneapolis, Milwaukee, and Chicago, Indian women usually lacked the family networks of the reservation, which made finding care for their children and supporting a family an increased burden.

When women did not receive support, financial or otherwise, from the father of their children, they had few alternatives other than to send them home to live with relatives or to enroll them at Indian boarding schools. This was the case for one Ojibwe mother living in Saint Paul, Minnesota, who left an abusive husband after he tried to assault their twelve-year-old daughter. In the aftermath of this crisis, the woman asked to send her daughter and another child to Flandreau while she looked for work.

In 1924, a single mother of several children labored in the linen room of the Ryan Hotel in Saint Paul while two of her sons attended school at Flandreau. As she explained,

> I have had the sole support of my three boys for the last six years. . . . I never had no help from their father . . . with the exception of the little he has sent for them this spring. I have had to care and work for them while they were small . . . but I am just like an old mother bear and will fight for my children.

Given her precarious economic situation, this parent felt boarding school was best for her boys and she was "real proud of the good work they have been doing this year."

Boarding school became a solution for many urban Indian women when they were not able to support a family. In 1925, a woman with two daughters, aged fourteen and eleven, living in Milwaukee asked to enroll her children at Flandreau. As she said, "I am living in the city, trying to keep my two little girls and sending them to school, but with what little funds I have I can not do justice to them or myself so I have been thinking of your school."

The following letter, written in 1925 by an Ojibwe woman who had relocated to Minneapolis, illustrates some of the problems Indians encountered as they moved to new, urban areas. The mother, originally from White Earth, felt that the urban environment was a bad influence on her child. As she explained to the administrator at Flandreau:

> I have my boy Herbert . . . from White Earth, with me and I have come to the conclusion that this city life is not conducive to his moral welfare. His grandmother . . . is not able to give him the proper care on account of [forgetfulness] or else I would send him back to the reservation. My sincere wish is that he enter your institution so that he may obtain the proper training to success. . . .

For a variety of sound reasons, students . . . often chose to attend off-reservation Indian schools. The small towns of northern Wisconsin and Minnesota have an unfortunate history of discrimination against Indians. When students felt unwelcome in nearby public institutions due to racism against Indians, government boarding schools offered a less threatening environment. Rural students had many serious issues to consider when deciding on a school, including their own proximity to public school facilities or the inability of some local schools to offer the upper grades.

Sometimes children were attracted to boarding schools when siblings or cousins were already students. At times boarding school students actively recruited new pupils when they came home for summer vacation. In August 1921, before the start of a new term, a young Lakota boy from Greenwood, South Dakota, wrote to his superintendent wondering if "you want a boy to go to school that is in third grade and another boy in second grade. If so let me know before Sept . . . both of these boys are 8 . . . years of age."

A few students, such as George White Bull, carefully considered their educational options before deciding on a particular school. In 1913, the young boy from Porcupine, South Dakota, wrote to ask to be enrolled at Flandreau, after attending Ogalalla boarding school for four years but saying he no longer got "much out of it."

> I am going to write to you and asked you how I can come to school and so wish you would give me the proportion to come I play in band for two or three years and I'm just in fifth grade and I am very glad to learned little more if I can I have looked over all the non-reservation schools but I dont think I can go any wheres but to come over to your Flandreau Indian School as I thought this School will give me a little more education so that I can make an honest living when I get out. I know several Indian boys from here that had been there before and as they tell me about how the School is over there and so I thought I will get my learning from you Well Sir I wish you would kindly send me some blanks so that I can fill them up The very first thing I want to do when I get over there is to join the band.

It was very common for siblings, cousins, or friends to attend the same boarding school, which alleviated some of the isolation most students encountered at off-reservation schools. In 1913, Simon Antelope of Greenwood, South Dakota, enrolled his fourteen-year-old son at Flandreau as well as a neighbor's son who "talks English and reads it." Mr. Antelope commented that the boys were "both full Indian but are used to work on farm." In a similar request made in June 1914, a North Dakota father sent the ten-dollar fare for the summer return of his son Waldo and asked to send another boy back with him in the fall who was "a little younger than him but smart and talk good English."

Some children, especially those with a poor family life, grew tired of their situation on the reservation and asked to be sent away to school. Josephine, a teenager from Wisconsin, was reportedly "anxious to go to school away from the reservation" and felt that the "classical courses offered at the local parochial school" did not "benefit" her, and "wanted to begin high school work with a vocation in mind." Josephine's family was poor and received support from their agency.

The complexity of Native American life and the multitude of problems Indians encountered throughout the boarding school era are all too obvious from the letters received at Flandreau and Haskell. In many cases, it is apparent that boarding schools created problems for Indians, but clearly in other instances the institutions provided a solution, however temporary, to some of their most crucial dilemmas. American Indians at times resented boarding schools, and rightly so, but they also found them useful. In times of family crisis or economic hardship, Indians could turn to boarding schools for help. Ojibwes and members of other tribes found a place for these institutions after the era of forced assimilation had passed.

Throughout the boarding school era, Indian parents and students hoped education would provide them with the skills to earn a living in order to cope with reservation conditions. After reservations were reduced in size or allotted, the most frequent result was poverty for Indians. When families could not earn an adequate living on the reservation or in the city, they often enrolled children in boarding schools as a temporary or long-term solution to some of their most pressing problems. Parents expected that in boarding school basic needs would be met in the form of food, clothing, a rudimentary education, and the opportunity to learn a trade. Even modest expectations on the part of parents were sometimes disappointed.

Reservation life proved to be a constant struggle for American Indians in the early twentieth century. Disease and poor health care combined to take the lives of many Indians at a young age. The high death rates reached a crisis point in many Indian communities. Traditional methods of absorbing needy individuals into the larger kinship network were not always possible as early death and increased poverty overwhelmed Ojibwe family life. In many instances Indian parents died young, and children were left without caretakers. Boarding schools often took in needy and orphaned children.

Ojibwe communities were situated in remote regions of the northern states. School facilities, especially high schools that were designed to serve the non-Indian community, were seldom conveniently located for Ojibwe students. During the notoriously harsh winters in these regions, it was nearly impossible to expect children to attend schools miles from home on a regular basis. Again, Indian students and their families had few alternatives other than education in a residential school.

Ojibwe students sometimes chose education in a government boarding school because of the familiarity and security of an all-Indian environment. Ojibwes from northern Wisconsin and Minnesota often complained of the discrimination they experienced in local white communities. There is little doubt that government boarding schools, although often antagonistic toward tribal cultures in many ways, also provided a friendly environment because of the intertribal composition of the student body. The decision to enter a government boarding school could be made by a reservation official, a struggling parent or guardian, or a personally motivated student. But, once reached, the boarding school path was frequently rocky, and there were few signs of an easy passage for beginners.

Crow Families in Transition

FREDERICK E. HOXIE

As Crow families struggled through the demographic pressures of the early twentieth century and looked about for a place to settle, they faced a crucial decision. How would they settle this new environment? The Northern Pacific Railroad's arrival in 1883 had brought the nearby city of Billings to life and had stimulated commercial agriculture along the length of the Yellowstone valley. In the 1890s, this process accelerated despite the onset of hard times. The army closed Fort Custer in 1898, marking the region's transfer to civilian authority, and the following year the sale of all the reservation lands between the fort and the Yellowstone opened additional farming and stock-raising areas to whites. During the decade of the 1890s two new rail lines cut through the reservation. The first, along Clark's Fork west of Pryor, and the second running the length of the Little Bighorn valley, from Sheridan, Wyoming, to the Yellowstone. (By the time the Clark's Fork line was completed, the sale of the tribe's western rangelands placed it outside the boundaries of the preserve.)

The availability of transportation increased the value of reservation lands and hastened a movement away from cattle ranching and towards farming. This transition also brought new legions of settlers to the area. By 1907 the combination of economic ambition and settler energy brought a town into being at the confluence of the Little Bighorn and Bighorn Rivers. Fittingly, the principal figure in the land company which controlled the real estate in the new hamlet of Hardin, Montana, was John Rankin, a man who developed his taste for Yellowstone valley rangeland a decade earlier during his service as allotment agent on the Crow Reservation. In 1912, Hardin became the seat of Bighorn County, a branch of state government which asserted its jurisdiction over the entire Crow Reservation.

As the non-Indian population rose in size and drew closer to their borders, the Crow residents of the reservation formed themselves into five major communities. While initiated by the Indians themselves, this process was supported by government action: a succession of agents subdivided the preserve into five districts and created agency branches in each. By 1920, this process had created five self-contained communities across the 350 square miles of what was now Crow country. The core of each was a collection of government offices, stores and supply shops.

The communities—and the districts which formed around them—began as camps gathered around an important leader or group of leaders. Along the western end of the preserve, for example, Plenty Coups had settled along the upper reaches of Pryor Creek even before the move to Crow Agency. Similarly, decisions by

Pretty Eagle and Iron Bull to settle near the mouth of Rotten Grass Creek in the Bighorn valley had brought others to the area. Further down the river—and at the lower end of the Little Bighorn valley—a community of River Crows and former scouts gathered near Fort Custer. Referred to as "Black Lodge," the tribal name for the River Crow bands, the people along this northern border of the reservation looked to headmen like Two Belly, Young Onion and Two Leggings for leadership. At the head of the Little Bighorn, Medicine Crow, Old Dog, Spotted Horse and Crazy Head attracted a number of families to the place where Lodge Grass Creek enters the river. A final district, called "Reno" after the creek where Custer's lieutenant scrambled for his life in 1876, surrounded the site of Crow Agency itself. Among the band leaders settled there were Bull Goes Hunting and Takes Wrinkle.

Agency personnel were assigned to these five communities as early as 1888, but it wasn't until 1892 that traders were licensed to operate at the mouth of Rotten Grass Creek and at Fort Custer, and not until 1894 that rations began to be issued at Pryor and in the Bighorn valley. In the ensuing decade schools were started at Pryor, Lodge Grass and at Rotten Grass Creek, adding to the sense that these communities were branches of the main reservation town at Crow Agency. In 1907, the tribe's agent reported that 450 Crows lived at Lodge Grass, 400 at Pryor, 400 at Bighorn, 200 at Black Lodge and 150 at Reno.

Settled originally by the 150 members of Plenty Coups's band in the early 1880s, the community of Pryor was sixty miles by horse or buggy from Crow Agency. Despite its distance from local authorities, however, Pryor was not isolated. It lay less than thirty miles from Billings, and following the sale of the tribe's western lands in 1890, it was adjacent to white-owned ranchland and a rail line leading south from the Yellowstone into Wyoming. The skill of the community's leader, together with its access to whites other than Indian Office personnel gave Pryor an independent air. When a subagent was appointed to take up permanent residence there in 1894, he was cautioned by his superiors that the Crows of Pryor "have been allowed greater liberty than those residing in other districts." The new officer should therefore be careful to see "that the changes in their management . . . shall not be too abrupt."

The center of the Pryor community was the two-story frame home built for Plenty Coups by the Indian Office shortly after the relocation of the agency to the Little Bighorn. Placed amidst a grove of cottonwoods overlooking Pryor Creek, the house was an ideal meeting place for both Indians and local ranchers. From his comments in the formal councils called to consider grazing leases, it was clear that Plenty Coups cultivated good relations with local cattlemen like Nelson Story and with the growing number of sheep men (such as Charles M. Bair) who were coming into the region. In addition, the chief operated a "store" at his home, a place where local residents could come for supplies and food. Since Plenty Coups had no trader's license or capital, his operation was more likely a kind of distribution center where presents from local ranchers and the leader's own crops and supplies could be retailed to the community. Surviving records suggest that Plenty Coups extended easy credit to his neighbors and followers; his goal did not appear to be the maximization of profit. In addition, Plenty Coups regularly intervened with the agent on questions arising from the allotment of land or the sale of livestock. It was not with too much exaggeration that a white visitor wrote in 1930 that the house "was the home of a great and famous man, the ruler of a people, an avowed sovereign." Not everyone was so enthusiastic. In 1912 the Crow agent had declared that the Indians of Pryor ("that bunch of Indians") had "grown impatient of all restraint."

In the years just prior to the relocation of the agency, Iron Bull, a former scout and respected tribal spokesman, had frequently expressed a desire to settle at the head of the Bighorn valley. He died shortly after the migration out of the mountains, however, and leadership in the valley generally passed to his comrade and fellow scout Pretty Eagle. For the first two decades of reservation life, Pretty Eagle played the role of the local chief as effectively in the Bighorn valley as Plenty Coups did at Pryor. From his home along Woody Creek, just ten miles over the nearby buttes from Crow Agency, the chief could communicate with local residents as well as government officials. Some flavor of his effectiveness is suggested by an order that went out to the local subagent in the spring of 1903. "Any time Pretty Eagle interferes with any orders that you give," Agent Reynolds wrote his man in the Bighorn, "send him to this agency." Referring to the chief's thirty-four-year-old son who was currently serving as a tribal policeman, Reynolds added, "And the first time Holds The Enemy disobeys an order you give him you send him to this agency also, and I will remove his star. . . ."

Despite the prominence of Pretty Eagle and Holds The Enemy, the 400 or more residents of the Bighorn valley spread themselves for twenty miles along the river, from the entrance of the Bighorn canyon in the south, to the flatland upstream from Fort Custer. This tendency to disperse accelerated after the elder chief's death in 1903. Among the variety of people to settle in the valley during the 1890s was Spotted Rabbit, a young man who had ridden through Crow Agency with Sword Bearer in 1887, but who had escaped imprisonment on the promise that he would avoid trouble and take up farming. Soon after his arrival, Spotted Rabbit married a young widow named Medicine Tobacco whose son and eighteen-year-old brother had just died. Medicine Tobacco's only surviving son, Philip Iron Head, came with her as she and Spotted Rabbit took an allotment near his father, within sight of the now-deserted Fort C. F. Smith. Closer to Pretty Eagle was Sits Down Spotted, only twenty-one when Crow Agency was founded in 1884 and still listed as a member of his stepfather's household. Within three years, however, two of Sits Down Spotted's four siblings would die and he would leave to begin farming along the Bighorn. By 1890 he was the owner of a house, a wagon, a plow and a variety of farming tools.

Among the River Crow families settling at Black Lodge, near Fort Custer at the lower end of the Bighorn and Little Bighorn valleys, was Three Irons, probably the same man who had become Tom Leforge's "brother" in 1868. As a member of Bear Wolf's band, Three Irons had been one of the last Crows to relocate to the reservation, preferring to travel with his kinsmen, visiting Sioux and Assiniboin camps in Montana and the Dakotas. A term in the Fort Custer guardhouse in 1883 probably persuaded him to stay put, and he apparently established a camp on the prairies between the army post and the new agency. During the 1890s, Three Irons' wife, mother-in-law and two of his three children died, leaving him alone with the care of a son. Nearby, another family with roots outside the reservation was making its home. Louis Bompard was the twenty-two-year-old son of an Assiniboin woman and a white man (perhaps a French-Canadian trader), when he first appeared on the agency records as a young horse raider in 1887. Like Three Irons, Bompard lost two family members during the 1890s, but he and his new wife, a Crow woman who took the confusing name Lois Bompard, had two children and began farming.

In addition to being the home of River Crows, former scouts and other relative newcomers to the Crow Reservation, Black Lodge also contained people who worked at Fort Custer or the new agency. Accusations of liquor selling—still relatively rare before 1900—were usually aimed in this direction, as were complaints that residents were begging for food from soldiers and traders. Agency policemen—most notably the River Crow officer Big Medicine—also were frequently drawn from Black Lodge.

South of Crow Agency lay the Reno district, a collection of Mountain Crow camps scattered across the rich bottomland of the Little Bighorn. Like Black Lodge, Reno was too close to the reservation headquarters to develop an independent leadership. Among its more prominent residents were Boy That Grabs, the chief of the agency police force until his death in 1903, and Bull Goes Hunting, a respected, older band leader and religious figure. As a young man, Bull Goes Hunting had married Medicine Crow's widowed mother and brought the young man into his home. The young leader considered the old man his father.

Like Bull Goes Hunting, many Reno residents had close ties to tribal members who lived further up the valley. The greatest concentration of these people appeared near the "Forty Mile" stage crossing where Lodge Grass Creek entered the Little Bighorn. People here were in easy reach of the Bighorn and Wolf Mountains and were less exposed to outsiders and government officials than their kinsmen down on the flatland of Reno and Black Lodge. Among them was Spotted Horse, who had always claimed the area as his own. Following Sword Bearer's death, Spotted Horse apparently decided to live at Lodge Grass in peace. The uprising had apparently convinced him that further resistance was futile. Medicine Crow, however, usually represented the area at tribal gatherings. A veteran war leader, Medicine Crow was only thirty-six when the Sword Bearer crisis ended. He seemed to lack Plenty Coups's ambition for tribal leadership, but he matched his contemporary from Pryor in his ability to unify the residents of his district.

The grasslands and river bottoms south of Lodge Grass also attracted a group of newcomers. These were mixed-blood families who had originally settled on the tribe's western lands near the city of Billings. When these lands were sold in 1890, and opened to white settlement two years later, tribal members had the option of remaining on their homesteads (now off the reservation) or claiming lands within the reduced boundaries of the preserve. Among those who relocated was the family of James B. Cooper, a white railroad worker from the East, and his Crow wife, Margaret Wallace. Their household also included three grown children of Margaret Wallace's prior marriage to Fellows D. Pease, a fur trader and an early Crow agent.

The local agent called Cooper and others like him "squaw men" and made every effort to exclude them from tribal life. The Cooper/Pease settlers in Lodge Grass were eager to exploit the farming and ranching country around them, however, and they quickly established themselves in the area. The Coopers ranched at the headwaters of Rottengrass Creek and were frequently involved in Lodge Grass affairs. As James Cooper passed from the scene, his eldest son, Joe—who had been one of the earliest students at the Crow Agency boarding school—took his place as outspoken defender of the family's interests. His half-brother, George Pease, settled near the Coopers for a time before moving on to Lodge Grass, where he opened the town's first store in 1900.

The mix of its location along the new rail line connecting Wyoming to the Yellowstone, the presence of tribal elders like Spotted Horse and young, relatively sophisticated mixed-blood leaders like Joe Cooper gave Lodge Grass a unique personality. While they did not reject the presence or activities of outsiders, community members were interested in charting their own course. There was little of the isolation of Pryor or Bighorn and perhaps less intimidation than was often felt by the residents of the two districts adjacent to Crow Agency itself. Not surprisingly, the residents of Lodge Grass were the first group on the reservation to submit a petition to Indian Office to protest the firing of a popular agent.

A final mark of Lodge Grass's independence was the formation by its residents of a sixth reservation community in the years just before World War I. Recognized as a promising agricultural area, the area near Pass Creek at the southern end of the Little Bighorn valley had few Crow residents before 1910. The local agent reported in 1909 that there were about thirty people in the area. During the next five years, however, a group which included both mixed-blood Crows and the son of Spotted Horse moved into the area near the rail station at Wyola. Before long they were petitioning for the creation of a subagency in their new district and electing their own representatives to attend meetings of the tribal council.

Like an empty stage set, a description of the early reservation's basic social geography tells us little until we observe the movement of families across it. Similarly, a roster of names cannot by itself reconstruct a family system. Like the Crows who searched in the early twentieth century for opportunities to maintain their social traditions in a modern setting, modern researchers must seek out the human decisions that shape the meanings embedded in a census report. Understanding what influenced such decisions—the decisions to take up residence in a particular location or to choose a particular mate—should help illuminate the social values that persisted into the reservation era. The object of such a search is a pattern of behavior that describes the social relationships that held Crow people together as they entered the twentieth century.

It is plain that households made up of grandparents, parents, children and other relatives formed the basis for Crow family life in the reservation era. Crows continued to gather in these traditional family groups even though conditions had changed. Nevertheless, it is less clear what the nature of these households was after 1884. It is necessary, then, to trace changes within these households during the first decades of the reservation in order to generate an accurate portrait of life in the reservation's five districts during the first decades of the twentieth century.

Census enumerations provide one way to track the behavior of Crow households through time. There are many reasons for this. First, they are numerous. Beginning in 1887, federal officials conducted an annual census of the tribe. In 1900 and 1920, the U.S. Census Bureau added special schedules for Indians to its regular inventory, providing modern researchers with a wealth of "extra" questions to examine. Second, very few tribal members left the reservation before World War II. (Indeed, as a legacy of the 1880s, Crows could be jailed for leaving their communities without the permission of their agent until World War I.) Viewed as a group, these censuses hold out the possibility of tracing individuals (or groups of individuals) through several enumerations and linking them to create a portrait of social behavior.

Two areas are most helpful in presenting a picture of Crow family and household life in the early reservation years: residence and marriage. Where did people settle when the reservation was established? Who settled with them? What kinds of structures emerged in their new settlements? Marriage can have many culturally specific meanings, but for purposes of analysis we can call it the process by which people select mates and form households. Whom did people marry and for how long did they remain together? What did Crows believe about marriage and household formation?

Five tribal enumerations provide some answers to these questions. The first of these censuses, undated but probably written in 1883 or 1884, is a "Record of Indian Bands." It is contained in four small notebooks that list 401 households. The "head" of each household is named along with a record of the number of men, women and children in the group. In addition, the census identifies each unit according to a list of twenty-seven "bands." The 1884 census provides a picture of prereservation social structure. We know that all the people listed by name in that census were the heads of households, and we know that at least some of the people grouped together in a band were affiliated in some way.

The second document is the 1900 federal census. While the federal census does not provide information regarding the location of individual residences, it does contain information on spouses, children and marital status.

Third is the roster of Crow allotments prepared following the completion of the first general division of the reservation into individual homesteads in 1905. This list provides the precise location of assigned residences as well as the location of allotments assigned to other family members. Agents frequently reported that Crows did not live on their allotments, but a family's allotments were generally made together and located in the district of their residence. The allotment list can therefore be used as a general indicator of family residence.

Fourth is the 1910 federal census, which contained information parallel to that in the 1900 enumeration. Fifth is a census of "Adult Crow Indians" prepared by the agency superintendent in 1920. This list indicated the home district of Crow adults and listed husbands and wives together.

As a set, these records provide five "snapshots" of Crow households taken at intervals over a thirty-six-year period. While sharing the flaws of any bureaucratic document prepared by outsiders, they can be checked against each other to eliminate many errors. Linking individuals in these records allows a modern observer to trace the consequences of a process by which individuals and other members of their households shifted from a migratory hunting subsistence to a pattern of permanent residence in an agricultural community.

An initial comparison of the 1884 and 1900 censuses produces a list of 183 individuals who appeared in both. That is, there were 183 Crows who were listed as heads of a household before the establishment of modern Crow Agency and who were still household heads in 1900. Of the 183 people who appeared in the first two censuses, 135 were identifiable on the 1905 allotment roll. These were the

"First Families of the Crow Reservation." They and their immediate kin can be identified in the federal census, their allotments can be located, and they can be tied to a prereservation social affiliation. Moreover, because they were heads of households throughout the first twenty years of reservation life, we can imagine they formed the backbone of Crow society in that period.

Several prereservation bands settled together and formed the core of a reservation district. The Plenty Coups band, for example, settled predominately along Pryor Creek, while Old Crow's and Spotted Horse's groups preferred the Little Bighorn. In addition, it appears that once settled in an area, families persisted there. . . .

The Back Of The Neck family presents a similar picture. Following Back Of The Neck's departure for Bighorn, his wife, Corn Woman, remained at Pryor with their children. In addition, Goes To House, listed as a member of their family in 1900, also remained in Pryor and married a local man. The women of the Back Of The Neck family stuck together and persisted in their original location. . . .

While one's band affiliation appears to have had varying degrees of influence on an individual's decision about where to settle, it is clear that once located in a district, a family remained there over time. Apparently, there was a structure, either in the Crow's nineteenth-century culture or in the emerging reservation community that fostered persistence in these separate districts. Several elements of this structure suggest themselves. First, in none of these cases—or in any dozens of other family genealogies—is there an example of members of one band marrying the offspring of fellow band members. These data confirm that Crow bands were exogamous. Children of the Crow first families—particularly the men who are most easily traced and are therefore overrepresented in the documents—sought spouses from outside their band but within their district. As a result, there was relatively little movement away from the places where first family members had originally settled.

It is also apparent from other sources that Crow bands in the 1880s generally contained members of more than one clan. The Plenty Coups band, for example, contained three prominent warriors in addition to its famous leader. Three Bears and Bell Rock belonged to the Without Shooting They Bring Game clan, while the headman and Hunts To Die were Sore Lips people. Similarly, Old Dog, the band leader who settled at Lodge Grass, was a member of the Sore Lips clan, while two other prominent leaders in his band belonged to two other kin groups. The Bread was a Whistling Waters clan member and Arm Around The Neck belonged to the Newly Made Lodges group.

Each newly settled district contained members of several Crow clans. Certain clans might predominate in one area (Not Mixed or Filth Eating at Black Lodge, Sore Lip or Burnt Mouth at Pryor, Whistling Waters at Lodge Grass), but members of other clans would also be present. What government agents saw as settled farming communities were actually re-creations of Crow band settlements. Nothing in the otherwise alien reservation environment disrupted the clan system. On the contrary, the clan system served to enforce the Crows' ties to their new districts by regulating marriage and providing a source of loyalty and support at a time of intense suffering. The traditional taboo against marrying within one's clan continued, thereby reinforcing old rules and ensuring that new marriages would continue to link a wide network of Crow households. While there was a great deal of visiting between districts on the reservation, there was no necessity for children of the community's first families to leave home to find a suitable spouse. Even though they might live in a crowded log cabin in a remote section of one district, household members could maintain their ties to kinsmen in every part of the reservation.

The preceding description of household formation and family persistence would have puzzled George W. Frost. When Frost was superintendent of the Crow Reservation in 1877, he reported that there was *no* structure to Crow social behavior. "Perhaps the worst feature of the Crow tribes," he wrote in his annual report that year, "is the almost perfect disregard of marital rights. Polygamy is common, a man taking all the wives that he can support, and, in their language, 'throwing them away' at pleasure. . . . They consider adultery no crime, and . . . for its commission there is no punishment." A decade later as the new Crow Agency boarding school was being established, one of Mr. Frost's successors, Henry E. Williamson, suggested that a twelve-foot-high board fence be erected around the new buildings. "There is now only a wire fence," he reported to Washington, so that "every Indian from the camp who wishes to can converse with the pupils and it cannot be prevented." The evil to be avoided was obvious: "The scenes of camp life . . . are detrimental to the pupils."

An analysis of the 1900 and 1910 federal census returns for the Crow Reservation presents a different view. Crows continued to marry within the tribe and to maintain their tribal language as the favored method of communication. While the percentage of the population reporting "100% Indian blood" declined from 91 to 77% between 1900 and 1910, the tribe continued to be overwhelmingly Crow in ancestry and orientation. Of all reservation residents, 98% were Crows, and two-thirds of them spoke only their tribal language.

When one turns to marriage statistics, there are two striking patterns. First, Crows valued marriage. (The term "marriage" is used here even though it is clear that the Crow respondents and federal census takers had different definitions of the term. Both understood the concept of stable, long-term unions of men and women.) Over 90% of all adult Crows were either married or widowed, according to the federal censuses of 1900 and 1910. Moreover, Crows appear to have married for long periods. Of the 53 people aged 60–69 who were married in 1900, they reported marriages lasting an average of more than thirty years.

Second, the census figures reveal that Crows married with extraordinary frequency. In an ear when some divorces still required legislative approval, 20% of the Crow tribe reported that they had been married four times or more. One might think that Agent Frost's condemnations were based on something concrete. But a careful examination of these data demonstrates Frost's myopia. For both men and women, the length of *last* marriage for individuals married in excess of five times indicates that the ideal of a long-term stable union had not been abandoned, even by those who married frequently. For men in their sixties, despite the fact that they had been married an average of eight times apiece, they had probably lived with their current spouse since sometime in their early forties.

Just as the persistence of district communities indicated the persistence of clan and family allegiances across the reservation, so the juxtaposition of outraged agents and extended marriages suggests a continuation of traditional Crow standards for individual conduct. Because Crow society was perceived as an amalgam of clans, marriages were more significant as alliances of extended families than they were as unions of individuals. For Crow men and women, the formation of a household brought together several generations and a large network of kin. When consolidated into an extended family containing children, this marriage created a complex web of social loyalties and social obligations. In the words of one modern anthropologist, "Crow women are not passive vehicles, but active *partners.*"

"Tell me of your marriage . . . Did you fall in love?" Montana historian Frank Linderman asked an elderly Crow woman in the 1920s. "No," she replied, "young women did not fall in love, and get married to please themselves, as they do now. They listened to their fathers, married the men selected for them." Other reports confirm Pretty Shield's answer. Suitors sought the approval of their intended's family through a process of gift giving which the girl's parents would control. In most cases these parents would play a major role in negotiating the terms of their daughter's marriage. If the marriage proved unsuccessful, the girl's parents would also supervise the dismissal of the man, even resorting in extreme cases to destroying their son-in-law's property and burning his lodge. The Anglo-American idea of romantic love—the idea that prompted Linderman's question in the first place—was not the central focus of Crow family life. Pretty Shield's reply suggests that in the twentieth century as in the nineteenth, other concerns took first priority.

While sexual intercourse would seal and confirm a Crow marriage, individual sexual behavior was as irrelevant to the negotiations that led to the formation of a household in the reservation context as it had been in Leforge's day. Marriage partners were generally expected to be faithful, but little premium was placed on abstinence or virginity. Crow children were encouraged to think of marriage partners at an early age, Crow girls were not condemned for sexual experimentation, and Crow boys were frequently told that "women were like a herd of buffalo." Indeed, one feature of the rivalry between Crow warrior societies in the nineteenth century was wife kidnapping. This practice—which Larocque had witnessed in 1805—was supported by a warrior ethic that encouraged stealth by attackers and stoicism among a raid's victims. Even though warrior societies declined in importance after the founding of Crow Agency, young men and women continued to participate in considerable sexual experimentation. In the tribal courts, virtually all prosecutions for "adultery" were of men and women under 25. That fact, coupled with the statistics of marriage and divorce, indicated that "traditional" practices continued into the reservation era.

The persistence of distinctively Crow concepts of gender provides a final indication of the nature of Crow family life in the reservation era. Thanks to the preference of the U.S. government for male political leaders and the dominance of men in the cash economy, Crow males were able to sustain an image of themselves as warriors and providers. Chiefs and headmen now rose before a general council and conducted verbal battles with the government—a faint echo of the old war parties, but still an opportunity to display bravado and win over younger followers. In a similar way, the Indian Office's preference for hiring males as teamsters and policemen and the neighboring cattlemen's need for cowboys provided men a chance to exercise economic independence and provide for their families. While Crow women had less support from external authorities, the tribe's traditional ideas about females were surprisingly evident in the twentieth century.

Unlike Europeans, Crows did not believe that the creator made women after men or that women were derived from men. Instead, all the versions of the tribal creation story that have been collected indicate that the two genders were made at the same time and from the same materials. One story has Old Man Coyote and his companion, "the little coyote," make "people," while another has Old Man Coyote make men and women out of mud before telling them "to have intercourse" to produce the first people. Crow mythology describes females as sharing equal status with men and having a comparable level of autonomy. Wives leave their husbands when neglected or mistreated, and women even dispute with mythical heroes like Old Man Coyote. In one famous story, two girls refuse to marry Old Man Coyote and trick him when he comes back to them to seek revenge. Being biologically female did not in itself prevent Crow women from participating in any activity.

Crow traditions made clear the distinction between biology and one's social role. Not only did the tribe accept men who dressed and lived as women, they acknowledged the achievements of women who chose to take on the male role of warrior. For example, when Pretty Shield was interviewed in the 1920s, she recalled two women who fought with the Crow warriors at the Battle of the Rosebud. After describing their exploits, she told her interviewer, "Ahh, the men did not tell you this; but I have. And it's the truth. Every old Crow, man or woman, knows that it is the truth." The anthropologist Robert Lowie reported a berdache living in the Bighorn district of the reservation in the first decade of the twentieth century. He reported that the government had repeatedly tried to have the man dress in male clothing but his neighbors refused, "saying that it was against his nature." In both instance, the successful fulfillment of one's social obligations was far more significant to the Crow community than an individual's anatomical makeup.

In the reservation setting, Crow women were expected to conform to Anglo-American standards of behavior. Not only were men considered preeminent in politics and economic activity, but government officials placed restrictions on the Crow tradition of shifting marriage partners frequently at a young age. Women were expected to conform to their husbands' desires rather than to maintain the level of autonomy they had enjoyed in the nineteenth century. Countering these pressures were the persistence of clan affiliation and the tradition of matrilineal descent within the clans, the pattern of frequent marriage and sexual experimentation noted above, and a personal sense of autonomy and individual power. While the latter is difficult to document, a set of twenty-three wills dictated by tribal members in the years just prior to World War I provide one kind of insight.

Fifteen of these wills—all filed with the agent between 1910 and 1914—were written or dictated by women. Of the fifteen women, only three left anything to their husbands; other relatives usually took precedence. But even for the three women who remembered their spouses, the meaning of the gift was not obvious. One woman, for example, Goes First, left 48 acres of land to her husband and 77 acres to another man "who has lived with me and helped care for me. . . ." Among the others who left their husbands nothing were three who added language similar to that in Sarah Shane Williams's will. "I do not wish my husband . . . to have any share in my estate," Mrs. Williams wrote, "For reason that he deserted me several years ago and has since given nothing toward my support." These statements provide powerful evidence that Crow women continued to believe that marriage was an alliance of equals.

Their allegiance to their family and clan relations did not require them to embrace Victorian mortality; they continued to inhabit and sustain a distinctively Crow set of social structures that functioned within the limits of the reservation environment.

During the first two decades of the twentieth century, the persistence of distinctively Crow patterns of kinship, marriage and family life established the underpinnings for community life. The "extensive" and "inclusive" relationships that Joseph Medicine Crow observed while growing up near Lodge Grass in the 1910s and 1920s were inherited from the people who had belonged to bands that had hunted buffalo in the Yellowstone country a century before. At the same time, the "harmony" and "tribal unity" Medicine Crow saw in his village were products of his relatives' ability to adapt inherited ideas about kinship to new conditions. The households he inhabited and visited, the relatives he counted within his extended family and the distinctive sense of social role and social obligation he carried into adulthood were all twentieth-century phenomena. They had been produced by men and women who lived as Crows despite the opposition of the government and the indifference of their white neighbors. Their achievement was no less a contribution to the new Crow nation than the council speeches of male politicians or the labors of the community's ranchers and farmers.

◈ *F U R T H E R   R E A D I N G*

David Wallace Adams, *Education for Extinction: American Indians and the Boarding School Experience, 1875–1928* (1995)

Brad A. Bays, *Townsite Settlement and Dispossession in the Cherokee Nation, 1866–1907* (1998)

Donald Berthrong, *The Cheyenne and Arapaho Ordeal: Reservation and Agency Life in the Indian Territory, 1875–1907* (1976)

Thomas A. Britten, *American Indians in World War I: At Home and at War* (1997)

Leonard Carlson, *Indians, Bureaucrats and the Land: The Dawes Act and the Decline of Indian Farming* (1981)

Brenda Child, *Boarding School Seasons: American Indian Families, 1900–1940* (1998)

Blue Clark, *Lone Wolf v. Hitchcock: Treaty Rights and Indian Law at the End of the Nineteenth Century* (1994)

Michael Coleman, *American Indian Children at School, 1850–1930* (1993)

Angie Debo, *And Still the Waters Run: The Betrayal of the Five Civilized Tribes* (1940)

Charles Eastman, *From the Deep Woods to Civilization: Chapters in the Autobiography of an Indian* (1916)

Clyde Ellis, *To Change Them Forever: Indian Education at the Rainy Mountain Boarding School, 1893–1920* (1996)

Robin Fisher, *Contact and Conflict: Indian-European Relations in British Columbia, 1774–1890* (1977)

Carolyn Gilman and Mary Jane Schneider, eds., *The Way to Independence: Memories of a Hidatsa Family, 1840–1920* (1987)

William T. Hagan, *Indian Police and Judges: Experiments in Acculturation and Control* (1966)

———, *The Indian Rights Association: The Herbert Welsh Years, 1882–1904* (1988)

———, *Quanah Parker, Comanche Chief* (1993)

———, *United States-Comanche Relations: The Reservation Years* (1976)

Sidney Harring, *Crow Dog's Case: American Indian Sovereignty, Tribal Law, and United States Law in the Nineteenth Century* (1994)

Markku Henriksson, *The Indian on Capitol Hill: Indian Legislation and the United States Congress, 1862–1907* (1988)

Hazel Hertzberg, *The Search for an American Indian Identity: Modern Pan-Indian Movements* (1971)

Linda Hogan, *Mean Spirit* (1990)

Brian C. Hosmer, *American Indians in the Marketplace: Persistence and Innovation Among the Menominees and Metlakatians, 1870–1920* (1999)

Frederick E. Hoxie, *A Final Promise: The Campaign to Assimilate the Indians, 1880–1920* (1988)

———, *Parading Through History: The Making of the Crow Nation in America, 1805–1935* (1995)

Phil Hughte, *A Zuni Artist Looks at Frank Hamilton Cushing* (1994)

Peter Iverson, *Carlos Montezuma and the Changing World of American Indians* (1982)

Helen Hunt Jackson, *A Century of Dishonor* (1886)

Robert Keller, *American Protestantism and United States Indian Policy, 1869–82* (1983)

Barbara Kramer, *Nampeyo and Her Pottery* (1996)

David LaVere, *Indian Life in Texas: The WPA Narratives* (1998)

Donal F. Lindsey, *Indians at Hampton Institute, 1877–1923* (1995)

Daniel F. Littlefield, Jr. and James W. Parins, *Native American Writing in the Southeast: An Anthology, 1875–1925* (1995)

K. Tsianina Lomawaima, *They Called It Prairie Light: The Story of Chilocco Indian School* (1994)

Henrietta Mann, *Cheyenne-Arapaho Education, 1871–1982* (1997)

Valerie Sherer Mathes, *Helen Hunt Jackson and Her Indian Reform Legacy* (1990)

John J. Mathews, *Sundown* (1934)

Janet A. McDonnell, *Dispossession of the Indian Estate, 1887–1934* (1991)

Melissa L. Meyer, *The White Earth Tragedy: Ethnicity and Dispossession at a Minnesota Anishinaabe Reservation, 1889–1920* (1994)

Devon A. Mihesuah, *Cultivating the Rosebuds: The Education of Women at the Cherokee Female Seminary, 1851–1909* (1993)

Clyde A. Milner II, *With Good Intentions: Quaker Work Among the Pawnees, Otos, and Omahas in the 1870s* (1982)

——— and Floyd A. O'Neil, eds., *Churchmen and the Western Indians, 1820–1920* (1985)

Craig Miner, *The Corporation and the Indian: Tribal Sovereignty and Industrial Civilization in Indian Territory, 1865–1907* (1976)

L. G. Moses, *The Indian Man: A Biography of James Mooney* (1984)

———, *Wild West Shows and the Images of American Indians, 1883–1933* (1996)

Francis Paul Prucha, ed., *Americanizing the American Indian: Writings by the "Friends of the Indian," 1880–1920* (1973)

———, *American Indian Policy in Crisis: Christian Reformers and the Indians, 1865–1900* (1976)

Scott D. Riney, *The Rapid City Indian School, 1898–1933* (1999)

John Shurts, *Indian Reserved Water Rights: The Winters Doctrine in Its Social and Legal Context, 1880s–1930s* (2000)

Luther Standing Bear, *My People, the Sioux* (1928)

Paul Stuart, *The Indian Office: Growth and Development of an American Institution, 1865–1900* (1979)

Robert A. Trennert, *The Phoenix Indian School: Forced Assimilation in Arizona, 1900–1935* (1988)

John Anthony Turcheneske, *The Chiricahua Apache Prisoners of War: Fort Sill, 1894–1914* (1997)

Peter Whiteley, *Deliberate Acts: Changing Hopi Culture Through the Oraibi Split* (1988)

Raymond Wilson, *Ohiyesa: Charles Eastman, Santee Sioux* (1983)

Zitkala-Sa, *American Indian Stories* (1921)

CHAPTER
12

Efforts at Reform,

1928–1941

◈

The 1920s saw the emergence of a new kind of reformer, one who began to under-stand what Indians across the country had understood for decades: that federal policy had failed, and failed badly. Native communities had lost most of their land. Trachoma, tuberculosis, and other diseases plagued the reservations. Board-ing schools separated children from their families. Tribal governments were either nonexistent or given remarkably limited powers. Tribal religions, languages, arts, and crafts continued to be discouraged by the Bureau of Indian Affairs. But a reform movement originating in Pueblo country at the beginning of the 1920s led to a full-scale investigation of Indian affairs.

By the start of the so-called Indian New Deal in 1933, the leader of this move-ment, a newcomer to Indian country, had been named Commissioner of Indian Affairs. John Collier held this position longer than any other person ever would. Although Congress and conservative forces in the West blocked some of his initia-tives, and Collier received mixed reviews from Indian communities, this era marked a turning-away from the assimilationist period. Why would there have been so much resistance to Collier's reforms?

The Indian New Deal mirrored the New Deal itself in emphasizing community, the arts, and more careful use of the land. In addition, Collier called for Indian religious freedom, advocated bilingual and bicultural education, and supported the right of Native communities to retain separate land bases. Indeed, Collier tried to add to and consolidate Indian reservation land holdings.

Like many reformers, Collier thought he knew best. He often imposed his own ideas. However, he did embrace cultural pluralism more fully than his predecessors. Collier remains a controversial figure in Indian country more than half a century after he resigned his position as Commissioner.

◈ *D O C U M E N T S*

The federal government, stung by widespread criticism of its Indian policy, eventually decided to ask Lewis Meriam and his associates to investigate conditions in Indian coun-try. This survey, published in 1928, became known informally as the Meriam report. Its criticisms helped to spur reforms during Herbert Hoover's administration and more extensive reforms during Franklin Delano Roosevelt's presidency. Document 1 is reprinted from the introduction to that report.

The primary piece of legislation passed during the Indian New Deal emerged as a compromise between Collier's aims and a cautious Congress. Document 2 is taken from that law, known as the Indian Reorganization Act (or the Wheeler-Howard Act, after its congressional sponsors). The remaining two selections speak to some of the initiatives and philosophies of the Collier commissionership. In Documents 3 and 4, Rupert Costo (Cahuilla) and Ben Reifel (Brule Lakota) offer contrasting judgments of Collier and the Indian New Deal. Costo and Reifel exchanged their views at a conference held in 1983 to mark the 50th anniversary of the Indian New Deal. Costo was a journalist and publisher while Reifel served as a congressman from South Dakota and as Commissioner of Indian Affairs.

1. Lewis Meriam Summarizes the Problems Facing American Indians, 1928

An overwhelming majority of the Indians are poor, even extremely poor, and they are not adjusted to the economic and social system of the dominant white civilization.

The poverty of the Indians and their lack of adjustment to the dominant economic and social systems produce the vicious circle ordinarily found among any people under such circumstances. Because of interrelationships, causes cannot be differentiated from effects. The only course is to state briefly the conditions found that are part of this vicious circle of poverty and maladjustment.

Health. The health of the Indians as compared with that of the general population is bad. Although accurate mortality and morbidity statistics are commonly lacking, the existing evidence warrants the statement that both the general death rate and the infant mortality rate are high. Tuberculosis is extremely prevalent. Trachoma, a communicable disease which produces blindness, is a major problem because of its great prevalence and the danger of its spreading among both the Indians and the whites.

Living Conditions. The prevailing living conditions among the great majority of the Indians are conducive to the development and spread of disease. With comparatively few exceptions the diet of the Indians is bad. It is generally insufficient in quantity, lacking in variety, and poorly prepared. The two great preventive elements in diet, milk, and fruits and green vegetables, are notably absent. Most tribes use fruits and vegetables in season, but even then the supply is ordinarily insufficient. The use of milk is rare, and it is generally not available even for infants. Babies, when weaned, are ordinarily put on substantially the same diet as older children and adults, a diet consisting mainly of meats and starches.

The housing conditions are likewise conducive to bad health. Both in the primitive dwellings and in the majority of more or less permanent homes which in some cases have replaced them, there is great overcrowding, so that all members of the

From Lewis Meriam, "Introduction," *The Problem of Indian Administration* (Baltimore: Johns Hopkins Press, 1928), 3–8. Reprinted by permission of The Johns Hopkins University Press.

family are exposed to any disease that develops, and it is virtually impossible in any way even partially to isolate a person suffering from a communicable disease. . . .

Sanitary facilities are generally lacking. Except among the relatively few well-to-do Indians the houses seldom have a private water supply or any toilet facilities whatever. Even privies are exceptional. Water is ordinarily carried considerable distances from natural springs or streams, or occasionally from wells. In many sections the supply is inadequate, although in some jurisdictions, notably in the desert country of the Southwest, the government has materially improved the situation, an activity that is appreciated by the Indians.

Economic Conditions. The income of the typical Indian family is low and the earned income extremely low. From the standpoint of the white man the typical Indian is not industrious, nor is he an effective worker when he does work. Much of his activity is expended in lines which produce a relatively small return either in goods or money. He generally ekes out an existence through unearned income from leases of his land, the sale of land, per capital payments from tribal funds, or in exceptional cases through rations given him by the government. The number of Indians who are supporting themselves through their own efforts, according to what a white man would regard as the minimum standard of health and decency, is extremely small. What little they secure from their own efforts or from other sources is rarely effectively used.

The main occupations of the men are some outdoor work, mostly of an agricultural nature, but the number of real farmers is comparatively small. A considerable proportion engage more or less casually in unskilled labor. By many Indians several different kinds of activity are followed spasmodically, a little agriculture, a little fishing, hunting, trapping, wood cutting, or gathering of native products, occasional labor and hauling, and a great deal of just idling. Very seldom do the Indians work about their homes as the typical white man does. Although the permanent structures in which they live after giving up primitive dwellings are simple and such as they might easily build and develop for themselves, little evidence of such activity was seen. Even where more advanced Indians occupied structures similar to those occupied by neighboring whites it was almost always possible to tell the Indian homes from the white by the fact that the white man did much more than the Indian in keeping his house in condition.

In justice to the Indians it should be said that many of them are living on lands from which a trained and experienced white man could scarcely wrest a reasonable living. In some instances the land originally set apart for the Indians was of little value for agricultural operations other than grazing. In other instances part of the land was excellent but the Indians did not appreciate its value. Often when individual allotments were made, they chose for themselves the poorer parts, because those parts were near a domestic water supply or a source of firewood, or because they furnished some native product important to the Indians in their primitive life. Frequently the better sections of the land originally set apart for the Indians have fallen into the hands of the whites, and the Indians have retreated to the poorer lands remote from markets.

In many places crops can be raised only by the practice of irrigation. Many Indians in the Southwest are successful in a small way with their own primitive systems of irrigation. When modern highly developed irrigation systems have been supplied by governmental activities, the Indians have rarely been ready to make effective use of the land and water. If the modern irrigation enterprise has been successful from an economic standpoint, the tendency has been for whites to gain possession of the land either by purchase or by leases. If the enterprise has not been economically a success, the Indians generally retain possession of the land, but they do not know how to use it effectively, and get much less out of it than a white man would.

The remoteness of their homes often prevents them from easily securing opportunities for wage earning, nor do they have many contacts with persons dwelling in urban communities where they might find employment. Even the boys and girls graduating from government schools have comparatively little vocational guidance or aid in finding profitable employment.

When all these factors are taken into consideration it is not surprising to find low incomes, low standards of living and poor health.

Suffering and Discontent. Some people assert that the Indians prefer to live as they do; that they are happier in their idleness and irresponsibility. The question may be raised whether these persons do not mistake for happiness and content an almost oriental fatalism and resignation. The survey staff found altogether too much evidence of real suffering and discontent to subscribe to the belief that the Indians are reasonable satisfied with their condition. The amount of serious illness and poverty is too great to permit of real contentment. The Indian is like the white man in his affection for his children and he feels keenly the sickness and the loss of his offspring.

The Causes of Poverty. The economic basis of the primitive culture of the Indians has been largely destroyed by the encroachment of white civilization. The Indians can no longer make a living as they did in the past by hunting, fishing, gathering wild products, and the extremely limited practice of primitive agriculture. The social system that evolved from their past economic life is ill suited to the conditions that now confront them, notably in the matter of the division of labor between the men and the women. They are by no means yet adjusted to the new economic and social conditions that confront them.

Several past policies adopted by the government in dealing with the Indians have been of a type which, if long continued, would tend to pauperize any race. Most notable was the practice of issuing rations to able-bodied Indians. Having moved the Indians from their ancestral lands to restricted reservations as a war measure, the government undertook to feed them and to perform certain services for them which a normal people do for themselves. The Indians at the outset had to accept this aid as a matter of necessity, but promptly they came to regard it as a matter of right, as indeed it was at the time and under the conditions of the inauguration of the ration system. They felt, and many of them still feel, that the government owes them a living, having taken their lands from them, and that they are under no obligation to support themselves. They have thus inevitably developed a pauper point of view.

When the government adopted the policy of individual ownership of the land on the reservations, the expectation was that the Indians would become farmers. Part of the plan was to instruct and aid them in agriculture, but this vital part was not pressed with vigor and intelligence. It almost seems as if the government assumed that some magic in individual ownership of property would in itself prove an educational civilizing factor, but unfortunately this policy has for the most part operated in the opposite direction. Individual ownership has in many instances permitted Indians to sell their allotments and to live for a time on the unearned income resulting from the sale. Individual ownership brought promptly all the details of inheritance, and frequently the sale of the property of the deceased Indians to whites so that the estate could be divided among the heirs. To the heirs the sale brought further unearned income, thereby lessening the necessity for self support. Many Indians were not ready to make effective use of their individual allotments. Some of the allotments were of such a character that they could not be effectively used by anyone in small units. The solution was to permit the Indians through the government to lease their lands to the whites. In some instances government officers encouraged leasing, as the whites were anxious for the use of the land and it was far easier to administer property leased to whites than to educate and stimulate Indians to use their own property. The lease money, though generally small in amount, gave the Indians further unearned income to permit the continuance of a life of idleness.

Surplus land remaining after allotments were made was often sold and the proceeds placed in a tribal fund. Natural resources, such as timber and oil, were sold and the money paid either into tribal funds or to individual Indians if the land had been allotted. From time to time per capita payments were made to the individual Indians from tribal funds. These policies all added to the unearned income of the Indian and postponed the day when it would be necessary for him to go to work to support himself.

Since the Indians were ignorant of money and its use, had little or no sense of values, and fell an easy victim to any white man who wanted to take away their property, the government, through its Indian Service employees, often took the easiest course of managing all the Indians' property for them. The government kept the Indians' money for them at the agency. When the Indians wanted something they would go to the government agent, as a child would go to his parents, and ask for it. The government agent would make all the decisions, and in many instances would either buy the thing requested or give the Indians a store order for it. Although money was sometimes given the Indians, the general belief was that the Indians could not be trusted to spend the money for the purpose agreed upon with the agent, and therefore they must not be given opportunity to misapply it. At some agencies this practice still exists, although it gives the Indians no education in the use of money, is irritating to them, and tends to decrease responsibility and increase the pauper attitude.

The typical Indian, however, has not yet advanced to the point where he has the knowledge of money and values, and of business methods that will permit him to control his own property without aid, advise, and some restrictions; nor is he ready to work consistently and regularly at more or less routine labor. . . .

2. The Indian Reorganization Act
(Wheeler-Howard Act), 1934

To conserve and develop Indian lands and resources; to extend to Indians the right to form business and other organizations; to establish a credit system for Indians; to grant certain rights of home rule to Indians; to provide for vocational education for Indians; and for other purposes.

Be it enacted by the Senate and House of Representatives of the United States of America in Congress assembled, That hereafter no land of any Indian reservation, created or set apart by treaty or agreement with the Indians, Act of Congress, Executive order, purchase, or otherwise, shall be allotted in severalty to any Indian.

Sec. 2. The existing periods of trust placed upon any Indian lands and any restriction on alienation thereof are hereby extended and continued until otherwise directed by Congress.

Sec. 3. The Secretary of the Interior, if he shall find it to be in the public interest, is hereby authorized to restore to tribal ownership the remaining surplus lands of any Indian reservation heretofore opened, or authorized to be opened, to sale, or any other form of disposal by Presidential proclamation, or by any of the public-land laws of the United States: *Provided, however,* That valid rights or claims of any persons to any lands so withdrawn existing on the date of the withdrawal shall not be affected by this Act: *Provided further,* That this section shall not apply to lands within any reclamation project heretofore authorized in any Indian reservation. . . .

Sec. 4. Except as herein provided, no sale, devise, gift, exchange or other transfer of restricted Indian lands or of shares in the assets of any Indian tribe or corporation organized hereunder, shall be made or approved: *Provided, however,* That such lands or interests may, with the approval of the Secretary of the Interior, be sold, devised, or otherwise transferred to the Indian tribe in which the lands or shares are located or from which the shares were derived or to a successor corporation; and in all instances such lands or interests shall descend or be devised, in accordance with the then existing laws of the State, or Federal laws where applicable, in which said lands are located or in which the subject matter of the corporation is located, to any member of such tribe or of such corporation or any heirs of such member: *Provided further,* That the Secretary of the Interior may authorize voluntary exchanges of lands of equal value and the voluntary exchange of shares of equal value whenever such exchange, in his judgment, is expedient and beneficial for or compatible with the proper consolidation of Indian lands and for the benefit of cooperative organizations.

Sec. 5. The Secretary of the Interior is hereby authorized, in his discretion, to acquire through purchase, relinquishment, gift, exchange, or assignment, any interest

---

This document is an excerpt from "Wheeler-Howard Act," June 18, 1934, *U.S. Statutes at Large* 48: 984.

in lands, water rights or surface rights to lands, within or without existing reservations, including trust or otherwise restricted allotments whether the allottee be living or deceased, for the purpose of providing land for Indians.

For the acquisition of such lands, interests in lands, water rights, and surface rights, and for expenses incident to such acquisition, there is hereby authorized to be appropriated, out of any funds in the Treasury not otherwise appropriated, a sum not to exceed $2,000,000 in any one fiscal year. . . .

Title to any lands or rights acquired pursuant to this Act shall be taken in the name of the United States in trust for the Indian tribe or the individual Indian for which the land is acquired, and such lands or rights shall be exempt from State and local taxation.

Sec. 6. The Secretary of the Interior is directed to make rules and regulations for the operation and management of Indian forestry units on the principle of sustained-yield management, to restrict the number of livestock grazed on Indian range units to the estimated carrying capacity of such ranges, and to promulgate such other rules and regulations as may be necessary to protect the range from deterioration, to prevent soil erosion, to assure full utilization of the range, and like purposes.

Sec. 7. The Secretary of the Interior is hereby authorized to proclaim new Indian reservations on lands acquired pursuant to any authority conferred by this Act, or to add such lands to existing reservations: *Provided,* That lands added to existing reservations shall be designated for the exclusive use of Indians entitled by enrollment or by tribal membership to residence at such reservations. . . .

Sec. 9. There is hereby authorized to be appropriated, out of any funds in the Treasury not otherwise appropriated, such sums as may be necessary, but not to exceed $250,000 in any fiscal year, to be expended at the order of the Secretary of the Interior, in defraying the expenses of organizing Indian chartered corporations or other organizations created under this Act.

Sec. 10. There is hereby authorized to be appropriated, out of any funds in the Treasury not otherwise appropriated, the sum of $10,000,000 to be established as a revolving fund from which the Secretary of the Interior, under such rules and regulations as he may prescribe, may make loans to Indian chartered corporations for the purpose of promoting the economic development of such tribes and of their members, and may defray the expenses of administering such loans. Repayment of amounts loaned under this authorization shall be credited to the revolving fund and shall be available for the purposes for which the fund is established. A report shall be made annually to Congress of transactions under this authorization.

Sec. 11. There is hereby authorized to be appropriated, out of any funds in the United States Treasury not otherwise appropriated, a sum not to exceed $250,000 annually, together with any unexpended balances of previous appropriations made pursuant to this section, for loans to Indians for the payment of tuition and other expenses in recognized vocational and trade schools: *Provided,* That not more than $50,000 of such sum shall be available for loans to Indian students in high schools and colleges. Such loans shall be reimbursable under rules established by the Commissioner of Indian Affairs. . . .

Sec. 16. Any Indian tribe, or tribes, residing on the same reservation, shall have the right to organize for its common welfare, and my adopt an appropriate constitution and bylaws, which shall become effective when ratified by a majority vote of the adult members of the tribe, or of the adult Indians residing on such reservation, as the case may be, at a special election authorized and called by the Secretary of the Interior under such rules and regulations as he may prescribe. Such constitution and bylaws when ratified as aforesaid and approved by the Secretary of the Interior shall be revocable by an election open to the same voters and conducted in the same manner as hereinabove provided. Amendments to the constitution and bylaws may be ratified and approved by the Secretary in the same manner as the original constitution and bylaws.

In addition to all powers vested in any Indian tribe or tribal council by existing law, the constitution adopted by said tribe shall also vest in such tribe or its tribal council the following rights and powers: To employ legal counsel, the choice of counsel and fixing of fees to be subject to the approval of the Secretary of the Interior; to prevent the sale, disposition, lease, or encumbrance of tribal lands, interests in lands, or other tribal assets without the consent of the tribe; and to negotiate with the Federal, State, and local Governments. The Secretary of the Interior shall advise such tribe or its tribal council of all appropriation estimates or Federal projects for the benefit of the tribe prior to the submission of such estimates to the Bureau of the Budget and the Congress.

Sec. 17. The Secretary of the Interior may, upon petition by at least one-third of the adult Indians, issue a charter of incorporation to such tribe: *Provided,* That such charter shall not become operative until ratified at a special election by a majority vote of the adult Indians living on the reservation. Such charter may convey to the incorporated tribe the power to purchase, take by gift, or bequest, or otherwise, own, hold, manage, operate, and dispose of property of every description, real and personal, including the power to purchase restricted Indian lands and to issue in exchange therefor interests in corporate property, and such further powers as may be incidental to the conduct of corporate business, not inconsistent with law, but no authority shall be granted to sell, mortgage, or lease for a period exceeding ten years any of the land included in the limits of the reservation. Any charter so issued shall not be revoked or surrended except by Act of Congress.

Sec. 18. This Act shall not apply to any reservation wherein a majority of the adult Indians, voting at a special election duly called by the Secretary of the Interior, shall vote against its application. It shall be the duty of the Secretary of the Interior, within one year after the passage and approval of this Act, to call such an election, which election shall be held by secret ballot upon thirty days' notice.

Sec. 19. The term "Indian" as used in this Act shall include all persons of Indian descent who are members of any recognized Indian tribe now under Federal jurisdiction, and all persons who are descendants of such members who were, on June 1,

1934, residing within the present boundaries of any Indian reservation, and shall further include all other persons of one-half or more Indian blood. For the purposes of this Act, Eskimos and other aboriginal peoples of Alaska shall be considered Indians. The term "tribe" wherever used in this Act shall be construed to refer to any Indian tribe, organized band, pueblo, or the Indians residing on one reservation. The words "adult Indians" wherever used in this Act shall be construed to refer to Indians who have attained the age of twenty-one years.

Approved, June 18, 1934.

3. Rupert Costo (Cahuilla) Condemns the Indian New Deal, 1986

. . . The IRA [Indian Reorganization Act of 1934] was the last great drive to assimilate the American Indian. It was also a program to colonialize the Indian tribes. All else had failed to liberate the Indians from their land: genocide, treaty-making and treaty-breaking, substandard education, disruption of Indian religion and culture, and the last and most oppressive of such measures, the Dawes Allotment Act. Assimilation into the dominant society, if by assimilation we mean the adoption of certain technologies and techniques, had already been underway for some hundred years. After all, the Indians were not and are not fools; we are always ready to improve our condition. But assimilation, meaning fading into the general society with a complete loss of our identity and our culture, was another thing entirely, and we had fought against this from the first coming of the white man.

This type of assimilation would be the foregone conclusion of the Indian Reorganization Act. Colonialization of the tribes was to be accomplished through communal enclaves subject to federal domination through the power of the secretary of the interior. Now this view of the IRA is now held by practically all of the historians who write the history of the IRA era.

The record shows otherwise. All one must do is to read and study the hearings held in the Congress, the testimony of Indian witnesses, the evidence of life itself, the statements of the Indian commissioner, and the practically identical tribal constitutions adopted by, or forced upon, the Indians under the IRA. In these constitutions the authority of the secretary of the interior is more powerful than it was before the so-called New Deal. No wonder the Indians called it the Indian Raw Deal.

The IRA did not allow the Indians their independence, which was guaranteed in treaties and agreements and confirmed in court decisions. It did not protect their sovereignty. Collier did not invent self-government: the right of Indians to make their own decisions, to make their own mistakes, to control their own destiny. The IRA had within it, in its wording and in its instruments, such as the tribal constitutions, the destruction of the treaties and of Indian self-government.

There are those who believe that most of the Indians who opposed the IRA were members of allotted tribes who had been economically successful with their allotments. This is a simplistic response, and one that displays a serious lack of

---

Rupert Costo remarks in Kenneth Philp, editor, *Indian Self Rule: First Hand Accounts of Indian-White Relations from Roosevelt to Reagan*, 1986, 48–52. Reprinted by permission of Howe Brothers.

understanding of Indian affairs and history. Allotments certainly did not originate with the Dawes Act. They also were established in treaties. The Dawes Act did, however, force Indians into the allotment system, with a guarantee that they would have to sell their land, either through taxation or by sheer physical force. Those who survived created what they had always wanted, an estate for themselves and their children, a type of insurance against being moved again like cattle to other lands and the chance to make a decent living on their own land. . . .

On May 17, 1934, in hearings before the Senate, the great Yakima nation, in a statement signed by their chiefs and councilmen, said, "We feel that the best interests of the Indians can be preserved by the continuance of treaty laws and carried out in conformity with the treaty of 1855 entered into by the fathers of some of the undersigned chiefs and Governor Stevens of the territory of Washington." Now these are only a few examples of some of the testimony given by Indian witnesses and by most of the tribes. Many refused to even consider the IRA and rejected it outright.

But the commissioner of Indian affairs reported to the House of Representatives on May 7, 1934, that, "I do not think that any study of the subject with all of the supporting petitions, reports, and referendums could leave any doubt that the Indian opinion is strongly for the bill." He then proceeded with this outright falsification of the facts, saying, "In Oklahoma I would say quite overwhelmingly they favor the bill." Both Congressmen Roy Ayres of Montana and Theodore Werner of South Dakota disputed those statements. They showed that Collier was falsifying the facts.

During April 1934, the tribes that had bitterly opposed the IRA attended some of the ten meetings held by the commissioner of Indian affairs throughout the country. Here, as evidence shows, they were subjected to Collier's manipulations. In May, they came before the House of Representatives and completely reversed themselves. In fact, they gave a blanket endorsement to the Indian Reorganization Act. The congressmen, in shocked disbelief, prodded them again and again. Finally they asked, "If the proposed legislation is completely changed into an entirely different act would you then also endorse it?" The Indian delegates, according to many of their tribesmen and tribeswomen said, without any authority of their people, "Yes. Even then we would endorse it." In short, at least two of the tribal delegates gave a blanket endorsement of the IRA in advance of the final legislation. How did this happen? I can tell you how it happened. They received promises that were never kept. They received some special considerations and they felt the arm of the enforcer ordering them to accept or be destroyed. That was Collier's way, as I very well know.

In California, at Riverside, forty tribes were assembled. All but three voted against the proposed bill. Collier then reported that most of the California tribes were for the proposed bill. The historical record was falsified, and his falsification was swallowed whole by Kenneth Philip who also stated in his book that "several mission Indians, led by Rupert Costo, agreed with an unsigned three-page circular sent around the reservation which claimed Collier's ideas were 'communistic and socialistic.'" The implication is that this was a sneaky, underhanded job. The truth is that there was a complete cover letter with that circular, signed by me and my tribe. We were outraged at the provisions of the proposed bill.

It is a curious fact that, in all the ten meetings held with Indians over the country, in not one meeting was there a copy of the proposed legislation put before the people. We were asked to vote on so-called explanations. The bill itself was with-held. We were told we need not vote but the meetings were only to discuss the Collier explanations. In the end, however, we were required to vote. And I sup-pose you would call this maneuvering self-rule. I call it fraud. The Hupa Indians of northern California had two petitions on this proposed bill. One was to be signed by those supporting it; the other, by those who opposed it. In neither case had anyone seen the actual bill, but they rejected it on a massive scale on the basis of explanations alone.

The Crow rejected the IRA and stated for the record in a letter to Senator Burton K. Wheeler, one of the sponsors of the bill, "That under the Collier-chartered community plan, which has been compared to a fifth-rate *poor farm* by newspapers in Indian country, the Indian is being led to believe that they, for the first time in history, would have self-government." But according to the bill, any plans the Indians might have for such self-government would have to be first sub-mitted to the interior secretary or commissioner of Indian affairs for supervision and approval. Self-government to this extent was already accomplished through the tribal councils and tribal business committees, which, by the way, were organ-ized and functioning long before Collier manifested his great interest in the Indians in general.

Now at these councils, Indians discuss matters they consider of vital interest and initiate measures for better management of their affairs, but no action may become effective without the approval of the commissioner of Indian affairs, or the secretary of the interior. Where is the advantage of an almost similar system bear-ing John Collier's name? Can we say that this power of the interior was forced upon the commissioner in the final proposed bill? No, not at all. His original bill contained not less than thirty-three references making it obligatory for the interior secretary to approve vital decisions of the tribes.

It is a matter of record that in California Indians were afraid to come to meet-ings for fear of losing their jobs if they showed disapproval of the Collier proposed bill. On the second day of the Riverside meeting, the Collier enforcers would not allow us to speak, and according to one report of an Indian organization, "they almost threw Rupert Costo out." Another element of the Collier enforcer policy is found in the warning to civil service employees in the BIA by Interior Secretary Ickes that they would be dismissed if they spoke out against Bureau policies on the proposed bill. . . .

4. Ben Reifel (Brulé Lakota) Praises the Legacy of John Collier, 1986

While I was a boy growing up on the Rosebud Indian Reservation, we had the most sickening poverty that one could imagine. Tuberculosis was a killer of Indians. The people on the Pine Ridge Reservation and at Oglala were eating their horses to sur-vive. Impoverishment was everywhere.

Ben Reifel remarks in Kenneth Philp, editor, *Indian Self Rule: First Hand Accounts of Indian-White Rela-tions from Roosevelt to Reagan,* 1986, 54–58. Reprinted by permission of Howe Brothers.

I remember going to Oglala in 1933 as a farm agent. The superintendent of the reservation, a gentleman by the name of James H. McGregor, looked to me almost as a son. After I graduated from college with a degree in agriculture, he recommended that the commissioner appoint me to be a farm agent. The reason he wanted me to be a farm agent was because, in this particular district on the Pine Ridge Reservation, all of the 1,300 people, except two or three mixed-blood families, had conducted their business with a farm agent who was a graduate of Carlisle by the name of Jake White Cow Killer. He talked Sioux and Lakota in all of his communications with these people. He was a member of the village in that area. McGregor wanted someone who could speak the language.

I was only twenty-five years of age, and the old timers would come in to have their dances. They could have dances only on Saturday night. Bert Hills Close to Lodge came in and said, "I want to get permission to have a dance tonight for our group in the village." I had just received a copy of a telegram signed by John Collier, Commissioner of Indian Affairs. It said, "If the Indian people want to have dances, dances all night, all week, that is their business." So I read it to him. Bert sat there, stroked his braids, looked off in the distance, and he said in Lakota, "Well, I'll be damned." The interesting part of it was, if they did not have the dance Saturday night, they would have a dance a month later, because they felt they were on their own. The Indian policemen were not going to police anybody, and it was just too much for them to have self-determination about their own dances.

Speaking of the benefits of the Indian Reorganization Act, we now have more young men and women in universities and colleges. Some of them are represented here. When I was in college in 1928, I could count the number of Indian students, at least from our reservation, on the fingers of your hand. Now they are in the hundreds and up to the thousands at universities and colleges around the country. We also have community colleges on five or six of our reservations.

The Flandreaux Santee Sioux Indian Tribe is made up of a group of about a hundred families that came into the Dakotas during the massacre in Minnesota [in 1862]. They homesteaded along with the whites around the Flandreaux Indian School. When the Indian Reorganization Act was finally passed, they got a leader and they went to us for assistance. They accepted the act and drafted a constitution, by-laws, and a charter. They also took advantage of the Indian land purchase provisions, and they bought farms around there. And then housing was made available under a rehabilitation program for the people who were needy. They got houses on their forty-acre tracts. Last month, under the Supreme Court decision for the Seminoles, they could have bingo. So they are now making good money playing bingo, and the state cannot touch them. This is because the Indian people have rights under the trust responsibility.

But getting back to the Indian Reorganization Act, there was in 1934 an Indian congress at Rapid City to discuss the Wheeler-Howard bill. Walter V. Woehlke, John Collier, and Henry Roe Cloud, a Winnebago Indian, were there. Henry Roe Cloud was probably one of the few Indians at the time that had a doctor's degree. I was quite impressed with him. Henry Roe Cloud had recently been appointed the first Indian to be the superintendent of the Haskell Institute.

And I remember Rev. Joseph Eagle Hawk, one of the dear friends of mine in the community. He was a fine gentleman and a Presbyterian minister. Speaking of

Indians not having a right to express themselves, we held this meeting at Rapid City for three or four days. I took leave to go up there because I wanted to see what it was all about. When Roe Cloud finished explaining part of the bill, Rev. Joe Eagle Hawk got up and said to Roe Cloud:

> You know, when we used to ship cattle to Omaha, Nebraska, they would go down to the slaughter house and they had a goat and they would lead a goat through the slaughter. The cattle would follow the goat in, the goat's life would be saved, and all the cattle would be killed. I think that is what you are, this Judas goat.

And he said that before the commissioner. I was impressed.

One of the things discussed at Rapid City was establishing some kind of official constitutional tribal government. When I grew up as a kid on the reservation, we had general tribal councils. What did they talk about when they came together? They passed a resolution asking the secretary of the interior, or the federal government, to allow them to have an attorney to represent them in their claims. When they had any tribal monies in place, the congressmen, about election time, would come around and say we will get you a per capita payment. They would then get a per capita payment, because at that time our Indian people, since 1921, even before that in South Dakota, were entitled to vote in the general election. If there was some of the tribal land to be leased, the general tribal council would come together and pass a resolution.

When I was a kid, there was also an old fellow called Chief High Bald Eagle. In those days we had an Indian trader store and a post office with counters and cages. Old High Bald Eagle was sitting up there with his legs crossed. He must have been about eighty or ninety years old; he looked like two hundred to me. We were having what we called a Scattergood dam constructed not too far away from our home. They were having a big tribal council meeting, and someone said to High Eagle in our language, "Why are you not up there at that big meeting?" He said, "When I was a young man years ago, when things were really important, then our leaders got together. But now, when a child gets constipated just about August eating chokecherries and it gets so his bowels are all stuck up, they have to have a council meeting on it." That is about as important as I thought the council meetings were on the Rosebud Reservation. That was also true at Pine Ridge. So I was impressed with Collier's idea that Indians would get together and form some kind of governmental operation where they would democratically elect their own people and select their own leaders.

I was also concerned over the years about the tribal courts. Tribal court judges were appointed by the superintendent or the Indian agent. There was no appeal from them. Before the Indian Reorganization Act came along, I remember my brother was thrown in jail because he lived close to where there was a big fight going on and they thought he was a part of it. My younger brother came in where I was working in a store, and he said, "Hey, our brother George is in jail." So what did I do? I knew the superintendent lived near by because I was a close friend of his son. I went over there, and he said, "What happened, Ben?" Well, I told him what happened, and he wrote out a little note which I gave to Andrew Night Pipe, who was the chief of police. Andrew Night Pipe unlocked the door and let my brother go home. That was the sort of thing that was going on, and I felt we needed a better judicial system.

I was really impressed with the original draft of the so-called Wheeler-Howard bill. In it was a section where there would be a circuit court that would move from one reservation to another. Funds would be provided for this court to operate. Under the federal system, there would be the right of appeal from the local court just like any other court. There would be none of this business that goes on where the judges are appointed by the superintendent or the tribal council. The revised bill was cut from forty or fifty pages to just about eleven pages. The court system and several other things were taken out.

After the Rapid City meeting, I asked the superintendent for permission to talk about the bill with the people; he agreed. But he felt that there was a little red tinge to all of this, because one of the remarks he made to me was "I do not mind the little red schoolhouses as long as they are not red on the inside." Nevertheless, he was very supportive of my going out and explaining this bill. Of course, there were those on the reservation who were very opposed to it. And there were those who were for it. Think of me, only twenty-five years old, getting up there arguing with the old timers such as American Horse. I do not know who all the rest of them were. I felt that this was something we could support.

Conditions have improved. Tribal councils have been organized. They are fighting among themselves, but as Floyd O'Neil said, this is no different than Congress. In South Dakota, some tribal councils cannot even write checks, because they are tied up in fussing over who is going to be in control. That is no different than in California where the governor was not going to make payments to employees. The legislative body would not go along. It took the Supreme Court of the United States or the federal court to order them to make payments to the employees. . . .

◈ *E S S A Y S*

A professor of history at the University of Tennessee, John R. Finger has written widely about the history of the Eastern Cherokees. His study of the Eastern Cherokees in the twentieth century, from which this first essay is excerpted, highlights some of the dilemmas posed by the Indian New Deal for Native communities where the gospel of individualism had won many adherents. By the 1930s, Indian lands were much less isolated and communities such as Eastern Cherokee also had to confront the mixed blessings brought by an influx of tourists. Collier's emphasis on tribalism earned praise from some members of the tribe while others, such as Fred Blythe Bauer, bitterly opposed the commissioner's initiatives.

D'Arcy McNickle was included on the tribal rolls of the Salish-Kutenai of Montana even though he was of Cree rather than of Salish-Kutenai descent. McNickle worked as an associate of Collier during the Indian New Deal. The author of several major works, including the acclaimed novel *The Surrounded* (1936), McNickle concluded his distinguished career by serving as the director of the Newberry Library's Center for the History of the American Indian (later renamed in his honor the McNickle Center). From his own vantage point, McNickle, as the second essay reveals, considered much of the criticism of Collier wide of the mark. Collier, he argued, not only represented a fundamental shift from the assimilationist period but also, in his support for cultural revitalization, day schools, religious freedom, and other crucial matters, helped to establish an early foundation for the modern Indian movement toward self-determination.

The Eastern Cherokees and the New Deal

JOHN R. FINGER

Franklin D. Roosevelt brought a jaunty optimism to the presidency and a bold New Deal featuring myriad agencies for coping with the depression. Amid these sweeping changes was an "Indian New Deal" designed by John Collier, Roosevelt's commissioner of Indian affairs. A native southerner and former New York City social worker, Collier had been impressed by the richness and variety of the immigrants' cultural heritage and had become a proponent of cultural pluralism. No longer should our nation strive for a homogenized, uniform citizen emerging from the melting pot of America. Instead, national culture should be a blend, reflecting certain common values—respect for equality under the law, for example—and varied ethnic attributes. By the 1920s Collier had developed a fascination with the Puebloan tribes of the Southwest and emerged as an impassioned spokesman for Indian rights. Extrapolating from his earlier experiences with immigrants, he believed Indians could be a vital part of American culture while retaining much of their tribal identity. His familiarity with Puebloan folkways had also given him respect for communalism as an agent of cultural bonding and cooperative change. Communalism or tribalism, he thought, might operate as an effective restraint on rampant American individualism.

Good progressive that he was, Collier also wished to address the Indians' many social, economic, and educational problems. A persistent critic of the Indian Office, he had supported the systematic analysis of reservation problems conducted by Lewis Meriam and applauded many of the conclusions in Meriam's published 1928 report. Thus Collier's background suggested that his approach as Indian commissioner would reflect both the fervor of progressivism and an appreciation of ethnic and cultural diversity.

The cornerstone of the Indian New Deal was the Wheeler-Howard Act of June 18, 1934, often called the Indian Reorganization Act (IRA). A decisive about-face from previous policy, it affirmed the validity of Indian cultures, formally abandoned the already discredited allotment policy, and promoted Indian progress within a modern tribal context. With the end of allotment the reservations would become sacrosanct communal societies. In some cases they would even be enlarged. Tribes were encouraged to write their own constitutions, organize as corporations, and apply for federal loans for economic development. Meanwhile the new administration would deemphasize off-reservation boarding schools and promote practical, socially responsible education among the Indians themselves. This included encouraging traditional crafts and skills as a means of preserving tribal culture and also earning money. Like many New Deal programs, then, the IRA combined old and new ideas with a bold willingness to experiment.

One of the most remarkable features of the IRA was a provision allowing tribes to vote on whether they would accept the new law and thus be eligible for its benefits. Never before had Indians been encouraged to exercise their own judgment in

John R. Finger, *Cherokee Americans: The Eastern Band of Cherokees in the Twentieth Century* (Lincoln, Nebr.: University of Nebraska Press, 1991), 75–98. Reprinted by permission of the University of Nebraska Press. Copyright © 1991 by the University of Nebraska Press.

policy matters relating to themselves, and a number of tribes disappointed Collier by voting against the IRA—in part for the novelty of saying no to the federal government and partly because of questions about how the new policy would actually be implemented. Initially, however, the Eastern Band had only mild objections. It was willing to incorporate under federal law, despite satisfaction with its state charter, but wanted certain practices to continue: state law enforcement on the reservation, tribal operation of a new handicraft guild, and heirship rights to possessory claims. Otherwise, agent Spalsbury noted, the concept of corporate self-government struck a responsive chord: "These Indians have been operating under a similar organization for many years and believe in it." In May 1934 the tribal council approved the pending Wheeler-Howard bill, and on December 20 the entire tribe likewise endorsed the recently passed act by a vote of 705 to 101. Counting absentee ballots, 806 out of an estimated 1,114 eligible voters went to the polls, better than 72 percent. Support was lopsided in all six communities as well as among the 60 absentee voters. Harold E. Foght, the current Cherokee agent, reported satisfaction "with the way the Indians turned out and voted, particularly as the mountain roads were in bad condition after several days of rain and snow." He anticipated quick adoption of a new tribal constitution and charter of incorporation to replace the existing 1889 state charter.

To many Eastern Cherokees, the most important facet of the Indian New Deal was the creation of new jobs on the reservation. Tribal unemployment had become particularly acute in the last months of Hoover's administration, and about the only income came from the agency's own limited road building. Fortunately, many of Roosevelt's famous "alphabet agencies" provided employment and relief to Indians as well as other Americans. One of John Collier's first steps as Indian commissioner was to establish the Indian Emergency Conservation Work Program (IECW), an adjunct of the Civilian Conservation Corps (CCC). Often called the Indian CCC, the IECW was, at Collier's insistence, "Indian-built, Indian-maintained, and Indian-used" and devoted exclusively to relief measures on reservations. It was quite prominent on Qualla Boundary and provided employment in reforestation, fire and erosion control, road building, and similar programs. More than 500 Eastern Cherokees applied for the 100 full-time positions, and to benefit the maximum number of Indians Harold Foght set up two shifts, each working two weeks a month. Later it became necessary to limit even further the hours any one individual could work. Other New Deal agencies like the Works Progress Administration (WPA) and the Public Works Administration (PWA) also allocated funds to the Department of the Interior for similar job programs on reservations. Even with all this, employment lagged badly. Late in 1936 only 135 out of about 650 eligible Eastern Cherokees had jobs—mostly on roads, the IECW, and a new hospital project. Yet the efforts at relief continued, and between 1933 and 1941 various New Deal agencies pumped a total of about $595,000 into the North Carolina reservation. Nationwide, the Indian CCC alone spent some $72 million among American Indians.

With passage of the Johnson-O'Malley Act in 1934, Collier's Indian Bureau encouraged state and local agencies to share in providing many Indian services. The state of North Carolina, for example, contracted with the United States Public Health Service and the Department of the Interior to furnish additional medical care for the Eastern Band. By 1938 the state had a district health unit operating out of

Waynesville and a resident field nurse on the reservation who visited even the most remote Cherokee homes. For the first time almost every Cherokee child received a medical examination and necessary immunizations, while prenatal care and treatment for venereal disease became readily available for adults. As in the past, state and county officials also continued to provide most tribal law enforcement, though sheriffs were sensitive to the fact that Indians paid no taxes. Less successful were federal efforts to interest white public school systems in admitting Cherokee pupils under the Johnson-O'Malley Act. As agents often pointed out, prejudice against Indians was simply too strong in Bryson City and Sylva.

Taking advantage of the IRA's desire to maintain and even enlarge reservations, the Eastern Band made an effort during the 1930s to acquire more tillable land to accommodate its inflated membership rolls. Some Indians talked about selling the more remote tracts in Graham and Cherokee counties and using the proceeds to buy better—and more defensible—property closer to Qualla Boundary. And on several occasions the tribe offered marginal though scenic property to the Great Smokey Mountains National Park in exchange for farmland, especially around Ravensford. The tribe was never able to make the exchanges it wanted, but it did eventually pay $25,000 for the 884-acre Boundary Tree Tract as a site for tribal tourist industries. While bargaining with the park service, the Cherokees also attempted to use New Deal agencies to acquire some 23,000 acres south of Qualla Boundary and in Graham County. Arrangements were nearly complete when, according to Harold Foght, the government dealt "a great blow" to Cherokee aspirations by deciding against it.

One revolutionary phase of the Indian New Deal of particular importance to the Eastern Band was its encouragement of Native American traditions, crafts, religion, and self-identity. In contrast to the early 1920s, when the Indian Office warned Indians to cease their "useless and harmful" dances and ceremonies, Collier explicitly encouraged Indian religious freedoms and preservation of tribal cultures. To the disgust of many missionaries and longtime reformers, he issued a circular in January 1934 directing the Indian Service to show an "affirmative, appreciative attitude toward Indian cultural values." Furthermore, "No interference with Indian religious life or ceremonial expression will hereafter be tolerated. The cultural liberty of Indians is in all respects to be considered equal to that of any non-Indian group." Tribal arts and crafts should be "prized, nourished, and honored."

Responding to this new directive, Harold Foght advocated teaching Indian history in Cherokee schools and creating a museum to exhibit craft work from other Indian schools in the United States. This "would lend an understanding and inspiration to the children that would be difficult to get in any other way." As for Cherokee religion and traditions, he later explained, "We are thus going out of our way to have meetings with the older Indians who are rapidly dying off to have them transmit in permanent form what they still retain from the ancient national epic of creation, their guiding supernatural spirit and the world hereafter as reward for noble deed and worthy living." Then, in a comment accurately reflecting the new ideology, he added, "Unfortunately, the Cherokees have not been a conservative religious group holding onto their ancient religion."

Cherokee crafts had been a matter of keen interest to Indian agents, tourists, and others well before the depression. Across the mountains in Gatlinburg, Tennessee, the predecessor of the Arrowmont School fostered traditional mountain crafts, an emphasis blending nicely with the new awareness of Indian culture. By spring 1932 R. L. Spalsbury was trying to organize a crafts guild among the Eastern Cherokees so they could become an auxiliary of the Southern Mountain Hand Craft Guild in Gatlinburg. Spalsbury confidently predicted that the new transmountain road from Knoxville and Gatlinburg would bring more tourists to Qualla Boundary and create greater demand for Cherokee crafts; the new Indian guild and its affiliation with the larger organization would help meet these demands. Unlike before, when Indians often bartered crafts for supplies at local stores, the new arrangement would allow them to bring their wares to the guild storehouse, where they would receive cash. The guild would then sell the crafts at enough of a markup to pay expenses and allow for future expansion. Using funds borrowed from the tribe, the guild was finally organized in the summer of 1933 and operated out of a storeroom in the new council house then nearing completion. It was the predecessor of the crafts guild that today handles much of the Cherokee artistic output.

Spalsbury and Harold Foght followed up these early efforts to promote Cherokee handicrafts. There were crafts classes in the tribal schools, an attempt to anticipate tourist demands, and frequent inquiries from the Indian Office regarding the state of Cherokee artistic creativity. Goingback Chiltoskey, a woodcarver and one of the most famous artists of the Eastern Band, received much of his instruction and encouragement during this period. Likewise, Roosevelt's New Deal gave a moral and financial boost to artists throughout America. On the other hand, the employment programs of the Indian New Deal sometimes detracted from Cherokee crafts. The government employed instructors in basketry and pottery part time at the boarding school but then lured them away with higher-paying opportunities elsewhere. Spalsbury advocated raising the instructors' salaries from twenty-five to fifty cents an hour, with at least fifteen hours of work a week. Yet New Deal programs continued to work at cross purposes. As Harold Foght noted in summer 1934, "I find that only a limited number of the reservation Indians are engaged in basketry and weaving, and very few in pottery making. This is probably due in part to the fact that the men have had remunerative work on Government projects in recent years."

Nourishing Indian handicrafts was simply one part of a larger program to transform Cherokee into a tourist center. As early as 1932 R. L. Spalsbury was anticipating future needs by advocating development of a plan for leasing attractive business sites in town and at Soco Gap. One problem was the number of whites already operating businesses under arrangements made with individual Indians before the government assumed trusteeship over the reservation. By spring 1933 the tribal council had decided that 10 percent of the consideration for all business leases would go into the tribal treasury to help with relief, and Spalsbury was requiring white businessmen to obtain traders' licenses from his office.

Completion of a modern highway system into Cherokee was of course critical, and by late 1935 the Appalachian Railroad had finally liquidated its holdings and surrendered its right-of-way for the new and more direct highway linking Bryson City and Cherokee. Whenever the long-discussed highway from Soco Gap was completed, Cherokee would also be a convenient gateway for motorists approaching from the east. In anticipation of these developments, the council voted to appropriate $50,000 of tribal funds to undertake an "industrial development" program in

Cherokee. Basically it entailed tearing down some of the old shacks and constructing new tourist-related facilities, including a hotel, trading post, craft shop, and service station. The council intended to oversee all phases of construction, the leasing of concessions, and landscaping. One objective was to drive out of business R. I. McLean, a white trader who operated a large general store and trading post on a small parcel of land in the heart of the business district; this had never been part of the reservation. Harold Foght said that McLean had long been "a thorn in the flesh" of other traders, whom he regularly outsmarted. The Indians at first were willing to start legal proceedings to force McLean to sell out, but Principal Chief Jarrett Blythe soon decided that if the tribe could open a new cooperative store as part of its industrial program, McLean would sell of his own volition. Little did Blythe realize that his program would soon come under attack by some fellow Cherokees as undemocratic and even subversive.

Whatever the accomplishments of the Indian New Deal, some Eastern Cherokees became disenchanted because it fostered tribalism at the expense of individualism, decisively eliminated the prospect of allotment, and appeared to be a "return to the blanket." They found themselves joining a rising chorus of opposition to Collier's programs among many acculturated Indians throughout the United States. Ironically, these dissenters found support among some poorly educated or conservative Indians who saw the Indian Reorganization Act not as an affirmation of tribal ways but as a suspicious new tactic adopted by an always devious federal government. What emerged on many reservations, then, was an alliance of convenience between certain acculturated and traditionalist Indians to resist the IRA. On the Eastern Band's reservation all that was required was an individual to crystallize such latent fears and resentment. Fred Blythe Bauer was the individual.

Bauer was born in December 1896, the son of Rachel Blythe Bauer, a Cherokee mixed-blood, and Adolphus Gustavus Bauer, a northern-born white architect who designed a number of important state buildings after moving to Raleigh. When his mother died just two weeks after his birth, Bauer was sent by his distraught father to Qualla Boundary to live with James and Josephine Blythe, who adopted him. Blythe was Rachel Bauer's brother, and his wife was the daughter of former principal chief Nimrod Jarrett Smith. Fred Bauer grew up with his cousin Jarrett Blythe (who was ten years older), attended Carlisle, and during World War I served with the army air corps in France. Afterward he taught and coached at various Indian institutions around the country.

By the early 1930s Bauer and his wife Catherine were employed at the school in Mount Pleasant, Michigan, and when it closed they returned to Qualla Boundary, where their intelligence and forceful personalities quickly ensured their prominence. R. L. Spalsbury was delighted to provide a teaching position on the reservation for Catherine, and her husband worked on a variety of relief projects, including construction of reservation highways. Before long, however, the couple became open and persistent critics of the Indian New Deal. Fred Bauer had always been a progressive who, culturally at least, was a "white Indian." To him full and unconditional Indian citizenship meant a good education, allotment of reservation lands, distribution of tribal assets, private initiative in business and government, and an end to Indian Office bureaucracy and paternalism. Anything less was un-American and unacceptable. In his eyes Collier's romantic notions of tribalism were not only un-American but communistic. Not surprisingly, Bauer quickly enlisted allies among other white Indians and suspicious conservatives willing to believe the worst about federal Indian policies. Of necessity they found themselves frequently at odds with the principal chief, who steadfastly backed most New Deal programs. That man was none other than Bauer's cousin and adoptive brother, Jarrett Blythe. It was a scenario befitting a Greek tragedy.

The catalyst for Bauer's campaign against Collier and the Indian New Deal was the new educational program on the Cherokee reservation. In September 1932, before Roosevelt's election, agent R. L. Spalsbury had posed a basic question: "What is the proper educational program for this reservation?" He had an answer. In line with the Meriam report and other critiques of Indian education, he called for "a complete reorganization" that would reduce the role of the boarding school at Cherokee and emphasize "close contacts between the school and the home" by means of day schools. Somewhat paradoxically, he finally concluded this could best be accomplished by improving the local road systems, closing the two existing day schools, converting the boarding school into a consolidated day facility, and busing in students who lived in Bird Town, Big Cove, and the Jackson County communities along Soco Creek. "This has all the merits of a consolidated school in any community," Spalsbury said. "It provides close daily contacts between the school and the home. It permits the children to maintain their home contacts while getting their education and suggests that the school might extend its influence easily by reason of these contacts to the improvement of the home life of the adults." It would also be cheaper than the current boarding system and would free several dormitories for other uses. For an indefinite period, however, Spalsbury admitted it would be necessary to retain boarding facilities for a few orphans, refugees from broken homes, and pupils from remote tracts in Graham and Cherokee counties. Whatever the merits of his proposals, the lame-duck Hoover administration had no intention of undertaking such costly changes on the Cherokee reservation. Instead, it authorized construction of a new day school in Soco Valley.

John Collier's regime likewise rejected the notion of a large consolidated Cherokee school and opted for expanding and improving existing day schools and making them more responsive to community needs. Spalsbury quickly proved himself a disciple of the new administration by defining tribal education in the broadest possible terms. Sketching the preliminary outlines of an idealized program for the Eastern Band, he said, "Our program of education will be wider than the classroom. It will take in the home, the fields, the forest, the churches, the tribal organization, and every individual entitled to participate in the tribe. Community wide in its ramifications, it will aim to better and improve the economic, social, sanitary and spiritual condition of these people." As he admitted, "This is a large order." Schoolwork would reflect the Cherokees' own environment and would not require such things as foreign languages or "higher mathematics." Spalsbury hoped to add grades eleven and twelve to the boarding-school curriculum during the next two years and, assuming the school could hire the necessary instructors, to teach both written and spoken Cherokee at those levels. As the agent put it, "On the background of [Cherokee] racial inheritance we should build a structure of knowledge, skill and attitudes dovetailing into their environment so that they will be able to make the best use of it without waste."

Spalsbury saw the "adult phase" of the new program "centering around the home and the family. These are the two primary social units that must be strengthened and developed." But the agent had only a vague idea of how this might be accomplished, and he acknowledged that everyone connected with the Indian New Deal would "have to attack and develop" the problem. One thing he knew for certain:

> Rugged individualism must give way to social cooperation. The social element is dominant. An individual can only develop in organized society. If this means anything, it means that the social organization of the community must receive major attention. The Cherokees have some most commendable features in their social life which should be preserved and extended. Their community club organizations for mutual help in times of trouble or need are examples of this. As their social stability rests on the strength of the home and family, every effort should be made to improve their economic and moral condition. Health and sanitation are important elements to be stressed throughout.

Spalsbury's successor, Harold Foght, was equally diligent but more practical in attempting to set up an educational system that conformed to the broad-gauged objectives of the Indian New Deal. He emphasized prevocational and vocational instruction in agriculture, forestry, and the mechanical arts. Basically he ignored curriculum formats and requirements in other North Carolina schools, thinking it "wasteful and positively foolish . . . to ape" them. An ominous foreshadowing of future events occurred when students at the boarding school and some Cherokee parents protested, to which Foght replied that they simply did not understand "the real situation." He was preparing Cherokee children for the realities of reservation life, but if there should be "a young Indian boy or girl who shows outstanding gift in certain cultural or professional fields, we would recommend such students for transfer from Cherokee to white high schools willing to accept Indian students."

Foght quickly found himself bewildered and beleaguered by a rising tide of opposition to the new school programs. In part it was a matter of his own "stern" personality, in part a reaction to the aggressive, radical nature of Collier's entire administration. The welter of anxieties and uncertainties relating to the Indian New Deal had suddenly coalesced and focused on the issue of education. And it was on this issue that Foght first directly confronted Fred and Catherine Bauer. Catherine had proved a very good substitute teacher in the spring of 1934, and Foght had had no qualms about recommending her for a full-time position at the new Soco Day School. By spring 1935, however, she and one or two other reservation teachers openly opposed the educational program. Her husband and a number of white Indians were meanwhile holding meetings and, according to Foght, making "insidious insinuations and false statements" and inducing many parents to sign a petition against the new programs. The exasperated agent dealt with his most immediate problem by firing Catherine Bauer, claiming she had been insubordinate and had "joined in the movement to discredit the new system of education." He asked the acting director of education within the Indian Office to investigate the matter himself, adding that "the Tribal Council, from the Chief down, is standing by us and look upon the whole matter as impertinent interference on the part of a few discontents."

Bauer meanwhile had gone at his own expense to Washington, conferred with Collier, and received no satisfaction. Back in Cherokee, he and others organized a "Cherokee Indian Rights Association," which held a strike against tribal schools; some parents were persuaded to protest the IRA educational program by withdrawing their children from classes. Amid the furor, the tribal council appointed a committee to look into the situation, and it prepared a report generally supporting Foght's educational program. For those favoring an education emphasizing assimilation rather than tribalism, Bauer made the case most cogently in a congressional hearing a few years later: "Suppose you, a white, born in a white community, see only white people, attend white schools, have only white associates. After you attain manhood you are suddenly dropped down in China, India, or Africa, with people of a different race, language, and social customs. Do you think you would be accepted without question into the social, economic, and political life of that community? And be happy there?" Cherokee children, Bauer argued, should attend public schools with white children to be better prepared for the "real world." The problem, as Bauer no doubt realized, was that schools in Swain and Jackson counties did not admit students who were phenotypically Indian. Withdrawal of the Cherokee reservation and the new national park from Swain County tax rolls had drastically reduced the local tax base, and quite apart from any racial animosity, county officials were not inclined to provide public services for the Cherokees.

A prominent ally of the Bauers was William Pearson McCoy, a white Indian from Bird Town who operated a small restaurant in Cherokee, where authorities seized two slot machines in summer 1934. Foght labeled him and Fred Bauer "the chronic trouble maker[s] of this reservation" and indeed they were to be persistent enemies of the Indian Office for years to come. But the list of Foght's critics went considerably beyond those two and included certain discontented parents and even a few teachers. Outsiders also had unkind things to say. A Tulsa woman, Mrs. R. M. Hill, appeared on the reservation during Foght's initial troubles with the Bauers and, according to the agent, seemed to be a religious crank who wanted the school day to begin and end with prayer. She also "launched upon a tirade against the teaching of Bolshevism and certain communistic practices in our schools, all of which was so preposterous that it was difficult for me to refrain from taking the whole matter in a jocular vein." Mrs. Hill's chief target was a teacher of industrial geography who had discussed the Soviet Union and had a pupil prepare a report on its economic system based on a book from the teacher's own library. A bit defensively, Foght acknowledged that "Communism and Bolshevism have no place in the report or in the book, but the word 'Russia' was evidently sufficient to set our objectors on edge. Anyhow, they had filled this woman with a lot of nonsense."

Charges that the IRA was promoting communism were reiterated by Fred Bauer and the American Indian Federation (AIF), an organization he had joined and whose assistance he solicited in the spring of 1935. The AIF was a national association of Indians of diverse backgrounds and viewpoints who happened to agree on three basic objectives: removal of John Collier from office; repeal of the IRA; and most important, abolition of the Office of Indian Affairs. Founded in Oklahoma in 1934 in response to the IRA, it was headed by Joseph Bruner, a wealthy, acculturated Creek who came from a traditionalist background. The "brains" of the AIF was its energetic publicist and Washington lobbyist Alice Lee Jemison, a Seneca who was also part Cherokee. Like Bauer, many AIF members perceived Collier and the Indian bureau as obstacles to Indian individualism and modernity. The IRA, they believed, fostered a bureaucracy and paternalism that stifled initiative and self-reliance. They argued forcefully for the Indian's "emancipation" and complete integration into white society. Others opposed the Indian New Deal because it seemed to violate treaty rights that guaranteed preservation of their identity as tribal Indians. A favorite attention-getting ploy of the AIF was a right-wing rhetoric that accused Collier and his program of being atheistic, communist inspired, and pawns of the American Civil Liberties Union.

In June 1935 the AIF asked the Senate Committee on Indian Affairs to investigate the situation in Cherokee and distributed a circular titled "Collierism and Communism in North Carolina" to every member of Congress. Eventually, at hearings before the committee in April 1936, the AIF charged that the "present Indian Bureau program involves 'atheism, communism and un-Americanism in the administration of Indian Affairs both at Cherokee and in general.'" Harold Foght and others at Cherokee were supposedly trying to destroy private ownership of property, promote collectivism, deny free speech, substitute social science for Christianity in the schools, and "subversively" teach sex.

Though the Senate committee proved unresponsive, the AIF continued its efforts to uproot the IRA on the Cherokee reservation. In January 1937 Alice Lee Jemison wrote North Carolina's Senator Josiah Bailey that "the regime at Cherokee" had become "autocratic and tyranical" as well as vindictive: "Those who have opposed their program at Cherokee have been denied work of any kind and every possible barrier has been thrown in their [way] to prevent them from earning a livelihood through individual enterprise." When Bailey asked Collier to respond, the Indian commissioner said Jemison's allegations were "arbitrary fictions in most cases. They are so wild and bizarre that an answer to them carries one into the realm of detective stories." On February 15 and 17 the Senate committee held additional hearings on the Cherokee case and focused on allegations about communist teachings in Cherokee schools, the IRA's support of native conjurers at the expense of modern medicine, and agency assaults on Christian belief. Similar accusations were made at hearings in 1938, 1939, and 1940, and Jemison claimed she spoke for about three hundred disgruntled Cherokees.

Amid these charges and countercharges, Fred Bauer was daily becoming more influential. Nowhere was this more apparent than in a tribal election of August 1935 on a proposed new constitution under the Indian Reorganization Act. Bauer and his allies waged what Foght characterized as "a campaign of falsehood and misrepresentation" that resulted in a decisive defeat of the constitution, 484 to 382. In Cherokee there were 74 votes for the constitution and 79 against; in Bird Town 54 for and 121 against; Paint Town 22 for and 92 opposed; Wolf Town 54 pro constitution and 129 con; Big Cove 97 for and 32 against; Graham County (Snowbird) 78 for and 2 against; and 2 absentee ballots in favor and 29 in opposition. Foght thought it significant that Graham County and Big Cove, "the two precincts inhabited by the full-blood Indians were the only two to vote right. . . . They seem still able to think for themselves. Birdtown, which is the stronghold of the white Indians gave a better vote for the Constitution than did either Painttown or Wolfetown, which ordinarily line up right on a proposition."

Foght had no trouble explaining why there had been such a remarkable turnabout after the overwhelming tribal support shown for the IRA less than a year before. In an obvious reference to the Bauer-Pearson McCoy group, he said "the real cause was after all a campaign of falsehood and misrepresentation that has been carried on by a certain faction well known to you for a long time. The only astonishing thing to me is that the propaganda used could so utterly mislead people who ordinarily do their own thinking." Despite his embarrassment, Foght said many Cherokees hoped for another election, "as it will not be long before these people will see the mistake they have made." But he was wrong. The Eastern Cherokees never adopted a new constitution and instead continued to operate under their amended 1889 state charter.

Just a few days after rejection of the constitution, Foght and the Collier program received another blow when Fred Bauer was elected vice chief of the Eastern Band. As an added insult, Pearson McCoy became a new councilman. The only real consolation to Foght was the reelection of Principal Chief Jarrett Blythe, a staunch IRA supporter. (Like many other Americans, the Eastern Cherokees have never shown much consistency in voting for their leaders.) Bauer's enemies attempted to block his swearing in because tribal law required the vice chief to have at least one-half Cherokee blood, and the Baker Roll listed him as three-eighths. The most persuasive evidence, however, suggests that Bauer was only one-quarter Cherokee. Part of the confusion over his ancestry resulted from the romantic tales surrounding his mother's marriage to Augustus Bauer, their supposed ostracism by Raleigh society, and Rachel's untimely death. According to stories circulating in the 1930s, she had been a full-blood Indian "princess." Perhaps these tales explain why several witnesses assured the tribal council that Rachel Bauer's son was a half-blood and therefore legally qualified for office. The council acquiesced, and the candidate quickly assumed his position as vice chief.

Bauer immediately made his presence felt by convincing the council to rescind the resolution of the preceding year appropriating $50,000 for construction of new tourist facilities. Foght almost sputtered with rage, but he was helpless to prevent reduction of the construction program to a face-saving standby basis. Bauer's obstructionism then took a different turn as he launched a campaign to halt plans for a new "park-to-park" highway across the reservation. This scenic mountain route, the Blue Ridge Parkway, would eventually stretch 469 miles from the Shenandoah National Park southwest of Washington, D.C., to the Great Smoky Mountains National Park. Late in 1934, after considerable controversy and lobbying, secretary of the interior Harold L. Ickes selected Cherokee as the terminus for the Smokies.

Originally the reservation section of the parkway was to be the long-needed state highway from Soco Gap to Cherokee, for which North Carolina had obtained a right-of-way sixty feet wide. The state then planned to reconvey the property to the United States. To the Cherokees' amazement, however, the National Park Service insisted on a much wider route along Soco Creek that would gobble up valuable farmland and potential business sites. It would also virtually wipe out the main street of Cherokee and necessitate moving back existing commercial buildings to the Oconaluftee's floodplain. Tribal access to the parkway, moreover, would be limited. Amid such revelations the Cherokees decided against the park demands, which Foght called "little less than confiscatory." Secretary Ickes pointed out the obvious benefits of such a road but said he would not force it on the Indians, who continued to hope the state would undertake construction of its own highway along the original right-of way. To this extent, at least, Foght and Blythe found themselves in rare agreement with Bauer. For a while it seemed the parkway would not cross the reservation at all.

By early 1937, however, negotiators had worked out a compromise proposal involving a land exchange between the tribe and the national park. The Cherokees would give the park some marginal acreage in return for long-coveted parkland near Ravensford. Then, in exchange for their properties along the necessary right-of-way, as well as North Carolina's promise of just compensation for damages, the affected Cherokees would receive part of the Ravensford lands. A bill allowing such an exchange was duly introduced in Congress, while Foght lined up a majority of councilmen to approve the plan. Then, to his shock and indignation, three of his staunchest supporters changed their minds during a Sunday adjournment and helped defeat the measure, six to five. Foght believed they had been threatened by the Bauer faction. Furious, he alluded to Bauer's lack of sufficient Cherokee blood to hold office, then asked, "Now would the Office of Indian Affairs sanction an attempt to displace him at this time, or shall the majority continue to suffer these unwarranted proceedings directed by him and two others[?]"

In an apparent effort to overcome Bauer's opposition, the House amended the pending bill to authorize the land exchanges if approved by secret ballot in a tribal election within sixty days of the bill's enactment. It was passed in August 1937, much to Chief Blythe's chagrin. He gave three reasons for opposing it. First, the Indians did not understand the act "and have been misinformed in regard to same"; second, because of past injustices the Cherokees were suspicious "of any proposition put to them by the Indian Office"; and third, section 2 of the bill stipulated that the results of the election would be final, "and since it is my belief that it will surely lose at this time, I do not think it wise to hold the election." The election never took place, probably saving the parkway from outright rejection by the Cherokees. Obviously Blythe recognized the potency of Bauer's opposition.

Finally, a new compromise emerged in 1938. Under this plan North Carolina would build a highway through Soco Valley, while the parkway would follow the mountain ridges surrounding Qualla Boundary and then descend to Ravensford, where it would connect with the road through the national park. This would give the Eastern Cherokees virtually everything they wanted: a new highway through Soco providing direct access to the park and leaving Indian tourist businesses intact, and a new parkway offering unobstructed views of mountain grandeur as well as alternative access to the park and reservation. Clyde M. Blair, Foght's successor as agent, canvassed all council members, including Fred Bauer, and expected unanimous approval. But much to his surprise, the council rejected the proposal nine to two. The only explanation given Blair was that some Cherokees feared the state would later turn control of the Soco highway over to the park service. In all likelihood Bauer was responsible for this misimpression. Both Blair and Chief Blythe were frustrated and disappointed.

George Stephens, publisher of the *Asheville Citizen*, was even more distressed, fearing Cherokee intransigence might mean loss of a parkway that promised millions of dollars for the regional economy. He believed that both Fred and Catherine Bauer had "inherited the ancient grudge of the Indians against the white man" and that their arguments had befuddled the average Cherokee. Furthermore, it was his understanding that the Bauers intended to ask North Carolina newspapers to publish articles they had written attacking the Indian Office. Stephens thought such diatribes would "so stir up the Cherokees that it will be impossible to ever get any cooperative action from the Indians on the Blue Ridge Parkway." He asked Curtis B. Johnson of the *Charlotte Observer* to delay publication of any such articles "until present negotiations are definitely settled." Johnson agreed to cooperate.

Congressman Zebulon Weaver was even more determined to have the parkway. He introduced a bill that would, if necessary, appropriate tribal lands for the project. The secretary of the interior would select lands for the parkway right-of-way in consultation with the tribal council but was not bound by its wishes. He would then convey those lands to North Carolina. In congressional hearings in July 1939, Weaver insisted he had no intention of harming the Eastern Band. "All I desire is to bring this road down there to them where more than a million people will pass over and through there during the year. Except for this roadway, they are isolated." Spokesmen for North Carolina said they were willing to pay the Band a total of $40,000 or $30 an acre, whichever was greater, for the compromise right-of-way; testimony demonstrated that this was much more than the land was worth. Under Weaver's bill, the Cherokees were allowed to use part of this money to buy more productive lands from the national park.

True to their sometimes exasperating tradition of playing both sides of an issue, the Band had delegated both Chief Blythe and Vice Chief Bauer to represent them. The former, predictably, favored the proposed compromise as "a very generous offer." Bauer, now a candidate for chief in the upcoming tribal elections, had a platform of not alienating any tribal lands and proposed a parkway route that would be entirely outside the reservation. When asked why two Cherokee representatives should have such different views, Bauer said Chief Blythe was a central figure in the tribe's "relief setup" whose "bread and butter comes from the Government pay check." But neither the testimony of Bauer nor that of Alice Lee Jemison could stop the parkway. The bill finally passed the House in early August without specifying a route. Then it awaited Senate action, leaving the Band a choice of taking immediate steps toward approving the compromise offer or running the risk that the secretary of the interior would select a route less attractive to the tribe.

This situation played into the hands of Jarrett Blythe, who was running against Bauer for reelection as principal chief. Blythe was probably the most popular political figure ever to hold office on the Cherokee reservation, a man Clyde Blair characterized as "very level-headed" and intelligent, "who has the best interest of the Indians as heart and who thoroughly understands the relationship between the Federal Government and the tribe." Against another opponent and in other circumstances, Fred Bauer might have been a more viable candidate. As Blair had conceded in 1938, Bauer exercised "a strong influence with the Council due largely to the fact that he is emotional, dramatic, clever and capable of very persuasive speech." But that had been a year earlier, when things were going Bauer's way. Now it was clear the parkway would be built on reservation land, with or without Cherokee approval—and possibly on terms far less generous than the compromise proposal. Blythe clearly favored the compromise, and the prospect of receiving a large sum of money for largely uninhabited, unproductive lands along that route must have swayed many Cherokees. Nor did it make matters easier for Bauer that he had recently coauthored a booklet published by William Dudley Pelly, head of the Silver Shirts of America, a pro-Nazi and virulently anticommunist and anti-Semitic organization. The booklet's title revealed its thesis: *Indians Aren't Red: The Inside Story of Administrative Attempts to Make Communists of the North Carolina Cherokees.* Although Clyde Blair doubted it would have much impact on the Indians, he reported that Congressman Weaver was asking for an investigation of Pelly's publishing company.

Whatever Bauer's problems, in all likelihood Jarrett Blythe would have beaten him—and anyone else—easily. One astute observer believed Bauer could have run against Blythe 150 times without winning. It was no contest. Not counting the Graham County returns, Blythe polled 707 votes in the September 1939 elections to 161 for his adoptive brother. Equally important, almost all of the new council members supported Blythe and the compromise right-of-way. Bauer's days of significant tribal authority were over, though his machinations and vocal opposition to the Indian Office would continue for another thirty years.

Besides losing the election, Bauer and his followers also failed in their efforts to promote a Cherokee education reflecting mainstream American culture. By 1939 the school system, although modernized in terms of its facilities and certain administrative procedures, unabashedly geared its education to reservation life rather than outside opportunities. The boarding school now had grades eleven and twelve but emphasized vocational education and Cherokee arts and crafts. More than previous administrations, the Collier regime had also attempted to provide elementary education for all reservation children without disrupting family ties. Access to expanded and modernized day schools at Big Cove, Bird Town, Soco, and Snowbird was much easier than in earlier days, and many children now attended classes who otherwise would have been overlooked. This in turn helped reduce the number of boarders at the central school to 140, while another 260 students—mostly older children—were bused in each day. For the present, at least, the Indian Office realized that few Cherokees would be allowed to attend public schools with whites. During the preceding decade, out of $2,351,000 of nonrelief federal money spent on the Band through the Bureau of Indian Affairs, more than $1,255,000 had been for education.

To Clyde Blair and other Indian Office employees, Bauer's eclipse and the unquestioned leadership of Jarrett Blythe must have brought enormous relief. Blair found the new tribal council to be diligent, cooperative, and willing to follow the advice of the chief. At the first meeting Blythe made it clear that he saw resolution of the right-of-way issue as a priority, and the council proved agreeable. In February 1940 it unanimously ratified what was essentially the compromise plan and, as a bonus to the Indian Office, denied that Alice Lee Jemison or any other outsider represented the Band. Congress promptly approved the new parkway route, and the Cherokees eventually had their Soco Valley highway as well.

Whatever one thinks of Bauer, his opposition to the initial parkway plans clearly had the support of a tribal majority, as well as Chief Blythe and agents Foght and Blair. Such a proposal would have strangled tribal business enterprise in both the Soco Valley and the town of Cherokee. For better or worse, the compromise allowed the present strip development of commercial enterprise along reservation highways. When the real tourist boom began after World War II, the Cherokees would be prepared. The most enduring legacy of the New Deal among the Eastern Cherokees was the groundwork it laid for that boom.

The Indian New Deal as Mirror of the Future

D'ARCY MCNICKLE (Salish-Kutenai)

We are moving far enough away from the 1930s and the reform movement commonly termed "the Indian New Deal" to view it dispassionately, without a sense of involvement. Strong lines were drawn up in those partisan days, each side charging its opposite with unworthy motives, each side dressing up its own purposes in seemly rhetoric. Now that the dust of combat has settled, one can begin to see what the true issues were, what the gains and what the losses.

First, a brief description of the social, economic, and political conditions which gave rise to programs of reform. One general set of circumstances prevailed during the period. It was a time of deep, seemingly inescapable depression—a time of long soup lines in the cities, of rioting farmers in the countryside, of bank closings, of unemployed businessmen selling apples at street corners. One does not always see behind the headlines and news broadcasts the reality of economic disaster. I walked to work in midtown Manhattan one morning just after a victim of the times had leaped from a tall apartment building and was spread all over the sidewalk. Even nature contrived to add to human misery, for that was a period of the dreadful duststorms, when the topsoil of the wheat-growing prairie states ascended into the jet streams and swirled out over the Atlantic. I saw that, too, standing in shock in a New York street. It was a time when men began to talk about ecological balance, and a documentary film, "The Plow That Broke the Plains," was viewed by hushed audiences. Men came face to face with themselves in those days and questioned the very society they had created, and which had created them.

A time of doom, but it was also a time of opportunity. Under the lash of the desperate emergency, social reform made giant strides. Banking methods were overhauled; the marketing of securities was regulated; vast holding company cartels were broken up; systems of social insurance and unemployment compensation were created. The management of national forests, grazing lands, wild life, water, and minerals was made responsive to the public interest. Vast public works projects were undertaken to repair some of the damage wrought through generations of heedless resource exploitation and abuse. Some of this concern for the environment, and some of the appropriated funds, managed to trickle down to the Indian community.

It is important to understand the conditions that prevailed in the Indian community. The older Indians of that period still lived with the defeats which many tribes experienced in the closing years of the 19th century. The tragedy of the first Wounded Knee affair was less than fifty years in the rear, a brief lifetime.

When Collier assumed the commissionership in 1933, the General Allotment Law had been operating for better than forty-five years, and in that interval some 90 million acres of land had passed out of Indian ownership; an estimate of 138 million acres, all owned in common in 1887, had been reduced to 48 million acres. For the most part, the alienated lands were the best lands: the river bottoms, rich grass lands, prime forests. But land losses tell only part of the story. The allotment process, the

D'Arcy McNickle, "The Indian New Deal as Mirror of the Future," in Ernest Schusky, editor, *Political Organization of Native North Americans,* University Press of America, 1980, 107–118.

individualizing of community-owned assets, created forces which had never before operated in Indian society. Families and individuals competed for choice lands, for water or other advantages. Outsiders intruded as homesteaders on so-called surplus lands, and inevitably meddled in the internal affairs of the tribe. Social structure was disoriented in many ways, as non-Indians married into a group, and kin groups were scattered throughout the reservation area. In each allotted reservation a class of landless, homeless individuals came into existence and, having no resources of their own, doubled up with relatives and intensified the poverty of all.

That, too, tells only part of the story. Tribes had been moved about like live-stock until, in some cases, the original homeland was no more than a legend in the minds of old men and women. Children had been forcefully removed from the family and kept in close custody until they lost their mother language and all knowledge of who they were, while the schooling to which they were subjected was conducted as an exercise in animal training. Tribal religious practices, when they were not proscribed outright, were treated as obscenities. The bureaucratic apparatus had penetrated the entire fabric of Indian life, usurping tribal decision-making, obtruding into the family, and demeaning local leadership. It was totally oblivious of its inadequacies and its inhumanity.

Part of John Collier's initial problem, as the incoming commissioner, was to remove some of the tar with which he himself had plastered the Bureau. He had been an outspoken and caustic critic of the Bureau, and suddenly he was in the position of asking Indians to have confidence in the institution. While he occupied the office for twelve years, he never entirely extricated himself from the awkward situation.

One of his first acts, intended to moderate the harsh image of the Bureau, was the issuance of an order (Office of Indian Affairs 1934) declaring: "No interference with Indian religious life will be hereafter tolerated. The cultural history of Indians is in all respects to be considered equal to that of any non-Indian group. And it is desirable that Indians be bilingual—fluent and literate in English, and fluent in their vital, beautiful, and efficient native languages."

In a further early effort to undo the past, he secured the repeal of twelve obsolete laws, some dating from as early as 1790, which collectively placed inordinate power over civil liberties in the hands of Bureau officials. The repeal of these laws, needless to say, was not enough to change the authoritarian nature of the Bureau.

Collier, of course, is associated with the Indian Reorganization Act, which in the context of the Roosevelt administration was known popularly as the Indian New Deal. The legislation had been adopted by a reluctant Congress in 1934, reluctant because the Act by open declaration was a denunciation of the policies followed by Congress and national administrations through the previous half-century. The reluctance moreover went deeper than bruised feelings. Most legislation as it emerges from the Congressional mill bears small resemblance to the bright promise that was fed into the hopper. The Indian Reorganization Act was no exception. Congress wanted the "Indian business" cleaned up, but it was not ready or willing to transfer real power to the Indian tribes. This unwillingness was emphasized by the rejection of four critical features: (1) an orderly procedure for transferring services and functions from the Bureau to an organized Indian community; (2) the creation of tribal corporations for the management of reservation resources, with power "to compel" the removal of any federal employee on grounds of inefficiency or "other causes";

(3) a training program to prepare Indians to take over and administer community services, including courses of study in Indian history and culture; and (4) the establishment of a tribal court system, with right of appeal to the federal appellate court and to the Supreme Court.

It was the first piece of major legislation dealing with Indian affairs ever taken into the Indian country and discussed in open meetings. And here the long history of bureaucratic misrule loomed as a major challenge to Collier's reform program. At every one of the regional meetings called to consider the pending bill, the motives and the purposes of the Bureau were questioned, heatedly at times. The distrust and suspicion voiced at these meetings, and in subsequent meetings in Washington, were reflected in the tribal elections that followed. By its terms, the act was not to apply on any reservation where a majority rejected it. Out of 258 tribes, bands, and rancherias voting in these elections, 77 voted against application. The Navajo was one of the tribes voting in the negative.

The bill as introduced in Congress was a document of some fifty typewritten pages, but what emerged was a scant six pages of print. The reduction in bulk was not critical, but what was stricken in the course of debate practically guaranteed that the nature of the bureaucracy would not be altered. By eliminating the provision giving the Indians a deciding role in the selection and retention of reservation employees, colonial rule was left intact. By deleting the articles creating a federal Indian court system, the control over the law and order was left in the hands of the Secretary of the Interior, and it encouraged the states, in later years, to seek to extend state law, and state taxation, to reservation lands. One other deletion deserves passing mention. If the article providing for courses of study in Indian history and culture and in administrative management had been retained, Indian studies programs might have been operating forty years ago.

The Indian Reorganization Act did retain two features central to Collier's reform program. The first of these was the prohibition against any future allotment of tribal lands; the other was a watered-down provision dealing with tribal government and property management. While the range of discretionary tribal action was greatly reduced from the original proposal, what remained was tacit recognition of the tribe as a surviving political entity with definable inherent powers. The Act referred specifically to "All powers vested in an Indian tribe or tribal council by existing law"; and that, of course, included treaty stipulations and court decisions, as well as statute law. In addition it recognized the right of a tribe to embody in a written constitution the power to "prevent the sale, disposition, lease or encumbrance of tribal lands." Within this legal framework it became possible for an Indian tribe to function as a municipal body and to exert the common law rights of a property owner.

The legislation was not the emancipating instrument that had been hoped for, and within less than a decade of its enactment the nation was at war, with the moneys authorized for salvaging the Indian community going elsewhere. But the Act did mark the way into the future—if there was to be an Indian future. In Collier's day that was not at all a certainty; indeed twenty years after the adoption of the Indian Reorganization Act, the Eisenhower administration almost closed out that possibility forever.

To go back a moment: The misgivings and outright opposition expressed by many Indians during the hearings on the Indian Reorganization Act were symptomatic of more basic trouble. Since the United States in 1871 renounced the policy of nego-tiating treaties with the tribes, a practice that had endured from colonial times, the Indians had not been consulted in any major decisions affecting their property, their family life, or the training of their children. All such matters came within reach of a bureaucratic structure, which developed attitudes and formalities impervious to Indian participation. And as the bureaucracy hardened, the Indian community with-drew deeper into itself and set up its own barriers to communication.

But Collier's problem did not come entirely from the fact that for those sixty-odd years since the renunciation of treaty-making the government had barred In-dians from assuming responsibility for their own lives. The unseen and, indeed, the larger problem had to do with the ethic of social intervention which, in the 1930s, still functioned as a tradition out of the 19th century—a heritage of colonial administration.

In a major crisis that developed early in his administration the reluctance or the inability of the bureaucracy to respond to human conditions had disastrous con-sequences. The occasion was the decision to reduce Navajo sheep herds, the prin-cipal subsistence base of the tribe, in order to bring the animal population into balance with deteriorating range lands. Studies carried out by professional agrono-mists demonstrated that top soil was blowing away, perennial grasses were being replaced by annual weeds of low nutrient value, summer rains were eroding deep gullies and carrying mountains of soil into newly constructed power and flood con-trol reservoirs, threatening to fill them with silt.

In designing a control program, Collier directed that reduction would be on a "sliding scale," with the largest reduction on the larger herds and a lesser reduction on the smaller herds, while herds of a minimum size would be left intact. The directive was later made specific in providing that herds of up to 100 head of sheep would not be reduced. Herds of that size were considered subsistence herds re-quired to provide family support. . . .

A report prepared soon after the reduction program was initiated in 1933 states that: "The larger owners flatly refused to make all the reductions from their herds. After an all-night session (at Tuba City, in November 1933) it was agreed . . . that every Navajo should sell 10 percent of his sheep. . . . This same agreement became widespread over the entire reservation, since the large owners consistently refused to make the total reduction from their flocks. . . ." In practice, the owners of small herds found themselves under greater economic pressure than the owners of large herds; they sold out their entire holdings and found themselves completely depend-ent on the emergency work programs financed by the government. When these pro-grams ran out of funds, real hardship followed.

Other complications quickly arose. The government had offered to buy sheep at prices ranging from $1.00 for ewes to $2.25–$3.00 for wethers. Chee Dodge, the respected leader of the tribe, argued that the government should concentrate on the purchase of good breeding ewes, at better prices; otherwise, the Navajo livestock owners would offer only old ewes and other non-productive stock and reduction would not be achieved. These prices, however, had been established in Washington by the emergency relief administration, the source of the funds, and they could not be altered in the field. The disappointing results confirmed what Chee Dodge had predicted.

Perhaps the most serious oversight was the failure to recognize the fact that women were in many instances the principal owners of the family herds. Women were not members of the tribal council, however, and they were not consulted as negotiations went forward between the government and the tribal leaders. When the leaders returned to their families and found the women opposed to plans for reductions, any agreements with the government became meaningless.

What Collier did not discover until it was too late to intervene was that field employees sometimes resorted to coercive action. This interference occurred specifically in the eastern Navajo area, where it was expected that legislation, then pending in Congress, would be enacted and would result in extending the eastern boundary of the reservation to include an additional two million acres. In anticipation of the increased acreage, the Navajos of the area were induced to sell their goats, with the idea of eventually replacing them with sheep. By the fall of 1935 formidable opposition had developed against the legislation, making it unlikely that it would be adopted. Nevertheless the goat reduction program went forward. As Collier reported to the Senate subcommittee in the summer of 1936: "In my judgment, we should not have carried out the goat purchase program within the eastern area . . . because we were no longer assured of the enactment of the boundary bill. . . . Why we did proceed with the goat purchases in this area, frankly, I don't know. . . . At the time we did not, at Washington, have any information, or evidence that duress was being, or was to be, employed anywhere. It was not directed to be employed, but on the contrary, all the sales were to be voluntary. However, before the close of the goat purchase operation, I began to receive . . . information that overpersuasion, and even duress, had in fact been employed in this area."

Elsewhere in his statement to the subcommittee, he commented: "The purchase was an error and I cannot, and do not desire, to evade responsibility for that error. . . . I am the Commissioner." . . .

Such episodes were possible because the bureaucracy was the instrument of an older view of the relationship with the Indian people. In that older view Indians were incompetent to make decisions, especially when questions of a technical nature were involved—and livestock management was considered to be of that nature, even though Navajos had been successful herdsmen for several centuries. Indeed, their very success in increasing their herds was in part responsible for their predicament. In a chain of command situation, such as characterizes bureaucratic structure, responsibility is diffused; one is never accountable for someone else's mistakes.

Collier's hope of restoring to the Indian community some measure of self-government was diminished by the same impersonal, insensate play of bureaucratic forces. Anyone who has worked in government knows that project financing is based on performance. If funds allocated to a field project are not expended within a time limit, usually the fiscal year, it is assumed by those who approve budget requests that the money was not needed. The amount approved for a subsequent operating period will likely be reduced. This leads to various strategems to keep ahead of the finance wizards, the commonest of which is to pile on expenditures before the end of the fiscal period, thus demonstrating the accuracy of the original estimate and the soundness of the project.

The Indian Reorganization Act authorized federal funds to assist tribes in formulating and voting on written constitutions and charters of incorporation. Collier intended that the organization documents should reflect a tribe's traditional ways of arriving at decisions and selecting leaders. To carry out this purpose he recruited a staff of cultural anthropologists, who were to work with the field employees engaged in the program. This move would appear to be one of the first attempts, if not the first, to use anthropologists as technical assistants by a government agency.

The planning came to grief on two counts. When it was discovered in Congress that the Commissioner was spending money on something called anthropology, the appropriation was promptly disallowed and the unit was abandoned although some anthropologists continued working for the Bureau under other titles. A more serious difficulty grew out of the fiscal year syndrome. To satisfy the budget watchers and the wardens of the Treasury, it was necessary to show progress in bringing the tribes under written constitutions. This involved sitting down in meeting after meeting and conducting a tribal drafting committee through a maze of *Whereas* clauses and *Therefore, be it enacted* resolutions. Leaders, who often were non-English-speaking or who had only a primary grade education, were exposed to the full battery of Anglo-Saxon parliamentary syntax, and they had to act before the end of the fiscal year. The result was the hurried adoption of tribal constitutions prepared in Washington and based on conventional political instruments with no provision for action by consensus or for the role of ritual leaders. The tribes were given tools, such as majority rule, for which they had no accustomed usage, and these became devices for community disruption and for petty demagoguery.

One should not conclude from this analysis of the Navajo that no positive gains were registered during the Collier administration. The long record of diminishing land and other resource holdings were halted. The total land base was actually enlarged by some four million acres, the first time in history that Indians gained instead of losing land. Credit financing was begun on a modest scale and made possible resource development and utilization, where previously Indians had leased out tribal and individual lands for lack of capital. A start was made, again modestly, in providing low cost housing. Day schools were built at a number of reservations as an alternative to the off-reservation boarding schools, and they were designed and operated as community centers, anticipating the movement of recent years to provide centers for recreation, adult education, and cultural activities.

These gains, modest as they were, were cut short by the crisis of war. When the shooting was over and Indian GIs and war industry workers came home, they found their reservations in ruins. Employment opportunities were gone, social services were severely curtailed (schools, hospitals, houses in disrepair or shut down entirely), and credit facilities denied. And presently, a hostile administration came to power committed to the ultimate extinguishment of tribal life.

What has come to the surface in tribal communities in recent years, notably at Wounded Knee and on the Pine Ridge reservation generally, is the anger that remained unuttered, but unappeased, for generations. It was an overwhelming anger growing out of the kinds of experiences suggested here; my account of these experiences has been mild and polite. Older Indians, still conscious of the defeats inflicted on their people in the closing years of the last century, withdrew from open challenge and tried passively to live with the white man's inscrutable ways. That former period seems to have come to a crashing end.

The generation of Indian leaders now emerging lacks that consciousness of defeat which inhibited their elders. More than that, as a consequence of international wars, the collapse of colonial empires, rioting and burning in urban ghettos, an economy that destroys the environment, the white man seems not as invincible as he once seemed.

It was possible at Wounded Knee in 1890 for an army unit—Custer's own 7th, Calvary, indeed—to slaughter a Sioux camp of men, women, and children. At that same site in the winter of 1973, armored vehicles and troop detachments surrounded another Indian camp, but no slaughter occurred. Two reasons suggest themselves. The surrounded Indians had access to the world beyond their lines, and they were able to verbalize their grievances to listeners who were sympathetic even though they might not understand what was going on. This access to public opinion was enough to discourage hasty action by gun-carrying troops. An even more compelling restraint was the changed circumstance behind that surrounding army. Men in power no longer had a mandate to kill Indians trying to protect their right to be themselves. Perhaps that is a measurable gain.

Where, then, have we come? One point certainly seems clear. Because Indians are discovering the uses of power in modern society, it is no longer possible to exclude them from the decision-making process in matters affecting their property, their families, the training of their children, or the nature of the accommodation they choose to make within the dominant society. John Collier helped to make these issues evident, but as a man of good will standing outside the Indian community, he was limited in what he could do. He could not substitute his will and vision for Indian will and vision. Nor can any man stand in the place of another.

That, too, is a discovery Indians have made in these very recent years. The simple demonstration of this discovery is the astonishing growth of news media operated by Indian groups reporting on conditions, and the equally remarkable growth of political and cultural organizations devoted to advancing Indian interests. The non-Indian "Friend of the Indian," that 19th-century image of altruistic involvement, is being told politely but firmly to stand aside.

Collier has been charged with turning the clock back on Indian advancement. The basis of the charge, of course, was his insistence on extending religious and cultural freedom to Indian groups and his commitment to the cause of revitalizing Indian society. A modern critic . . . asserts that Collier mistakenly assumed, from his knowledge of Indians of the Southwest, "that Indians everywhere would wish to return to tribal, communal life, if given the opportunity."

What this writer fails to recognize, even in this late day, is that Indians "everywhere" have always been, and remain, more tribal, communal if you will, or conscious of ethnic boundaries, than observers from the outside generally realize. Already in Collier's day the studies of A. Irving Hallowell and others were offering evidence that culturally-wrought personality persists even in circumstances where the outward forms of behavior have accommodated to the dominant society.

Other critics of Collier's effort to build upon the tribal past were people whose ideas had been formed largely in the 19th century, who saw Native society as incapable of development into modern forms. In this view, the Native American existed in a world devoid of logic, or sentiment, or dynamics. Indian life came from nowhere and went nowhere.

Collier challenged this view in many published statements and in his public career. He saw Indian society as "not fossilized, unadaptive, not sealed in the past, but plastic, adaptive, assimilative, while yet faithful to . . . ancient values." And again he . . . wrote: "Societies are living things, sources of the power and values of their members; to be and to function in a consciously living, aspiring, striving society is to be a personality fulfilled."

Whether or not they are aware of John Collier's insight in this matter, Indians today are discovering the truth that lies in this vision. This discovery accounts, in part, for the Indian studies centers that have come into existence at major institutions across the country. The Navajo Community College springs from this vision. In a harsher mode, it accounts for the incidents at Wounded Knee.

Indians were not held back by Collier's efforts to build upon the tribal past. Instead, they have plunged affirmatively into the twentieth century, asserting their identity, and acquiring the skills that will enable them to survive as Indians and members of an Indian community.

◈ *F U R T H E R   R E A D I N G*

David F. Aberle, *The Peyote Religion Among the Navajo* (1966)
John Adair, *The Navajo and Pueblo Silversmiths* (1944)
Thomas Biolsi, *Organizing the Lakota: The Political Economy of the New Deal on the Pine Ridge and Rosebud Reservations* (1992)
Peter Blaine, Sr., with Michael S. Adams, *Papagos and Politics* (1981)
John Collier, *From Every Zenith: A Memoir and Some Essays on Life and Thought* (1963)
Vine R. Deloria, Jr., and Clifford Lytle, *The Nations Within: The Past and Future of American Indian Sovereignty* (1984)
William E. Farr, *The Reservation Blackfeet, 1882–1945: A Photographic History of Cultural Survival* (1984)
Edward T. Hall, *West of the Thirties: Discoveries Among the Navajo and Hopi* (1994)
Laurence M. Hauptman, *The Iroquois and the New Deal* (1981)
Esther Burnett Horne and Sally McBeth, *Essie's Story: The Life and Legacy of a Shoshone Teacher* (1998)
Lawrence C. Kelly, *The Assault on Assimilation: John Collier and the Origins of Indian Policy Reform* (1983)
Oliver La Farge, ed., *The Changing Indian* (1942)
Alexander Leighton and Dorothea Leighton, *The Navaho Door: An Introduction to Navaho Life* (1944)
D'Arcy McNickle, *The Surrounded* (1935)
Katherine M. B. Osburn, *Southern Ute Women: Autonomy and Assimilation on the Reservation, 1887–1934* (1998)
Dorothy R. Parker, *Singing an Indian Song: A Biography of D'Arcy McNickle* (1992)
Donald L. Parman, *The Navajos and the New Deal* (1976)
Kenneth R. Philip, *John Collier's Crusade for Indian Reform, 1920–1954* (1977)
———, ed., *Indian Self-Rule: First-Hand Accounts from Roosevelt to Reagan* (1986)
John Lloyd Purdy, *The Legacy of D'Arcy McNickle: Writer, Historian, Activist* (1996)
Ruth Roessel, ed., *Navajo Livestock Reduction: A National Disgrace* (1974)
Robert F. Schrader, *The Indian Arts and Crafts Board: An Aspect of Indian New Deal Policy* (1983)
Leo Simmons, ed., *Sun Chief: The Autobiography of a Hopi Indian* (1942)
Graham D. Taylor, *The New Deal and American Indian Tribalism: The Administration of the Indian Reorganization Act, 1934–1945* (1980)
Ruth Murray Underhill, *Singing for Power: The Song Magic of the Papago Indians* (1938)

CHAPTER
13

World War II, Termination, and the Foundation for Self-Determination, 1941–1960

◈

When World War II began, the Indian New Deal already had lost its impetus, as had the New Deal itself. The nation's attention turned to the international conflict. Indians responded to the war, with thousands of Native men and women serving in the armed forces and thousands more working in war-related industries. Many people were affected deeply by these experiences, which altered how they saw their communities and themselves. Indians took collective pride in the achievements of people such as Clarence Tinker (Osage) and Ira Hayes (Pima), as well as the accomplishments of the Navajo codetalkers during the Pacific campaign. The codetalkers based a code on the Navajo language and relayed messages with speed and accuracy. The code was never broken. Indian success in adapting to the exigencies of wartime encouraged others to see them as just like everyone else.

This perception proved to be a double-edged sword, for if it encouraged greater respect it also promoted a renewed push for assimilation. The passage in 1946 of the Indian Claims Commission Act seemed to promise a redress of past injustices. However, many claims were denied or were recognized with very limited compensation, and most Indian communities were disappointed with the results. The ICC was part of the process by which the federal government attempted to end its involvement with Indian communities. The effort to end federal trust responsibilities for Indian reservations—a movement generally labeled termination—initially gained some support from Native people who were tired of Bureau mismanagement and constraints. Unfortunately, the form that termination took differed drastically from what most Indians had in mind. At the same time, some Indians moved from rural areas or reservations into urban centers. This movement was sometimes voluntary and sometimes pushed by Bureau officials who saw reservations as economic dead ends. The shock waves of this period also had the ironic consequence of catalyzing Indians' political activism and their development of their own economies on their own terms. As with the earlier assimilationist period of the late nineteenth and early twentieth centuries, this era proved to be a complex time, one that historians are only now beginning to comprehend more fully. What is the legacy of this time period?

◈ *D O C U M E N T S*

World War II certainly promoted significant change in Indian country. Ella Deloria, the Yankton Dakota anthropologist and linguist, recognized the significance of these years. In *Speaking of Indians*, published in 1944, she perceptively addressed the impact of the war. Document 1 is excerpted from this book. Ruth Muskrat Bronson, a western Cherokee who played a vital role in the newly-established Congress of American Indians, spoke out strongly against termination. Her protest against the end of federal trusteeship comprises Document 2. Northern Cheyenne leader John Wooden Legs emphasized the importance of the tribal land base. "Back on the War Ponies," composed in 1960, furnishes Document 3. In Document 4, Mary Jacobs (Lumbee) explains how the city of Chicago could become home for her family.

1. Ella Deloria (Yankton Dakota) on Indian Experiences During World War II, 1944

All the Indians today may be thought of as divided into the same three groupings found among any other class of citizens—those who are left at home, the men and women in the services, and the workers in war industries. Let me tell you about them.

First, some glimpses of the people at home, who carry on there, praying, working, and comforting one another as they meet the inevitable hardships and sorrows that come to all in war. I receive many letters from my Dakota kith and kin telling me what goes on among that particular tribe. One says quite naturally, in speaking of a recent drive from Rosebud to Rapid City, "Of course it was a long slow ride in the cold, at thirty-five miles an hour, but we made it all right." I know that road. It is long, monotonous, and deserted. Nobody on earth would ever know if they speeded along, as usual, at fifty miles an hour. But they had been asked not to do so in order to conserve gas and tires for the sake of the boys; so they obeyed. It was not smart to cheat.

Then I have the story of a woman whose only son was the first from that reservation to be killed in action. In her intense grief, she reverted to ancient customs, so long given up, and demeaned herself by cutting off her hair, wearing her oldest clothes, and wandering over the hills, wailing incessantly. Nor would she be comforted. Did the people do anything? Certainly. In the old-time manner, which they now carry over into their church, they made a feast and invited the bereaved mother. After a memorial service in the church they went down to the guild hall. There the elder men and women, strong in their faith and given to such exhortation, made speeches addressed to her, as is the traditional manner of condoling with those who mourn. "I do not presume to make light of your great sorrow, my relative," said one

From Ella Deloria, *Speaking of Indians,* 137–148. Copyright © 1944. Published by the University of Nebraska Press.

earnest Christian woman, "but to remind you of God's love." And so the woman's silent weeping subsided. They washed her tear-stained face and partook of food with her, all in decent quiet, for this was a ceremony. "Then they all collected gifts for her, mostly food," the letter ends, "and she told them she felt lots stronger now because they had talked to her and comforted her."

Another letter tells what happened after a four-engine bomber burst into flames high over a little Dakota chapel and fell blazing and crashing to the ground not far off. Everyone in it was lost. The Dakota catechist immediately rang the bell and the people came running. When he saw that all hope of rescue was gone he said to them, "My relatives, let us go into the church." They took their places, some weeping softly for the nameless victims. Then he read prayers from the burial office in the native tongue amid a stillness that was absolute but for the fire still crackling outside. The families of the boys in that plane might like to know that prayers were offered for them first by Christian Dakotas.

In no line of any letter is there the least sign of discouragement or despondency over their hardships. The people see singly: "There's a job to be done. So let's get at it. Never mind about *us* now."

Next, the second group: the young men and women in the services. The reports come thick and fast about them and their record shows that they are more than doing their best. They are constantly being cited for heroism and given the various army and navy decorations. The Secretary of the Interior, Harold L. Ickes, writes of them:

> The inherited talents of the Indian make him uniquely valuable. He has endurance, rhythm, a feeling for timing, coordination, sense perception, an uncanny ability for getting over any kind of terrain at night, and, better than all else, an enthusiasm for fighting. He takes a rough job and makes a game of it. Rigors of combat hold no terrors for him; severe discipline and hard duties do not deter him.

That is a generous and, I believe, fair appraisal, but for one word that may strike a false note, "an enthusiasm for fighting." For me that flavors too much of the old notion of savage bloodthirstiness, consciously or unconsciously imputed indiscriminately to all Indians. It does not seem a fair way to represent modern Indian boys who had known only peace. "An enthusiasm for action when the aim is plain" would be truer.

I see a little paper each month, *Victory News*, edited by a talented Dakota girl, an A.B. from Carleton College. Her staff are all Dakotas. It is mimeographed by them on the reservation and is the organ of the Victory Club of Rosebud, through which the people work together to send cheer and home news to the boys all over the world. Think of it, a little Indian paper with a mailing list that covers the globe! There are similar papers at other places. These clubs prepare army kits and write personal letters to the boys without parents and to those whose parents cannot write.

Here are a few random excerpts from service men's letters, which *Victory News* quotes monthly:

Pfc. Anthony Omaha-Boy is "glad for God's protection." Pfc. Laverne Iron Wing is studying French and Italian between times! Robert Schmidt is a gunner on one of Uncle Sam's flying forts. Sgt. Gilbert Feather asks "that we all pray God to bring us safely back to the good old U.S.A." Pvt. Albert Bad Hand ends, "I haven't seen my Indian pals since I came over. I am aching to see one so that I can chat with him in Dakota."

The *Martin Messenger Weekly*, of Martin, South Dakota, carried this letter from Paddy Starr, in Hawaii, addressed to his catechist. It shows that the boys feel responsible for their home church: "You may think I have forgotten everything back home. No. I bear every one of you in my heart. I'm enclosing a money order for $15.00, of which $5.00 is for the Men's Society, $5.00 for the Women's Auxiliary, and $5.00 for the Young People's Fellowship. I'm doing my part over here. In prayers I want every one of you to do your part."

Indian boys are in every branch of service. From General Tinker, who lost his life at the very start of the war, down to the last private, they qualify for any post and are serving everywhere, courageously.

Indian girls are Red Cross nurses, WACS, and WAVES. They, too, are every-where. When a missionary's wife asked where his sister was now, a little full-blood boy answered quite casually, "In Iceland." Iceland was now part of his world.

These new experiences of Indian youth raise some vital questions about their training, and this may be a good place to stop and consider them.

Before the war some of the educational planning was directed to a very special kind of life. It was predicated on the common statement, "Ninety per cent of the Indians return to the reservation anyway," the assumption always being that there is little need of training them for the outside world since they will not be in it. The course of study and training was thus devised for the limited, expectable needs of reservation life. And now, see where the young people are! How well prepared were they for the world at large? It seemed a good idea at the time, no doubt. But in future a course of study that corresponds in all essentials to the requirements of the various state boards of education might be safer—and fairer to the Indians in the long run.

We might well ask ourselves, "Why do they return to the reservation, any-way?" Well, partly it is that pull toward home and family, a universal human need but peculiarly accentuated in the Indian nature from centuries of close family and clan and *tiyoṡpaye* life. But that is not all. It is also because Indian young people had not been prepared to get into American general society and feel at home in it. If they had known the ordinary, commonplace things that other American youth take for granted, they would not have felt ill at ease and lonely there. If one is not familiar with the allusions and casual references that pepper the conversation of a particular group, one is bound to feel left out. Indian people are by nature reticent and retiring; when they feel a lack of social ease and self-confidence, they want to run away from the crowd, knowing they are ill-prepared to hold their own. It is not enough to be a good mechanic or a well trained stenographer at such times.

I sometimes listen to quiz programs on the radio to see if I can answer the ques-tions. It challenges me to find out the things I miss. I don't like *not* to know the an-swers. Some Americans know them; why not I? That is the way I think other Indians feel. That is how some parents have been feeling of late. They have been saying they want their children to learn what the other children in their state are required to learn. They can teach them all the Indian lore and language they themselves choose, they say, and do a better job of it. They want the schools to concentrate on things the children cannot learn at home. I think they have something there.

The war has indeed wrought an overnight change in the outlook, horizon, and even habits of the Indian people—a change that might not have come about for many years yet. For weal or woe, the former reservation life has been altered radically. As it looks now, that idea of a special course of study set up for Indians alone shows up a bit negatively as a kind of race discrimination. What is right and necessary for the majority of American school children and is made available to them ought not to be denied to other American children. It is a challenge, moreover, to be expected to measure up, the same as anyone else, rather than to have allowances continually made on the basis of race.

The third group we are considering here, the workers in industry, are numerous and important. Whole families have moved into the cities and are meeting problems they have never faced before. As workers they are valuable. Skillful with their hands at tasks requiring meticulous care, they are extremely accurate, patient, dependable. If they are a split second more deliberate than some others, they make correspondingly fewer mistakes that might prove fatal. They will not stop to bargain for themselves; it is not in their tradition to think of self first; and they will not grumble. They will never do anything to hinder the war effort. They are too peculiarly American for that.

One of their problems is that of paying rent. They find it an irksome concomitant to living away from their own homes. They have never paid rent before. Naturally they try to find the least expensive places—with the result that they sometimes find themselves among undesirable neighbors. And of course there are numerous other problems. What to do with their children and adolescent girls in these surroundings is one of the hardest problems. How to get wholesome entertainment is another, and where to go to church, a third.

These Indians are earning "big money" now, and for many of them it is their first experience. They like it and will want to keep on earning and being able to buy, out of their own efforts entirely, what they desire, instead of waiting endlessly for their money from leases handled by the agency.

But do they all know how to take care of their money? What knowledge have they of practical business? Can they budget wisely? Many of them have till now had little chance to handle money, since the agency office has always managed even personal accounts for the majority of them.

And then what of the great problem they share with people on every continent—the new ordering of their life when their sons and daughters return from the armed services and the war industries are closed?

What will the workers in war plants do then? Many will doubtless want to stay in the cities, having become urbanized and liking it. Some will doubtless get on there; but others may quite possibly force out of work. Reticent and uncompetitive, as some of their tribal societies have made their people, perhaps they will have their jobs snatched by the aggressive and blatant type of workers who are used to competition.

The vast majority will probably want to go home. It is natural to want to be near one's own people. Many Indians cannot yet feel complete with just their little family, their spouse and children. They have been used to thinking in terms of the larger family groups for many generations. Even while they work their hearts turn homeward. "This is transitory," they think. "We will soon be home again." For many, that means the reservation, and it seems very good to them, however drab and bare it may look to outsiders. It will be good it get into their own homes, be they ever so humble. At least they won't have to feel beholden to landlords and will be able once again to reckon without rent. Owning one's own home will take on a new meaning.

The boys and girls in distant lands must be thinking of home, too. Perhaps for the first time they really appreciate having lands and houses. Their own sojourn in areas of great destruction where they see throngs of pitiful refugees will make them extra thankful for America and for their reservation homes.

Numbers of these young people will want to get back and do something about the life in their old communities. For now they have seen things, not only pitiful but also thought-provoking things: how people get along; how they work without letup to improve their places; how they manage to own some livestock and take good care of it; and how they grow things on every spare inch of ground and garner every berry and grain, loath to lose even one. Wonderful object lessons! Those who have been away will want to copy them when they come home.

Being with other people is indeed an eye opener to many things. The boys and girls have had a chance to see how they measure up in the life of average American communities, and they have begun to realize what their churches and schools have done for them. They went to school in the past because it seemed they must, and they occupied themselves with whatever was taught them. They had no choice about it; but then they had no basis for making a choice anyway. Some of it has certainly stood them in good stead, but other parts of it looks now like so much waste. They might have learned certain other things, instead, for which they now feel a definite lack. They know now, too, that they never went far enough in any one thing, nor deep enough into fundamentals. That was why they disqualified for this or that type of specialized training, even though they knew they could do it because they had a natural feel for it.

They will come back with perspective. They will see their churches and schools in a new light. They will appreciate what those agencies have tried to do for them. Now they will be able to say just what they require of them. There will be a new call to government to help them with their land and economic problems, since they will be ready and eager for help. There will be a new call for schools, for now they know what they need, what they missed in the past, and what their children must not miss in the future. They have fought and suffered for their country. They are Americans, and they will want to be treated as such. . . .

2. Ruth Muskrat Bronson (Cherokee) Criticizes the Proposed Termination of Federal Trusteeship, 1955

If the official policies of the Federal Government, as reflected by the current policies of the Bureau of Indian Affairs and the actions of the 83rd Congress, continue to be pursued the American Indian (like that other living creature associated with him in history, the buffalo) is likely, similarly, to continue to exist only on the American nickel.

From Ruth M. Bronson (Cherokee) on Termination, National Congress of American Indians Papers.

The tragedy is that this may come about through misunderstanding of the issues involved in the proposed termination of Federal trusteeship over the Indian. These issues have been almost completely obscured in a miasma of confusion caused by conflicting financial interests, conflicting opinions on proper psychological solutions, and of justice itself. And, most important of all, caused by uninformed sentiment.

The average American is noted for his sympathy with the underdog. He is also apt to have romantic sentiment for the American Indian. Add to these two admirable qualities a vague sense of guilt for the actions of his forebears in ousting the original inhabitants of the rich land they adopted and for the long and shameful history of broken treaties with these dispossessed, and you have a tendency toward impulsive action based on a desire to make amends. If this action is founded on superficial or inaccurate knowledge rather than on thoughtful study or familiarity with fact and reality the result can be exceedingly serious, even disastrous, for the Indian. This is true in the case of the termination bills since these jeopardize the Indian's very existence and unquestionably would lead to his eventual—literal—extinction.

There is even widespread misconception as to what is involved in the Federal trusteeship. The casually informed citizen, dedicated to fair play, feels there is something definitely insulting in labeling an adult a ward of the government, as though he were being branded as too incompetent to function without a guardian. Actually, today's Indian enjoys all the major rights and obligations of every American citizen: the right to vote, for instance; to move freely about the country (that is, to live on a reservation or not, as he chooses); the right to sue in court and to make contracts, to hold office; the obligation to pay taxes, and to fight and die for his country in the armed forces.

In addition, he has special privileges, which is what trusteeship boils down to, which he gained by bargaining with his conquerors. In the not so distant past the Indians agreed to end their fighting and cede land to white settlers in exchange for certain defined, inalienable lands and specified services which the Indians could not provide for themselves and which are provided by the States and local communities for non-Indian citizens. It is hard to see how benefits make a "second class" citizen out of an Indian, especially when preferential treatment seems not to jeopardize the status of veterans, farmers, subsidized airlines and steamship companies, manufacturers protected by tariffs, or the businessmen with rapid tax write-offs.

On the contrary, it would seem to be our established political philosophy that the economic well-being of particular groups is a legitimate concern of the Federal government—all this aside from the fact that, in the case of the Indians, it is a matter of solemn treaty.

In addition to the treaties which established reservations as the property and home of the Indian people, the Reorganization Act of 1934 affirmed the partnership of Indian tribes and the Federal Government. Consolidating numerous individual treaties that had been effected with Indian tribes over the years, the Indians were granted by this Act the right to exist as distinct communities, with their own properties, culture, and religion, and the promise of certain services to be furnished by the Federal Government normally furnished [to] other citizens by the states was reaffirmed and enlarged upon.

In the 83rd Congress there was a concerted effort to abrogate this Act, by means of over 100 bills claiming to "free" Indians. Tens of those bills proposed termination of trusteeship over specific tribes. Five of them were passed and signed by the President. All of the bills follow the same pattern. They were introduced by less than a handful of men, but were designed to cut down the Indian on many fronts: the family, the band, the tribe and at State level. They would destroy the tribal organizations, abolish tribal constitutions and corporations formed under the Act of 1934 and void Federal-Indian treaties. Government supervision of the sale of Indian property and expert guidance on the development of natural resources which has been provided up to now would also be cut off, thus exposing the individual Indian, the weak as well as the strong, to exploitation by the unscrupulous and those more knowledgeable in the commercial ways of a highly complex and competitive society. This would take away from him the protection that was preventing further depletion of his last remaining resources. Such a loss would be the country's as well as the Indian's, since conservation along with guided expert development would cease.

In addition, there would be a cessation of education, health and welfare services now supplied by the Federal Government, guaranteed by treaty and sorely needed, without assurance that these would be provided by the States or local communities. . . .

Actually very few voices are raised against eventual termination of trusteeship over the Indians. The Indian people themselves, the friends of the Indians, and the authorities on Indian affairs who are deeply concerned about the trend toward termination are frightened and deeply disturbed, not only because of the inequities contained in the legislation proposed in the 83rd Congress, but at the haste, without proper safeguards or study in relation to the conditions of individual tribes.

And most of all, we are deeply concerned that termination is being decided upon *without the consent,* nay, over the protests, of the Indians concerned. Too often when Indian consent is given it has been obtained by unfair pressures amounting to nothing less than administrative blackmail, as in the case of two tribes which accepted termination bills because they were denied their own funds until they consented. This seems to them a shocking violation of faith.

The informed feel that there should be an attack on the major forces that are keeping the Indian from realizing his potentialities: ill health, lack of educational opportunities, widespread poverty. By attacking these problems at the root, they feel the day will be hastened when the Indian people will no longer need the protection of a special relationship with the Federal Government.

Termination of trusteeship, they believe (if it should be undertaken at all), should be carefully planned-for well ahead of the event, after thorough study, with the agreement of the Indians, the Federal agencies involved, the States and local government units, and the other organizations who would assume responsibility for providing the services now given by the Federal Government. Maintenance of the tribal integrity, if this is what the Indians want, must be assured in any program looking toward their future healthy integration into the American way of life. The consent of the Indians, moreover, should not be obtained by pressure amounting to duress such as was used last year in the cases of Menominee and

Klamath when it was made clear to these two tribes that they would be permitted to withdraw their own money in the United States Treasury only if that withdrawal was coupled with "termination."

More than one theorist has stated that "the solution to the Indian problem" is the absorption of the Indian into the culture, race and society of the European-oriented American way. Shouldn't the Indian have something to say about this? Should the Indian be forced to give up his beliefs, his way of conducting his affairs, his method of organized living, his kind of life on the land he is a part of, if he chooses not to? Shouldn't the Indians have the same right to self-determination that our government has stated, often and officially, is the inalienable right of peoples in far parts of the world? Do we apply a different set of principles, of ethics, to the people within our own borders? . . .

3. John Wooden Legs (Northern Cheyenne) Outlines the Fight to Save the Land, 1960

I am not proud of myself for anything. I am a humble man. But I am proud to be a Cheyenne.

In the old days my people fought hard to defend their homeland. The Cheyennes were a small tribe—but fast on horseback. They came and went like a tornado. That is why the soldiers shot down old people and children when defeat came. The soldiers did not stop until my people were helpless.

Sixty years my people stood looking down at the ground. Hope was running out of them the way blood runs. I heard an Indian Bureau employee say, "The Northern Cheyenne Tribe is in the process of dissolution." He said that in front of me. He thought I did not know what he meant. . . .

I will tell you what it means to be a Cheyenne. Then you will understand what it means to my people to be back on the war ponies—going somewhere.

The white people living near us call the Cheyennes "those poor devils over on the reservation." Sometimes they call us "no-good Indians" and say we do not know how to use our land and the sooner we sell it to white men the better. Even our Bureau Area Director thinks that about us. He wrote me a letter that said my people should not try to keep their land. He said we should let white men buy all over our reservation, so that the Cheyennes could live next door to these white men and learn to be just like them.

To us, to be Cheyenne means being one tribe—living on our own land—in America, where we are citizens.

Our land is everything to us. It is the only place in the world where Cheyennes talk the Cheyenne language to each other. It is the only place where Cheyennes remember same things together.

I will tell you one of the things we remember on our land.

We remember our grandfathers paid for it—with their life. My people and the Sioux defeated General Custer at the Little Big Horn. There never was an Indian

---

From John Wooden Legs, "Back on the War Ponies," *Indian Affairs,* 1960, 3–4. Reprinted by permission of the Association on American Indian Affairs.

victory after that. But the Army hated us. I think they were a little afraid of us too. They took my people away from Montana. They took them to Oklahoma Indian Territory. The people were sick there in all that heat and dust. They asked to go home again, but they were locked up in a military prison instead. Then Little Wolf and Dull Knife broke out of the prison, and they led the people on the long walk home. Montana is far away from Oklahoma, and they had no horses. They had no warm clothes, and many froze to death in the snow. They had nothing to fight with, and most of them were shot by the soldiers. A whole Army hunted them all the way. My grandmother told me she walked holding a little girl by the hand on each side. She had to keep pulling them out of the line of the soldiers' bullets. 300 of my people left Oklahoma. 100 came home. After that the Government gave us the reservation we live on now.

Now you can understand why we are fighting to save our land today. This fight is not against soldiers. It is a fight to stop land sales.

The General Allotment Act was passed in 1887. It is said that the Government could take away any reservation, and give every member of the tribe a piece of it, with the right to sell it to white men in twenty five years. In the southwest the Apache and other tribes never had their land allotted. These tribes have good economic development programs today. Their people are not turning into landless gypsies. . . .

Our Cheyenne land is cattle country. Sensible people knew it would be wrong to take cattle land like ours and divide it up into little pieces—big enough for grazing rabbits, but not cattle. Allotment was held off for the Cheyennes until 1926. My people did not know what allotment was. 25 years had to go by before individual Cheyennes could sell their pieces of our homeland out of Cheyenne ownership. Nobody worried until 1955—except white ranchers and speculators. They were waiting to defeat my hungry people with dollars the way soldiers defeated them with bullets. Then in 1955 the life and death fight of our Northern Cheyenne Tribe started.

When I tell you about the fight remember this. Cheyennes don't sell pieces of our homeland because they want to take their land sale money and go away from the people to life. They spend their land sale money on food—clothes—old cars to get around in. . . .

In 1955 the first tracts of Northern Cheyenne land were put up for sale by the Indian Bureau. Our people told us, the tribal council, to save the reservation any way we could—by asking the Bureau to stop Cheyenne land sales, by having the tribe buy up any land that was going to be sold. The tribal council liquidated our tribal steer enterprise, and we wanted to use $40,000 from this to keep the first Cheyenne land from being sold. The Bureau would not release our money to us in time for us to bid on the land. And they refused to hold up the land sale until our money was released. The Bixby Tracts were 1,340 acres of our best grazing and with water, and they were sold to a Mr. Norris for $22,458. A year later Mr. Norris offered to sell the land back to us again—for $47,736, a $25,278 profit. By then the tribe couldn't afford to buy back the Bixby Tracts, because the Billings Area Office of the Bureau was putting other tracts of our land up for sale as fast as they could. We had to bid on those tracts with the money we had. So far—from 1958 to 1959—the tribal council managed to hold our reservation together by bidding on every piece of land that went up for sale. In 1959 we borrowed $50,000 from the Indian Revolving Loan Fund at 4% interest. We knew this money will not be enough to buy all the land that ever comes up for sale. We thought we could save our home-land for a little while longer—and then the end would come.

The tribal council remembered the people told us to save the reservation. We prayed and thought. Then we wrote a plan to save the land the Cheyennes came home to from the Oklahoma. The people approved the plan. The Keeper of the Sacred Hat blessed it, and he is our holiest man.

Our plan is the Northern Cheyenne 50-Year Unallotment Program. It is a plan to make our reservation unallotted again in 50 years. The plan asks the Bureau to make us a 50-year loan of $500,000 at 2½% interest for land purchase. We have proved that we can repay this loan in 50 years or less out of income from the land the tribe will be buying. In the 50 years that the plan will be going on, we asked the Bureau to stop all Cheyenne land sales except to the tribe, and the tribe obligates itself to buy all land that individual Cheyennes want to sell. We also asked the Bu-reau to stop the approval of all fee patents during the period of the plan—and we asked them to allow members of the tribe to buy, sell and trade land among them-selves without being forced to take it out of trust.

That plan could save our land. It will not cost the Government anything. The Government divided up our land so that it could be sold to white men in pieces. Now we are willing to buy every piece back again out of our own money.

We took our plan to the Interior Department—to Assistant Secretary Roger Ernst. He congratulated us for planning for ourselves. He said the plan would be approved if we could show that we could repay the loan we asked for.

We asked the Indian Bureau to stop all land sales on our reservation imme-diately, so that our lands would not be slipping away while we waited to get our loan. The Interior Department said the Bureau would do that. Right after we heard this good news, the Billings Area Office of the Bureau advertised 13 tracts of land for sale. The Association on American Indian Affairs told us to trust the Interior Department because Secretary Seaton and Secretary Ernst were men of their word. The Association was right. My people will tell the story of a thing that happened for a long time.

The land sale was advertised. Certain white men were wheeling around like buzzards waiting for the bidding to start. The Cheyennes could not talk—they were so angry and sad. Then all at once the land sale was called off—by a telephone call from Washington. You would have to be a Cheyenne to know what it meant when the Government in Washington kept its word—helped us against the Bureau in Montana. At first the people whispered the news to each other. Then they said it out loud. I never saw the Cheyennes as happy as that. I was never as happy myself in my whole life. I think all of us had a picture of the Government helping us save our land, then helping us with a plan to make our Cheyenne community a good part of America.

It is good for us to have that picture of how life can be for us. It will keep us strong in the fight ahead. . . .

My people are fighting to save their land. They are not fighting Congress or the Interior Department. . . . .

4. Mary Jacobs (Lumbee) Relates How Her Family Made a Home in Chicago, n.d.

On Christmas day in 1952 my parents, Willard Cummings and Lora Neil Brooks, were married in Dillon, South Carolina. On the next day, my parents left Robeson County to make Chicago their new home. As a child I never thought about the courage or sense of self that my parents must have had to complete that seemingly simple act of moving away from home for the first time. They had come from very simple beginnings. My dad was 22 when he married my mom. He was the third child of Newton Cummings and Flora Ann Lowry. My father's parents were share-croppers moving up from a one-mule farm to a two-mule farm. Finally my grand-parents were able to realize a dream and bought their own 100-acre farm in the Prospect community. They had fourteen children; seven girls and seven boys. All but one of my father's siblings (a brother) would live to adulthood.

My mother was 18 when she married my father. She was the second-youngest child of Andrew Worth Brooks and Mary Jane Locklear. My mother's father operated a crane, and he helped build highways across several states, including Oklahoma and Virginia. My grandmother, my mom's mother, stayed in Pembroke raising their twelve children; only nine would survive to adulthood.

My parents were born during the Depression and their schooling took place in segregated schools. Everyone was poor and few people had the opportunity to better themselves through higher education. During my parents' school years there were the three school buses that rode through Pembroke: one for whites, one for blacks, and one for Indians. My father had attended both of the local high schools for Indians in Robeson County, Pembroke and Prospect High School, but never completed the degree. My mother did graduate from Pembroke High School and even attended a semester of college at Pembroke State University.

Now re-named the University of North Carolina at Pembroke (UNCP), UNCP has the distinction of being the only state-supported college created for the educa-tion of Indians. UNCP was established in 1887. It was called the Croatan Normal School. Croatan was one of many names by which the state recognized Robeson County Indians. The legislation that created the Normal school stated that Lumbee people had to purchase the land and erect a building for their school; both of which were completed within the legislative two-year deadline.

While my parents were growing up, Pembroke State represented the only chance for higher education in Lumbees in North Carolina. The college was a school for teachers and teaching represented one of the few career paths open to Lumbees at that time; the career options were preaching and farming. For those Lumbee men without the required education, the military offered a good alternative.

My father went into the army during the Korean War. He served one term (three and half years), during which he wrote to my mother. He had had dreams of being a veterinarian and during the war he served as a medic. Going to medical school was

---

From Mary Jacobs, "Coming Around Again," in Terry Straus and Grant P. Arndt, eds., *Native Chicago* (Chicago: Chicago Indian Community, n.d.), 311–317. Reprinted with permission.

not in his future since no school in North Carolina would accept him and he did not have the money to go out of state. After the war he returned to Robeson County and began working doing carpentry work. Today carpentry work (hanging sheet rock and finishing work) is still a popular area for young men with little education in Robeson County. The work was and is seasonal and sporadic at best.

While working, my father heard about a school in Chicago from Peter Dial, a young Indian man from the Prospect area who had attended there. The school was the Allied Institute of Technology, a trade school, on Michigan Avenue. Peter also gave my father the address of a boarding house where he had lived while he had attended the school. So my parents left Robeson County with the address of the school and the name and address for a place to live.

My mother said that she recalled feeling very apprehensive about moving to Chicago. She had never lived outside Robeson County and wondered if she and my father would be accepted by their neighbors, because Indians were not accepted by whites in and around Robeson County at that time.

They spent New Year's weekend with my great uncle Coolidge Mack Cummings (my father's paternal uncle), his wife Van, and their children in Louisville, Kentucky. Coolidge was a pastor in a "white" church there. It would be several years before he would return to Robeson County to pastor an Indian church. Over the years in Chicago, my parents would visit Uncle Coolidge in Kentucky often.

On the last day of 1952 my parents drove into Chicago. They had an address for an apartment house that Peter Dial had given them; it was 1418 West Jackson. My father said that the woman who ran the apartment house just happened to have an available apartment. They signed the lease. That same week my father went to Allied Institute to sign up for classes. Since he had not contacted the school earlier, he did not know that the school term had already started and he would have to wait one term before he could enroll. Meanwhile, both he and my mother looked for work.

First Jobs

My father's first job in Chicago was at a plant that made coils for bedsprings. The plant was on Pulaski, but since my parents had a car he was able to get from their apartment to work until he was in an accident. My father recalled that a "drunk" ran into him and the car was totaled. After that he found a job closer to their apartment. That job was in a tool and die shop on Madison, at about the 1200 block west.

My mother worked for a catalog company, the Alden catalog, across the street from the apartment. She was able to do the work, but felt that the management was too overbearing. None of the workers in the shop were allowed to speak to each other and all of their breaks were timed. She felt as though every minute was regulated. She left the first job and then went to a small company that printed bank certificates and hunting licenses. She proofread the materials after they were printed. But after getting pregnant, she stopped working because the fumes from the ink made her ill. She would not work again until all of her children were in school.

About a month after moving to the city, my father began attending school at the Allied Institute. He was able to use his GI benefits to pay for school and completed his A.A. degree in Industrial Engineering. Immediately after completing the degree, he got a job with Scully-Jones, a family owned company that designed and made tools for other industries. Later Scully-Jones became a part of Bendix Corporation. My father would stay with the company for twenty-four years before leaving that job to move back to Robeson County.

Keeping in Touch with Home

Mom said that most of their neighbors in Chicago were poor whites from the south: Kentucky, Tennessee, and Mississippi. She recalled that poor southern whites were most of the people that they met, but whenever they heard about another Lumbee person in the city they would make an effort to meet them and visit with them. My mother said that both her parents and my dad's parents would write them and let them know about other Indians (Lumbees) from home living in or traveling through Chicago.

My mother recalled visiting H. B. Jacobs (she could not remember his full name), a Lumbee man who had served in World War II and married a woman he met in Germany. The Jacobs lived on Adams, near my parents' apartment. There was also Morrison and Odessa Maynor, who lived just north of Kimball Avenue. Then in 1958, my mother's nephew Samuel Brooks came to Oak Park to attend college at Emais Bible College, a brethren college located in that suburb (my mother's family attended the brethren church in Pembroke). My mother's elder brother, Venus Brooks, was pastor of the brethren church in Pembroke and he wanted his son, Sam, to attend a brethren school. Samuel would marry a white woman from Oak Park and live in that suburb for most of his life.

My parents were able to meet a lot of Lumbee people moving to Detroit or living in Chicago for brief periods who were there for work. While my parents knew of Indians from other tribes living in the city, they did not make much effort to seek them out. My parents grew up in a generation of Lumbee that did not consider themselves "real Indians" because "real Indians like the ones in the movies wore feathers and lived on reservations in the west."

Before there was a real movement among the Lumbee to recover lost traditions and consider themselves a tribe, the people relied on familial ties for identity. That is, your family group (large groupings of families descended from some major figure) determined your identity as an Indian.

My father recalled that few people asked him about his race, but when they did he said he was a Cherokee Indian from Robeson County. He recalled "that's what they told us we were." Cherokee Indians from Robeson County was one of the many names that the Lumbees had to use until the state and federal government would allow the Lumbees to name themselves in 1956.

But my parents did not rely on a tribal identity to know who was Lumbee; rather people were known only by "who their people were." At that time (and to an extent this is still true), when Lumbee people first met they introduce themselves by telling who their parents and grandparents (and sometimes other relatives who might have been well known in the community) were. Knowing who another Indian's "people" were placed that person in their proper context. With that information you knew where they probably lived in the county, went to school, and which familial church they attended. It also gave information about what kind of work they probably did and, to an extent, the familial reputation (being smart or other personal characteristics) that might extend to that individual as well. That is why my parents were able to keep in touch with events and people from "home" that they might not have known otherwise.

But my parents did return to Robeson County after moving to Chicago. For all of the twenty-five years that they lived in Chicago and later Maywood, they returned "home" almost every summer. I remember well leaving home at 2 or 3 A.M. to begin the trip to Pembroke. It would usually take us 18 or more hours of driving and we would not stop until we reached "home." To all Lumbees of my parents' generation and to most today, Robeson County is always called "home." When I returned there people usually ask "How long will you be home this time?" And my parents and in-laws usually want to know "when are you coming home?" They are referring to our family home in Pembroke, but they are also referring to Robeson County as a larger home for Indian (Lumbee) people.

My Return to Chicago

My parents had eight children. I was their last child; the youngest or "baby" of the family. I was born in Chicago, like all my brothers and sisters, but considered Pembroke my home. My parents moved back to Robeson County when I was thirteen years old and I attended junior high, high school, and college in North Carolina. I met my husband (another Lumbee person) there and we were married in my mother-in-law's living room.

I decided to move to Chicago after being accepted into the doctoral program in Social Work at the University of Chicago. I really had mixed feelings about moving here. After my husband and I were married we moved to Southern California and had been living there for six years. I did not know a lot about the U. of Chicago before moving there and I was not sure that I would like it. I did know that Chicago had an Indian community, but I did not know any Lumbee people here except my sister.

My sister, Stephana, was the third eldest child in our family and she never moved to Robeson County with the family. She was already married to a white man she has met at church, and they stayed in Illinois after we moved. All of my other siblings and family were living in Robeson County (and still are).

However, after moving here, I did meet other Indian people, but my sister and I are the only Lumbee people here that we know. My first cousin Samuel Brooks passed away in the mid-1980s and his widow and children still live near Oak Park. My sister and I do visit with them. In addition to school, I work with a group in the Indian community in Chicago who are trying to create more Indian foster parent homes for Indian children, the Native American Foster Parent Association (NAFPA).

I, unlike my parents, grew up during a period of great traditional recovery in Robeson County. Lumbees were more in touch and aware of themselves as a tribal group and were a growing political force in national tribal politics as well. Although Lumbees are still not federally recognized, we do have a national reputation because of all the work that individual Lumbee people do at a national level with various Indian communities and in Washington, D. C. Upon moving to Chicago, I told people here in the Indian community I was Lumbee; they recognized my tribe and I felt very welcomed by the Indian community here.

Today, my parents do not come to Chicago often, but do visit here with my sister and me and our families on occasion. I think their hope is that we will finally return to Robeson County to live permanently, but they understand that returning is not always possible. There are still rather limited employment opportunities in Robeson and the surrounding counties. In addition, they jobs there do not pay well and there are still a lot of racial tensions in the community, especially between whites and Indians.

I hope that I will return to Robeson County or at least the state of North Carolina someday, but for now I am happy to be living and attending school in Chicago. I, like my parents, consider Chicago a temporary stop on the way back home.

◈ E S S A Y S

Florida Atlantic University professor Harry A. Kersey's *An Assumption of Sovereignty: Social and Political Transformation among the Florida Seminoles, 1953–1979* (1996), from which the first selection is taken, is an important study of a significant southern Indian community. Kersey presents a carefully drawn portrait of the effort to end federal trusteeship for this Florida group. Although we tend to think primarily of the impact of the termination upon reservations that were terminated, such as Menominee in Wisconsin or Klamath in Oregon, Kersey's essay reminds us that other Indian nations were targeted as well. Florida offers an example of local Native and non-Native opposition preventing termination from being realized.

Peter Iverson's essay represents an early revisionist view of the termination period. A professor of history at Arizona State University, Iverson argues here that despite the many problems posed by the era, and sometimes because of those very dilemmas, Indian individuals and communities began to establish the foundation for the movement for self-determination. This essay was one of the first reinterpretations of the era, one that moved away from a total emphasis on victimization and paid more attention to the ability of Indians to respond creatively and productively to the demands of this time.

The Florida Seminoles Confront Termination

HARRY A. KERSEY, JR.

The Eighty-third Congress, which convened in January 1953, became notorious to those in Indian affairs as the "termination Congress" for its initiation of legislation directly threatening the existence of tribal communities. In general, its members reflected a sentiment building since the end of World War II that American Indians were ready to stand on their own without support or supervision from Washington. Thus they assumed that federal expenditures could be radically reduced by eliminating services to the tribes, while at the same time allowing Indians freedom from government restrictions in order to pursue their own economic interests. To that

From Harry A. Kersey, Jr., *An Assumption of Sovereignty: Social and Political Transformation among the Florida Seminoles, 1953–1979* (Lincoln, Nebr.: University of Nebraska Press, 1996), 23–50. Reprinted by permission of the University of Nebraska Press. Copyright © 1996 by the University of Nebraska Press.

end, over two hundred bills and resolutions pertaining to Indians were introduced and forty-six became law, including House Concurrent Resolution 108.

Although the 1946 elections had returned Republican majorities in both houses, the determination to force assimilation of the American Indian crossed party lines. As a rule, Indian affairs held little interest for most members, so conservatives of both parties were able to secure their program with little opposition. An unusual level of agreement existed between Democrats and Republicans on the issue of termination, although generally for different reasons. Liberal Democrats subscribed to the position that a paternalistic Bureau of Indian Affairs oppressed Indians by keeping them in a status that restricted their social and economic progress. They sought to ensure Indian civil liberties, end social segregation, and promote economic self-development. For example, when Representative Henry Jackson of Washington introduced legislation in 1945 to create an Indian Claims Commission, it was with the understanding that funds thus derived would enable tribes to improve economic opportunities for their people. Conservatives, on the other hand, viewed the bill as an opportunity to discharge federal obligations to the tribes and get out of the Indian business altogether. In 1953 Jackson, then a senator and still convinced that termination held the best hope for assuring Indian prosperity, sponsored HCR 108 in the Senate. He and other western Democrats, such as Clinton Anderson of New Mexico and Frank Church of Idaho, accepted the conservatives' interpretation of events when they became members of the Senate Interior Committee and remained strong supporters of termination.

At the opposite end of the political spectrum was Senator Arthur Watkins, an archconservative Republican from Utah and the leading proponent of Indian termination. Watkins won election to the Senate in 1946 and served for two terms. A Mormon, he strongly believed in hard work and self-reliance and abhorred governmental assistance or interference with the free enterprise system. Far from considering that tribes were stifled on the reservations, Watkins believed the Indians had been coddled and given too much support for their own good; moreover, he thought the BIA services on the reservations were a fiscal burden which American taxpayers should not have to bear. He did not recognize the possibility that Indian cultural values and psychological conditioning might impede their assimilation and saw no reason to retain any of the reservations. As chairman of the Senate Subcommittee on Indian Affairs, Watkins took an aggressive role in the passage of termination bills for a number of tribes; he then exerted political pressure to overcome Indian resistance to the legislation. Conservatives were convinced that Indians who objected to termination were trying to avoid taxation and refusing to accept responsibility for their own future, and that the Indian rights organizations which protested termination did so to justify their own continued existence.

Each tribe had to approve its termination bill in some manner, and Watkins seized upon small assimilated minorities willing to leave the reservation as a sign that all Indians desired this course. Appealing to his liberal colleagues, the senator from Utah compared termination with the Emancipation Proclamation in its liberating impact on the Indian. With support from Congressman E. Y. Berry of South Dakota, the staunchest proponent of termination in the House, Watkins coerced the Menominee tribe into accepting termination with about eight percent of the tribe voting on the issue. In other cases, merely the consent of the tribal council, often dominated by acculturated Indians, was taken as assent by an entire tribe. With such relentless antagonists leading the attack, it would be very difficult for a small, unsophisticated tribe like the Seminoles to resist being swept away by the rising tide of assimilationist sentiment.

Fortunately for the Seminoles, two influential congressional figures from Florida, both of whom became increasingly sympathetic to the tribe's position, served on the subcommittees which dealt with Indian affairs during the termination era. Senator George Smathers, a first-term Democrat, held one of five seats on the Senate Subcommittee on Indian Affairs. In 1950 Smathers, a Marine Corps veteran and popular congressman from Miami, unseated the incumbent New Deal liberal Claude Pepper by advocating fiscal conservatism and exploiting anti-Communist sentiment. As Florida's junior senator he sought appointment to the interior committee primarily because it dealt with national parks and other public lands, accepting a place on its Indian Affairs subcommittee almost as an afterthought.

Historians of Indian termination agree that Smathers had originally been a supporter of HCR 108 but later reversed his position. However, they disagree somewhat as to his motivation in breaking with Watkins. Donald Fixico holds that Smathers modified his position after he became familiar with the problems of termination and the poor living conditions in Indian communities. "Senator Smathers," he wrote, "sympathized with Native Americans for he believed they lacked the capability to take advantage of the federal government and did not yet have the capacity to live successfully among other Americans." By contrast, Larry Burt links Smathers' concern directly to the impact such a bill would have on the Seminoles: "Florida Senator George Smathers generally went along with Watkins's termination policy, but in this case he feared that unscrupulous outsiders would exploit the land and resources of these inexperienced people." Smathers enjoyed good relations with the Seminoles dating from high school days in Florida when he played football with a member of the tribe, and after he became a congressman Indians often visited his Washington office. As a result, he claimed to have kept an open mind on the termination issue.

Representative James Haley, Democrat of Florida, served as a member and later chairman of the House Subcommittee on Indian Affairs. . . . In 1952, Haley won election to represent the seventh (later eighth) congressional district, one of the most conservative constituencies in Florida. He served in the House from the Eighty-third through the Ninety-fourth Congresses. His arrival in Washington coincided with the height of Republican control in the Congress; the conservative Haley received an assignment to the Committee on Interior and Insular Affairs and in 1954 became chairman of the Subcommittee on Indian Affairs. Rarely had an easterner held this position, which was usually reserved for representatives from western states with large Indian populations. Haley filled the position with distinction. Even Vine Deloria, a critic of federal Indian policy, praised the chairman's defense of Indian lands against outside development during the Kennedy and Johnson administrations. However, Haley remained an ardent fiscal conservative who subscribed to the underlying philosophy of the terminationists, and it now appears likely that he engineered placement of the Seminoles on the list of tribes to be terminated. A former colleague in the Florida congressional delegation ventured an opinion that Haley subjected Seminoles to the same scrutiny which he demanded for other tribes, assuming that investigation would reveal they were not ready for termination. If so, he took a gamble given the protermination tenor of the Congress.

Termination bills for the thirteen tribes identified in HCR 108 were to be introduced in both the House and Senate. Each tribe would have two options for disposing of its properties: it could organize into a corporation for continued management under a trustee of its choice, or it could sell all properties and assets and distribute the proceeds among tribal members. Eventually, termination bills were approved for only six tribes—the Menominee in Wisconsin, Klamath and western Oregon bands, Utes of Utah, mixed-blood Paiutes in Nevada, and the Alabama-Coushattas in Texas—while other small, disorganized groups seemed headed for a similar fate. For the first time in history the two subcommittees sat in joint session to consider the bills that were drawn. This would prevent efforts to forestall legislation by assuring that the language in both versions was identical, eliminating the necessity for a conference to reconcile differences. Conference committees had traditionally been the place where compromises were struck and tribes were able to kill legislation.

On 18 January 1954, Rep. A. L. Miller of Nebraska, a member of the House Subcommittee on Indian Affairs, introduced a package of termination bills. One of the bills, HR7321, would "provide for the termination of Federal supervision over the property of the Seminole Tribe of Indians in the State of Florida and the individual members thereof, and for other purposes." A companion measure, s2747, was introduced in the Senate. The bills had been drafted by the Bureau of Indian Affairs and were identical in content. They were submitted to the Speaker of the House and president of the Senate with a request for immediate action.

The joint subcommittee hearings on Seminole termination convened in Washington on 1 March 1954, with Senator Watkins presiding. Smathers was the only other member of the Senate subcommittee present for the session. Those representing the House subcommittee included Chairman E. Y. Berry of South Dakota, as well as Haley of Florida and George Shuford of North Carolina. Congressman Dwight Rogers also attended, and the subcommittee invited him to participate in its deliberations. Rogers, a Democrat, represented the sprawling eleven-county sixth district, which extended from the Atlantic Ocean to the Gulf of Mexico in southern Florida. All of the Seminole reservations were located in his district, and Rogers often intervened on their behalf with state and federal officials. After introductory remarks, the hearings focused on the termination bill's impact on the tribe. The key provision of the legislation authorized the secretary of the interior to transfer within three years all property of the tribe to a corporation established by the tribe or its elected trustees for liquidating or management. The proceeds of this liquidation or management were to be vested in those Seminoles whose name appeared on the official tribal roll. It authorized the secretary, after disposing of the lands, to publish a proclamation in the *Federal Register* declaring the federal trust relationship in affairs of the tribe had been terminated. However, the BIA report accompanying this legislation cautioned that "wide differences of opinion were expressed as to the length of time that Federal supervision should be continued." Underscoring this concern, over twenty individuals testified or had statements entered into the record, and all but three opposed immediate or rapid termination of supervision for the Florida Seminoles.

The first to testify before the joint subcommittee were Associate H. Rex Lee and Kenneth Marmon, superintendent of the Seminole agency. Marmon, who had served in Florida since 1942, provided an account of the Seminole reservations, resources and people. Under questioning from Senator Smathers, who appeared intent on establishing whether the Seminoles were ready for termination, he confirmed that the tribal population was 918, sixty percent of whom lived on the federal reservations or had affiliations with them through owning cattle; an estimated 640 Indians, about seventy percent of the tribe, were non-English speaking and could neither read nor write; only ninety-six Seminoles were enrolled in public school while forty-seven attended reservation schools; the Seminoles were scattered throughout five south Florida counties, and since there was no tribal government it was necessary to work with leaders chosen by each of the Indian communities; although eighty-eight Indian families owned about fifty cattle each, most Seminoles were employed only seasonally. The annual federal appropriation for the tribe amounted to $137,000, and most of that went to building roads; it provided nothing for unemployed Seminoles.

When Smathers inquired what would happen to the non-English-speaking Indians if the bill was adopted, Marmon admitted that even though contacts with the white world had improved, it would be a good many years before the Seminoles were ready or able to assimilate into the larger community. Smathers then asked, "If there were a referendum, if all of the Indians were permitted to vote on what they wanted insofar as ending Federal control, what do you think the result would be?" The superintendent offered that over seventy-five percent would vote against it, primarily because they would be afraid of losing their land to property taxes if they became independent. Rogers also stressed the Seminole readiness issue, asking Marmon directly, "in your experience with the Indians from 1942 until now, do you think they are prepared for the termination of Federal supervision?" Marmon replied, "No; I do not. I think there should be additional time given them in order that they may progress as they are going at the present time."

Representative Berry, intent on establishing that the Seminoles were self-sufficient, asked Rex Lee if the government had done much for these Indians in the past or had they pretty much taken care of themselves; also, if the government intervened wouldn't that just make them more dependent?" When Lee, the bureau's leading termination advocate, answered that possibly the Seminoles could become more dependent, Senator Smathers launched into a long discourse by asking Lee if he had heard of the Point Four program and the Marshall Plan which the federal government initiated in countries around the world to help people become strong and independent. He suggested that it had been the goal of federal policy to move the Seminoles toward self-sufficiency and protect them; with three-fourths of the Indians unable to speak English, the possibility of exploitation was great unless the government set up a corporation that would guarantee title to Indian lands. Lee replied that tribes had the responsibility to set up such a legal entity and, under the bill, the secretary of the interior had the right to approve or disapprove it and appoint trustees to liquidate the land. "But," he noted, "I have more faith in the Secretary than that. I don't think he is looking toward liquidation. He is trying to put these people on their feet and to give them the type of organization and the type of protection that they want."

Watkins interjected that under the Marshall Plan aid had not gone directly to individuals but to their government, and as for the Point Four program, he was not sure it had been all that successful. He stated, "I wanted to call your attention to that because my good friend from Florida rather bore down on that just a bit. It doesn't get to the individual people. I would be just as much against giving the Europeans a dole direct to individuals as I would be to giving the Indians that sort of thing." Smathers countered that nothing in the bill would give the Seminoles a direct dole; what they were talking about was federal supervision over Indian lands and health and education programs. He disagreed with Watkins about the effectiveness of Point Four and Marshall Plans in making people independent, noting that is what federal supervision over Indians was supposed to do, but had failed. This exchange between Watkins and Smathers set the tone for the remainder of the session; the assimilationists exploited every point that would signal Seminole readiness for termination, while Smathers, Rogers, and to a lesser degree Haley took the opposite tack.

Prominent among those scheduled to testify was a delegation of eight Seminoles chosen by their people. On 9 October 1953, the Seminole agency hosted a meeting in which government officials from the bureau's Muskogee Area Office— at that time Florida Seminole affairs were still administered from Oklahoma—discussed the implications of HCR 108 with a large number of reservation Seminoles, as well as a few from the Tamiami Trail. As a result, the Seminoles present decided that each Indian community would select two representatives to attend the upcoming Washington hearings on the Seminole termination bill. The delegates from Dania were Sam Tommie and Laura Mae Osceola; from the Brighton Reservation, Billy Osceola and Toby Johns; Joseph Billy and Jimmy Cypress were sent by the Big Cypress Reservation; Henry Cypress and Curtis Osceola represented an off-reservation group. This delegation spoke for approximately sixty percent of the Florida Indian population; most important, these were people who would be directly affected by the withdrawal of federal services and protection. They entered a prepared statement into the record which made the plea, "We, the Seminole Indians of Florida, request that no action be taken on the termination of Federal supervision over the property of the Seminole Indians for a period of 25 years."

The Seminole statement outlined a number of reasons why termination should not take place. A lack of formal education meant that the Seminoles needed time to develop a leadership cadre which could administer their property. They feared that their lands, particularly pasturage, were insufficiently developed to become income producing, and if they failed to meet tax obligations, the property would be lost. The general state of Seminole health was poor, and the delegation recognized that the people had much to learn about proper sanitation, infant care, disease prevention, and so on, which could come about only if public health services were continued. They needed better housing on the reservations, along with council houses to help develop community spirit in the Indian settlements. Rural reservations such as Big Cypress and Brighton had much acreage that needed to be drained before the land could be used for pasturage or other agriculture. The delegates thought this could be best achieved through federal cooperation with state drainage and conservation projects in Florida. In conclusion, the Indians stated that "during the past 20 years our advancement has been rapid, but we need guidance for a longer period and we look to the Federal Government for continuance of their supervision."

Obviously the Seminoles feared losing their reservation lands; nor did they want them placed under the trusteeship of a bank or other nongovernment institution. Billy Osceola, a Baptist lay minister and cattle owner from the Brighton

Reservation, stated, "These Indian want more time to get better education in that period of 25 years. At that time the Indians want to take over; they don't want to turn it over to some other organization. They want to control it. They want to handle their own affairs." An early spirit of Indian self-assurance could be sensed in a response by the Seminoles' highly respected interpreter, Laura Mae Osceola. She was the only woman in the delegation, and its youngest and best educated member. A twenty-two-year-old housewife with young children, she had worked diligently to ensure that Seminoles would be present at the Washington hearings, often appearing before church and civic groups in the Fort Lauderdale area to solicit funds for the trip. When Representative Berry challenged her on how far she thought the Seminole people could be expected to progress, her retort was spirited and optimistic: "In twenty-five years they won't need your help. We will be giving you help!" . . .

Congressman Rogers submitted his own statement in support of the federal trusteeship over the Seminole lands and people; he suggested: "It seems to me that when this bill was drawn up one essential point was forgotten—the Seminoles' ignorance of the ownership of real estate or its handling, or of mortgaging, or of foreclosure, or of taxes, or of its value. How can their property be handled properly when they do not have the knowledge to protect their own interests? . . . Since this legislation is so vital to so many Indians, there is no need for hasty, ill-considered action which will only serve to multiply the problems of our Seminoles, not to solve them."

William Sturtevant, an anthropologist who later became curator of North American ethnology at the Smithsonian Institution, had conducted extensive fieldwork among the Florida Indians. His opinion would weigh heavily in subcommittee deliberations. He estimated that 625 were opposed to termination and 275 were in favor, but also cautioned, "The Seminoles are so dividend into factions that it will be impossible to turn the tribal property over intact to a tribal organization. . . . I would say that for this tribe at least, termination of Federal supervision at this time would cause great hardships."

Bertram Scott, executive secretary of the politically active Seminole Indian Association, based in the Orlando area, also spoke. He offered a brief review of the Seminole cattle industry which developed in the 1930s after the government provided the starter herd. The business had originally operated as a tribal project but recently had been shifted to individual ownership, with eighty-eight Indians each owning about fifty head. The tribe held a $261,040 mortgage for the cattle that had to be repaid in eight years. Scott took this as a clear indication that Indians were moving in the direction of the self-sufficiency which Watkins, Berry, and others advocated. He believed Seminoles would eventually be capable of managing their own affairs; however, the tribal cattlemen, nearly all of whom were illiterate, still needed help from the agricultural agent and agency superintendent to run their business. If federal control of the reservations was withdrawn and the lands were taxed, the Indian cattlemen could lose everything. Scott also dismissed Watkins's suggestion that the State of Florida might serve as trustee for the tribe, citing massive Everglades drainage projects that threatened to inundate the reservations before the BIA and Seminole Indian Association intervened. Finally, he declared, "I really do not know why this bill was ever drawn concerning the Seminole Indians . . . but if there was ever a tribe that is not ready to go on its own, and will not be for some time, it is the Seminole Tribe of Florida." To which Senator Watkins, in the first sign that he might concede the point, replied, "I will admit that it is not nearly as strong a case as the cases that have been made for other Indian tribes."

An overwhelming majority of the statements submitted to the subcommittee by concerned citizens, civic groups, and experts on national Indian issues such as the Association on American Indian Affairs, emphasized the need for federal control and guidance to preserve the reservations. But in the hearings it became obvious that not all Florida Indians lived on federal lands, nor did they share common social and economic interests. About a third of them—the Miccosukee-speaking Trail Indians—lived in the Everglades and shunned the outside world. To complicate matters, the Trail Indians themselves were divided into several factions. These had been identified by a bureau official who traveled in Florida during February 1953 to investigate reports of Indian rights violations. He visited the camp of Mike Osceola and his father, William McKinley Osceola, the recognized leader of the Osceola band. Later he met with Jimmie Tiger who, with the medicine man Ingraham Billie, headed the other faction. These two groups followed diametrically opposite lifestyles. Mike Osceola owned a piece of land just west of Miami where he operated a store. He believed in educating Indian children and in complying with state and federal laws. The Tiger-Billie group believed Indian people were the rightful owners of any land they wanted to occupy in South Florida; it opposed education for Indian children and refused to recognize state hunting and fishing laws. So great were the differences between the two groups, the official noted, "that they now have two 'Green Corn Dances' or Councils." Both Trail Indian groups had representation at the Washington hearings.

Larry Mike Osceola (generally called Mike), an articulate Indian entrepreneur claiming to represent seventy-seven Indians living on the east end of the Tamiami Trail, spoke forcefully for an immediate end to government control of Seminole affairs. He recounted his own experiences in public high school in Miami (where he had known Senator Smathers) and later training as an aircraft mechanic. In addition, he operated a business selling merchandise to tourists on the Tamiami Trail and owned cattle pastured at the Brighton Reservation. Osceola questioned the statement of Superintendent Marmon that over six hundred Indians spoke no English, claiming that he knew of only ten or so who could not converse with outsiders. He felt that Indians were capable of managing their own financial affairs without federal assistance, and therefore endorsed setting up a corporation to manage Indian lands. An attorney with close ties to the Osceola group, O. B. White, of Miami, submitted a statement recommending immediate termination of government supervision and establishment of an eleemosynary corporation to handle Indian property. He and Osceola also questioned the legitimacy of Miccosukee Seminoles in the "official" delegation who claimed to speak for off-reservation Indians.

Rogers and Haley assailed the credibility of Mike Osceola, questioning whether he spent much time on the reservations or knew the people in the tribe well enough to state that most spoke English; furthermore, Smathers charged that Osceola might want termination because it would make him important to the tribe due to his connections in the white community. Osceola denied this accusation, claiming that he only wanted the best for his people. That was good enough for Senator Watkins, who told Osceola, "I think you are a splendid example of what can be accomplished when people are given their opportunity to do as you have done, to work, and particularly to stand on your own feet and develop. I congratulate you upon the success you have made. And I think instead of criticizing you for wanting to help your people, you ought to be complimented for that. The Seminoles would be much better off if they had a hundred just like you, who could lead the way out and help them with their problems."

The Miccosukee General Council was represented by attorney Morton Silver and spokesman Buffalo Tiger. Silver had written to the secretary of the interior in October 1953 announcing that he represented the "General Council of the Seminole Indians of the State of Florida"—the name would evolve to become Miccosukee General Council—and it was the first time federal authorities realized such a group existed. The BIA initially suspected the "council" to be a numerically insignificant rump group of malcontents whose claims were spurious and possibly inflated by an unscrupulous attorney. Silver spoke first, claiming that the General Council represented a majority of Seminole adults in Florida. His clients had lived peacefully in the Everglades, never recognizing federal authority over their land, and sent representatives to the hearings only to ensure that the government did nothing to affect their independence. But when Watkins noted, "I failed to see how much damage we are going to do them by withdrawing Federal supervision that they never had," the attorney then claimed that the council also represented many Indian people on the reservations and was protecting their interests as well; he also pointed out that the number of reservation Seminole delegates present was disproportionate to their true constituency. Silver's abrasive advocacy and evasive answers to questions about how long federal supervision should be retained obviously irritated some members of the subcommittee.

By contrast, when the low-key Buffalo Tiger testified, he was less confrontational. Although he lived in Hialeah, had a non-Indian wife, and sent his children to public school, Tiger claimed to speak for three hundred Miccosukee Indians who were opposed to any federal action that would impair their existing way of life. He estimated that six hundred Seminoles could not speak English. When asked if his people would consider sending their children to school, Tiger replied that Miccosukees were upset over the bill because they thought it would change their law and way of life: "It is a little too involved for Indians. I think they would be unhappy to do it right away."

Senator Smathers sought to identify conditions under which the Indians might accept termination. He asked if they would object if the government assured them that their land could not be stolen, if their land was placed in an Indian corporation to be used for the general benefit of all their people. When Tiger still demurred, Smathers asked, "You say we should do nothing. Is that what you are saying, to leave everything as it is?" Tiger replied calmly, "It would be easier for you, I imagine."

Smathers never convinced Buffalo Tiger that the bill could protect his people by vesting title to the land in the Indians themselves. Watkins, too, pursued the theme that the Indians would have ownership of the land, something that their children could inherit. He totally missed the point that the Indians believed they already had a right to the land through treaties and prior usage; they had no interest in the concept of property in severalty. "I will tell you now," Tiger replied, "I am pretty sure my people won't like that . . . this bill you are speaking about now is just a bad thing for the Seminoles." . . .

Following the congressional hearing that spring, Stranahan, Scott, and other Seminole partisans continued their lobbying against federal plans to withdraw services from the tribe. They emphasized that no matter what the outcome of the termination issue, additional lands should be secured for the Seminoles as provided for in the termination bill. As an inducement to gain Seminole acceptance of the bill, a provision had been inserted that transferred 27,086 acres of submarginal land at the Brighton Reservation to the tribe. Brighton encompassed 35,000 acres, 6,700 of which were secured with Indian Reorganization Act funds and 1,920 through exchange with the State of Florida, and the submarginal land was the carrot which assimilationists hoped would induce Seminoles to accept termination. The Resettlement Administration, a New Deal agency, originally purchased this tract in the 1930s for Seminole use. Title subsequently passed to the Department of Agriculture, with supervision transferred to the Department of the Interior by Executive Order 7868 on 15 April 1938. If the Seminole termination bill passed, the entire 35,000 acres at Brighton would be placed in an Indian corporation, or liquidated if the tribe chose to do so. But antitermination advocates warned that the tribe could lose its land to taxes unless federal trusteeship protection continued for at least another quarter century. . . .

When the Eighty-fourth Congress convened in January 1955, the sentiment for termination remained strong, and there was a possibility that the Seminole bill would be reintroduced. The House Subcommittee on Indian Affairs scheduled additional hearings to be held in Florida, and on 5 April 1955 Representative Haley, who had assumed the subcommittee chairmanship, presided at a day-long session in Clewiston, a town approximately equidistant from the Brighton and Big Cypress communities. Many who had testified at the Washington hearings in 1954 were again present. Haley opened the session by recalling that a year earlier he had brought members of the House subcommittee to Florida to investigate Seminole problems—although they held no public hearings—and there were still several matters that required study and clarification. "We hope to gather information," he noted, "which will help in preparing termination time schedules, if termination is desirable, information which will guide our thinking on the question of State trusteeship, and on the timing and basis for state assumption of welfare, law and order." The latter issues were particularly important because Florida would become one of twelve states to claim civil and criminal jurisdiction over offenses committed by or against Indians under the provisions of Public Law 280 enacted by Congress during 1953. Following Haley's statement, longtime subcommittee member A. L. Miller, of Nebraska, acknowledged the presence of Congressman Paul Rogers, who had been elected to replace his recently deceased father, Dwight Rogers. The new congressman from the sixth district welcomed the subcommittee, saying, "I think we are very fortunate to have this committee take the time when the rest of the members of Congress are taking a vacation, to come down here because they are interested, deeply interested, in the conditions of our Indians." At the subcommittee's invitation Rogers remained and participated in the proceedings.

Strong statements came from several local officials—a superintendent of schools, three county commissioners, and a county attorney—who agreed that taxpayers would expect the government to reimburse localities for the expenses of education and road maintenance, as well as medical and welfare services to the Indian population. When Haley asked an official whether the termination bill and attempts to interrupt government trusteeship over the Seminole Indians should be delayed until the present younger generation had reached adulthood and received a good education, the response was resoundingly affirmative. Agnes Denver, a Seminole living with her family in Utah, also made a statement. Denver, one of the first Seminoles to complete high school at the Cherokee Indian School in North Carolina, represented a progressive element within the tribe. She was living proof of an Indian's ability to function away from the reservation, yet she unequivocally declared, "The Seminole Indians are ready to be terminated."

Bill Osceola, acting as chairman of the board of directors for the three reservations, entered a statement reiterating the tribe's desire to extend federal protection for twenty-five more years. Even that sounded unacceptable to Reverend Henry Cypress, a member of the delegation sent to Washington the previous spring; he expressed the sentiment of his small off-reservation group: "Some people said 25 more years extended, but I have said in Washington I want a lifetime." Mike Osceola reiterated his position favoring termination. Initially he testified that the Seminoles should not be turned loose without a legally chartered organization to protect their interests. Questioning by Haley and Rogers disclosed that Mike Osceola had educational and economic advantages which either Indians did not enjoy, and he then became defensive. He declared that he did not believe in socialism, and if the federal trusteeship remained for twenty-five more years it would subconsciously indoctrinate the Indian people to socialism.

This struck a responsive chord with conservative Congressman Miller, who considered Mike Osceola to be a "fine example" of what Indians should achieve on their own. He, too, questioned the seemingly arbitrary request for extending federal supervision over the Seminoles: "This 25 years puzzled me. I think if we make them wards and give them something every day and feed, and house and clothe them, and they make no efforts on their own, it will still be that way 25 years from now." This, in turn, drew a strong rebuttal from Haley, who detailed federal neglect of the Florida Indians; he concluded by saying, "Of course, I take now the position that I have taken all along: I too want to see the Seminoles where they will fit in the economy and the social life of my State and their own community. I do not know whether 25 years is too much, but I do know, and I think it is plain to be seen, that 3 years is not the proper time, or 2 years. So I just hope that the gentlemen will assist me in maintaining a program that will bring the Seminole Indians of Florida some of the things that they should have been receiving many years ago." This strong statement from the chairman—which provided the first public indication of his intent in the matter—drew applause from the largely antitermination audience. . . .

The favorable tenor of these hearings convinced the antitermination forces that they had won the day. On 20 April, Bertram Scott informed Emmons that he had written to Haley requesting introduction of legislation to immediately transfer submarginal lands at Brighton Reservation to the Seminole Indians. . . . Following Scott's suggestion . . . [Haley] introduced a bill transferring approximately thirty thousand acres of land from the Department of Agriculture to the Bureau of Indian Affairs and officially creating the Brighton Reservation, which became law on 20 July 1956. . . .

Congress saw no Seminole termination bill introduced in the Eighty-fourth Congress or thereafter, thanks in great part to the determined opposition of Floridians . . . , as well as the Seminoles themselves . . . .

Building Toward Self-Determination:
Plains and Southwestern Indians
in the 1940s and 1950s

PETER IVERSON

Within the past decade, more students of Indian history have turned their attention to the twentieth century. Until very recently, the topical focus of this work has been primarily in the area of federal Indian policy, and the chronological focus, for the most part, has been on the years before World War II. This article represents a change in both topic and time. It attempts to analyze the period from World War II until the beginning of the 1960s, with specific consideration given to Indians of the Plains and the Southwest.

This era is often referred to in the literature as the era of termination. During this time, many members of Congress and the Truman and Eisenhower administrations made sporadic but persistent efforts to reduce or eliminate federal services and protection for American Indians. The public rhetoric spoke of liberating the Indians by reducing governmental interference. Termination sought to immerse Indians in the mainstreams of their counties and states. This crusade resulted in significant hardships for many Indians. Tribes such as Menominees in Wisconsin or the Klamaths in Oregon saw their reservation status ended. Indians who relocated to cities, with or without federal sponsorship, confronted many dilemmas. State and local agencies proved unwilling or unable to shoulder responsibilities previously bestowed upon the federal government. Economic development programs on reservations usually did not markedly improve unemployment, housing, and other critical problems.

Yet to label these years as the termination era and to emphasize so exclusively the negative aspects of this generation is to present an incomplete picture. We cannot ignore federal policy in our consideration of any period, for it always has an important effect. But the 1940s and 1950s are more than a time of troubles. Just as new research is starting to reveal the late nineteenth and early twentieth centuries as a time when Indians in many areas made important and necessary adjustments to continue their lives as Indians, so too a closer examination of this more recent era shows it to be a period in which tribalism and Indian nationalism were reinforced. Indeed, to a significant degree, the threat and the enactment of terminationist policy often strengthened rather than weakened Indian institutions and associations. In addition, the attitudes of state and local officials, as well as the perspectives of urban residents, encouraged Indians throughout the nation to recognize increasingly their common bonds and needs.

During the 1940s and 1950s, then, Indians in growing numbers tried to identify and take advantage of their own economic resources and tried to affirm their identities as members of tribes and as Indians. They rejected the conventional wisdom that they would be "less Indian" if they gained more education, acquired new jobs, or moved to a new residence. Actually, greater contact with the larger American

---

From Peter Iverson, "Building Toward Self-Determination in the 1940s and 1950s," *Western Historical Quarterly,* vol. 16, no. 2 (April 1985), 163–173. Copyright by Western History Association. Reprinted by permission.

society promoted greater awareness that the English language, new technological skills, and other elements of the American culture could be used to promote a continuing, if changing, Indian America.

A review of Indian actions in two important regions—the Plains and the Southwest—reveals a vital maturation in Indian leadership and a reaffirmation of Indian identity in the 1940s and 1950s. Far from vanishing, Indians emerged from this generation more determined than ever to be recognized on their own terms. The more publicized activism of the late 1960s and 1970s thus may trace its origins to these ostensibly more quiet years.

World War II marks a critical turning point in modern American Indian history. Indians took great pride in their involvement in the war effort. For example, Cecil Horse, a Kiowa, remembered his son John winning a bronze star and a purple heart and in turn receiving from his people a war bonnet and a give away ceremony in his honor. Navajos celebrated their Codetalkers' role in the Pacific. In a publication of November 1945, the Office of Indian Affairs recorded the military honors earned by Indians and the investment by Indians in more than $17 million of restricted funds in war bonds. It quoted the instructions of Private Clarence Spotted Wolf, a Gros Ventre killed on December 21, 1944, in Luxembourg:

> If I should be killed, I want you to bury me on one of the hills east of the place where my grandparents and brothers and sisters and other relatives are buried. If you have a memorial service, I want the soldiers to go ahead with the American flag. I want cowboys to follow, all on horseback. I want one of the cowboys to lead one of the wildest of the T over X horses with saddle and bridle on. I will be riding that horse.

The war generated more than memories and emotions. It meant that Indians had become more a part of the larger world in which they lived. As Ella Deloria, the Dakota linguist, wrote in 1944: "The war has indeed wrought an overnight change in the outlook, horizon, and even the habits of the Indian people—a change that might not have come for many years yet." Through the service, through off-reservation experiences, and through wage work, Indian perspectives and Indian economies began to change. Returning veterans and other participants in the war effort recognized the significance of better educational opportunities. Navajo Scott Preston put it simply: "We have to change and we have to be educated."

Change also demanded organization. Indian delegates from fifty tribes, hailing from twenty-seven states, met November 15–18, 1944, in Denver to organize the National Congress of American Indians. In the words of one of the congress's first presidents, N. B. Johnson, the delegates set "an example for speed, diplomacy and harmony." Within four days, they "adopted a constitution and formally launched the organization in an effort to bring all Indians together for the purpose of enlightening the public, preserving Indian cultural values, seeking an equitable adjustment of tribal affairs, securing and preserving their rights under treaties with the United States, and streamlining the administration of Indian affairs." In subsequent meetings in Browning, Montana, in 1945 and Oklahoma City in 1946, those in attendance proved to be, according to Johnson, "a cross-section of Indian population: old and young, full-bloods, mixed-bloods, educated and uneducated Indians from allotted areas and others from reservations," all of whom "were dissatisfied with many phases of the government's administration of Indian affairs." Improved health care and educational opportunities, protection of Indian land rights, and increased Indian veterans' benefits were advocated. The National Congress of American Indians urged the U.S. Congress and the current administration "not to enact legislation or promulgate rules and regulations thereunder affecting the Indians without first consulting the Tribes affected."

Such, of course, would not be the case. In both the Truman and Eisenhower administrations, the federal government proceeded to pass legislation and carry out policies contrary to the will of the vast majority of American Indians. For many Americans, the Indian war record had prompted concern that Indians be treated fairly. O. K. Armstrong's influential article in the August 1945 *Reader's Digest* urged America to "Set the American Indians Free!" House of Representatives Majority Leader John W. McCormack read Armstrong's piece advocating the removal of "restrictions" from Indians and wrote to his colleague, W. G. Stigler, that he was "interested in seeing justice done for all—and this applies with great force to our fine American Indians." Cherokee/Creek historian Tom Holm has properly summarized what happened: "In the end, fighting the White man's war gained sympathy for American Indians but it also fueled a fire that they did not want and eventually found difficult to extinguish."

While they were not without effective allies, Indians had to lead the fight against Public Law 280, House Concurrent Resolution 108, and other features of termination. Protests against such measures soon resounded throughout the West. Through a variety of means, Indians attempted to ward off the implementation of a policy they realized could bring them great harm. In the early years, voices from tribal councils and business committees rang out against a specific action in a particular locale. For example, Richard Boynton, Sr., and George Levi of the Cheyenne-Arapaho business committee telegrammed Oklahoma congressman Toby Morris to protest against the impending closing of the Cheyenne-Arapaho school in El Reno. Kiowa leader Robert Goombi argued that abolishing the Concho Indian School would be counterproductive. Yet, as the wider pattern of era emerged, multitribal associations were strengthened as a more effective means of presenting a more powerful Indian voice.

The National Congress of American Indians (NCAI) therefore continued to expand in its influence in the years that followed its establishment in 1944. Plains and Southwestern Indian peoples remained active in the executive ranks of the organization throughout the 1940s and 1950s. In the mid-1950s over half the elected members of the executive council would come from regional tribes, including the Osages, Gros Ventres, Gila River Pimas, Taos Pueblos, Blackfeet, Oglala Sioux, and Cheyenne-Arapahoes. Colorado River tribes, Hualapais, Omahas, and the San Carlos Apaches appointed additional representatives. Oglala Sioux Helen Peterson served as executive director; Papago Thomas Segundo was regional representative.

The NCAI filled two critical functions. It helped Indians speak out against termination, but it also advocated programs that would contribute to Indian social, political, and economic revitalization. Through publicity releases from its Washington office, specially called tribal forums, and other means, the congress directly confronted the forces favoring termination. John Rainer from Taos Pueblo thus in 1950 attacked Commissioner of Indian Affairs Dillon Myer for imposing "drum head justice" upon Indians by denying tribes the power to choose their own attorneys.

The organization did more than criticize. It manifested a maturing capacity to articulate counterproposals when it offered suggestions to reduce Indian poverty, improvements for health care and educational facilities, and provisions to use reservation resources more effectively. A specific example—the Point Nine Program—was formulated and adopted by the congress in November 1954. It addressed critical questions relating to such matters as land and water resources, planning, credit, land purchase, and job training. Pointing to the assistance provided by the United States to underdeveloped countries around the world, Helen Peterson and other leaders demanded that this country apply the same principles within its borders.

Indians addressed the issues of the day through other forums as well. The Association on American Indian Affairs, under the direction of Oliver La Farge, helped publicize both the dangers of federal policy and Indian moves to oppose it. Thus when the NCAI mobilized Indian representatives from twenty-one states and Alaska to come to Washington, D.C., on February 25–28, 1954, to protest impending legislation, *Indian Affairs*, the newsletter of AAIA, not only gave extensive coverage but also proper credit to NCAI for its actions. Other institutions and organizations put together symposia for the examination of contemporary Indian well-being. Tribal spokesmen from the Plains and the Southwest participated vigorously in such gatherings, be it the annual meeting of the American Anthropological Association in Tucson in 1954 or the annual conference on Indian affairs at the University of South Dakota's Institute of Indian Studies.

By the end of the era, new forums had been sought for the expression of Indian views. In 1961 representatives from sixty-four tribes, totaling approximately seven hundred delegates, met in Chicago to create the Declaration of Indian Purpose. They did not all agree with one another, but the so-called Chicago Conference was an important landmark in modern Indian affairs because of its size and its impact upon many of the participants.

Another example is the National Indian Youth Council (NIYC), which came into being soon thereafter. The NIYC had its roots in the annual conferences of the Southwest Association on Indian Affairs, beginning in 1956. This one-day session at the St. Francis Auditorium in Santa Fe brought Indian community people together with high school and college students, with the latter speaking to the former about their studies and the applicability of these studies to the communities. From this local beginning, the conference became regional in its focus in 1957 and was called the Southwest Regional Indian Youth Council. The council held annual conferences in the spring until April 1961 when the last meeting was held in Norman, Oklahoma. According to the Tewa anthropologist Alfonso Ortiz, "It was a core group from these youth councils, augmented later by alumni of D'Arcy McNickle's Indian Leadership Training Programs, who founded the NIYC in Gallup after the American Indian Chicago Conference was held in June."

Other experiences and associations prompted heightened pan-Indian feelings. Relocation programs to American cities brought Indians into contact with non-Indians indifferent to tribal distinctions. Prejudice sometimes spurred pan-Indian identification. The formation of Indian communities and intertribal marriages in the cities also could foster such sentiments.

The Cherokee anthropologist Robert K. Thomas and other observers have noted that this movement frequently had a "pan-Plains" quality to it. Thomas also suggested that within the Southwest something of a "pan-Puebloism" could be perceived. Pan-Indianism, as it continued to evolve during this time, could be "very productive, as nationalist movements often are, in literature and the arts," but it also developed institutions dealing with non-Indians. One such development was the growth of powwows—a source of pleasure and pride for participants and enjoyment and education for spectators.

A final example of the pan-Indian movements in the 1940s and 1950s that should be cited is the Native American Church. It found significant support within the Plains and the Southwest, and leaders for the organization frequently hailed from these regions. At the tribal level, the Native American Church increased its membership during this period. Many Indians looked to participation within the peyote religion as a way of accommodating the various demands of modern life and reaffirming their identities as Indians. In Montana perhaps half the Crows and many Cheyennes embraced the church. Adherents included prominent tribal leaders such as Robert Yellowtail, Crow, and Johnnie Woodenlegs, Northern Cheyenne. Frank Takes Gun also emerged as an important, if controversial, church leader.

Attitudes toward the practice of the faith varied considerably, to be sure, from one Indian community to another and within communities. In the Navajo nation, the peyote religion grew considerably in its membership during the 1950s, despite an antagonistic stance taken against it by the tribal chairperson, Paul Jones. Raymond Nakai gained the chairmanship in 1963 in part because he pledged to stop harassing the Native American Church. On the Wind River reservation in Wyoming, Northern Arapahoe political and traditional leaders became more conciliatory toward the well-established practice. As was true in many tribes, the Arapahoes often added the Native American Church to prior participation in other religious ceremonies, be they Christian or traditional.

The reservation continued in the 1940s and 1950s as a centrally important place for religious observances, but for other reasons as well. The guiding philosophy of federal policy dictated that reservations were economic dead ends. After all, people were supposed to relocate because there were not enough jobs being generated at home. Since the land, families, familiarity, and, indeed, everything that went into the definition of home continued to be valued so deeply, Indian communities within the Plains and the Southwest endeavored to keep more of their citizens at home. While organizations such as the NCAI could advocate local development of resources, such development had to be prompted and managed.

Navajo economic and political development has been described elsewhere in some detail. In the face of termination, Navajos who distrusted state governments and desired to maintain a working ethnic between themselves and whites had little choice during the era but to pursue a more nationalistic approach. With large sums newly available to the tribal treasury from mineral revenues, the Navajo tribal government became far more ambitious. Federal assistance through the long-range rehabilitation program also assisted internal Navajo development. While the 1960s and 1970s would bring more fully to fruition some of these plans and programs, the 1940s and 1950s were crucial in the reinforcement of a working tribal identity and a commitment to a revitalized tribal economy.

Arts and crafts came to command a more important place in many tribal economies in the Southwest. For the Navajos, silversmithing and weaving continued to be vital sources of income. Pottery also gained widening acclaim, particularly at San Ildefonso, but also in other Pueblo communities along the Rio Grande and at some of the Hopi villages. Silverwork at the Hopi and Zuni pueblos, basket weaving especially among the Papagos and Walapais, the paintings of such artists as Fred Kabotie, Hopi, and Harrison Begay, Navajo, and the sculpture of Alan Hauser, Apache, also found appreciative audiences. Though the boom in Indian art had yet to arrive, a kind of foundation had been established.

Cattle ranching represented another important element in economic development. On the San Carlos Apache reservation, the cattle industry underwent significant alteration. The tribal council in October 1956 approved Ordinance No. 5-56 to reorganize and consolidate existing associations and implement various reforms in grazing regulations and practices. Improved range management could be combined with maintenance of cooperative efforts among the people of San Carlos. Cattle sales created some income for most families in the tribe. The quality of the Apaches' Herefords consistently attracted cattle buyers from throughout the West and generated a positive image of the Apaches to the non-Indian residents of Arizona.

Similarly, the Northern Arapahoes gained greater control over their tribal ranch established during the Indian New Deal. With the assistance of an attorney, the tribe eventually was able to hire a ranch manager and to have the ranch trustees be Arapahoes appointed by the Arapahoe business council. This sizable operation returned a consistent profit to each Arapahoe. As with the San Carlos Apaches, the ranching enterprise contributed to tribal self-esteem, the status of the tribal government, and an enhanced view of the Arapahoes among outsiders, including the Shoshones who shared the Wind River reservation.

In 1950 the tribal council of the Pine Ridge reservation in South Dakota passed a tax of three cents per acre for grazing privileges on tribal lands. The tax met with strenuous objections by white cattle ranchers. In the face of such opposition, the Department of the Interior quickly assigned responsibility of collecting the tax to the Sioux. By 1956 white ranchers had challenged the tax in court, but in the following year the U.S. District Court judge ruled against them, contending that Indian tribes were "sovereign powers and as sovereign powers can levy taxes."

Greater assertion of Sioux power was not limited to Pine Ridge. Under the leadership of Chairman Frank Ducheneaux, the Cheyenne River tribal council approved a firm resolution against Public Law 280. Both on Rosebud and on Pine Ridge, tribal voters in 1957 overwhelmingly defeated the assumption of state jurisdiction in South Dakota on Indian reservations. Opposition to repeated efforts to institute state jurisdiction led in 1963 to the formal organization of the United Sioux Tribes.

By 1959 the Rosebud Sioux tribal chairman, Robert Burnette, had filed complaints of discrimination under the Civil Rights Act of 1957 before the Civil Rights Commission. Burnette contended that Indian in South Dakota had been excluded from juries, had been beaten and chained in prisons, and generally had been greeted as people without equal rights in the state. While the commission was not very responsive to Burnette's allegations, the very act of publicly challenging local conditions indicated that a more activist stance would be assumed in the 1960s.

In the Dakotas, Wyoming, Arizona, and elsewhere, then, the growing importance of attorneys could be observed. For many tribes the establishment of the

Indian Claims Commission in 1945 had prompted their first acquisition of some form of legal counsel. While the Bureau of Indian Affairs in the 1950s had often discouraged tribal use of attorneys or tired to dictate the choice of a specific firm, by decade's end it was clear that legal assistance would play a vital role in many realms of tribal life.

Williams v. *Lee* is a useful example of this evolution. Called by Chemehuevi attorney Fred Ragsdale "the first modern Indian law case," *Williams* v. *Lee* involved a non-Indian trader on the Navajo reservation who sued a Navajo in the state court to collect for goods sold on credit. While the Arizona Supreme Court ruled in favor of the trader, the U.S. Supreme Court reversed this decision. Justice Hugo Black, on behalf of the Court, stated: "There can be no doubt that to allow the exercise of state jurisdiction here would undermine the authority of the tribal courts over Reservation affairs and hence would infringe on the right of the Indians to govern themselves." This landmark decision served as a crucial statement in support of tribal sovereignty, presaging additional legal battles to be waged in the years to come.

In any reappraisal of the 1940s and 1950s, it is important to not overstate the case. The negative aspects of the period remain, even with the vital developments outlined above. And in a treatment of this length, some events of magnitude must be slighted. For example, the damming of the Missouri River created great hardship for the Indian peoples of that area. Scholars have correctly underlined the problems that seemed to exist everywhere, from the most isolated reservations to the largest city.

Nonetheless, a more careful examination yields a more balanced picture. In overdramatizing the difficulties of the time, we may not give sufficient credit to the enduring nature of Indians in this country. By the end of the 1950s, tribal resources were more studied and better understood; tribal council leadership was often more effective. The Salish scholar and writer D'Arcy McNickle appreciated the transition that had taken place. He spoke in 1960 of the growing Indian movement toward self-determination. Indians in the future, he suggested, would "probably use the white man's technical skills for Indian purposes." McNickle affirmed that "Indians are going to remain Indian . . . a way of looking at things and a way of acting which will be original, which will be a compound of these different influences."

The 1940s and 1950s witnessed not only change in Indian policy and a resurgence of pressures to assimilate Indians into the larger society, but they also saw maturation and growth of Indian leadership at the local and national levels and efforts to develop tribal institutions as well as a reaffirmation of identity, and a willingness to adapt and change in the face of new conditions. In the immediate future, seemingly new demands would resound for self-determination. Yet these demands were firmly based upon a foundation gradually constructed in the previous generation.

◈ *F U R T H E R   R E A D I N G*

John Adair, Kurt Deuschle, and Walsh McDermott, *The People's Health: Anthropology and Medicine in a Navajo Community* (1970)

Alison R. Bernstein, *American Indians and World War II: Toward a New Era in Indian Affairs* (1991)

Margaret B. Blackman, *Sadie Brower Neakok: An Inupiaq Woman* (1989)

Karen Blu, *The Lumbee Problem: The Making of an American Indian People* (1980)

George A. Boyce, *When the Navajos Had Too Many Sheep: The 1940s* (1973)

William Brophy and Sophie Aberle, eds., *The Indian: America's Unfinished Business* (1966)

Larry Burt, *Tribalism in Crisis: Federal Indian Policy, 1953–1961* (1982)

Thomas W. Cowger, *The National Congress of American Indians: The Founding Years* (1999)

Ella Deloria, *Speaking of Indians* (1944)

Richard Drinnon, *Keeper of Concentration Camps: Dillon S. Myer and American Race Relations* (1987)

Donald L. Fixico, *Termination and Relocation: Federal Indian Policy, 1945–1960* (1986)

Laurence M. Hauptman, *The Iroquois Struggle for Survival: World War II to Red Power* (1986)

Broderick Johnson, ed., *Navajos and World War II* (1977)

William F. Kelly, ed., *Indian Affairs and the Indian Reorganization Act: The Twenty Year Record* (1954)

Kirke Kickingbird and Karen Ducheneaux, *One Hundred Million Acres* (1973)

Dean Kohlhoff, *When the Wind Was a River: Aleut Evacuation in World War II* (1995)

Michael L. Lawson, *Dammed Indians: The Pick-Sloan and the Missouri River Sioux, 1944–1980* (1982)

Donald Craig Mitchell, *Sold American: The Story of Alaska's Natives and Their Land 1867–1959: The Army to Statehood* (1997)

Elaine Neils, *Reservation to City: Indian Migration and Forced Relocation* (1971)

Gary Orfield, *A Study of the Termination Policy* (1965)

Nicholas C. Peroff, *Menominee Drums: Tribal Termination and Restoration, 1954–1974* (1982)

Kenneth R. Philp, *Termination Revisited: American Indians on the Trail to Self-Determination, 1933–1953* (1999)

Mark St. Pierre, *Madonna Swan: A Lakota Woman's Story* (1991)

Robert A. Trennert, *White Men's Medicine: Government Doctors and the Navajo, 1863–1955* (1998)

Edmund Wilson, *Apologies to the Iroquois* (1960)

Taking Control of Lives and

Lands, 1961–1980

◈

During the 1960s and the 1970s, American Indians became increasingly urban and more visible to the larger American society. Protest movements, including the occupation of Alcatraz Island in 1969 and of the village of Wounded Knee in 1973, gave prominence to younger activists. At the same time, reservation communities sought new ways to revitalize their economies and safeguard their rights. It is crucial for us to realize that the significance of this period was not regional but national and affected not only large federally recognized entities but also smaller communities throughout the United States, many of them in the East and the South, who sought full recognition from the federal government. Indian groups attempted to regain control over sacred sites, such as Blue Lake for Taos Pueblo; they pushed for realization of traditional hunting and fishing rights, especially in the Pacific Northwest and the Upper Midwest. Why did Indian individuals and communities feel so strongly about these matters?

The existence of television and the creation of new Indian newspapers, which quickly gained national readerships, allowed for a new degree of publicity to be given to what had once been localized struggles for change. Indians became adept at creating and utilizing the attention of the media. At the same time, tribal newspapers sometimes were able to offer a forum for the discussion of vital issues. Indian writers, artists, and musicians gained unprecedented audiences for their work. As more and more Indian students were able to attend colleges and universities, they gained new training that better equipped them, and often their home communities, to face the future. Beginning with the establishment of Navajo Community College (now Diné College) in 1968, tribal colleges began to be founded on many reservations. New legal service programs, Head Start, and other initiatives yielded other possibilities for meaningful, lasting change. Why would such new programs be important?

◈ *D O C U M E N T S*

Clyde Warrior (Ponca) was a fiery young Indian leader of the 1960s, who had little patience with others who equivocated in the face of the challenges facing Native peoples. In Document 1, the president of the National Indian Youth Council presents a critique and a call to arms. By decade's end, Indian activism had entered a new phase. The "Proclamation of All Tribes" on Alcatraz Island in 1969, Document 2, underscored Native dissatisfaction with federal trusteeship. Occupation of the famous island brought international attention to the Indians' grievances, even if the island could not be held in the long run. Alaska constituted another contested area. Oil discoveries and development and a rapidly increasing non-Native presence put unprecedented demands and pressures upon traditional Native subsistence economies. The *Tundra Times,* founded by Inuit journalist Howard Rock, provided an important indigenous voice in the ongoing struggles by Native peoples. In Document 3, the newspaper's editorial writer Philip Guy assumes the role of the land itself and speaks eloquently to the contemporary situation. In Wisconsin, the Menominees launched a drive in 1961 to restore their lands to reservation status. After a twelve-year battle, their success in 1973 in overturning the termination of their reservation marked an important victory for American Indians everywhere. Ada Deer, who later headed the Bureau of Indian Affairs, led the fight for restoration. She explains in Document 4 how this triumph was achieved.

1. Clyde Warrior (Ponca) Delineates Five Types of Indians, 1965

Among American Indian youth today there exists a rather pathetic scene, in fact, a very sick, sad, sorry scene. This scene consists of the various types of Indian students found in various institutions of learning throughout American society. It is vary sad that these institutions, and whatever conditioning takes place, creates these types. For these types are just what they are, types, and not full, real human beings, or people.

Many of you probably already know these types. Many of you probably know the reasons why these types exist. This writer does not pretend to know why. This writer can only offer an opinion as to names and types, define their characteristics, and offer a possible alternative; notice alternative—not a definite solution. All this writer is merely saying is he does not like Indian youth being turned into something that is not real, and that somebody needs to offer a better alternative:

Type A—SLOB or HOOD. This is the individual who receives his definition of self from the dominant society, and unfortunately, sees this kind in his daily relationships and associations with his own kind. Thus, he becomes this type by dropping out of school, becomes a wino, steals, eventually becomes a court case, and is usually sent off. If lucky, he marries, mistreats his family, and becomes a real pain to his tribal community as he attempts to cram that definition [of himself] down the society's throat. In doing this, he becomes a Super-Slob. Another Indian hits the dust through no fault of his own.

Type B—JOKER. This type has defined himself that to be an Indian is a joke. An Indian does stupid, funny things. After defining himself, from cues society gave him, he proceeds to act as such. Sometimes he accidentally goofs-up, sometimes unconsciously on purpose, after which he laughs, and usually says, "Well, that's Indian." And he goes through life a bungling clown.

From Clyde Warrior, "Which One Are You?: Five Types of Young Indians," in *ABC: Americans Before Columbus,* II, No. 4, December, 1964. Reprinted with permission.

Type C—REDSKIN "WHITE-NOSER" or THE SELL-OUT. This type has accepted and sold out to the dominant society. He has accepted that definition that anything Indian is dumb, usually filthy, and immoral, and to avoid this is to become a "LITTLE BROWN AMERICAN" by associating with everything that is white. He may mingle with Indians, but only when it is to his advantage, and not a second longer than is necessary. Thus, society has created the fink of finks.

Type D—ULTRA-PSEUDO-INDIAN. This type is proud that he is Indian, but for some reason does not know how one acts. Therefore he takes his cues from non-Indian sources, books, shows, etc., and proceeds to act "Indian." With each action, which is phony, we have a person becoming unconsciously phonier and phonier. Hence, we have a proud, phony Indian.

Type E—ANGRY NATIONALIST. Although abstract and ideological, this type is generally closer to true Indianness than the other types, and he resents the others for being ashamed of their own kind. Also, this type tends to dislike the older generation for being "Uncle Tomahawks" and "yes men" to the Bureau of Indian Affairs and whites in general. The "Angry Nationalist" wants to stop the current trend toward personality disappearance, and institute changes that will bring Indians into contemporary society as real human beings; but he views this, and other problems, with bitter abstract and ideological thinking. For thinking this [he] is termed radical, and [he] tends to alienate himself from the general masses of Indians, for speaking what appears, to him, to be truths.

None of these types is the ideal Indian. . . .

It appears that what is needed is genuine contemporary creative thinking, democratic leadership to set guidelines, cues and goals for the average Indian. The guidelines and cues have to be *based on true Indian philosophy geared to modern times.* This will not come about without nationalistic pride in one's self and one's own kind.

This group can evolve only from today's college youth. Not from those who are ashamed, or those who have sold out, or those who do not understand true Indianism. Only from those with pride and love and understanding of the People and the People's ways from which they come can this evolve. And this appears to be the major task of the National Indian Youth Council—for without a people, how can one have a cause?

This writer says this because he is fed up with religious workers and education-alists incapable of understanding, and pseudo-social scientists who are consciously creating social and cultural genocide among American Indian youth.

I am fed up with bureaucrats who try to pass off "rules and regulations" for organizational programs that will bring progress.

I am sick and tired of seeing my elders stripped of dignity and low-rated in the eyes of their young.

I am disturbed to the point of screaming when I see American Indian youth accepting the horror of "American conformity," as being the only way for Indian progress. While those who do not join the great American mainstream of personal-ityless neurotics are regarded as "incompetents and problems."

The National Indian Youth Council must introduce to this sick room of stench and anonymity some fresh air of new Indianness. A fresh air of new honesty, and integrity, a fresh air of new Indian idealism, a fresh air of a new Greater Indian America.

How about it? Let's raise some hell!

2. A Proclamation from the Indians of All Tribes, Alcatraz Island, 1969

To the Great White Father and All His People—

We, the native Americans, re-claim the land known as Alcatraz Island in the name of all American Indians by right of discovery.

We wish to be fair and honorable in our dealings with the Caucasian inhabitants of this land, and hereby offer the following treaty:

We will purchase said Alcatraz Island for twenty-four dollars (24) in glass beads and red cloth, a precedent set by the white man's purchase of a similar island about 300 years ago. We know that $24 in trade goods for these 16 acres is more than was paid when Manhattan Island was sold, but we know that land values have risen over the years. Our offer of $1.24 per acre is greater than the 47 cents per acre the white men are now paying the California Indians for their land.

We will give to the inhabitants of this island a portion of the land for their own to be held in trust by the American Indian Affairs and by the bureau of Caucasian Affairs to hold in perpetuity—for as long as the sun shall rise and the rivers go down to the sea. We will further guide the inhabitants in the proper way of living. We will offer them our religion, our education, our life-ways, in order to help them achieve our level of civilization and thus raise them and all their white brothers up from their savage and unhappy state. We offer this treaty in good faith and wish to be fair and honorable in our dealings with all white men.

We feel that this so-called Alcatraz Island is more than suitable for an Indian reservation, as determined by the white man's own standards. By this we mean that this place resembles most Indian reservations in that:

1. It is isolated from modern facilities, and without adequate means of transportation.
2. It has no fresh running water.
3. It has inadequate sanitation facilities.
4. There are no oil or mineral rights.
5. There is no industry and so unemployment is very great.
6. There are no health care facilities.
7. The soil is rocky and non-productive, and the land does not support game.
8. There are no educational facilities.
9. The population has always exceeded the land base.
10. The population has always been held as prisoners and kept dependent upon others.

Further, it would be fitting and symbolic that ships from all over the world, entering the Golden Gate, would first see Indian land, and thus be reminded of the true history of this nation. This tiny island would be a symbol of the great lands once ruled by free and noble Indians.

What use will we make of this land?

This document can be found in Peter Blue Cloud, ed., *Alcatraz Is Not an Island* (Berkeley, Calif.: Wingbow Press, 1972).

Since the San Francisco Indian Center burned down, there is no place for Indians to assemble and carry on tribal life here in the white man's city. Therefore, we plan to develop on this island several Indian institutions:

1. A Center for Native American Studies which will educate them to the skills and knowledge relevant to improve the lives and spirits of all Indian peoples.
2. An American Indian Spiritual Center which will practice our ancient tribal religious and sacred healing ceremonies. . . .
3. An Indian Center of Ecology which will train and support our young people in scientific research and practice to restore our lands and waters to their pure and natural state. . . .
4. A Great Indian Training School will be developed to teach our people how to make a living in the world, improve our standard of living, and to end hunger and unemployment among all our people. . . .

Some of the present buildings will be taken over to develop an American Indian Museum which will depict our native food & other cultural contributions we have given to the world. Another part of the museum will present some of the things the white man has given to the Indians in return for the land and life he took: disease, alcohol, poverty and cultural decimation (As symbolized by old tin cans, barbed wire, rubber tires, plastic containers, etc.). . . .

In the name of all Indians, therefore, we re-claim this island for our Indian nations. . . .

> Signed,
> Indians of All Tribes
> November 1969
> San Francisco, California

3. The Native Alaskan Land Speaks, 1969

My master, the Native People, have depended upon me for his existence beginning from the time unknown to any living man. My master, before the advent of this so-called disturbing civilization, used me for shelter, used my collection of rocks for weapons such as, spears or arrow points, clubs, even used my ignescent rocks for starting his protective quills the firewood, for warmth and cooking.

He has been and still is dependent on my precious pets the moose, caribou, reindeer, bear, mountain squirrels, sea mammals, and many, many more too numerous to name, for his livelihood. He not only used them for food but he used their skins for clothing, their bones for weapons. He quenches his thirst from my precious blood streams. And when he discovered I had more resources, namely varieties of fish which he utilized to help him survive, he was further elated.

My master did not squander my collection of riches. He made use of what he could get in a manner respectable to my pride. My master in his struggle for survival has traveled over me, many most fertile areas so that he could pass me on to

---

From Philip Guy, "The Native Land Speaks," *Tundra Times*, October 13, 1969, 2.

his sons, grandsons, daughters and granddaughters along with the knowledge he has gained for eternities to come.

If my master, the Native People, documents his activities, the various hunting techniques, whereabouts of his fishcamps, fallcamps, wintercamps, and spring-camps, the rivers and creeks he fished, the ponds and lakes from which he hunted variety of furred animals, the mountains from which he hunts various land animals, the timber areas from which he gets his firewood aside from hunting wildlife which roams in them.

My ornaments, the variety of berries he picks off from my insulated fertile coat, the tundra, he would have all the documentation to substantiate that I am his property without argument.

Lately in his endeavors to improve himself; to adjust himself, in this transitional period to alien form of government by gaining village incorporation status in order that he may become eligible for federal and state programs.

In his efforts to conform to alien policies by becoming an incorporated village or city of fourth class, my master, the Native, has outlined the boundaries of his village including my most fertile areas on which he depends for his existence. Some examples of my fertile areas are the rivers, the tundra and the ponds and lakes, timber areas, the creeks. The other areas inside the boundaries as outlined by my Native master, included are their hunting, fishing and camping areas.

My Native master in his strive to better himself, in his effort conformed to: his government's principles; the established unrealistic regulations, has again been wronged. These wrongs can be seen in the communities of Alakanuk, the twin villages of Upper and Lower Kalskag, Akolmuit (Nunapitchuk, Kasigluk, and Almauluak) and Mekoryuk on the Univak Island.

My master's government has once again made use of vicious tentacles, the Legal Boundary Commission, by having or allowing its servants to reduce to absurd size my master's selected land areas in his applications to become an incorporated community.

This practice is not RIGHT—it is absolutely WRONG when my Native master has endured so many eons and centuries of hardship living off me. It is my confirmed opinion that my Native master can make his own decisions just as well, or even better than the man at a desk in Juneau especially when it involves the boundaries of his hunting, fishing and camping land areas.

4. Ada Deer (Menominee) Explains How Her People Overturned Termination, 1974

. . . Termination occurred in 1954, it became finalized in 1961. Our people have had a strong sense of identity as a group, also a strong adherence to the land. We live in one of the most beautiful areas in this entire country, even if I have to admit it myself. But, we have beautiful lakes, streams and forests. Senator Nelson, who is a great environmentalist, became so concerned about the development [building and selling cabins and land to outsiders] that was starting to take place that he introduced

From Ada Deer, "How the Good Guys Won," *Journal of Intergroup Relations* 3 (1974), 41–50.

and pushed through Congress the Wild Rivers Act, and made the Wolfe River which runs through our area part of this, so the development would stop. In 1961, our tribe, which at that time was composed of 3,270 members, had 10 million dollars in the treasury. We were one of the wealthiest tribes in the country and paid for almost all of our services that were provided by the Bureau of Indian Affairs. We had a lumber mill and our land was intact. This changed. First of all, our land and assets were taken out of trust. Our areas are approximately 234,000 acres. This became a separate county in the state of Wisconsin. We are now the poorest county in the state and the poorest in the nation. Again, to make the story short, it's been an economic, political, a cultural disaster, and instead of taking away federal supervision and giving tribal supervision, as you would think by looking at the resolution, and at the termination law, this did not occur. The trust was taken away; all the protection and services of the Bureau of Indian Affairs were taken away, and a very oppressive and private trust was thrust upon us. First of all, we became a county. Our people had no experience in county government, did not understand how a county functioned, what the responsibilities, the obligations of county government were. Many people had no experience in business enterprise. A separate tribal corporation called MEI, Menominee Enterprises Incorporated, was established. However, this was not controlled by the Menominees because we had another group called the Menominee Common Stock and Voting Trust which was established. This consisted of seven members, four white and three Indians. Now, in most corporations, the individual owners elect the board of directors but this did not occur here. The board of directors was elected by the Menominee Common Stock and Voting Trust. Now, to add insult to injury, there were many people declared incompetent. For example, we had a man who was blind who was declared incompetent without due process of law. Some people ran around and made a big list, shipped it to the Bureau of Indian Affairs and it was authorized, so we have many people who are incompetent, we also have the minors, the children under 18. These votes were controlled by the First Wisconsin Trust Company of Milwaukee. So from 1961 to 1970, we were controlled by white banking and financial institutions. The only participation that the Menominees were able to have in the tribal affairs was to elect one trustee per year at the annual meeting. It was very frustrating. The hospital was closed, many of the youngsters were consolidated into attending one school, the dropout rate has been phenomenal, we've had many serious problems as a result of termination. It has accentuated the values of competitiveness, selfishness, greed, and it's had a disastrous effect not only on our people as a group, but on many individuals. Many people have gone off to Milwaukee, Chicago and other areas across the country.

However, that thing that galvanized us into action was the fact that our board of directors got into a partnership with land developers. Land developers are not only a problem to the Indians but to every single person in this country, because we don't have enough land that's beautiful that we can preserve for everyone. I think that every one of us ought to be concerned about this. . . . To increase the tax base, we had some fast-talking developers coming up there. We have an area of over 80 natural lakes; they created an artificial lake. They channeled some of these; it's an ecological disaster. The lakes are continually changing. They're pumping water from one to another. The shoreline trees have been destroyed in many areas. We've got motor boats, snowmobiles, pollution, terrible situations. Two thousand lots were slotted for sale and we started demonstrating. We demonstrated, we marched, we started to use the press, we formed a grass roots group called DRUMS, "Determination of Rights and Unity for Menominee Shareholders." This is a real grass roots group, because there were several of us that got together in 1970 and decided that no matter what we felt, it was important to fight for our land and people. . . .

Restoration has three points: (1) putting our land assets into trust, (2) making us eligible for federal services, such as education and health services, and (3) giving us federal recognition as a tribe. Our bill was introduced last year, but we didn't get through the entire legislative process because of the presidential campaign. It was re-introduced again this year in May. . . .

I especially tell this to Indian people because it's a typical response of bureaucrats and other people that work with you. They say, "You can't do it , it's going to take a lot of work and there's no way you can change the system." This is not really true. We have chosen another path and this is to beat the system. Now it's taken four years, and in a way, I feel like I've been preparing for this all my life, because my background is a social worker, community action person, and in social action every now and then you have to put your money where your mouth is, and I feel that we as Indians have to practice our Indian values, which is concern for your tribe, and be involved when it's of vital importance. Now, this has meant that several of us have had to change our lives around. I was in law school; the people that I was starting with are going to be graduating this year and will be joining the legal profession. My car is falling apart, some of the others' cars are falling apart, but along with this we are about to achieve the most significant victory in all of American Indian history. On Tuesday of this week, the House passed our act, the Menominee Restoration Act, with a vote of 404 to 3; everybody wants to know who the three that voted against it and how did I let them get away. . . .

We started, first of all, tracking every single Menominee that we could. We called people, we made home visits. First we got two people elected into the Voting Trust. The second year we got four people. Even with four of eleven, they elected me the chairperson of the group. They decided then to proceed with this lobbying effort. Now, the platform we ran on was the stopping of land sales, restoration and Menominee Restoration. Last year, we took over and have been working very hard since that time. We have gone around to all Indian groups, major Indian groups in the country, conducted extensive speaking campaigns—we're learning how to use the media too—and it's been very exciting to be a part of this. It's also very exhausting, but on the other hand, it's worth fighting for. It was such a great pleasure to meet and sit in the House gallery last Tuesday to see the whole United States Congress voting on something that one small Indian tribe brought to their attention. I think it's very significant not only for the Menominee tribe, for all Indian tribes, but for American people as a whole, because I was mentioning to Senator Mondale last evening, we were talking about our legislation that we were about to win, and he said, "Yes, it looks like the good guys are going to win," and we are. Now we've done this in a very interesting way and approach. We decided to approach this on a bi-partisan basis, because we feel that everyone's to blame for Indian problems. We went to the Republican Party platform hearing last year in Miami and we got a statement from the Republican platform stating their recognition of Menominee problems and promising a complete and sympathetic hearing of our plea. We received a good reception at the Democratic Party convention, and in the Democratic platform there was a statement opposing the policy of termination. Then we conducted a drive to get as many people of both parties as we could on our legislation, and it was very interesting to see. We've got about 50 people as sponsors from the House and we have everyone from Bella Abzug to Collins, from Illinois. We did the same thing in the Senate, we have people like Senator Goldwater and Senator Kennedy, and all the Republican members of the Senate Interior and Insular Affairs Committee as sponsors of our legislation. Again, this is an incredible accomplishment which can only be attributed to making the system work. I assume that people are on our side until they prove themselves. I think it's very important to understand that people will take different positions depending on the issue and then of course, you kind of blitz them and you use a little humor in your lobby. I learned a lot. I didn't start out being a lobbyist, but if you care enough—I've told everybody that I would do anything to promote the legislation. So one day it was, I decided, be-kind-to-BIA day. I went out and bought two pounds of candy and started out with the headquarters—this was before it was taken over—I said to the guard, "I'm starting out with headquarters here and I'm going to sweeten you up a little," and I gave him some candy. Of course, he'd been letting me park there in the BIA parking lot, and usually you have to get all kinds of permits and permissions, etc. I smiled at him and he smiles at me, and every now and then it does, even though we live in a chauvinist society which we're changing, every now and then it does help to use some of your feminine wiles. Anyway, he was very nice and he allowed me to park there, so then I went to see all the secretaries. By the time I got to the top floor, I only had two or three pieces of candy left. So you have to use kind of a light touch in all of this lobbying, and we do have some bumper stickers which we have been selling and distributing around the country. We have to have visibility, and I feel that there is not enough of us Indians, so we have to make our presence count. We feel that it is important to keep our issue before the public, and I've met many interesting people on airplanes and in airports as a result of this. Now, I've given you kind of the highlights, the problems that has engendered this, what we've done about it and in essence, I would say that any citizen in this country can take action on an issue if you're ready to get involved and ready to move on it. . . .

◈ *E S S A Y S*

Laurence Hauptman, a history professor at the State University of New York at New Paltz, and anthropologist Jack Campisi have been two of the most important scholars examining the status of eastern Native peoples in the past and the present. In the first essay, Hauptman and Campisi underscore the significance of the Indian communities located east of the Mississippi River. The authors address the efforts by many Indian peoples to gain federal recognition of their proper status. In addition, the essay emphasizes the influence of the famous Chicago conference of 1961, organized by University of Chicago anthropology professor Sol Tax. Troy Johnson, a professor of American Indian studies at California State University, Long Beach, has written widely about contemporary Indian activism. In the second essay, Johnson looks to this era to analyze the roots and development of this vital movement.

Eastern Indian Communities Strive for Recognition

LAURENCE M. HAUPTMAN AND JACK CAMPISI

Much of the modern impetus for federal recognition among eastern Native American communities emanated from the American Indian Chicago Conference of June 1961 and its preliminary meetings. Organized by Sol Tax, this convocation, described in this chapter, was designed to provide a forum for all Native American communities, East and West, federally and nonfederally recognized, concerning a wide variety of issues affecting Indian affairs in the United States.

Today, federal recognition can be achieved in three ways: (1) a Native American tribe may take action in court to force the United States to recognize its trust responsibilities; (2) it may be deemed a federally recognized tribe by congressional legislation; or (3) it may follow a bureaucratic and often convoluted process established by the Department of the Interior. To long-neglected Indian communities, attaining federally recognized status fosters community pride and allows eastern Native Americans to gain a more equal footing in the Native American world. In most cases, it provides them with access to federal Indian programs and allows these newly recognized Indian nations the right to sue for land in federal court as well as to seek other federal protections against the willful actions of states. In more recent times, federally recognized status often, but not in all cases, allows Indian nations to put purchased lands into trust, with the secretary of the interior's approval, giving special tax advantages to them. This strategy has been used effectively in more recent years by Indian nations intent on entrepreneurial activities such as gaming.

As of January 1994, seven criteria had to be "satisfied" in the petition for federal recognition sent to the Federal Acknowledgment Branch of the Bureau of Indian Affairs:

a. establish that they have been identified from historical times to the present on a substantially continuous basis as American Indian or aboriginal;

b. establish that a substantial portion of the group inhabits a specific area or lives in a community viewed as American Indian, distinct from other populations in the area . . . ;

c. furnish a statement of facts which establishes that the group has maintained tribal political influence or other authority over its members as an autonomous entity throughout history until the present;

d. furnish a copy of the group's present governing document . . . describing in full the membership criteria and the procedures through which the group currently governs its affairs and its members;

e. furnish a list of all known current members . . . based on the group's own defined criteria. The membership must consist of individuals who have established, using evidence acceptable to the Secretary of the Interior, descendancy from a tribe which existed historically or from historical tribes which combined and functioned as a single autonomous entity;

From Laurence M. Hauptman and Jack Campisi, "There Are No Indians East of the Mississippi," in Laurence Hauptman, *Tribes and Tribulations: Misconceptions About American Indians and Their Histories* (Albuquerque, N. Mex.: University of New Mexico Press, 1995), 94–108. Reprinted with permission.

f. establish that the membership of the group is composed principally of persons who are not members of any other North American Indian tribe;

g. [demonstrate] that the group or its members are not the subject of congressional legislation which has expressly terminated or forbidden the Federal Relationship. (25 CRF 83.7)

The petition route through the Department of the Interior was established in 1978. Seven eastern Native American communities have won recognition—the Grand Traverse Band of Ottawa and Chippewa; the Tunica-Biloxi Indian Tribe of Louisiana; the Narragansett Indian Tribe; the Poarch Band of Creeks; the Wampanoag Tribe of Gay Head; the Micmac Tribe of Maine; and the Mohegan Tribe of Connecticut. An eighth eastern Native American community, the Mashantucket Pequot Tribe of Connecticut, achieved federal recognition through congressional legislation.

In the East as well as in the West, many Native American communities have not yet been able to secure federal recognition because it is a time-consuming, expensive, and politically charged, as well as demeaning, process. Congressional politics and budget cutting, BIA stonewalling, and racist perceptions . . . are all roadblocks on the route to federal recognition. Moreover, certain Native American leaders themselves do not want Washington to recognize more Indian communities, such as the populous but nonfederally recognized Lumbee of North Carolina, since they fear the further shrinking of the federal pie to Indian communities.

The American Indian Chicago Conference (AICC) was a major watershed in the history of contemporary Native peoples. Between June 13 and 20, 1961, 467 American Indians from ninety separate communities met at the University of Chicago, at a convocation organized by anthropologist Sol Tax, to voice their opinions about a wide variety of concerns affecting Indian affairs in the United States. This convocation drafted the *Declaration of Indian Purpose,* an elaborate policy statement, which, among other things, asked for a reversal of the federal government's termination policies; for increased Indian educational opportunities, more economic development programs, and better health-care-delivery systems; for the abolition of ten BIA area offices; for the protection of Indian water rights; and for presidential reevaluation of federal plans to build the Kinzua Dam. The Indians insisted in the *Declaration:* "What we ask of America is not charity, not paternalism, even when benevolent. We ask only that the nature of our situation be recognized and made the basis of policy and action." Although the conference has been credited with promoting the development of a new awareness of American Indian concerns, a new national Indian organization—the National Indian Youth Council (NIYC)—and a more radical turn in the formation of Indian political strategy, scholars have totally ignored the meeting's specific impact on eastern Indians.

In 1968, Nancy Lurie, who assisted Tax in his efforts, reflected on the AICC and its influence: "Certainly, it had a profound influence on a number of tribes in offering a model of action and a good deal of moral support for what in 1961 were, as far as the general public is concerned, unpopular and incomprehensible goals." One of these "unpopular and incomprehensible goals," which was pushed by Tax from the beginning, was his aim of bringing eastern Indian concerns to the fore. Besides a conscious effort to bring public attention to the plight of the Seneca Indians, whose lands were being inundated by the Kinzua Dam, the conference organizers focused on Indian communities east of the Mississippi whose primary concern was federal and state recognition. This conscious decision, which went against much of the anthropological, policymaking, and reservation Indian thinking of the time, contributed significantly to increased efforts by the Abenaki, Gay Head Wampanoag, Haliwa, Houma, Lumbee, Mashpee Wampanoag, and Narragansett in seeking federal recognition over the past quarter-century.

In 1960, Tax, after discussions with members of the Schwartzhaupt Foundation, developed a proposal to update the Meriam Report, a comprehensive analysis of American Indian conditions and federal Indian policies undertaken by scholars for the Institute of Government Research and published in 1928. According to Carl Tjerandsen, the executive secretary of the foundation, Tax insisted that, unlike the Meriam Report, the Indians should have the "central role" in producing a document assessing the current scene. Having been initially awarded ten thousand dollars by the Schwartzhaupt Foundation, Tax then approached the leaders of the National Congress of American Indians (NCAI) for support of his idea. At a time of significant Indian land loss, as a result of federal hydroelectric and/or flood control projects and major efforts to terminate federal treaty and trust responsibilities to Indian nations, Tax's proposal received a favorable response from the NCAI leadership. It also endorsed Tax's only stipulation, namely, that any and all Indians have the opportunity to participate in all deliberations.

Tax had long prepared for the inclusion of eastern Indian groups at the AICC. While spending much of his time in the late 1950s as an "action anthropologist" among the Fox in Iowa, he had worked with Robert K. Thomas, Samuel Stanley, Bruce MacLachlan, and Myron Rosenberg in mapping North American Indian populations. From 1956 to 1961, he revised this map four times and included on it, unlike BIA maps of the period, communities that claimed Indian heritage but which, at that time, were not recognized by federal or state agencies. These Indians included the Haliwa, Houma, Lumbee, Mashpee Wampanoag, Mohegan, Narragansett, Pequot, and Tunica-Biloxi. Later, this revealing map, although criticized by federally recognized Indians and some anthropologists, was distributed at the AICC meetings and subsequently reprinted in one of Lurie's publications.

Tax also was in direct correspondence with Indian-rights advocates, as well as with anthropologists and sociologists, in order to identify and ascertain the needs of these eastern groups. From the beginning, his intention was to get as wide a representation of American Indian people as possible. After being sent three separate reprints from sociologist Brewton Berry about these southern communities, Tax noted on top of one of Berry's articles that it "may prove useful documentation in [the] Eastern Area." Significantly, Tax, unlike Berry and other academics, never referred to these populations as "racial hybrids," "mestizos," "almost white," "triracial isolates," or "marginal groups." Indeed, he and Lurie would frequently refer to these groups as "self-identified Indians." Lurie later expounded upon Tax's thinking, writing about a preliminary AICC planning meeting held in Chicago: "Sol invited 20 people and got a good representation about groupings (org. and unorg. tribes; urban Indians, nonfederal recognized; intertribal groups—NCAI, Longhouse, etc. and Native American Church) and good geographic spread." Consequently, nine hundred American Indians from the East received AICC mailings, and seven Indians from this region were appointed to the AICC rules committee of twenty-four members, including Chief W. R. Richardson, the Haliwa leader, and Judge Lacy R. Maynor, a prominent Lumbee and town justice of the Maxton, North Carolina, recorder court.

In order to pursue this "eastern strategy," Tax had to balance diplomatically the interests of competing Indian groups and organizations. He had worked almost from the beginning with the leadership of the National Congress of American Indians (NCAI). Through D'Arcy McNickle, Clarence Wesley, and Helen Peterson, Tax received the NCAI's formal endorsement. Although this endorsement proved useful in the West, many eastern Indians viewed the NCAI as too conservative, too much aligned with the BIA, and too opposed to eastern Indian interests, including federal recognition efforts. Thus, Tax and Lurie, although relying on the skills of McNickle, nevertheless attempted to prevent the AICC from appearing to be merely a carbon copy of a NCAI convention.

Two eastern American Indians played key roles in the planning and development of the AICC: (1) William Rickard (Tuscarora) and (2) Lacy W. Maynor (Lumbee). Rickard, the son of well-respected Chief Clinton Rickard who had aided eastern Indians through the Indian Defense League, had come to public attention in the late 1950s as a prominent activist fighting against Robert Moses and the New York State Power Authority's efforts to expropriate Tuscarora lands. Historian Barbara Graymont has described the qualities of William and Clinton Rickard that made them leaders of the Indian Defense League and eastern Indians:

> William and his father [Clinton] were always very close and in many ways very similar. They were alike in their interest in Indian rights, in their Indian conservatism, and in their personalities. Both were men of brilliance and native genius, easygoing nature, selfless devotion to others, and tenacious actions. Both were deeply religious men but revealed this trait in different ways. Clinton always preferred the church. William, though he had been voluntarily baptized as an adult and had passed through the "Christian degrees" of Masonry, came to be a devoted follower of the Longhouse religion, much preferring it to Christianity.

On January 26, 1961, Tax extended an invitation to William Rickard, explaining the goals and agenda of the AICC meeting. Tax insisted that instead "of having 'experts' plan for communities of people, we have learned that people have to plan for themselves." He continued by indicating that any "plan for American Indians is a bad plan if the Indians who have to live with it do not understand it or do not want it," adding that improvement could not take place "unless the Indian point of view is fully expressed and honored." Tax assured Rickard that he was the coordinator, not the czar, of the meetings, and that he was attempting to bring all Indian viewpoints together. Yet he conceded to Rickard that he had limited knowledge of the diversity of positions: "But who are 'all Indians' and how can such a national discussion be carried through?" Tax then appointed Rickard to the planning committee of "12 or 15" Indian leaders from all over the United States to meet him at the University of Chicago for four days beginning on February 10. Rickard, as representative of the Iroquois Defense League and the Iroquois Longhouse, was subsequently chosen as a member of the Indian steering committee of the planned Chicago conference and chairman of the eastern regional meeting at Haverford

College, leading up to the major convocation in Chicago. Rickard, who checked out all his statements beforehand with the chiefs of the Onondaga Longhouse, realized that the Iroquois were not as open-minded and sympathetic to the aims and aspirations of nonfederally recognized Indian groups as he was. In writing a summary report of an early AICC planning meeting, he feared that the Iroquois might not "work with the East coast Indians, Shinacooks [*sic*], Naragansetts [*sic*], etc. I might have to have two meetings, one for each. I hope not." In the end, Rickard nevertheless was able to convince the Iroquois of the importance of participation in the AICC at the regional and national levels.

From the inception of his involvement in the AICC, Rickard was at odds with many of the sentiments expressed by other Indian representatives. After an early planning session in February, Rickard wrote: "I was not at all satisfied the way the Chicago meeting was conducted by the National Congress of American Indians. If their plans is [*sic*] to be followed, the venture is doomed to failure. They talk of a 'new frontier' but it is the same old muddle that has got our Indian people in such a deplorable state." In typical Iroquois fashion, he added that his aim was to "initiate the True [*sic*] course for our Indian people at Haverford" and, obviously later, at Chicago. As a result, he suggested that more effort be made to broaden the representation. He recommended that invitations be sent to Indians with nonfederally recognized status, including Mary Red Wing Congdon, a prominent Narragansett, as well as representatives of traditionalist perspectives such as Iroquois Tadodaho George A. Thomas. Rickard's involvement in AICC was no easy task for Tax and Lurie. In February, Lurie wrote McNickle that "Helen Peterson [an NCAI leader] will be just as happy to have Rickard out of the picture," but that Lurie hoped to straighten out any misunderstandings with him in order to avoid later complications in Chicago. Since Rickard had sizable influence over traditionalists, or "Longhouses" (Lurie's words), involved in the AICC process, Lurie worked hard to keep the channels of communication open to Rickard and his followers.

At the February strategy meeting held in Chicago, Rickard was one of thirteen Indians in attendance. Three represented eastern Indians: Rickard, Judge Lacy Maynor (Lumbee), and George Heron (Seneca). Rickard and Heron recounted the troubles that each of their Iroquois nations was facing at the time. Heron described the Kinzua Dam controversy that threatened over 9,000 acres of Seneca lands in Pennsylvania and New York, and Rickard recalled the Tuscarora loss of 556 acres of tribal reservation land to a New York State Power Authority's reservoir and hydroelectric project along the Niagara River. Judge Maynor sadly indicated that his people had no federal recognition, but proudly insisted that they had retained a sense of Indian identity and distinctive community, despite the "racially complicated picture of the Southern states, since colonial times." It was at this meeting and at subsequent ones that an eastern alliance was formed that proved useful at the Chicago convocation six months later. The Maynors impressed Rickard, leading the Tuscarora to praise the judge. Rickard later wrote that the Lumbee did not have a reservation; but they did have the "same status as other people," and "they are sticking together and are not being pushed around to any great extent." In appreciation, Judge Maynor was supportive of Rickard's causes—protecting treaty rights and reaffirming Indian sovereignty—and Rickard believed that "he [Judge Maynor] and his people would help in any way possible."

Tax and Lurie set up regional meetings around the country, leading up to the final conclave in Chicago. One of the coordinators of these meetings explained the reasons for this administrative structure: "Tax thought that [Indian] people ought to get warmed up and think their problems over and get things formulated in advance so that the Chicago experience would be more profitable." Because of this format, Judge Maynor proved to be invaluable in promoting the AICC in the South, especially when a hitch occurred at the last moment over the site of the southeastern regional meeting. When the University of North Carolina at Chapel Hill turned down the AICC's organizers' request to host a regional meeting because the university's administrators found a southern conference on the race issue "too touchy," Tax and Lurie approached Maynor to have Pembroke State College (now Pembroke State University) hold the conference. Lurie also wrote Maynor, asking him to promote the AICC as far away as Alabama and Louisiana in order to get widespread support in Indian communities for the regional and Chicago meetings. Through a committee of thirty-two Lumbees, Maynor and his daughter Helen organized the Pembroke meeting.

The site selection for this southeastern meeting is quite significant. Coming less than three years the Lumbee won public attention by driving the Ku Klux Klan out of Robeson County, North Carolina, this decision was not merely by chance. The Lumbee, the largest Indian population east of the Mississippi, had founded Pembroke State College, their own institution of higher learning, in the 1880s. Moreover, as highly educated, numerous, and powerful as they were, compared to other nonfederally recognized Indians, the Lumbee offered a protected enclave in the South, during a time of racial tensions, where Indian issues could be discussed. Since one of the goals of the AICC was to develop Indian leadership, the availability of an Indian-founded, Indian-administered college as the host institution is noteworthy. Although no full transcript of the Pembroke meeting has been found, the regional conference held in April focused on educational problems facing American Indians and, in particular, southeastern communities, as well as racial discrimination, media stereotyping, housing problems, and concerns for economic development. Since the Lumbee had sought federal recognition since the 1930s and had come close to achieving it in 1956, one could surmise that this issue also received attention at Pembroke. It is also significant to note that one prominent anthropologist, who attended the meeting, observed that "reservation groups were badly underrepresented" at Pembroke since nonfederally recognized Indian groups were in the vast majority.

A second regional meeting was held at Haverford College and organized by Theodore B. Hetzel, professor of engineering and longtime Indian-rights advocate. In order to prepare for the conference, Hetzel wrote Lurie to inquire about Nanticoke and Lumbee participation and adding names to the AICC mailing list, including state-recognized Pamunkey and Mattaponi chiefs, two Catawbas and the Indian governors at the Penobscot and Passamaquoddy reservations in Maine. Besides Hetzel, Heron, and Rickard, the Indian committee organizing the Haverford College regional meeting included a Narragansett and a Mohawk-Cherokee married to a Narragansett Indian. As a result of Rickard's influence, the Haverford meeting included federally recognized as well as nonrecognized reservations, and urban Indians. Besides Rickard, his father Clinton, and other Iroquois, the registration list included a "who's who" of off-reservation and/or nonfederally recognized Indians: Lewis Mofsie, Clarence Wood, and Mimi Hines, leaders in the New York City Indian community; Mary Red Wing Congdon and Tall Oak, a future leader of the Red Power movement among the Narragansett of Rhode Island; Gladys Widdiss, the former tribal chair among the Gay Head Wampanoag; Earl Mills, a prominent Mashpee; as well as delegates from the Abenaki, Penobscot, and Shinnecock.

For three full days, the conferees talked about Indian sovereignty and communicated about common problems. William Rickard, who served as the chairman of the meeting held on April 7–11, 1961, once again expressed his concern that Indian sovereignty was being eroded by such actions as those by the New York State Power Authority. Rickard then went on to discuss his spiritual visit to the traditional people of the Hopi Nation. Penobscot Richard Bounding Elk insisted that the United States must provide a "Marshall Plan for Indians." He joined in an appeal with a Mohawk conferee urging President Kennedy to recognize the Six Nations as a sovereign nation just like Italy viewed San Marino. Importantly, at Haverford, Bounding Elk and other Indians insisted that the United States government recognize the federal status of Indians' reservation lands in Maine. Francis McCall, another Penobscot, recounted the prejudice and economic problems faced by Indians in Maine. He maintained that the state was the major problem and that its supervision of Indian affairs was abominable. Later, McCall insisted that the Penobscot were beyond the jurisdiction of Maine's laws since they were foreign nations and that treaties made with these Indians were more than just documents housed in the Maine state house.

Not all of the AICC regional meetings supported the concept of an open convocation with nonfederally recognized Indian communities in attendance. This issue came to a head at the Oklahoma regional meeting held at the University of Oklahoma in the early spring of 1961. Alice Marriott and Carol Rachlin reported to Tax that the meeting focused its attention on the meaning of "self-identified Indians" and that these words produced great concern among the leadership among the Five Civilized Tribes. The two anthropologists, who had been working on behalf of the AICC, were asked to explain the term. When they were unable to do so, the regional meeting, with the support of Marriott and Rachlin, adopted a resolution insisting that "only members of federally-recognized Indian tribes who can so identify themselves in Chicago, be recognized at the June conference." The Oklahoma conferees, fearing the influence of what it claimed were individuals of questionable Indian heritage, also criticized the AICC map for including nonfederally recognized communities and suggested that the "identity of Indian tribes" be "based upon the estimates of a Federal agency, such as the Bureau of Indian Affairs." The attack on so-called self-identified Indians, a code name for Afro-Indians in the minds of some of the leaders of the Five Civilized Tribes, was because of rampant discrimination since, in Rachlin's words, these Indians (leaders of Five Civilized Tribes at AICC), "REPRESENT THE OLD SOUTH IN OKLAHOMA." Indian disdain and intolerance of these communities was long-standing and pervasive especially in Oklahoma and in the South, and was largely based on the white man's taboos against white and Indian miscegenation with blacks since the age of slavery.

After the regional meetings, the AICC organizers solicited follow-up responses from those in attendance. One respondent, Richard Gaffney, an Abenaki Indian, emphasized that the AICC should take up "Federal 'recognition' of the legal existence of certain tribes east of the Mississippi who are on state reservations or not at all." Helen Attaquin, a Wampanoag from Middleboro, Massachusetts, suggested that the AICC should encourage a realization that nonreservation Indians can aid reservation Indians and be "their biggest and best spokesmen." An Oneida and several Rappahannocks insisted that the AICC focus on claims to lands lost; one Tuscarora stressed the need to focus on treaties; while a Houma asked to serve on the education and law committees of AICC. Karen Rickard, William's sister and a founder of NIYC, hoped that the AICC would promote the preservation of Native arts. Importantly, she added that the AICC should avoid breaking down into small groups right away at the approaching Chicago meeting. She concluded by asserting that what "the Indians needs is unity, which can be done during the first days—then break up later in the week." Yet, unlike Rickard, Emmanuel Many Deeds, a Standing Rock Sioux and NCAI member, stressed the need for a committee on screening that would limit seating at the Chicago conclave to those who could document their Indian heritage.

In one of the most ambitious endeavors, Zara Ciscoe Brough, a Nipmuck, from her home at Grafton, Massachusetts, drafted a detailed plan for the complete overhaul of Indian affairs in the United States. She suggested abolishing the BIA and its civil-service structure and establishing an "Indian Board Committee Government" in the Interior Department, composed of a chairman and four board members selected by the president of the United States. The Indian Board, funded by the federal government, would allocate funds to tribal projects through four regional district offices. In each district, there would be a governor, the Indian district chairman, who would be responsible to both reservation and nonreservation Indians in his/her district. At the bottom of this new structure would be reservation and nonreservation tribal committees with proportional representation according to the size of reservation or individual groups. Importantly, nowhere in this elaborate plan were federally recognized and nonfederally recognized Indians set apart.

Eastern Indians hoped that the AICC would bring a new day to their communities. Despite outright racism expressed against them by other Indians and warnings about their seating at the Chicago conclave, Brough wrote Tax that the Indians in Connecticut, Massachusetts, and Rhode Island were "very enthusiastic about the conference" and were "anxiously awaiting the outcome of the conference." Mary Red Wing Congdon talked up the significance of the AICC among the Mohegans and Narragansetts, attended a strategy meeting at Mashpee, and discussed her findings about the matter with local New England Indian nationalist organizations. In writing Tax, she went so far as to volunteer her services at Chicago and requested that Tax allow her to address the full convention about "Our Golden Heritage," Indian affairs in general, and the Narragansetts' survival as Indian people.

Tax carefully tried to win acceptance of these groups prior to the Chicago conclave. In a major article written for the *Chicago Sun Times,* Tax wrote:

> It is sometimes argued that the crippling effects of governmental paternalism could have been avoided if the government had simply "stayed out of the Indian business." But this has not worked either. There are many Indian communities which are not recognized by the government which face problems as acute as those of the overregulated communities. These "non-reservation" settlements, even when they no longer "own" their land,

are identifiable as communities whose members are as attached to their territories as any other Indians, and with pressing problems comparable to others. Their problems cannot be wished away by refusing to recognize them. These are communities without paternalistic control but also without the needed subsidization to begin to carry out choices they would like to make for their own benefit.

Despite Tax's efforts, internal disputes erupted in Chicago over the participation by these Indians. In fact, the entire week-long convocation in Chicago was marred by intense conflict. According to McNickle:

> Even in the presence of a common danger, however, collaboration was not spontaneously achieved. Indians from traditionalist communities were fearful of finding themselves associated with ideas or actions which might betray their interests. Reservation Indians were especially distrustful of their urbanized kinsmen, whom they suspected of scheming to liquidate tribal resources and claim their share. In the absence of traditional channels for intertribal communication, the conferees had as their only guiding experience their generations of negotiating with the white man, an experience that had taught extreme wariness and distrust. At several critical moments the conference stood ready to dissolve, but on each such occasion an acceptable base for continuing discussion was found.

McNickle was vague in his description and failed to elaborate on the friction over the nonfederally recognized Indians' role at the Chicago meeting; however, Lurie clarified the nature of this conflict by specifying that non-reservation Indians in general, "and the presence of non-federally recognized tribes, also evoked their [the delegates of federally recognized groups] anxiety." By favoring and establishing a "60%–70% arrangement, in which the federally recognized communities would have the larger share of votes, these Indians held the power at the Chicago conclave. Moreover, these federally recognized communities further alienated some Indians, but mostly urban and nonfederally recognized groups, by pushing through a resolution allowing them to use their 60 percent as a bloc vote at the convocation! Despite these power plays, the voices of Indians east of the Mississippi were not silenced at Chicago. Once again, William Rickard's influence was apparent.

Rickard, who participated and addressed the convocation in Chicago, caused a commotion when he objected to a pamphlet prepared by Sophie Aberle and William Brophy, entitled "A Program for Indian Citizens," which had been distributed prior to the June meeting. Since the Iroquois considered themselves as citizens of their individual Indian nations or of the Iroquois Confederacy, the Tuscarora interpretation of the Aberle-Brophy pamphlet was as government design to assimilate the Indians. In Chicago, after hearing McNickle read the *Declaration of Indian Purpose,* Rickard pointed out that some Indians did not come to an American Indian conference to be told that "ALL INDIANS ARE U.S. CITIZENS." Rickard explained that Iroquois traditionalist views did not recognize the 1924 Indian citizenship act and that there was nothing wrong with the requirements before 1924, when an Indian had to qualify, be educated, and become a citizen of his own free will and accord. Rickard concluded by blaming the NCAI, who "is influenced mainly by white politicians and lobbyists and that they have not worked for the best interests of the Indians," "Indian Bureau politicians," and misguided academics, diplomatically excluding his hosts, Tax and Lurie. Yet after the AICC, the Tuscarora activist later insisted, in

Iroquois metaphorical style, that the voice of eastern Indians, "supposedly assimilated, terminated or relocated and are not federally recognized," had, despite efforts to silence them, been heard. They had questioned the dangerous parts of various proposals, "symbolically screaming a warning to other Nations and Tribes of Indians of approaching danger as is the duty of the eagle atop the Iroquois tree of peace." No longer, according to Rickard, could the NCAI ignore the existence of Indian groups and Indian organizations east of the Mississippi.

Rickard later claimed that the AICC was not an open conference and that the convocation had insulted Indians east of the Mississippi:

> We who were from the east were permitted to speak and serve on the various committees, but for the most part, it was only a token courtesy. Several times in a discussion group I heard the phrase used, "You are not from the federally recognized tribes" when an eastern Indian spoke. You would be allowed to talk. When you finished, they paid no attention to any suggestions you might have made.

Yet Rickard was only partially correct. Although open discrimination against non-federally recognized Indians was clearly practiced, much to the embarrassment of Tax, Lurie, and many Indians in attendance, Indians east of the Mississippi without federal status achieved some notable results. Without question, the AICC's *Declaration of Indian Purpose* showed no inkling of this internal battle and reflected true concern for these Indian communities:

> Mention has not been made in the above categories of the situation of those Indian groups, mostly in the East and the South, for whom no lands were ever reserved under federal law and for whom no federal services have ever been provided. Yet, they remain Indian, and they remain isolated. We say emphatically that the problems of health, education, economic distress and social nonacceptance rest as heavily on all the Indians in these categories as they do on the reservation Indians, and possibly more heavily. Therefore, in all the recommendations herein, it is to be understood that even where non-reservation or off-reservation are not specified, it is our purpose to insist that their needs be taken into account.

Equally astounding, the *Declaration* contained no distinctions in its text about federally recognized and nonrecognized Indians and made no attempt to define *Indian* or *tribe*.

Perhaps more importantly, the AICC gave renewed hope to Indians east of the Mississippi to push for federal recognition. Helen Maynor (Schierbeck), who subsequently became a leading Indian educator, wrote Tax a month after the AICC that "many good things happened at the Chicago Conference." Citing the group discussions and the acquaintances she made, Maynor insisted that "Indian thinking as a national group grew." At a time when federal recognition of Maynor's Lumbee community had recently been denied, she was apparently reacting to the realization that other eastern Indians experienced the same frustrations as well as aspirations. In this vein, Chief Calvin W. McGee, an Alabama Creek, told Nancy Lurie in Chicago that he could not believe there were "so many Indians in the same boat." The AICC, to be sure, had contributed to networking American Indian communities, including those eastern groups who had long aspired for federal recognition. Defended by prominent anthropologists and receiving attention on a national scale for the first time, these Indians went back to their communities more confident about their future and more committed to pushing for recognition of their Indian status. It was no coincidence that two of the Houma delegates, after attending the AICC in Chicago, went back to their community in the Louisiana bayou country and began a major effort to achieve federal recognition.

Perhaps the most extraordinary impact of the AICC on eastern Indians was its effect on the Haliwa of North Carolina. Chief W. R. Richardson, who is still the leader of the Haliwa, had actively participated in the planning sessions leading up to the Chicago meeting. In the process, he became acquainted with William Rickard and his family. This friendship made at Chicago had significant results. Twice between June 1961 and early 1963, William, his father Clinton, and other family members, as well as Chief Elton Greene and Walter Printup of the Tuscarora, visited the Haliwa. On one of these visits, the Tuscarora, after learning of the history and customs of these North Carolina peoples, gave their formal tribal recognition to the Haliwa. Rickard stated the following in an affidavit to Chief Richardson: "It is my observation that the Indians of the Haliwa Indian Community are the direct descendants of remnant groups of Tuscarora, Cherokee, and other Indian tribes and nations occupying their territory many years ago." One year after William Rickard's death in 1964, North Carolina granted the Haliwas state recognition as an Indian community. Since that time, Chief Richardson and the Haliwa have pressed for federal recognition and are currently preparing a petition of status clarification for the Department of the Interior.

On August 15, 1962, thirty-two Indians active in AICC presented the *Declaration of Indian Purpose* to President John F. Kennedy at a special ceremony at the White House. Nine Indians from nonfederally recognized communities attended the ceremony, including two Chickahominy, four Alabama Creeks, one Lumbee, one Narragansett, and one Ottawa. Helen Maynor [Schierbeck] of the Lumbee and Chief Calvin W. McGhee of the Alabama Creek, both of whom had played important roles in the acceptance of the AICC in the South, were there along with Robert Burnette, executive director of the NCAI, to push for improvement of Indian conditions in the United States. After the White House gathering, the Indians met with Vice President Lyndon Johnson, Senator Sam J. Ervin, Jr., and Congressman Ben Riefel, himself of Lakota Indian ancestry and a founder of NCAI, in order to discuss a legislative program suggested by the *Declaration of Indian Purpose.*

The seeds sown at Chicago were generally slow to reach harvest. In 1976, the American Indian Policy Review Committee Task Force 10 covered much of the same ground that Tax and Lurie had initiated a decade and a half earlier, mapping Indian populations east of the Mississippi and identifying their needs. With the establishment of the Federal Acknowledgment Branch in the Department of the Interior in the late 1970s and increased congressional sensitivity to these Indian communities came federal recognition for the Alabama Creek (Poarch Band), the Narragansett, the Ottawa, the Tunica-Biloxi, the Mashantucket Pequot, and other groups as well as the reinstitution of federal status for all of the Indian nations of Maine.

By allowing a forum for eastern American Indians and their concerns, the AICC stimulated the movement for federal recognition. Tax and his staff should also be credited with helping to instill a new pride, confidence, and direction to the leaders of these long-neglected communities who, for the first time, shared the podium with tribal chiefs and chairmen from around the country. Tax, in an interview in 1982, was correct in his assessment that "we [the AICC] started this movement for federal recognition." The AICC was truly a vast experiment in action anthropology, whose overall significance to eastern Indians is becoming easier to comprehend more than three decades later.

The Roots of Contemporary Native American Activism

TROY R. JOHNSON

. . . The lessons of the civil rights movement were not missed by Indian people. As civil rights issues and rhetoric dominated the headlines, some Indian groups adopted the vocabulary and techniques of the Blacks in order to get Indian issues covered by the media and attract the attention of the American public. The National Indian Youth Council (NIYC), a group of young college-educated Indians who had organized following the American Indian Charter Convention held in Chicago in 1961, adopted some of the ideas of the civil rights movement and held numerous fish-ins in the Pacific Northwest, where Washington State was attempting to use state laws to restrict Indian fishing rights guaranteed by federal treaties. Earlier Indian protest groups such as the National Congress of American Indians (NCAI), founded in 1944, had lobbied in Washington against the Termination Act of 1953. The NCAI was joined by organizations such as the Indian Rights Association and the American Friends Services Committee in its fight against termination. During the fish-ins, however, physical confrontation rather than lobbying became the protest tool. Indian people risked their boats, their nets, and their lives in confrontation with state authorities.

When Isaac Stevens was appointed governor of the new Washington Territory in 1853, he concluded the Medicine Creek (1854) and Point Elliott (1855) treaties, which guaranteed the Indians' rights to fish both on and off reservation and to take fish at their usual and accustomed grounds and stations. In the mid-1950s, the Washington authorities tried to control Indian fishing in off-reservation areas on the Puyallup River. The Indians protested, arguing that these were "usual and accustomed grounds and stations" within the meaning of the 1854 and 1855 treaties. In 1963 the U.S. Court of Appeals upheld the rights of Indian people to fish in accordance with the guaranteed treaty rights. In 1964, in defiance of the Supreme Court decision, the Washington State courts closed the Nisqually River to Indian fishermen in areas off of the Nisqually Reservation. In the same year, the Survival of American Indians Association (SAIA) was formed as a protest organization to assert and preserve off-reservation fishing rights. SAIA organized fish-ins at Frank's Landing on the Nisqually River to protest the state's latest attempt to deny Indian treaty rights. A large force of state and local officers raided Frank's Landing in 1965, smashing boats and fishing gear, slashing nets, and brutalizing Indian people, including Indian women and children. Seven Indian people were arrested in this particular incident, and in an incident in 1970 at Frank's Landing, sixty Indian

From Troy R. Johnson, "The Roots of Contemporary Native American Activism," *American Indian Culture and Research Journal,* vol. 20, no. 2 (1996), 127–154. Reprinted by permission of the American Indian Studies Center, UCLA. Copyright © Regents of the University of California.

persons were arrested. SAIA members, led by Janet McCloud, a Tulalip Indian, gathered in Seattle and marched in protest at the federal courthouse. Protests, raids, and arrests continued throughout the remainder of the 1960s and into early 1970. In January 1971 Hank Adams, a former member of NIYC and now a member of SAIA who had participated in a decade of fish-ins, was shot in the stomach by two white sport fishermen as he slept in his pickup truck. Adams had been tending a set of fish nets for a friend on the Puyallup River. Although Adams survived the shooting, police disputed his account of the incident. In February 1974 in *United States* v. *Washington*, Judge George Boldt upheld the treaty rights of Indian people to fish at their usual and accustomed grounds and stations off-reservation and "in common with" other citizens. The fish-ins and demonstrations came at a time when protest marches and political activism were common throughout the country.

Of equal concern to Indian people was the Vietnam War, where Indian men and women fought to defend a freedom that they themselves had never experienced. Although American Indians may have been the forgotten Americans in the minds of many politicians and bureaucrats during peacetime, this was not the case in time of war or national emergency. American Indians were required to serve and did serve honorably; 1,000 in World War I, 44,500 in World War II, and 29,700 during the Korean conflict. The Vietnam war proved no exception. A total of 61,100 American Indians served during the Vietnam era.

Beginning with the commitment of troops to Vietnam in 1963, American Indians either served voluntarily or were drafted into military service. In the minds of some Indian servicemen, this undeclared war was fought against a people who were an oppressed minority in much the same manner as American Indians. Wallace "Mad Bear" Anderson, a Tuscarora Indian who visited Vietnam seven times, stated, "When I walk down the streets of Saigon those people look like my brothers and sisters." Robert Thomas, a Cherokee anthropologist, stated that Indian people understood the war in Vietnam better than his university colleagues did. The conflict in Vietnam was tribal in origin, and the Vietnamese were tired of the war machine flattening their crops.

American Indians returning from Vietnam faced difficult choices. Those who returned, or attempted to return, to life on the reservation confronted high unemployment rates, poor health facilities, and substandard housing conditions, just as Indian veterans who had returned from World War II had experienced. Those who elected to relocate or settle in urban areas encountered what can best be described as "double discrimination." First, they had to deal with the continuing discrimination against Indian people, which resulted in high unemployment, policy brutality, and, very often, alcoholism and death. Second, they experienced the discrimination being felt by other Vietnam veterans who were participants in an unpopular war. Rather than being hailed as heroes or shown some measure of respect for their sacrifice, they were considered third-rate citizens and were treated as outcasts of society. In an attempt to retreat for a period of time, to adjust to a changing society, or perhaps simply to acquire skills for future employment, many of these returning Indian veterans utilized their GI bill educational benefits and enrolled in colleges and universities in the Bay Area. Indian students from these colleges, many of them Vietnam veterans, filled the ranks of the rising Indian activism movement now emerging as Red Power.

The movement consisted of disillusioned Indian youth from reservations, urban centers, and universities who called for Red Power in their crusade to reform the conditions of their people. These disillusioned urban Indians were speaking out against the treatment they were receiving from the local, the state, and the federal government, both in the cities and on the reservations. In *Behind the Trail of Broken Treaties,* Native American scholar Vine Deloria, Jr., states, "The power movements which had sprung up after 1966 now began to affect Indians, and the center of action was the urban areas on the West Coast, where there was a large Indian population." These Red Power groups strongly advocated the policy of Indian self-determination, used here as meaning, the right to real self-government or autonomy. The NIYC emphasized the psychological impact of powerlessness on Indian youth in connection with the need for self-determination. Powerlessness and lack of self-determination were explained by Clyde Warrior, a Ponca Indian and co-founder of NIYC, when he told government officials in Washington in 1967, "We are not allowed to make those basic human choices and decisions about our personal life and about the destiny of our communities which is the mark of free mature people. We sit on our front porch or in our yards, and the world and our lives in it pass us by without our desires or aspirations having any effect." An article in *Warpath,* the first militant, pan-Indian newspaper in the United States, established in 1968 by United Native Americans (UNA), summed up the attitude of the Bay Area Indian community:

> The "Stoic, Silent Redman" of the past who turned the other cheek to white injustice is dead. (He died of frustration and heartbreak.) And in his place is an angry group of Indians who dare to speak up and voice their dissatisfaction at the world around them. Hate and despair have taken their toll and only action can quiet this smoldering anger that has fused this new Indian movement into being.

The rhetoric of Indian self-determination can be traced to the early 1960s, when Melvin Thom, a Paiute Indian from Walker River, Nevada, cofounder and president of the NIYC, recognized the need to alleviate the poverty, unemployment, and degrading lifestyles forced on both urban and reservation Indians. Thom realized that it was essential that Indian people, Indian tribes, and Indian sovereign rights not be compromised in the search for solutions to the many problems. Thom said, "Our recognition as Indian people and Indian tribes is very dear to us. We cannot work to destroy our lives as Indian people." Thom recognized that family, tribalism, and sovereignty had sustained Indian people through the many U.S. government programs designed to destroy them as a people and to nationalize Indian traditional lands. The official policy of the federal government, dating back to 1953, was termination of the relationship between the federal government and Indian communities. Termination would mean that Indian tribes would eventually lose any special relationship they had under federal law. They would lose the tax-exempt status of their lands; the federal government no longer would be responsible for their economic and social well-being; and the tribes themselves would be effectively destroyed. Thom described the termination policy as a "cold war" fought against Indian people:

> The opposition to Indians is a monstrosity which cannot be beaten by any single action, unless we as Indian people could literally rise up, in unison, and take what is ours by force. . . . We know the odds are against us, but we also realize that we are fighting for

the lives of future Indian generations. . . . We are convinced, more than ever, that this is a real war. No people in this world ever has been exterminated without putting up a last resistance. The Indians are gathering.

Indian people wanted self-determination rather than termination. This included the right to assume control of their own lives independent of federal control; the creation of conditions for a new era in which the Indian future would be determined by Indian acts and Indian decisions; and the assurance that Indian people would not be separated involuntarily from their tribal groups. . . .

[A]ctivism . . . actually began to build in the 1950s, with more than twenty major demonstrations or nonviolent protests by Indian people. The demonstrations were aimed at ending further reductions of the Indian land base, stopping the termination of Indian tribes, and halting brutality and insensitivity toward Indian people. This rise in Indian activism was largely tribal in nature, however; very little, if any, pan-Indian or supratribal activity occurred. The militancy was primarily a phenomenon of traditional people typified by the participation of elders, medicine people, and entire communities, not the forging of alliances outside of tribal boundaries such as would later occur during the Alcatraz occupation.

In the 1950s, the Six Nations used passive resistance and militant protests to block various New York State projects. Tuscarora and Mohawk people demonstrated in opposition to the building of power projects such as the Fort Randall Dam on the Missouri River and the Kinzua Dam in upstate New York, which required the displacement of Indians and the flooding of Indian land. In 1957, Anderson, a Tuscarora Indian, helped the Mohawk fend off a New York State income tax, on the grounds of Indian sovereignty on Indian reservations. Anderson led a protest group of several hundred Indians from the St. Regis Reservation to the Massena, New York, courthouse, where they tore up summonses for nonpayment of state taxes.

In April 1958, Mad Bear Anderson led a stand against the tide of land seizures, a move that ultimately brought armed troops onto Indian land. The New York Power Authority, directed by chairman Robert Moses, planned to expropriate 1,383 acres of Tuscarora land to build a reservoir and back-flood of Indian lands. Anderson and others blocked surveyors' transits and deflated vehicle tires as harassment tactics. When Power Authority workers tapped the Indian leaders' telephones, Tuscarora people switched to speaking their tribal language. When the Tuscarora refused to accept the state's offer to purchase the land, one hundred armed state troopers and police invaded Tuscarora lands. The troops were met by a nonviolent front of 150 men, women, and children, led by Anderson, blocking the road by lying down or standing in front of government trucks. At the same time, Seneca and Mohawk people set up camps on the disputed land, challenging the state to remove them. Anderson and other leaders were arrested, but the media attention forced the power company to back down. The Federal Power Commission ruled that the Indians did not have to sell the land and the tribe did not sell. The *Buffalo Courier Express* reported that Mad Bear Anderson, more than anyone else, was responsible for the tribe's decision.

Following the Six Nations' success in New York State, the Miccosukee Indian Nation of Florida summoned Anderson to help fight the federal government's attempt to take land from them as part of the Everglades Reclamation Project. In 1959, several hundred Indian people marched on BIA headquarters in Washington,

D.C., protesting the government policy of termination of Indian tribes and attempting a citizen's arrest of the Indian commissioner. In California, Nevada, and Utah, the Pit River Indians, led by Chief Ray Johnson, refused $29.1 million of claims case money awarded by the government and demanded return of their traditional lands. The Pit River Indian people carried on their battle for return of their lands until 1972, at which time they reached a negotiated settlement for partial restoration of land, along with monetary compensation.

The 1960s witnessed a continuation of localized Indian protest actions such as the brief Indian occupation of Alcatraz Island in 1964. Preceding this event, however, and attracting more of a national audience were the "fish-ins" along the rivers of Washington State. The fish-in demonstrations provided Washington Indian youth with an opportunity to express their disillusionment and dissatisfaction with American society and also to actively protest the social conditions endured by their people. Celebrities such as Marlon Brando lent their names to bring national media coverage of the protest actions. Indian people who participate in the fish-ins would later lend their assistance to the occupiers on Alcatraz Island.

In the summer of 1968, UNA was founded in the San Francisco Bay Area. Many of the Indian occupiers of Alcatraz Island were, or had been, members of UNA; many more were strongly influenced by the organization. UNA had a pan-Indian focus and sought to unify all persons of Indian blood throughout the Americas and to develop a democratic, grassroots organization. Its goal was to promote self-determination through Indian control of Indian affairs at every level. Lehman Brightman was the first president of UNA.

Nineteen-sixty-eight closed with a confrontation between Canada, the United States, and members of the Iroquois Nation. Canada had been restricting the free movement of Mohawk Indians (members of the Iroquois Nation) between the United States and Canada, demanding that the Mohawk pay tolls to use the bridge and pay customs on goods brought back from the United States. Members of the Iroquois League felt that this was an infringement of their treaty rights granted by Great Britain, and members of the Mohawk tribe confronted Canadian officials as a means of forcing the issues of tolls and customs collection on the Cornwall International Bridge (the St. Lawrence Seaway International Bridge) between the two countries. The protest was specifically over Canadian failure to honor the Jay Treaty of 1794 between Canada and the United States.

A number of Mohawk Indians were arrested for blockading the Cornwall Bridge on 18 December 1968, but when they pressed for presentation of their case in the court system, the Canadian government dismissed the charges. This protest action was not without precedent, however. In 1928, the Indian Defense League, founded in 1926, had argued that unrestricted rights for Indians to trade and travel across the U.S.-Canadian border existed based on the Jay Treaty of 1794 and the Treaty of Ghent in 1814. But it was not until the 1969 concession that the Canadian government formally recognized these rights, under Article III of the treaty, and allowed Indians to exchange goods across the border, duty-free, and permitted unrestricted travel between the countries.

The 1968–69 Cornwall Bridge confrontation also brought about the creation of an Indian newspaper called *Akwesasne Notes,* which began as an effort to bring news to Indian people regarding the international bridge crisis by reprinted articles from diverse newspapers. Edited by Jerry Gambill, a non-Indian employed by the Canadian Department of Indian Affairs, *Akwesasne Notes* developed into a national Indian newspaper with a circulation of nearly fifty thousand and providing full coverage of the Cornwall Bridge incident. As a result, Cornwall Bridge became a prominent discussion topic of Indians across the nation. The influence of the Iroquois power movement of December 1968 and January 1969 that occurred on the Saint Regis Mohawk Reservation in New York and Canada is considerable. Out of this confrontation grew not only *Akwesasne Notes,* which would provide the Alcatraz occupation an Indian media voice, but two other influences as well, both of considerable import. In addition to founding *Akwesasne Notes,* Jerry Gambill assisted Ernest Benedict, a Mohawk Indian, in establishing the North American Indian Traveling College and the White Roots of Peace, a Mohawk group committed to the preservation of leadership in the Mohawk Longhouse. The White Roots of Peace harked back to an earlier Mohawk group, Akwesasne Counselor Organization, founded by Ray Fadden, a Mohawk Indian, in the mid 1930s. The counselor organization had "traveled far and wide inculcating Indian pride among Mohawk youth . . . hoping to influence a group of young Mohawk . . . to take up leadership roles in the Mohawk Longhouse." This was largely an attempt by Fadden and other Mohawk people to preserve and revive Iroquois lifeways. Seeing the spiritual crisis caused by the death of key elders and the movement of many young Indians away from the faith, Gambill founded this organization, which was committed, through speaking engagements to Indian and non-Indian communities and school audiences, to preserving tradition by bringing back the Great Binding Law.

In addition to the rise in activism among the Mohawk, the Miccosukee, the Pit River Indians, and the Bay Area Indians mentioned above, the Taos Pueblo Indians of New Mexico also reasserted their claims to ancestral lands in the 1960s. In 1906, the United States government appropriated the Taos Blue Lake area, a sacred site belonging to the Taos Pueblo Indians, and incorporated it into the Carson National Forest. In 1926, the Taos Indians, in reply to a compensation offer made by the U.S. government, waived the award, seeking return of Blue Lake instead. As a result, they got neither the compensation nor Blue Lake. On 31 May 1933, the Senate Indian Affairs Committee recommended that the Taos Indians be issued a permit to use Blue Lake for religious purposes. The permit was finally issued in 1940. On 13 August 1951, Taos Indians filed a suit before the Indian Claims Commission, seeking judicial support for the validity of title to the lake. On 8 September 1965, the Indian Claims Commission affirmed that the U.S. government had taken the area unjustly from its rightful owners, the Taos Pueblo Indians. On 15 March 1966, legislation was introduced to return Blue Lake to the Taos Indians; however, the bill died without action in the Senate Interior and Insular Affairs Subcommittee. On 10 May 1968, House Bill 3306 was introduced to restore the sacred area to the Taos Indians. Although it passed the House of Representatives unanimously, it once again died in the Senate Interior and Insular Affairs Subcommittee.

The return of Taos Blue Lake would become the centerpiece of the Indian policy for the incoming Nixon presidential administration. Two other significant events also had a strong effect on Nixon's developing policy of Indian self-determination. The first was the receipt of Alvin M. Josephy, Jr.'s study of the BIA entitled *The American Indian and the Bureau of Indian Affairs—1969, A Study with*

Recommendations. Josephy's report, completed on 24 February 1969, chastises the federal government for its ineptitude in the handling of Indian affairs. Specifically, the report condemns the failure of the various presidencies to affect any change in the multilayered, bureaucratically inept BIA, the failure of the government policy in Indian education, and the high rates of unemployment, disease, and death on Indian reservations that resulted from neglect of Indian people by the federal government. The second significant event that affected Nixon's developing policy of Indian self-determination was the publication of Edgar S. Cahn's edited book *Our Brother's Keeper: The Indian in White America.* Published in 1969, *Our Brother's Keeper* is a study of the ineptitude of the BIA and an indictment of the agency for its failure to carry out its responsibilities to the American Indian people. Recognizing that Indian people have been studied to death, *Our Brother's Keeper* highlights the numerous studies, all conducted by non-Indians with one exception, and states that "recommendations have come to have a special non-meaning for Indians. They are part of a tradition in which policy and programs are dictated by non-Indians even when dialogue and consultation have been promised."

Nixon's announced policy of self-determination would also be tested in California, particularly the Bay Area, which had become the hotbed for the newly developing Indian activism. Jack Forbes, a Powhatan/Lenape Indian and a professor of Native American studies and anthropology at the University of California, Davis, became advisor and mentor to many of the new Indian students. In the spring of 1969, Forbes drafted a proposal for a College of Native American Studies to be created on one of the University of California campuses. American Indian or Native American studies programs were already being formed on the various college campuses in California, such as the University of California at Berkeley, the University of California, Los Angeles, and San Francisco State College. These programs grew out of the Third World student strikes in progress on the various campuses and included Indian students who would soon be intimately involved in the Alcatraz occupation: Richard Oakes, Ross Harden, Joe Bill, Dennis Turner, LaNada Boyer, and Horace Spencer.

On 30 June 1969, the California legislature endorsed Forbes's proposal for the creation of a separate Indian-controlled university. Forbes wrote to John G. Veneman, assistant secretary, Health, Education, and Welfare, and requested that Veneman look into the availability of a 650-acre site between Winter and Davis, California, as a possible site for an Indian-controlled university. Additionally, in 1969, the Native American Student Union was formed in California, creating a pan-Indian alliance between the newly emerging Native American studies program on the various campuses. In San Francisco members of the Native American Student Union prepared to test Nixon's commitment to his stated policy of self-determination before a national audience by occupying Alcatraz Island. For Indian people of the Bay Area, the social movements of the 1960s had not only come to full maturity but now would include Indian people. The heightened social awareness generated by the highly unpopular war in Vietnam, the Black Panther movement, the New Left generation, the Third World strikes, the emerging LaRaza movement, and the nascent feminist movement provided a sympathetic national audience for a new Indian activism. In November 1969, Indian people moved onto the national scene of ethnic unrest as active participants in a war of their own. Alcatraz Island was the battlefield.

In actuality, there were three separate occupations of Alcatraz Island. The first was a brief, four-hour occupation on 9 March 1964, during which five Sioux Indians, representing the urban Indians of the Bay Area, occupied the island. The event was planned by Belva Cottier, the wife of one of the occupiers. The federal penitentiary on the island had been closed in 1963, and the government was in the process of transferring the island to the city of San Francisco for development. Meanwhile, Belva Cottier and her Sioux cousin developed plans of their own. They recalled having heard of a provision in the 1868 Sioux treaty with the federal government stating that all abandoned federal lands reverted to ownership by the Sioux people. Using this interpretation of the treaty, they encouraged five Sioux men to occupy Alcatraz Island and claim it for the Sioux people. They issued press releases claiming the island in accordance with the 1868 Sioux treaty and demanded better treatment for urban Indians. Richard McKenzie, the most outspoken of the group, pressed the claim for title to the island through the court system, only to have the courts rule against him. More importantly, however, the Indians of the Bay Area were becoming vocal and united in their efforts to improve their lives.

The 1964 occupation of Alcatraz Island was a forewarning of the unrest that was fermenting, quietly but surely, in the urban Indian population. Prior to the 1964 occupation, Bay Area newspapers contained a large number of articles about the federal government's abandonment of urban Indians and the state and local governments' refusal to meet their needs. The social clubs that had been formed for support became meeting places for Indian people to discuss the discrimination they were facing in schools, housing, employment, and health care. They also talked about the police, who, like law officers in other areas of the country, would wait outside of Indian bars at closing time to harass, beat, and arrest Indian patrons. Indian centers began to appear in all the urban relocation areas and became nesting grounds for new pan-Indian, and eventually activist, organizations.

The second Alcatraz occupation came out of the Bay Area colleges and universities and other California college campuses, where young, educated Indian students joined with other minority groups during the 1969 Third World Liberation Front strike and began demanding that colleges offer courses relevant to Indian students. Indian history written and taught by non-Indian instructors was no longer acceptable to these young students, who were awakened to the possibility of social protest to bring attention to the shameful treatment of Indian people.

Among the Indian students at San Francisco State was a young Mohawk named Richard Oakes. Oakes came from the St. Regis Reservation, had worked on high steel in New York, and had traveled across the United States, visiting various Indian reservations. He eventually had reached California, where he married a Kashia Pomo woman who had five children from a previous marriage. Oakes worked in an Indian bar in Oakland for a period of time and eventually was admitted to San Francisco State. In September 1969, he and several other Indian students began discussing the possibility of occupying Alcatraz Island as a symbolic protest, a call for Indian self-determination. Preliminary plans were made for a symbolic occupation to take place in the summer of 1970, but other events caused an earlier execution of the plan.

The catalyst for the occupation was the destruction of the San Francisco Indian Center by fire in late October 1969. The center had become a meeting place for Bay Area Indian organizations and the newly formed United Bay Area Indian Council, which had brought the thirty private clubs together into one large organization headed by Adam Nordwall (later to be known as Adam Fortunate Eagle). The destruction of the Indian center united the council and the American Indian student organizations as never before. The council needed a new meeting place, and the students needed a forum for their new activist voice.

After the fire, the second occupation of Alcatraz Island was planned for 9 November 1969. Richard Oakes and the other Indian college students, along with a group of people from the San Francisco Indian Center, chartered a boat and headed for Alcatraz Island. Since many different tribes were represented, the group adopted the name *Indians of All Tribes.*

The initial plan was to circle the island and symbolically claim it for Indian people. During the circling maneuver, however, Richard and four others jumped from the boat and swam to the island. They claimed Alcatraz in the name of Indians of All Tribes and left the island after meeting with the caretaker, who asked them to leave. Later that same evening, Oakes and fourteen others returned to the island with sleeping bags and food sufficient for two or three days; they left the island the following morning without incident.

In meetings following the 9 November occupation, Oakes and his fellow students realized that a prolonged occupation was possible. It was clear that the federal government had only a token force on the island and that no physical harm had come to anyone involved. A new plan began to emerge.

Following the brief 9 November occupation, Oakes traveled to UCLA, where he met with Ray Spang and Edward Castillo and asked for their assistance in recruiting Indian students for what would become the longest Indian occupation of a federal facility to this very day. Spang, Castillo, and Oakes met in UCLA's Campbell Hall, now the home of the American Indian Studies Center and the editorial offices of the *American Indian Culture and Research Journal,* in private homes, and in Indian bars in Los Angeles. On 20 November 1969, the eighty Indian people who occupied Alcatraz Island included seventy Indian students from UCLA.

The occupation of Alcatraz would last nineteen months and would bring together Indian people from across the United States, Alaska, Canada, Mexico, and South America. Most importantly, Alcatraz would force the federal government to take a new look at the situation faced by urban Indian people, the long-forgotten victims of a failed relocation program.

The federal government, for its part, insisted that the Indian people leave and placed an ineffective coast guard barricade around the island. Eventually, the government agreed to the Indian council's demands for formal negotiations, but, from the Indians' side, the demands were nonnegotiable. They wanted the deed to the island; they wanted to establish an Indian university, a cultural center, and a museum; and they wanted federal funding to establish all of these. The government negotiators turned down their demands and insisted that they leave the island.

By the end of 1969, the Indian organization on the island began to fall into disarray. Two groups rose in opposition to Richard Oakes, and, as the Indian students began returning to school in January 1970, they were replaced by Indian people from urban areas and reservations who had not been involved in the initial occupation. Where Oakes and the other students claimed title to the island by right of discovery, the new arrivals harked back to the rhetoric of the 1964 occupation and the Sioux treaty, a claim that had been passed through the court system by Richard McKenzie and had been found invalid. Additionally, some non-Indians now began taking up residency on the island, many from the San Francisco hippie and drug culture. Drugs and liquor had been banned from the island by the original occupiers, but they now became commonplace.

The final blow to the early student occupation occurred on 5 January 1970, when Richard Oakes's twelve-year-old stepdaughter fell three floors down a stairwell to her death. Yvonne Oakes and some other children apparently had been playing unsupervised near an open stairwell when she slipped and fell. Following Yvonne's death, the Oakes family left the island, and the two remaining groups maneuvered back and forth for leadership. Despite changes of leadership, however, the demands of the occupiers remained consistent: title to Alcatraz Island, the development of an Indian university, and the construction of a museum and cultural center that would display and teach the valuable contributions of Indian people to the non-Indian society.

By this time, the attention of the federal government had shifted from negotiations with the island occupants to restoration of navigational aids to the Bay Area—aids that had been discontinued as the result of a fire on Alcatraz Island and the discontinuance of electrical service. The government's inability to restore the navigational aids brought criticism from the coast guard, the Bay Area Pilot's Association, and local newspapers. The federal government now became impatient. On 11 June 1971, the message went out to end the occupation of Alcatraz Island that had begun on 20 November 1969.

The success or failure of the Indian occupation of Alcatraz Island should not be judged by whether the demands for title to the island and the establishment of educational and cultural institutions were realized. If one were to make such a judgment, the only possible answer would be that the occupation was a failure. Such is not the case, however. The underlying goals of the Indians on Alcatraz were to awaken the American public to the reality of the plight of the First Americans and to assert the need for Indian self-determination. In this they were indeed successful. Additionally, the occupation of Alcatraz Island was a springboard for Indian activism, inspiring the large number of takeovers and demonstrations that began shortly after the 20 November 1969 landing and continued into the late 1970s. Many of the approximately seventy-four occupations that followed Alcatraz were either planned by or included people who had been involved in the Alcatraz occupation or who certainly had gained their strength from the new "Indianness" that grew out of that movement.

American Indian activism and broken Indian treaties once again grabbed the newspaper headlines and America's attention in October and November 1972 when more than five hundred Indian protesters participated in the "Trail of Broken Treaties" (the march on Washington and the occupation of the BIA building). The idea for a Trail of Broken Treaties began at the Sioux Rosebud Reservation in 1972 as an attempt to sensitize both the Republican and Democratic parties to the problems faced by Indian people. Although there was enthusiastic support in every section of Indian Country for such a protest march, a catalyst was needed to serve as the focal point. On 21 September 1972, Richard Oakes was shot to death by a YMCA guard in northern California. AIM leaders, including Russell Means, Hank Adams, and Sid Mills, held a press conference in Seattle to denounce the killing of Oakes. One week following Oakes's death, approximately fifty Indians gathered at the New Albany Hotel in Denver to formalize the concept of the Indian pilgrimage to Washington, D.C. Plans called for one part of the caravan to begin on the West Coast. Those coming from the Southeast followed the Cherokee Trail of Tears; the Sioux passed by Wounded Knee, the site of the massacre in 1890. When the caravan arrived in Washington and found that the accommodations promised them were not available, the group moved to the BIA headquarters building. On 2 November 1972, in a disagreement over housing and food provisions, members of the Trail of Broken Treaties occupied and barricaded the BIA building and presented a list of twenty civil rights demands that had been drawn up during the march. The Indians occupied the BIA building for seven days. Eventually, the government promised to review the demands, refrain from making arrests, and pay the Indians' expenses home. The occupation was a great moral victory for the Indians, who, for the first time, faced white America as a united people. The two governmental negotiators were Brad Patterson and Leonard Garment, who had overseen the Alcatraz occupation for the government. Although many of the Alcatraz occupiers participated in the Trail of Broken Treaties, the occupation was directed by AIM and NIYC. Other sponsoring groups included the National Indian Brotherhood of Canada, Survival of American Indians, National American Indian Council, Native American Rights Fund, National Council on Indian Work, American Indian Commission of Alcohol and Drug Abuse, and National Indian Leadership Training.

Following the BIA takeover, AIM members led by Dennis Banks and Russell Means responded to an invitation from traditional members of the Oglala Sioux to investigate corruption and mistreatment of tribal members by the Indian Reorganization Act (IRA) tribal government led by Richard "Dicky" Wilson. Charges were made that Wilson and his appointed council misused tribal funds, awarded reservation jobs to Wilson's cronies, and maintained a "goon squad" to intimidate those who opposed him. AIM leaders allied themselves with the traditionalists. Tensions began to mount on 21 January 1973, when Wesley Bad Heart Bull, a local Oglala, was stabbed to death. The white man accused of his death was charged with second-degree manslaughter. On 6 February 1973, as part of an effort to protest the leniency of the charges, Indian demonstrators stormed the courthouse in Custer, South Dakota, and set the courthouse on fire. National guardsmen were called to active duty as tensions mounted and Indian people clashed with national guard troops and local police, including Wilson's goon squad.

On the afternoon of 27 February 1973, approximately two hundred members and supporters of AIM gathered at Calico Hall, near the community of Pine Ridge, some carrying rifles, pistols, and knives. That evening a car caravan departed Calico Hall and slowly wound its way to Wounded Knee, South Dakota, the site of the 1890 Wounded Knee Massacre. Tensions between the protesters and the local authorities grew until the situation became a siege of the town, which lasted for seventy-one days. The Indian occupiers were surrounded by three hundred federal marshals and FBI agents, equipped with armored personnel carriers (APCs), M-16s, automatic infantry weapons, chemical weapons, steel helmets, gas masks, body armor, illuminating flares, military clothing, and rations. The army's 82nd airborne division provided leadership and logistical support for the government "peace-keeping" force. On 12 March 1973 the Indian occupiers declared Wounded Knee a sovereign territory of the new Oglala Sioux Nation according to the Laramie Treaty of 1868, which recognized the Sioux as an independent nation. The siege finally ended on the morning of 8 May, when the two sides began firing on each other and two Indians, Frank Clearwater and Lawrence (Buddy) Lamont, were shot and killed, an act that called national attention to the Native American civil rights movement. Two hundred thirty-seven arrests were made during the course of the seventy-one-day occupation, and thirty-five weapons were confiscated. The primary leaders of the Wounded Knee takeover were members of AIM, supported by a coalition of organizations including former occupiers of Alcatraz Island.

The murder of Wesley Bad Heart Bull and the occupation of Wounded Knee were symptomatic of the problems faced by Indian people on reservations throughout the United States, with Pine Ridge being perhaps the most violent. The corruption and protest did not end with the Wounded Knee occupation however. Following the end of the occupation, terror stalked the small community. While AIM leaders sat in jails and prisons, went into hiding, or awaited trial, atrocities continued. It is estimated that, following the Wounded Knee occupation, some 250 Oglala people, many of whom were AIM members or participants in the Wounded Knee occupation, disappeared from the face of the earth. The IRA tribal police, under Wilson's control, and the FBI refused to investigate the disappearances, and newspapers failed to cover the stories. It was not until June 1975 that events on Pine Ridge again captured national attention.

On 26 June 1975, a shootout occurred on the Pine Ridge Reservation between AIM members and the FBI, resulting in the death of an Indian man, Joseph Stuntz, and two FBI agents, Jack Coler and Ronald Williams. Following the incident, the FBI reported that the agents had been ambushed from sophisticated bunkers and were riddled with bullets as they attempted to serve arrest warrants. Officials later admitted that the initial reports were false and that it was unclear exactly what had happened. An FBI spokesman in Washington told newsmen, "We're going to make sure that the people who killed our agents don't get out of there."

The original reports that the two FBI agents were ambushed and killed with repeated blasts of gunfire were later found to be inflammatory, distorted, and inaccurate. FBI agents claimed that they were serving arrest warrants, but AIM members state that "they came in shooting." Falling on the heels of the large number of disappearances, the FBI decided to investigate; two of their own had been killed. As a result, FBI agents swarmed all over the reservation. The U.S. Commission on Civil Rights later condemned the FBI's "full-scale military-style invasion" of the Pine Ridge Reservation.

Despite conflicting evidence and the withholding of evidence by the FBI, Leonard Peltier was arrested, charged, and convicted for the murder of the FBI agents and is currently serving two life prison sentences. American Indian people continue to protest against the imprisonment of Peltier. They have demanded that the case against Peltier be reopened based on new information that allegedly proves FBI involvement in the manufacturing and withholding of evidence used to convict Peltier. The death of Joseph Stuntz went unpunished.

The years following 1975 saw a shift in American Indian activism away from a national agenda led by AIM to a focus on specific issues and local problems, some with national implications. These included the continuing fight over treaty fishing rights, protection of sacred sites for the practice of traditional religions, the repatriation of human skeletal remains and associated funerary objects, as well as the protection of gaming on Indian reservations as a function of tribal sovereignty. As a result of federal government infiltration under the CONTERINTELPRO program and internal dissension among leaders, AIM split into smaller regional chapters with no national organization. Dennis Banks, Russell Means, and Clyde Bellecourt pursued different agendas that prevented them from coming together as a unified force. In 1982 Dennis Banks called for a meeting to be held in San Francisco. His goal was to pull AIM together as a national organization once again. Although some consensus was reached and 250 people responded to AIM's call for a Walk for Religious Freedom, no sustaining national organization emerged. AIM continues to represent Indian people today when called upon and to press for fair treatment and recognition of rights guaranteed by U.S. Indian treaties. The organization continues to do this primarily from state or local chapters rather than a strong national organization with the charismatic leadership of people such as Banks, Means, Bellecourt, and John Trudell. . . .

◈ *F U R T H E R   R E A D I N G*

Akwesasne Notes, *Trail of Broken Treaties: BIA, I'm Not Your Indian Any More* (1974)
———, *Voices From Wounded Knee, 1973, in the Words of the Participants* (1974)
Thomas R. Berger, *Village Journey: The Report of the Alaska Native Review Commission* (1985)
Joy A. Bilharz, *The Allegany Senecas and Kinzua Dam: Forced Relocation Through Two Generations* (1998)
Peter Blue Cloud, *Alcatraz Is Not An Island* (1972)
Paul Brodeur, *Restitution: The Land Claims of the Mashpee, Passamaquoddy, and Penobscot Indians of New England* (1985)
David M. Brugge, *The Navajo-Hopi Land Dispute: An American Tragedy* (1994)
Robert Burnette and John Koster, *The Road to Wounded Knee* (1974)
Jack Campisi, *The Mashpee Indians: Tribe on Trial* (1991)
George P. Castile, *To Show Heart: Native American Self-Determination and Federal Indian Policy, 1960–1975* (1998)
Fay G. Cohen, *Treaties on Trial: The Continuing Controversy Over Northwest Fishing Rights* (1986)
Stephen E. Cornell, *The Return of the Native: American Indian Political Resurgence* (1988)
Philip J. Delona, *Playing Indian* (1998)
Vine Deloria, Jr., *Behind the Trail of Broken Treaties: An Indian Declaration of Independence* (1974)
———, *Custer Died For Your Sins: An Indian Manifesto* (1969)
———, *We Talk, You Listen: New Tribes, New Turf* (1970)
Estelle Fuchs and Robert Havighurst, *To Live On This Earth: American Indian Education* (1972)
Mario Gonzalez and Elizabeth Cook-Lynn, *The Politics of Hallowed Ground: Wounded Knee and the Struggle for Indian Sovereignty* (1998)
R. C. Gordon-McCutchan, *The Taos Indians and the Battle for Blue Lake* (1991)
Alexandra Harmon, *Indians in the Making: Ethnic Relations and Indian Identities Around Puget Sound* (1998)

Laurence M. Hauptman, *Formulation of American Indian Policy in New York State, 1970–1986* (1988)

Peter Iverson, *The Navajo Nation* (1981)

Troy R. Johnson, *The Occupation of Alcatraz Island: Indian Self-Determination and the Rise of Indian Activism* (1996)

———, Joane Nagel and Duane Champagne, eds., *American Indian Activism: Alcatraz to the Longest Walk* (1997)

Alvin M. Josephy, Jr., ed., *Red Power: The American Indians' Fight for Freedom* (1971)

Jerry Kammer, *The Second Long Walk: The Navajo-Hopi Land Dispute* (1980)

Stuart Levine and Nancy Lurie, eds., *The American Indian Today* (1966)

D'Arcy McNickle, *Wind From an Enemy Sky* (1978)

N. Scott Momaday, *House Made of Dawn* (1968)

Joane Nagel, *American Indian Ethnic Renewal: Red Power and the Resurgence of Identity and Culture* (1996)

John William Sayer, *Ghost Dancing the Law: The Wounded Knee Trials* (1997)

Leslie Marmon Silko, *Ceremony* (1977)

Paul Chaat Smith and Robert Allen Warrior, *Like a Hurricane: The Indian Movement From Alcatraz to Wounded Knee* (1996)

Sam Stanley, ed., *American Indian Economic Development* (1978)

Stan Steiner, *The New Indians* (1968)

Kenneth S. Stern, *Loud Hawk: The United States Versus the American Indian Movement* (1994)

Jack O. Waddell and O. Michael Watson, eds., *The American Indian in Urban Society* (1971)

James Welch, *The Death of Jim Loney* (1979)

———, *Winter in the Blood* (1974)

Robert White, *Tribal Assets: The Rebirth of Indian America* (1990)

CHAPTER

15

Continuing Challenges, Continuing Peoples, 1981–1999

◈

If the final two decades of the twentieth century reflected challenges for American Indians, they also demonstrated conclusively that in many ways a new century could be faced with optimism. Individually and collectively, Native peoples confront complex and central questions about schooling for their children, health care, employment, housing, and their relationship to other Americans. Gaming, mineral and water resources, tourism, and other concerns create opportunities as well as dilemmas. In some ways, Indian communities have faced challenges comparable to those in other rural American communities; yet in other respects, because of their unique historical and legal standing and experience, they are indeed separate. Why do so many Americans resist the notion of a unique historical and legal standing for American Indians?

Although debate goes on about Indians' place and status in America, there was no doubt, as the twentieth century drew to a close, that the image of the vanishing Indian has proved a myth. In fact there were far more Native Americans in 1999 than there had been in 1899. In 1999, Richard West (Cheyenne), director, and other associates broke ground for a new National Museum of the American Indian to be constructed on the mall in Washington, D.C. Native art, music, and literature have flourished. An unprecedented number of contemporary Indians have entered medicine, law, engineering, and other professions. Powwows, rodeos, and other forums have evolved to permit people from different tribes the chance to be with, compete with, and learn from one another. Five hundred years and more after Columbus, American Indians remain as distinct entities within North American life.

◈ D O C U M E N T S

Economic development has always been a pressing concern within Indian communities. One of the contemporary Indian communities to have enjoyed significant success in this regard has been the Mississippi Band of Choctaw. The long-time leader of this group, Philip Martin, presents in Document 1 his assessment of some of the key issues facing his people and other Indian nations in regard to economic development.

James Riding In (Pawnee), a professor of justice studies at Arizona State University, has gained national prominence for his role in pushing for the repatriation of sacred and secular objects to their proper place within Indian communities. In Document 2, Riding In offers his perspective on this vital concern.

Charlene Teters (Spokane) has been outspoken in her concern over the symbols and images of Native people. She has campaigned tirelessly in an effort to educate non-Indian individuals about the offensiveness of employing Indians a mascots for athletic teams. In Document 3, she raises a question about what kind of history we should (and should not) celebrate.

In 1998 a major new Indian museum opened in the Mashantucket Pequot community of southeastern Connecticut. This remarkable facility was made possible through the profits gleaned from the community's enormously successful casino. In Document 4, Ben Winton (Yaqui) addresses the significance of the new museum.

One of the most pressing cultural concerns for most Native communities concerned the preservation and revitalization of their languages. In Document 5, Liz Dominguez (Chumash/Yokuts/Luiseño) considers this issue in an especially poignant way.

1. Philip Martin (Choctaw) Discusses the Challenges of Economic Development, 1988

I intend to speak to you . . . as a person who has been actively involved in a tribal government for 30 years, and who more recently has overseen the creation of over 1200 private sector manufacturing jobs on the Mississippi Choctaw reservation. This economic take-off for our tribe has been accomplished both through negotiations with present-day major national corporations . . . and through internal economic planning involving a choice of strategies. . . .

First, some background on the Mississippi Band of Choctaw Indians. The 4,500 members of the tribe, descendants of the Choctaw people who resisted the forced removals to Oklahoma between 1830 and 1907, live on and near 22,000 acres of reservation land scattered over eight counties in rural, east central Mississippi. Our region is hilly, remote, and agrarian, though it has never been an area for large crop production—the main natural resource is timber. The region as a whole is economically underdeveloped; and for many years the Choctaw people were at the bottom of the economic and social ladders, practically all of them subsisting as sharecroppers during the period between the Civil War and the 1960's, when agriculture was mechanized. Throughout, the tribe's culture was zealously preserved, so that even today 95 per cent of tribal households speak exclusively Choctaw in the home.

The tribe organized itself under the provisions of the Indian Reorganization Act in 1945, at which time a Tribal Council was established and the tribe became self-governing, at least on paper. In reality, the tribal government exercised few formal powers, and was ruled by the local Bureau of Indian Affairs staff. . . .

By the late 1950's, though, large numbers of tribal members had been hit by the agricultural decline, the unemployment rate was reaching toward 80 per cent,

From Philip Martin, "Comments on Economic Dependency in Indian Communities," in D'Arcy McNickle Center for the History of the American Indian, *Overcoming Economic Dependency,* Occasional Papers in Curriculum Series, no. 9 (1988), 58–61. Copyright © 1988 by D'Arcy McNickle Center for American Indian History.

and the local leaders who began to emerge, many of them veterans of the military services, began to look toward the tribal government as an instrument for change. This change was facilitated by two major pieces of federal legislation from 1964; the Civil Rights Act, which opened the local job market to some extent to member of the tribe; and the Economic Opportunity Act, which granted us the resources to start local community action programs that could begin to address the basic needs of our people that had long been denied, including inadequate nutrition, lack of income, low educational levels, and lack of employment. At around the same time, the first high school opened on the reservation; and our students were no longer required to travel to Oklahoma or North Carolina for their secondary educations.

Based upon an accumulation of these federal programs, first from the Office of Economic Opportunity, then from the traditional Indian agencies, the BIA and IHS, and other federal discretionary grants, the tribal government developed itself into a strong and creative institution. Early on, we centralized administrative functions, established definitive policies and procedures for a wide range of tribal governmental activities (finance, personnel, elections), and were the first tribe to obtain a federal indirect cost rate to finance the management of the tribal government. The strengthening of the tribal government was a gradual process that took place between the late 60's and 1979, perhaps the most important step of which was a revision of the Tribal Constitution in 1975, which separated the tribal executive and legislative branches, and increased the terms for tribal officials, including members of the Tribal Council, from two years to four. It also staggered the terms of Council members, so that at any one time there were always at least eight of the 16 total who had experience in governmental service.

Once efficiency and stability had been brought to the tribal government, and the unemployment rate had been lowered somewhat through the creation of jobs in the tribal social programs, we were ready to begin to address the overall unemployment problem and the reservation economy.

Actually, we had tried some economic development in the late 60's and early 70's, and were notably unsuccessful—our tribal industrial park produced nothing but hay for about a decade. We fired off letters to major corporations throughout the country, and some even came to visit . . . but none showed any interest. At that time, of course, the tribal government had barely begun to develop, and our reservation was devoid of infrastructure—these and the underdeveloped nature of the entire region meant we really had nothing of significance to offer to the American business establishment.

After we had strengthened the tribal government and had a means to marshall our only resource, the human resource, though, we did have something to offer. . . . [W]e had established a tribal sovereignty which had not existed before, and major corporations were able to perceive that they were dealing with an entity that exercised powers, and, as such, could deliver what they wanted. In all this we had only one environmental advantage that I can think of over some other reservations; because our land base is so small, our work force is concentrated geographically—a prerequisite for manufacturing activity not present on the larger reservations out West, with dispersed populations.

Still, our first, large step forward, was really a gamble on the part of our corporate associates. All economic development involves risk, but the Packard Electric

Division of General Motors, in agreeing to assist us in opening a wiring harness assembly plant on the reservation, was taking a very large risk, because we had no track record. Frankly, they were attracted by what they considered the cheap labor available on the reservation. What they ended up with was a supplier with the highest quality rating of any of their suppliers—one which got them quality products, on time, and at a reasonable price. I firmly believe that at least a part of the cause of this first of our tribal successes was that the plant was wholly tribally owned, operated by a board of directors appointed by the Tribal Council; it was, and continues to be, an extension of the tribal government. Had this first plant been one operated by outsiders, I do not believe we would have succeeded.

Success breeds success. From that start in 1979, we have gone on to build and operate five additional manufacturing plants, and we are working on a sixth. Once the corporations we now call our customers—these include the Ford Motor Company, Chrysler Corporation, Westinghouse, Xerox, Navistar, and (ten years after their first visit to the reservation) American Greeting Corporation—saw our productivity and quality levels at that first plant, they were ready to do business with us. Of course, there continued to be obstacles along the way, especially the necessary but sluggish involvement of the Bureau of Indian Affairs, which continues to exercise its "'patriarchal' and 'dictatorial' rules over tribes. . . ."

Another major reason for our success is that we have pursued a conscious policy of involving our non-Indian neighbors in our industrial development. Our enterprises, which follow a policy of Indian preference in employment, all have work forces of around 70 per cent Choctaws, 15 per cent blacks, and 15 per cent whites. In this way, we have made sure that our economic success is tied to the economic improvement of the entire east central Mississippi region; and it has done much to bind the wounds that Mississippians suffer as a result of the state's former social policies.

I need to tell you something about the tribe's relationship with our corporate customers. . . . Corporate America has not changed all that much—their interest in the bottom line is supreme, and most of their representatives' knowledge of Indian Affairs is limited to stereotypes. Charity is not a part of their action plan; unemployment only interests them insofar as it affects labor force availability. But once you realize that profit is their sole concern, developing a working relationship is not difficult, as long as you have something to offer them.

With Indian people, this is usually labor. But there is another strength we have, that I alluded to before, and this is the quality of our work. There is a sense of cooperation among Indian people that a few centuries of rugged individualism may have diluted in other Americans, which, if managed right, produces high quality results, something that should be used by tribes talking with corporations in their efforts to improve tribal economies. It is an important attribute that does not manifest itself so much in natural resources development or retail sales as it does in the making of things.

. . . We do derive a little income from the sale of our forest products; and we are currently working on a project to establish a chipper plant for on- and off-reservation timber. We are also constructing a shopping center on the reservation. . . . But our primary strategy has been manufacturing based upon competitive bidding for corporate customers on the open market.

Although there has been significant planning and feasibility determination involved with all of this, I must emphasize to you that our activities in this area have been based on the crucial question of survival—of the tribe and of its individual members. It is not as though we have the leisure to really pick and choose our development strategies; whatever will be most productive for us and produce the largest number of jobs, we must pursue. We are, however, now approaching the point where we may be able to spin-off from our labor-intensive concerns, and begin to move into high tech and higher-paying technical jobs; that is, to diversify our economy. Recently, we have begun receiving large numbers of inquiries from smaller, regional concerns interested in doing business with us, which will someday provide our economy with some independence from the upturns and downturns of the large corporations. Already our wage rates on the average are in excess of those paid by other labor-intensive manufacturers in our immediate area. . . .

2. James Riding In Presents a Pawnee Perspective on Repatriation, 1996

The acts committed against deceased Indians have had profound, even harmful, effects on the living. Therefore, as an activist and historian, I have had to develop a conceptual framework for giving meaning and order to the conflict. The foundation of my perspective concerning repatriation is derived from a combination of cultural, personal, and academic experiences. An understanding of Pawnee religious and philosophical beliefs about death, gained through oral tradition, dreams, and research, informs my view that repatriation is a social justice movement, supported by native spirituality and sovereignty, committed to the amelioration of the twin evils of oppression and scientific racism. Yet, I am neither a religious fundamentalist nor a left- or right-wing reactionary. Concerning repatriation, I simply advocate that American Indians receive what virtually every other group of American enjoys; that is, the right to religious freedom and a lasting burial.

My training as critical scholar provides another cornerstone of my beliefs about the nature of "imperial archaeology." My writings cast the legacy of scientific body snatching within the realm of oppression. Oppression occurs when a set or sets of individuals within the dominant population behave in ways that infringe on the beliefs, cultures, and political structures of other groups of people. Acts of stealing bodies, infringing on spirituality, and resisting repatriation efforts represent classic examples of oppression.

Although exposed to years of secular interpretations about the nature of the world and the significance of archaeology for understanding the past through formal Euroamerican education, I have continued to accept Pawnee beliefs about the afterlife. To adopt any other perspective regarding this matter would deny my cultural heritage. I cannot reconcile archaeology with tradition because of the secular orientation of the former as well as its intrusive practices. Unlike archaeologists

From James Riding In, "Repatriation: A Pawnee's Perspective." Reprinted from *American Indian Quarterly,* vol. 20, no. 2 (Spring 1996), 238–250, by permission of the University of Nebraska Press. Copyright © 1996 by the University of Nebraska Press.

who see Native remains as specimens for study, my people view the bodies of deceased loved ones as representing human life with sacred qualities. Death merely marks the passage of the human spirit to another state of being. In a 1988 statement, then Pawnee President Lawrence Goodfox Jr. expressed a common perspective stressing the negative consequences of grave desecration on our dead: "When our people die and go on to the spirit world, sacred rituals and ceremonies are performed. We believe that if the body is disturbed, the spirit becomes restless and cannot be at peace."

Wandering spirits often beset the living with psychological and health problems. Since time immemorial, Pawnees have ceremoniously buried our dead within Mother Earth. Disinterment can occur only for a compelling religious reason. Equally critical to our perspective are cultural norms that stressed that those who tampered with the dead did so with profane, evil, or demented intentions. From this vantage point, the study of stolen remains constitutes abominable acts of sacrilege, desecration, and depravity. But racist attitudes, complete with such axioms as "The only good Indian is a dead Indian," have long conditioned white society to view Indians (as other non-whites) as intellectually inferior subhumans who lacked a right to equal treatment under legal and moral codes. Complicating matters, value judgments about the alleged superiority of the white race became interlocked with scientific thought, leading to the development of oppressive practices and policies.

Consequently, orgies of grave looting occurred without remorse. After the Pawnees removed from Nebraska to Oklahoma during the 1870s, local settlers, followed by amateur and professional archaeologists, looted virtually every Pawnee cemetery they could find, taking remains and burial offerings. Much of the "booty" was placed in an array of institutions including the Nebraska State Historical Society (NSHS) and the Smithsonian Institution.

We have a right to be angry at those who dug our dead from the ground, those who established and maintained curatorial policies, and those who denied our repatriation requests. Last year, my elderly grandmother chastised white society in her typically reserved, but direct fashion for its treatment of our dead. After pointing to an Oklahoma bluff where many Pawnee relatives are buried, she declared, "It is not right, that they dug up all of those bodies in Nebraska." What she referred to can be labeled a spiritual holocaust. When anyone denies us our fundamental human rights, we cannot sit idly by and wait for America to reform itself. It will never happen. We have a duty not only to ourselves, but also to our relatives, our unborn generations, and our ancestors to act. Concerning repatriation, we had no choice but to work for retrieval of our ancestral remains for proper reburial and for legislation that provided penalties for those who disrupted the graves of our relatives.

Yet our initiatives sought redress in a peaceful manner. In 1988, Lawrence Goodfox expressed our goals, declaring "All we want is [the] reburial of the remains of our ancestors and to let them finally rest in peace and for all people in Nebraska to refrain from, forever, any excavation of any Native American graves or burial sites." In our view, reburying the disturbed spirits within Mother Earth equalizes the imbalance between the spiritual and physical worlds caused by the desecration. . . .

3. Charlene Teters (Spokane) Asks "Whose History Do We Celebrate?" 1998

"We took the liberty of removing Don Juan de Oñate's right foot on behalf of our brothers and sisters at Acoma Pueblo."
—*Anonymous letter to the* Albuquerque Journal, *Jan. 8, 1998*

This year marks the Cuartocentenario, the 400th anniversary of the incursion of the Spanish conquistador Don Juan de Oñate from Mexico into what is now Texas, Arizona, and New Mexico. Recently, however, New Mexicans on the verge of a year-long series of celebrations were shocked by the action of an unidentified group whose members sawed off the right foot of a bronze statue of Oñate in the Española Valley north of Santa Fe.

New Mexico, home to one of the largest contemporary American Indian populations, was quickly reminded that Indian people are still here—and that we are not always docile. The disfiguring of the statue also resulted in a quick and powerful history lesson for mainstream America. One of many brutal truths selectively omitted from most history books is this: in 1599, Oñate attacked Acoma Pueblo in retaliation for the death of his nephew, ordering that the right feet of all men in the pueblo above the age of 25 be chopped off.

History is very powerful. The manner in which it is presented has the ability to inspire or deflate, to move nations to love, joy, anger, or hatred. The vast majority of Americans know very little about how this continent—originally peopled by thousands of diverse Indian nations—came to be what is now the United States. This ignorance serves to perpetuate the doctrine of Manifest Destiny, the supposedly inevitable conquest of North America and the islands of the Pacific and the Caribbean. Twenty-five years ago, from Wounded Knee, South Dakota, the American Indian Movement decried the absence of American Indian history in the nation's classrooms. Even today, many remain willfully ignorant of it.

I embrace the concept of personal destiny. I am a survivor, not a victim. And yet during my public school experience, the presentation of American history deeply influenced my self-esteem, as it did for many Native children. I remember trying to become invisible as teachers told stories of brave settlers, untamed lands, and savage, uncivilized Indians. Washington State history simply did not include American Indian history. To this day, it remains largely ignored or distorted in most American schools.

While growing up in Washington State, I also felt the impact of a powerful mural portraying the explorers Lewis and Clark pointing to the western horizon in the direction of my homeland in Washington State. That same mural depicts Indians and other people of color bowed in an all-too-typical posture of servitude before the two glorified travelers. The caption beneath it reads, "The first civilized men to look upon the Inland Empire."

Now, many year later, I still feel the sting of ethnocentric propaganda in public art. As an artist, I know the power of art used to reinforce heroes, icons, and political

From Charlene Teters, "Whose History Do We Celebrate?," in *Indian Artist,* vol. 4, no. 3 (Summer 1998), 14–15. Reprinted with permission. Copyright © 1998 Indian Artist, Inc.

ideology. All across the United States, bronze statues, monuments, and murals celebrate conquests and commemorate the fulfillment of Manifest Destiny.

Art also has a history of effective use in social activism. As the nation celebrates numerous anniversaries—the Quincentennial of Columbus's landing in America, the Oklahoma Land Rush, the California Gold Rush, and the Cuartocentenario—the question is: how do we Indians find appropriate ways to mark these events in our collective history? How do we reconcile that some of America's heroes are not *our* heroes? Glorifying Indian killers feels to us like glorifying Hitler.

Cutting the foot off the Oñate statue in the face of public celebrations forces the issue that there is another side to the notion of conquest. Native artists have often used art to express their own reactions to historical events. But such expression often appears in subversive forms, as our dissenting voices are still largely unwelcome in such national festivities.

Another dissenting voice is Edgar Heap of Birds, a Cheyenne-Arapaho conceptual artist, who responded to Oklahoma's 1989 Land Rush celebrations with a series of five billboards that spelled out the words, "RUN OVER INDIAN NATIONS, APARTHEID OKLAHOMA." Like the sawing off of Oñate's foot, Heap of Birds's caustic message didn't stand in the way of reenactments, parades, and speeches, but it gave voice to a strong and widespread sentiment that was missing in the state-sanctioned celebrations.

Art also provides more mainstream ways of expressing dissent. In a break from tradition this year, the Oakland Museum in California is presenting a series of programs giving expression to California's untold stories. With the museum's blessing, Maidu artist Harry Fonseca has created a body of work entitled *The Discovery of Gold in California,* which explores the impact of the Gold rush on California's Indian population. Similarly, the American Indian House Gallery in New York City is planning a summer exhibition that will express two histories simultaneously: that of the Indians and that of the colonizers.

These two exhibitions are steps in the right direction, because our history is very different from that of the colonizers. For Indians to celebrate many events in American history requires either that we have historical amnesia or that we grant amnesty for the atrocities committed on our populations. The cost of either of these alternatives is too great to pay. It is time we all began acknowledging a more balanced history than that provided by schoolbooks and supermarket tabloids. Together, let us find more ways to honor the victims and survivors of the legacy of conquest, who are also American citizens.

4. Ben Winton (Yaqui) Delineates the Significance of the Mashantucket Pequot Museum, 1998

Dozens of faces peer into the camera. They are friendly, smiling. A man in a business suit stands in the center; to his left women in buckskin dresses hold eagle feathers; young men in tennis shoes and T-shirts relax on the lawn. Some are fair-haired and light-skinned. Others bear the physical traits of their African ancestors

Reprinted with permission from "Ben Winton Delineates the Significance of the Mashuntucket Pequot Museum, 1998," from *Native Peoples,* Fall 1998, 56–60.

who escaped slavery in the southern United States nearly two hundred years ago. A wood-frame house sits in the background, its shingles faded from the wet Connecticut winters. The house is central in the life of this family—yes, they are related—where matriarch Elizabeth George lived until she died in 1973. From this place, she launched the effort to rebuild the great Mashantucket Pequot Nation.

Three hundred and sixty-one years after British soldiers and allied Indian tribes nearly wiped out the Pequots in a predawn raid, members of the Mashantucket Pequot Nation stand proudly for a portrait. These are the descendants of the survivors. For some, their ancestors had escaped into the woodlands. Many had been given to neighboring tribes allied with the British, such as the Mohegans. Others had been given as slaves to non-Indian settlers. This portrait is one small way the Pequots, like so many other Native peoples, are saying, "We are still here."

But the other way they are saying it is much grander. The portrait greets visitors to the 308,000 square-foot Mashantucket Pequot Museum & Research Center, the largest Native-owned and -operated of its kind in North America. It is a place that many are hailing as sacred and scholarly, a place that will set the historical record straight about the Pequots and other Eastern Woodlands peoples, whom the history books had asserted were extinct.

Wilma Mankiller, former principal chief of the Cherokee Nation and a Medal of Honor recipient, says the museum and research center is an eloquent way to fulfill a basic obligation of Native peoples to preserve and advance their cultures. She says, "So, much of who we are as Native peoples has to do with how we remember ourselves. There is little distinction between past and present."

Native elders' lessons nurture the next generation, informing its members how to live. These lessons are reminders of a responsibility to keep the culture alive, Mankiller says. Then, the elders pass on, becoming ancestors. But they are not gone.

"Our ancestors can no longer speak for themselves. It is up to us to speak for them," Mankiller says. "If they could speak today, they would say, 'Look at this museum. They have not forgotten us. We have survived.'"

Indeed, this center honors the ancestors, with life-like re-creations of the land at virtually the beginning of time and of the first peoples to inhabit coastal New England. The journey begins 18,000 years ago, when a mile-thick sheet of ice was beginning to melt and break up, allowing life to spring forth. Visitors to the museum travel through a glacier, feeling the chilly air and an occasional drip of water. Then, they begin their journey forward through time, as life springs forth, observing artistic representations of other tribes' creation stories—Kiowa, Tlingit, Mohave.

At least nine thousand years ago, the first peoples to inhabit what is now coastal New England appeared. They hunted caribou, using all of the animal for food, clothing and shelter. Archaeologists have found pit houses, projectile point flakes and other evidence in the rocky soil just feet from the museum and research center. A lifelike diorama depicts a hunting scene. An interactive computer answers visitors' questions.

Barely three months since it opened August 11, the center has altered scientific views about the first peoples to inhabit the New England area. Evidence of human habitation at the end of the last ice age was unimagined before the discoveries on Mashantucket Pequot lands. More than 250 archaeological sites have been found on Pequot land near the museum and research center, including the remnants of a 17th-century fort. The Mashantucket Pequots, then, would be among the oldest tribes to continually inhabit the same area in North America, says archaeologist Kevin McBride, the museum's research director.

But more significant, McBride says, is that these discoveries are being made in partnership with Native peoples, who are having a significant impact on how scientists interpret their findings. "Native people, in general, are seeking to influence to a greater extent the way their history and past is being portrayed and being researched," McBride says. "They're saying, 'Let us tell our stories.'"

More than fifty tribes and two hundred Native individuals helped develop the museum and research center. Among them is Cheryl Metoyer, a Cherokee who is director of information resources. Metoyer is a nationally known scholar and pioneer in library development. She retains her position as senior staff researcher at UCLA's American Indian Studies Research Center.

"Never in my dreams did I think I would see this kind of opportunity. Here was a tribe that had the commitment and resources to build an absolutely state-of-the-art museum and library and archives. If we continue to do this right, we will really make an incredible difference," Metoyer says. The research center has a 250,000-volume capacity devoted to Native histories and cultures. Classrooms, laboratories and study areas are designated for children, students and scholars-in-residence.

By allowing Native peoples to do just that, tribal histories are being rewritten.

"We have benefited greatly from that relationship. It's not just the information we are getting. It's the new perspectives on the past," McBride says. "We used to have one way of looking at the past. It was not necessarily through Western eyes, but through certain methodologies. But any time you engage in dialogue with people looking at things with a different perspective, you're bound to see something new. For example, at Mashantucket, the traditional approach to the study of Native peoples in the historic period had been to look at it through the study of the acculturation. But, now, it is from a perspective of continuity and resistance. The people are saying, 'We have made decisions. We have maintained certain aspects of our identity and culture.'"

N. Scott Momaday, the Pulitzer Prize-winning novelist, poet and artist, says tribal involvement in connecting past and present is an essential part of celebrating life and perpetuating the culture. He is involved in one such project, called the Buffalo Trust, which seeks to build Native cultural centers throughout North America. These centers would interpret life from a Native perspective, teaching Native languages, beliefs and traditions, including that of his own Kiowa heritage. What the Pequots are doing, Momaday says, will pave the way for many other tribes to tell their stories in their own unique ways.

"It sounds to me as if it's a very important institution and a very important expression on the part of the tribe to celebrate itself, its pride and to call attention to the values of the Native American people in general," Momaday says.

For the Pequots, the $193-million museum is a dream-come-true, says Chairman Richard "Skip" Hayward. In the early 1970s, Elizabeth George and other tribal members learned that Connecticut planned to convert tribal lands into a state park. George sprang into action, urging her grandchildren to return to the land and revitalize the tribe. Hayward, then 27, and a handful of others came home. They began developing businesses that would lure more tribal members back to the land.

In those early days, they tried everything from tapping maple trees, to cutting cordwood, to hydroponic lettuce-growing, to community gardening, to pig farming.

Economically, they survived, but it was a struggle. The pig farming project collapsed after tribal members got attached to the animals and gave them all names, rather than send them to slaughter.

Members were exasperated but not defeated. Restoring the tribe kept them going, and talk often focused on building a museum. As the talk continued, the tribe ventured into high-stakes bingo in the late 1980s. Although bingo was a huge success, three years of discussions ensued before the tribe decided to develop Foxwoods Resort and Casino in 1992. The wild success of Foxwoods enabled the tribe to build a world-class museum and research center—a center that Robert Anderson, Director of the British Museum in London, said "will be able to take its place immediately among its more well-established museum counterparts around the world."

W. Richard West, founding director of the National Museum of the American Indian and chairman of the American Association of Museums, goes further. "This building is a technological wonder. It serves as a model in the museum community," West says. But West says the museum speaks more of people.

"This building is only metaphor for something more powerful and profound— the life and spirit of a living people," West says. The Pequots were among the first Native peoples to suffer devastation at the hands of new European arrivals. "Yet, they refused to die. They persisted because, ultimately, they remembered. We Native people always have known who we are, what we have done and why we are here."

It is no different for Hayward and others, who remember the early days of bringing the tribe back together. "We had no running water. The floors got so cold your feet would stick to the floor. Aunt Eva was born in [grandmother's] house. She was a preemie. They put her in a codfish box and put her on the oven door to keep her warm. It was fairly rugged living on the land," Hayward says.

What kept tribal members going were the stories of Elizabeth George, particularly on thunderstorm-laden nights. "We'd stay up all night. That's when granny would spin some of her best yarns," Hayward says.

George acted in the true sense of a Native elder, passing down traditional Pequot stories in the oral tradition. The stories she told about the Mashantucket Pequots went back hundreds of years. Many of them now are illustrated in the museum's elaborate exhibits, complete with interactive computer displays, full restorations and hundreds of heirlooms and artifacts dating to the 17th century. A 70 mm film depicts the massacre by British soldiers and their Indian allies from neighboring tribes of the Pequots on May 26, 1637. Visitors can walk through a 22,000 square-foot Pequot village of the 17th century. The village includes wigwams built a year before the museum opened by the Mashpee people of Cape Cod, a re-creation of the forests and rivers in the area, a myriad sounds and even the smell of campfires.

Museum workers cast lifelike figures from Native peoples of the area, including Pequot tribal members. Similarly, trees and other plant life specific to the area but now vanished were cast from forests in Connecticut and Wisconsin consistent with the times of 360 years ago.

A focal point of the museum is its 20,000 square-foot glass-and-steel Gathering Space. The space is the entry to the exhibitions, where visitors can look onto the archaeological excavation where the Pequots built a fort and took refuge from their enemies in the Great Cedar Swamp. The Gathering Space is constructed of two offset semicircles patterned after the fort. Its blue floor is embedded with seashells as a reminder of the Pequots' traditional relationship with the sea.

Such reminders are important to Theresa Hayward Bell, executive director. A granddaughter of George, Bell recalls being told by a schoolteacher that she was, essentially, extinct. Education will be a primary focus of the center, Bell says.

"In our area and our region, education about Native peoples has been needed for many many years. In this region, you're not recognized as being Native. You're out of sight and out of mind. Historically, there's always been that struggle to say we still exist. I think the museum will help strengthen our presence even more, not just for us but all Algonquian-speaking Woodlands people," Bell says.

Schools and colleges are clamoring for information. This past summer, before the museum and research center opened, a workshop for educators had to be expanded, said Trudi Lamb Richmond, program manager for education, and a member of the Schaghticoke tribe of northwestern Connecticut.

Steve Dennin, director of marketing for the museum and research center, also is feeling the heightened interest from the public. "We're at a point in time where people are understanding what it means to be indigenous," Dennin says. Like many museums, the Mashantucket Pequot museum is seeking business sponsors, partners and members. Such measures ensure that the museum benefits the larger community. For its first year, the museum and research center will offer charter memberships for both businesses and individuals. Corporate memberships range from $2,500 to $25,000 annually. Individual memberships range from $35 to $55 for a family. Benefits include free admission, the use of museum facilities for private events and behind-the-scenes tours.

Joan Thomas, collections manager, is counting on such partnerships to build a diverse representation of Native peoples.

"We're not static. We're evolving like everybody else," says Thomas, who is Kiowa. "We deal with the same pressures that other groups do and we work them through like everybody else. We're not stuck back in the 19th century, like those black-and-white pictures of yesteryear."

5. Liz Dominguez (Chumash/Yokuts/Luiseño) Hears Ishi's Voice, 1998

I would like to introduce myself to those of you who don't know me. My name is Onok'ok Colocutayuit. Most people know me as Liz Dominguez. I am Chumash from the Santa Ynez band, and am also Yowlumni/Tachi Yokuts and Luiseño. I would like to share with you my vision of a living language.

My vision began four years ago, when I came upon a cassette tape of songs sung by Ishi, the last of the Yahi people. It was a wax-cylinder recording done in the twenties by an anthropologist named Kroeber. It brought chills to me when I listened to the songs and stories that Ishi shared. It was as if he was trying so hard to leave

From Liz Dominguez, "A Vision of a Living Language," *News From Native California,* vol. 12, no. 1 (Fall 1998), 17. Reprinted by permission of the author.

something behind, to say to all that he and his people had been here; as if he was leaving a legacy in exactly the way he had been taught to do, that being oral tradition. It then saddened me to think that there wasn't any Yahi left to learn from this legacy left behind by this courageous man. Not only were there no Yahi left, there wasn't anyone around that could translate anything Ishi was saying! After Ishi learned a little English, he was able to translate some of the words of his language. Then he succumbed to European diseases, taking with him a culture to never be taught again.

I then began to think how wonderful it would be if one of my ancestors had left behind a legacy like this for me and my people. I did some research, and lo and behold! I got copies of the Chumash wax-cylinder recordings! And what was even more of a gift was that my great-great-great-grandmother Maria Solares was one of the singers on the tapes! The first time I heard her sweet, shy voice, and at the same time looked at a photo of her, it was as if she were alive again! To live again! Yes, Yes!! It all made sense to me right then and there. I saw my grandmother sitting on her porch looking at all the young ones running around. She was reminiscing about when she was young, and all the things she used to do, and the things she witnessed and was told. It brought a smile to her face to remember those days, and then shortly after that smile came a frown: a frown because no one cared anymore about the old ways, the songs they used to dance to all night long, the stories they would share in a language that belonged to them, a culture full and complete in every aspect. No, no one cared anymore to listen. Everyone was too excited about all the new things that this new way of life had brought with it.

It was then that a man named John Harrington approached her with a five-dollar bill in his hand, and asked her if she could share with him all of her memories of her culture. Yes, that five dollars sure would come in handy, but most of all John said that everything she said would be preserved for generations to come. Bingo! Maria thought. Maybe one day, as sure as the circle will complete itself, there will be one of my relations that will find these treasures, and all that has passed, and all that has been held dearest to the ancestors. The blood, sweat, and tears that the ancestors endured to keep this culture alive will not have been in vain, and we can finally smile from where we be. I know she and the others are smiling when they hear me singing the songs. May their journey be complete.

That was four years ago. Today I am a beginning speaker of two Chumash languages, a singer of over one hundred songs, a dancer in the fashion of the old ways. Someone once told me I live *in* the past. They had it a little wrong. I live *for* the past. Now it has become my responsibility to carry on the legacy my grandmother and the others left behind, to share as I learn with all others, in hopes that one day, when the cycle of the circle has come to its completion, we will all be in it together, a living language, a living culture. Thank you, Ishi, your message came through.

◈ *E S S A Y S*

Although gaming is far from a panacea, many Indian communities have employed it to achieve unprecedented opportunities for their citizens. In the first essay, *New Mexico Magazine* writer Steve Larese provides a clear and concise depiction of how gaming and other economic development projects have made it more likely that tribal governments can achieve long-standing culturally conservative ends. Education can pull a student away from his or her roots, but it can also create a new chance for an individual to truly learn about his or her identity. The second essay presents a remarkable life journey of a Kiowa-Comanche man, who through hard work and opportunity was able to come home. Arvo Quoetone Mikkanen grew up in New England but is now an attorney in Oklahoma. The third essay reveals the significance of oral history and the importance that so many Indian families place on the obligations and responsibilities that bind the generations together. Angela Cavender Wilson (Wahpatonwan Dakota) eloquently explains the ties between grandmother and granddaughter. In 2000, Cavender Wilson became the first American Indian to complete a Ph.D. in history at Cornell University and joined the history department at Arizona State University.

Contemporary Indian Economies in New Mexico

STEVE LARESE

"We haven't renovated since this was built in 1978," [Judy] Tenorio says between calls inquiring about visiting Sky City, Ácoma's traditional pueblo. "But we're getting so many people. . . ."

Outside, threatening storm clouds don't deter tourists from traipsing behind guide Damian Garcia as he highlights the history of Sky City. Commanding all it surveys atop a 367-foot windswept mesa, the impressive ancestral home of the Ácoma sees an average of 100,000 tourists a year from all over the planet.

The expansion of Ácoma's visitors' center is just one sign of the boon many of New Mexico's 22 tribes are experiencing—or would like to experience—in the state's changing economy.

New Mexico's Native American tribes—from Ácoma to Zia—say they have always felt used as a source of revenue by non-Indians. But by aggressively pursuing tourism and business themselves, New Mexico's tribal governments are striving for strong, independent and diverse economies for their people in the coming millennium.

"Look in any tourism brochure here and you'll see Indians," says Lorentino Lalio, a Zuni tribal member and New Mexico's director of Indian Tourism. "Indians have been very generous in opening their communities to outsiders, yet we haven't seen the benefits."

Tourism stokes a $3.5 billion industry in New Mexico—the state's second largest industry next to natural resources—according to the state's Department of Tourism. Surveyed visitors say scenic landscapes and Indian culture are the top two reasons why they chose to vacation in The Land of Enchantment.

"Why are reservations compared to Third World countries when we're the source of a multibillion dollar industry?" Lalio asks. "It's because it's hard to make money when you don't have any."

Infrastructure, he says, remains the tallest hurdle in the tribes' efforts to keep more tourism dollars on tribal lands. Tourists visit pueblos, pay the admission fee if

From Steve Larese, "Awakening the Giant: Tribal Governments See Business as Means to Preserve Way of Life," *New Mexico Magazine*, August 1999, 49–57. Reprinted by permission of the author.

there is one, buy a piece of jewelry and take photographs, he says. But they then leave for hotels, restaurants, museums and shops off reservation. Tribes are left with hassles, dust and a couple of bucks. Federal resources, tribes say, don't adequately cover basic utilities, let alone museums.

"People couldn't understand the big deal of a gas station going in at Zuni," Lalio says. "They don't realize that until then we had to drive 32 miles off reservation to fill up. Now our money stays on our land. It's small, but it's a source of pride."

When Sandía Pueblo opened table games at its casino in 1994, it opened a new era of opportunity for New Mexico's tribes. Nine other pueblos and the Jicarilla and Mescalero Apaches have since opened casinos. Some are housed in elaborate tents. Others, like the casinos at Ácoma and Santa Ana pueblos, are already expanding and remodeling their buildings with state-of-the-art upgrades. The millions of dollars that have flowed into tribal coffers are being used to build restaurants, truck stops, golf courses and resorts, as well as fund schools, scholarships, homes, roads and other necessities.

But the newfound wealth hasn't come easily. After years of legal wrangling with the state, the tribes and New Mexico signed gaming compacts in 1997. The state promised not to allow non-tribal entities to establish Class 3 gaming (table games) in exchange for 16 percent of the tribes' slot machine earnings on a quarterly basis. Also, the tribes must pay $300 per slot machine, $750 per table game and $6,250 per casino quarterly in regulatory fees. In essence, the tribes bought a monopoly from the state. And though they signed the compacts, some tribes pay less than the 16 percent in protest, and the Mescalero and Jicarilla Apaches tribes refuse to pay anything, claiming it is illegal for the state to collect the fees. The state is expected to renegotiate the compacts, however, and possibly lower the fees—good news for tribes like Santa Ana, which paid $1,070,081 for its slots alone last quarter.

Many non-Native American business owners say they are being hit hard by the loss of finite dollars in New Mexico's economy to tribal casinos. Competition is one thing, they say, but competing against businesses not restricted by the same state laws is like running a race with your shoelaces tied together.

"The argument that casinos bring money into the state's economy doesn't wash," says Richard Buratti, executive vice president of the New Mexico Restaurant Association. "Gaming only benefits other businesses if over 50 percent of the money coming in is from out of state. Tourists aren't the ones spending in casinos, it's the locals."

Less than 10 percent of out-of-state visitors say they gamble while here, according to the New Mexico Department of Tourism. A 1998 New Mexico Taxation and Revenue report estimates Indian gaming has taken roughly $350 million directly and $1 billion indirectly out of New Mexico's non-Indian economy.

"We're a force to be reckoned with now, and some people don't like that," says Phil Tsosie, tribal planner for Isleta Pueblo. "They liked having us selling pots on the side of the highway. They want us to look like Hollywood Indians for the tourists while their businesses make all the money."

Tsosie and other tribal economic development officers say they realize gambling on gaming for the long haul isn't wise. Eventually, casinos will start competing with one another.

"Gaming has been great, and we'll take advantage of it as long as we can," he says. "But we realize it's not here forever. It's just allowing us to establish an economic base we've never had."

While the future of gaming on New Mexico's reservations may be uncertain, the opportunities it's brought to the tribes aren't. With money in hand, beautiful land and federal tax incentives, tribes are attracting private businesses that until a few years ago wouldn't dream of entering into deals with tribal governments. Combining hot tubs with heritage could turn some reservations into tourist meccas.

Santa Ana's tribal administrator Roy Montoya says that's the driving philosophy behind the $80 million, 350-room Hyatt Regency Tamaya luxury golf resort slated to open next fall on tribal land. The tribe will own the resort and Hyatt will manage it. The Mescalero Apaches have their successful Inn of the Mountain Gods, and Santa Clara and San Juan pueblos are in the process of building resorts and golf courses.

"We have the land, we have the location, so why not," Montoya asks. "Why shouldn't we get into the game?"

Santa Ana is one example of a tribe that is playing the game and winning. With 690 registered members, the pueblo employs 504—almost 100-percent employment for tribal members able to work—at its Santa Ana Star Casino, four-star Prairie Star Restaurant, 27-hole golf course, Warrior Apparel wholesale clothing, native plant nursery and other tribally owned enterprises. Santa Ana also employs 393 non-tribal members, a number that is expected to increase significantly once Tamaya opens.

"Tax breaks didn't factor into our decision to pursue this," says Dale Moulton, vice president of development for Hyatt. "But providing a unique experience for our guests and the tribe's ability to afford the hotel sure did."

Tsosie says Isleta is also being taken seriously by investors and believes the pueblo's independence is strengthening.

"Before we were dependent on federal grants," he says, adding grant money and loan guarantees have been severely cut in the past few years. "But now, with the influx of gaming money, we can fund our own multiple projects."

Non-tribal businesses operating on tribal lands still must pay New Mexico gross receipts tax, usually in addition to tribal taxes. This dual taxation keeps many businesses off the reservations. To counter this, Pueblo of Santa Clara tribal administrator Calvin Tafoya says his tribe in 1997 proposed House Bill 141, which allows the Pueblo to share the New Mexico gross receipts tax non-tribal businesses must pay. The Pueblo wouldn't have to additionally tax business to benefit. The bill passed, and now Santa Clara is seeing a six-screen theater being built, as well as a hotel, casino and resort on the drawing boards.

The Navajo Nation, with a population estimated at more than 200,000, is seeing slow but steady economic progress on its West Virginia-sized reservation.

"We're seeing more of our members buying into franchises or at least joint ventures," says Ed Richards, director of small business development for the Navajo Nation. "A lot of money is still going off reservation to towns like Farmington and Gallup, but it's getting better."

The largest tribe in the U.S., the Navajo Nation has battled high double-digit unemployment for decades. But by better managing their abundant natural resources and marketing tourism, private and tribal businesses are gaining significant footholds on the reservation without gaming money.

Compromising or contaminating their culture through business concerns many tribes. All of New Mexico's tribes value their way of life and have gone to great lengths to protect and insulate it. But in this changing world, they understand in order to preserve the old, they must embrace part of the new.

To protect their traditional religious-based governments, many tribes have formed separate business offices and have incorporated themselves. This keeps the traditional governments from becoming tangled in secular conflicts, and it's also good for business. Many non-Indian businesses fear if something should go sour with a deal, they won't have any legal recourse because of the tribes' unique sovereignty. Some tribal officials change yearly. Arrangements made between a governor and private business one year can completely change the next. By creating a separate corporate entity, tribes create a constant with which non-Native businesses can deal, regardless of what happens in the complicated and "foreign" tribal governments.

"I wouldn't say non-Indians were a little leery of doing business with us, I'd say they were a lot leery," says Montoya, who also chairs Santa Ana Hospitality Corp., which was established in 1998. "But now we're up to our ears with people wanting to do business with us."

But the biggest concern many tribes have is how development and instant cash will affect their way of life. Tribes must open themselves up to pursue business when for centuries they've worked hard to close off outside influences.

Ray Trujillo, tribal planner for the Pueblo de Cochití, says that's why his tribal council has decided not to pursue gaming. "We're a very traditional pueblo," he says. "You give up a lot when you enter into gaming. Priorities are shifted to the casino and away from traditional matters."

Cochití's main tribal enterprise is the Pueblo de Cochití Golf Course, one of the top-ranked in the nation. They plan to add nine additional holes to the 18-hole course in the near future. From there, Trujillo says, they might expand the clubhouse and even look at a resort. "We're looking at several possible projects, but we're in no rush," he says. "We want to look at everything and make sure everything is done right."

Like Cochití, Zia has chosen not to enter into gaming for fear it might upset the traditional balance of the village.

"If tourists come, they come," says Peter Pino of Zia Pueblo. "We have a small cultural center, but we also enjoy our privacy." Still, Zia has nothing against making money. Currently the pueblo leases small sites on its land to gypsum mining, pipeline right-of-way and communication towers. Other plans include developing land the tribe owns in San Ysidro and Bernalillo. Pino, who is CEO of the tribe's Zia Realty and Investment Enterprise, says Zia is currently looking for private investors for the off-reservation developments. By keeping development away from Zia, the pueblo hopes to benefit without impacting the traditional lives of its 650 members.

Many tribal officials see engaging in business as the way to protect their communities.

"When a pueblo has the ability to keep members on the reservation and has flexible work schedules for religious and family leave, the pueblo strengthens itself and its culture," says Santa Ana's Montoya.

He explains sometimes tribal members must return to their pueblo for religious reasons or clan duties. They may be absent from their jobs for days. "Indians can't always live in a 9 to 5, Monday through Friday world."

And while each tribal government is an independent entity that is approaching the coming years differently, many of New Mexico's Native Americans agree with Santa Clara's Tafoya when he says no matter what tribal governments decide to do, the end goal is to strengthen their people and culture.

"We have a serenity here that the rest of the world is looking for," says Tafoya. "Everything we do is to protect this for us and our future generations. We're a giant that's been asleep because we've been fed through our veins by the federal government. But now that's ending, and we're waking up and flexing muscles we never knew we had. And no one knows what we're capable of."

Coming Home

ARVO QUOETONE MIKKANEN (Kiowa-Comanche)

The clarity of the air, along with the brightness of the sky both during the day and at night, is something that makes the Wichita Mountains otherworldly to me. Rising out of the plains like great mounds of rough, rounded boulders, the Wichitas have been an important and even magical place to me since childhood. I remember my fascination as I watched a mother buffalo and her calf lumbering along, unbound by fences and corrals, and recall my amusement when I tried to sneak up on the prairie dogs in the prairie dog town before they jumped into their burrows. I remember that, sometimes, when it was very quiet, I could hear their shrill barks in the distance over the whistling wind through the knee-high grass in the fields surrounding the mountains. I always enjoyed visiting the Wichitas when I returned to Oklahoma in the summertime for visits with my family.

It is also curious that these mountains have such beauty not only in the spring when the grasses are lush and green, but also in the winter when the grasses are golden brown and dry. When driving through the refuge that surrounds these mountains, one cannot look out across the fields without imagining what they must have been like a hundred and fifty years ago when the plains were still open and there were no fences, electric wires, or roads.

These mountains have always been an important place for the Kiowas and Comanches, not only because they were primary landmarks in the last tribal reservation, but also because so many of our ancestors are buried in the mountains in unmarked graves under the heavy rocks and boulders and down in crevices— places where no one has trodden since they were placed there hundreds of years ago. I also wondered how it was that the Kiowas and Comanches lost these lands. My curiosity about this was sparked by conversations with my grandfather about the old treaties and the many laws affecting the tribes.

From Arvo Quoetone Mikkanen, "Coming Home," in Andrew Garrod and Colleen Larimore, eds., *First Person, First Peoples: Native American College Graduates Tell Their Life Stories* (Ithaca, N.Y.: Cornell University Press, 1997), 171–188. Copyright © 1997 by Cornell University. Used by permission of the publisher, Cornell University Press.

Today, when I return to the Wichitas, it reminds me of my childhood visits to Oklahoma and the time spent exploring the lakes, rocks, and fields of the entire area. Sometimes I also recall how it came to pass that I am now here in Oklahoma. I guess I just could not get enough of the Wichitas and the rolling plains of Oklahoma; or maybe it was an inner longing for a place where I felt that I belonged or that was meaningful or significant to me. I was a bit lost in high school and looking for a direction in my life—something that would be important for me to do—and it took some time to find that goal. Ironically, I think it was primarily an education at a small liberal arts college on the border of New Hampshire and Vermont that brought me back to Oklahoma. This is the story of that journey.

The journey began during the summer immediately before my senior year in high school, when a subtle panic began to set in. Everyone I spoke to inquired, "What are you going to do after you graduate? . . . Where are you going to college? . . . What are you going to do with your life?" I did not have a definite answer. I assume that in the back of my mind, I thought planning for my future could be put off for a while. However, the closer I got to graduation, the more I realized that the time to act was now upon me and I had some important decisions to make. During my senior year, I spent a lot of time working in my high school's closed-circuit television station. From the time I was a freshman, I had worked in the television production facility in a variety of technical positions. Falmouth High School, in Massachusetts, was built in the mid-1970s and was a modern "high-tech" school equipped with a three-channel television studio that provided programming, news shows, announcements, and special productions to the faculty and students. The station was connected to the community cable network, and its broadcasts could be seen by the public as well.

Eventually, my long hours of after-school work at the TV studio, as well as my training and interest in creating different types of TV programs, resulted in my being selected to be the general manager of the station. At that point, it seemed that television would play a big part in my future. When the time for graduation came, I really had no idea what to do for a career other than to pursue a position connected with television production.

Unfortunately, my guidance counselor did little, if any, "guiding" during our few sporadic meetings throughout my high school years. I actually felt at times that I was nothing more to him than a number on some manila file folder. I don't really blame him—I felt that he was a good person who had some interest in my future, but he didn't know me well enough to suggest what would be in my best interest from an educational and career standpoint. Needless to say, I didn't receive much direction from him.

Unlike many parents, who push and prod their children into a particular field, my mother and father were very open and supportive of my interests and life goals. The issue of what I would do after high school was, therefore, squarely "in my court." I appreciated that sense of freedom, but without a definite path set out for me, it was that much harder to make a decision about something so vague as "the future."

While I was still in high school, I had secured a part-time job working for a private television production company, relying upon my experience in video production. The company originally started in a local entrepreneur's basement with a home video recorder and a hand-held-mini-camera, and quickly grew into a substantial business with a half-dozen employees. I ended up doing almost all of the camera shooting, editing, and composition of the various productions ranging from sports events to travel documentaries. This work first made me realize that not only could I have fun working in television production, but I could possibly make a living at it as well. I also preferred working in the air-conditioned videotape editing studio at fifteen dollars an hour to working for minimum wage in the hot sun at the golf driving range where I had previously been employed. As a result, most of the universities that I looked at, and considered applying to, were those that had an active program in television production.

Unlike many other students, I didn't really have a concrete plan from the beginning that I would go to college. I guess I always assumed that I would go to college, although I never made a specific decision until right before my senior year in high school. A big concern I had was where to get the money for a college education. Both of my parents worked—my dad as an electronics technician and my mom as a nurse—but we were an average middle-class family, without a trust fund or a tremendous amount of savings to pay for my education. In fact, we had only moved into our first house when I was a junior in high school. Before that, we had lived in either an apartment or a mobile home. Moving into our own house was a big step for us, primarily because it was the first time that we had a permanent place that we could call our own.

After I decided that I would go to college, I set out to try to research every scholarship, grant, and fellowship that I could find so that I could accumulate enough money to help me pay for my education. My mom and I had a Saturday morning ritual where I would go to the local public library and read for a few hours while she went grocery shopping. It was during one of these many research sessions in search of college funds that I discovered the path that led me to my college.

I sorted through tattered boxes, dog-eared books, brochures, and flyers piled in stacks describing countless scholarships and fellowships available for everyone from professional bowling league members to the descendants of Civil War veterans. I recall reading a publication dealing with scholarships available to Native Americans, and remember something catching my eye. It described a small, liberal arts, Ivy league college that was looking for Native American applicants who could "adjust to a small-town New England environment." I thought to myself, "Well, that sounds like me." I was a Kiowa/Comanche living in a small town on Cape Cod, Massachusetts. I figured that I had adjusted fairly well to a New England environment, since that's where I had lived since third grade, except for the summers and holidays that I spent with my extended family in Oklahoma. The union of my dad, of Finnish descent from Massachusetts, and my mother, a full blood Kiowa/Comanche Indian from Oklahoma, led to the unusual situation of my being a Plains Indian on Cape Cod, Massachusetts, of all places.

Although I was proud of my Finnish background and was familiar with that side of my family, it was somewhat difficult for me to forge a Native American identity since I was only immersed in Indian culture on those occasions when I returned to Oklahoma. It just so happened that we lived near a small Massachusetts community called Mashpee, home to a Wampanoag Indian community. While I had some classmates and friends who were descendants of individuals from this tribe, I really didn't feel all that close to their tribal culture, since it was so different from the Plains culture that I was familiar with. Moreover, the Wampanoags, through almost 500 years of acculturation and intermarriage, had very little left of their own traditional culture. While I did go to some pow wows and other events in Mashpee, it felt somewhat foreign to me as a Kiowa/Comanche.

I ultimately applied to several universities known for their television production programs. Almost as an afterthought, I completed my application to Dartmouth College, even though it didn't fit my "mold" of being a school with a known degree program in television production and it cost two or three times the amount of other schools I had considered. I sent off the application and really didn't know what to expect.

To my surprise, I was accepted to Dartmouth in the spring of 1979. Fortunately, my searching for funds had also paid off and I received several scholarships from private foundations, from the Kiowa Tribe, and from the federal government. Of course, I had saved some money from my old job at the golf driving range and from my video production position. My parents had also saved some money to help me, and I sold my rusted-out, 1966 4-wheel-drive truck to help pay for some of the expenses.

I traveled to Hanover, New Hampshire, on a spring day and visited the campus. Dave Bonga, a Chippewa and the outgoing director of the Native American Program, gave my mother and me the grand tour of the campus. This visit was the first time I had actually seen the Dartmouth College that was not on the glossy cover of a brochure. In actuality, it looked much like a brochure, with all of the scenic beauty, bright white buildings, and foliage. It seemed unreal and fantasy-like. I decided to accept the offer and enroll. With this step, I had made the plunge, not knowing what to expect.

Not long afterward, my mother shared with me the fact that her dream had always been for me to go to Dartmouth. I was somewhat surprised and perplexed by this, especially since she had never told me, nor had she encouraged me to apply specifically to that institution. In any event, it was clear to me, as it as to her, that this was an opportunity that I could not let pass; despite the expense, I figured that I would go and try my best.

During that initial visit, I also had arranged an informal internship with a local television station in the nearby town of White River Junction, Vermont. After my visit to this backwoods broadcasting facility located in the basement of an old motel complex, I felt I could still hold fast to my goal of going into some aspect of television production. Like the old cliché, I felt like I could have my cake and eat it too.

My first experience with college life was the freshman trip that took twenty of us on a three-day hiking excursion through the White Mountains of New Hampshire. I enjoyed this experience with the outdoors and despite my mosquito bites, calluses, and sore back, I joined in with the hundreds of other students in a rendezvous with the various other freshman trip groups at a lodge at the foot of one of the mountains.

The rendezvous at the college's mountain lodge was the culmination of our trip and the opportunity to eat our first home-cooked meal after three days of hiking and surviving on powdered soup, canned meat, and crackers. Our long-awaited meal consisted of scrambled eggs dyed green (in honor of Dr. Seuss, an alumnus of the college), green orange juice, and burned sausages. Somehow, despite the unusual color, we all appreciated having some real food. We were introduced to many of our classmates in this rather unusual fashion, and it served to draw us closer together. Afterward I felt that this was preferable to the bland introductory lecture you might expect in a traditional university orientation.

When I arrived on campus to begin classes, I was relegated to one of the groups of dormitories with an early 1960s-style cinder-block decor which was certainly at the bottom of any student's preference list. Not surprisingly, these dorms were primarily occupied by freshmen and a few unlucky sophomores. During my freshman year, I attempted to adapt to this environment with other students from various cities, regions, and states. However, by spring term, I came to the conclusion that I had little in common with these students and sought housing elsewhere.

Our dorm was a curious mix of jocks, computer whizzes, and hard-core "partiers" who could stay up half the night reveling and then pass a three-hour midterm the next day with flying colors. I had a somewhat difficult time adopting the mentality of the so-called popular people in our dorm who, perhaps because this was their first opportunity to be away from home, displayed what may politely be described as the worst aspects of their personalities. I guess one could call it a "pack" mentality, where people would do things to be "part of the group" that they would not do alone—such as drinking all night long, being critical and obnoxious to those who were "different" or who were overly studious, performing devious pranks and practical jokes, and ignoring their neighbors by blasting music at 200 decibels well into the early morning hours.

I stayed in this environment most of my freshman year, and, initially succumbing to peer pressure, even joined one of the local fraternities—although I never became fully active in fraternity life and eventually only marginally participated in its activities. In reflection, I think that the only reason I thought about joining was that everyone else around me was going through the process of being recruited by fraternities. Although the fraternity and sorority system had a positive side in that it provided some sense of camaraderie for many students, it also brought to the surface the worst aspects of student life. Blatant abuse of alcohol, rude and inappropriate behavior, and fostering the "us" versus "them" attitude was common in the fraternity system. Fortunately, the fraternity I joined was less along these lines than some others. However, that proved to be its ultimate doom as well. People were attracted to other, more traditional houses, and the population of our fraternity house continued to decline over time. It seemed sad to me to realize that in order to attract active members, some of the brothers were drawn into more destructive and outrageous behavior to fit in with the frat image. That trend was what ultimately turned me off, and over time I stopped going to meetings and eventually drifted away. In the end, the strategy of being more "fraternity-like" did not save that house, and it has recently been sold to a new sorority.

The fraternity that I joined was one of the few that actually had some Indian members. The fraternity system's undying support of the unofficial "Indian symbol" mascot turned the stomachs of most Indian students, who did not want to be associated with the part of the student body that supported the Indian symbol. As a result, few Indian students were fraternity members—at least of the more popular fraternities that sought the return of the Indian as the school mascot and bemoaned the loss of all of the associated cheers, outfits, and related offensive sporting paraphernalia. The use of "the Indian" as a mascot for the College was officially discouraged by the administration, but its return was the rallying cry for those rebels without a cause and for some of the more aged alumni who tenaciously clung to memories of the different and now bygone era when they were in school.

The Indian symbol, or simply "the symbol" as we knew it, was the source of most of my negative experiences while in college. The use of the symbol was opposed by most Native American students because we did not appreciate having the cheerleaders lead the crowd in "war whoops," fake scalpings, and hatchet throwing during the football halftimes as they had done in the past. I remember looking at some of the photos and memorabilia from the "good old" days, including such items as fake tom-toms, "Indian chief" headdresses, souvenirs, diaper pants with an Indian head insignia, and huge drums that were pounded by wild green, bare-chested Dartmouth "braves" with Mohawk wigs at the football games.

I was always very puzzled when people would attempt to change my mind to support the Indian symbol, telling me, "You should be proud that we are honoring Indians in this fashion." I would doubt very seriously if any other minority group would tolerate being treated in such a way. For example, running out on the football field in blackface with a watermelon and doing a tap dance at halftime would hardly be considered to be "honoring" African American culture. In any event, few of the older, non-Indian Dartmouth alumni wanted to hear that, and instead became incensed when the real Indians did not similarly embrace the college's unofficial symbol. In their minds, I guess we were the living incarnations of their mascot, and they simply could not understand why we did not run out on the field ourselves or appreciate being held up as the school's mascot. We clearly did not choose or want that role. I presume that they wanted us to act appreciative—for what, I still don't know. In return, we objected to any use of the symbol and were consequently attacked, criticized, and labeled "too sensitive."

I remember one traditional Indian song that was sung at one of the Dartmouth Pow Wows which clearly embodied the students' sentiment. That song, called a '49 song, is sung along with a drum at night after a pow wow. The lyrics were a variation of a popular, traditional Kiowa '49 song, "I'm from Oklahoma." Our version instead began "I'm from Dartmouth College" and concluded with the phrase, "We are not *your* Indians, we are not *your* symbols anymore." That's how the students felt—we were not the symbols of the majority population—we refused to be *their* Indians. We were who we were, not who the alumni wanted us to be—not the drunken, bare-chested, green Indians who pounded on the big drum in feathers at football games in the '50s. None of that was real.

While the Indian symbol was a blatant example of tensions between racial groups, other well-intentioned and supposedly knowledgeable persons committed less obvious faux pas. Like many other Indian students, I was constantly bombarded with myriad questions and statements from peers on every topic from the innocuous "Does your mother wear leather dresses?" to the often-repeated "Did you know *my* great-grandmother was an Indian princess?" I remember vividly one incident when someone asked an Eskimo friend of mine whether he and his family lived in an igloo. I thought to myself, "and these are supposed to be educated people." After about three years of effort, I eventually became tired of continually fighting and trying to educate the entire campus about the Indian symbol. Although it was a challenge and the Indian students appreciated those individuals who wanted to learn more, after countless seminars, rallies, and classes where one's consciousness was raised through the roof, I eventually became tired of functioning as the ambassador and expert for every tribe from the Bering Strait to Tierra Del Fuego—especially when I had my normal class schedule and other academic assignments to keep up with. Like many Native American students, I eventually became worn out by the effort of trying to educate my peers about Indians and why one group of people should not be forced to be the mascots of another.

About the same time that I realized I did not feel totally comfortable with the dorm and fraternity life, I began to become more interested in participating in the Native American Program on campus. Since I did not come from a classic "reservation" background, at first I felt a little reluctant to become involved with the Indian student organization. After my initial contact, however, I felt that the Indian students were more friendly and supportive and that I had much more in common with them than with any other students at Dartmouth, particularly those students in my dorm and fraternity. Although most of my contact with other Indians had been with Indians from Oklahoma, I felt a common bond with other Indian students even though they came from places like Alaska, New York, New Mexico, and Arizona.

When the student group Native Americans at Dartmouth (a.k.a NAD) chose an Indian design I had drawn as a freshman as the official logo of the organization, I felt as though I was officially "accepted" by my peers. My close association with the native American students for the next three years gave me much of the incentive to continue on with school despite the academic pressure and the rigorous class schedule. Being from a public high school, as opposed to a prep school, I did not feel as adequately prepared for the academic assignments as some of my classmates. I felt, at times, like I had to spend twice as much time as my classmates to get things done. For all I know, I was spending no more time on my classwork than anyone else, but I guess because I came from a public school, I thought my preparation must have been inferior.

My close association with the Native American students ultimately provided me with the motivation to go on to law school and, in a real sense, gave me some purpose for my education. The other event triggering my interest in Indian law was a class that I took in Native American studies during my freshman year. In particular, there was one final lecture in an introductory course taught by Professor Michael Dorris that in some sense changed my whole outlook on how Indians fared in and fit into American society.

This course had explored the rich culture of the Pueblo tribes, the unique and complicated Maya cosmology, the intricate Natchez system of marriage and class mobility, and the balance and stability of the Iroquois system of government. For the first time, I learned in an academic setting about all of the fascinating and unique characteristics of American Indian peoples in the western hemisphere. The class covered a vast period of time and had taken us all the way from 40,000 B.C. to 1492 and contact with the Europeans.

With this background, Professor Dorris summarized the class by describing the modern, post-contact history of one tribe, the Cherokee Nation. Unlike many other tribes, the Cherokee ultimately accepted many aspects of the non-Indian culture and did not strongly resist the adoption of European systems of government and social organization. Unlike the Kiowa and Comanche, who were classic horse-mounted Plains Indian tribes that were described in most books as "warlike and tenacious," the Cherokee were, for the most part, a peaceful people who cooperated with the U.S. government. As I sat there in class, I wondered to myself, "What was their history? How did their story end? Was it any better than that of the other tribes? Since they cooperated with the United States, are they in a better position today? Were they an example for other Indian tribes to emulate?" Not knowing their history and not being Cherokee, I really had no idea.

It was during this lecture that I hoped the culmination of the class and the history of Indian-white relations would end on a positive note. Unfortunately, as I guess I should have expected, it did not. Instead, the feeling I was left with was shock bordering on genuine outrage about the treatment of the Cherokee people. Although the Cherokee had repeatedly done everything that had been requested of them, including giving up huge parcels of land, removing their entire population thousands of miles to west of the Mississippi, adopting Western constitutions and court systems, wearing European-style dress, and adopting many "American" customs, in the end they fared no better than any of the other tribes. In fact, they ultimately were much *worse* off because they were so powerful, educated, and influential. In an ironic twist of fate, they were, through various Congressional acts, legally stripped of their tribal property, power, and authority because they were too successful as a separate nation. In order to cripple their power and influence at the turn of the century, their courts were shut down and their power to tax and raise funds for continued operation of the tribal government was abolished. Their lands were opened to non-Indian land settlement and their towns and villages were overrun, despite the fact that such actions violated numerous promises guaranteed by treaties. In the end, they lost almost ninety-five percent of their reservation to the "boomers" and "sooners" who claimed and grabbed their land. Many Cherokee ceremonies and religious practices were outlawed, as were traditional customs and languages. I wondered to myself, "Where was the justice in what was done? How could the American system of laws authorize such a complete destruction and utter dispossession of a people?"

I still remember sitting there in my seat with my head spinning and stepping outside the lecture hall into the sunshine thinking, "My God, why didn't someone do something? How could this have happened?" At that point, I felt the need to learn as much as I could so that I could understand what had happened. I felt that Indian people in general were vulnerable because there was no one to understand their desires or to speak for them. I hoped that at least I could learn more about the law and maybe someday, in some fashion, do something to have an impact on the recognition and development of tribal sovereignty.

Several Dartmouth students had participated in internships with various Indian organizations and I, too, wanted to find some work connected with Indian law that would bring me back home where my relatives lived in Oklahoma. I had always enjoyed talking to my grandfather about treaties and various agreements that the United States government had made with the Kiowas and Comanches. I recall when I spoke to him at times, his normally calm exterior would give way to a quiet excitement of sorts. I knew that he had served as an elected tribal leader and as a commissioner for the tribal housing authority. He had also been one of the original drafters of our tribal constitution. Although he never said it, I subtly felt that he had always wanted to be a lawyer or at least gain some background in law.

He often spoke to me about his older brother, Guy Quoetone, who had been instrumental in testifying for and implementing various pieces of legislation dealing with the Kiowa-Comanche-Apache land claims with the United States government. If ever there was a modern-day delegate and spokesperson for the Kiowa Nation in Washington, D.C., he was it. My relatives used to call him "Senator Guy" since he had made so many trips to the nation's capital to work on various issues of importance for the Kiowas.

Sometimes my grandfather would close his eyes, lean back, and tell me about various legal questions that had bothered him, or recount how various parcels of tribal land had mysteriously ended up being sold or claimed by businessmen or the nearby Army base. Often, he would pull out a big, tattered old expandable leather briefcase that was about to burst because it was stuffed so full of papers, newspaper articles, and documents. My grandfather used to call it his archives. From his own memory and those of other tribal members, he recounted different stories of certain fence boundaries that had been changed, certain laws that had been passed, and certain promises that were made but not fulfilled. By the way he spoke to me, in some instances I got the impression that he felt a little anxious, but hopeful that the legal questions that he had always wondered about could perhaps now be answered. At other times, I felt like he wanted to tell me everything he could remember about various concerns that he had so at least there would be someone who would be able to research and uncover what had happened years ago. Because of my courses in Native American policy, I, too, began to ask questions. I wondered to myself, "Why hasn't anyone done anything to protect tribal sovereignty? Why haven't any Indian lawyers been involved? Can't someone do something?"

In late 1980, while I was visiting relatives, this growing interest in Indian law led me to visit a local Bureau of Indian Affairs office in Anadarko, Oklahoma. After speaking with several employees, I met a friendly paralegal who was a fellow tribal member and who indicated that the newly established tribal court system was interested in an intern to assist in the tribal prosecutor's office.

The Court of Indian Offenses, located in Anadarko, Oklahoma, served as a tribal court for seven tribes in the area, including the Kiowas and Comanches. It had been set up only a year before, when a federal court case had upheld the tribes' continuing rights to exercise authority over several hundreds of thousands of acres of land in the original reservation boundaries. In Oklahoma, for decades the Indian tribes had been told that they did not have the right to function as a separate government or that they had no land under their jurisdiction. The status of tribal jurisdiction had been in limbo since statehood in 1907, and for the first time in modern history in Oklahoma, the tribes' rights to self-government were reaffirmed.

When I began working with the tribal court, I realized the practical importance of tribal jurisdiction and was influenced by the support of fellow tribal members in the legal field such as Frances Oheltoint and George Tah-Bone, Jr. For the first time, I recognized not only the cultural and historical elements that a tribe possesses, but also the powers that a tribe has as a government. I was fascinated with this concept of a nation existing within nation, having its own laws, police, court systems, and authority over designated lands. It was during this internship with the court system, arranged through Dartmouth's Native American studies department, that I first set foot in a courtroom. I so thoroughly enjoyed working with the tribal court system that I returned to Dartmouth with a new goal and understanding that the law, particularly Indian law, would play a part in my future. Little did I know that not even a decade after graduation, I would be serving as the chief judge for ten tribes in the very same court system that I had served as an intern.

About the time of my internship in the tribal court, I had abandoned my idea of going into television production and changed my major to government, with certification in Native American studies. The government major was viewed as a rigorous undertaking. Nevertheless, I wanted to have a proper foundation and background for law school. After my internship, the Native American Studies Program continued to give me some direction in focusing my energies, since I felt that I now had at least some sense of purpose for my education.

I later went on to take several classes from Professor Dorris, who opened an entire world of understanding to me about Native Americans from all over the United States and Canada. I thought I knew about Indians before going to college, but I came to realize that many different tribes had vastly different histories, traditions, and cultures. I found that Navajos, Eskimos, and Mohawks were almost as different from Kiowas and Comanches, and from one another, as people from different nations. Of course, as I now understand, we *are* from different nations.

After graduation from Dartmouth, I went on to Yale Law School and received my law degree. While in law school, I worked one summer for the Kiowa Tribe, and another summer for the Native American Rights Fund, a nationwide public interest law firm located in Boulder, Colorado. With this background, I came to appreciate the intricacies of Indian law more fully. I also realized that I wanted to return to the traditional homelands of my own tribes and be involved in some fashion in the legal field.

I am thankful that my education led me back to Oklahoma and drew me into Indian law because I feel as though my legal education has had a positive effect on others in understanding the unique status that tribes hold. After my graduation from Yale, I spent a year working for a federal judge on Indian law cases at the United States Claims Court in Washington, D.C., and then spent another year working for a federal judge in a United States District Court in east Texas. After working for these judges, I returned to Oklahoma permanently and accepted employment with a private law firm in Oklahoma City, to litigate cases and assist tribes in legal problems. Fortunately, the law firm permitted me to pursue my interests by developing this practice and allowed me to continue to serve as a tribal judge for over a dozen tribes and also to work as an adjunct professor in Oklahoma City University Law School's Native American Legal Assistance Clinic. The clinic helps law students acquire practical experience working with Indians and other poor people who need legal services through local legal aid offices.

In 1994, I accepted a position as an Assistant United States Attorney with the United States Department of Justice for the Western District of Oklahoma. As the first person to hold the position of Special Assistant for Tribal Relations, I have primary responsibility for handling all Indian affairs, bringing suits to protect tribal assets and properties, and prosecuting crimes committed on Indian lands. As the first Kiowa tribal member and one of the first Indian persons ever to hold such a position in the state, I am thankful to be given this opportunity by the local United States Attorney. In a sense, appointment to this position has fulfilled a dream for me, permitting me to return to Oklahoma, to practice law, and to be directly involved in legal matters affecting the tribes.

I recall an essay entitled "Coming Home" that I wrote for a Native American studies class at Dartmouth. It chronicled my trek up a small creek to get some spring water requested by some Kiowa elders for an upcoming meeting. In a larger sense, the essay described my return to Oklahoma and my Indian roots. I had traveled back to Oklahoma during one of my breaks from Dartmouth to a place north of the Wichita Mountains in the southwestern part of Oklahoma, where my ancestors had lived and where my maternal great-grandfather Jimmy Quoetone raised his family:

> The creek winds like a snake down through the Wichitas, in a twisting and winding path and all the green is drawn to it like some great magnet. From Mount Scott's summit you can see the trees that surround it, that draw life from it. In the driest of seasons, when every river and lake dries up to reveal their muddy bottoms and smooth flat rocks, this creek still flows. These waters nourish, even in the scalding rays of the summer; the ice-cold currents give life to the land. This is Jimmy Creek, this is where it all began.
>
> The old Kiowas wanted some spring water for their next get-together so they asked me to get some for them. We began our journey on foot, to follow the waters that bear my great-grandfather's name—Jimmy Quoetone, whose last name means "wolf tail."
>
> On we walked up the stream, its cool waters forming deep pools along the curves of the bank. Water spiders zipped across the glassy surface like ice skaters as small fish broke the surface trying to catch them.
>
> From the creek, we could see where the old house used to be. It was Jimmy's house, the one he built himself. There was the climbing tree and over there was the swimming hole. My mother grew up here and she can still remember. They always had a big arbor up to shade themselves from the hot August sun. Jimmy was always there, telling stories of how it used to be. There always seemed to be someone stopping by to visit, to share the fry bread, corn soup, and boiled meat. They would stay and talk, and Jimmy would sit under his medicine bundle.
>
> In his later years, he would wait, wait for the return of Kiowas who came back from Wyoming with water from the springs. They got the water near the place where a great rock formation came out of the ground; it was called Devil's Tower. My mother was but a young girl, but she remembers. He would take the water and sprinkle it all over his body. He said it revitalized him and made him stronger. It must have worked, for Jimmy Quoetone lived to be 101 years old.
>
> We continued to walk on, just beyond where the house once stood, following the bend of the stream as it carved its way through twisted roots and trees that had fallen. We finally reached the end of the creek. It was a circular pool of deep blue water, a kind of oasis on the prairie. The reflections of the sun streaming through the trees danced on its surface as it trickled over the cool stones into the creek. The pool seemed bottomless, and its underwater form merged with the shadows. This was it, the source of Jimmy Creek, where it all began—the flow of water, the flow of time, and the point of origin. I had come nearly 2,000 miles to this spot, a place that I had always heard about and imagined in my mind. This is where Quo-yoit, my great-great-grandfather, had first settled, where Jimmy Quoetone built his house, where my grandparents brought up all of their kids, where my parents came after they were married, and where I now stood.
>
> This place symbolized the beginning of my family. In the same way we drew strength, power, and the will to survive from my great-grandfather, so too does this land from the waters which bear his name. As I looked down into the waters I could

almost imagine looking into time. I wondered if Quoetone ever looked into these same waters and reflected on his own past, and also hoped for the future of his people, in the only place that they could truly call home.

For me, this place is significant not only because it is where we hold our family reunions and where I swam as a child on countless occasions, but also because it's where my mother and father first went after they were married, and is near the spot where I was married to my wife Tracey on the top of one of the Wichita Mountains.

Like the journey I described in the essay, that pulled me back to a little stream named after my great-grandfather in Oklahoma, my education has had a lot to do with where I find myself today. It is curious to think that the experiences I had at a small college on the border of Vermont and New Hampshire could have led me to become an Indian attorney, professor, and judge in Oklahoma. These experiences helped me "come home" to the traditional tribal homeland of the Kiowas and Comanches, and appreciate that much more the value of family while also giving me the opportunity to use my education to positively affect the future of Indian people. I sometimes wonder where I would be today had I not made that journey. Now, I'm just glad that I did.

Grandmother to Granddaughter: Generations of Oral History in a Dakota Family

ANGELA CAVENDER WILSON (Wahpatonwan Dakota)

The intimate hours I spent with my grandmother listening to her stories are reflections of more than a simple educational process. The stories handed down from grandmother to granddaughter are rooted in a deep sense of kinship responsibility, a responsibility that relays a culture, an identity, and a sense of belonging essential to my life. It is through the stories of my grandmother, my grandmother's grandmother, and my grandmother's grandmother's grandmother and their lives that I learned what it means to be a Dakota woman, and the responsibility, pain, and pride associated with such a role. These stories in our oral tradition, then, must be appreciated by historians not simply for the illumination they bring to the broader historical picture but also as an essential component in the survival of culture.

Maza Okiye Win (Woman Who Talks To Iron) was ten years old at the time of the United States–Dakota Conflict of 1862. She saw her father, Chief Mazomani (Walking Iron), die from wounds suffered in the Battle of Wood Lake. White soldiers wounded him while he was carrying a white flag of truce, She also witnessed the fatal stabbing of her grandmother by a soldier during the force marched to Fort Snelling in the first phase of the Dakota removal to Crow Creek, South Dakota. For three years Maza Okiye Win stayed in Crow Creek before she moved to Sisseton, South Dakota. Finally, after more than twenty-five years of banishment from Minnesota, she returned with her second husband, Inyangmani Hoksida (Running

From Angela Cavender Wilson, "Grandmother to Granddaughter: Generations of Oral History in a Dakota Family," *American Indian Quarterly,* vol. 20, no. 1 (Winter 1996), 7–13. Reprinted by permission of the University of Nebraska Press. Copyright © 1996 by the University of Nebraska Press.

Walker Boy) to the ancient Dakota homeland of Mni-Sota Makoce, or Land Where The Waters Reflect The Heavens. By this time both she and her husband had become Christians and were known in English as John and Isabel Roberts. There they raised their children and three of their grandchildren.

Elsie Two Bear Cavender was born in Pezihuta zizi village in 1906 to Anna Roberts and Joseph Two Bear. She was raised by her grandparents, John and Isabel Roberts. Her Dakota name was Wiko (Beautiful), given to her by one of her great aunts when she was just a girl. Grandma always seemed embarrassed by that name—as though she didn't believe she was Beautiful enough to possess it and certainly too modest to introduce herself that way. But now that she is gone, I can use what I perceive to be a fitting name without embarrassing her. To me, she was always *Kunsi,* or Grandma. She had eight children, four of whom she buried in her lifetime. She was well known for her generosity, her wonderful pies and rolls, and her stories.

Grandma grew up in a rich oral tradition. Not only was she well acquainted with many of the myths and legends of our people, she also possessed an amazing comprehension of our history, and many of her stories revolved around the events of the United States–Dakota Conflict of 1862. Her grandmother, in particular, had carried vivid, painful memories of those traumatic times. Over time, those painful memories of my great-great-grandmother became the memories of my grandmother, and then, they became my memories.

Early on, when I first began thinking about these stories in an academic context, I realized my understanding of oral tradition and oral history were incompatible with those I was finding in other texts. This incompatibility was largely because of terminology. David Henige, in his book *Oral Historiography,* differentiates between oral history and oral tradition, conveying an understanding that seems to be representative of most scholars in the field, when he says, "As normally used nowadays, 'oral history' refers to the study of the recent past by means of life histories or personal recollections, where informants speak about their own experiences . . . oral tradition should be widely practiced or understood in a society and it must be handed down for at least a few generations." These definitions are applicable to Native American oral history and oral tradition only in a very limited way. Native peoples' life histories, for example, often incorporate the experiences of both human and non-human beings. In addition, this definition would not allow for the incorporation of new materials because it would then be outside the "tradition."

From a Native perspective, I would suggest instead that oral history is contained within oral tradition. For the Dakota, "oral tradition" refers to the way in which information is passed on rather than the length of time something has been told. Personal experiences, pieces of information, events, incidents, etc., can become a part of the oral tradition at the moment it happens or the moment it is told, as long as the person adopting the memory is part of an oral tradition.

Who belongs to an oral tradition? Charles Eastman, a Wahpetonwan Dakota, reveals in his autobiography *Indian Boyhood* the distinct way in which the oral tradition was developed:

> Very early, the Indian boy assumed the task of preserving and transmitting the legends of his ancestors and his race. Almost every evening a myth, or a true story of some deed done in the past, was narrated by one of the parents or grandparents, while the boy listened with parted lips and glistening eyes. On the following evening, he was usually

required to repeat it. If he was not an apt scholar, he struggled long with his task; but as a rule, the Indian boy is a good listener and has a good memory, so that his stories are tolerably well mastered. The household became his audience, by which he was alternately criticized and applauded.

This excerpt highlights the rigorous and extensive training required of young Dakota people. The Dakota oral tradition is based on the assumption that the ability to remember is an acquired skill—one that may be acutely developed or neglected. Eastman also describes the differentiation between myths and true stories, necessitating an understanding of history as being encompassed in oral tradition. However, few scholars working in oral history make any distinction between oral information collected from those belonging to a written culture and those belonging to an oral tradition. This is an area that is yet to be explored.

My grandmother, Elsie Cavender, received this type of training. She had much to tell about some of our more popular characters, stories starring our mythical trickster figure, Unktomi, as well as stories about Dakota men and women—mostly belonging to my lineage—who lived and died long before I was born.

In my own family, the importance of specific stories as interpreted by my grandmother was expressed by the frequency with which those were told. As a girl I was acquainted with an assortment of stories from these categories, and I remember having to request specifically those which were not in the historical realm. But I didn't have to request the stories we classify as "history." Those she offered freely and frequently. Especially in the last years of her life, on every visit she would tell stories about the Conflict of 1862, as if to reassure herself that she had fulfilled her obligations and that these stories would not be forgotten.

One of these stories has become particularly important to me since my grandmother's death because it deals with grandmothers and granddaughters, of which I am the seventh generation. Aspects of this story have helped shape my perception of what my responsibility is, as a mother and eventual grandmother, and as a Dakota. This particular story is an excerpt taken from an oral history project I began with my grandmother in 1990. This is an edited version with much of the repetition cut for the sake of clarity and conciseness in this presentation. However, under usual storytelling circumstances, the repetition is part of the storytelling procedure, often added for emphasis. Grandmother titled this portion of the United States–Dakota Conflict "Death March," consciously drawing on the similarities between the removal of Dakota from the Lower Sioux Agency, first to Fort Snelling and then on to Crow Creek, South Dakota, with the Bataan Death March in World War II. After one of our Dakota relatives who had participated in that march related to her his experiences she saw many parallels with 1862 and thought "Death March" a fitting title. This passage is in my grandmother's voice:

> Right after the 1862 Conflict, most of the Sioux people were driven out of Minnesota. A lot of our people left to other states. This must have been heartbreaking for them, as this valley had always been their home.
>
> My grandmother, Isabel Roberts (Maza Okiye Win is her Indian name), and her family were taken as captives down to Fort Snelling. On the way most of them [the people] walked, but some of the older ones and the children rode on a cart. In Indian the cart was called *canpahmihma-kawitkotkoka*. That means crazy cart in Indian. The reason they called the cart that is because it had one big wheel that didn't have any spokes.

It was just one big round board. When they went they didn't grease it just right so it squeaked. You could just hear that noise about a mile away. The poor men, women, old people, and children who had to listen to it got sick from it. They would get headaches real bad. It carried the old people and the children so they wouldn't have to walk.

They passed through a lot of towns and they went through some where the people were real hostile to them. They would throw rocks, cans, sticks, and everything they could think of: potatoes, even rotten tomatoes and eggs. New Ulm was one of the worst towns they had to go through.

When they came through there they threw cans, potatoes, and sticks. They went on through the town anyway. The old people were in the cart. They were coming to the end of the town and they thought they were out of trouble. Then there was a big building at the end of the street. The windows were open. Someone threw hot, scalding water on them. The children were all burned and the old people too. As soon as they started to rub their arms the skin just peeled off. Their faces were like that, too. The children were all crying, even the old ladies started to cry, too. It was so hard it really hurt them but they went on.

They would camp someplace at night. They would feed them, giving them meat, potatoes, or bread. But they brought the bread in on big lumber wagons with no wrapping on them. They had to eat food like that. So, they would just brush off the dust and eat it that way. The meat was the same way. They had to wash it and eat it. A lot of them got sick. They would get dysentery and diarrhea and some had cases of whooping cough and small pox. This went on for several days. A lot of them were complaining that they drank the water and got sick. It was just like a nightmare going on this trip.

It was on this trip that my maternal grandmother's grandmother was killed by white soldiers. My grandmother, Maza Okiye Win, was ten years old at the time and she remembers everything that happened on this journey. The killing took place when they came to a bridge that had no guard rails. The horses or stock were getting restless and were very thirsty. So, when they saw water they wanted to get down to the water right away, and they couldn't hold them still. So, the women and children all got out, including my grandmother, her mother, and her grandmother.

When all this commotion started the soldiers came running to the scene and demanded to know what was wrong. But most of them [the Dakota] couldn't speak English and so couldn't talk. This irritated them and right away they wanted to get rough and tried to push my grandmother's mother and her grandmother off the bridge, but they only succeeded in pushing the older one off and she fell in the water. Her daughter ran down and got her out and she was all wet, so she took her shawl off and put it around her. After this they both got back up on the bridge with the help of the others who were waiting there, including the small daughter, Maza Okiye Win.

She was going to put her mother in the wagon, but it was gone. They stood there not knowing what to do. She wanted to put her mother someplace where she could be warm, but before they could get away, the soldier came again and stabbed her mother with a saber. She screamed and hollered in pain, so she [her daughter] stooped down to help her. But, her mother said, "Please daughter, go. Don't mind me. Take your daughter and go before they do the same thing to you. I'm done for anyway. If they kill you the children will have no one." Though she was in pain and dying she was still concerned about her daughter and little granddaughter who was standing there and witnessed all this. The daughter left her mother there at the mercy of the soldiers, as she knew she had a responsibility as a mother to take care of her small daughter.

"Up to today we don't even know where my grandmother's body is. If only they had given the body back to us we could have given her a decent funeral," Grandma said. They didn't though. So, at night, Grandma's mother had gone back to the bridge where her mother had fallen. She went there but there was no body. There was blood all over the bridge but the body was gone. She went down to the bank. She walked up and down the bank. She even waded across to see if she could see anything on the other side, but no body, nothing. So she came back up. She went on from there not knowing what happened to her or what they did with the body. So she really felt bad about it. When we were small Grandma used to talk about it. She used to cry. We used to cry with her.

Things happened like this but they always say the Indians are ruthless killers and that they massacred white people. The white people are just as bad, even worse. You never hear about the things that happened to our people because it was never written in the history books. They say it is always the Indians who are at fault.

An excerpt such as this challenges the emphasis of the *status quo*. This account does not contradict the many written texts on the subject, but contributes details not seen elsewhere, details that shift the focus from the "Indian atrocities," which are provided in rich detail in histories written by non-Indians, to "white atrocities" and Indian courage. It exemplifies the nature of the oral tradition in Dakota culture, as it is the story of one family, one lineage, reflecting the ancient village structure and the community that united those with a collective identity and memory. This account by itself will not change the course of American history, or create a theory for or framework from which the rest of the Plains wars may be interpreted. It is not even representative of the "Dakota perspective." Instead, it is one family's perspective that in combination with other families' stories might help to create an understanding of Dakota views on this event and time period. Certainly these stories shed light on the behavior and actions of members of my family that have led up to the present moment.

As I listened to my grandmother telling the last words spoken by her great-great-great-grandmother, and my grandmother's interpretation, "Though she was in pain and dying, she was still concerned about her daughter and little granddaughter who was standing there and witnessed all this," I understood that our most important role as women is making sure our young ones are taken care of so that our future as Dakota people is assured. I learned that sometimes that means self-sacrifice and putting the interests of others above your own. It also was clear through this story and others that although these were and continue to be hard memories to deal with, always there is pride and dignity in the actions of our women.

In addition, my connection to land and place is solidified with each telling of the story. As a Dakota I understand that not only is Mni-sota a homeland worth defending, but through the stories I learn where the blood of my ancestors was spilt for the sake of the future generations, for me, my children, and grandchildren.

Because these stories are typically not told in the history texts, we also must recognize we are responsible for their repetition. The written archival records will not produce this information. These stories are not told by people who have been "conquered," but by people who have a great desire to survive as a nation, as Dakota people. Consequently, these are not merely interesting stories or even the simple dissemination of historical facts. They are, more important, transmissions of culture upon which our survival as a people depends. When our stories die, so will we.

In my last real visit with my grandmother, several months before she was hospitalized in her final days, she recited this story again. I was moving to New York to begin my graduate education, and it was as if she were reminding me where I come from. In the same way, these stories served to validate my identity in a positive way when, as a girl, I was confronted with contrasting negative images of the

"Sioux" in school texts. These stories have stabilized me through graduate school and reminded me why I am involved in this sometimes painful process. One of the last video clips we have of my grandmother is of her telling one of our Unktomi stories to my daughter in Dakota. When I watch that scene it becomes apparent to me that the learning of these stories is a lifelong process and, likewise, the rewards of that process last a lifetime.

The contributions of stories such as this should be recognized as celebrations of culture, as declarations of the amazing resiliency and tenacity of a people who have survived horrible circumstances and destructive forces. Some of the greatest stories are those told by Native people and serve as challenges to the rest of the world to be so strong. Native people have an unbreakable belief in the beauty and the significance of our cultures, and this is reflected in our stories. They are testimony to the richness, variety, detail, and complexity of the interpretations of history. Our role as historians should be to examine as many perspectives of the past as possible—not to become the validators or verifiers of stories, but instead to put forth as many perspectives as possible. But, the greatest lessons of these stories are to the young people, the children, and grandchildren of the elders and storytellers, who will gain an understanding of where they came from, who they are, and what is expected of them as a Diné, as an Apache, as a Laguna, as a Choctaw, and as a Dakota.

◈ *F U R T H E R   R E A D I N G*

Lawrence Abbott, ed., *I Stand in the Center of the Good: Interviews with Contemporary Native American Artists* (1994)

Sherman Alexie, *Indian Killer* (1996)

———, *Lone Ranger and Tonto Fistfight in Heaven* (1993)

———, *Reservation Blues* (1995)

Marjane Ambler, *Breaking the Iron Bonds: Indian Control of Energy Development* (1990)

James H. Barker, *Always Getting Ready: Yup'ik Eskimo Subsistence in Southwest Alaska* (1993)

Joseph Bruchac, ed., *Songs From This Earth on Turtle's Back: Contemporary American Indian Poetry* (1983)

———, ed., *Survival This Way: Interviews With American Indian Poets* (1987)

Stephen E. Cornell and Joseph P. Kalt, eds., *What Can Tribes Do?: Strategies and Institutions in Indian Economic Development* (1992)

Michael Dorris, *A Yellow Raft in Blue Water* (1987)

———, *The Broken Cord* (1989)

Peter H. Eichstaedt, *If You Poison Us: Uranium and Native Americans* (1994)

Louise Erdrich, *Love Medicine* (1984)

———, *Tracks* (1988)

Donald L. Fixico, *The Invasion of Indian Country in the Twentieth Century: American Capitalism and Tribal National Resources* (1998)

John Gattuso, ed., *A Circle of Nations: Voices and Visions of American Indians* (1993)

Rayna Green, ed., *That's What She Said: Contemporary Poetry and Fiction by Native American Women* (1984)

Elizabeth S. Grobsmith, *Indians in Prison: Incarcerated Native Americans in Nebraska* (1994)

Janet Campbell Hale, *Bloodlines: Odyssey of a Native Daughter* (1993)

Joy Harjo and Gloria Bird, eds., *Reinventing the Enemy's Language: Contemporary Native Women's Writings of North America* (1997)

LaDonna Harris, *A Comanche Life* (2000)

E. Richard Hart, *Zuni and the Courts: A Struggle for Sovereign Land Rights* (1995)

Charlotte Heth, ed., *Native American Dance: Ceremonies and Social Traditions* (1992)

Bruce W. Hodgins and Jamiue Benidickson, *The Tenagami Experience* (1989)

Tom Holm, *Strong Hearts, Wounded Souls: Native American Veterans of the Vietnam War* (1996)

Bruce Hucko, *Where There Is No Name for Art: The Art of Tewa Pueblo Children* (1996)

Peter Iverson, *Riders Of the West: Portraits From Indian Rodeo* (1999)

Michael C. Keith, *Signals in the Air: Native Broadcasting in America* (1995)

Thomas King, *Green Grass, Running Water* (1993)

————, *Medicine River* (1990)

Carol Herselle Krinsky, *Contemporary Native American Architecture: Cultural Regeneration and Creativity* (1996)

Wilma Mankiller, with Michael Wallis, *Mankiller: A Chief and Her People* (1993)

W. Dale Mason, *Indian Gaming: Tribal Sovereignty and American Politics* (2000)

Thomas McGuire, et al., eds., *Indian Water for a New West* (1994)

Vincent L. Mendoza, *Son of Two Bloods* (1996)

Phyllis Mauch Messenger, ed., *The Ethics of Collecting Cultural Property: Whose Culture? Whose Property?* (1989)

Frank Pommersheim, *Braid of Feathers: American Indian Law and Contemporary Tribal Life* (1995)

Susan Power, *Grass Dancer* (1994)

Luana Ross, *Inventing the Savage: The Social Construction of Native American Criminality* (1998)

Greg Sarris, *Grand Avenue* (1994)

C. Matthew Snipp, *American Indians: The First of This Land* (1989)

Luci Tapahonso, *Saanii Dahataal: The Women Are Singing: Poems and Stories* (1993)

James Welch, *The Indian Lawyer* (1990)

Robert N. Wells, Jr., ed., *Native American Resurgence and Renewal* (1994)

Rick Whaley, with Walter Bresette, *Walleye Warriors: An Effective Alliance Against Racism and for the Earth* (1994)

Geoffrey York, *The Dispossessed: Life and Death in Native Canada* (1989)